Praise for *Head First HTML with CSS & XHTML*

"*Head First HTML with CSS & XHTML* is a thoroughly modern introduction to forward-looking practices in Web page markup and presentation. It correctly anticipates readers' puzzlements and handles them just in time. The highly graphic and incremental approach precisely mimics the best way to learn this stuff: make a small change and see it in the browser to understand what each new item means."

> — **Danny Goodman, author of *Dynamic HTML: The Definitive Guide***

"Eric and Elisabeth Freeman clearly know their stuff. As the Internet becomes more complex, inspired construction of web pages becomes increasingly critical. Elegant design is at the core of every chapter here, each concept conveyed with equal doses of pragmatism and wit."

> — **Ken Goldstein, Executive Vice President &**
> **Managing Director, Disney Online**

"The Web would be a much better place if every HTML author started off by reading this book."

> — **L. David Baron, Technical Lead, Layout & CSS, Mozilla Corporation**
> **http://dbaron.org/**

"I've been writing HTML and CSS for ten years now, and what used to be a long trial and error learning process has now been reduced neatly into an engaging paperback. HTML used to be something you could just hack away at until things looked okay on screen, but with the advent of web standards and the movement towards accessibility, sloppy coding practice is not acceptable anymore... from a business standpoint or a social responsibility standpoint. *Head First HTML with CSS & XHTML* teaches you how to do things right from the beginning without making the whole process seem overwhelming. HTML, when properly explained, is no more complicated than plain English, and the Freemans do an excellent job of keeping every concept at eye-level."

> **Mike Davidson, President & CEO, Newsvine, Inc.**

"The information covered in this book is the same material the pros know, but taught in an educational and humorous manner that doesn't ever make you think the material is impossible to learn or you are out of your element."

> — **Christopher Schmitt, Author of The CSS Cookbook**
> **and Professional CSS, schmitt@christopher.org**

Oh, great. You made an XHTML book simple enough a CEO can understand it. What will you do next? Accounting simple enough my developer can understand it? Next thing you know we'll be collaborating as a team or something.

> —**Janice Fraser, CEO, Adaptive Path**

More Praise for *Head First HTML with CSS & XHTML*

"I *heart* *Head First HTML with CSS & XHTML* – it teaches you everything you need to learn in a 'fun coated' format!"

— **Sally Applin, UI Designer and Fine Artist, http://sally.com.**

"This book has humor, and charm, but most importantly, it has heart. I know that sounds ridiculous to say about a technical book, but I really sense that at its core, this book (or at least its authors) really care that the reader learn the material. This comes across in the style, the language, and the techniques. Learning – real understanding and comprehension – on the part of the reader is clearly top most in the minds of the Freemans. And thank you, thank you, thank you, for the book's strong, and sensible advocacy of standards compliance. It's great to see an entry level book, that I think will be widely read and studied, campaign so eloquently and persuasively on behalf of the value of standards compliance in web page code. I even found in here a few great arguments I had not thought of – ones I can remember and use when I am asked – as I still am – 'what's the deal with compliance and why should we care?' I'll have more ammo now! I also liked that the book sprinkles in some basics about the mechanics of actually getting a web page live - FTP, web server basics, file structures, etc."

— **Robert Neer, Director of Product Development, Movies.com**

"Freeman's *Head First HTML with CSS & XHTML* is a most entertaining book for learning how to build a great web page. It not only covers everything you need to know about HTML, CSS, and XHTML, it also excels in explaining everything in layman's terms with a lot of great examples. I found the book truly enjoyable to read, and I learned something new!"

— **Newton Lee, Editor-in-Chief, ACM Computers in Entertainment http://www.acmcie.org**

"My wife stole the book. She's never done any web design, so she needed a book like *Head First HTML with CSS & XHTML* to take her from beginning to end. She now has a list of web sites she wants to build – for our son's class, our family, ... If I'm lucky, I'll get the book back when she's done."

— **David Kaminsky, Master Inventor, IBM**

"Beware. If you're someone who reads at night before falling asleep, you'll have to restrict *Head First HTML with CSS & XHTML* to daytime reading. This book wakes up your brain."

— **Pauline McNamara, Center for New Technologies and Education, Fribourg University, Switzerland**

Previous Praise for books by *the authors*

From the awesome Head First Java folks, this book uses every conceivable trick to help you understand and remember. Not just loads of pictures: pictures of humans, which tend to interest other humans. Surprises everywhere. Stories, because humans love narrative. (Stories about things like pizza and chocolate. Need we say more?) Plus, it's darned funny.

> **— Bill Camarda, READ ONLY**

"This book's admirable clarity, humor and substantial doses of clever make it the sort of book that helps even non-programmers think well about problem-solving."

> **— Cory Doctorow, co-editor of Boing Boing**
> **and author of "Down and Out in the Magic Kingdom"**
> **and "Someone Comes to Town, Someone Leaves Town"**

"I feel like a thousand pounds of books have just been lifted off of my head."

> **— Ward Cunningham, inventor of the Wiki**
> **and founder of the Hillside Group**

"This book is close to perfect, because of the way it combines expertise and readability. It speaks with authority and it reads beautifully. It's one of the very few software books I've ever read that strikes me as indispensable. (I'd put maybe 10 books in this category, at the outside.)"

> **— David Gelernter, Professor of Computer Science,**
> **Yale University and author of "Mirror Worlds" and "Machine Beauty"**

"A Nose Dive into the realm of patterns, a land where complex things become simple, but where simple things can also become complex. I can think of no better tour guides than the Freemans."

> **— Miko Matsumura, Industry Analyst, The Middleware Company**
> **Former Chief Java Evangelist, Sun Microsystems**

"I laughed, I cried, it moved me."

> **— Daniel Steinberg, Editor-in-Chief, java.net**

"Just the right tone for the geeked-out, casual-cool guru coder in all of us. The right reference for practical development strategies—gets my brain going without having to slog through a bunch of tired, stale professor-speak."

> **— Travis Kalanick, Founder of Scour and Red Swoosh**
> **Member of the MIT TR100**

"I literally love this book. In fact, I kissed this book in front of my wife."

> **— Satish Kumar**

Other related books from O'Reilly

HTML Pocket Reference

CSS Pocket Reference

CSS Cookbook

Cascading Style Sheets: The Definitive Guide

HTML & XHTML: The Definitive Guide

Dynamic HTML: The Definitive Reference

Learning Web Design: A Beginner's Guide to HTML, Graphics, and Beyond

Other books in O'Reilly's *Head First* series

Head First Java

Head First Object-Oriented Analysis and Design (OOA&D)

Head Rush Ajax

Head First HTML with CSS and XHTML

Head First Design Patterns

Head First Servlets and JSP

Head First EJB

Head First PMP

Head First SQL

Head First Software Development

Head First JavaScript

Head First Ajax

Head First Statistics

Head First Physics (2008)

Head First Programming (2008)

Head First Ruby on Rails (2008)

Head First PHP & MySQL (2008)

Head First HTML
with CSS & XHTML

> Wouldn't it be dreamy
> if there was an HTML book
> that didn't assume you knew what
> elements, attributes, validation,
> selectors, and pseudo-classes were,
> all by page three? It's probably just
> a fantasy...

Elisabeth Freeman
Eric Freeman

O'REILLY®

Beijing • Cambridge • Köln • Sebastopol • Taipei • Tokyo

Head First HTML with CSS and XHTML

by Elisabeth Freeman and Eric Freeman

Copyright © 2006 O'Reilly Media, Inc. All rights reserved.

Printed in the United States of America.

Published by O'Reilly Media, Inc., 1005 Gravenstein Highway North, Sebastopol, CA 95472.

O'Reilly Media books may be purchased for educational, business, or sales promotional use. Online editions are also available for most titles (safari.oreilly.com). For more information, contact our corporate/institutional sales department: (800) 998-9938 or corporate@oreilly.com.

Associate Publisher:	Mike Hendrickson
Series Creators:	Kathy Sierra, Bert Bates
Series Advisors:	Elisabeth Freeman, Eric Freeman
Editor:	Brett McLaughlin
Cover Designers:	Ellie Volckhausen, Karen Montgomery
HTML Wranglers:	Elisabeth Freeman, Eric Freeman
Structure:	Elisabeth Freeman
Style:	Eric Freeman
Page Viewer:	Oliver

Printing History:

December 2005: First Edition.

ISBN: 978-0-596-10197-8

[C]

[14/10]

Browser wars? You'll find out in Chapter 6.

To the W3C, for saving us from the browser wars and for their brilliance in separating structure (HTML) from presentation (CSS)...

And for making HTML, CSS, and XHTML complex enough that people need a book to learn it.

Authors of Head First HTML with CSS & XHTML

Elisabeth Freeman →

← Eric Freeman

Elisabeth is an author and software developer. She's been involved with the Internet since the early days, having co-founded The Ada Project (TAP), an award winning web site for women in computing now adopted by the ACM. More recently Elisabeth led research and development efforts in digital media at the Walt Disney Company where she co-invented Motion, a content system that delivers terabytes of video every day to Disney, ESPN, and Movies.com users.

Elisabeth is a computer scientist at heart and holds graduate degrees in Computer Science from Yale University and Indiana University. She's worked in a variety of areas including visual languages, RSS syndication, and Internet systems. She's also been an active advocate for women in computing, developing programs that encourage woman to enter the field. These days you'll find her sipping some Java or Cocoa on her Mac, although she dreams of a day when the whole world is using Scheme.

Elisabeth has loved hiking and the outdoors since her days growing up in Scotland. When she's outdoors her camera is never far away. She's also an avid cyclist, vegetarian, and animal lover.

You can send her email at beth@wickedlysmart.com

Eric is a computer scientist with a passion for media and software architectures. He just wrapped up four years at a dream job – directing Internet broadband and wireless efforts at Disney – and is now back to writing, creating cool software, and hacking Java and Macs.

Eric spent a lot of the '90s working on alternatives to the desktop metaphor with David Gelernter (and they're both *still* asking the question "why do I have to give a file a name?"). Based on this work, Eric landed a Ph.D. at Yale University in '97. He also co-founded Mirror Worlds Technologies (now acquired) to create a commercial version of his thesis work, Lifestreams.

In a previous life, Eric built software for networks and supercomputers. You might know him from such books as *JavaSpaces Principles Patterns and Practice*. Eric has fond memories of implementing tuple-space systems on Thinking Machine CM-5s and creating some of the first Internet information systems for NASA in the late 80s.

Eric is currently living on Bainbridge Island. When he's not writing text or code you'll find him spending more time tweaking than watching his home theater and trying to restoring a circa 1980s Dragon's Lair video game. He also wouldn't mind moonlighting as an electronica DJ.

Write to him at eric@wickedlysmart.com or visit his blog at http://www.ericfreeman.com

Table of Contents (summary)

Table of Contents (the real thing)

Intro

Your brain on HTML & CSS.

Here *you* are trying to *learn* something, while here your *brain* is doing you a favor by making sure the learning doesn't *stick*. Your brain's thinking, "Better leave room for more important things, like which wild animals to avoid and whether naked snowboarding is a bad idea." So how *do* you trick your brain into thinking that your life depends on knowing HTML & CSS?

getting to know html

1 The Language of the Web

The only thing that is standing between you and getting yourself on the Web is learning to speak the lingo:
HyperText Markup Language, or HTML for short. So, get ready for some language lessons. After this chapter, not only are you going to understand some basic **elements** of HTML, but you'll also be able to speak HTML with a little **style.** Heck, by the end of this book you'll be talking HTML like you grew up in Webville.

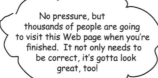

No pressure, but thousands of people are going to visit this Web page when you're finished. It not only needs to be correct, it's gotta look great, too!

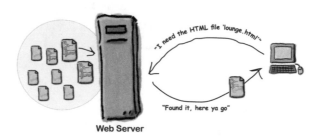

Web Server

2

Meeting the 'HT' in HTML

Did someone say "hypertext?" What's that? Oh, only the *entire basis* of the Web. In Chapter 1 we kicked the tires of HTML and found it to be a nice *markup language* (the 'ML' in HTML) for describing the structure of Web pages. Now we're going to check out the 'HT' in HTML, *hypertext*, which will let us break free of a single page and link to other pages. Along the way we're going to meet a powerful new element, the <a> element, and learn how being "relative" is a groovy thing. So, fasten your seat belts – you're about to learn some hypertext.

building blocks

3 Web Page Construction

I was told I'd actually be creating Web pages in this book?

You've certainly learned a lot already: tags, elements, links, paths... but it's all for nothing if you don't create some killer Web pages with that knowledge. In this chapter we're going to ramp up construction: you're going to take a Web page from conception to blueprint, pour the foundation, build it, and even put on some finishing touches. All you need is your hard hat and your tool belt, as we'll be adding some new tools and giving you some insider knowledge that would make Tim "The Toolman" Taylor proud.

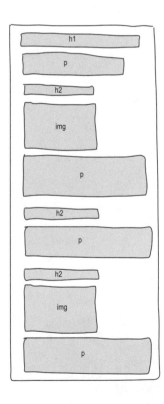

getting connected

4 A Trip to Webville

Web pages are a dish best served on the Internet.
So far you've only created HTML pages that live on your own computer. You've also only linked to pages that are on your own computer. We're about to change all that. In this chapter we'll encourage you to get those Web pages on the Internet where all your friends, fans, and customers can actually see them. We'll also reveal the mysteries of linking to other pages by cracking the code of the h, t, t, p, :, /, /, w, w, w. So, gather your belongings; our next stop is Webville.

CONTENTS:
HTML and Images

LOCATION:
Root folder

adding images to your pages

Meeting the Media

Smile and say "cheese." Actually, smile and say "gif", "jpg", or "png" — these are going to be your choices when "developing pictures" for the Web. In this chapter you're going to learn all about adding your first media type to your pages: images. Got some digital photos you need to get online? No problem. Got a logo you need to get on your page? Got it covered. But before we get into all that, don't you still need to be formally introduced to the <img> element? So sorry, we weren't being rude, we just never saw the right opening. To make up for it, here's an entire chapter devoted to <img>. By the end of the chapter you're going to know all the ins and outs of how to use the <img> element and its attributes. You're also going to see exactly how this little element causes the browser to do a lot extra work to retrieve and display your images.

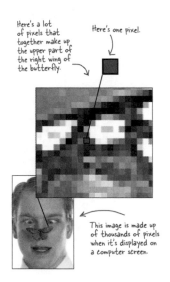

Here's a lot of pixels that together make up the upper part of the right wing of the butterfly.

Here's one pixel.

This image is made up of thousands of pixels when it's displayed on a computer screen.

standards, compliance, and all that jazz

6

Serious HTML

What else is there to know about HTML?
You're well on your way to mastering HTML. In fact, isn't it about time we move on to CSS and learn how to make all this bland markup look fabulous? Before we do, we need to make sure your HTML is really tight (you know... buttoned up, ship shape, nailed down) and we're going to do that by getting serious about the way we write our HTML. Don't get us wrong, you've been writing first-class HTML all along, but there's a few things you can do to help the browser faithfully display your pages and to make sure that little mistakes don't creep into your markup. What's in it for you? Pages that display more uniformly across browsers (and are readable on mobile devices and screen readers for the visually impaired), pages that load faster, and pages that are guaranteed to play well with CSS. Get ready, this is the chapter where you move from Web tinkerer to Web professional.

moving to xhtml

7 Putting the 'X' into HTML

We've been keeping a dirty secret from you. We know you

thought you bought an HTML book, but this is really an XHTML book in disguise. In fact, we've been teaching you mostly XHTML all along. You're probably wondering, just what the heck is XHTML? Well, meet eXtensible HTML – otherwise known as XHTML – the next evolution of HTML. It's leaner, meaner, and even more tuned for compatibility with a wide range of devices beyond browsers. In this short little chapter we're going to get you from HTML to XHTML in three simple steps. So, turn the page, you're almost there... (and then we're on to CSS).

I like keeping up with trends and technologies. XHTML is the future, and since it's almost exactly like HTML, why not go with the better technology?

Maintains her own blog.

8 Adding a Little Style

I was told there'd be CSS in this book. So far you've been concentrating on learning XHTML to create the structure of your Web pages. But as you can see, the browser's idea of style leaves a lot to be desired. Sure, we could call the fashion police, but we don't need to. With CSS, you're going to completely control the presentation of your pages, often without even changing your XHTML. Could it really be so easy? Well, you *are* going to have to learn a new language; after all, Webville is a bilingual town. After reading this chapter's guide to learning the language of CSS, you're going to be able to stand on *either* side of Main Street and hold a conversation.

Five-Minute Mystery

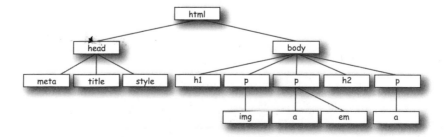

styling with fonts and colors

9 Expanding your Vocabulary

Your CSS language lessons are coming along nicely.

You already have the basics of CSS down and you know how to create CSS rules to select and determine the style of the elements. Now what you need is to increase your vocabulary, and that means picking up some new properties and learning about what they can do for you. In this chapter we're going to work through some of the most common properties that affect the display of text. To do that, you'll need to learn a few things about fonts and color. You're going to see you don't have to be stuck with the fonts everyone else uses, or the clunky sizes and styles the browser uses as the defaults for paragraphs and headings. You're also going to see there is a lot more to color than meets the eye.

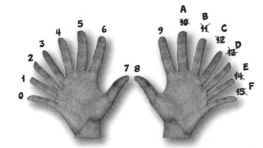

the box model

Getting Intimate with Elements

10

To do advanced Web construction you really need to know your building materials. In this chapter we're going to take a close look at our building materials: the XHTML elements. We're going to put block and inline elements right under the microscope and see what they're made of. You're going to see how you can control just about every aspect of how an element is constructed with CSS. But we're not going to stop there; you're also going to see how you can give elements unique identities. And, if that weren't enough, you're going to discover why you might want to use multiple style sheets.

11

divs and spans

Advanced Web Construction

It's time to get ready for heavy construction. In this chapter
we're going to roll out two new XHTML elements, called <div> and <span>. These
are no simple "two by fours;" these are full blown steel beams. With <div> and
<span>, you're going to build some serious supporting structures, and once you've
got those structures in place, you're going to be able to style them all in new and
powerful ways. Now, we couldn't help but notice that your CSS toolbelt is really
starting to fill up, so it's time to show you a few shortcuts that will make specifying all
these properties a lot easier. And, we've also got some special guests in this chapter,
the *pseudo-classes*, which are going to allow you to create some very interesting
selectors. (But, if you're thinking that "pseudo-classes" would make a great name for
your next band; too late, we beat you to it.)

layout and positioning

Arranging Elements

12

It's time to teach your XHTML elements new tricks. We're not going to let those XHTML elements just sit there anymore; it's about time they get up and help us create some pages with real *layouts*. How? Well, you've got a good feel for the <div> and <span> structural elements and you know all about how the box model works, right? So, now it's time to use all that knowledge to craft some real designs. No, we're not just talking about more background and font colors, we're talking about full blown professional designs using multi-column layouts. This is the chapter where everything you've learned comes together.

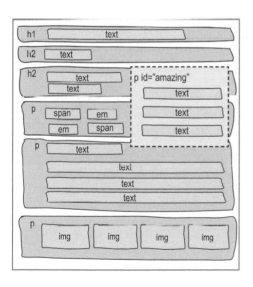

tables and more lists

13

Getting Tabular

If it walks like a table and talks like a table...
There comes a time in life when we have to deal with the dreaded *tabular data*. Whether you need to create a page representing your company's inventory over the last year, or a catalog of your Beanie Babies collection (don't worry, we won't tell), you know you need to do it in HTML; but how? Well, have we got a deal for you: order now and in a single chapter we'll reveal the secrets of tables that will allow you to put your very own data right inside HTML tables. But there's more: with every order we'll throw in our exclusive guide to styling HTML tables. And, if you act now, as a special bonus, we'll throw in our guide to styling HTML lists. Don't hesitate, call now!

xhtml forms

14

Getting Interactive

So far all your Web communication has been one way: from *your page* to *your visitors*. Golly, wouldn't it be nice if your visitors could talk back? That's where HTML forms come in: once you enable your pages with forms (along with a little help from a Web server), your pages are going to be able to gather customer feedback, take an online order, get the next move in an online game, or collect the votes in a "hot or not" contest. In this chapter you're going to meet a whole team of XHTML elements that work together to create Web forms. You'll also learn a bit about what goes on behind the scenes in the server to support forms, and we'll even talk about keeping those forms stylish (a controversial topic – read on and see why).

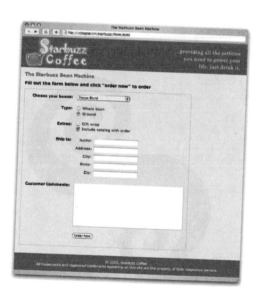

15

appendix: leftovers

The Top Ten Topics (we didn't cover)

We covered a lot of ground, and you're almost finished with this book. We'll miss you, but before we let you go, we wouldn't feel right about sending you out into the world without a little more preparation. We can't possibly fit everything you'll need to know into this relatively small chapter. Actually, we *did* originally include everything you need to know about XHTML and CSS (not already covered by the other chapters), by reducing the type point size to .00004. It all fit, but nobody could read it. So, we threw most of it away, and kept the best bits for this Top Ten chapter.

 **Index**

Intro

In this section, we answer the burning question:
"So, why DID they put that in an HTML book?"

Who is this book for?

If you can answer "yes" to all of these:

1 Do you have access to a computer with a **Web browser** and a **text editor**?

2 Do you want to **learn, understand,** and **remember** how to **create** Web pages using the best techniques and the most recent standards?

3 Do you prefer **stimulating dinner party conversation** to **dry, dull, academic lectures?**

this book is for you.

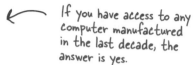

← *If you have access to any computer manufactured in the last decade, the answer is yes.*

Who should probably back away from this book?

If you can answer "yes" to any one of these:

1 **Are you <u>completely</u> new to computers?**

(You don't need to be advanced, but you should understand folders and files, simple text editing applications, and how to use a Web browser.)

2 Are you a kick-butt Web developer looking for a *reference* **book?**

3 Are you **afraid to try something different?** Would you rather have a root canal than mix stripes with plaid? Do you believe that a technical book can't be serious if HTML tags are anthropomorphized?

this book is not for you.

[Note from marketing: this book is for anyone with a credit card.]

We know what you're thinking.

"How can this be a serious book?"

"What's with all the graphics?"

"Can I actually learn it this way?"

And we know what your *brain* is thinking.

Your brain craves novelty. It's always searching, scanning, *waiting* for something unusual. It was built that way, and it helps you stay alive.

Today, you're less likely to be a tiger snack. But your brain's still looking. You just never know.

So what does your brain do with all the routine, ordinary, normal things you encounter? Everything it *can* to stop them from interfering with the brain's *real* job—recording things that *matter*. It doesn't bother saving the boring things; they never make it past the "this is obviously not important" filter.

How does your brain *know* what's important? Suppose you're out for a day hike and a tiger jumps in front of you, what happens inside your head and body?

Neurons fire. Emotions crank up. *Chemicals surge.*

And that's how your brain knows...

This must be important! Don't forget it!

But imagine you're at home, or in a library. It's a safe, warm, tiger-free zone. You're studying. Getting ready for an exam. Or trying to learn some tough technical topic your boss thinks will take a week, ten days at the most.

Just one problem. Your brain's trying to do you a big favor. It's trying to make sure that this *obviously* non-important content doesn't clutter up scarce resources. Resources that are better spent storing the really *big* things. Like tigers. Like the danger of fire. Like how you should never again snowboard in shorts.

And there's no simple way to tell your brain, "Hey brain, thank you very much, but no matter how dull this book is, and how little I'm registering on the emotional Richter scale right now, I really *do* want you to keep this stuff around."

Your brain thinks THIS is important.

Great. Only 637 more dull, dry, boring pages.

Your brain thinks THIS isn't worth saving.

We think of a "Head First" reader as a <u>learner</u>.

So what does it take to *learn* something? First, you have to *get* it, then make sure you don't *forget* it. It's not about pushing facts into your head. Based on the latest research in cognitive science, neurobiology, and educational psychology, *learning* takes a lot more than text on a page. We know what turns your brain on.

Some of the Head First learning principles:

Browsers make requests for HTML pages or other resources, like images.

Web Server   "Found it, here ya go"

Make it visual. Images are far more memorable than words alone, and make learning much more effective (up to 89% improvement in recall and transfer studies). It also makes things more understandable.
Put the words within or near the graphics they relate to, rather than on the bottom or on another page, and learners will be up to *twice* as likely to solve problems related to the content.

Use a conversational and personalized style. In recent studies, students performed up to 40% better on post-learning tests if the content spoke directly to the reader, using a first-person, conversational style rather than taking a formal tone. Tell stories instead of lecturing. Use casual language. Don't take yourself too seriously. Which would *you* pay more attention to: a stimulating dinner party companion, or a lecture?

It really sucks to forget your <body> element.

Get the learner to think more deeply. In other words, unless you actively flex your neurons, nothing much happens in your head. A reader has to be motivated, engaged, curious, and inspired to solve problems, draw conclusions, and generate new knowledge. And for that, you need challenges, exercises, and thought-provoking questions, and activities that involve both sides of the brain, and multiple senses.

The head element is where you put things <u>about</u> your page.

Does it make sense to create a bathtub class for my style, or just to style the whole bathroom?

Get—and keep—the reader's attention. We've all had the "I really want to learn this but I can't stay awake past page one" experience. Your brain pays attention to things that are out of the ordinary, interesting, strange, eye-catching, unexpected. Learning a new, tough, technical topic doesn't have to be boring. Your brain will learn much more quickly if it's not.

Touch their emotions. We now know that your ability to remember something is largely dependent on its emotional content. You remember what you *care* about. You remember when you *feel* something. No, we're not talking heart-wrenching stories about a boy and his dog. We're talking emotions like surprise, curiosity, fun, "what the...?", and the feeling of "I Rule!" that comes when you solve a puzzle, learn something everybody else thinks is hard, or realize you know something that "I'm more technical than thou" Bob from engineering *doesn't*.

Metacognition: thinking about thinking

If you really want to learn, and you want to learn more quickly and more deeply, pay attention to how you pay attention. Think about how you think. Learn how you learn.

Most of us did not take courses on metacognition or learning theory when we were growing up. We were *expected* to learn, but rarely *taught* how to learn.

But we assume that if you're holding this book, you really want to learn how to create Web pages. And you probably don't want to spend a lot of time. And you want to *remember* what you read, and be able to apply it. And for that, you've got to *understand* it. To get the most from this book, or *any* book or learning experience, take responsibility for your brain. Your brain on *this* content.

The trick is to get your brain to see the new material you're learning as Really Important. Crucial to your well-being. As important as a tiger. Otherwise, you're in for a constant battle, with your brain doing its best to keep the new content from sticking.

I wonder how I can trick my brain into remembering this stuff...

So how *DO* you get your brain to think HTML & CSS are as important as a tiger?

There's the slow, tedious way, or the faster, more effective way. The slow way is about sheer repetition. You obviously know that you *are* able to learn and remember even the dullest of topics, if you keep pounding on the same thing. With enough repetition, your brain says, "This doesn't *feel* important to him, but he keeps looking at the same thing *over* and *over* and *over*, so I suppose it must be."

The faster way is to do **anything that increases brain activity,** especially different *types* of brain activity. The things on the previous page are a big part of the solution, and they're all things that have been proven to help your brain work in your favor. For example, studies show that putting words *within* the pictures they describe (as opposed to somewhere else in the page, like a caption or in the body text) causes your brain to try to make sense of how the words and picture relate, and this causes more neurons to fire. More neurons firing = more chances for your brain to *get* that this is something worth paying attention to, and possibly recording.

A conversational style helps because people tend to pay more attention when they perceive that they're in a conversation, since they're expected to follow along and hold up their end. The amazing thing is, your brain doesn't necessarily *care* that the "conversation" is between you and a book! On the other hand, if the writing style is formal and dry, your brain perceives it the same way you experience being lectured to while sitting in a roomful of passive attendees. No need to stay awake.

But pictures and conversational style are just the beginning.

Here's what WE did:

We used **pictures**, because your brain is tuned for visuals, not text. As far as your brain's concerned, a picture really *is* worth 1024 words. And when text and pictures work together, we embedded the text *in* the pictures because your brain works more effectively when the text is *within* the thing the text refers to, as opposed to in a caption or buried in the text somewhere.

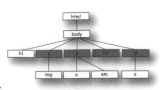

We used **redundancy**, saying the same thing in *different* ways and with different media types, and *multiple senses*, to increase the chance that the content gets coded into more than one area of your brain.

We used concepts and pictures in **unexpected** ways because your brain is tuned for novelty, and we used pictures and ideas with at least *some* **emotional** *content*, because your brain is tuned to pay attention to the biochemistry of emotions. That which causes you to *feel* something is more likely to be remembered, even if that feeling is nothing more than a little **humor**, **surprise**, or **interest.**

Be the Browser

We used a personalized, **conversational style**, because your brain is tuned to pay more attention when it believes you're in a conversation than if it thinks you're passively listening to a presentation. Your brain does this even when you're *reading*.

We included more than 100 **activities**, because your brain is tuned to learn and remember more when you **do** things than when you *read* about things. And we made the exercises challenging-yet-do-able, because that's what most *people* prefer.

BULLET POINTS

We used **multiple learning styles**, because *you* might prefer step-by-step procedures, while someone else wants to understand the big picture first, while someone else just wants to see a code example. But regardless of your own learning preference, *everyone* benefits from seeing the same content represented in multiple ways.

We include content for **both sides of your brain**, because the more of your brain you engage, the more likely you are to learn and remember, and the longer you can stay focused. Since working one side of the brain often means giving the other side a chance to rest, you can be more productive at learning for a longer period of time.

Puzzles

And we included **stories** and exercises that present **more than one point of view,** because your brain is tuned to learn more deeply when it's forced to make evaluations and judgements.

We included **challenges**, with exercises, and by asking **questions** that don't always have a straight answer, because your brain is tuned to learn and remember when it has to *work* at something. Think about it—you can't get your *body* in shape just by *watching* people at the gym. But we did our best to make sure that when you're working hard, it's on the *right* things. That **you're not spending one extra dendrite** processing a hard-to-understand example, or parsing difficult, jargon-laden, or overly terse text.

We used **people**. In stories, examples, pictures, etc., because, well, because *you're* a person. And your brain pays more attention to *people* than it does to *things*.

We used an **80/20** approach. We assume that if you're going to be a kick-butt Web developer, this won't be your only book. So we don't talk about *everything*. Just the stuff you'll actually *need*.

cut this out and stick it on your refrigerator.

Here's what YOU can do to bend your brain into submission

So, we did our part. The rest is up to you. These tips are a starting point; listen to your brain and figure out what works for you and what doesn't. Try new things.

----

(1) Slow down. The more you understand, the less you have to memorize.

Don't just *read*. Stop and think. When the book asks you a question, don't just skip to the answer. Imagine that someone really *is* asking the question. The more deeply you force your brain to think, the better chance you have of learning and remembering.

(2) Do the exercises. Write your own notes.

We put them in, but if we did them for you, that would be like having someone else do your workouts for you. And don't just *look* at the exercises. **Use a pencil.** There's plenty of evidence that physical activity *while* learning can increase the learning.

(3) Read the "There are No Dumb Questions"

That means all of them. They're not optional sidebars—*they're part of the core content!* Don't skip them.

(4) Make this the last thing you read before bed. Or at least the last *challenging* thing.

Part of the learning (especially the transfer to long-term memory) happens *after* you put the book down. Your brain needs time on its own, to do more processing. If you put in something new during that processing-time, some of what you just learned will be lost.

(5) Drink water. Lots of it.

Your brain works best in a nice bath of fluid. Dehydration (which can happen before you ever feel thirsty) decreases cognitive function.

(6) Talk about it. Out loud.

Speaking activates a different part of the brain. If you're trying to understand something, or increase your chance of remembering it later, say it out loud. Better still, try to explain it out loud to someone else. You'll learn more quickly, and you might uncover ideas you hadn't known were there when you were reading about it.

(7) Listen to your brain.

Pay attention to whether your brain is getting overloaded. If you find yourself starting to skim the surface or forget what you just read, it's time for a break. Once you go past a certain point, you won't learn faster by trying to shove more in, and you might even hurt the process.

(8) *Feel* something!

Your brain needs to know that this *matters*. Get involved with the stories. Make up your own captions for the photos. Groaning over a bad joke is *still* better than feeling nothing at all.

(9) *Create* something!

Apply this to something new you're designing, or rework an older project. Just do *something* to get some experience beyond the exercises and activities in this book. All you need is a pencil and a problem to solve... a problem that might benefit from using HTML and CSS.

Read Me

This is a learning experience, not a reference book. We deliberately stripped out everything that might get in the way of learning whatever it is we're working on at that point in the book. And the first time through, you need to begin at the beginning, because the book makes assumptions about what you've already seen and learned.

We begin by teaching basic HTML, then standards-based HTML 4.01, and then on to XHTML.

To write standards-based HTML or XHTML, there are a lot of technical details you need to understand that aren't helpful when you're trying to learn the basics of HTML. Our approach is to have you learn the basic concepts of HTML first (without worrying about these details), and then, when you have a solid understanding of HTML, teach you to write standards compliant HTML and XHTML. This has the added benefit that the technical details are more meaningful after you've already learned the basics.

It's also important that you be writing compliant HTML or XHTML when you start using CSS, so, we make a point of getting you to standards-based HTML and XHTML before you begin any serious work with CSS.

We don't cover every single HTML element or attribute or CSS property ever created.

There are a *lot* of HTML elements, *a lot* of attributes, and *a lot* of CSS properties. Sure, they're all interesting, but our goal was to write a book that weighs less than the person reading it, so we don't cover them all here. Our focus is on the core HTML elements and CSS properties that *matter* to you, the beginner, and making sure that you really, truly, deeply understand how and when to use them. In any case, once you're done with Head First HTML & CSS, you'll be able to pick up any reference book and get up to speed quickly on all the elements and properties we left out.

This book advocates a clean separation between the structure of your pages and the presentation of your pages.

Today, serious Web pages use HTML and XHTML to structure their content, and CSS for style and presentation. 1990s-era pages often used a different model, one where HTML was used for both structure and style. This book teaches you to use HTML for structure and CSS for style; we see no reason to teach you out-dated bad habits.

We encourage you to use more than one browser with this book.

While we teach you to write HTML, CSS, and XHTML that is based on standards, you'll still (and probably always) encounter minor differences in the way Web browsers display pages. So, we encourage you to pick at least two up-to-date browsers and test your pages using them. This will give you experience in seeing the differences among browsers and in creating pages that work well in a variety of browsers.

We often use tag names for element names.

Rather than saying "the a element", or "the 'a' element", we use a tag name, like "the **<a>** element". While this may not be technically correct (because **<a>** is an opening tag, not a full blown element), it does make the text more readable, and we always follow the name with the word "element" to avoid confusion.

The activities are NOT optional.

The exercises and activities are not add-ons; they're part of the core content of the book. Some of them are to help with memory, some are for understanding, and some will help you apply what you've learned. ***Don't skip the exercises.*** The crossword puzzles are the only things you don't *have* to do, but they're good for giving your brain a chance to think about the words in a different context.

The redundancy is intentional and important.

One distinct difference in a Head First book is that we want you to *really* get it. And we want you to finish the book remembering what you've learned. Most reference books don't have retention and recall as a goal, but this book is about *learning*, so you'll see some of the same concepts come up more than once.

The examples are as lean as possible.

Our readers tell us that it's frustrating to wade through 200 lines of an example looking for the two lines they need to understand. Most examples in this book are shown within the smallest possible context, so that the part you're trying to learn is clear and simple. Don't expect all of the examples to be robust, or even complete—they are written specifically for learning, and aren't always fully-functional.

We've placed all the example files on the Web so you can download them. You'll find them at **http://www.headfirstlabs.com/books/hfhtml/**

The 'Brain Power' exercises don't have answers.

For some of them, there is no right answer, and for others, part of the learning experience of the Brain Power activities is for you to decide if and when your answers are right. In some of the Brain Power exercises you will find hints to point you in the right direction.

Tech Reviewers

Louise Barr

Joe Konior

Valentin Crettaz

Corey McGlone

Barney Marispini

Eiffel Tower

Fearless leader of the Extreme Review Team.

Marcus Green

Johannes de Jong

Pauline McNamara

Pauline gets the "kick ass reviewer" award.

Ike Van Atta

David O'Meara

Our reviewers:

We're extremely grateful for our technical review team. **Johannes de Jong** organized and led the whole effort, acted as "series dad," and made it all work smoothly. **Pauline McNamara**, "co-manager" of the effort, held things together and was the first to point out when our examples were a little more "baby boomer" than hip. The whole team proved how much we needed their technical expertise and attention to detail. **Valentin Crettaz**, **Barney Marispini**, **Marcus Green**, **Ike Van Atta**, **David O'Meara**, **Joe Konior**, and **Corey McGlone** left no stone unturned in their review and the book is a much better book for it. You guys rock! And further thanks to Corey and Pauline for never letting us slide on our often too formal (or we should just say it, incorrect) punctuation. A shout out to JavaRanch as well for hosting the whole thing.

A big thanks to **Louise Barr**, our token Web designer, who kept us honest on our designs and on our use of XHTML & CSS (although you'll have to blame us for the actual designs).

Acknowledgments*

Even more technical review:

We're also extremely grateful to our esteemed technical reviewer **David Powers**. We have a real love/hate relationship with David because he made us work so hard, but the result was *oh so worth it*. The truth be told, based on David's comments, we made significant changes to this book and it is technically twice the book it was before. Thank you, David.

Esteemed Reviewer, David Powers

Don't let the sweater fool you, this guy is hard core (technically of course).

At O'Reilly:

Our biggest thanks to our editor, **Brett McLaughlin**, who cleared the path for this book, removed every obstacle to its completion, and sacrificed family time to get it done. Brett also did hard editing time on this book (not an easy task for a Head First title). Thanks Brett, this book wouldn't have happened without you.

Our sincerest thanks to the whole O'Reilly team: **Greg Corrin, Glenn Bisignani, Tony Artuso,** and **Kyle Hart** all led the way on marketing and we appreciate their out-of-the-box approach. Thanks to **Ellie Volkhausen** for her inspired cover design that continues to serve us well, and to **Karen Montgomery** for stepping in and bringing life to this book's cover. Thank you, as always, to **Colleen Gorman** for her hardcore copyedit (and for keeping it all fun). And, we couldn't have pulled off a color book like this without **Sue Willing** and **Claire Cloutier**.

Brett McLaughlin

No Head First acknowledgment would be complete without thanking **Mike Loukides** for shaping the Head First concept into a series, and to **Tim O'Reilly** for always being there and his continued support. Finally, thanks to **Mike Hendrickson** for bringing us into the Head First family and having the faith to let us run with it.

Kathy Sierra and Bert Bates:

Last, and anything but least, to **Kathy Sierra** and **Bert Bates**, our partners in crime and the BRAINS who created the series. Thanks guys for trusting us *even more* with your baby. We hope once again we've done it justice. The three-day jam session was the highlight of writing the book, we hope to repeat it soon. Oh, and next time around can you give LTJ a call and tell him he's just going to have to make a trip back to Seattle?

Bert Bates

Kathy Sierra

Hard at work researching Head First Parelli.

Kara

*The large number of acknowledgments is because we're testing the theory that everyone mentioned in a book acknowledgment will buy at least one copy, probably more, what with relatives and everything. If you'd like to be in the acknowledgment of our *next* book, and you have a large family, write to us.

1 getting to know HTML

The Language of the Web

Not so fast... to get to know me you've got to speak the **universal language**. You know, HTML and CSS.

The only thing that is standing between you and getting yourself on the Web is learning to speak the lingo:

HyperText Markup Language, or HTML for short. So, get ready for some language lessons. After this chapter, not only are you going to understand some basic **elements** of HTML, but you'll also be able to speak HTML with a little **style**. Heck, by the end of this book you'll be talking HTML like you grew up in Webville.

The Web
~~Video~~ killed the radio star

Want to get an idea out there? Sell something? Just need a creative outlet? Turn to the Web – we don't need to tell you it has become the universal form of communication. Even better, it's a form of communication **YOU** can participate in.

But, if you really want to use the Web effectively, you've got to know a few things about **HTML**, not to mention how the Web works. Let's take a look from 30,000 feet:

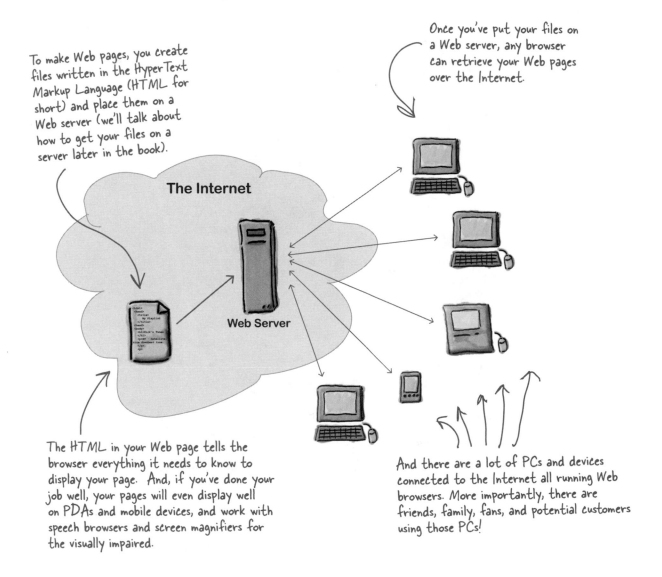

To make Web pages, you create files written in the HyperText Markup Language (HTML for short) and place them on a Web server (we'll talk about how to get your files on a server later in the book).

Once you've put your files on a Web server, any browser can retrieve your Web pages over the Internet.

The Internet

Web Server

The HTML in your Web page tells the browser everything it needs to know to display your page. And, if you've done your job well, your pages will even display well on PDAs and mobile devices, and work with speech browsers and screen magnifiers for the visually impaired.

And there are a lot of PCs and devices connected to the Internet all running Web browsers. More importantly, there are friends, family, fans, and potential customers using those PCs!

What does the Web <u>server</u> do?

Web servers have a full time job on the Internet, tirelessly waiting for requests from Web browsers. What kinds of requests? Requests for Web pages, images, sounds, or maybe even a movie. When a server gets a request for any of these resources, the server finds the resource, and then sends it back to the browser.

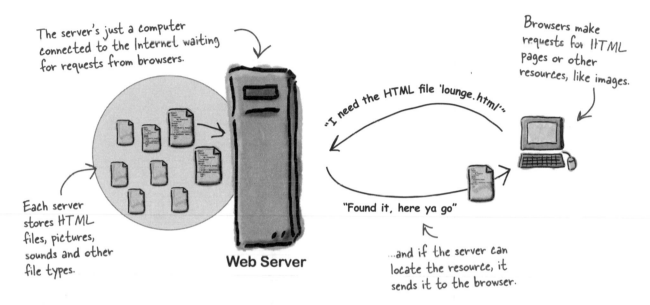

The server's just a computer connected to the Internet waiting for requests from browsers.

Each server stores HTML files, pictures, sounds and other file types.

Web Server

"I need the HTML file 'lounge.html'"

"Found it, here ya go"

...and if the server can locate the resource, it sends it to the browser.

Browsers make requests for HTML pages or other resources, like images.

What does the Web <u>browser</u> do?

You already know how a browser works: you're surfing around the Web and you click on a link to visit a page. That click causes your browser to request an HTML page from a Web server, retrieve it, and display the page in your browser window.

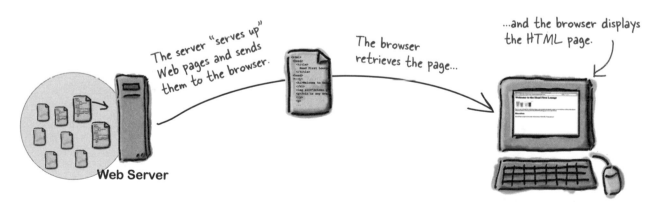

The server "serves up" Web pages and sends them to the browser.

The browser retrieves the page...

...and the browser displays the HTML page.

Web Server

But, how does the browser know how to display a page? That's where HTML comes in. HTML tells the browser all about the content and structure of the page. Let's see how that works...

What you write (the HTML)...

So, you know HTML is the key to getting a browser to display your pages, but, what exactly does HTML look like? And, what does it do?

Let's have a look at a little HTML... imagine you're going to create a Web page to advertise the *Head First Lounge*, a local hangout with some good tunes, refreshing elixirs, and wireless access. Here's what you'd write in HTML:

```html
<html>
  <head>
    <title>Head First Lounge</title>          Ⓐ
  </head>
  <body>
    <h1>Welcome to the Head First Lounge</h1>  Ⓑ
    <img src="drinks.gif">                     Ⓒ
    <p>
Ⓓ     Join us any evening for refreshing elixirs,
       conversation and maybe a game or
       two of <em>Dance Dance Revolution</em>.  Ⓔ
       Wireless access is always provided;
       BYOWS (Bring your own web server).
    </p>
    <h2>Directions</h2>  Ⓕ
    <p>
Ⓖ     You'll find us right in the center of
       downtown Webville. Come join us!
    </p>
  </body>
</html>
```

We don't expect you to know HTML, yet.

Relax

At this point you should just be getting a feel for what HTML looks like; we're going to cover everything in detail in a bit. For now, study the HTML and see how it gets represented in the browser on the next page. Be sure to pay careful attention to each letter annotation and how and where it is displayed in the browser.

What the browser creates...

When the browser reads your HTML, it interprets all the *tags* that surround your text. Tags are just words or characters in angle brackets, like **<head>**, **<p>**, **<h1>**, and so on. The tags tell the browser about the *structure and meaning* of your text. So rather than just giving the browser a bunch of text, with HTML you can use tags to tell the browser what text is in a heading, what text is a paragraph, what text needs to be emphasized, or even where images need to be placed.

Let's check out how the browser interprets the tags in the Head First Lounge:

Notice how each tag in the HTML maps to what the browser displays.

Head First Lounge Ⓐ

http://lounge.headfirstlabs.com/

Welcome to the Head First Lounge Ⓑ

Ⓒ

Ⓓ Join us any evening for refreshing elixirs, conversation and maybe a game or two of *Dance Dance Revolution*. Ⓔ Wireless access is always provided; BYOWS (Bring your own web server).

Directions Ⓕ

Ⓖ You'll find us right in the center of downtown Webville. Come join us!

Q: So HTML is just a bunch of tags that I put around my text?

A: For starters. Remember that HTML stands for HyperText *Markup* Language, so HTML gives you a way to "mark up" your text with *tags* that tell the browser how your text is structured. But there is also the *HyperText* aspect of HTML, which we'll talk about a little later in the book.

Q: How does the browser decide how to display the HTML?

A: HTML tells your browser about the structure of your document: where the headings are, where the paragraphs are, what text needs emphasis, and so on. Given this information, browsers have built-in default rules for how to display each of these elements.

But, you don't have to settle for the default settings. You can add your own style and formatting rules with CSS that determine font, colors, size, and a lot of other characteristics of your page. We'll get back to CSS later in the chapter.

Q: The HTML for the Head First Lounge has all kinds of indentation and spacing, and yet I don't see that when it is displayed in the browser. How come?

A: Correct, and good catch. Browsers ignore tabs, returns, and most spaces in HTML documents. Instead, they rely on your markup to determine where line and paragraph breaks occur.

So why did we insert our own formatting if the browser is just going to ignore it? To help us more easily read the document when we're editing the HTML. As your HTML documents become more complicated, you'll find a few spaces, returns, and tabs here and there really help to improve the readability of the HTML.

Q: So there are two levels of headings, <h1> and a subheading <h2>?

A: Actually there are six, <h1> through <h6>, which the browser typically displays in successively smaller font sizes. Unless you are creating a complex and large document, you typically won't use headings beyond <h3>.

Q: Why do I need the <html> tag? Isn't it obvious this is a HTML document?

A: The <html> tag tells the browser your document is actually HTML. While some browsers will forgive you if you omit it, some won't, and as we move toward "industrial strength HTML" later in the book, you'll see it is quite important to include this tag.

Q: What makes a file an HTML file?

A: Basically an HTML file is a simple text file. Unlike a word processing file, there is no special formatting embedded in it. By convention we add a ".html" or ".htm" (on systems that only support three letter file extensions) to the end of the file name to

give the operating system a better idea of what the file is. But, as you've seen, what really matters is what we put inside the file.

Q: Markup seems silly. What-you-see-is-what-you-get applications have been around since, what, the '70s? Why isn't the Web based on a format like Microsoft Word or a similar application?

A: The Web is created out of text files without any special formatting characters. This enables any browser in any part of the world to retrieve a Web page and understand its contents. You'll see that on the Web, in many ways HTML is more powerful than using a proprietary document format.

Q: Is there any way to put comments to myself in HTML?

A: Yes, if you place your comments in between <!-- and --> the browser will totally ignore them. Say you wanted to write a comment "Here's the beginning of the lounge content". You'd do that like this:

```
<!-- Here's the beginning of
        the lounge content -->
```

Notice that you can put comments on multiple lines. Keep in mind anything you put between the "<!--" and the "-->", even HTML, will be ignored by the browser.

Sharpen your pencil

You're closer to learning HTML than you think...

Here's the HTML for the Head First Lounge again. Take a look at the tags and see if you can guess what they tell the browser about the content. Write your answers in the space on the right; we've already done the first couple for you.

```
<html>
  <head>
    <title>Head First Lounge</title>
  </head>
  <body>
    <h1>Welcome to the Head First Lounge</h1>
    <img src="drinks.gif">
    <p>
      Join us any evening for refreshing elixirs,
      conversation and maybe a game or
      two of <em>Dance Dance Revolution</em>.
      Wireless access is always provided;
      BYOWS (Bring your own web server).
    </p>
    <h2>Directions</h2>
    <p>
      You'll find us right in the center of
      downtown Webville. Come join us!
    </p>
  </body>
</html>
```

Tells the browser this is the start of HTML...

Starts the page "head" (more about this later).

_____

_____

_____

_____

_____

_____

_____

_____

_____

_____

_____

_____

Sharpen your pencil

answers

```
<html>                                          Tells the browser this is the start of HTML.

  <head>                                        Starts the page "head".

    <title>Head First Lounge</title>            Gives the page a title.

  </head>                                        End of the header.

  <body>                                         Start of the body of page.

    <h1>Welcome to the Head First Lounge</h1>   Tells browser that "Welcome to..." is a heading.

    <img src="drinks.gif">                       Places the image "drinks.gif" here.

    <p>                                          Start of a paragraph.

      Join us any evening for refreshing elixirs,
      conversation and maybe a game or
      two of <em>Dance Dance Revolution</em>.    Puts emphasis on Dance Dance Revolution.
      Wireless access is always provided;
      BYOWS (Bring your own web server).

    </p>                                          End of paragraph.

    <h2>Directions</h2>                          Tells the browser that "Directions" is a subheading.

    <p>                                          Start of another paragraph.

      You'll find us right in the center of
      downtown Webville. Come join us!

    </p>                                          End of paragraph.

  </body>                                         End of the body.

</html>                                           Tells the browser this is the end of the HTML.
```

Your big break at Starbuzz Coffee

Starbuzz Coffee has made a name for itself as the fastest growing coffee shop around. If you've seen one on your local corner, look across the street – you'll see another one.

In fact, they've grown so quickly, they haven't even managed to put up a web page, yet... and therein lies your big break: By chance, while buying your Starbuzz Chai Tea, you run into the Starbuzz CEO...

Word has it you know a little about HTML. We really need a Web page that features the Starbuzz offerings. Can you help?

The Starbuzz CEO

Decisions, decisions.
Check your first priority below (choose only one):

❏ A. Give dog a bath.

❏ B. Finally get my checking account balanced.

❏ C. Take the Starbuzz gig and launch BIG-TIME Web career.

❏ D. Schedule dentist appointment.

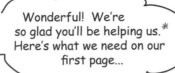

Wonderful! We're so glad you'll be helping us.* Here's what we need on our first page...

The CEO scribbles something on a napkin and hands it to you...

Starbuzz Coffee Coffee Starbuzz Coffee

Thanks for giving us a hand! On the Web page we just need something simple (see below) that includes the beverage names, prices, and descriptions.

House Blend, ƒ1.49
A smooth, mild blend of coffees from Mexico, Bolivia and Guatemala.

Mocha Cafe Latte, ƒ2.35
Espresso, steamed milk and chocolate syrup.

Cappuccino, ƒ1.89
A mixture of espresso, steamed milk and foam.

Chai Tea, ƒ1.05
A spicy drink made with black tea, spices, milk and honey.

Sharpen your pencil

Take a look at the napkin. Can you determine the *structure* of it? In other words, are there obvious headings? Paragraphs? Is it missing anything like a title?

Go ahead and mark up the napkin (using your pencil) with any structure you see, and add anything that is missing.

You'll find our answers at the end of Chapter 1.

* If by chance you chose options A, B, or D on the previous page, we recommend you donate this book to a good library, use it as kindling this winter, or what the hell, go ahead and sell it on Amazon and make some cash.

Creating the Starbuzz Web page

Of course, the only problem with all this is that you haven't actually created any Web pages, yet. But, that's why you decided to dive head first into HTML, right?

No worries, here's what you're going to do on the next few pages:

❶ Create an HTML file using your favorite text editor.

❷ Type in the menu the Starbuzz CEO wrote on the napkin.

❸ Save the file as "index.html".

❹ Open the file "index.html" in your favorite browser, step back, and watch the magic happen.

No pressure, but thousands of people are going to visit this Web page when you're finished. It not only needs to be correct, it's gotta look great, too!

Creating an HTML file (Mac)

All HTML files are text files. To create a text file you need an application that allows you to create plain text without throwing in a lot of fancy formatting and special characters. You just need plain, pure text.

We'll use TextEdit on the Mac in this book; however, if you prefer another text editor, that should work fine as well. And, if you're running Windows, you'll want to skip ahead a couple of pages to the Windows instructions.

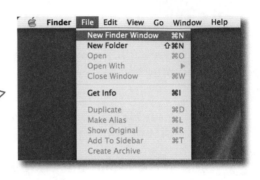

Step one:

Navigate to your **Applications** folder

The TextEdit application is in the Applications folder. The easiest way to get there is to choose "New Finder Window" from the Finder's File menu and then look for the Application directly in your shortcuts. When you've found it, click on Applications.

Here's TextEdit.

Your Finder shortcuts.

Step two:

Locate and run **TextEdit**

You'll probably have lots of applications listed in your applications folder, so scroll down until you see TextEdit. To run the application, double click on the TextEdit icon.

Step three (optional):

Keep **TextEdit** in your **Dock**

If you want to make your life easier, click and hold on the TextEdit icon in the Dock (this icon appears once the application is running). When it displays a popup menu, choose "Keep in Dock." That way, the TextEdit icon will always appear in your Dock and you won't have to hunt it down in the Applications folder every time you need to use it.

Step four:

Change your TextEdit **Preferences**

By default, TextEdit is in "rich text" mode, which means it will add its own formatting and special characters to your file when you save it – not what you want. So, you'll need to change your TextEdit Preferences so that TextEdit saves your work as a pure text file. To do this, first choose the "Preferences" menu item from the TextEdit menu.

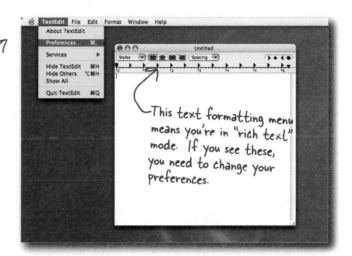

This text formatting menu means you're in "rich text" mode. If you see these, you need to change your preferences.

Step five:

Set Preferences for **Plain text**

Once you see the Preferences dialog box, there are three things you need to do.

First, choose "Plain text" as the default editor mode in the New Document tab.

Second, in the "Open and Save" tab, make sure that the "Add .txt extension to plain text files" is **un**checked.

Last, make sure "Ignore rich text commands in HTML files" is checked.

That's it; to close the dialog box click on the red button in the top left corner.

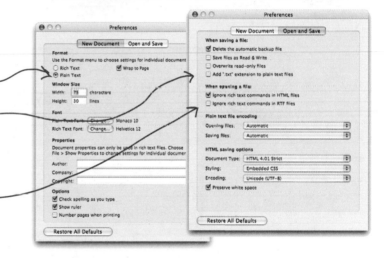

Step six:

Quit and **restart**

Now quit out of TextEdit by choosing Quit from the TextEdit menu, and then restart the application. This time, you'll see a window with no fancy text formatting menus at the top of the window. You're now ready to create some HTML.

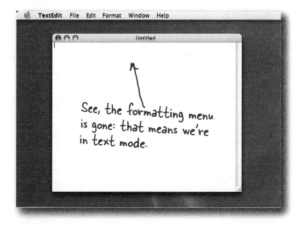

See, the formatting menu is gone: that means we're in text mode.

Creating an HTML file (Windows)

If you're reading this page you must be a Windows XP user. If not, you might want to skip a couple of pages ahead. Or, if you just want to sit in the back and not ask questions, we're okay with that too.

Or another version of Windows.

To create HTML files in XP we're going to use Notepad – it ships with every copy of Windows, the price is right, and it's easy to use. If you've got your own favorite editor that runs on XP, that's fine too; just make sure you can create a plain text file with an ".html" extension.

If you're using another version of Windows you'll find Notepad there as well.

Assuming you're using Notepad, here's how you're going to create your first HTML file.

Step one:

Open the **Start** menu and navigate to Notepad

You'll find the Notepad application in Accessories. The easiest way to get there is to click on the "Start" menu, then on "All Programs", then "Accessories". You'll see Notepad listed there.

Step two:

Open **Notepad**

Once you've located Notepad in the Accessories folder, go ahead and click on it. You'll see a blank window ready for you to start typing HTML.

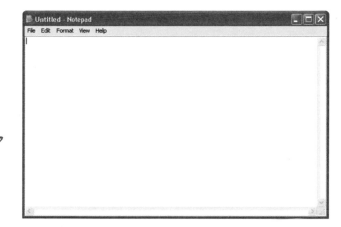

But recommended.

Step three (optional):

Don't hide extensions of well known file types.

By default XP's File Explorer hides the file extensions of well known file types. For example, a file named, "Irule.html" will be shown in the Explorer as "Irule" without its ".html" extension.

It's much less confusing if XP shows you these extensions, so let's change your folder options so you can see the file extensions.

First, in any Explorer window select "Folder Options..." from the Tools menu.

Next, in the "View" tab, under "Advanced settings", scroll down until you see "Hide extensions for known file types" and *uncheck* this option.

That's it. Click on the OK button to save the preference and you'll now see the file extensions in the Explorer.

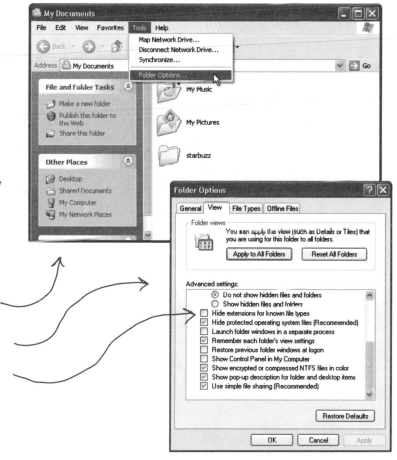

there are no
Dumb Questions

Q: **Why am I using a simple text editor? Aren't there powerful tools like Dreamweaver, FrontPage and GoLive for creating Web pages?**

A: You're reading this book because you want to understand the true technologies used for Web pages, right? Now those are all great tools, but they do a lot of the work for you, and until you are a master of HTML and CSS you want to learn this stuff without a big tool getting in your way.

Once you're a master, however, these tools do provide some nice features like syntax checking and previews. At that point, when you view the "code" window, you'll understand everything in it, and you'll find that changes to the raw HTML and CSS are often a lot faster than going through a user interface. You'll also find that as standards change, these tools aren't always updated right away and may not support the most recent standards until their next release cycle. Since you'll know how to change the HTML and CSS without the tool, you'll be able to keep up with the latest and greatest all the time.

Q: **I get the editor, but what browser am I supposed to be using? There are so many – Internet Explorer, Firefox, Opera, Safari – what's the deal?**

A: The simple answer: use whatever browser you like. HTML and CSS are industry standards, which means that all browsers try to support HTML and CSS in the same way (just make sure you are using the newest version of the browser for the best support).

The complex answer: in reality there are slight differences in the way browsers handle your pages. If you've got users who will be accessing your pages in a variety of browsers, then always test your web page in several different browsers. Some pages will look exactly the same; some won't. The more advanced you become with HTML and CSS, the more these slight differences may matter to you, and we'll get into some of these subtleties throughout the book.

If you're looking for a good browser, give Mozilla's Firefox a try; it has very good HTML and CSS support.

Q: **I'm creating these files on my own computer – how am I going to view these on the Web/Internet?**

A: That's one great thing about HTML: you can create files and test them on your own computer and then later publish them on the Web. Right now we're going to worry about how to create the files and what goes in them. We'll come back to getting them on the Web a bit later.

Meanwhile, back at Starbuzz Coffee...

Okay, now that you know the basics of creating a plain text file, you just need to get some content into your text editor, save it, and then load it into your browser.

Start by typing in the beverages straight from the CEO's napkin; these beverages are the content for your page. You'll be adding some HTML markup to give the content some structure in a bit, but for now, just get the basic content typed in. While you're at it, go ahead and add "Starbuzz Coffee Beverages" at the top of the file.

Type in the info from the napkin like this.

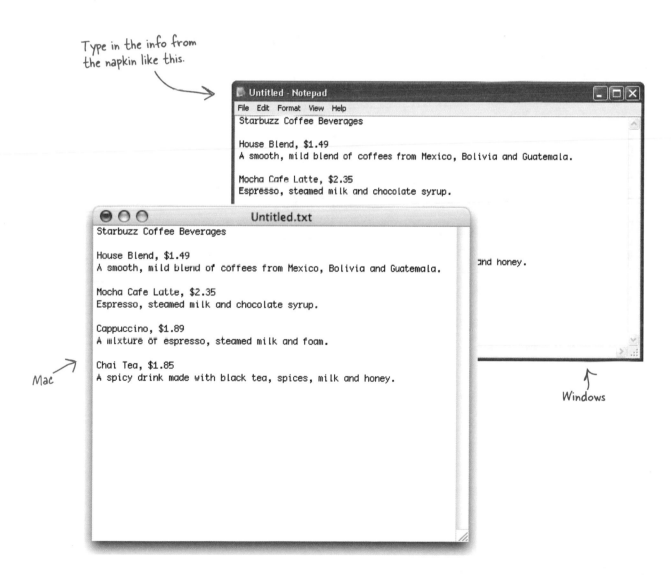

Mac

Windows

Saving your work...

Once you've typed in the beverages from the CEO's napkin, you're going to save your work in a file called "index.html". Before you do that, you'll want to create a folder named "starbuzz" to hold the site's files.

To get this all started, choose "Save" from the File menu and you'll see a "Save As" dialog box. Then, here's what you need to do:

Windows

① First, create a "starbuzz" folder for all your Starbuzz related files. You can do this with the New Folder button.

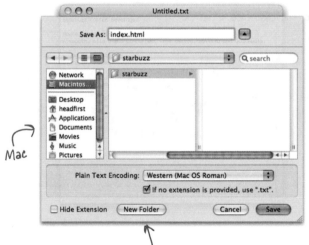

Create a new folder here.

Mac

Create a new folder here.

Using Windows you need to also choose "All Files" as your type, otherwise Notepad will add a ".txt" to your filename.

② Next, click on the newly created "starbuzz" folder and then enter "index.html" as the file name and click on the Save button.

Opening your Web page in a browser

Are you ready to open your first Web page? Using your favorite browser, choose "Open File..." (or "Open..." using Windows XP and Internet Explorer) from the File menu and navigate to your "index.html" file. Select it and click "Open".

Mac

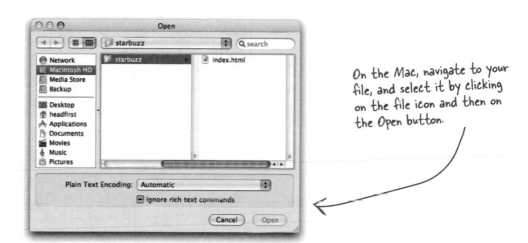

On the Mac, navigate to your file, and select it by clicking on the file icon and then on the Open button.

In Windows Internet Explorer it's a two step process. First you'll get the open dialog box.

Windows →

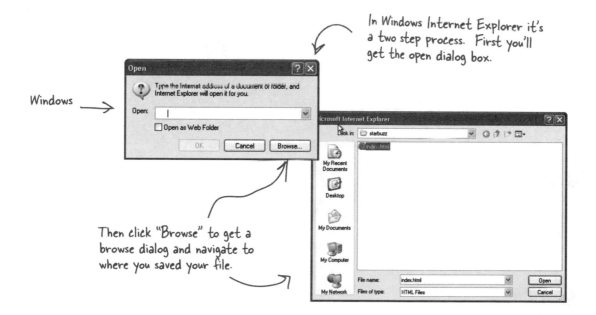

Then click "Browse" to get a browse dialog and navigate to where you saved your file.

Taking your page for a test drive...

Success! You've got the page loaded in the browser, although the results are a little... uh... unsatisfying. But that's just because all you've done so far is go through the mechanics of creating a page and viewing it in the browser. And, so far, you've only typed in the *content* of the Web page. That's where HTML comes in. HTML gives you a way to tell the browser about the *structure* of your page. What's structure? As you've already seen, it is a way of marking up your text so that the browser knows what's a heading, what text is in a paragraph, what text is a subheading, and so on. Once the browser knows a little about the structure, it can display your page in a more meaningful and readable manner.

Windows

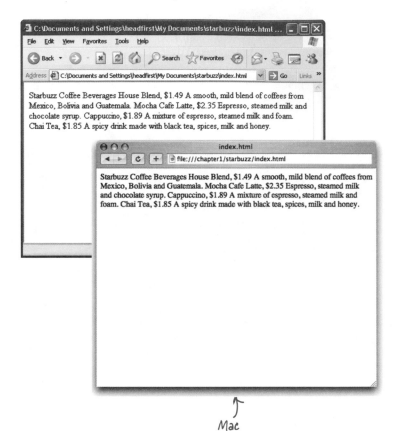

Mac

Depending on your operating system and browser, often you can just double-click the HTML file or drag it on top of the browser icon to open it. Much simpler.

Markup Magnets

So, let's add that structure...

Your job is to add structure to the text from the Starbuzz napkin. Use the fridge magnets at the bottom of the page to mark up the text so that you've indicated which parts are headings, subheadings and paragraph text. We've already done a few to get you started. You won't need all the magnets below to complete the job; some will be left over.

 `<h1>` Starbuzz Coffee Beverages `</h1>`

House Blend, $1.49
A smooth, mild blend of coffees from Mexico, Bolivia and Guatemala.

 `<h2>` Mocha Cafe Latte, $2.35 `</h2>`
`<p>` Espresso, steamed milk and chocolate syrup. `</p>`

Cappuccino, $1.89
A mixture of espresso, steamed milk and foam.

Chai Tea, $1.85
A spicy drink made with black tea, spices, milk and honey.

`<h1>`
Use this magnet to start a heading.

`</h1>`
Use this magnet to end a heading.

`<h2>`
Use this magnet to start a subheading.

`</h2>`
Use this magnet to end a subheading.

`<p>`
Use this magnet to start a paragraph.

`</p>`
Use this magnet to end a paragraph.

Congratulations, you've just written your first HTML!

They might have looked like fridge magnets, but you were really marking up your text with HTML. Only, as you know, we usually refer to the magnets as *tags*. Check out the markup below and compare it to your magnets on the previous page.

Use the <h1> and </h1> tags to mark headings. All the text in between is the actual content of the heading.

`<h1>Starbuzz Coffee Beverages</h1>`

`<h2>House Blend, $1.49</h2>`
`<p>A smooth, mild blend of coffees from Mexico, Bolivia and Guatemala.</p>`

The <h2> and </h2> tags go around a subheading. Think of an <h2> heading as a subheading of an <h1> heading.

`<h2>Mocha Cafe Latte, $2.35</h2>`
`<p>Espresso, steamed milk and chocolate syrup.</p>`

The <p> and </p> tags go around a block of text that is a paragraph. That can be one or many sentences.

`<h2>Cappuccino, $1.89</h2>`
`<p>A mixture of espresso, steamed milk and foam.</p>`

`<h2>Chai Tea, $1.85</h2>`
`<p>A spicy drink made with black tea, spices, milk and honey.</p>`

Notice that you don't have to put matching tags on the same line. You can put as much content as you like between them.

Are we there yet?

You have an HTML file with markup – does that make a Web page? Almost. You've already seen the **<html>**, **<head>**, **<title>**, and **<body>** tags, and we just need to add those to make this a first class HTML page...

First, surround your HTML with <html> & </html> tags. This tells the browser the content of the file is HTML.

Next add <head> and </head> tags. The head contains information about your Web page, like its title. For now, think about it this way: the head allows you to tell the browser things *about* the Web page.

Go ahead and put a title inside the head. The title usually appears at the top of the browser window.

```
<html>
```

```
    <head>
            <title>Starbuzz Coffee</title>
    </head>
```

The head consists of the <head> & </head> tags and everything in between.

```
    <body>
            <h1>Starbuzz Coffee Beverages</h1>
            <h2>House Blend, $1.49</h2>
            <p>A smooth, mild blend of coffees from Mexico,
                    Bolivia and Guatemala.</p>

            <h2>Mocha Cafe Latte, $2.35</h2>
            <p>Espresso, steamed milk and chocolate syrup.</p>

            <h2>Cappuccino, $1.89</h2>
            <p>A mixture of espresso, steamed milk and foam.</p>

            <h2>Chai Tea, $1.85</h2>
            <p>A spicy drink made with black tea, spices,
                    milk and honey.</p>

    </body>
```

```
</html>
```

The body consists of the <body> & </body> tags and everything in between.

The body contains all the content and structure of your Web page – the parts of the Web page that you <u>see</u> in your browser.

Keep your head and body separate when writing HTML.

Another test drive...

Go ahead and change your "index.html" file by adding in the <head>, </head>, <title>, </title>, <body> and </body> tags. Once you've done that, save your changes and reload the file into your browser.

Notice that the title, which you specified in the <head> element, shows up here.

You can reload the index.html file by selecting the "Open File" menu item again, or by using your browser's reload button.

Now things look a bit better. The browser has interpreted your tags and created a display for the page that is not only more structured but also more readable.

Starbuzz Coffee Beverages

House Blend, $1.49

A smooth, mild blend of coffees from Mexico, Bolivia and Guatemala.

Mocha Cafe Latte, $2.35

Espresso, steamed milk and chocolate syrup.

Cappuccino, $1.89

A mixture of espresso, steamed milk and foam.

Chai Tea, $1.85

A spicy drink made with black tea, spices, milk and honey.

Sweet!

Tags dissected...

Okay, you've seen a bit of markup, so let's zoom in and take a look at how tags really work...

You usually put tags around some piece of content. Here we're using tags to tell the browser that our content, "Starbuzz Coffee Beverages", is a top level heading (that is, heading level one).

This is the closing tag that ends the heading; in this case the `</h1>` tag is ending an `<h1>` heading. You know it's a closing tag because it comes after the content, and it's got a "/" before the "h1". All closing tags have a "/" in them.

Here's the **opening tag** that begins the heading.

`<h1>` Starbuzz Coffee Beverages `</h1>`

Tags consist of the tag name surrounded by angle brackets; that is, the < and > characters.

The whole shebang is called an **element**. In this case we can call it the `<h1>` element. An element consists of the enclosing tags and the content in between.

We call an opening tag and its closing tag **matching tags**.

To tell the browser about the structure of your page, use pairs of tags around your content.

Remember,

Element = Opening Tag + Content + Closing Tag

there are no Dumb Questions

Q: So matching tags don't have to be on the same line?

A: No; remember the browser doesn't really care about tabs, returns, and most spaces. So, your tags can start and end anywhere on the same line or they can start and end on different lines. Just make sure you start with an opening tag, like <h2>, and end with a closing tag, like </h2>.

Q: Why do the closing tags have that extra "/"?

A: That "/" in the closing tag is to help both you and the browser know where a particular piece of structured content ends. Otherwise, the closing tags would look just like the opening tags, right?

Q: I've noticed the HTML in some pages doesn't always match opening tags with closing tags.

A: Well, the tags are *supposed* to match. In general, browsers do a pretty good job of figuring out what you mean if you write incorrect HTML. But, as you're going to see, these days there are big benefits to writing totally correct HTML. If you're worried you'll never be able to write perfect HTML, don't be; there are plenty of tools to verify your code before you put it on a Web server so the whole world can see it. For now, just get in the habit of always matching your opening tags with closing tags.

Q: Well, what about that <img src="drinks.gif"> tag in the lounge example? Did you forget the closing tag?

A: Wow, sharp eye. There are some elements that use a shorthand notation with only one tag. Keep that in the back of your mind for now and we'll come back to it in a later chapter.

Q: An element is an opening tag + content + closing tag, but can't you have tags inside other tags? Like the head and body are inside an <html> tag?

A: Yes, HTML tags are often "nested" like that. If you think about it, it's natural for an HTML page to have a body, which contains a paragraph, and so on. So many HTML elements have other HTML elements between their tags. We'll take a good look at this kind of thing in later chapters, but for now just get your mind noticing how the elements relate to each other in a page.

 **BRAIN POWER**

Tags can be a little more interesting than what you've seen so far. Here's the paragraph tag with a little extra added to it. What do you think this does?

```
<p id="houseblend">A smooth, mild
blend of coffees from Mexico, Bolivia
and Guatemala.</p>
```

Exercise

Oh, I forgot to mention, we need our company mission on a page, too. Grab the mission statement off one of our coffee cups and create another page for it...

Starbuzz Coffee's Mission

To provide all the caffeine that you need to power your life.

Just drink it.

mission.html

❶ Write the HTML for the new "mission.html" page here.

❷ Type in your HTML using a text editor, and save it as "mission.html" in the same folder as your "index.html" file.

❸ Once you've done that, open "mission.html" in your browser.

❹ Check your work at the end of the chapter before moving on...

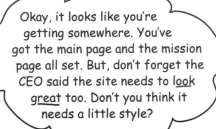

Okay, it looks like you're getting somewhere. You've got the main page and the mission page all set. But, don't forget the CEO said the site needs to look great too. Don't you think it needs a little style?

Right. We have the structure down, so now we're going to concentrate on its <u>presentation</u>.

You already know that HTML gives you a way to describe the structure of the content in your files. When the browser displays your HTML, it uses its own built-in default style to present this structure. But, relying on the browser for style obviously isn't going to win you any "designer of the month" awards.

That's where CSS comes in. CSS gives you a way to describe how your content should be presented. Let's get our feet wet by creating some CSS that makes the Starbuzz page look a little more presentable (and launch your Web career in the process).

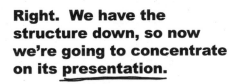

CSS is an abbreviation for Cascading Style Sheets. We'll get into what that all means later, but for now just know that CSS gives you a way to tell the browser how elements in your page should look.

Meet the style element

To add style, you add a new (say it with us) E-L-E-M-E-N-T to your page – the **<style>** element. Let's go back to the main Starbuzz page and add some style. Check it out...

The <style> element is placed inside the head of your HTML.

Just like other elements, the <style> element has an opening tag, <style>, and a closing tag, </style>

*...but, the <style> tag also requires an **attribute**, called type, which tells the browser the kind of style you're using. Because you're going to use CSS, you need to specify the "text/css" type.*

And, here's where you're going to define the styles for the page.

```
<html>
    <head>
        <title>Starbuzz Coffee</title>
        <style type="text/css">

        </style>
    </head>

    <body>
        <h1>Starbuzz Coffee Beverages</h1>

        <h2>House Blend, $1.49</h2>
        <p>A smooth, mild blend of coffees from Mexico, Bolivia and
            Guatemala.</p>

        <h2>Mocha Caffe Latte, $2.35</h2>
        <p>Espresso, steamed milk and chocolate syrup.</p>

        <h2>Cappuccino, $1.89</h2>
        <p>A mixture of espresso, steamed milk and milk foam.</p>

        <h2>Chai Tea, $1.85</h2>
        <p>A spicy drink made with black tea, spices, milk and honey.</p>
    </body>
</html>
```

there are no Dumb Questions

Q: An element can have an "attribute?" What does that mean?

A: Attributes give you a way to provide additional information about an element. Like, if you have a style element, the attribute allows you to say exactly what kind of style you're talking about. You'll be seeing a lot more attributes for various elements; just remember they give you some extra info about the element.

Q: Why do I have to specify the type of the style, "text/css", as an attribute of the style? Are there other kinds of style?

A: There aren't currently any other styles that work with today's browsers, but those designers of HTML are always planning ahead and anticipate that there may be other types of style in the future. Personally, we're holding our breath for the <style type="50sKitsch"> style.

Giving Starbuzz some style...

Now that you've got a **<style>** element in the HTML head, all you need to do is supply some CSS to give the page a little pizazz. Below you'll find some CSS already "baked" for you. Whenever you see the  logo, you're seeing HTML and CSS that you should type in as-is. Trust us. You'll learn how the markup works *later*, after you've seen what it can do.

So, take a look at the CSS and then add it to your "index.html" file. Once you've got it typed in, save your file.

Ready Bake CSS

```html
<html>
    <head>
        <title>Starbuzz Coffee</title>
        <style type="text/css">
            body {
                background-color: #d2b48c;
                margin-left: 20%;
                margin-right: 20%;
                border: 1px dotted gray;
                padding: 10px 10px 10px 10px;
                font-family: sans-serif;
            }
        </style>
    </head>

    <body>
        <h1>Starbuzz Coffee Beverages</h1>

        <h2>House Blend, $1.49</h2>
        <p>A smooth, mild blend of coffees from Mexico, Bolivia and
            Guatemala.</p>

        <h2>Mocha Caffe Latte, $2.35</h2>
        <p>Espresso, steamed milk and chocolate syrup.</p>

        <h2>Cappuccino, $1.89</h2>
        <p>A mixture of espresso, steamed milk and milk foam.</p>

        <h2>Chai Tea, $1.85</h2>
        <p>A spicy drink made with black tea, spices, milk and honey.</p>
    </body>
</html>
```

CSS uses a syntax that is totally different from HTML.

Cruisin' with style...

It's time for another test drive, so reload your "index.html" file again.
This time you'll see the Starbuzz Web page has a whole new look.

Background color is now tan.

Now we have margins around the content.

We've got a gray border around the content as well...

There's now some padding between the content and the border (on all sides).

We're using a different font for a cleaner look.

Margin

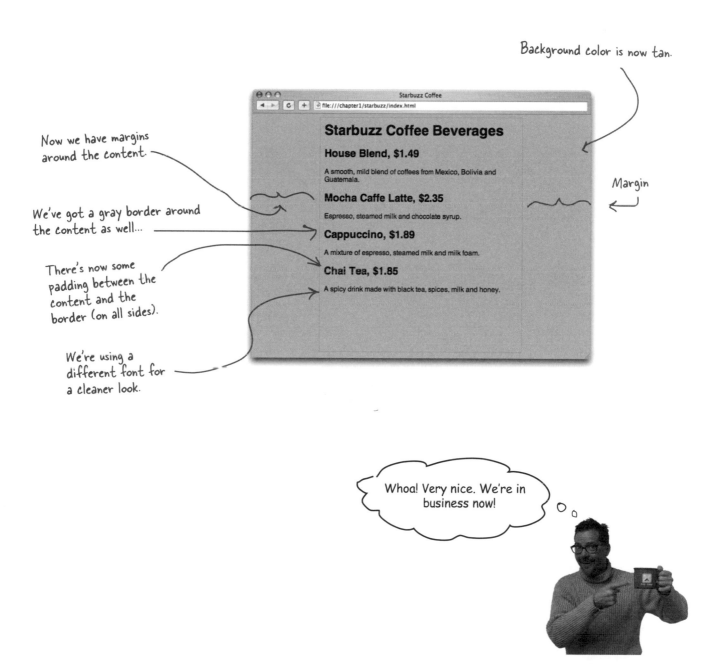

Whoa! Very nice. We're in business now!

WHO DOES WHAT?

Even though you've just glanced at CSS, you've already begun to see what it can do. Match each line in the style definition to what it does.

`background-color: #d2b48c;`

Defines the font to use for text.

`margin-left: 20%;`
`margin-right: 20%;`

Defines a border around the body that is dotted and the color gray.

`border: 1px dotted gray;`

Sets the left and right margins to take up 20% of the page each.

`padding: 10px 10px 10px 10px;`

Sets the background color to a tan color.

`font-family: sans-serif;`

Creates some padding around the body of the page.

there are no Dumb Questions

Q: **CSS looks like a totally different language than HTML. Why have two languages? That's just more for me to learn, right?**

A: You are quite right that HTML and CSS are completely different languages, but that is because they have very different jobs. Just like you wouldn't use English to balance your checkbook, or Math to write a poem, you don't use CSS to create structure or HTML to create style because that's not what they were designed for. While it does mean you need to learn two languages, you'll discover that because each language is good at what it does, this is actually easier than if you had to use one language to do both jobs.

Q: **#d2b48c doesn't look like a color. How is #d2b48c the color "tan"?**

A: There are a few different ways to specify colors with CSS. The most popular is called a "hex code", which is what #d2b48c is. This really is a tan color. For now, just go with it, and we'll be showing you exactly how #d2b48c is a color a little later.

Q: **Why is there a "body" in front of the CSS rules? What does that mean?**

A: The "body" in the CSS means that all the CSS between the "{" and "}" applies to content within the HTML **<body>** element. So when you set the font to sans-serif, you're saying that the default font within the body of your page should be sans-serif.

We'll go into a lot more detail about how CSS works shortly, so keep reading. Soon, you'll see that you can be a lot more specific about how you apply these rules, and by doing so you can create some pretty cool designs.

Exercise

Now that you've put a little style in the Starbuzz "index.html" page, go ahead and update your "mission.html" page to have the same style.

1 Write the HTML for the "mission.html" page below, and then add the new CSS.

2 Update your "mission.html" file to include the new CSS.

3 Once you've done that, reload "mission.html" in your browser.

4 Make sure your mission page looks like ours, at the end of the chapter.

Fireside Chats

HTML

Greetings CSS; I'm glad you're here because I've been wanting to clear up some confusion about us.

Lots of people think that my tags tell the browsers how to *display* the content. It's just not true! I'm all about *structure*, not presentation.

Well, you can see how some people might get confused; after all, it's possible to use HTML without CSS and still get a decent-looking page.

Hey, I'm pretty powerful too. Having your content structured is much more important than having it look good. Style is so superficial; it's the structure of the content that matters.

Whoa, what an ego! Well I guess I shouldn't expect anything else from you – you're just trying to make a fashion statement with all that style you keep talking about.

CSS

Really? What kind of confusion?

Heck yeah - I don't want people giving you credit for my work!

"Decent" might be overstating it a bit, don't you think? I mean, the way most browsers display straight HTML looks kinda crappy. People need to learn how powerful CSS is and how easily I can give their web pages great style.

Get real! Without me web pages would be pretty damn boring. Not only that, take away the ability to style pages and no one is going to take your pages seriously. Everything is going to look clumsy and unprofessional.

HTML

CSS

Fashion statement? Good design and layout can have a huge effect on how readable and usable pages are. And you should be happy that my flexible style rules allow designers to do all kinds of interesting things with your elements without messing up your structure.

Right. In fact we're totally different languages, which is good because I wouldn't want any of your style designers messing with my structure elements.

Don't worry, we're living in separate universes.

Yea, that is obvious to me any time I look at CSS – talk about an alien language.

Yeah, like HTML can be called a language? Who has ever seen such a clunky thing with all those tags?

Millions of web writers would disagree with you. I've got a nice clean syntax that fits right in with the content.

Just take a look at CSS; it's so elegant and simple, no goofy angle brackets <around> <everything>. <See> <I> <can><talk> <just><like><Mr.><HTML><,><look><at> <me><!>

Hey stupid, ever heard of closing tags?

Just notice that no matter where you go, I've got you surrounded by <style> tags. Good luck escaping!

Ha! I'll show you... because, guess what? I *can* escape...

Not only is this one fine cup of House Blend, but now we've got a web page to tell all our customers about our coffees. Excellent work.

I've got some bigger ideas for the future; in the meantime, can you start thinking about how we are going to get these pages on the Internet so other people can see them?

BULLET POINTS

- HTML and CSS are the languages we use to create web pages.

- Web servers store and serve Web pages, which are created from HTML and CSS. Browsers retrieve pages and render their content based on the HTML and CSS.

- HTML is an abbreviation for HyperText Markup Language and is used to structure your web page.

- CSS is an abbreviation for Cascading Style Sheets, and is used to control the presentation of your HTML.

- Using HTML we mark up content with tags to provide structure. We call matching tags, and their enclosed content, elements.

- An element is composed of three parts: an opening tag, content and a closing tag. There are a few elements, like <img>, that are an exception to this rule.

- Opening tags can have attributes. We've seen one already: type.

- Closing tags have a "/" after the left angle bracket, in front of the tag name to distinguish them as closing tags.

- Your pages should always have an <html> element along with a <head> element and a <body> element.

- Information about the Web page goes into the <head> element.

- What you put into the <body> element is what you see in the browser.

- Most whitespace (tabs, returns, spaces) are ignored by the browser, but you can use these to make your HTML more readable (to you).

- CSS can be added to an HTML Web page by putting the CSS rules inside the <style> element. The <style> element should always be inside the <head> element.

- You specify the style characteristics of the elements in your HTML using CSS.

HTMLcross

It's time to sit back and give your left brain something to do. It's your standard crossword; all of the solution words are from this chapter.

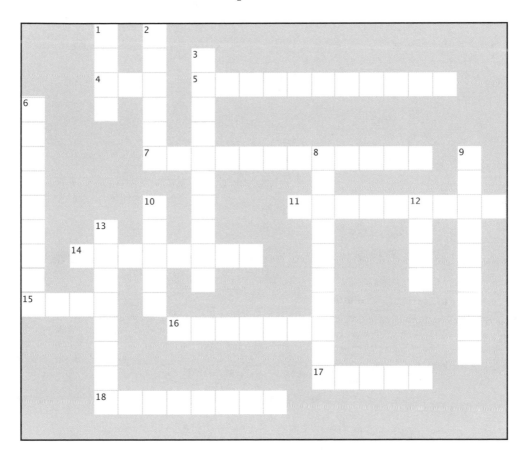

Across

4. We emphasized this.
5. Always separate these in HTML.
7. CSS is used when you need to control this.
11. You markup content to provide this.
14. Only style available.
15. About your web page.
16. Two tags and content.
17. You define presentation through this tag.
18. Company that launched your web career.

Down

1. What you see in your page.
2. The "M" in HTML.
3. Browsers ignore this.
6. Style we're all waiting on.
8. Tags can have these to provide additional information.
9. Purpose of <p> element.
10. Appears at the top of the browser for each page.
12. Opening and closing.
13. There are six of these.

Sharpen your pencil
Solution

Go ahead and mark up the napkin (using your pencil) with any structure you see, and add anything that is missing.

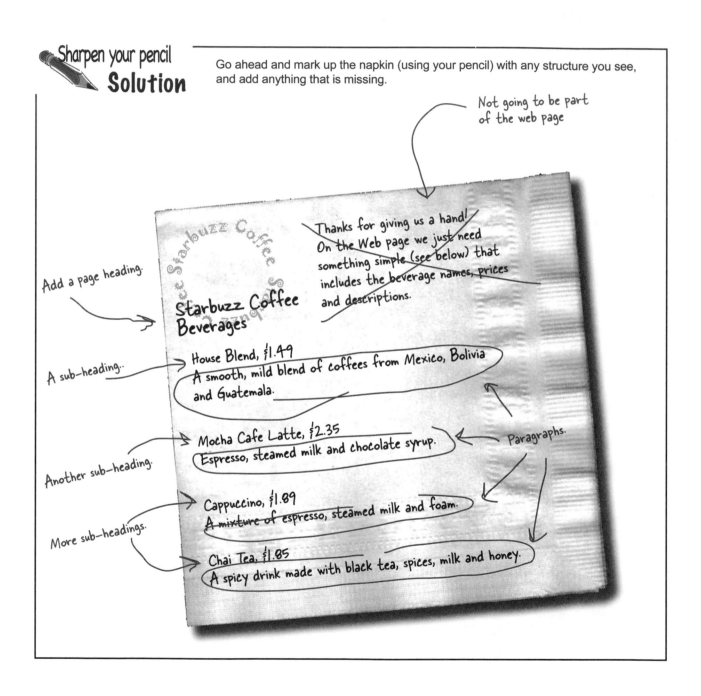

Not going to be part of the web page

Add a page heading.

A sub-heading.

Another sub-heading.

More sub-headings.

Paragraphs.

~~Thanks for giving us a hand! On the Web page we just need something simple (see below) that includes the beverage names, prices and descriptions.~~

Starbuzz Coffee Beverages

House Blend, $1.49
A smooth, mild blend of coffees from Mexico, Bolivia and Guatemala.

Mocha Cafe Latte, $2.35
Espresso, steamed milk and chocolate syrup.

Cappuccino, $1.89
A mixture of espresso, steamed milk and foam.

Chai Tea, $1.85
A spicy drink made with black tea, spices, milk and honey.

Markup Magnets Solution

Your job is to add some structure to the text from the Starbuzz napkin. Use the fridge magnets at the bottom of the page to mark up the text so that you've indicated which parts are headings, subheadings and paragraph text. We've already done a few to get you started. You won't need all the magnets below to complete the job; some will be left over.

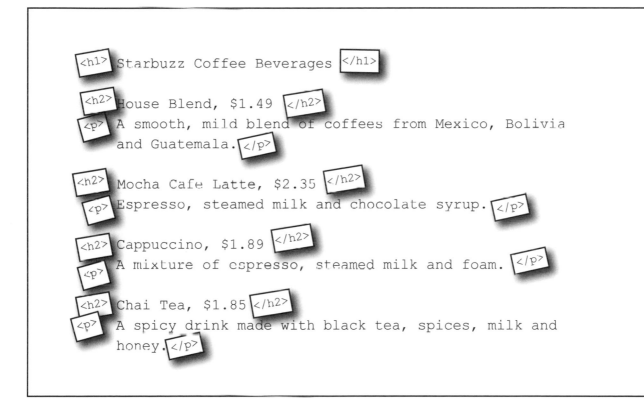

```
<h1> Starbuzz Coffee Beverages </h1>

<h2> House Blend, $1.49 </h2>
<p> A smooth, mild blend of coffees from Mexico, Bolivia
and Guatemala. </p>

<h2> Mocha Cafe Latte, $2.35 </h2>
<p> Espresso, steamed milk and chocolate syrup. </p>

<h2> Cappuccino, $1.89 </h2>
<p> A mixture of espresso, steamed milk and foam. </p>

<h2> Chai Tea, $1.85 </h2>
<p> A spicy drink made with black tea, spices, milk and
honey. </p>
```

`<h1>` `</h1>`

Exercise
Solutions

```
<html>
  <head>
    <title>Starbuzz Coffee's Mission</title>
  </head>
  <body>
    <h1>Starbuzz Coffee's Mission</h1>
    <p>To provide all the caffeine that you need to
power your life.</p>
    <p>Just drink it.</p>
  </body>
</html>
```

Here's the HTML.

Starbuzz Coffee's Mission

To provide all the caffeine that you need to power your life.

Just drink it.

Here's the HTML
displayed in a browser.

Exercise Solutions

mission.html

```html
<html>

  <head>

    <title>Starbuzz Coffee's Mission</title>
    <style type="text/css">
      body {
            background-color: #d2b48c;
            margin-left: 20%;
            margin-right: 20%;
            border: 1px dotted gray;
            padding: 10px 10px 10px 10px;
            font-family: sans-serif;
      }
    </style>

  </head>

  <body>

    <h1>Starbuzz Coffee's Mission</h1>

    <p>To provide all the caffeine that you need to power your life.</p>

    <p>Just drink it.</p>

  </body>

</html>
```

Exercise Solutions

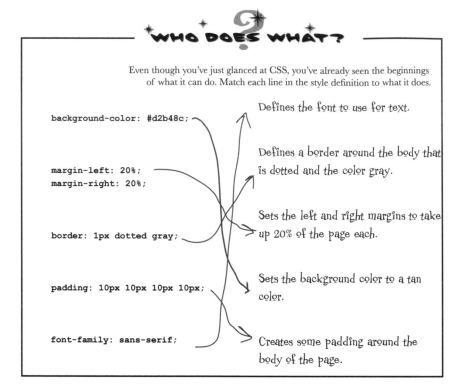

Even though you've just glanced at CSS, you've already seen the beginnings of what it can do. Match each line in the style definition to what it does.

```
background-color: #d2b48c;
```

```
margin-left: 20%;
margin-right: 20%;
```

```
border: 1px dotted gray;
```

```
padding: 10px 10px 10px 10px;
```

```
font-family: sans-serif;
```

Defines the font to use for text.

Defines a border around the body that is dotted and the color gray.

Sets the left and right margins to take up 20% of the page each.

Sets the background color to a tan color.

Creates some padding around the body of the page.

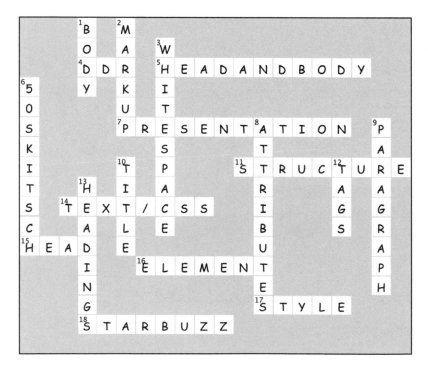

		¹B	²M		³W							
		O	A		W							
		⁴D D R	⁵H E A D A N D B O D Y
	⁶S	Y	K	I
	O		U	I
	S		⁷P R E S E N T ⁸A T I O N	⁹P
	K		S	T	A
	I	¹⁰T	P	¹¹S T R U C ¹²T U R E
	T	¹³H I	A	R	A	A
¹⁴T E X T / C S S	A	T	C	I	G	G
	C	L	E	B	S	R
¹⁵H E A D	E	U	A
	I	¹⁶E L E M E N T	P
	N	E	H
	G	¹⁷S T Y L E
¹⁸S T A R B U Z Z

Meeting the 'HT' in HTML

Did someone say "hypertext?" What's that? Oh, only the *entire basis* of the Web. In Chapter 1 we kicked the tires of HTML and found it to be a nice *markup language* (the 'ML' in HTML) for describing the structure of Web pages. Now we're going to check out the 'HT' in HTML, *hypertext*, which will let us break free of a single page and link to other pages. Along the way we're going to meet a powerful new element, the <a> element, and learn how being "relative" is a groovy thing. So, fasten your seat belts – you're about to learn some hypertext.

Head First Lounge, New and Improved

Remember the Head First Lounge? Great site, but wouldn't it be nice if customers could view a list of the refreshing elixirs? Even better, we should give customers some real driving directions so they can find the place.

Here's the new and improved page.

The "elixirs" link points to a page with a full list of elixir selections.

We've added links to two new pages, one for elixirs and one for driving directions.

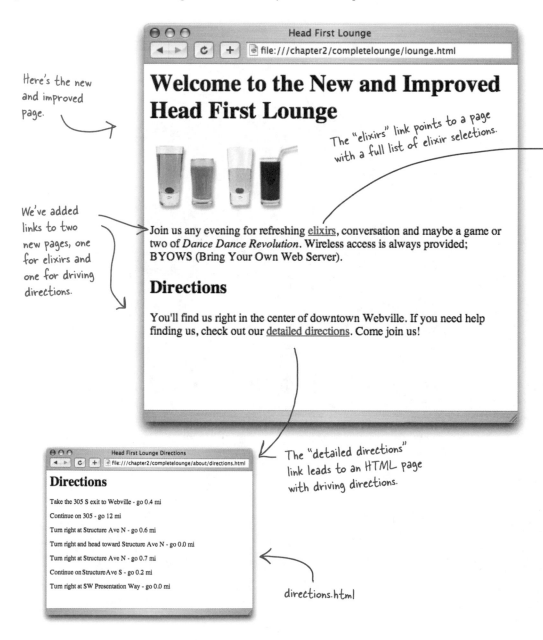

The "detailed directions" link leads to an HTML page with driving directions.

directions.html

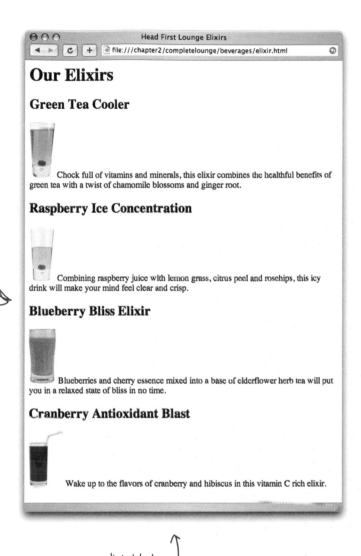

A page listing some refreshing and healthy drinks. Feel free to grab one before going on.

elixir.html

Creating the new and improved lounge in three steps...

Let's rework the original Head First Lounge page so it links to the two new pages.

1 The first step is easy because we've already created the "directions.html" and "elixir.html" files for you. You'll find them in the source files for the book, which are available at http://www.headfirstlabs.com.

2 Next you're going to edit the "lounge.html" file and add in the HTML needed to link to "directions.html" and "elixir.html".

3 Last, you'll give the pages a test drive and try out your new links. When you get back we'll sit down and look at how it all works.

Flip the page and let's get started...

Creating the new lounge

❶ Grab the source files

Go ahead and grab the source files from http://www.headfirstlabs.com. Once you've downloaded them, look under the folder "chapter2/lounge" and you'll find "lounge.html", "elixir.html", and "directions.html" (and a bunch of image files).

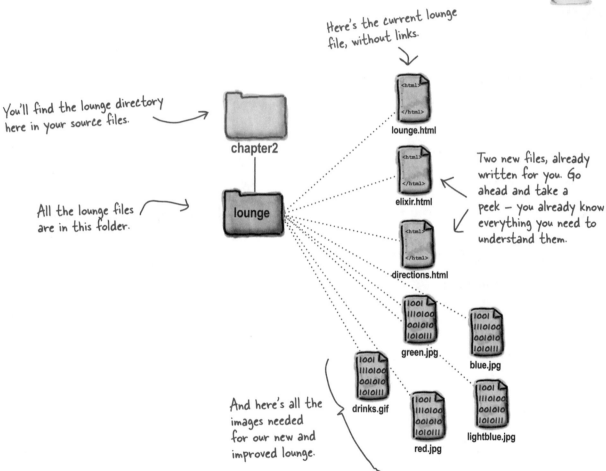

Here's the current lounge file, without links.

You'll find the lounge directory here in your source files.

All the lounge files are in this folder.

Two new files, already written for you. Go ahead and take a peek — you already know everything you need to understand them.

And here's all the images needed for our new and improved lounge.

chapter2

lounge

lounge.html

elixir.html

directions.html

green.jpg

blue.jpg

drinks.gif

red.jpg

lightblue.jpg

⚛ **BRAIN POWER**

The Head First Lounge is already growing; do you think that keeping all the site's files in a single directory is a good way to organize the site? What would you do differently?

❷ Edit lounge.html

Open "lounge.html" in your editor. Add the new text and HTML that is highlighted below.
Go ahead and type this in; we'll come back and see how it all works on the next page.

```
<html>
  <head>
    <title>Head First Lounge</title>
  </head>
  <body>
    <h1>Welcome to the New and Improved Head First Lounge</h1>
    <img src="drinks.gif">
    <p>
        Join us any evening for
        refreshing <a href="elixir.html">elixirs</a>,
        conversation and maybe a game or two of
        <em>Dance Dance Revolution</em>.
        Wireless access is always provided;
        BYOWS (Bring your own web server).
    </p>
    <h2>Directions</h2>
    <p>
        You'll find us right in the center of downtown Webville.
        If you need help finding us, check out
        our <a href="directions.html">detailed directions</a>.
        Come join us!
    </p>
  </body>
</html>
```

Let's add "New and Improved" to the heading.

Here's where we add the HTML for the link to the elixirs.

To create links we use the <a> element; we'll take a look at how this element works in just a sec...

We need to add some text here to point customers to the new directions.

And here's where we add the link to the directions, again using an <a> element.

❸ Save lounge.html and give it a test drive.

When you're finished with the changes, save the file "lounge.html" and open it in
your browser. Here are a few things to try...

❶ Click on the elixir link and the new elixir page will display.

**❷ Click on the browser's back button and "lounge.html"
should be displayed again.**

**❸ Click on the directions link and the new directions page
will display.**

Okay, I've loaded the new lounge page, clicked the links, and everything worked. But, I want to make sure I understand how the HTML works.

What did we do?

1 Let's step through creating the HTML links. First we need to put the text we want for the link in an <a> element, like this:

<a>elixirs</a>   <a>driving directions</a>

The <a> element is used to create a link to another page.

The content of the <a> element acts as a label for the link. In the browser the label appears with an underline to indicate you can click on it.

2 Now that we have a label for each link, we need to add some HTML to tell the browser where the link points to:

For this link, the browser will display an "elixirs" label that, when clicked, will take the user to the "elixir.html" page.

<a href="elixir.html">elixirs</a>

The href attribute is how you specify the destination of the link.

And for this link, the browser will display a "driving directions" link that, when clicked, will take the user to the "directions.html" page.

<a href="directions.html">driving directions</a>

What does the browser do?

1 First, as the browser renders the page, if it encounters an <a> element, it takes the content of the element and displays it as a clickable link.

```
<a href="elixir.html">elixirs</a>
```

Both "elixirs" and "detailed directions" are between the opening and closing <a> tags, so they end up being clickable labels in the web page.

```
○ ○ ○                    Head First Lounge
◄ ► C +  file:///chapter2/lounge/lounge.html
```

Welcome to the New and Improved Head First Lounge

Join us any evening for refreshing elixirs, conversation and maybe a game or two of *Dance Dance Revolution*. Wireless access is always provided; BYOWS (Bring Your Own Web Server).

Directions

You'll find us right in the center of downtown Webville. If you need help finding us, check out our detailed directions. Come join us!

```
<a href="directions.html">detailed directions</a>
```

> Use the <a> element to create a hypertext link to another web page.
>
> The content of the <a> element becomes clickable in the web page.
>
> The href attribute tells the browser the destination of the link.

Behind the Scenes

2 Next, when a user clicks on a link, the browser uses the "href" attribute to determine the page the link points to.

The user clicks on either the elixirs link or...

...on detailed directions.

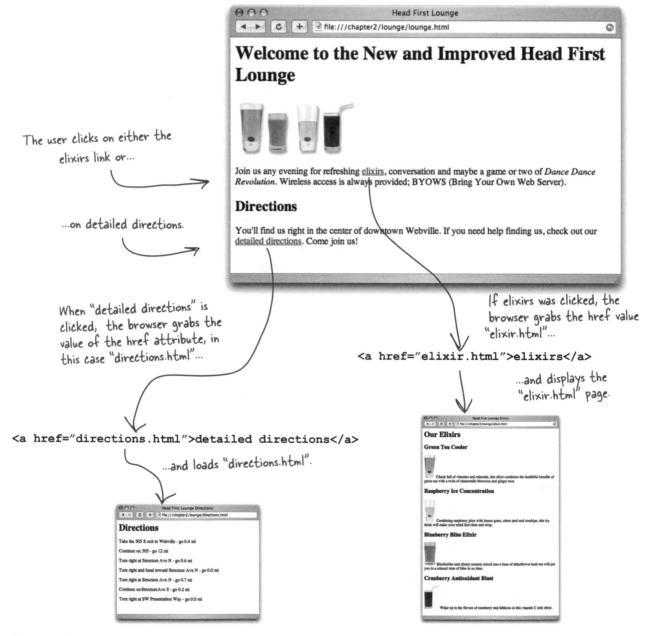

When "detailed directions" is clicked, the browser grabs the value of the href attribute, in this case "directions.html"...

If elixirs was clicked, the browser grabs the href value "elixir.html"...

`<a href="elixir.html">elixirs</a>`

...and displays the "elixir.html" page.

`<a href="directions.html">detailed directions</a>`

...and loads "directions.html".

Understanding attributes

Attributes give you a way to specify additional information about an element. While we haven't looked at attributes in detail, you've already seen a few examples of them:

```
<style type="text/css">
```
The type attribute specifies which style language we're using, in this case CSS.

```
<a href="irule.html">
```
The href attribute tells us the destination of a hyperlink.

```
<img src="sweetphoto.gif">
```
The src attribute specifies the filename of the picture an img tag displays.

Let's cook up an example to give you an even better feel for how attributes work:

What if <car> was an element?

If **<car>** was an element, then you'd naturally want to write some markup like this:

```
<car>My Red Mini</car>
```
With no attributes, all we can supply is a descriptive name for the car.

But this **<car>** element only gives a descriptive name for your car – it doesn't tell us the make, precise model, whether it is a convertible, or a zillion other details we might want to know. So, if **<car>** were really an element, we might use attributes like this:

But with attributes, we can customize the element with all kinds of information.

```
<car make="BMW" model="Mini Cooper" convertible="no">My Red Mini</car>
```

Better, right? Now this markup tells us a lot more information in an easy to write, convenient form.

SAFETY FIRST

Attributes are always written the same way: first comes the attribute name, followed by an equals sign, and then the attribute value surrounded in double quotes.

You may see some sloppy HTML on the Web that leaves off the double quotes, but don't get lazy yourself. Being sloppy can cause you a lot of problems down the road (as we'll see later in the book).

Do this (correct form)

```
<a href="top10.html">Great Movies</a>
```

attribute name   equals sign   double quote   attribute value   double quote

Not this (incorrect form)

```
<a href=top10.html>Great Movies</a>
```

WRONG – no double quotes around the attribute value.

The "href" attribute is pronounced "h - ref"...

...rhymes with "space chef".

there are no Dumb Questions

Q: Can I just make up new attributes for an HTML element?

A: No, because Web browsers only know about a predefined set of attributes for each element. If you just made up attributes, then Web browsers wouldn't know what to do with them, and as you'll see later in the book, doing this will very likely get you into trouble. When a browser recognizes an element or an attribute, we like to say that it "supports" that element or attribute. You should only use attributes that you know are supported.

Q: Who decides what is "supported?"

A: There are standards committees that worry about the elements and attributes of HTML. These committees are made up of people ~~with nothing better to do~~ who generously give their time and energy to make sure there's a common HTML roadmap that all companies can use to implement their browsers.

Q: How do I know what attributes and elements are supported? Or, can all attributes be applied to any element?

A: Only certain attributes can be used with a given element. Think about it this way: you wouldn't use an attribute "convertible" with the element <toaster>, would you? So, you only want to use attributes that make sense and are supported by the element.

We're going to be learning which attributes are supported by which elements as we make our way through the book. After you've finished the book there are lots of great references you can use to refresh your memory, such as *HTML & XHTML: The Definitive Guide* (O'Reilly).

Attributes Exposed

This week's interview:
Confessions of the href attribute

HeadFirst: Welcome, href. It's certainly a pleasure to interview as big an attribute as you.

href: Thanks. It's good to be here and get away from all the linking; it can wear an attribute out. Every time someone clicks on a link, guess who gets to tell the browser where to go next? That would be me.

HeadFirst: We're glad you could work us into your busy schedule. Why don't you take us back to the beginning... What does it mean to be an attribute?

href: Sure. Well, attributes are used to customize an element. It's easy to wrap some **<a>** tags around a piece of content, like "Sign up now!" – we do it like this: **<a>Sign up now!</a>** – but without me, the href attribute, you have no way to tell the **<a>** element the destination of the link.

HeadFirst: Got it so far...

href: ...but with an attribute you can provide additional information about the element. In my case, that's where the link points to:
<a href="signup.html">Sign up now!</a>. This says that the **<a>** element, which is labeled "Sign up now!", links to the "signup.html" page. Now, there are lots of other attributes in the world, but I'm the one you use with the **<a>** element to tell it where it points to.

HeadFirst: Nice. Now, I have to ask, and I hope you aren't offended, but what is with the name? href? What's with that?

href: It's an old Internet family name. It means "hypertext reference", but all my friends just call me "href" for short.

HeadFirst: Which is?

href: A hypertext reference is just another name for a resource that is on the Internet or your computer. Usually the resource is a Web page, but I can also point to audio, video... all kinds of things.

HeadFirst: Interesting. All our readers have seen so far are links to their own pages; how do we link to other pages and resources on the Web?

href: Hey, I gotta get back to work, the whole Web is getting gunked up without me. Besides, isn't it your job to teach them this stuff?

HeadFirst: Okay okay, yes, we're getting to that in a bit... thanks for joining us, href.

Exercise

You've created links to go from "lounge.html" to "elixir.html" and "directions.html"; now we're going to go back the other way. Below you'll find the HTML for "elixir.html". Add a link with the label "Back to the Lounge" at the bottom of the elixir page that points back to "lounge.html".

```html
<html>
  <head>
    <title>Head First Lounge Elixirs</title>
  </head>
  <body>
    <h1>Our Elixirs</h1>

    <h2>Green Tea Cooler</h2>
    <p>
            <img src="green.jpg">
            Chock full of vitamins and minerals, this elixir
            combines the healthful benefits of green tea with
            a twist of chamomile blossoms and ginger root.
    </p>
    <h2>Raspberry Ice Concentration</h2>
    <p>
            <img src="lightblue.jpg">
            Combining raspberry juice with lemon grass,
            citrus peel and rosehips, this icy drink
            will make your mind feel clear and crisp.
    </p>
    <h2>Blueberry Bliss Elixir</h2>
    <p>
            <img src="blue.jpg">
            Blueberries and cherry essence mixed into a base
            of elderflower herb tea will put you in a relaxed
            state of bliss in no time.
    </p>
    <h2>Cranberry Antioxidant Blast</h2>
    <p>
            <img src="red.jpg">
            Wake up to the flavors of cranberry and hibiscus
            in this vitamin C rich elixir.
    </p>




  </body>
</html>
```

Your new HTML goes here. ⤷

When you are done, go ahead and do the same with "directions.html" as well.

We need some help constructing and deconstructing <a> elements. Given your new knowledge of the <a> element, we're hoping you can help. In each row below you'll find some combination of the label, destination, and the complete <a> element. Fill in any information that is missing. The first row is done for you.

Label	Destination	What you write in HTML
Hot or Not?	hot.html	`<a href="hot.html">Hot or Not?</a>`
Resume	cv.html	
	candy.html	`<a href="_____">Eye Candy</a>`
See my mini	mini-cooper.html	
let's play		`<a href="millionaire.html">_____</a>`

there are no Dumb Questions

Q: I've seen many pages where I can click on an image rather than text. Can I use the <a> element for that?

A: Yes, if you put an **<img>** element between the **<a>** tags then your image will be clickable just like text. We're not going to talk about images in depth for a few chapters, but they work just fine as links.

Q: So I can put anything between the <a> tags and it will be clickable? Like, say, a paragraph?

A: Whoa now. Not so fast. Not every element can be placed inside an **<a>** element. In general you'll just be using text and images (or both) within the **<a>** element. What tags will go inside other tags is a whole other topic, but don't worry; we'll get there soon enough.

> Your work on the Head First Lounge has really paid off. With those enticing elixirs and directions, lots of people are frequenting the place and visiting the Web site. Now we've got plans for expanding the lounge's online content in all sorts of directions.

Getting organized

Before you start creating more HTML pages, it's time to get things organized. So far, we've been putting all our files and images in one folder. You'll find that even for modestly-sized Web sites, things are much more manageable if you organize your Web pages, graphics, and other resources into a set of folders. Here's what we've got now:

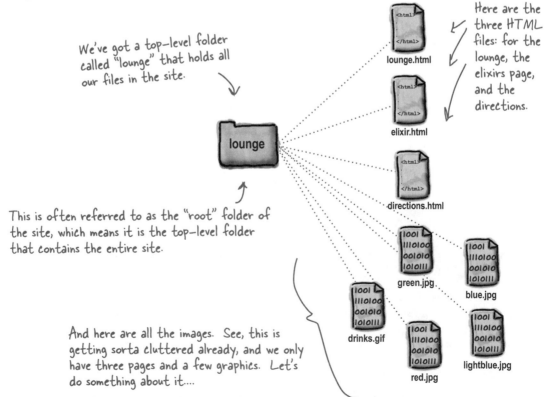

We've got a top-level folder called "lounge" that holds all our files in the site.

Here are the three HTML files: for the lounge, the elixirs page, and the directions.

lounge.html

elixir.html

directions.html

This is often referred to as the "root" folder of the site, which means it is the top-level folder that contains the entire site.

green.jpg

blue.jpg

drinks.gif

And here are all the images. See, this is getting sorta cluttered already, and we only have three pages and a few graphics. Let's do something about it....

red.jpg

lightblue.jpg

Organizing the lounge...

Let's give the lounge site some meaningful organization now.
Keep in mind there are lots of ways to organize any site; we're
going to start simple and create a couple of folders for pages.
We'll also group all those images into one place.

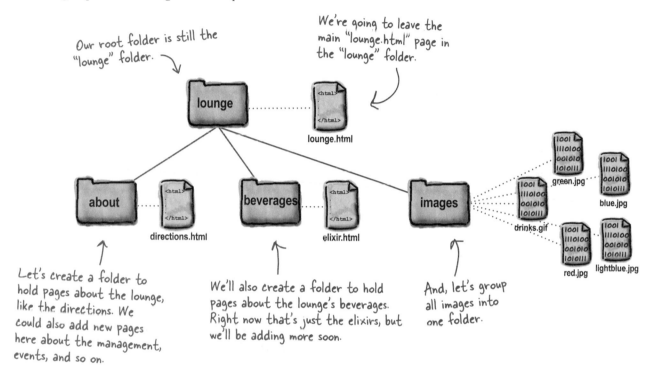

Our root folder is still the "lounge" folder.

We're going to leave the main "lounge.html" page in the "lounge" folder.

lounge

lounge.html

about

directions.html

beverages

elixir.html

images

green.jpg

blue.jpg

drinks.gif

red.jpg

lightblue.jpg

Let's create a folder to hold pages about the lounge, like the directions. We could also add new pages here about the management, events, and so on.

We'll also create a folder to hold pages about the lounge's beverages. Right now that's just the elixirs, but we'll be adding more soon.

And, let's group all images into one folder.

there are no Dumb Questions

Q: Since you have a folder for images, why not have another one called "html" and put all the HTML in that folder?

A: You could. There aren't any "correct" ways to organize your files; rather, you want to organize them in a way that works best for you and your users. As with most design decisions, you want to choose an organization scheme that is flexible enough to grow, while keeping things as simple as you can.

Q: Or, why not put an images folder in each other folder, like "about" and "beverages."

A: Again, we could have. We expect that some of the images will be reused among several pages, so we put images in a folder at the root (the top level) to keep them all together. If you have a site that needs lots of images in different parts of the site, you might want each branch to have its own image folder.

Q: "Each branch"?

A: You can understand the way folders are described by looking at them as upside down trees. At the top is the root and each path down to a file or folder is a branch.

Exercise

Now you need to create the file and folder structure shown on the previous page. Here's exactly what you need to do:

1. Locate your "lounge" folder and create three new subfolders named "about", "beverages", and "images".

2. Move the file "directions.html" into the "about" folder.

3. Move the file "elixir.html" into the "beverages" folder.

4. Move all the images into the "images" folder.

5. Finally, load your "lounge.html" file and try out the links. Compare with how ours worked below.

Technical difficulties

It looks like we've got a few problems with the lounge page after moving things around.

We've got an image that isn't displaying. We usually call this a "broken image".

And, when you click on elixirs (or detailed directions) things get much worse: we get an error saying the page can't be found.

Some browsers display this error as a web page rather than a dialog box.

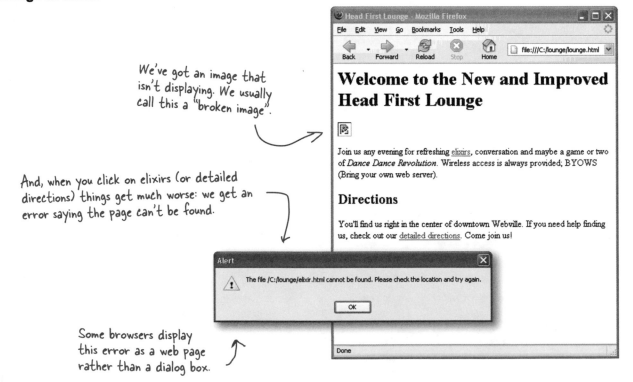

I think the problem is that the browser thinks the files are still in the same folder as "lounge.html". We need to change the links so they point to the files in their new folders.

Right. We need to tell the browser the new location of the pages.

So far you've used **href** values that point to pages in the *same folder*. Sites are usually a little more complicated, though, and you need to be able to point to pages that are in *other folders*.

To do that, you trace the path from your page to the destination file. That might mean going down a folder or two, or up a folder or two, but either way we end up with a *relative path* that we can put in the **href**.

Planning your paths...

What do you do when you're planning that vacation in the family truckster? You get out a map and start at your current location, and then trace a path to the destination. The directions themselves are *relative* to your location – if you were in another city, they'd be different directions, right?

Okay, you'd really go to Google maps, but work with us here!

To figure out a relative path for your links, it's the same deal: you start from the page which has the link, and then you trace a path through your folders until you find the file you need to point to.

There are other kinds of paths too. We'll get to those in later chapters.

Let's work through a couple of relative paths (and fix the lounge at the same time):

Linking down into a subfolder

① Linking from "lounge.html" to "elixir.html".

We need to fix the elixirs link in the "lounge.html" page. Here's what the **<a>** element looks like now:

Right now we're just using the filename "elixir.html", which tells the browser to look in the same folder as "lounge.html".

```
<a  href="elixir.html">elixirs</a>
```

② Identify the source and the destination.

When we re-organized the lounge, we left "lounge.html" in the "lounge" folder, and we put "elixir.html" in the "beverages" folder, which is a subfolder of "lounge".

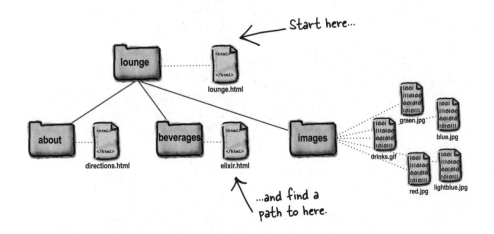

Start here...

lounge
lounge.html

about
directions.html

beverages
elixir.html

images
drinks.gif

green.jpg
blue.jpg
red.jpg
lightblue.jpg

...and find a path to here.

③ **Trace a path from the source to the destination.**

Let's trace the path. To get from the "lounge.html" file to "elixir.html", we need to go into the "beverages" folder first, and then we'll find "elixir.html" in that folder.

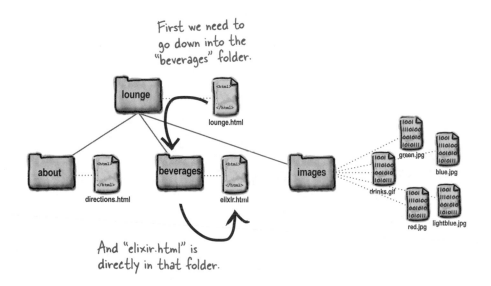

First we need to go down into the "beverages" folder.

And "elixir.html" is directly in that folder.

④ **Create an href to represent the path we traced.**

Now that we know the path, we need to get it into a format the browser understands. Here's how you write the path:

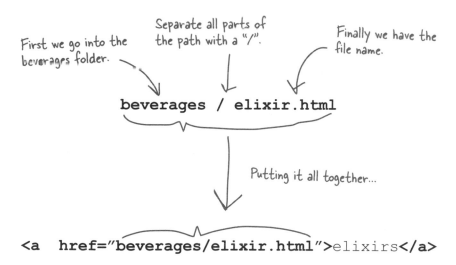

First we go into the beverages folder.

Separate all parts of the path with a "/".

Finally we have the file name.

beverages / elixir.html

Putting it all together...

`<a href="beverages/elixir.html">elixirs</a>`

We put the relative path into the href value. Now when the link is clicked on, the browser will look for the "elixir.html" file in the "beverages" folder.

Sharpen your pencil

Your turn: trace the relative path from "lounge.html" to "directions.html". When you've discovered it, complete the **\<a\>** element below. Check your answer in the back of the chapter, and then go ahead and change both **\<a\>** elements in "lounge.html."

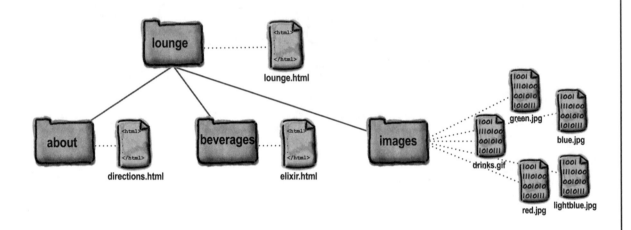

```
<a  href="_____">detailed directions</a>
```
            YOUR ANSWER HERE ⤴

Going the other way; linking up into a "parent" folder

① **Linking from "directions.html" to "lounge.html".**

Now we need to fix those "Back to the Lounge" links. Here's what the **<a>** element looks like in the "directions.html" file:

```
<a  href="lounge.html">Back to the Lounge</a>
```

Right now we're just using the filename "lounge.html", which tells the browser to look in the same folder as "directions.html". That's not going to work.

② **Identify the source and the destination.**

Let's take a look at the source and destination. The source is now the "directions.html" file, which is down in the "about" folder. The destination is the "lounge.html" file that sits above the "about" folder, where "directions.html" is located.

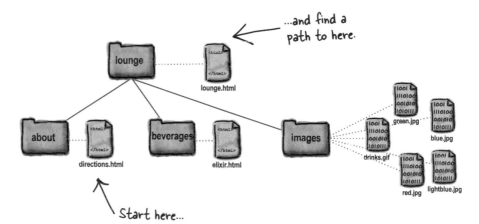

...and find a path to here.

Start here...

③ **Trace a path from the source to the destination.**

Let's trace the path. To get from the "directions.html" file to "lounge.html", we need to go up one folder into the "lounge" folder, and then we'll find "lounge.html" in that folder.

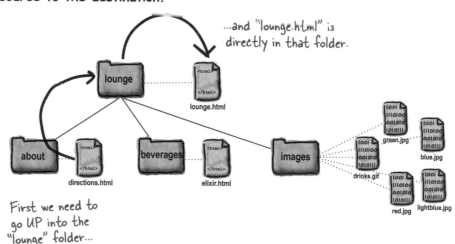

...and "lounge.html" is directly in that folder.

First we need to go UP into the "lounge" folder...

④ **Create an href to represent the path we traced.**

We're almost there. Now that you know the path, you need to get it into a format the browser understands. Let's work through this:

First you need to go up one folder. How do you do that? With a "..". That's right, two periods. Go with it, we'll explain in a sec.

Separate all parts of the path with a "/".

Finally you have the file name.

.. / lounge.html

Pronounce ".." as "dot dot".

Putting it all together...

`<a href="../lounge.html">Back to the Lounge</a>`

Now when you click on the link, the browser will look for the "lounge.html" file in the folder above.

Dot dot ~~Up~~, down, housewares, lingerie?

there are no
Dumb Questions

Q: What's a parent folder? If I have a folder "apples" inside a folder "fruit", is "fruit" the parent of "apples"?

A: Exactly. Folders (you might have heard these called directories) are often described in terms of family relationships. For instance, using your example, "fruit" is the parent of "apples", and "apples" is the child of "fruit". If you had another folder "pears" that was a child of "fruit", it would be a sibling of "apples." Just think of a family tree.

Q: Okay, parent makes sense, but what is ".."?

A: When you need to tell the browser that the file you're linking to is in the parent folder, you use ".." to mean "move UP to the parent folder." In other words, it's browser-speak for parent.

In our example, we wanted to link from "directions.html", which is in the "about" folder, to "lounge.html", which is in the "lounge" folder, the parent of "about". So we had to tell the browser to look UP one folder. ".." is the way we tell the browser to go UP.

Q: What do you do if you need to go up two folders instead of just one?

A: You can use ".." for each parent folder you want to go up. Each time you use ".." you're going up by one parent folder. So, if you want to go up two folders, you'd type "../..". You still have to separate each part with the "/", so don't forget to do that (the browser won't know what "...." means!).

Q: Once I'm up two folders, how do I tell the browser where to find the file?

A: You combine the "../.." with the filename. So, if you're linking to a file called "fruit.html" in a folder that's two folders up, you'd write "../../fruit.html". You might expect that we'd call "../.." the "grandparent" folder, but we don't usually talk about them that way, and instead say, "the parent of the parent folder," or "../.." for short.

Q: Is there a limit to how far up I can go?

A: You can go up until you're at the root of your Web site. In our example, the root was the "lounge" folder. So, you could only go up as far as "lounge".

Q: What about in the other direction – is there a limit to how many folders I can go down?

A: Well, you can only go down as many folders as you have created. If you create folders that are 10 deep, then you can write a path that takes you down 10 folders. But we don't recommend that – when you have that many folder levels, it probably means your website organization is *too* complicated!

In addition, there is a limit to the number of characters you can have in a path: 255 characters. That's a lot of characters, so it's unlikely you'll ever need that many, but if you have a large site, it's something to be aware of.

Q: My operating system uses "\" as a separator; shouldn't I be using that instead of "/"?

A: No; in Web pages you always use "/". Don't use "\". Various operating systems use different file separators (for instance, Windows uses "\" instead of "/") but when it comes to the Web, we pick a common separator and all stick to it. So, whether you're using Mac, Windows, Linux, or something else, always use "/" in the paths in your HTML.

 **BRAIN POWER**

Your turn: trace the relative path from "elixir.html" to "lounge.html" from the "Back to the Lounge" link. How does it differ from the same link in the "directions.html" file?

Answer: It doesn't, it is exactly the same.

Fixing those broken images...

You've almost got the lounge back in working order; all you need to do now is fix those images that aren't displaying.

We haven't looked at the **<img>** element in detail yet (we will in a couple of chapters), but all you need to know for now is that the **<img>** element's **src** attribute takes a relative path, just like the **href** attribute.

Here's the image element from the "lounge.html" file:

`<img src="drinks.gif">`

Here's the relative path, which tells the browser where the image is located. We specify this just like we do with the href attribute in the <a> element.

Finding the path from "lounge.html" to "drinks.gif"

To find the path, we need to go from the "lounge.html" file to where the images are located, in the "images" folder.

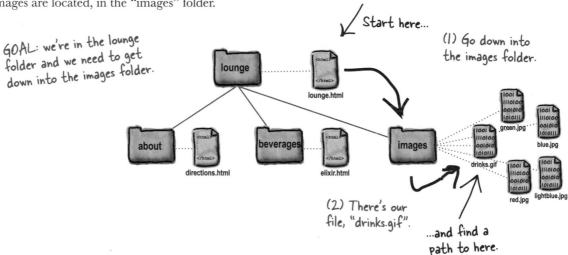

GOAL: we're in the lounge folder and we need to get down into the images folder.

Start here...

(1) Go down into the images folder.

(2) There's our file, "drinks.gif".

...and find a path to here.

So putting (1) and (2) together our path looks like "images/drinks.gif", or:

`<img src="images/drinks.gif">`

Finding the path from "elixir.html" to "red.jpg"

The elixirs page contains images of several drinks: "red.jpg",
"green.jpg", "blue.jpg", and so on. Let's figure out the path to
"red.jpg" and then the rest will have a similar path because they
are all in the same folder:

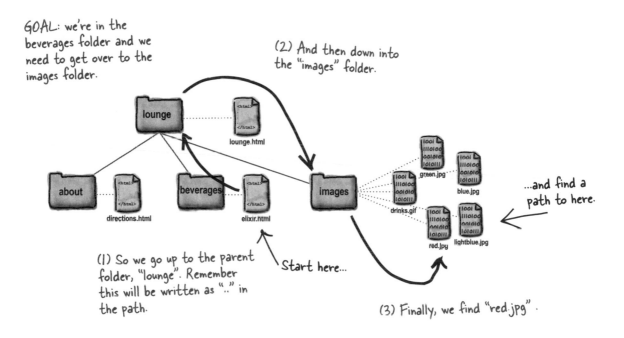

GOAL: we're in the beverages folder and we need to get over to the images folder.

(2) And then down into the "images" folder.

(1) So we go up to the parent folder, "lounge". Remember this will be written as ".." in the path.

...and find a path to here.

Start here...

(3) Finally, we find "red.jpg".

So putting (1), (2), and (3) together we get:

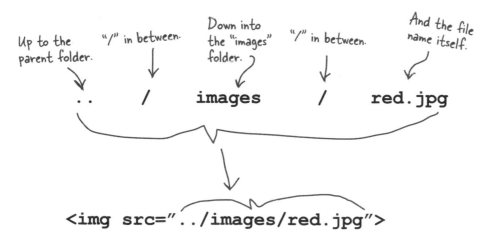

Up to the parent folder.

"/" in between.

Down into the "images" folder.

"/" in between.

And the file name itself.

`..`   `/`   `images`   `/`   `red.jpg`

`<img src="../images/red.jpg">`

Exercise

That covers all the links we broke when we reorganized the lounge, although you still need to fix the images in your "lounge.html" and "elixir.html" files. Here's exactly what you need to do:

❶ In "lounge.html", update the image **src** attribute to have the value "images/drinks.gif".

❷ In "elixir.html", update the image **src** attribute so that "../images/" comes before each image name.

❸ Save both files and load "lounge.html" in your browser. You'll now be able to navigate between all the pages and view the images.

P.S. If you're having any trouble, the folder "chapter2/completelounge" contains a working version of the lounge. Double-check your work against it.

> You did it! Now we've got organization and all our links are working. Time to celebrate. Join us and have a green tea cooler.

> And then we can take the site to the next level!

BULLET POINTS

- When you want to link from one page to another, use the **<a>** element.

- The **href** attribute of the **<a>** element specifies the destination of the link.

- The content of the **<a>** element is the label for the link. The label is what you see on the Web page. By default, it's underlined to indicate you can click on it.

- You can use words or an image as the label for a link.

- When you click on a link, the browser loads the Web page that's specified in the **href** attribute.

- You can link to files in the same folder, or files in other folders.

- A relative path is a link that points to other files on your Web site relative to the Web page you're linking from. Just like on a map, the destination is relative to the starting point.

- Use ".." to link to a file that's one folder above the file you're linking from.

- ".." means "parent folder."

- Remember to separate the parts of your path with the "/" character.

- When your path to an image is incorrect, you'll see a broken image on your Web page.

- Don't use spaces in names when you're choosing names for files and folders for your Web site.

- It's a good idea to organize your Web site files early on in the process of building your site, so you don't have to change a bunch of paths later when the Web site grows.

- There are many ways to organize a Web site; how you do it is up to you.

The Relativity Grand Challenge

Here's your chance to put your relativity skills to the test. We've got a Web site for the top 100 albums in a folder named "music". In this folder you'll find HTML files, other folders and images. Your challenge is to find the relative paths we need so we can link from our Web pages to other Web pages and files.

On this page, you'll see the Web site structure; on the next page you'll find the tasks to test your skills. For each source file and destination file, it's your job to make the correct relative path. If you succeed, you will truly be champion of relative paths.

Good luck!

Feel free to draw right on this Web site picture to figure out the paths.

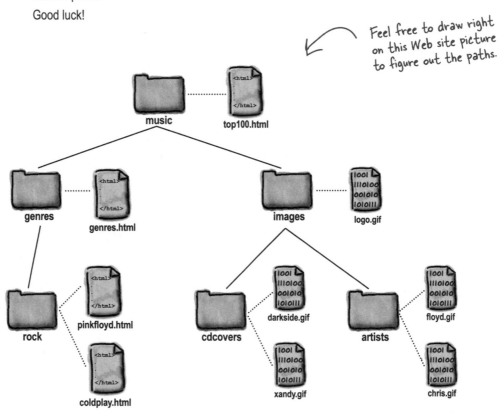

It's time for the competition to begin. Ready... set... write!

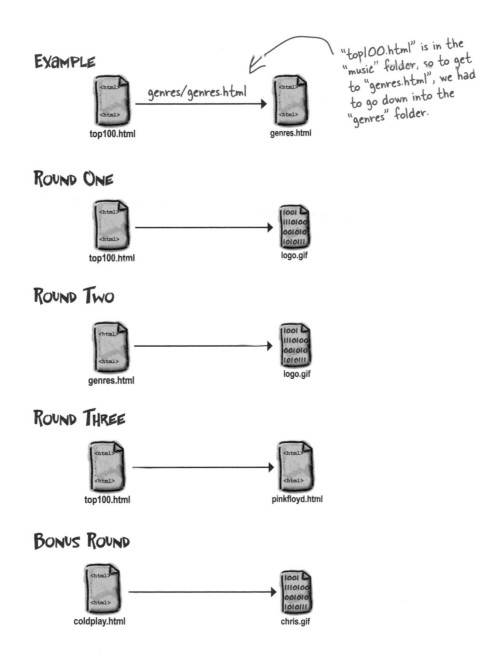

EXAMPLE

top100.html — genres/genres.html → genres.html

"top100.html" is in the "music" folder, so to get to "genres.html", we had to go down into the "genres" folder.

ROUND ONE

top100.html → logo.gif

ROUND TWO

genres.html → logo.gif

ROUND THREE

top100.html → pinkfloyd.html

BONUS ROUND

coldplay.html → chris.gif

HTMLcross

How does a crossword help you learn HTML? Well, all the words are HTML-related and from this chapter. In addition, the clues provide the mental twist and turns that will help you burn alternative routes to HTML right into your brain!

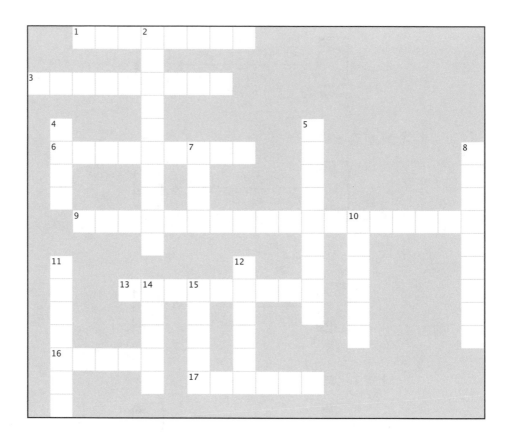

Across

1. ../myfiles/index.html is this kind of link.
3. Another name for a folder.
6. Flavor of blue drink.
9. what href stands for.
13. Everything between the <a> and </a> is this.
16. Can go in an <a> element, just like text.
17. Pronounced "..".

Down

2. href and src are two of these.
4. Hardest working attribute on the web.
5. Rhymes with href.
7. Top folder of your site.
8. The "HT" in HTML.
10. Healthy drink.
11. A folder at the same level.
12. Use .. to reach this kind of directory.
14. Text between the <a> tags acts as a _____.
15. A subfolder is also called this.

Exercise Solutions

```
<html>
  <head>
    <title>Head First Lounge Elixirs</title>
  </head>
  <body>
    <h1>Our Elixirs</h1>

    <h2>Green Tea Cooler</h2>
    <p>
            <img src="green.jpg">
            Chock full of vitamins and minera
            combines the healthful benefits of
            a twist of chamomile blossoms and
    </p>
    <h2>Raspberry Ice Concentration</h2>
    <p>
            <img src="lightblue.jpg">
            Combining raspberry juice with le
            citrus peel and rosehips, this icy
            will make your mind feel clear and
    </p>
    <h2>Blueberry Bliss Elixir</h2>
    <p>
            <img src="blue.jpg">
            Blueberries and cherry essence mixed into a base
            of elderflower herb tea will put you in a relaxed
            state of bliss in no time.
    </p>
    <h2>Cranberry Antioxidant Blast</h2>
    <p>
            <img src="red.jpg">
            Wake up to the flavors of cranberry and hibiscus
            in this vitamin C rich elixir.
    </p>
    <p>
        <a href="lounge.html">Back to the Lounge</a>
    </p>
  </body>
</html>
```

Here's the new <a> element pointing back to the lounge.

We put the link inside its own paragraph to keep things tidy. We'll talk more about this in the next chapter.

Browser window:

Our Elixirs

Green Tea Cooler

Chock full of vitamins and minerals, this elixir combines the healthful benefits of green tea with a twist of chamomile blossoms and ginger root.

Raspberry Ice Concentration

Combining raspberry juice with lemon grass, citrus peel and rosehips, this icy drink will make your mind feel clear and crisp.

Blueberry Bliss Elixir

Blueberries and cherry essence mixed into a base of elderflower herb tea will put you in a relaxed state of bliss in no time.

Cranberry Antioxidant Blast

Wake up to the flavors of cranberry and hibiscus in this vitamin C rich elixir.

Back to the Lounge

Exercise solutions

Label	Destination	Element
Hot or Not?	hot.html	`<a href="hot.html">Hot or Not?</a>`
Resume	cv.html	`<a href="cv.html">Resume</a>`
Eye Candy	candy.html	`<a href="` candy.html `">Eye Candy</a>`
See my mini	mini-cooper.html	`<a href="mini-cooper.html">See my mini</a>`
let's play	millionaire.html	`<a href="millionaire.html">` let's play `</a>`

Crossword solution:

```
   ¹R E L ²A T I V E
         T
   ³D I R E C T O R Y
         R
   ⁴H    I           ⁵S                    ⁸H
   ⁶R A S P B E ⁷R R Y    P                Y
   E       U   O         A                P
   F       T   O         C                E
         ⁹H Y P E R T E X T R E F ¹⁰E R E N C E R
         S            C    L              T
   ¹¹S          ¹²P   H    I              E
      ¹³C ¹⁴L I ¹⁵C K A B L E    X        X
   I   A    H   R        F    I        T
   B   B    I   E             R
   L ¹⁶I M A G E    L   N
   N   L        ¹⁷D O T D O T
   G
```

Sharpen your pencil
Solution

Trace the relative path from "lounge.html" to "directions.html". When you've discovered it, complete the **<a>** element below.

Here's the solution. Did you change both **<a>** elements in "lounge.html"?

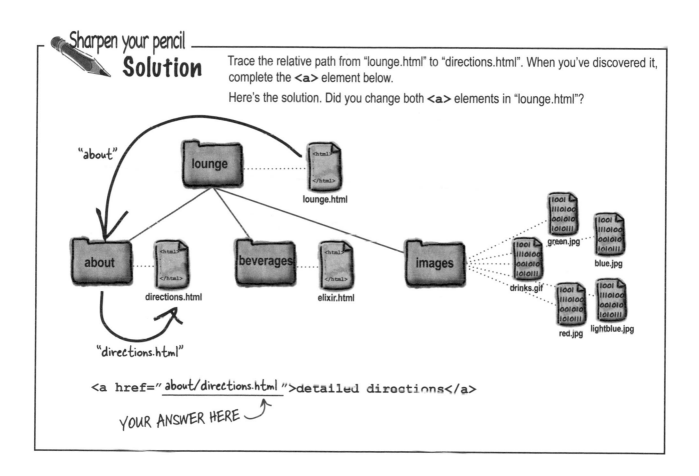

"about"

"directions.html"

<a href=" about/directions.html ">detailed directions</a>

YOUR ANSWER HERE

The Relativity Grand Challenge Solution

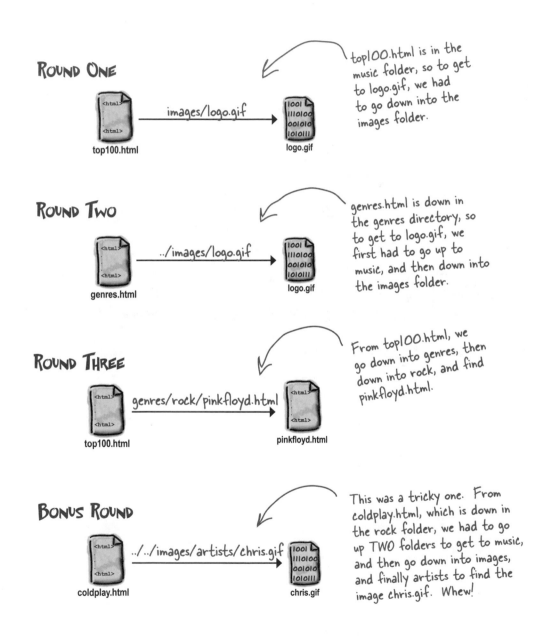

ROUND ONE

top100.html → images/logo.gif → logo.gif

top100.html is in the music folder, so to get to logo.gif, we had to go down into the images folder.

ROUND TWO

genres.html → ../images/logo.gif → logo.gif

genres.html is down in the genres directory, so to get to logo.gif, we first had to go up to music, and then down into the images folder.

ROUND THREE

top100.html → genres/rock/pinkfloyd.html → pinkfloyd.html

From top100.html, we go down into genres, then down into rock, and find pinkfloyd.html.

BONUS ROUND

coldplay.html → ../../images/artists/chris.gif → chris.gif

This was a tricky one. From coldplay.html, which is down in the rock folder, we had to go up TWO folders to get to music, and then go down into images, and finally artists to find the image chris.gif. Whew!

3 building blocks

Web Page Construction

We better find some hard hats, Betty. It's a real construction zone around here, and these Web pages are going up fast!

I was told I'd actually be creating Web pages in this book?

You've certainly learned a lot already: tags, elements, links, paths... but it's all for nothing if you don't create some killer Web pages with that knowledge. In this chapter we're going to ramp up construction: you're going to take a Web page from conception to blueprint, pour the foundation, build it, and even put on some finishing touches. All you need is your hard hat and your tool belt, as we'll be adding some new tools and giving you some insider knowledge that would make Tim "The Toolman" Taylor proud.

Tony →

What better way to enjoy my new Segway than to hit the open road? I'm riding it across the entire USA and I've been documenting my travels in my journal. What I really need to do is get this in a Web page so my friends and family can see it.

↑
Tony's Segway

Tony's Journal →

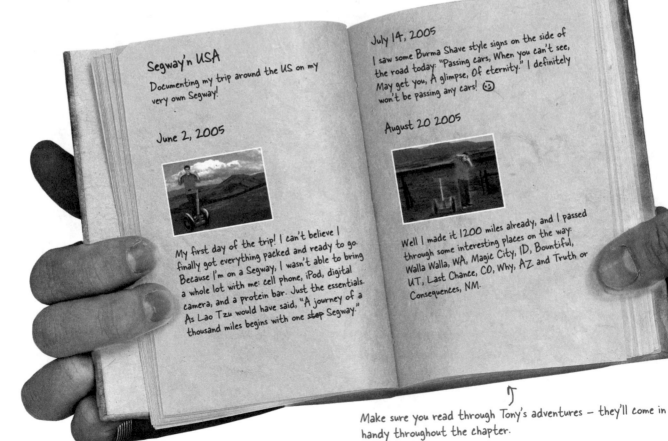

Segway'n USA
Documenting my trip around the US on my very own Segway!

June 2, 2005

My first day of the trip! I can't believe I finally got everything packed and ready to go. Because I'm on a Segway, I wasn't able to bring a whole lot with me: cell phone, iPod, digital camera, and a protein bar. Just the essentials. As Lao Tzu would have said, "A journey of a thousand miles begins with one ~~step~~ Segway."

July 14, 2005

I saw some Burma Shave style signs on the side of the road today: "Passing cars, When you can't see, May get you, A glimpse, Of eternity." I definitely won't be passing any cars! ☺

August 20 2005

Well I made it 1200 miles already, and I passed through some interesting places on the way: Walla Walla, WA, Magic City, ID, Bountiful, UT, Last Chance, CO, Why, AZ and Truth or Consequences, NM.

Make sure you read through Tony's adventures — they'll come in handy throughout the chapter.

From Journal to Web site, at 12mph

The Segway's ^recommended top speed.

Tony's got his hands full driving across the United States on his Segway. Why don't you give him a hand and create a Web page for him.

Here's what you're going to do:

1 First, you're going to create a rough sketch of the journal that is the basis for your page design.

2 Next, you'll use the basic building blocks of HTML (**\<h1>**, **\<h2>**, **\<h3>**, **\<p>**, and so on) to translate your sketch into an outline (or blueprint) for the HTML page.

3 Once you have the outline, then you're going to translate it into real HTML.

4 Finally, with the basic page done, you'll add some enhancements and meet some new HTML elements along the way.

Sharpen your pencil

STOP! Do this exercise before turning the page.

Take a close look at Tony's journal and think about how you'd present the same information in a Web page.

Draw a picture of that page on the right. No need to get too fancy, you're just creating a rough sketch. Assume all his journal entries will be on one page.

Your sketch goes here. →

Things to think about:

- Think of the page in terms of large structural elements: headings, paragraphs, images, and so on.

- Are there ways his journal might be changed to be more appropriate for the Web?

The rough design sketch

Tony's journal looks a lot like a Web page; all we need to do to create the design sketch is to get all his entries on one page and map out the general organization. It looks like, for each day that Tony creates an entry, he has a date heading, an optional picture, and a description of what happened that day. Let's look at the sketch...

Tony gave his journal a title, "Segway'n USA", so let's get that right at the top as a heading.

He also gave his journal a description. We'll capture that here as a small paragraph at the top.

Each day, Tony creates an entry that includes the date, usually a picture, and a description of the day's adventures. So, that's a heading, an image, and another paragraph of text.

Sometimes he doesn't include a picture. In this entry he just has a heading (the date) and a description of the day's events.

The third entry should look just like the first one: a heading, an image, and a paragraph.

Unlike Tony's paper journal, our page length isn't limited, so we can fit many entries on one Web page. His friends and family can just use the scroll bar to scroll through his entries...

However, notice that we reversed the order of the journal entries from newest to oldest. That way the most recent entries appear at the top where users can see them without scrolling.

Segway'n USA

Documenting my trip around the US on my very own Segway!

August 20, 2005

Well I made it 1200 miles already, and I passed through some interesting places on the way: Walla Walla, WA, Magic City, ID, Bountiful, UT, Last Chance, CO, Why, AZ and Truth or Consequences, NM.

July 14, 2005

I saw some Burma Shave style signs on the side of the road today: "Passing cars, When you can't see, May get you, A glimpse, Of eternity". I definitely won't be passing any cars!

June 2, 2005

My first day of the trip! I can't believe finally got everything packed and ready to go. Because I'm on a Segway, I wasn't able to bring a whole lot with me: cellphone, iPod, digital camera, and a protein bar. Just the essentials. As Lao Tzu would have said, "A journey of a thousand miles begins with one Segway."

From a sketch to an outline

Now that you've got a sketch of the page, you can take each section and draw something that looks more like an outline or blueprint for the HTML page...

Here we've taken each area of the sketch and created a corresponding block in our blueprint

All you need to do now is figure out which HTML element maps to each content area, and then you can start writing the HTML.

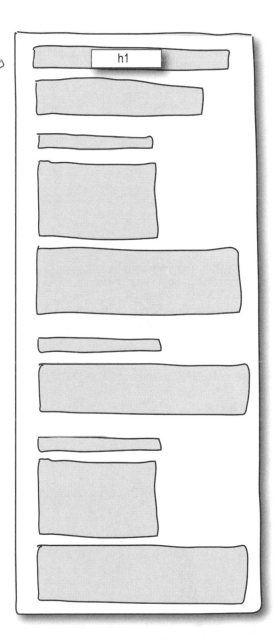

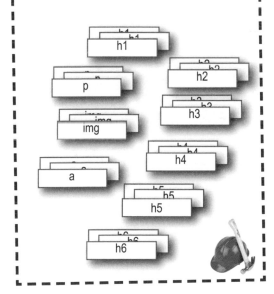

EXERCISE: WEB CONSTRUCTION

You've already figured out the major architectural areas of the page; now you just need to nail down the building materials. Use the elements below to label each area. You won't use them all, so don't worry if you have some building materials left over. And don't forget to wear your hard hat.

From the outline to a Web page

You're almost there. You've created an outline of
Tony's Web page. Now all you need to do is create
the corresponding HTML to represent the page
and fill in Tony's text.

Before you begin, remember that every Web page
needs to start with the **<html>** element and include
the **<head>** and **<body>** elements.

> Now that you know
> what "building blocks" make up
> each part of the page, you can
> translate this blueprint directly
> into HTML.

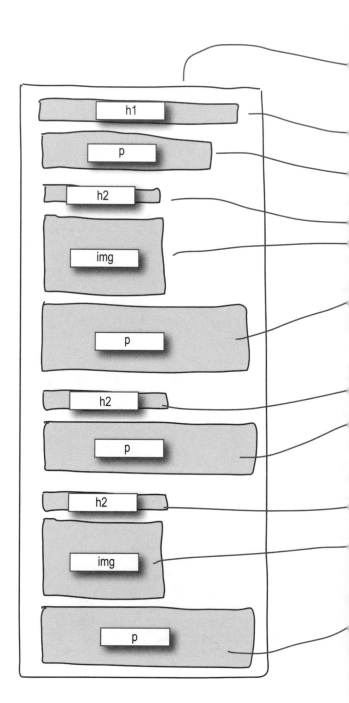

Don't forget, you always need the <html>, <head>, <title> and <body> elements.

We're using the title of the journal as the title of the Web page.

```html
<html>
  <head>
    <title>My Trip Around the USA on a Segway</title>
  </head>
  <body>

    <h1>Segway'n USA</h1>
    <p>
        Documenting my trip around the US on my very own Segway!
    </p>

    <h2>August 20, 2005</h2>
    <img src="images/segway2.jpg">
    <p>
        Well I made it 1200 miles already, and I passed
        through some interesting places on the way: Walla Walla,
        WA, Magic City, ID, Bountiful, UT, Last Chance, CO,
        Why, AZ and Truth or Consequences, NM.
    </p>

    <h2>July 14, 2005</h2>
    <p>
        I saw some Burma Shave style signs on the side of the
        road today: "Passing cars, When you can't see, May get
        you, A glimpse, Of eternity." I definitely won't be passing
        any cars.
    </p>

    <h2>June 2, 2005</h2>
    <img src="images/segway1.jpg">
    <p>
        My first day of the trip!  I can't believe I finally got
        everything packed and ready to go.  Because I'm on a Segway,
        I wasn't able to bring a whole lot with me: cellphone, iPod,
        digital camera, and a protein bar. Just the essentials.  As
        Lao Tzu would have said, "A journey of a thousand miles begins
        with one Segway."
    </p>

  </body>
</html>
```

Here's the heading and description of Tony's journal.

heading
image
description

Here's Tony's most recent entry.

Here's his second entry, which doesn't have an image.

And at the bottom, Tony's first entry, with the image "segway1.jpg".

Last, but not least, don't forget to close your <body> and <html> elements.

Go ahead and type this in. Save your file to the "chapter3/journal" folder as "journal.html". You'll find the images "segway1.jpg" and "segway2.jpg" already in the "images" folder. When you're done, give this page a test drive.

Test driving Tony's Web page

Segway'n USA

Documenting my trip around the US on my very own Segway!

August 20, 2005

Well I made it 1200 miles already, and I passed through some interesting places on the way: Walla Walla, WA, Magic City, ID, Bountiful, UT, Last Chance, CO, Why, AZ and Truth or Consequences, NM.

July 14, 2005

I saw some Burma Shave style signs on the side of the road today: "Passing cars, When you can't see, May get you, A glimpse, Of eternity." I definitely won't be passing any cars.

June 2, 2005

My first day of the trip! I can't believe I finally got everything packed and ready to go. Because I'm on a Segway, I wasn't able to bring a whole lot with me: cellphone, iPod, digital camera, and a protein bar. Just the essentials. As Lao Tzu would have said, "A journey of a thousand miles begins with one Segway."

Look how well this page has come together. You've put everything in Tony's journal into a readable and well-structured Web page.

Fantastic! This looks great; I can't wait to add more entries to my page.

Tony's calling in from the road...

Adding some new elements

You have the basic elements of HTML down. You've gone from a hand-written journal to an online version in just a few steps using the basic HTML elements **<p>**, **<h1>**, **<h2>**, and **<img>**.

Now we're going to s-t-r-e-t-c-h your brain a little and add a few more common elements. Let's take another look at Tony's journal and see where we can spruce things up a bit...

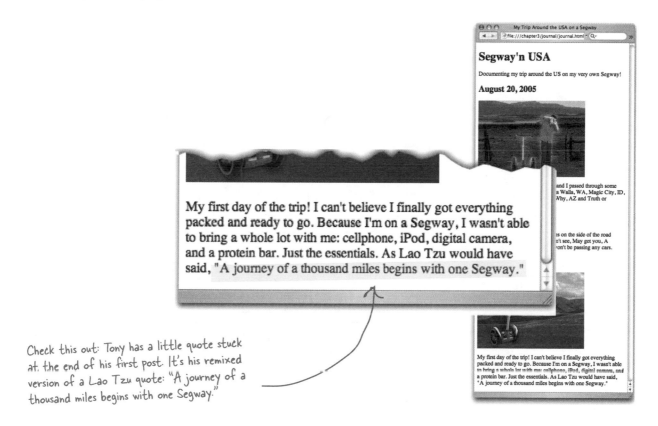

My first day of the trip! I can't believe I finally got everything packed and ready to go. Because I'm on a Segway, I wasn't able to bring a whole lot with me: cellphone, iPod, digital camera, and a protein bar. Just the essentials. As Lao Tzu would have said, "A journey of a thousand miles begins with one Segway."

Check this out: Tony has a little quote stuck at the end of his first post. It's his remixed version of a Lao Tzu quote: "A journey of a thousand miles begins with one Segway."

HTML has an element, <q>, for just that kind of thing. Let's take a look on the next page...

Meet the <q> element

Got a short quote in your HTML? The **<q>** element is just what
you need. Here's a little test HTML to show you how it works:

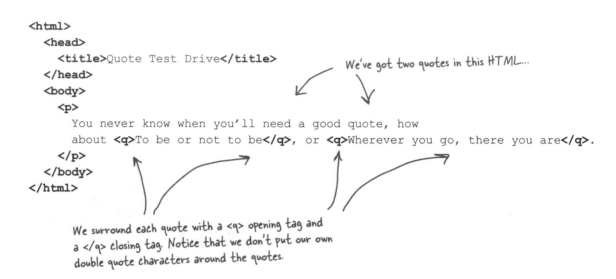

```
<html>
  <head>
    <title>Quote Test Drive</title>
  </head>
  <body>
    <p>
      You never know when you'll need a good quote, how
      about <q>To be or not to be</q>, or <q>Wherever you go, there you are</q>.
    </p>
  </body>
</html>
```

We've got two quotes in this HTML...

We surround each quote with a <q> opening tag and
a </q> closing tag. Notice that we don't put our own
double quote characters around the quotes.

...and check out the test drive...

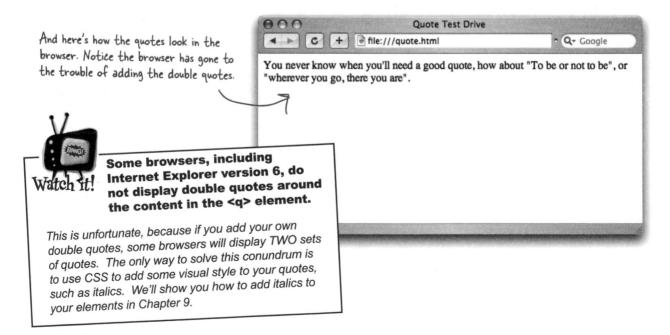

And here's how the quotes look in the
browser. Notice the browser has gone to
the trouble of adding the double quotes.

Quote Test Drive

file:///quote.html

You never know when you'll need a good quote, how about "To be or not to be", or
"wherever you go, there you are".

Watch it!

**Some browsers, including
Internet Explorer version 6, do
not display double quotes around
the content in the <q> element.**

*This is unfortunate, because if you add your own
double quotes, some browsers will display TWO sets
of quotes. The only way to solve this conundrum is
to use CSS to add some visual style to your quotes,
such as italics. We'll show you how to add italics to
your elements in Chapter 9.*

Wait a sec... you removed the double quotes and substituted a **<q>** element, which just displays double quotes? Am I supposed to be impressed? Are you *trying* to make things more complicated?

No. We're trying to make things more <u>structured</u> and <u>meaningful</u>.

There are lots of reasons people use double quotes in text, but when we use **<q>** that means something specific – it means the text of an *actual quote* (in Tony's case, a "remixed" quote).

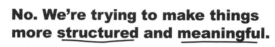

See! Using double quotes doesn't make something an actual quote.

In other words what we've done is to add some additional meaning by marking up the quote. Before we added the **<q>** element, the browser just knew it had a paragraph of text with a few double quote characters in it. Now, because we're using the **<q>** element, the browser *knows* that some of that text is a real quote.

So what? Well, now that the browser knows this is a quote it can display it in the best way possible. Some browsers will display double quotes around the text, some won't, and in instances where browsers are using non-English languages, other methods might be used. And don't forget mobile devices, like cell phones, or audio HTML browsers for the visually impaired. It's also useful in other situations, such as a search engine that scours the Web looking for Web pages with quotes. Structure and meaning in your pages are Good Things.

One of the best reasons (as you'll see when we get back to presentation and CSS later in the book) is that you'll be able to style quotes to look just the way you want. Suppose you want quoted text to be displayed in italics and colored gray? If you've used the **<q>** element to structure the quoted content in your Web pages, you'll be able to do just that.

Exercise

Here's Tony's journal. Go ahead and rework his Lao Tzu quote to use the <q> element. After you've done it on paper, make the changes in your "journal.html" file and give it a test drive. You'll find the solution in the back of the chapter.

```
<html>
  <head>
    <title>Segway'n USA</title>
  </head>
  <body>

    <h1>Segway'n USA</h1>
    <p>
        Documenting my trip around the US on my very own Segway!
    </p>

    <h2>August 20, 2005</h2>
    <img src="images/segway2.jpg">
    <p>
      Well I made it 1200 miles already, and I passed
      through some interesting places on the way: Walla Walla,
      WA, Magic City, ID, Bountiful, UT, Last Chance, CO,
      Why, AZ and Truth or Consequences, NM.
    </p>

    <h2>July 14, 2005</h2>
    <p>
      I saw some Burma Shave style signs on the side of the
      road today: "Passing cars, When you can't see, May get
      you, A glimpse, Of eternity." I definitely won't be passing
      any cars.
    </p>

    <h2>June 2, 2005</h2>
    <img src="images/segway1.jpg">
    <p>
      My first day of the trip!  I can't believe I finally got
      everything packed and ready to go.  Because I'm on a Segway,
      I wasn't able to bring a whole lot with me: cellphone, iPod,
      digital camera, and a protein bar. Just the essentials.  As
      Lao Tzu would have said, "A journey of a thousand miles begins
      with one Segway."
    </p>
  </body>
</html>
```

The Case of the Elements Separated at Birth

Identical twins were born in Webville a number of years ago and by a freak accident involving an Internet router malfunction, the twins were separated shortly after birth. Both grew up without knowledge of the other, and only through another set of freak circumstances did they later meet and discover their identity, which they decided to keep secret.

Five-Minute Mystery

After the discovery, they quickly learned that they shared a surprising number of things in common. Both were married to wives named Citation. They also both had a love for quotations. The first twin, the `<q>` element, loved short, pithy quotes, while the second, `<blockquote>`, loved longer quotes, often memorizing complete passages from books or poems.

Being identical twins, they bore a strong resemblance to each other, and so they decided to put together an evil scheme whereby they might stand in for each other now and then. They first tested this on their wives (the details of which we won't go into) and they passed with flying colors – their wives had no idea (or at least pretended not to).

Next they wanted to test their switching scheme in the work place where, as another coincidence, they both performed the same job: marking up quotes in HTML documents. So, on the chosen day, the brothers went to the other's work place fully confident they'd pull off their evil plan (after all, if their wives couldn't tell, how could their bosses?), and that's when things turned bad. Within 10 minutes of starting the work day, the brothers had both been found to be imposters and the standards authorities were immediately alerted.

How were the twins caught in the act?
Keep reading for more clues...

Looooong Quotes

Now that you know how to do short quotes, let's tackle long ones. Tony's given us a long quote with the Burma Shave jingle.

In his journal Tony just put the Burma Shave quote right inside his paragraph, but wouldn't it be better if we pulled this quote out into a "block" of its own, like this:

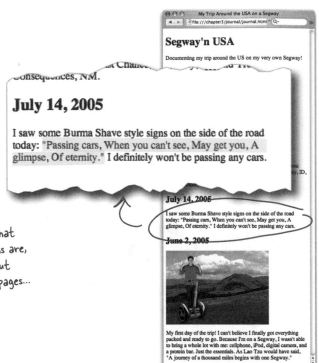

I saw some Burma Shave style signs on the side of the road today:

> Passing cars,
> When you can't see,
> May get you,
> A glimpse,
> Of eternity.

I definitely won't be passing any cars.

If you don't know what "Burma Shave" slogans are, we'll tell you all about them in just a few pages...

That's where the **\<blockquote\>** element comes in. Unlike the **\<q\>** element, which is meant for short quotes that are part of an existing paragraph, the **\<blockquote\>** element is meant for longer quotes that need to be displayed on their own.

It's important to use the right tool for the job, and the \<blockquote\> element is perfect for this job.

Adding a <blockquote>

Let's get a **<blockquote>** into Tony's online journal.

1 Open your "journal.html" file and locate the July 14th entry. Rework the paragraph to look like this:

```
<h2>July 14, 2005</h2>
<p>
    I saw some Burma Shave style signs on the
    side of the road today:
</p>
<blockquote>
    Passing cars,
    When you can't see,
    May get you,
    A glimpse,
    Of eternity.
</blockquote>
<p>
    I definitely won't be passing any cars.
</p>
```

To insert the <blockquote> element, we need to and this paragraph first.

Next we put the Burma Shave text in the <blockquote> element.

We also put each line of text on a separate line so it reads more like a Burma Shave slogan.

And finally, we need to add a <p> tag to start this paragraph after the <blockquote>.

2 Time for another test drive. Open "journal.html" in your browser and take a look at the results of your work:

<blockquote> creates a separate block (like <p> does), plus it indents the text a bit to make it look more like a quote. Just what we wanted...

But our quote isn't looking quite like we wanted because all the lines are running together. We really wanted them on different lines. Hmmm. Let's come back to that in a bit...

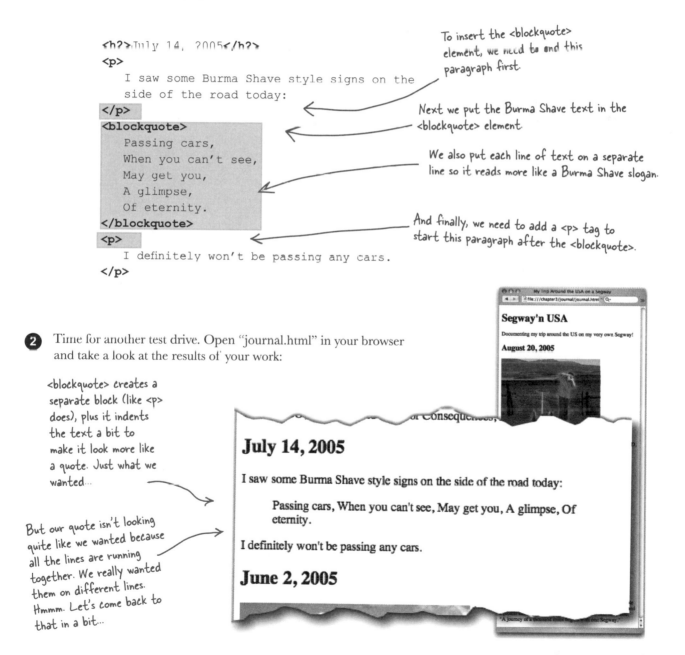

July 14, 2005

I saw some Burma Shave style signs on the side of the road today:

> Passing cars, When you can't see, May get you, A glimpse, Of eternity.

I definitely won't be passing any cars.

June 2, 2005

Q: So let me see if I have this right: I use <q> when I just want to have some quote in with the rest of my paragraph, and I use <blockquote> when I have a quote that I want to break out on its own in my Web page?

A: You've got it. In general you'll use <blockquote> if you want to quote something that was a paragraph or more, while you can use <q> anytime you just want to throw in a quote as part of your running text.

Q: Multiple paragraphs in a block quote? How do I do that?

A: Easy. Just put paragraph elements inside your <blockquote>, one for each paragraph. *Do* try this at home.

Q: How do I know what my quotes or block quotes will look like in other browsers? It sounds like they may handle it differently.

A: Yes. Welcome to the World Wide Web. You don't really know what your quotes will look like without trying them out in different browsers. Some browsers use double quotes, some use italics and some use nothing at all. The only way to really determine how they'll look is to style them yourself, and we'll certainly be doing that later.

Q: I get that the <blockquote> breaks its text out into a little block of its own and indents it, so why isn't the <blockquote> inside the paragraph, just like the <q> element is?

A: Because the <blockquote> really is like a *new* paragraph. Think about this as if you were typing it into a word processor. When you finish one paragraph you hit the return key twice and start a new paragraph. To type a block quote you'd do the same thing and indent the quote. Put this in the back of your mind for a moment; it's an important point and we're going to come back to it in a sec.

Also, remember that the indenting is just the way some browsers display a <blockquote>. Not all browsers use indentation for <blockquote>, and those that do might not in new versions. So, don't rely on a <blockquote> to look the same in all browsers.

Q: Can I combine quote elements? For instance, could I use the <q> element inside the <blockquote> element?

A: Sure. Just like you can put a <q> element inside the <p> element, you can put <q> inside <blockquote>. You might do this if you're quoting someone who quoted someone else. But, a <blockquote> inside a <q> doesn't really make sense, does it?

Q: You said that we can style these elements with CSS, so if I want to make the text in my <q> element italics and gray, I can do that with CSS. But couldn't I just use the <em> element to italicize my quotes?

A: Well, you could, but it wouldn't be the right way to do it, because you'd be using the <em> element for its effect on the display rather than because you're really writing emphasized text. If the person you were quoting really did emphasize a word, or you want to add emphasis to make a strong point about the quote, then go right ahead and use the <em> element inside your quote. But don't do it simply for the italics. There are easier and better ways to get the look you want for your elements with CSS.

Solved: The Case of the Elements Separated at Birth

How were the identical quote twins found to be imposters so quickly?

As you've no doubt guessed by now, **<q>** and **<blockquote>** were discovered as soon as they went to work and began to mark up text. **<q>**'s normally unobtrusive little quotes were popping out into blocks of their own, while **<blockquote>**'s quotes were suddenly being lost inside regular paragraphs of text. In follow-up interviews with the victims of the pranks, one editor complained, "I lost an entire page of liner quotes thanks to these wackos." After being reprimanded and sent back to their respective jobs, **<blockquote>** and **<q>** fessed up to their wives, who immediately left town together in a T-Bird convertible. But that's a whole 'nother story (it didn't end well).

The <u>real</u> truth behind the <q> and <blockquote> mystery

Okay, it's time to stop the charade: **<blockquote>** and **<q>** are actually different types of elements. The **<blockquote>** element is a *block* element and the **<q>** element is an *inline* element. What's the difference? Block elements are always displayed as if they have a linebreak before and after them, while inline elements appear "in line" within the flow of the text in your page.

Block: stands on its own

<h1>, <h2>, ..., <h6>, <p>, and <blockquote> are all block elements.

Inline: goes with the flow

<q>, <a>, and <em> are inline elements.

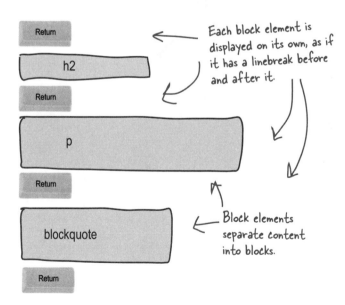

Each block element is displayed on its own, as if it has a linebreak before and after it.

Block elements separate content into blocks.

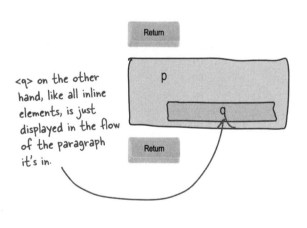

<q> on the other hand, like all inline elements, is just displayed in the flow of the paragraph it's in.

Remember: block elements stand on their own;
inline elements go with the flow.

there are no
Dumb Questions

Q: I think I know what a linebreak is; it's like hitting the carriage return on a typewriter or the return key on a computer keyboard. Right?

A: Pretty much. A linebreak is literally a "break in the line," like this, and happens when you hit the Return key, or on some computers, the Enter key. You already know that linebreaks in HTML files don't show up visually when the browser displays a page, right? But now you've also seen that any time you use a block element, the browser uses linebreaks to separate each "block".

Once again, this all sounds great, but why is all this talk of linebreaks, blocks, and inline elements useful? Can we get back to Web pages?

Don't underestimate the power of knowing how HTML works. You're soon going to see that the way you combine elements in a page has a lot to do with whether elements are block or inline. We'll get to all that.

In the meantime, you can also think about block versus inline this way: block elements are used as the major building blocks of your Web page, while inline elements mark up small pieces of content. When you're designing a page, you typically start with the bigger chunks (the block elements) and then add in the inline elements as you refine the page.

The real payoff is going to come when we get to controlling the presentation of HTML with CSS. If you know the difference between inline and block, you're going to be sipping martinis while everyone else is still trying to get their layout right.

Fireside Chats

Tonight's talk: **Inline and Block air their differences.**

Inline

Hey there, Block. I'm kind of surprised to see you here.

Because you're kind of a loner. You've always got those linebreaks hanging around keeping everyone away from you, like they're your body guards or something.

Don't get too big on yourself over there. Yeah, you're great, but where would you be without inline content? Paragraphs and headings and all that are kind of pointless without text and inline content like links.

I'll tell you right now **<a>** isn't going anywhere. He's born and bred inline. And if your pages don't have **<a>**, **<em>**, **<q>**, and all the other inline elements, you're not going to have very interesting pages, even if you have a good foundation.

Block

Why's that?

I'm just a busy guy. Block elements are really the major building blocks of all these Web sites. If you didn't have me, these pages would just crumble.

I agree **<a>** is an important element, and we've actually been trying to recruit him over to our side. But the most important part of a page is that it be designed well at the foundation, and that takes block elements. You can't just take a bunch of links and make a *real* page, now can you?

Inline

Block

We may not get **\<a\>**, but I've been telling **\<img\>** he should come over to our side for years. He'd make a great block element.

Well, a lot of people do think at first that the **\<img\>** element is block, but he's not, and he makes much more sense as an inline element. People like images mixed in with all their text and links.

We'll see about that. I'll tell you another thing, this **\<blockquote\>** versus **\<q\>** thing is silly. We've got a perfectly good block quote; why do we need **\<q\>**?

Because people like to use small quotes *inline* with their text. I've got no issue with **\<blockquote\>**, so why are you picking on **\<q\>**? You know, for thinking inline elements aren't very important, you sure are recruiting a lot of them.

Where are those linebreak body guards when I need them? Look how behind I am now I gotta get back to building some pages.

Oh, how convenient. Let me know how all that page building goes without any inline elements. I'm sure those are going to be some useful pages. Not!

I've been thinking about the Burma Shave lines. I wasn't surprised that they weren't broken up because we've said from the beginning that whitespace and linebreaks aren't displayed by the browser...

... but the only way I can think of to fix this is to put each one in a block element like a paragraph. Otherwise, how can you get the browser to add linebreaks?

What if you had an element whose only job was to give you a linebreak when you needed one?

Wouldn't that be nice? You'd actually be able to make the browser pay attention and insert some carriage returns for a change.

Turns out there is an element, the **
** element, just for that purpose. Here's how you use it:

```
<h2>July 14, 2005</h2>
<p>
    I saw some Burma Shave style signs on the
    side of the road today:
</p>
<blockquote>
    Passing cars, <br>
    When you can't see, <br>
    May get you, <br>
    A glimpse, <br>
    Of eternity. <br>
</blockquote>
<p>
    I definitely won't be passing any cars.
</p>
```

Here's the July 14th snippet from Tony's page.

Add a <br> element to any line when you want to break the flow and insert a "linebreak."

Exercise

Go ahead and add the `<br>` elements to Tony's journal. After you make the changes, save the file, and give it a test drive.

Here's what the changes should look like. Now it reads like a Burma Shave slogan should read!

Each line now has a linebreak after it.

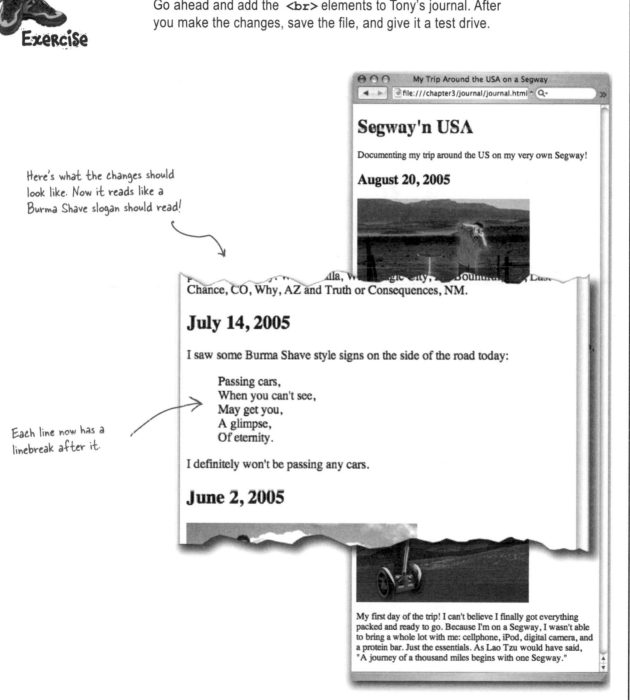

In Chapter 1 we said that an element is an opening tag + content + closing tag. So how is <br> an element? It doesn't have any content, and it doesn't even have a closing tag.

Exactly, it doesn't have any content.

The **
** element is an element that doesn't have any content. Why? Because it's just meant to be a linebreak, nothing else. So, when an element doesn't have any real content by design, we just use a shorthand to represent the element and it ends up looking like **
**. After all, if we didn't have this shorthand, you'd be writing **
</br>** every time you needed a linebreak, and how much sense does that make?

 **
** isn't the only element like this; there are others, and we have a name for them: *empty elements*. In fact, we've already seen another empty element, the **<img>** element. We'll be coming back to look at the **<img>** element in detail in a couple chapters.

Keep in mind, the reason for the shorthand isn't laziness so much as it is efficiency. It's more efficient to represent empty elements this way (efficient in typing, in the number of characters that end up in a page, and so on). In fact, after reading HTML for a while, you'll find that it is easier on your eyes too.

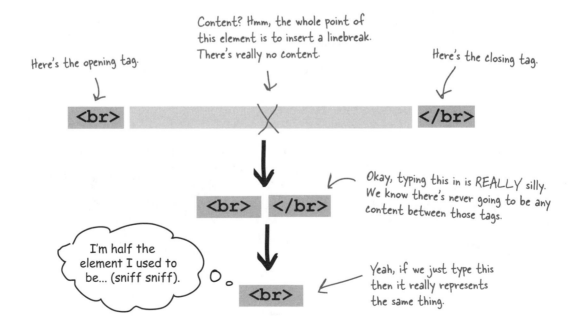

Here's the opening tag.

Content? Hmm, the whole point of this element is to insert a linebreak. There's really no content.

Here's the closing tag.

`<br>` `</br>`

Okay, typing this in is REALLY silly. We know there's never going to be any content between those tags.

`<br>` `</br>`

I'm half the element I used to be... (sniff sniff).

Yeah, if we just type this then it really represents the same thing.

`<br>`

there are no
Dumb Questions

Q: So, the only purpose of <br> is to insert a linebreak?

A: Right; the only place the browser typically inserts breaks in your content is when you start a new block element (like <p>, <h1>, and so on). If you want to insert a linebreak into your text, then you use the <br> element.

Q: Why is <br> called an "empty" element?

A: Because it has no content, as in **element = opening tag + content + closing tag**. So, it's empty because there's no content.

Q: I still don't get it. Explain why the <br> element is "empty"?

A: Think about an element like <h1> (or <p> or <a>). The whole point of the element is to tag some content, like:

<h1>Don't wait, order now</h1>

With the <br> element, the point is just to insert a linebreak into your HTML. There is no content you are trying to mark up, so it's empty. Since it is empty, we don't need all the extra brackets and markup, so we just shorten it into a more convenient form.

If an element doesn't need to mark up some text, then it is probably an empty element.

Q: Are there any other empty elements? I think <img> must be an empty element, too, right?

A: Yes, there are a few of them. You've already seen us use the <img> element, and we'll be getting to the details of this element soon.

Q: Can I make any element empty? For instance if I have a link, and don't want to give it any content, can I just write <a href="mypage.html"> instead?

A: No. There are two types of elements in the world: normal elements, like <p>, <h1>, and <a>, and then there are empty elements, like <br> and <img>. You don't switch back and forth between the two. For instance, if you just typed <a href="mypage.html">, that's not an empty element – it's an opening tag without content and a closing tag.

Elements that don't have any HTML content by design are called empty elements. When you need to use an empty element, like <br> or <img>, you only use an opening tag. This is a convenient shorthand that reduces the amount of markup in your HTML.

Meanwhile, back at Tony's site...

You've come a long way already in this chapter: you've designed and created Tony's site, you've met a few new elements, and you've learned a few things about elements that most people creating pages on the Web don't even know (like block and inline elements, which are really going to come in handy in later chapters).

But you're not done yet. We can take Tony's site from good to great by looking for a few more opportunities to add some markup.

Like what? How about lists? Check this out:

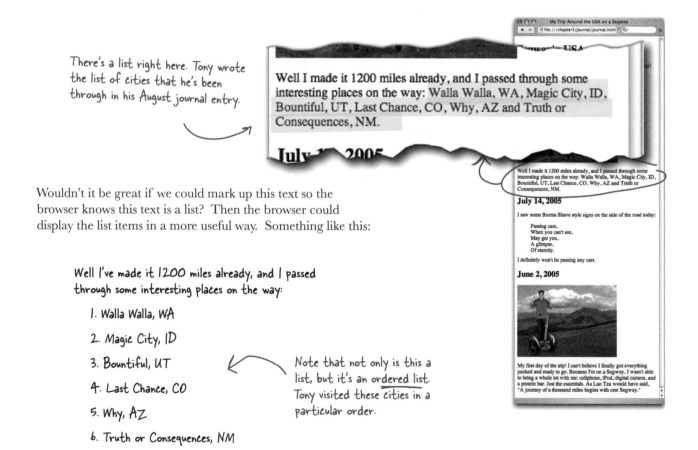

There's a list right here. Tony wrote the list of cities that he's been through in his August journal entry.

Wouldn't it be great if we could mark up this text so the browser knows this text is a list? Then the browser could display the list items in a more useful way. Something like this:

Well I've made it 1200 miles already, and I passed through some interesting places on the way:

1. Walla Walla, WA
2. Magic City, ID
3. Bountiful, UT
4. Last Chance, CO
5. Why, AZ
6. Truth or Consequences, NM

Note that not only is this a list, but it's an ordered list. Tony visited these cities in a particular order.

Of course, you <u>could</u> use the <p> element to make a list...

It wouldn't be hard to make a list using the **<p>** element. It would end up looking something like this:

```
<p>
1. Red Segway
</p>
<p>
2. Blue Segway
</p>
```

Top two preferred colors for Segway.

But there are lots of reasons <u>not</u> to.

You should be sensing a common theme by now. You always want to choose the HTML element that is closest in meaning to the structure of your content. If this is a list, let's use a list element. Doing so gives the browser and you (as you'll see later in the book) the most power and flexibility to display the content in a useful manner.

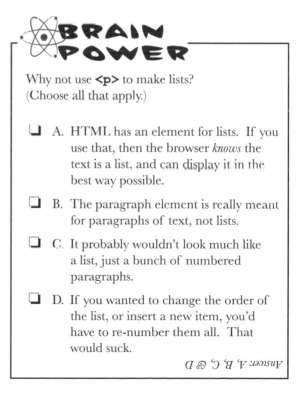

BRAIN POWER

Why not use **<p>** to make lists? (Choose all that apply.)

❏ A. HTML has an element for lists. If you use that, then the browser *knows* the text is a list, and can display it in the best way possible.

❏ B. The paragraph element is really meant for paragraphs of text, not lists.

❏ C. It probably wouldn't look much like a list, just a bunch of numbered paragraphs.

❏ D. If you wanted to change the order of the list, or insert a new item, you'd have to re-number them all. That would suck.

Answer: A, B, C, & D

Remember, it's important to use the right tool for the job, and the <p> element is NOT the right tool for this job.

Constructing HTML lists in two easy steps

Creating an HTML list requires two elements that, when used together, form the list. The first element is used to mark up each *list item*. The second determines what kind of list you're creating: *ordered* or *unordered*.

Let's step through creating Tony's list of cities in HTML.

Step One:

Put each list item in an <li> element.

To create a list, you put each list item in its own **<li>** element, which means enclosing the content in an opening **<li>** tag and a closing **</li>** tag. As with any other HTML element, the content between the tags can be as short or as long as you like and broken over multiple lines.

We're just showing a fragment of the HTML from Tony's journal here.

Locate this HTML in your "journal.html" file and keep up with the changes as we make them.

```
<h2>August 20, 2005</h2>
    <img src="images/segway2.jpg" />
<p>
Well I've made it 1200 miles already, and I passed
through some interesting places on the way:

</p>

<li>Walla Walla, WA</li>
<li>Magic City, ID</li>
<li>Bountiful, UT</li>
<li>Last Chance, CO</li>
<li>Why, AZ</li>
<li>Truth or Consequences, NM</li>

<h2>July 14, 2005</h2>

<p>
I saw some Burma Shave style signs on the side of
the road today:
</p>
```

First move the list items outside of the paragraph. The list is going to stand on its own.

...and then enclose each list item with an <li>, </li> set of tags.

Each of these <li> elements will become an item in the list.

Step Two:

Enclose your list items with either the <ol> or <ul> element.

If you use an **<ol>** element to enclose your list items, then the items will be displayed as an ordered list; if you use **<ul>**, the list will be displayed as an unordered list. Here's how you enclose your items in an **<ol>** element.

Again, we're just showing a fragment of the HTML from Tony's journal here.

```
<h2>August 20, 2005</h2>
    <img src="images/segway2.jpg" />
<p>
Well I've made it 1200 miles already, and I passed
through some interesting places on the way:
</p>

<ol>
    <li>Walla Walla, WA</li>
    <li>Magic City, ID</li>
    <li>Bountiful, UT</li>
    <li>Last Chance, CO</li>
    <li>Why, AZ</li>
    <li>Truth or Consequences, NM</li>
</ol>
```

We want this to be an ordered list, because Tony visited the cities in a specific order. So we use an <ol> opening tag.

All the list items sit in the middle of the <ol> element and become its content.

And here we close the <ol> element.

```
<h2>July 14, 2005</h2>

<p>
I saw some Burma Shave style signs on the side of
the road today:
</p>
```

BRAIN POWER

Is **<ol>** a block element or inline? What about **<li>**?

Make it Stick

HTML is for structure

Use ul or ol for lists

Wash the cat

unordered **l**ist = ul

ordered **l**ist = ol

list **i**tem = li

Taking a test drive through the cities

Make sure you've added all the HTML for the list, reload your "journal.html" file and you should see something like this:

Segway'n USA

Documenting my trip around the US on my very own Segway!

August 20, 2005

Well I made it 1200 miles already, and I passed through some interesting places on the way:

1. Walla Walla, WA
2. Magic City, ID
3. Bountiful, UT
4. Last Chance, CO
5. Why, AZ
6. Truth or Consequences, NM

Here's the new and improved list of cities.

There's a linebreak before the list starts, so <ol> must be a block element.

But there's also a linebreak after each item, so <li> must be a block element too!

Notice that the browser takes care of automatically numbering each list item (so you don't have to).

July

I saw so...

When you can't...
May get you,
A glimpse,
Of eternity.

I definitely won't be passing any cars.

June 2, 2005

My first day of the trip! I can't believe I finally got everything packed and ready to go. Because I'm on a Segway, I wasn't able to bring a whole lot with me: cellphone, iPod, digital camera, and a protein bar. Just the essentials. As Lao Tzu would have said, "A journey of a thousand miles begins with one Segway."

Sharpen your pencil

It turns out Tony actually visited Arizona *after* New Mexico. Can you rework the list so the numbering is correct?

Exercise

Here's another list from Tony's journal: cell phone, iPod, digital camera, and a protein bar. You'll find it in his June 2nd entry. This is an *unordered* list of items.

The HTML for this entry is typed below. Go ahead and add the HTML to change the items into an HTML unordered list (remember, you use **<ul>** for unordered lists). We've already reformatted some of the text for you.

When you've finished, check your answers in the back of the chapter. Then make these changes in your "journal.html" file and test.

```
<h2>June 2, 2005</h2>
<img src="segway1.jpg">
<p>
  My first day of the trip!  I can't believe I finally got
  everything packed and ready to go.  Because I'm on a Segway,
  I wasn't able to bring a whole lot with me:


      cell phone
      iPod
      digital camera
      and a protein bar


  Just the essentials.  As
  Lao Tzu would have said, <q>A journey of a
  thousand miles begins with one Segway.</q>
</p>
```

Q: Do I always have to use <ol> and <li> together?

A: Yes, you should always use <ol> and <li> together (or <ul> and <li>). Neither one of these elements really makes sense without the other. Remember, a list is really a group of items: the <li> element is used to identify each item, and the <ol> element is used to group them together.

Q: Can I put text or other elements inside an <ol> or <ul> element?

A: No, the <ol> and <ul> elements are designed to work only with the <li> element.

Q: What about unordered lists? Can I make the bullet look different?

A: Yes. But hold that thought. We'll come back to that when we're talking about CSS and presentation.

Q: What if I wanted to put a list inside a list? Can I do that?

A: Yes, you sure can. Make the content of any <li> either <ol> or <ul> and you'll have a list within a list (what we call a nested list).

```
<ol>
    <li>Charge Segway</li>          Nested list
    <li>Pack for trip
        <ul>                        Here's the
            <li>cell phone</li>     <li>. It
            <li>iPod</li>           encloses
            <li>digital camera</li> the nested
            <li>a protein bar</li>  list.
        </ul>
    </li>
    <li>Call mom</li>
</ol>
```

Q: I think I basically understand block elements and inline elements, but I'm totally confused about what elements can go inside other elements, or, as you say, what can be "nested" inside of what.

A: That's one of the hardest things to get straight with HTML. This is something you're going to be learning for a few chapters, and we'll show you a few ways to make sure you can keep the relationships straight. But, we're going to back up and talk about nesting a little more first. In fact, since you brought it up, we'll do that next.

Q: So HTML has ordered and unordered lists. Are there any other list types?

A: Actually there is another type: definition lists. A definition list looks like this:

Each item in the list has a term, <dt>, and a description, <dd>.

```
<dl>
    <dt>Burma Shave Signs</dt>
    <dd>Road signs common in the U.S. in the 1920s
and 1930s advertising shaving products.</dd>
    <dt>Route 66</dt>
    <dd>Most famous road in the U.S. highway
system.</dd>
</dl>
```

Type this in and give it a try.

Q: Burma Shave?

A: Burma Shave was a company that made brushless shaving cream in the early part of the 20th century. They began advertising their product using roadside signs in 1925, and these signs proved to be very popular (if somewhat distracting for drivers).

The signs were grouped in bunches of four, five or six, each with one line from the slogan. At one point, there were 7,000 of these signs on roadsides throughout the United States. Most are gone now, but there are still a few left, here and there.

Putting one element inside another is called "nesting"

When we put one element inside another element, we call that *nesting*. We say, "the **<p>** element is nested inside the **<body>** element." At this point, you've already seen lots of elements nested inside other elements. You've put a **<body>** element inside an **<html>** element, a **<p>** element inside a **<body>** element, a **<q>** element inside a **<p>** element, and so on. You've also put a **<head>** element inside the **<html>** element, and a **<title>** element inside the **<head>**. That's the way HTML pages get constructed.

The more you learn about HTML, the more important having this nesting in your brain becomes. But no worries – before long you'll naturally think about elements this way.

<q> nested inside <p>,
nested inside <body>,
nested inside <html>.

To understand the nesting relationships, draw a picture

Drawing the nesting of elements in a Web page is kind of like drawing a family tree. At the top you've got the great-grandparents, and then all their children and grandchildren below. Here's an example...

Simple Web page.

```
<html>
  <head>
    <title>Musings</title>
  </head>
  <body>
    <p>
        To quote Buckaroo,
      <q>The only reason
        for time is so
        that everything
        doesn't happen
        at once.</q>
    </p>
  </body>
</html>
```

Let's translate this into a diagram, where each element becomes a box, and each line connects the element to another element that is nested within it.

<html> is always the element at the root of the tree.

<html> has two nested elements: <head> and <body>. You can call them both "children" of <html>.

<body> is nested within the <html> element, so we say <body> is the "child" of <html>.

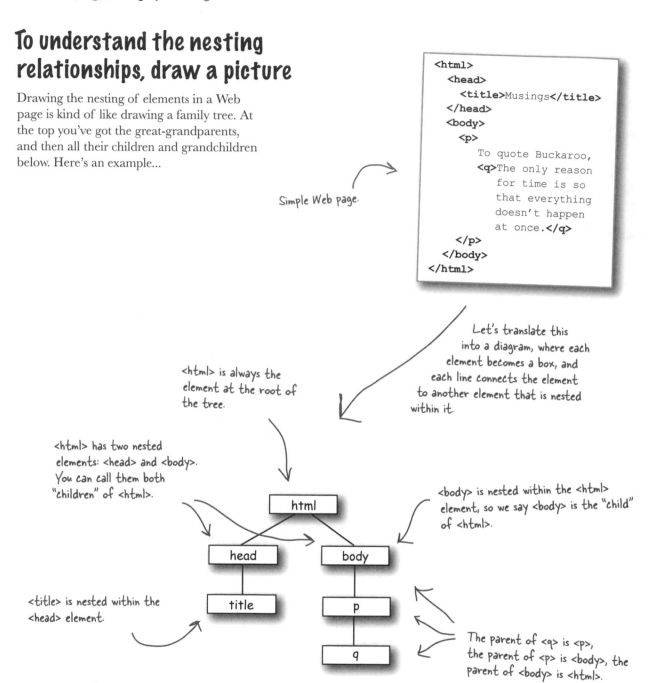

<title> is nested within the <head> element.

The parent of <q> is <p>, the parent of <p> is <body>, the parent of <body> is <html>.

Using nesting to make sure your tags match

Your first payoff for understanding how elements are nested is that you can avoid mismatching your tags. (And there's gonna be more payoff later, just wait.)

What does "mismatching your tags" mean and how could that happen? Take a look at this example:

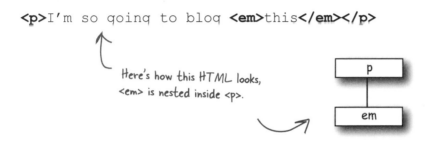

`<p>I'm so going to blog <em>this</em></p>`

Here's how this HTML looks, <em> is nested inside <p>.

So far, so good, but it's also easy to get sloppy and write some HTML that looks more like this:

`<p>I'm so going to blog <em>this</p></em>`

WRONG: the <p> tag ends before the <em> tag! The <em> element is supposed to be inside the <p> element.

Given what you now know about nesting, you know the **<em>** element needs to be nested fully within, or contained in, the **<p>** element.

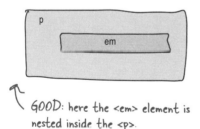

GOOD: here the <em> element is nested inside the <p>.

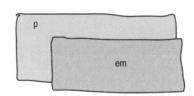

BAD: here the <em> element has leaked outside of the <p> element, which means it's not properly nested inside it.

So what?

It's okay to mess up your nesting if you like playing Russian roulette. If you write HTML without properly nesting your elements, your pages may work on some browsers but not on others. By keeping nesting in mind, you can avoid mismatching your tags and be sure that your HTML will work in all browsers. This is going to become even more important as we get more into "industrial strength HTML" in later chapters.

BE the Browser

Below, you'll find an HTML file with some mismatched tags in it. Your job is to play like you're the browser and locate all the errors. After you've done the exercise look at the end of the chapter to see if you caught all the errors.

```html
<html>
<head>
    <title>Top 100</title>
<body>
<h1>Top 100
<h2>Dark Side of the Moon</h2>
<h3>Pink Floyd</h3>
<p>
    There's no dark side of the moon; matter of fact <q>it's all dark.
</p></q>
<ul>
    <li>Speak to Me / Breathe</li>
    <li>On The Run</li>
    <li>Time</li>
    <li>The Great Gig in The Sky</li>
    <li>Money</li>
    <li>Us And Them</em>
    <li>Any Colour You Like</li>
    <li>Brain Damage</li>
    <li>Eclipse</li>
</ul>
</p>
<h2>XandY</h3>
<h3>Coldplay</h2>
<ol>
    <li>Square One
    <li>What If?
    <li>White Shadows
    <li>Fix You
    <li>Talk
    <li>XandY
    <li>Speed of Sound
    <li>A Message
    <li>Low
    <li>Hardest Part
    <li>Swallowed In The Sea
    <li>Twisted Logic
</ul>
</body>
</head>
```

Who am I?

A bunch of HTML elements, in full costume, are playing a party game, "Who am I?" They'll give you a clue – you try to guess who they are based on what they say. Assume they always tell the truth about themselves. Fill in the blanks to the right to identify the attendees. Also, for each attendee, write down whether or not the element is inline or block.

Tonight's attendees:

Any of the charming HTML elements you've seen so far just might show up!

Clue	Name	Inline or block?
I'm the #1 heading.	_____	_____
I'm all ready to link to another page.	_____	_____
Emphasize text with me.	_____	_____
I'm a list, but I don't have my affairs in order.	_____	_____
I'm a real linebreaker.	_____	_____
I'm an item that lives inside a list.	_____	_____
I keep my list items in order.	_____	_____
I'm all about image.	_____	_____
Quote inside a paragraph with me.	_____	_____
Use me to quote text that stands on its own.	_____	_____

I was just creating a Web page explaining everything I was learning from this book, and I wanted to mention the <html> element inside my page. Isn't that going to mess up the nesting? Do I need to put double quotes around it or something?

You're right, that can cause problems.

Because browsers use **<** and **>** to begin and end tags, using them in the content of your HTML can cause problems. But, HTML gives you an easy way to specify these and other special characters using a simple abbreviation called a *character entity*. Here's how it works: for any character that is considered "special" or that you'd like to use in your Web page, but that may not be a typeable character in your editor (like a copyright symbol), you just look up the abbreviation and then type it into your HTML. For example, the **>** character's abbreviation is **>** and the **<** character's is **<**.

So, say you wanted to type "The <html> element rocks." in your page. Using the character entities, you'd type this instead:

```
The &lt;html&gt; element rocks.
```

Another important special character you should know about is the **&** character. If you'd like to have an **&** in your HTML content, use the character entity **&** instead of the **&** character itself.

So what about the copyright symbol? And all those other symbols and foreign characters? You can look common ones up at this URL:

```
http://www.w3schools.com/tags/ref_entities.asp
```

or, for a more exhaustive list, use this URL:

```
http://www.unicode.org/charts/
```

there are no Dumb Questions

Q: Wow, I never knew the browser could display so many different characters. There are a ton of different characters and languages at the www.unicode.org site.

A: Be careful. Your browser will only display all these characters if your computer or device has the appropriate fonts installed. So, while you can probably count on the basic entities from the www.w3schools.com page to be available on any browser, there is no guarantee that you can display all these entities. But, assuming you know something about your users, you should have a good idea of what kind of foreign language characters are going to be common on their machine.

Q: You said that & is special and I need to use the entity & in its place, but to type in any entity I have to use a &. So for, say, the > entity, do I need to type &gt;?

A: No, no! The reason & is special is precisely because it is the first character of any entity. So, it's perfectly fine to use & in your entity names, just not by itself. Just remember to use & anytime you type in an entity, and if you really need an & in your content, use & instead.

Q: When I looked up the entities at the www.w3cschools.com, I noticed that each entity has a number too. What do I use that for?

A: You can use either the number, like &#100 or the name of an entity in your HTML (they do the same thing). However, not all entities have names, so in those cases your only choice is to use the number.

Crack the Location Challenge

Dr. Evel, in his quest for world domination, has put up a private Web page to be used by his evil henchmen. You've just received a snippet of intercepted HTML that may contain a clue to his whereabouts. Given your expert knowledge of HIML, you've been asked to crack the code and discover his location. Here's a bit of the text from his home page:

```
There's going to be an evil henchman meetup
next month at my underground lair in
&#208;&epsilon;&tau;&#114;&ouml;&igrave;&tau;.
Come join us.
```

Hint: visit http://www.w3schools.com/tags/ref_entities.asp and/or type in the HTML and see what your browser displays.

Element Soup

Use this element to mark up text you want emphasized. **<em>**

<strong> Use this element to mark up text you want emphasized with extra strength.

Whenever you want to make a link, you'll need the <a> element.

<a>

<address> This element tells the browser that the content is an address, like your contact info.

<pre> Use this element for formatted text when you want the browser to show your text exactly as you typed it.

Use this element for short quotes... you know, like "to be or not to be", or "No matter where you go, there you are."

<q>

<ul> Need to display a list? Say, a list of ingredients in a recipe or a todo list? Use the <ul> element.

An empty element for making linebreaks...

**
**

... and another one for making horizontal lines (called "horizontal rules"), like to start a new section without a heading.

<hr>

Just give me a paragraph, please. **<p>**

<ol> If you need an ordered list instead, use the <ol> element.

The code element is used for displaying code from a computer program.

For items in lists, like chocolate, hot chocolate, chocolate syrup ...

Blockquote is for lengthy quotations. Something that you want to highlight as a longer passage, say, from a book.

<code>

<li>

<blockquote>

Here's a bunch of elements you already know, and a few you don't.

Remember, half the fun of HTML is experimenting! So make some files of your own and try these out.

Rockin' page. It's perfect for my trip and it really does a good job of providing an online version of my journal. You've got the HTML well-organized too, so I should be able to add new material myself. So, when can we actually get this off your computer and onto the Web?

BULLET POINTS

- Plan the structure of your Web pages before you start typing in the content. Start with a sketch, then create an outline, and finally write the HTML.

- Plan your page starting with the large, block elements, and then refine with inline elements.

- Remember, whenever possible, use elements to tell the browser what your content means.

- Always use the element that most closely matches the meaning of your content. For example, never use a paragraph when you need a list.

- <p>, <blockquote>, <ol>, <ul>, and <li> are all block elements. They stand on their own and are displayed with space above and below the content within them.

- <q>, <em>, and <a> are all inline elements. The content in these elements flows in line with the rest of the content in the containing element.

- Use the <br> element when you need to insert your own linebreaks.

-
 is an "empty element."

- Empty elements have no content.

- An empty element consists of only one tag.

- A nested element is an element contained completely within another element. If your elements are nested properly, all your tags will match correctly.

- You make an HTML list using two elements in combination: use <ol> with <li> for an ordered list; use <ul> with <li> for an unordered list.

- When the browser displays an ordered list, it creates the numbers for the list so you don't have to.

- You can specify your own ordering in an ordered list with the start attribute. To change the values of the individual items, use the value attribute.

- You can build nested lists within lists by putting <ol> or <ul> elements inside your <li> elements.

- Use entities for special characters in your HTML content.

HTMLcross

It's time to give your right brain a break and put that left brain to work: all the words are HTML-related and from this chapter.

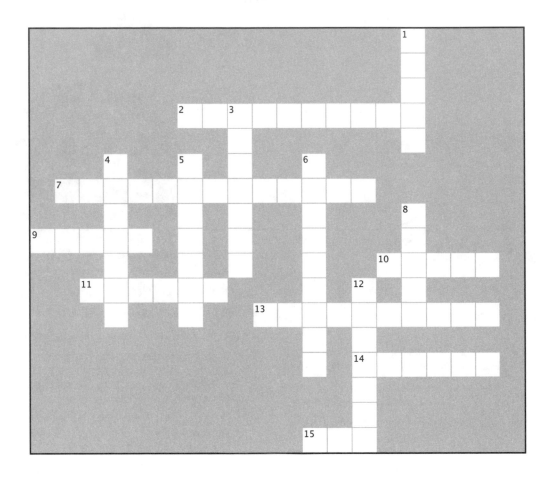

Across

2. Block element for quotes.
7. Major building blocks of your pages.
9. Requires two elements.
10. Element without content.
11. <q> is this type of element.
13. Famous catchy road signs.
14. Tony's transportation.
15. Another empty tag.

Down

1. Left together in a T-Bird.
3. Use <ol> for these kinds of lists.
4. Empty elements have none.
5. Putting one element inside another is called this.
6. Use <ul> for these kinds of lists.
8. Max speed of Segway.
12. Tony won't be doing any of this.

Exercise
Solutions

Here's the rework of Tony's Lao Tzu quote using the <q> element.
Did you give your solution a test drive?

Here's the part that changes...

```
<p>
    My first day of the trip!  I can't believe I finally got
    everything packed and ready to go.  Because I'm on a
    Segway, I wasn't able to bring a whole lot with me:
    cellphone, iPod, digital camera, and a protein bar. Just
    the essentials.  As Lao Tzu would have said, <q>A journey
    of a thousand miles begins with one Segway.</q>
</p>
```

We've added the <q> opening tag
before the start of the quote
and the </q> closing tag at the
very end.

Notice that we also
removed the double quotes.

And, here's the test drive...

Okay, it doesn't LOOK any
different, but don't you FEEL
better now?

My first day of the trip! I can't believe I finally got everything
packed and ready to go. Because I'm on a Segway, I wasn't able
to bring a whole lot with me: cellphone, iPod, digital camera,
and a protein bar. Just the essentials. As Lao Tzu would have
said, "A journey of a thousand miles begins with one Segway."

Exercise Solutions

Here's another list from Tony's journal: cell phone, iPod, digital camera, and a protein bar. You'll find it in his July 14th entry. This is an *unordered* list of items.

Make these changes in your "journal.html" file, too. Does it look like you expected?

```html
<h2>June 2, 2005</h2>
<img src="segway1.jpg">
<p>
   My first day of the trip!  I can't believe I finally got
   everything packed and ready to go.  Because I'm on a Segway,
   I wasn't able to bring a whole lot with me:
</p>
<ul>
      <li>cell phone</li>
      <li>iPod </li>
      <li>digital camera</li>
      <li>and a protein bar</li>
</ul>
<p>
   Just the essentials.  As
   Lao Tzu would have said, <q>A journey of a
   thousand miles begins with one Segway.</q>
</p>
```

First end the previous paragraph.

Start the unordered list.

Put each item into an <li> element.

End the unordered list.

And, we need to start a new paragraph.

BE the Browser
Solution

```
<html>
<head>
    <title>Top 100</title>          ⟵ Missing </head> closing tag.
<body>
<h1>Top 100                ⟵ Missing </h1> closing tag.
<h2>Dark Side of the Moon</h2>
<h3>Pink Floyd</h3>
<p>
    There's no dark side of the moon; matter of fact <q>it's all dark.
</p></q>                                    ⟵  <p> and <q> are not nested properly:
<ul>                                            the </p> tag should come after the
    <li>Speak to Me / Breathe</li>              </q> tag.
    <li>On The Run</li>
    <li>Time</li>
    <li>The Great Gig in The Sky</li>
    <li>Money</li>
    <li>Us And Them</em>      ⟵  We have a closing </em> where we should
    <li>Any Colour You Like</li>     have a closing </li> tag.
    <li>Brain Damage</li>
    <li>Eclipse</li>
</ul>                           Here's a closing </p> that doesn't match
</p>                    ⟵       any opening <p> tag.
<h2>XandY</h3>          ⟵  We mixed up the closing </h2> and </h3> tags on these headings.
<h3>Coldplay</h2>
<ol>                    ⟵  We started an <ol> list, but it's matched
    <li>Square One          with a closing </ul> tag.
    <li>What If?
    <li>White Shadows
    <li>Fix You
    <li>Talk                ⟵  We're missing all our
    <li>XandY                  closing </li> tags.
    <li>Speed of Sound
    <li>A Message
    <li>Low
    <li>Hardest Part
    <li>Swallowed In The Sea
    <li>Twisted Logic
</ul>     ⟵  This doesn't match the opening <ol> tag at the start of the list, above.
</body>
</head>  ⟵  Here's our missing </head> tag; but we're missing a closing </html> tag.
```

Exercise Solutions

A bunch of HTML elements, in full costume, are playing a party game "Who am I?" They gave you a clue – you tried to guess who they were based on what they said.

Tonight's attendees:

Quite a few of the charming HTML elements you've seen so far showed up for the party!

Clue	Name	Inline or block?
I'm the #1 heading.	h1	block
I'm all ready to link to another page.	a	inline
Emphasize text with me.	em	inline
I'm a list, but I don't have my affairs in order.	ul	block
I'm a real linebreaker.	br	↙
I'm an item that lives inside a list.	li	block
I keep my list items in order.	ol	block
I'm all about image.	img	inline
Quote inside a paragraph with me.	q	inline
Use me to quote text that stands on its own.	blockquote	block

Stumped?
 is in limbo land between block and inline. It does create a linebreak, but isn't typically displayed with space above and below it, like block elements are.

We haven't talked about this in detail yet, but, yes, <img> is inline. Give it some thought and we'll come back to this in Chapter 5.

Exercise
Solutions

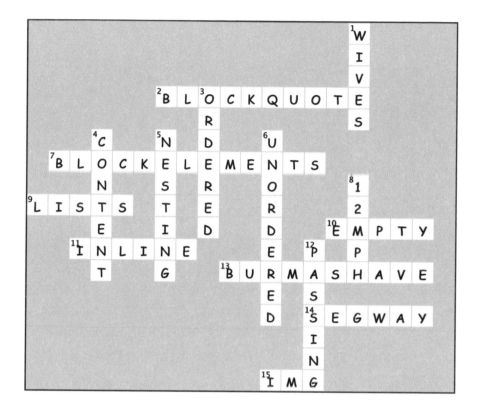

Crack the Location Challenge

You could have looked up each entity, or typed them in. In either case, the answer looks like Detroit!

```
There's going to be an evil henchman meetup
next month at my underground lair in
&#208;&epsilon;&tau;&#114;&ouml;&igrave;&tau;.
Come join us.
```

evel.html

There's going to be an evil henchman meetup next month at my underground lair in Ðετröὶτ. Come join us.

A Trip to Webville

Web pages are a dish best served on the Internet. So far you've only created HTML pages that live on your own computer. You've also only linked to pages that are on your own computer. We're about to change all that. In this chapter we'll encourage you to get those Web pages on the Internet where all your friends, fans, and customers can actually see them. We'll also reveal the mysteries of linking to other pages by cracking the code of the h, t, t, p, :, /, /, w, w, w. So, gather your belongings; our next stop is Webville.

WARNING: once you get to Webville, you may never come back. Send us a postcard.

Remember me from way back in Chapter 1? You were going to get the Starbuzz Web site online so our customers could actually see it.

Getting Starbuzz (or yourself) onto the Web

You're closer to getting Starbuzz – or even better, your own site – on the Web than you might think. All you need to do is find a "Web Hosting Company" (we'll call this a "hosting company" from now on) to host your pages on their servers, and then copy your pages from your computer to one of those servers.

Of course it helps to understand how your local folders are going to "map" to the server's folders, and once you put your pages on the server, how you point a browser to them. But we'll get to all that. For now, let's talk about getting you on the Web. Here's what you're going to need to do:

① **Find yourself an hosting company.**

② **Choose a name for your site (like "www.starbuzzcoffee.com").**

③ **Find a way to get your files from your computer to a server at the hosting company (there are a few ways).**

④ **Point your friends, family, and fans to your new site and let the fun begin.**

We're going to take you through each of these steps, and even if you're not going to set up a Web site online *right now*, follow along because you'll learn some important things you'll need to know later. So, get ready for a quick detour from HTML...

A Web Detour

Finding a hosting company

To get your pages on the Web, you need a server that actually lives on the Web *full-time*. Your best bet is to find a hosting company and let them worry about the details of keeping a server running. No worries, though; finding a hosting company is fairly straightforward and inexpensive.

Which company? Well, we'd *love* to sign you up for Web hosting at **Head First Hip Web Hosting, Inc.**, but that doesn't really exist. So, you're going to have to do a little homework on your own. While finding a company to host your pages isn't difficult, it's kind of like choosing a cable TV company: there are lots of options and plans. You really have to shop around for the best deals and for the service that works for you.

The good news is that you should be able to get started for almost nothing out of your pocket, and you can always upgrade later if you need additional features. While we can't suggest a particular provider, we can tell you a few things to look for in a provider, and we also list a few of the more popular providers at:

`http://www.headfirstlabs.com/providers.html`

Note from marketing: if a hosting company writes a big enough check we can!

You don't have to get your pages on the Web to finish this book.

While it's a lot more fun if your pages are actually *on the Web*, you can finish the rest of this book by working on your own computer.

In either case, follow along for the next few pages so you know how everything fits together.

One minute hosting guide

We can't tell you everything you need to know about getting a hosting company (after all, this book is about HTML and CSS), but we're going to give you a good push in the right direction. Here are some features to think about while you're shopping.

- *Technical support:* Does the hosting company have a good system for handling your technical questions? The better ones will answer your questions quickly either over the phone or via email.

- *Data transfer:* This is a measure of the amount of pages and data the hosting company will let you send to your visitors during a given month. Most hosting companies offer reasonable amounts of data transfer for small sites in their most basic plans. If you're creating a site that you expect will have lots of visitors, you may want to carefully look into this.

- *Backups:* Does the hosting company regularly make a backup of your pages and data that can be recovered in the event that the server has a hardware failure?

- *Domain names:* Does the hosting company include a domain name in its pricing? More about these on the next page.

- *Reliability:* Most hosting companies report keeping Web sites up 99% of the time or better.

- *Goodies:* Does your package include other goodies such as email addresses, forums, or support for scripting languages (something that may become important to you in the future)?

HELLO, my ^domain name is...

Even if you've never heard of a *domain name*, you've seen and used a zillion of them; you know... google.com, yahoo.com, amazon.com, disney.com, and a maybe a few you wouldn't want us to mention.

So what is a domain name? Just a unique name that is used to locate your site. Here's an example:

This part is the domain name.

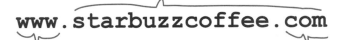

www.starbuzzcoffee.com

This part is the name of a specific server IN the domain.

There are different domain "endings" for different purposes: .com, .org, .gov, .edu; and also for different countries: .co.uk, .co.jp, and so on. When choosing a domain, pick the one that best fits you.

There are a couple of reasons you should care about domain names. If you want a unique name for your site, you're going to need your own domain name. Domain names are also used to link your pages to other Web sites (we'll get to that in a few pages).

There is one other thing you should know. Domain names are controlled by a centralized authority (called ICANN) to make sure that only one person at a time uses a domain name. Also (you knew it was coming), you pay a small annual registration fee to keep your domain name.

After years of struggling, we finally have our very own domain name.

How can you get a domain name?

The easy answer is to let your hosting company worry about it. They'll often throw in your domain name registration with one of their package deals. However, there are hundreds of companies that would be glad to help – you can find a list of them at

```
http://www.internic.net/regist.html
```

As with finding a hosting company, we're afraid we'll have to leave you to find and register your own domain name. You'll probably find that going through your hosting company is the easiest way to get that done.

A Web Detour

there are no
Dumb Questions

Q: Why is it called a "domain name" rather than a "Web site name"?

A: Because they are different things. If you look at www.starbuzzcoffee.com, that's a Web site name, but only the "starbuzzcoffee.com" part is the domain name. You could also create other Web sites that use the same domain name, like corporate.starbuzzcoffee.com or employees.starbuzzcoffee.com. So the domain name is something you can use for a lot of Web sites.

Q: If I were going to get the domain name for Starbuzz, wouldn't I want to get the name www.starbuzzcoffee.com? Everyone seems to use Web sites with the www at the front.

A: Again, don't confuse a domain name with a Web site name: starbuzzcoffee.com is a domain name, while www.starbuzzcoffee.com is the name of a Web site. Buying a domain is like buying a piece of land, let's say, 100mainstreet.com. On that land you can build as many Web sites as you like, for example: home.100mainstreet.com, toolshed.100mainstreet.com and outhouse.100mainstreet.com. So www.starbuzzcoffee.com is just one Web site in the starbuzzcoffee.com domain.

Q: What's so great about a domain name anyway? Do I really need one? My hosting company says I can just use their name, "www.dirtcheaphosting.com"?

A: If that meets your needs there is nothing wrong with using their name. But (and it's a *big but*) here's the disadvantage:

should you ever want to choose another hosting company, or should that hosting company go out of business, then everyone who knows your site will no longer be able to easily find it. If, on the other hand, you have a domain name, you can just take that with you to your new hosting company (and your users will never even know you've switched).

Q: If domain names are unique, that means someone might already have mine. How can I find out?

A: Good question. Most companies that provide registration services for domain names allow you to search to see if a name is taken (kind of like searching for vanity license plates). You'll find a list of these companies at http://www.internic.net/regist.html

---

Here's an exercise you really need to go off and do on your own. We'd love to personally help but there's only so much you can ask of book authors (and feeding the cat while you're on vacation is probably out too).

DO try this at home

It's time to seek out a hosting company and grab a domain name for your site. Remember, you can visit Head First Labs for some suggestions and resources. Also, remember that you can complete the book without doing this (even though you really should!).

My Web Hosting Company: _____

My Domain Name: _____

A Web Detour

Moving in

Congratulations! You've got your hosting company lined up, you've found a domain name, and you've got a server all ready for your Web pages. (Even if you don't, keep following along because this is important stuff.)

Now what? Well, it's time to move in, of course. So, take that For Sale sign down and gather up all those files, we're going to get them moved to the new server. Like any move, the goal is to get things moved from, say, the kitchen of your old place to the kitchen of your new place. On the Web, we're just worried about getting things from your own root folder to the root folder on the Web server. Let's get back to Starbuzz and step through how we do this. Here's what things look like now:

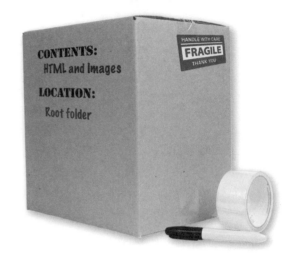

CONTENTS:
HTML and Images

LOCATION:
Root folder

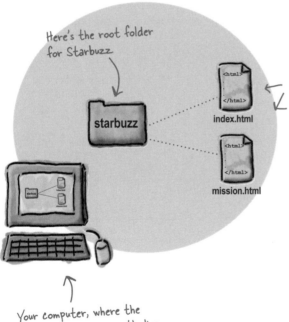

Here's the root folder for Starbuzz

Remember your Starbuzz pages? There are two: the main page (index.html) and the page that contains the mission statement (mission.html).

index.html

mission.html

Your computer, where the Starbuzz pages currently live.

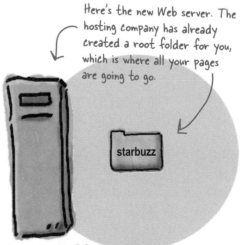

Here's the new Web server. The hosting company has already created a root folder for you, which is where all your pages are going to go.

starbuzz

Here's the new Web site name. We're using the starbuzzcoffee.com domain (since we beat you to it, you'll have to use your own domain name instead).

www.starbuzzcoffee.com

there are no Dumb Questions

Q: Wait a sec, what's the "root folder" again?

A: Up until now the root folder has just been the top-level folder for your pages. On the Web server, the root folder becomes even more important because anything inside the root folder is going to be accessible on the Web.

Q: My hosting company seems to have called my root folder "mydomain_com". Is that a problem?

A: Not at all. Hosting companies call root folders lots of different things. The important thing is that you know where your root folder is located on the server, and that you can copy your files to it (we'll get to that in a sec).

Q: So let me make sure I understand. We've been putting all our pages for the site in one folder, which we call the root folder. Now we're going to copy all that over to the server's root folder?

A: Exactly. You're going to take all the pages on your own computer, and put them all inside your site's root folder on the hosting company server.

Q: What about subfolders, like the "images" folder. Do I copy those too?

A: Yes, you're basically going to replicate all the pages, files, and folders in your own root folder onto the server. So if you've got an "images" folder on your computer, you'll have one on the server too.

Getting your files to the root folder

You're now one step away from getting Starbuzz Coffee on the Web: you've identified the root folder on your hosting company's server and all you need to do is copy your pages over to that folder. But how do you transfer files to a Web server? There are a variety of ways, but most hosting companies support a method of file transfer called FTP, which stands for File Transfer Protocol. You'll find a number of applications out there that will allow you to transfer your files via FTP; we'll take a look at how that works on the next page.

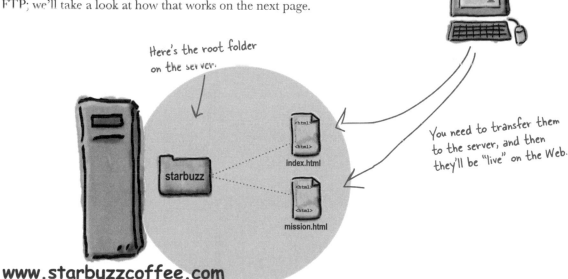

The files are sitting on your computer.

Here's the root folder on the server.

index.html

starbuzz

mission.html

You need to transfer them to the server, and then they'll be "live" on the Web.

www.starbuzzcoffee.com

A Web Detour

As much FTP as you can possibly fit in two pages

Seriously, this really is an HTML and CSS book, but we didn't want to leave you up a creek without a paddle. So, here's a very quick guide to using FTP to get your files on the Web. Keep in mind your hosting company might have a few suggestions for the best way to transfer your files to their servers (and since you are paying them, get their help). After the next few pages, we're off our detour and back to HTML and CSS until we reach the end of the book (we promise).

We'll assume you've found an FTP application. Some are command-line driven, some have complete graphical interfaces, and some are even built into applications like Dreamweaver and GoLive. They all use the same commands, but with some applications you type them in yourself, while in others you use a graphical interface. Here's how FTP works from 10,000 feet:

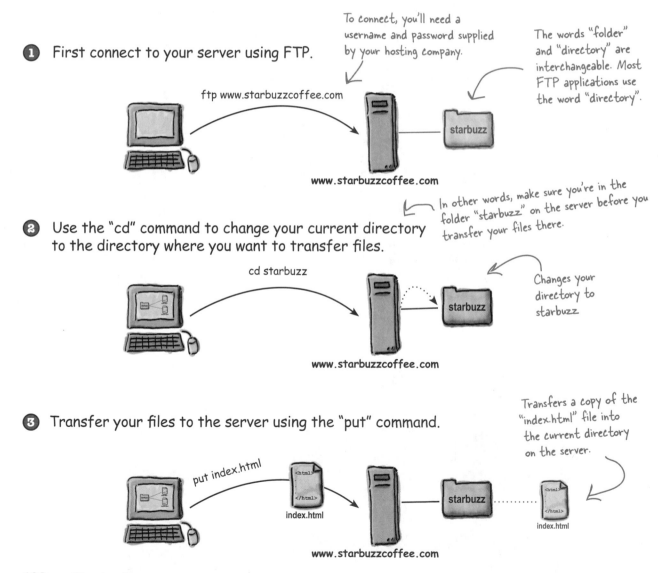

① First connect to your server using FTP.

To connect, you'll need a username and password supplied by your hosting company.

The words "folder" and "directory" are interchangeable. Most FTP applications use the word "directory".

ftp www.starbuzzcoffee.com

starbuzz

www.starbuzzcoffee.com

In other words, make sure you're in the folder "starbuzz" on the server before you transfer your files there.

② Use the "cd" command to change your current directory to the directory where you want to transfer files.

cd starbuzz

starbuzz

Changes your directory to starbuzz

www.starbuzzcoffee.com

Transfers a copy of the "index.html" file into the current directory on the server.

③ Transfer your files to the server using the "put" command.

put index.html

index.html

starbuzz

index.html

www.starbuzzcoffee.com

④ You can also make a new directory on the server with the "mkdir" command.

This is just like making a new folder, only you're doing it on the server, not your own computer.

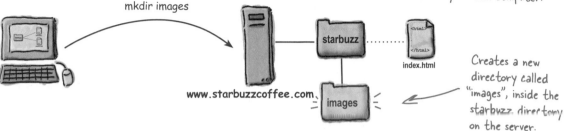

mkdir images

www.starbuzzcoffee.com

starbuzz

index.html

images

Creates a new directory called "images", inside the starbuzz directory on the server.

⑤ You can retrieve files too, with the "get" command.

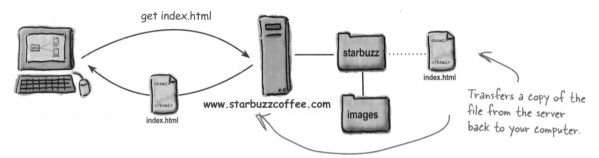

get index.html

www.starbuzzcoffee.com

starbuzz

index.html

images

index.html

Transfers a copy of the file from the server back to your computer.

Let's put all that together. Here's an example of FTP being used from a command-line application:

Most FTP applications come with much friendlier graphical interfaces, so feel free to skip right over this if you're using one of those.

```
File Edit Window Help Jam
%ftp www.starbuzzcoffee.com
Connected to www.starbuzzcoffee.com          Connect and login.
Name: headfirst
Password:******                              Get a directory of
230 User headfirst logged in.                what is there.      One
ftp> dir                                                         directory
drwx------   4096 Sep  5 15:07 starbuzz                          called
ftp> cd starbuzz            Change to the                        starbuzz
CWD command successful      starbuzz directory.
ftp> put index.html
Transfer complete.                    Transfer index.html
ftp> dir                              there.
-rw-------   1022 Sep  5 15:07 index.html
ftp> mkdir images                            Look at the
Directory successfully created               directory, there's
ftp> cd images                               index.html.
CWD command successful
ftp> bye            Make a directory for images, and
                    then quit using the bye command
```

FTP commands

Whether you're typing in FTP commands on the command-line, or using an FTP application with a graphical interface, the commands or operations you can perform are pretty much the same.

- *dir:* get a listing of the current directory.

- *cd:* change to another directory. ".." means up one directory here, too.

- *pwd:* display the current directory you're in.

- *put <filename>:* transfers the specified filename to the server.

- *get <filename>:* retrieves the specified filename from the server, back to your computer.

there are no
Dumb Questions

Q: My hosting company told me to use SFTP, not FTP. What's the difference?

A: SFTP, or Secure File Transfer Protocol, is a more secure version of FTP, but works mostly the same way. Just make sure your FTP application supports SFTP before you make a purchase.

Q: So do I edit my files on my computer and then transfer them each time I want to update my site?

A: Yes, for small sites, that is normally the way you do things. Use your computer to test your changes and make sure things are working the way you want before transferring your files to the server. For larger Web sites, organizations often create a test site and a live site so that they can preview changes on the test site before they are moved to the live site.

If you're using a tool like Dreamweaver or GoLive, these tools will allow you to test your changes on your own computer, and then when you save your files, they are automatically transferred to the Web site.

Q: Can I edit my files directly on the Web server?

A: That usually isn't a good idea because your visitors will see all your changes and errors before you have time to preview and fix them.

That said, some hosting companies will allow you to log into the server and make changes on the server. To do that you usually need to know your way around a DOS or Linux command prompt, depending on what kind of operating system your server is running.

Popular FTP applications

Here's a few of the most popular FTP applications for Mac and Windows:

For Mac OS X:

- Fetch (http://fetchsoftworks.com/) is one of the most popular FTP applications for Mac. $

- Transmit (http://www.panic.com/transmit/) $

- Cyberduck (http://cyberduck.ch/) FREE

For Windows:

- Smart FTP (http://www.smartftp.com/download/) $

- WS_FTP (http://www.ipswitch.com/products/file-transfer.asp). FREE for the basic version, $ for the Pro version

Most FTP applications have a trial version you can download to try before you buy.

DO try this at home

It's another homework assignment for you (check each item as you do it):

☐ Make sure you know where your root folder is on the server at your hosting company.

☐ Figure out the best way (and the best tool to use) to transfer files from your computer to the server.

☐ For now, go ahead and transfer the Starbuzz "index.html" and "mission.html" files to the root folder of the server.

End of Web Detour

Back to business...

That's the end of the detour and we're back on the Web superhighway. At this point you should have the two Starbuzz pages, "index.html" and "mission.html", sitting under your root folder on a server (or if not, you're at least following along).

After all this work, wouldn't it be satisfying to make your browser retrieve those pages over the Internet and display them for you? Let's figure out the right address to type into your browser...

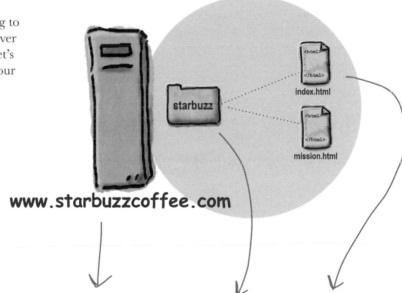

www.starbuzzcoffee.com

All Web page addresses start with this, right? We'll look into what http means in a sec.

```
http://   www.starbuzzcoffee.com   /   index.html
```

Here's the Web site name.

For the root folder we just use "/".

And here's the page file name.

Mainstreet, ~~USA~~ URL

You've probably heard the familiar "h" "t" "t" "p" "colon" "slash" "slash" a zillion times, but what does it mean? First, of all, the Web addresses you type into the browser are called *URLs* or Uniform Resource Locators.

If it were up to us we would have called them "Web addresses," but no one asked, so we're stuck with Uniform Resource Locators. Here's how to decipher a URL:

`http://www.starbuzzcoffee.com/index.html`

The first part of the URL tells you the <u>protocol</u> that needs to be used to retrieve the resource.

The second part is the Web site name. At this point you know all about that.

And the third part is the <u>absolute path</u> to the resource from the root folder.

To locate anything on the Web, as long as you know the server that hosts it, and an *absolute path* to the resource, you can create a URL and most likely get a Web browser to retrieve it for you using some *protocol* – usually HTTP.

A Uniform Resource Locator (URL) is a <u>global address</u> that can be used to locate anything on the Web, including HTML pages, audio, video, and many other forms of Web content.

In addition to specifying the location of the resource, a URL also names the <u>protocol</u> that you can use to retrieve that resource.

Come on down to http://www.earlsautos.com

$100

What is the HTTP Protocol?

HTTP is also known as the *HyperText Transfer Protocol*. In other words, it's an agreed-upon method (a protocol) for transferring hypertext documents around the Web. While "hypertext documents" are usually just HTML pages, the protocol can also be used to transfer images, or any other file that a Web page might need.

HTTP is a simple request and response protocol. Here's how it works:

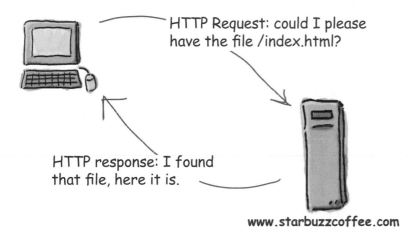

HTTP Request: could I please have the file /index.html?

HTTP response: I found that file, here it is.

www.starbuzzcoffee.com

So each time you type a URL into your browser's address bar, the browser asks the server for the corresponding resource using the HTTP protocol. If the server finds the resource, it returns it to the browser and the browser displays it. What happens if the server doesn't find it?

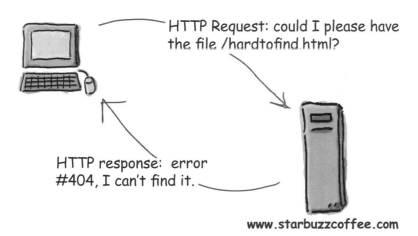

HTTP Request: could I please have the file /hardtofind.html?

HTTP response: error #404, I can't find it.

www.starbuzzcoffee.com

If the resource can't be found, you'll get the familiar "404 Error", which the server reports back to your browser.

Whatever you do, don't pronounce URL as "Earl," because that's my name. It's pronounced U-R-L.

What's an Absolute Path?

The last time we talked about paths we were writing HTML to make links with the **<a>** element. The path we're going to look at now is the absolute path part of a URL, the last part that comes after the protocol (http) and the Web site name (www.starbuzzcoffee.com).

 An absolute path tells the server how to get from your root folder to a particular page or file. Take Earl's Autos site, for example. Say you want to look in Earl's inventory to see if your new Mini Cooper has come in. To do that, you'll need to figure out the absolute path to the file "inventory.html" that is in the "new" folder. All you have to do is trace through the folders, starting at the root, to get to the "new" folder where his "inventory.html" file is located. The path is made up of all the folders you go through to get there.

So, that looks like root (we represent root with a "/"), "cars", "new", and finally, the file itself, "inventory.html". Here's how you put that all together:

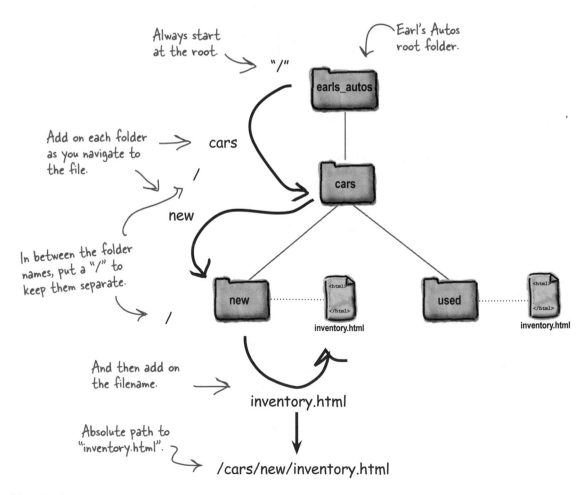

there are no
Dumb Questions

Q: What is important about the absolute path?

A: The absolute path is what a server needs to locate the file you are requesting. If the server didn't have an absolute path, it wouldn't know where to look.

Q: I feel like I understood the pieces (protocols, servers, Web sites, and absolute paths), but I'm having trouble connecting them.

A: If you add all those things together you have a URL, and with a URL you can ask a browser to retrieve a page (or other kinds of resources) from the Web. How? The protocol part tells the browser the method it should use to retrieve the resource (in most cases, this is HTTP). The Web site part (which consists of the server name and the domain name) tells the browser which computer on the Internet to get the resource from. And the absolute path tells the server what page you're after.

Q: We learned to put relative paths in the href attribute of our <a> elements. How can the server find those links if they aren't absolute?

A: Wow, great question. When you click on a link that is relative, behind the scenes the browser creates an absolute path out of that relative path and the path of the page that you click on. So, all the Web server ever sees are absolute paths, thanks to your browser.

Q: Would it help the browser if I put absolute paths in my HTML?

A: Ah, another good question, but hold that thought, we'll get back to that in a sec.

Sharpen your pencil

You've waited long enough. It's time to give your new URL a spin. Before you do, fill in the blanks below and then type in the URL (like you haven't already). If you're having any problems, this is the time to work with your hosting company to get things sorted out. If you haven't set up an hosting company, fill in the blanks for www.starbuzzcoffee.com, and type the URL into your browser anyway.

_____ :// _____ _____
    protocol   Web site name   absolute path

> I'd like my visitors to be able to type "http://www.starbuzzcoffee.com" and not have to type the "index.html". Is there a way to do that?

Remember, when we're talking about Web servers or FTP, we usually use the term "directory" instead of "folder." But they're really the same thing.

Yes, there is. One thing we haven't talked about is what happens if a browser asks for a directory rather than a file from a Web server. For instance, a browser might ask for:

`http://www.starbuzzcoffee.com/images/`

The images directory in the root directory.

or

`http://www.starbuzzcoffee.com/`

The root directory itself.

When a Web server receives a request like this, it tries to locate a *default* file in that directory. Typically a default file is called "index.html" or "default.htm" and if the server finds one of these files, it returns the file to the browser to display.

So, to return a file by default from your root directory (or any other directory), just name the file "index.html" or "default.htm".

But, you need to find out what your hosting company wants you to name your default file, because it depends on the type of server they use.

> But I asked about "http://www.starbuzzcoffee.com", which looks a little different. It doesn't have the ending "/".

Oops, you sure did. When a server receives a request like yours without the trailing "/" and there is a directory with that name, then the server will add a trailing slash for you. So if the server gets a request for:

`http://www.starbuzzcoffee.com`

it will change it to:

`http://www.starbuzzcoffee.com/`

which will cause the server to look for a default file, and in the end it will return the file as if you'd originally typed:

`http://www.starbuzzcoffee.com/index.html`

How default pages work

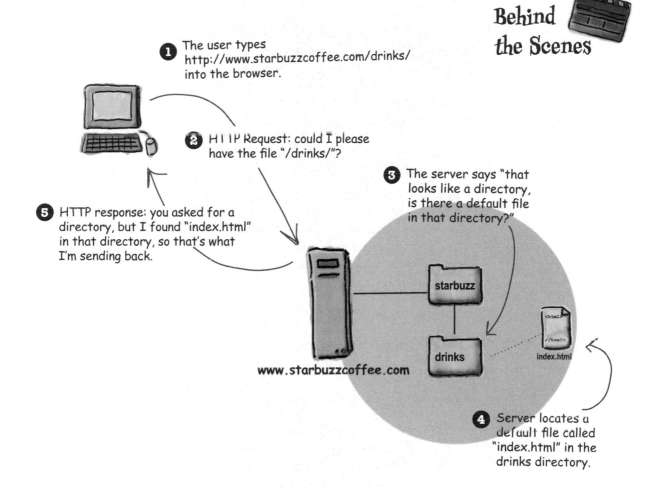

Behind the Scenes

1 The user types http://www.starbuzzcoffee.com/drinks/ into the browser.

2 HTTP Request: could I please have the file "/drinks/"?

3 The server says "that looks like a directory, is there a default file in that directory?"

5 HTTP response: you asked for a directory, but I found "index.html" in that directory, so that's what I'm sending back.

starbuzz

drinks

index.html

www.starbuzzcoffee.com

4 Server locates a default file called "index.html" in the drinks directory.

---

there are no Dumb Questions

Q: **So anyone who comes to my site with the URL http://www.mysite.com is going to see my "index.html" page?**

A: Right. Or, possibly "default.htm" depending on which kind of Web server your hosting company is using. (Note that "default.htm" usually has no "l" on the end. This is a Microsoft Web Server oddity.)

There are other possible default filenames, like "index.php", that come into play if you start writing scripts to generate your pages. That's way beyond this book, but that doesn't mean you won't be doing it in the future.

Q: **So when I'm giving someone my URL, is it better to include the "index.html" part or not?**

A: Not. It's always better to leave it off. What if, in the future, you change to another Web server and it uses another default file name like "default.htm"? Or you start writing scripts and use the name "index.php"? Then the URL you originally gave out would no longer be valid.

Earl needs a little help with his URLs

Earl may know Earl, but he doesn't know U-R-L. He needs a little help figuring out the URL for each of the files below, labeled A, B, C, D, and E. On the right, write in the URL needed to retrieve each corresponding file from www.earlsautos.com.

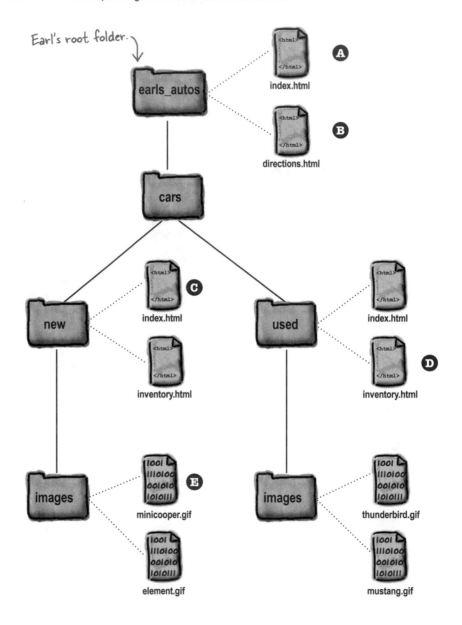

Write the URL here.

A Earls Autos

B Earls Autos

C Earls Autos

D Earls Autos

E Earls Autos

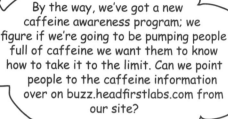

How do we link to other Web sites?

URLs aren't just for typing into browsers; you can use them right in your HTML. And, of course, right on cue, the Starbuzz CEO has a new task for you: make a link from the main Starbuzz page over to the caffeine information at **http://buzz.headfirstlabs.com**. As you can probably guess, we're going to throw that URL right into an **<a>** element. Here's how:

```
<a href="http://buzz.headfirstlabs.com">Caffeine Buzz</a>
```

An everyday, normal, garden-variety <a> element.

We've put a URL in the href. Clicking on the label "Caffeine Buzz" will retrieve a page from buzz.headfirstlabs.com.

That's all there is to it. To link to any resource on the Web, all you need is its Uniform Resource Locator, which goes in the **<a>** element as the value of the **href** attribute. Let's go ahead and add this in the Starbuzz "index.html" page.

Linking to Caffeine Buzz

Open your Starbuzz "index.html" file in the "chapter4/starbuzz" folder, and scan down to the bottom. Let's add two new links: a relative link to the mission statement in "mission.html", and a link to Caffeine Buzz. Make the changes below, then save and load your "index.html" file in your browser. Click on the link and enjoy the Caffeine Buzz.

```html
<html>
    <head>
        <title>Starbuzz Coffee</title>
        <style type="text/css">
            body {
                    background-color: #d2b48c;
                    margin-left: 20%;
                    margin-right: 20%;
                    border: 1px dotted gray;
                    padding: 10px 10px 10px 10px;
                    font-family: sans-serif;
            }
        </style>
    </head>

    <body>
        <h1>Starbuzz Coffee Beverages</h1>
        <h2>House Blend, $1.49</h2>
        <p>A smooth, mild blend of coffees from Mexico,
            Bolivia and Guatemala.</p>

        <h2>Mocha Cafe Latte, $2.35</h2>
        <p>Espresso, steamed milk and chocolate syrup.</p>

        <h2>Cappuccino, $1.89</h2>
        <p>A mixture of espresso, steamed milk and foam.</p>

        <h2>Chai Tea, $1.85</h2>
        <p>A spicy drink made with black tea, spices,
            milk and honey.
        </p>
        <p>
            <a href="mission.html">Read about our Mission</a>
            <br>
            Read the <a href="http://buzz.headfirstlabs.com">Caffeine Buzz</a>
        </p>
    </body>
</html>
```

Here's the link to the "mission.html" file. This uses a relative path to link to "mission.html".

We added a <br> to put the links on two different lines.

Here's where we've added the link to the buzz.headfirstlabs.com page.

And we've added some structure here by grouping the links and text into a paragraph.

And now for the test drive...

Here's the page with the new link, just as we planned.

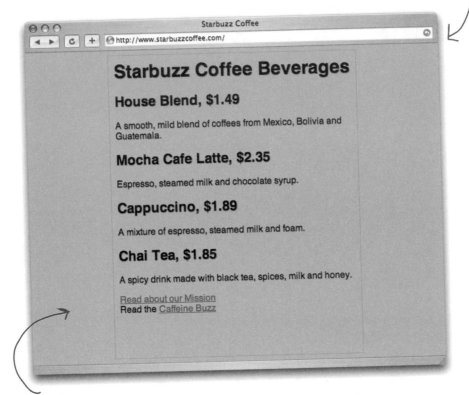

Here's the new link. Notice, we only linked the words "Caffeine Buzz" so it looks a little different from the other link.

And when you click on the link, your browser will make an HTTP request to buzz.headfirstlabs.com and then display the result.

At Caffeine Buzz we use relative links to other pages on our site, and URLs to link offsite, like www.caffeineanonymous.com.

there are no Dumb Questions

Q: **It seems like there are two ways to link to pages now: relative paths and URLs.**

A: Well, relative paths can only be used to link to pages *within* the same Web site, while URLs are typically used to link to other Web sites.

Q: **Wouldn't it be easier if I just stuck with URLs for links to my own pages *and* outside pages? That would work wouldn't it?**

A: Sure, it would work, but there's a couple of reasons you don't want to go there. One problem is that URLs are hard to manage when you have a lot of them in a Web page: they're long, difficult to edit, and they make HTML more difficult to read (for you, the page author).

Also, if you have a site with nothing but URLs that link to local pages and you move the site or change its name, you have to go change all those URLs to reflect the new location. If you use relative paths, as long as your pages stay in the same set of folders – because the links are all relative – you don't have to make any changes to your <a> element href attributes.

So, use relative links to link to your own pages in the same site, and URLs to link to pages at other sites.

Q: **Haven't we seen one other protocol? I kept seeing "file://" before we started using a Web server.**

A: Yes; good catch. The file protocol is used when the browser is reading files right off your computer. The file URL,

for example, "file:///chapter4/starbuzz/index.html", tells the browser that the file "index.html" is located at the path "/chapter4/starbuzz/". This path may look different depending on your operating system.

One important thing to notice in case you try to type in a file URL is that the file URL has three slashes, not two, like HTTP. Remember it this way: if you take an HTTP URL and delete the Web site name you'll have three slashes, too.

Q: **Are there other protocols?**

A: Yes, many browsers can support retrieval of pages with the FTP protocol, and there is a mail protocol that can send data via email. HTTP is the protocol you'll be using most of the time.

Q: **I've seen URLs that look like this: http://www.mydomain.com:8000/index.html. Why is there a ":8000" in there?**

A: The ":8000" is an optional "port" that you can put in an HTTP URL. Think of a port like this: the Web site name is like an address, and the port is like a mailbox number at an address (say, in an apartment complex). Normally everything on the Web is delivered to a default port (which is 80), but sometimes Web servers are configured to receive requests at a different port (like 8000). You'll most likely see this on test servers. Regular Web servers almost always accept requests on port 80. If you don't specify a port, it defaults to 80.

The Case of Relatives and Absolutes

PlanetRobots, Inc., faced with the task of developing a Web site for each of its two company divisions – PlanetRobot Home and PlanetRobot Garden – decided to contract with two firms to get the work done. RadWebDesign, a seemingly experienced firm, took on the Home division's Web site and proceeded to write the site's internal links using only URLs (after all, they're more complicated, they must be better). A less experienced, but well-schooled firm, CorrectWebDesign, was tasked with PlanetRobot's Garden site, and used relative paths for links between all the pages within the site.

Just as both projects neared completion, PlanetRobots called with an urgent message: "We've been sued for trademark infringement, so we're changing our domain name to RobotsRUs. Our new Web server is going to be **www.robotsrus.com**." CorrectWebDesign made a couple of small changes that took all of five minutes and was ready for the site's unveiling at the RobotsRUs corporate headquarters. RadWebDesign, on the other hand, worked until 4 a.m. to fix their pages but luckily completed the work just in time for the unveiling. However, during a demo at the unveiling, the horror-of-horrors occurred: as the team leader for RadWebDesign demonstrated the site he clicked on a link that resulted in a "404 - Page Not Found" error. Displeased, the CEO of RobotsRUs suggested that RadWebDesign might want to consider changing *their* name to BadWebDesign and asked CorrectWebDesign if they were available to consult on fixing the Home site.

What happened? How did RadWebDesign flub things up so badly when all that changed was the name of the Web server?

Web page fit and finish

Can you say "Web career?" You've certainly delivered everything the Starbuzz CEO has asked for, and you've now got a high profile Web site under your belt (and in your portfolio).

But you're not going to stop there. You want your Web sites to have that professional "fit and finish" that makes good sites into great ones. You're going to see lots of ways to give your sites that extra "polish" in the rest of this book, but let's start here with a way to improve your links.

Improving accessibility by adding a title to your links

Wouldn't it be nice if there was a way to get more information about the link you're about to click on? This is especially important for the visually impaired using screen readers because they often don't want the entire URL spoken to them: ("h" "t" "t" p" ":" "slash" "slash" "w" "w" "w" "dot") and yet the link's label usually only gives a limited description, like "Caffeine Buzz".

The **<a>** element has an attribute called **title** just for this purpose. Some people are confused by this attribute name because there's an *element* called **<title>** that goes in the **<head>**. They have the same name because they are related – it is often suggested that the value of the **title** attribute be the same as value of the **<title>** element of the Web page you are linking to. But that isn't a requirement and often it makes more sense to provide your own, more relevant description in the **title** attribute.

Here's how you add a **title** attribute to the **<a>** element:

```
Read the <a href="http://buzz.headfirstlabs.com"
```
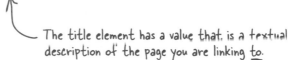
```
          title="Read all about caffeine on the Buzz">Caffeine Buzz</a>
```

The title element has a value that is a textual description of the page you are linking <u>to</u>.

Exercise

Now that we've got a title attribute, let's see how your visitors would make use of it. Different browsers make different use of the title, but many display a tool tip. Add the changes above to your "index.html" file and reload the page to see how it works in your browser.

The title test drive...

For most browsers, the title is displayed as a "tool tip" when you pass the mouse over a link. Remember that browsers for the visually impaired may read the link title aloud to a visitor.

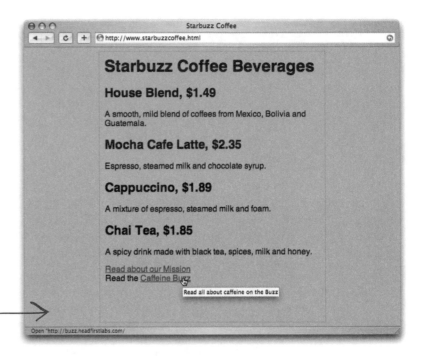

The title is displayed as a "tool tip" in most browsers. Just pass your mouse over the link and hold it there a second to see the tool tip.

The Head First Guide to Better Links

Here are a few tips to keep in mind to further improve the fit and finish of your links:

☞ *Keep your link labels concise. Don't make entire sentences or large pieces of text into links. In general, keep them to a few words. Provide additional information in the title attribute.*

☞ *Keep your link labels meaningful. Never use link labels like "click here" or "this page". Users tend to scan pages for links first, and then read pages second. So, providing meaningful links improves the usability of your page. Test your page by reading just the links on it; do they make sense? Or do you need to read the text around them?*

☞ *Avoid placing links right next to each other; users have trouble distinguishing between links that are placed closely together.*

Exercise

Open your Starbuzz "index.html" file and add a title to the link to "mission.html" with the text "Read more about Starbuzz Coffee's important mission". Notice that we didn't make the mission link's label as concise as it should be. Shorten the link label to "our Mission". Check the back of the chapter for the answer, and test your changes.

> Great job on the links. I'd really like for people to link directly to the coffee section of the Buzz site. Is that possible?

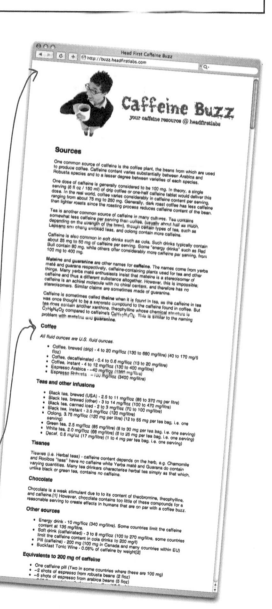

Linking Into a page

So far, whenever you've linked to another page, the page loads and your browser displays it from the top.

But, the CEO's asking you to *link into* a particular spot in the page: the Coffee section.

Sound impossible? Come on, this is Head First – we've got the technology. How? Well, we haven't told you everything about the **<a>** element yet. Turns out the **<a>** element can play *two roles*: you've already seen it act as the jumping off point for traveling from one page to another, but it can also act as a *landing point* or *destination* of a link.

Using the <a> element to create a destination

When you use an **<a>** element to create a destination, we call that a "destination anchor." Creating a destination anchor is straightforward. Here's how you can do it in three short steps:

1 Find the location in the page where you'd like to create a landing spot. This can be any text on the page, but often is just a short piece of text in a heading.

2 Wrap the text within an **<a>** element.

3 Choose a identifier name for the destination, like "coffee" or "summary" or "bio", and insert an **id** attribute into your **<a>** element.

Let's give it a try. Say you want to provide a way to link to the Chai Tea item on the Starbuzz page. Here's what it looks like now:

Here's the snippet from "index.html" with the Chai heading and description.

```
<h2>Chai Tea, $1.85</h2>
<p>A spicy drink made with black tea, spices, milk and
honey.</p>
```

Following the three steps above, we get this:

Add the <a> opening tag before the text.

And we'll give this destination the identifier "chai".

And then end the element with a closing tag.

Make sure your <a> element is properly nested inside your <h2> element.

```
<h2><a id="chai">Chai Tea, $1.85</a></h2>
<p>A spicy drink made with black tea, spices, milk and
honey.</p>
```

You've made a destination anchor out of the Chai Tea heading in the "index.html" page.

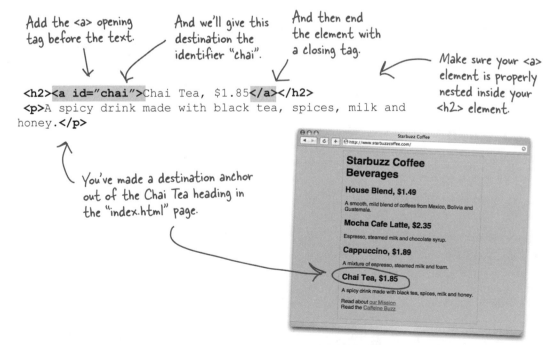

How to link to destination anchors

You already know how to link to pages using either relative links or URLs. In either case, to link more specifically to a destination anchor in a page, just add a **#** on the end of your link, followed by the destination anchor identifier. So if you wanted to link from any Starbuzz Coffee Web page to the "chai" destination anchor you'd write your **<a>** element link this:

```
<a href="index.html#chai">See Chai Tea</a>
```

Unfortunately, linking to Chai Tea with a destination anchor isn't very impressive because the whole page is small enough that it easily fits in the browser. Let's link to the Coffee section of http://buzz.headfirstlabs.com instead. Here's what you're going to do:

> The main benefit of destination anchors is to link to locations in long files so your visitors don't have to scroll through the file looking for the right section.

1 Figure out the id of the destination anchor.

2 Alter the existing **<a>** element in the Starbuzz Coffee "index.html" file to point to the destination anchor.

3 Reload your "index.html" page and test out the link.

Finding the destination anchor

To find the destination anchor, you're going to have to look at the buzz.headfirstlabs.com page and view their HTML. How? Almost all browsers have a "View Source" option. So, visit the page and when it is fully loaded, choose the "View Source" option, and you'll see the markup for the page.

In most browsers, you can right-click to "View Source". You'll also find "View Source" in the browser menu, usually under "View".

Now that you've got your hands on their HTML...

Scroll down until you see the Coffee section; it looks like this:

Just a small snippet from the Caffeine Buzz page.

```
This is similar to the naming problem
with <b>mateine</b> and <b>guaranine</b>.
</p>

<h3><a id="Coffee">Coffee</a></h3>
<p>
<i>All fluid ounces are U.S. fluid ounces.</i>
</p>
```

Here's the Coffee section. You can see the heading for it along with the start of the paragraph below.

Ahhh, and here is the destination anchor. It has the name "Coffee".

Reworking the link in "index.html"

Now all you need to do is revisit the link to Caffeine Buzz
and add on the destination anchor name, like this:

This is a snippet from the Starbuzz "index.html" file.

Add # along with the destination anchor id to your href.

```
Read the <a href="http://buzz.headfirstlabs.com#Coffee"
         title="Read all about caffeine on the Buzz">Caffeine Buzz</a>
```

Exercise

Make this change to your Starbuzz
"index.html" file. Reload and click on
the "Caffeine Buzz" link. You should be
taken directly to the Coffee section of
Caffeine Buzz's front page.

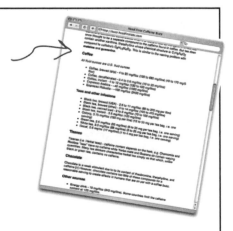

Dumb Questions

Q: When I have two attributes in an element, is the order important? For example, should the title attribute always come after the href?

A: The order of attributes is not important in any element (if it were we'd all have headaches 24/7). So, use any ordering you like.

Q: Normally when I use an <a> element the browser underlines the text, but when I used the id attribute instead of href, it doesn't.

A: Right. When you use the id attribute it has no effect on the look of the text the <a> element surrounds. Remember, the point of the destination anchor (<a> with the id attribute) is just to mark the location within the page, not to create a link, so there isn't any need to display it visually.

Q: Why is it called an anchor? What's anchor-like about it?

A: On this one we're just going to say it like it is: "anchor" was a bad choice of names and has confused tens of thousands before you, if not millions. We're not even going to try to give you a cute metaphor to understand how it could possibly be an anchor. Basically we're all stuck with the name, but now you do know what it does, and before long you won't even give the name a second thought.

Q: Well even with the bad name, why use the same element to do such different things? Why not have separate linking and destination elements?

A: Think of it this way: you have to link *from* something *to* something else. The <a> element with an href provides a way to describe the *from* something. And the *to* something has always been just the top of the other Web page – in other words, you got the *to* something for free. With the destination anchor you can also define the *to* something yourself. So, while confusing, there is some sanity to the naming.

Q: I noticed in the anchor id names, you used "chai" with all lowercase letters and Caffeine Buzz used "Coffee" with a upper case "C". Does it matter?

A: You can use any combination of upper- and lowercase characters in your id attributes. Just make sure you are consistent and always use the same upper- and lowercase letters in your hrefs and destination anchor id (which is why it is often easier to make these names entirely lowercase every time). If you aren't consistent, don't expect your links to work correctly on every browser.

Q: Can I put a link to a destination anchor from within the same document?

A: Sure. In fact, it is common to define a destination anchor "top" at the top of a page and have a link at the bottom of the page saying "Back to top". It is also common in long documents to have a table of contents for the entire page. For instance, to link to the "top" destination anchor in the same page, you would write <a href="#top">Back to top</a>.

Q: If a Web page doesn't provide a destination anchor and I still need to link to a specific part of the page, how can I?

A: You can't. If there is no destination anchor then you can't direct the browser to go to a specific location in a Web page. You might try to contact the page author and ask them to add one (even better, tell them how!).

Q: Can I have a destination anchor id like "Jedi Mindtrick" or does an id have to be only one word?

A: To work consistently with the most browsers, always start your id with a letter (A-Z or a-z) and follow it with any letter, digit, hyphen, underscore, colon, or period. So, since you can't use a space, you can't have a name like "Jedi Mindtrick", but that isn't much of a restriction because you can always have "Jedi-Mindtrick", "Jedi_Mindtrick", "JediMindtrick", and so on.

Q: How can I tell others what destination anchors they can link to?

A: There is no established way of doing this, and in fact, "View Source" remains the oldest and best technique for discovering the destination anchors you can link to.

The Case of Relatives and Absolutes

So, how did RadWebDesign flub up the demo? Well, because they used URLs for their **href**s instead of relative links, they had to edit and change *every single link* from http://www.planetrobots.com to http://www.robotsrus.com. Can you say error-prone? At 3:00 a.m., someone yawned and accidentally typed http://www.robutsru.com (and as fate has it, that was the same link that the CEO clicked on at the demo).

Oops... someone forgot an "s" on the end of the name.

CorrectWebDesign, on the other hand, used relative paths for all internal links. For example, the link from the company's mission statement to the products page, `<a href="../products.html">`, works whether the site is called PlanetRobots or RobotsRUs. So, all CorrectWebDesign had to do was update the company name on a few pages.

So RadWebDesign left the demo sleep-deprived and with a little egg on their face, while CorrectWebDesign left the meeting with even more business. But, the story doesn't end there. It turns out that RadWebDesign dropped by a little coffeehouse/ bookstore after the demo and, determined not to be outdone, picked up a certain book on HTML & CSS. What happened? Join us in a few chapters for "The Case of Brute Force versus Style."

Five-Minute Mystery Solved

Awesome job linking
to the Buzz site... I know I keep
asking for changes, but really, this
is the last one. Can you make the Buzz site
come up in a separate window when I click
on the link? I don't want the Starbuzz
page to go away.

Linking to a new window

We have another new requirement from the
Starbuzz CEO (there are *always* new requirements
for Web sites). What he wants is this: when you
click on the "Caffeine Buzz" link in the Starbuzz
Coffee page, the Starbuzz Coffee page shouldn't go
away. Instead a whole new window should open
up with the Caffeine Buzz page in it, like this:

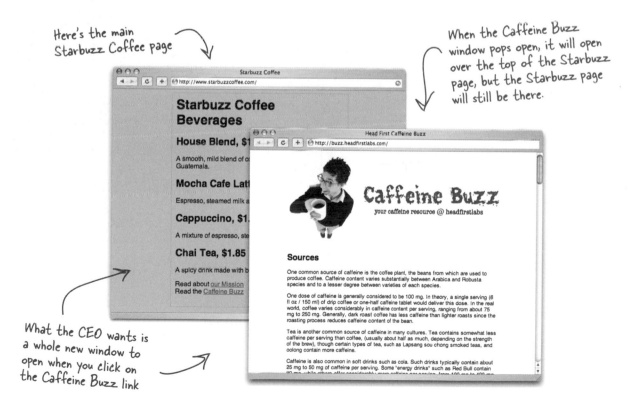

Here's the main
Starbuzz Coffee page

When the Caffeine Buzz
window pops open, it will open
over the top of the Starbuzz
page, but the Starbuzz page
will still be there.

What the CEO wants is
a whole new window to
open when you click on
the Caffeine Buzz link

Opening a new window using target

To open a page in a new window, you need to tell the browser the name of the window in which to open it. If you don't tell the browser a specific window to use, the browser just opens the page in the *same* window. You can tell the browser to use a *different* window by adding a **target** attribute to the **<a>** element. The value of the **target** attribute tells the browser the "target window" for the page. If you use "_blank" for the target, the browser will *always* open a new window to display the page. Let's take a closer look:

```
<a target="_blank" href="http://buzz.headfirstlabs.com"
   title="Read all about caffeine on the Buzz">Caffeine Buzz</a>
```

The target attribute tells the browser where to open the Web page that is at the link in the href attribute. If there is no target, then the browser opens the link in the <u>same</u> window. If the target is "_blank" then the browser opens the link in a <u>new</u> window.

Exercise

Open your Starbuzz "index.html" file. Add the **target** attribute to the <a> tag that links to the Caffeine Buzz page. Now give it a try – did you get a new window?

BRAIN POWER

Can you think of some advantages and some disadvantages to using the target attribute to open a page in a new window?

Q: What if I have more than one <a> element with a target? If there's already a "_blank" new window open, will it open in the window that's already open? Or will it open in a new "_blank" window?

A: If you give the name "_blank" to the targets in all your <a> elements, then each link will open in a new blank window. However, this is a good question because it brings up an important point: you don't actually have to name your target "_blank". If you give it another name, say, "coffee", then all links with the target name "coffee" will open in the same window. The reason is that when you give your target a specific name, like "coffee", you are really naming the new window that will be used to display the page at the link. "_blank" is a special case that tells the browser to *always* use a new window.

The Target Attribute Exposed

This week's interview:
Using target considered bad?

Head First: Hello target, we're so glad you could join us.

Target Attribute: I'm glad to be here. It's nice to know you're still interested in hearing about me.

Head First: Why do you say that?

Target: Well, to be honest, I'm not as popular as I used to be.

Head First: Why do you think that is?

Target: I think it's because users want to be in control of when a window opens. They don't always like new windows popping open at unexpected times.

Head First: Well, it can be very confusing – we've had complaints from people who end up with so many windows on their screens, they can't find the original page.

Target: But it's not like it's difficult to get rid of the windows... just click on the little close button. What's so hard about that?!

Head First: True, but if users don't know a new window has opened then they can get confused. Sometimes the new window completely covers the old window and it's hard to tell what's happening. That can be confusing for anyone, but especially for someone with a visual impairment.

Target: Oh, I never thought of that.

Head First: Well, think about it: if someone's got their browser window magnified, and a whole new window opens on top of the one they're reading, it can be very confusing for them. It's hard to tell what's going on when you're not looking at the whole screen at once.

Target: Yeah I suppose it would be. It's probably difficult for using screen readers, too.

Head First: Yup. Some screen readers play a sound when a new window opens, but others just ignore the new window completely, or else they jump right to the new window immediately. Either way, it's gotta be confusing for someone who can't see what's going on. And of course, since the page is in a whole new window, there's no way to use the back button to get back to the original window.

Target: [Sigh] I'm starting to see why I'm not as popular as I used to be.

Head First: Don't get too depressed; there *are* times when it's nice to have a new window open, right?

Target: Yes, I always thought having those little informational windows for "extra information" was handy, and I'm especially proud when people use me to open large versions of images. That way, the user can view the large image and then go right back to the main page.

Head First: Okay, see, you do come in handy at times. We've just got to remember to use you when it's appropriate, but to keep in mind those people who might be visually impaired and not overuse you.

Target: Right!

HTMLcross

Here are some mind benders for your left brain.

Across

2. Wrong way to pronounce URL.
4. Attribute used to anchor an <a> element to a page.
7. Earl sold these.
8. Web address to a resource.
9. Protocol we've been using up until this chapter.
11. Unique name on the Web.
12. Always use these kinds of links when linking to pages on the same server.
13. Request/response protocol.
14. Most popular Mac FTP application.

Down

1. People scan these rather than reading text.
3. Path from the root.
5. What are you supposed to send back from Webville?
6. Informative caffeine site.
7. Keep your link labels _____.
10. Controls domain names.
11. _____ file you get when you ask for a directory.
12. Top directory of your Web site.

BULLET POINTS

- Typically the best way to get on the Web is to find a hosting company to host your Web pages.

- A domain name is a unique name, like amazon.com or starbuzzcoffee.com, that is used to identify a site.

- A hosting company can create one or more Web servers in your domain. Servers are often named "www".

- The File Transfer Protocol (FTP) is a common means of transferring your Web pages and content to a server.

- FTP applications, like Fetch for Mac or WS_FTP for Windows, can make using FTP easier by providing a graphical user interface.

- A URL is a Uniform Resource Locator, or Web address, that can be used to identify any resource on the Web.

- A typical URL consists of a protocol, a Web site name, and an absolute path to the resource.

- HTTP is a request and response protocol used to transfer Web pages between a Web server and your browser.

- The file protocol is used by the browser to read pages from your computer.

- An absolute path is the path from the root folder to a file.

- "index.html" and "default.htm" are examples of default pages. If you specify a directory without a filename, the Web server will look for a default page to return to the browser.

- You can use relative paths or URLs in your <a> element's href attribute to link to other Web pages. For other pages in your site, it's best to use relative paths, and use URLs for external links.

- Use the id attribute to create a destination anchor in a page. Use '#' followed by a destination anchor id to link to that location in a page.

- To help accessibility, use the title attribute to provide a description of the link in <a> elements.

- Use the target attribute to open a link in another browser window. Don't forget that the target attribute can be problematic for users on a variety of devices and alternative browsers.

> Wait, wait! Before you go, we need our logo on the Web page! Hello? Oh, I guess they've already gone on to Chapter 5...

Sharpen your pencil

Solution

http	:// www.starbuzzcoffee.com	/index.html
protocol	Web site name	absolute path

Your Web site name here.

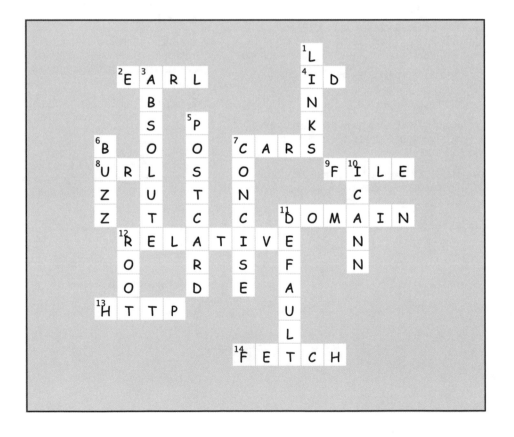

Earl needs a little help with his URLs

Solution

A Earls Autos
http://www.earlsautos.com/

B Earls Autos
http://www.earlsautos.com/directions.html

C Earls Autos
http://www.earlsautos.com/cars/new/

D Earls Autos
http://www.earlsautos.com/cars/used/inventory.html

E Earls Autos
http://www.earlsautos.com/cars/new/images/minicooper.gif

Exercise Solutions

Add a title to the link to "mission.html" with the text "Read more about Starbuzz Coffee's important mission". Notice that we didn't make the mission link's label as concise as it should be. Shorten the link label to "our Mission". Here's the solution; did you test your changes?

```html
<html>
    <head>
        <title>Starbuzz Coffee</title>
        <style type="text/css">
            body {
                    background-color: #d2b48c;
                    margin-left: 20%;
                    margin-right: 20%;
                    border: 1px dotted gray;
                    padding: 10px 10px 10px 10px;
                    font-family: sans-serif;
            }
        </style>
    </head>

    <body>
        <h1>Starbuzz Coffee Beverages</h1>
        <h2>House Blend, $1.49</h2>
        <p>A smooth, mild blend of coffees from Mexico,
            Bolivia and Guatemala.</p>

        <h2>Mocha Cafe Latte, $2.35</h2>
        <p>Espresso, steamed milk and chocolate syrup.</p>

        <h2>Cappuccino, $1.89</h2>
        <p>A mixture of espresso, steamed milk and foam.</p>

        <h2>Chai Tea, $1.85</h2>
        <p>A spicy drink made with black tea, spices,
            milk and honey.
        </p>
        <p>
            Read about <a href="mission.html"
title="Read more about Starbuzz Coffee's important mission">our Mission</a>
            <br>
            Read the <a href="http://buzz.headfirstlabs.com"
                title="Read all about caffeine on the Buzz">Caffeine Buzz</a>
        </p>
    </body>
</html>
```

Add a title attribute to the mission link.

Move the "Read about" outside the <a> element.

5 adding images to your pages

Meeting the Media

Smile and say "cheese." Actually, smile and say "gif", "jpg", or "png"

– these are going to be your choices when "developing pictures" for the Web. In this chapter you're going to learn all about adding your first media type to your pages: images. Got some digital photos you need to get online? No problem. Got a logo you need to get on your page? Got it covered. But before we get into all that, don't you still need to be formally introduced to the <img> element? So sorry, we weren't being rude, we just never saw the "right opening." To make up for it, here's an entire chapter devoted to <img>. By the end of the chapter you're going to know all the ins and outs of how to use the <img> element and its attributes. You're also going to see exactly how this little element causes the browser to do extra work to retrieve and display your images.

How the browser works with images

Browsers handle **`<img>`** elements a little differently than other elements. Take an element like an **`<h1>`** or a **`<p>`**. When the browser sees these tags in a page, all it needs to do is display them. Pretty simple. But, when a browser sees an **`<img>`** element something very different happens: the browser has to retrieve the image before it can be displayed in a page.

The best way to understand this is to look at an example. Let's take a quick look back at the elixirs page from the Head First Lounge, which has four **`<img>`** elements:

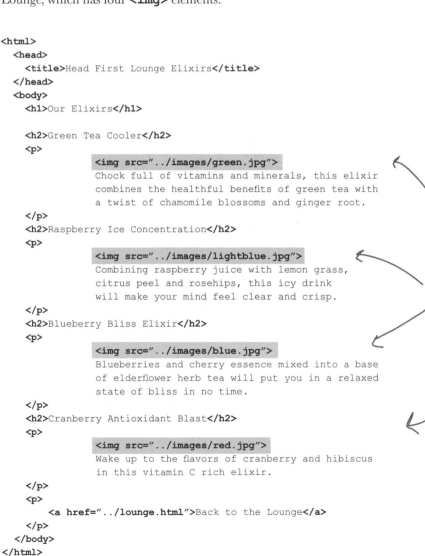

```
<html>
  <head>
    <title>Head First Lounge Elixirs</title>
  </head>
  <body>
    <h1>Our Elixirs</h1>

    <h2>Green Tea Cooler</h2>
    <p>
            <img src="../images/green.jpg">
            Chock full of vitamins and minerals, this elixir
            combines the healthful benefits of green tea with
            a twist of chamomile blossoms and ginger root.
    </p>
    <h2>Raspberry Ice Concentration</h2>
    <p>
            <img src="../images/lightblue.jpg">
            Combining raspberry juice with lemon grass,
            citrus peel and rosehips, this icy drink
            will make your mind feel clear and crisp.
    </p>
    <h2>Blueberry Bliss Elixir</h2>
    <p>
            <img src="../images/blue.jpg">
            Blueberries and cherry essence mixed into a base
            of elderflower herb tea will put you in a relaxed
            state of bliss in no time.
    </p>
    <h2>Cranberry Antioxidant Blast</h2>
    <p>
            <img src="../images/red.jpg">
            Wake up to the flavors of cranberry and hibiscus
            in this vitamin C rich elixir.
    </p>
    <p>
        <a href="../lounge.html">Back to the Lounge</a>
    </p>
  </body>
</html>
```

We've got four images in this HTML.

Now let's take a look behind the scenes and step through how the browser retrieves and displays this page when it is requested from http://lounge.headfirstlabs.com:

Behind
the Scenes

1 First the browser retrieves the file "elixir.html" from the server.

Empty browser window, nothing retrieved yet.

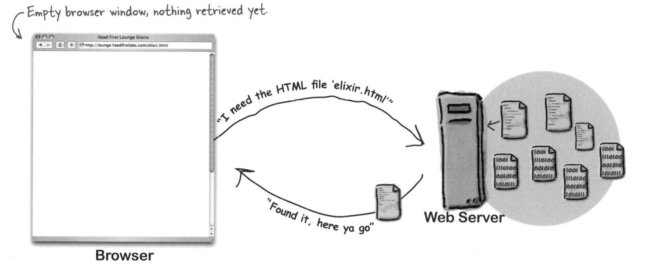

Browser

"I need the HTML file 'elixir.html'"

"Found it, here ya go"

Web Server

---

2 Next the browser reads the "elixir.html" file, displays it, and sees it has four images to retrieve. So, it needs to get each one from the Web server, starting with "green.jpg".

The HTML page is retrieved, but the browser still needs to get the images.

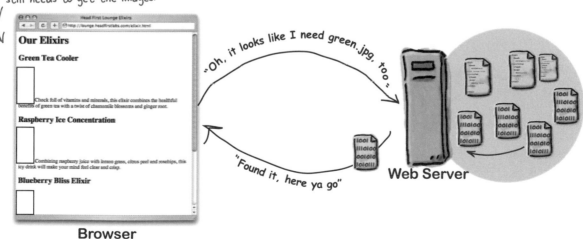

Browser

"Oh, it looks like I need green.jpg, too"

"Found it, here ya go"

Web Server

3 Having just retrieved "green.jpg", the browser displays it and then moves on to the next image: "lightblue.jpg".

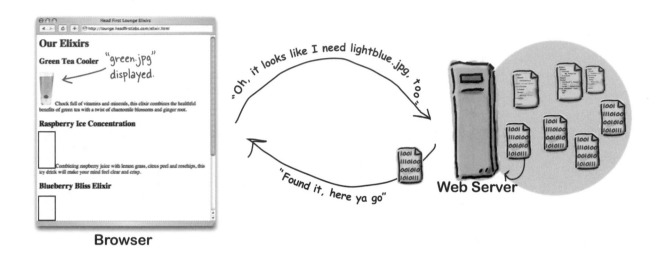

4 Now the browser has retrieved "lightblue.jpg", so it displays that image and then moves on to the next image, "blue.jpg". This process continues for each image in the page.

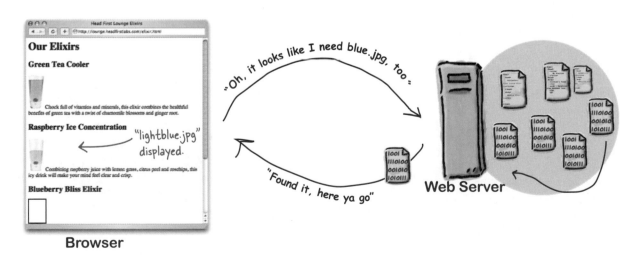

How images work

Images are just images, right? Well, actually there are a zillion formats for images out there in the world, all with their own strengths and weaknesses. But luckily, only two of those formats are commonly used on the Web: JPEG and GIF. The only tricky part is deciding which to use when.

What's the difference between JPEG and GIF?

Use JPEG for photos and complex graphics

Use GIF for images with solid colors, logos, and geometric shapes.

Works best for continuous tone images, like photographs.	Works best for images with a few solid colors, and images with lines, like logos, clip art, and small text in images.
Can represent images with up to 16 million different colors.	Can represent images with up to 256 different colors.
Is a "lossy" format because to reduce the file size, it throws away some information about the image.	GIF also compresses the file to reduce its size, but doesn't throw anything way. So, it is a "lossless" format.
Does not support transparency.	Allows one background color to be set to "transparent" so that anything underneath the image will show through.

Fireside Chats

Tonight's talk: **JPEG and GIF compare their images.**

JPEG

Hello again, GIF. Didn't I just see you on a Web page?

Hah. As soon as you get good at representing complex images, like photos, I'm sure people will be happy to stick with you, but you still don't know how to represent anything that needs more than a puny 256 colors.

You wanna talk to me about quality? I let my users choose exactly how much quality they want.

That's true, but most people are more than happy with that. Not everyone needs super high-resolution images on their pages. With me, users can usually choose a quality setting of low or medium and they are just fine with the quality of the images. And, if they used you instead, they'd have huge files for the same image.

GIF

Yeah... wouldn't it be nice if everyone just stuck to GIF? Then I wouldn't have to run into you so often.

Hey, representing photos is easy if you're willing to *lose quality*. But I'm all about quality. If I can't represent an image fully, I won't do it. Just take a look at some of the logos you've tried to represent ... Yuck.

Yeah, but at what cost? Face it, to get a photo down to a size that is reasonable to transmit over the Web, you have to lose a little quality in the image.

Sure, sure, but have you ever looked at lines, logos, small text, solid colors? They don't look so great with JPEG.

JPEG

Yeah, sure, GIF works great for those, but only as long as there are a small number of those colors. You're just like a lesser version of me. I can do anything you can.

Say what? GIF? We're doing a show here. Where'd you go?

I think you make way too much of this transparency thing – I say, just build that background color into the image.

Well, I'm not too worried about it; there aren't many photos without backgrounds.

When would that ever happen?

Yeah, right. Stick to your logos and simple text images, and I'll stick to photos and complex images. Everyone knows I'm better for handling complexity.

GIF

{GIF disappears, literally}

{GIF reappears}

Don't panic. I'm just proving a point. If JPEG is so great, how come you can't make parts of your images transparent like I can? With transparency, what is underneath the image shows through. If my users want a logo on a Web page, and the page has a colored background, they'll use me because they know I'll let the background show through the parts of the logo without any color.

Sure, and then someone changes the Web page color. No way. Transparency is the way to go, and to get it, you gotta use me.

Oh yeah? How about if you want to cut out a picture of a person, or even a tree, and use it on a Web page without a background?

You'd be surprised how often I get to represent photos just because my users want that transparent background.

Hey, someone is asking me to do transparency... gotta run.

WHICH IMAGE FORMAT?

Congratulations: you've been elected "Grand Image Format Chooser" of the day. For each image below, choose the format that would best represent it for the Web.

JPEG   or   GIF

☐   ☐

☐   ☐

☐   ☐

☐   ☐

☐   ☐

Uh, I don't mean to be rude, but we're on the ninth page of the IMAGES chapter and you STILL haven't introduced me! JPEG, GIF, blah, blah, blah... could you get on with it?

And now for the formal introduction: meet the <img> element.

We've held off on the introductions long enough. As you can see, there's more to dealing with images than just the HTML markup. Anyway, enough of that for now... it's time to meet the **<img>** element.

Let's start by taking a closer look at the element (although you've probably already picked up on most of how **<img>** works by now):

Here's the <img> element.

The <img> element is an inline element. It doesn't cause linebreaks to be inserted before or after it.

```
<img src="images/drinks.gif">
```

The src attribute specifies the location of an image file to be included in the display of the Web page.

You already know <img> is an empty element.

So, is that it? Not quite. There are a couple of attributes you'll want to know about. And of course you'll also want to know how to use the **<img>** element to reference images on the Web that aren't on your own site. But really, you already know the basics of using the **<img>** element.

Let's work through a few of the finer points of using the **<img>** element, and then put all this knowledge to work.

<img>: it's not just relative links anymore

The **src** attribute can be used for more than just relative links; you can also put a URL in your **src** attribute. Images are stored on Web servers right alongside HTML pages, so every image on the Web has its own URL, just like Web pages do.

You'll generally want to use a URL for an image if you're pointing to an image at a *different* Web site (remember, for links and images on the *same* site, it's better to use relative paths).

Here's how you link to an image using a URL:

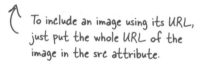

```
<img src="http://www.starbuzzcoffee.com/images/corporate/ceo.jpg">
```

To include an image using its URL, just put the whole URL of the image in the src attribute.

The URL is the path to the image, so the filename at the end is always the filename of an image. There's no such thing as a default image like there is for Web pages.

✏️ Sharpen your pencil

Here's a "Sharpen your pencil" that is actually about pencils (oh, and images too). This exercise involves a bit of trivia: *Given a typical, brand-new pencil, if you drew one continuous line with it, using the entire pencil up, how long would the line be?*

What's that got to do with images? To find the answer you're going to have to write some HTML. The answer to this trivia is contained in the image that is at the URL: http://www.headfirstlabs.com/trivia/pencil.gif. Your job is to add an image to this HTML and retrieve the answer:

```
<html>
    <head>
        <title>Sharpen your pencil trivia</title>
    </head>
    <body>
        <p>How long a line can you draw with the typical pencil?</p>
        <p>
                                    ← Put your image element here.
        </p>
    </body>
</html>
```

Q: So the <img> element is quite simple – it just provides a way to specify the location of the image that needs to be displayed in the page?

A: Yes, that about sums it up. We'll talk about a couple of attributes you can add to the element. Later, you'll see a number of ways to use CSS to change the visual style of an image.

But there's a lot to know about the images themselves. What are the different image formats for? When should I use one over the other? How big should they be? How do I prepare images for use in a Web page?

Q: We've learned that empty elements are elements without content. We've also learned that the <img> element is empty. But, doesn't it have content (the Image)?

A: Well, to be more precise, an empty element is an element that doesn't have any content *in the HTML page* to put the open and closing tags around. True, an image is content, but the <img> element refers to the image. The image isn't part of the HTML page itself. Instead, the image *replaces* the <img> element when the browser displays the page. And remember, HTML pages are purely text, so the image could never be directly part of the page. It's always a separate thing.

Q: Back in the example of a Web page loading with images... when I load a Web page, I don't see the images loading one after the other. Why?

A: Browsers often retrieve the images *concurrently*. That is, the browser makes requests for multiple images at the same time. Given the speed of computers and networks, this all happens fast enough that you usually see a page display along with its images.

Q: If I see an image on a Web page, how do I determine its URL so that I can link to it?

A: Most browsers allow you to "right-click" on an image, which brings up a contextual menu with some choices. In these choices you should see "Copy Image Address" or "Copy Image Link", which will place the URL in your clipboard. Another way to find the URL is to right-click and choose "Open Image in New Window", which will open the image in a browser window. Then you can get the URL of the image from the browser's address bar. A last option is to use your browser's "View Source" menu option and look through the HTML. Keep in mind, though, you might find a relative link to the image, so you'll have to "reconstruct" the URL using the Web site domain name and the path of the image.

Q: What makes a JPEG photo better than a GIF photo, or a GIF logo better than a JPEG logo?

A: "Better" is usually defined as some combination of image quality and file size. A JPEG photo will usually be much smaller than an equivalent quality GIF, while a GIF logo will usually look better, and have a smaller file size than in JPEG format.

Q: I've heard about the PNG image format too. Why didn't you mention that?

A: PNG is the latest newcomer in graphic formats, and an interesting one as it can support both JPEG and GIF styles of images. It also has more advanced transparency features than GIF. Right now, PNG is a little on the cutting edge because not all browsers support it. But its popularity is growing quickly. You should feel free to use PNG, but just be aware that it won't work on every browser.

Always provide an alternative

One thing you can be sure of on the Web is that you never know exactly which browsers and devices will be used to view your pages. Visitors are likely to show up with mobile devices, screen readers for the visually impaired, browsers that are running over very slow Internet connections (and may retrieve only the text, not the images, of a site), cell phones, Internet-enabled toasters... Who knows?

But in the middle of all this uncertainty *you can be prepared*. Even if a browser can't display the images on your page, there is an alternative. You can give the visitor some indication of what information is in the image using the **<img>** element's **alt** attribute. Here's how it works:

```
<img src="http://www.headfirstlabs.com/trivia/pencil.gif"
     alt="Pencil line 35 miles long">
```

The alt attribute just requires a short bit of text that describes the image.

If the image can't be displayed, then this text is used in its place.

Exercise

In this exercise you're going to see how your browser handles the alt attribute when you have a broken image. The theory goes that if an image can't be found, the alt attribute is displayed instead. But not all browsers implement this, so your results may vary. Here's what you need to do:

1 Take your HTML from the previous exercise.

2 Update the image element to include the `alt` attribute "Pencil line 35 miles long".

3 Change the image name of "pencil.gif" to "broken.gif". This image doesn't actually exist, so you'll get a broken image.

4 Reload the page in your browser.

5 Finally, download a couple of other browsers and give this a try. Did you get different results?

For instance, you could try Firefox (http://www.mozilla.org/) or Opera (http://www.opera.com/).

Look at the end of the chapter to see our results...

Sizing up your images

There's one last attribute of the **<img>** element you should know about – actually, they're a pair of attributes: **width** and **height**. You can use these attributes to tell the browser, up front, the size of an image in your page.

Here's how you use **width** and **height**:

```
<img src="images/drinks.gif" width="48" height="100">
```

The width attribute tells the browser how wide the image should appear in the page.

The height attribute tells the browser how tall the image should appear in the page.

Both width and height are specified using the number of pixels. If you're not familiar with pixels, we'll go into what they are in a little more detail later in this chapter. You can add width and height attributes to any image; if you don't, the browser will automatically determine the size of the image before displaying it in the page.

there are no
Dumb Questions

Q: **Why would I ever use these attributes if the browser just figures it out anyway?**

A: On many browsers, if you supply the width and height in your HTML, then the browser can get a head start laying out the page before displaying it. If you don't, the browser often has to readjust the page layout after it knows the size of an image. Remember, the browser downloads images *after* it downloads the HTML file and begins to display the page. The browser can't know the size of the images before it downloads them unless you tell it.

You can also supply width and height values that are larger or smaller than the size of the image and the browser will scale the image

to fit those dimensions. Many people do this when they need to display an existing image at a size that is larger or smaller than its original dimensions. As you'll see later, however, there are many reasons not to use width and height for this purpose.

Q: **Do I have to use these attributes in pairs? Can I just specify a width or a height?**

A: You can, but if you're going to go to the trouble to tell the browser one dimension, supplying the second dimension is about the same amount of work (and there isn't a lot to be gained by supplying just a width or a height unless you're scaling the image to a particular width or height).

Q: **We've said many times that we are supposed to use HTML for structure, and not for presentation. These feel like presentation attributes. Am I wrong?**

A: It depends on how you are using these attributes. If you're setting the image width and height to the correct dimensions, then it is really just informational. However, if you are using the width and height to resize the image in the browser, then you *are* using these attributes for presentation. In that case, it's probably better to consider using CSS to achieve the same result.

Creating the ultimate fan site: myPod

iPod owners love their iPods, and they take them everywhere. Imagine creating a new site called "myPod" to display pictures of your friends and their iPods from their favorite locations, all around the world.

What do you need to get started? Just some knowledge of HTML, some images, and a love for your iPod.

We've already written some of the HTML for this site, but we haven't added the images yet – that's where you come in. But before you get to the images, let's get things set up; look for the "chapter5" folder in the sample source for the book. There you'll find a folder named "mypod". Open the "mypod" folder and here's what you'll see inside:

My iPod in Seattle! You can see rain clouds and the Space Needle. You can't see the 628 coffee shops.

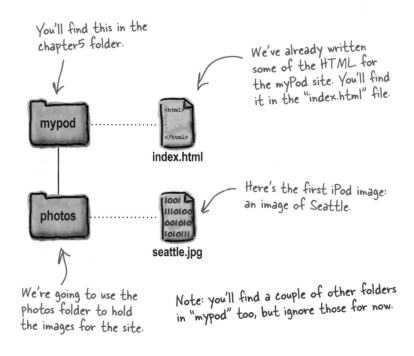

You'll find this in the chapter5 folder.

We've already written some of the HTML for the myPod site. You'll find it in the "index.html" file.

index.html

Here's the first iPod image: an image of Seattle.

seattle.jpg

We're going to use the photos folder to hold the images for the site.

Note: you'll find a couple of other folders in "mypod" too, but ignore those for now.

Check out myPod's "index.html" file

Open up the file "index.html" and you'll see work has already begun on myPod. Here's the HTML so far:

```html
<html>
    <head>
        <title>myPod</title>
        <style type="text/css">
            body { background-color: #eaf3da; }
        </style>
    </head>
    <body>

        <h1>Welcome to myPod</h1>
        <p>
            Welcome to the place to show off your iPod, wherever you might be.
            Wanna join the fun! All you need is any iPod from the early classic
            iPod to the latest iPod Nano, the smallest iPod Shuffle to the largest
            iPod Photo, and a digital camera.  Just take a snapshot of your iPod in
            your favorite location and we'll be glad to post it on myPod. So, what
            are you waiting for?
        </p>

        <h2>Seattle, Washington</h2>
        <p>
            Me and my iPod in Seattle!  You can see rain clouds and the
            Space Needle.  You can't see the 628 coffee shops.
        </p>


    </body>
</html>
```

We threw in some **Ready Bake CSS** here. Just type this in for now — all it does is give the page a light green background. We'll be getting to CSS in a few chapters — promise!

This HTML should look familiar, as we're using the basic building blocks: <h1>, <h2>, and <p>.

And here's how it looks in the browser. Not bad, but we need images.

Sharpen your pencil

As you can see, a lot of the HTML is already written to get myPod up and running. All you need to do is add an **<img>** element for each photo you want to include. There's one photo so far, "seattle.jpg", so go ahead and add an element to place that image in the page below. When you've finished, load the page in your browser and check out the view of Seattle.

This is where you need to place the first photo.

```html
<html>
    <head>
        <title>myPod</title>
        <style type="text/css">
            body { background-color: #eaf3da;}
        </style>
    </head>
    <body>

        <h1>Welcome to myPod</h1>
        <p>
            Welcome to the place to show off your iPod, wherever you might be.
            Wanna join the fun? All you need is any iPod from, the early classic
            iPod to the latest iPod Nano, the smallest iPod Shuffle to the largest
            iPod Photo, and a digital camera.  Just take a snapshot of your iPod in
            your favorite location and we'll be glad to post it on myPod. So, what
            are you waiting for?
        </p>

        <h2>Seattle, Washington</h2>
        <p>
            Me and my iPod in Seattle!  You can see rain clouds and the
            Space Needle.   You can't see the 628 coffee shops.
        </p>
```

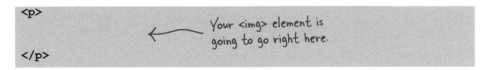

```html
        <p>


        </p>
```

Your <img> element is going to go right here.

```html

    </body>
</html>
```

Whoa! The image is way too large

Well, the image is right there where it should be, but that is one *large* image. Then again, most of the images that come from digital cameras these days are that large (or larger). Should we just leave the image like it is and let visitors use the scroll bar? You're going to see there are a couple of reasons why that's a bad idea.

Let's take a look at the image and the browser and see just how bad this situation is...

If the image fits nicely in your browser window, then your browser may have an "auto image resize" option turned on. More on this in just a sec...

Here's our browser. It's about the size of the typical browser window.

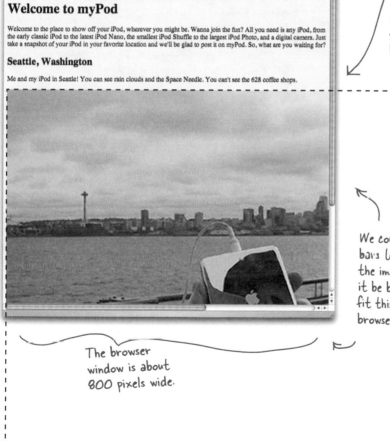

Welcome to myPod

Welcome to the place to show off your iPod, wherever you might be. Wanna join the fun? All you need is any iPod, from the early classic iPod to the latest iPod Nano, the smallest iPod Shuffle to the largest iPod Photo, and a digital camera. Just take a snapshot of your iPod in your favorite location and we'll be glad to post it on myPod. So, what are you waiting for?

Seattle, Washington

Me and my iPod in Seattle! You can see rain clouds and the Space Needle. You can't see the 628 coffee shops.

And here's the "seattle.jpg" image you added to "index.html."

Here's the full size of the image, which is bigger than the size of the browser window... much bigger.

We could use the scroll bars to see the rest of the image, but wouldn't it be better if we could fit this image into the browser window?

The browser window is about 800 pixels wide.

The image is 1200 pixels wide.

there are no
Dumb Questions

Q: **What's wrong with having the user just use the scroll bar to see the image?**

A: In general, Web pages with large images are hard to use. Not only can your visitors not see the entire image at once, but using scroll bars is cumbersome. Large images also require more data to be transferred between the server and your browser, which takes a lot of time and may result in your page being very slow to display, particularly for users on dialup or other slow connections.

Q: **Why can't I just use the width and height attribute to resize the images on the page?**

A: Because the browser still has to retrieve the entire large image before it scales it down to fit your page.

Q: **You said the browser window is 800 pixels wide; what exactly does that mean?**

A: Your computer's display is made up of millions of dots called pixels. If you look very closely at your display you'll see them:

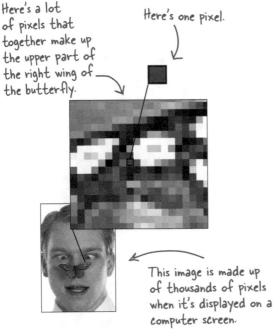

Here's a lot of pixels that together make up the upper part of the right wing of the butterfly.

Here's one pixel.

This image is made up of thousands of pixels when it's displayed on a computer screen.

And, while screen sizes and resolutions tend to vary (some people have small monitors, some large), 800 pixels is the typical width that most people set their browsers to. So, 800 pixels is a good rule of thumb for the *maximum* width of your images (and your Web pages too, but we'll get to that in a later chapter).

Q: **How do the number of pixels relate to the size of the image on the screen?**

A: A good rule of thumb is 72 pixels to every inch, although depending on your monitor, you can have up to 120 pixels in an inch. Assuming your monitor has 72 pixels per inch, if you want an image to be approximately 3" wide and high, you'd make it 72 (pixels) times 3 (inches) = 246 pixels, or, rounding up, 250 by 250 pixels.

Q: **Well, how large should I make my images then?**

A: In general, you want to keep the width of your image to less than 800 pixels. Of course, you may want your images to be significantly smaller depending on what you're using the image for. What if the image is a logo for your page? You probably want that small, but still readable. After all, you don't need a logo the width of the entire Web page. Logos tend to run between 100 and 200 pixels wide. So, ultimately, the answer to your question depends on the design of your page. For photos – which you usually do want to view as large as possible – you may want to have a page of small thumbnail images that load quickly, and then allow the user to click on each thumbnail to see a larger version of the image. We'll get to all that shortly.

Q: **I think my browser automatically resized the image of Seattle, because it fits perfectly in the window. Why did my browser do this?**

A: Some browsers have a feature that resizes any image that doesn't fit within the width of your browser. But many browsers don't do this, so you don't want to rely on it. Even if every browser *did* have this feature, you'd still be transferring a lot more data than necessary between the server and browser, which would make your page slow to load and less usable.

Resize the image to fit in the browser

Let's fix up this image so it fits the browser page better. Right now this image
is 1200 pixels wide by 800 pixels tall (you'll see how to determine that in a sec).
Because we want the width of the image to be less than 800 pixels, we need to
decide on a width that would fit our myPod Web page nicely. The whole point
of myPod is viewing photos of iPods in their surroundings, so we probably
want to have reasonably large images. If we reduce this image size by one
half to 600 pixels wide by 400 pixels high, that will still take up most of the
browser width, while still allowing for a little space on the sides. Sound good?
Let's get this image resized...

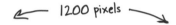

1200 pixels

600 pixels

800
pixels

400
pixels

We need to resize the
image so that it's still
reasonably large, but
is less than 800 pixels
wide. 600 seems like a
nice width that happens
to be one half the
current size.

Here's what you're going to do:

1 Open the image using a photo editing application.

2 Reduce the image size by one half (to 600 pixels by 400 pixels).

3 Save the image as "seattle_med.jpg".

Before we get started, which photo editing application are we going to use to resize the image? I have Photoshop Elements. Will that work?

Good question – there are lots of photo editing applications on the market (some freely available), which are all quite similar. We're going to use Adobe's Photoshop Elements to resize the images, because it is one of the most popular photo editing applications, and is available on both Windows and the Macintosh. If you own another photo editing application, you should have no problem following along and translating each editing task to your own application.

If you don't yet have a photo editing application, you might first check to see if there was one included with your operating system. If you have a Mac, you can use iPhoto to edit your photos. If you're a Windows user, you might find Microsoft's Digital Image Suite on your computer already. If you still don't have an editing application available to you, follow along and and for each step you can use the HTML and images included in the example folders.

If you don't have Adobe Photoshop Elements, but you'd like to follow along for the rest of the chapter with it, you can download it and try it out free for 30 days. The URL to download it is: http://www.adobe.com/products/tryadobe/main.jsp

Open the image

First, start your photo editing application and open the "seattle.jpg" image. In Photoshop Elements, you'll want to choose the "Browse Folders..." menu option under the "File" menu, which will open the "File Browser" dialog box. You're going to use this to navigate to the image "seattle.jpg" in the "chapter5/mypod/photos" folder.

Or, if you're using Windows, use the File > Open menu to open the "seattle.jpg" image directly.

Here's the File Browser dialog box. Use this dialog to navigate to the "seattle.jpg" image.

As you navigate through folders, you'll see a preview of the images in those folders here.

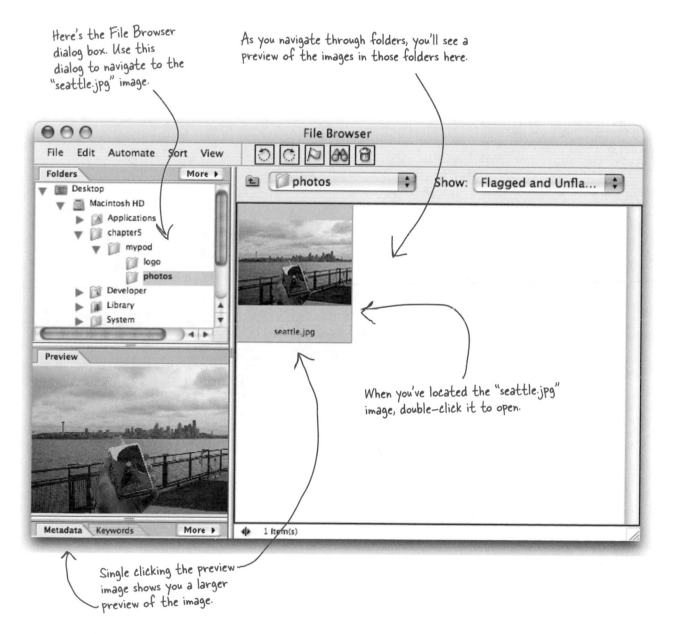

When you've located the "seattle.jpg" image, double-click it to open.

Single clicking the preview image shows you a larger preview of the image.

Resizing the image

Now that "seattle.jpg" is open, we're going to use the "Save for Web" dialog
to both resize the image and save it. To get to that dialog box, just choose the
"Save for Web" menu option from the "File" menu.

To resize the image, choose "Save
for Web" from the File menu.

Here's the "seattle.jpg" image
in Photoshop Elements.

Resizing the image, continued...

After you've selected the "Save for Web" menu option, you should see the dialog box below; let's get acquainted with it before we use it.

This dialog lets you do all kinds of interesting things. For now, we're going to focus on how to use it to resize and save images in JPEG format for Web pages.

Here's where you choose the format to save your file. Currently it's set to save as GIF; we're going to change this to JPEG in a couple of pages...

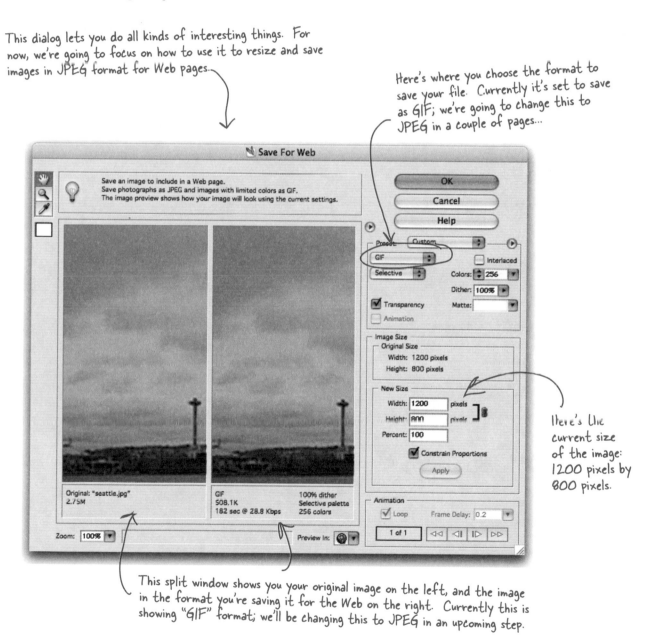

Here's the current size of the image: 1200 pixels by 800 pixels.

This split window shows you your original image on the left, and the image in the format you're saving it for the Web on the right. Currently this is showing "GIF" format; we'll be changing this to JPEG in an upcoming step.

As you can see, there's a lot of functionality built into this dialog. Let's put it to good use. To resize the image, you need to change the width to 600 pixels and the height to 400 pixels. Then you need to save the image in JPEG format. Let's start with the resize...

(1) Change the image size here to a width of 600 and a height of 400. If you have "Constrain Proportions" checked, then all you have to do is type the new width, 600, and Elements will change the height to 400 for you.

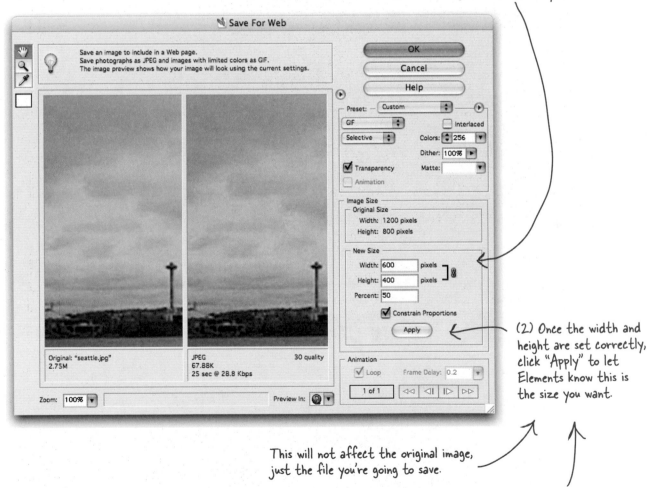

(2) Once the width and height are set correctly, click "Apply" to let Elements know this is the size you want.

This will not affect the original image, just the file you're going to save.

You must click Apply to reduce the image size; otherwise, the image will be saved at its original width and height.

You've resized - now save

Now you just need to save the image in the correct format (JPEG). To do that, you need to choose JPEG format and set the quality to "Medium". We'll talk more about quality in a sec.

(1) Now that the image size is set, you just need to choose the format for the image. Currently it's set to save as GIF; change this to JPEG like we've done here.

(2) Set the quality to "Medium".

(3) That's it; click "OK" and go to the next page.

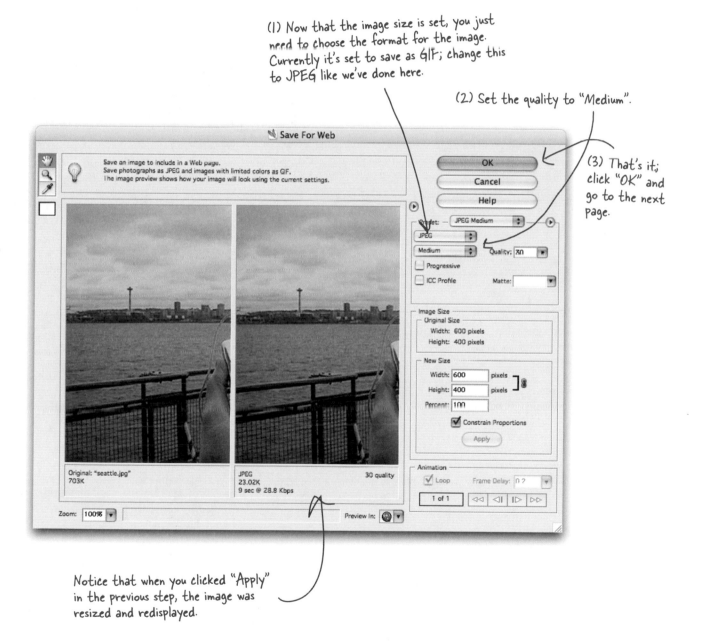

Notice that when you clicked "Apply" in the previous step, the image was resized and redisplayed.

Save the image

After you click OK, you'll get a Save dialog. Save the image as "seattle_med.jpg" so you don't overwrite the original photo.

Change the filename to seattle_med.jpg.

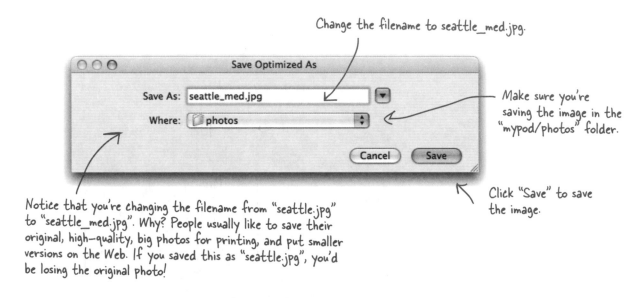

Make sure you're saving the image in the "mypod/photos" folder.

Click "Save" to save the image.

Notice that you're changing the filename from "seattle.jpg" to "seattle_med.jpg". Why? People usually like to save their original, high-quality, big photos for printing, and put smaller versions on the Web. If you saved this as "seattle.jpg", you'd be losing the original photo!

---

there are no Dumb Questions

Q: **Can you say more about the quality setting in "Save for Web"?**

A: The JPEG format allows you to specify the level of image quality you need. The lower the quality, the smaller the file size. If you look at the preview pane in the "Save for Web" dialog you can see both the quality and file size change as you change the quality settings.

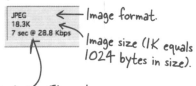

Image format.

Image size (1K equals 1024 bytes in size).

Photoshop Elements even tells you how long it would take to transfer over a dialup modem to a browser.

The best way to get a feel for quality settings and the various image formats is to experiment with them on your own images. You'll soon figure out what quality levels are needed for your image and the type of Web page you're developing. You'll also get to know when to use JPEG versus other formats.

Q: **What is the number 30 next to the Quality label in the JPEG Options dialog box?**

A: 30 is a number that Photoshop Elements considers "Medium" quality. JPEG actually uses a scale of 1-100%, and Low, Medium, High, etc. are just preset values that many photo editing applications use.

Q: **Couldn't I just use the <img> element's width and height attributes to resize my image instead?**

A: You could use the width and height attributes to resize an image, but that's not a good idea. Why? Because if you do that, you're still downloading the full-size image, and making the browser do the work to resize the image (just like when you have the auto resize option on in browsers that support that feature). The width and height attributes are really there to help the browser figure out how much space to reserve for the image; if you use them, they should match the actual width and height of the image.

Fixing up the myPod HTML

Once you've saved the image, you can quit out of Photoshop Elements. Now all you need to do is change the myPod "index.html" page to include the new version of the photo, "seattle_med.jpg". Here's a snippet of the "index.html" file, showing only the parts you need to change.

```
<html>
  <head>
    <title>myPod</title>
    <style type="text/css">
      body { background-color: #eaf3da; }
    </style>
  </head>
  <body>
    .
    .
    .
    <h2>Seattle, Washington</h2>
    <p>
      Me and my iPod in Seattle!  You can see rain clouds and the
      Space Needle.  You can't see the 628 coffee shops.
    </p>

    <p>
      <img src="photos/seattle_med.jpg" alt="My iPod in Seattle, WA">
    </p>

  </body>
</html>
```

The rest of the HTML goes here. You've already got it in your "index.html" file.

All you need to do is change the filename in the <img> element to the name of the image you just made: "seattle_med.jpg".

And now for the test drive...

Go ahead and make the changes, save them, and reload "index.html" in your browser. Things should look much better. Now the image is sized just right to give your visitors a good view – without overwhelming them with a large photo.

Now the image fits nicely in the browser window.

WHICH IMAGE FORMAT?²

Your task this time: open the file "chapter5/testimage/eye.jpg" in Photoshop Elements. Open the "Save for Web" dialog and fill in the blanks below by choosing each quality setting for JPEG (low, medium, high, etc.). You'll find this information in the preview pane below the image. Once you've finished, determine which setting makes the most sense for this image.

```
JPEG          ←── Format.
18.3K         ←── Size of image.
7 sec @ 28.8 Kbps ←── Time to transfer over
                       dialup modem.
```

Format	Quality	Size	Time	Winner
JPEG	Maximum	_____	_____	☐
JPEG	Very High	_____	_____	☐
JPEG	High	_____	_____	☐
JPEG	Medium	_____	_____	☐
JPEG	Low	_____	_____	☐
GIF	N/A	_____	_____	☐

More photos for myPod

A new batch of photos has arrived for myPod: two more from Seattle and
a few from a friend in Britain. The photos have already been resized to less
than 800 pixels wide. Add the **<img>** elements for them (you'll find the
images already in the photos folder):

```
<html>
   <head>
      <title>myPod</title>
      <style type="text/css">
         body { background-color: #eaf3da;}
      </style>
   </head>
   <body>

      <h1>Welcome to myPod</h1>
      <p>
         Welcome to the place to show off your iPod, wherever you might be.
         Wanna join the fun? All you need is any iPod, from the early classic
         iPod to the latest iPod Nano, the smallest iPod Shuffle to the largest
         iPod Photo, and a digital camera.  Just take a snapshot of your iPod in
         your favorite location and we'll be glad to post it on myPod. So, what
         are you waiting for?
      </p>

      <h2>Seattle, Washington</h2>
      <p>
         Me and my iPod in Seattle!  You can see rain clouds and the
         Space Needle.  You can't see the 628 coffee shops.
      </p>

      <p>
         <img src="photos/seattle_med.jpg" alt="My iPod in Seattle, WA">
         <img src="photos/seattle_shuffle.jpg" alt="An iPod Shuffle in Seattle, WA">
         <img src="photos/seattle_downtown.jpg" alt="An iPod in downtown Seattle, WA">
      </p>

      <h2>Birmingham, England</h2>
      <p>
         Here are some iPod photos around Birmingham. We've obviously got some
         passionate folks over here who love their iPods. Check out the classic
         red British telephone box!
      </p>

      <p>
         <img src="photos/britain.jpg" alt="An iPod in Birmingham at a telephone box">
         <img src="photos/applestore.jpg" alt="An iPod at the Birmingham Apple store">
      </p>
   </body>
</html>
```

Feel free to add some of your own photos here as well. Just remember to resize them first.

Let's keep all the Seattle photos together.

Same with the Birmingham photos...

Taking myPod for another test drive

At this point we don't need to tell you to reload the page in your browser; we're sure you're way ahead of us. Wow, what a difference a few images make, don't you think? This page is starting to look downright interesting.

But that doesn't mean you're there yet. While you've got a great set of images on the page, and even though you've already resized them, the images are still quite large. Not only is the page going to load more and more slowly as you add more images, but the user has to do a lot of scrolling to see them all. Wouldn't it be better if users could see a small "thumbnail" image for each photo, and then click on the thumbnail to see the larger image?

Here's what the whole page looks like now, with all the images.

And, here's what the page looks like now, close up.

Reworking the site to use thumbnails

You're now going to make this page more usable by substituting a smaller image (which we'll call a *thumbnail*) for each photo, and then you'll create a link from that thumbnail to each of the larger photos. Here's how you're going to do this, one step at a time:

1. Create a new directory for the thumbnails.

2. Resize each photo to 150 by 100 pixels and save it in a "thumbnail" folder.

3. Set the **src** of each **<img>** element in "index.html" to the thumbnail version of the photo.

4. Add a link from each thumbnail to a new page containing the larger photo.

Create a new directory for thumbnails

To keep things organized, create a separate folder for the thumbnail images. Otherwise, you'll end up with a folder of larger images and small thumbnails all lumped together, which could get quite cluttered after you've added a significant number of photos.

Create a folder called "thumbnails" under the "mypod" folder. If you're working from the book example files, you'll find this folder already in there.

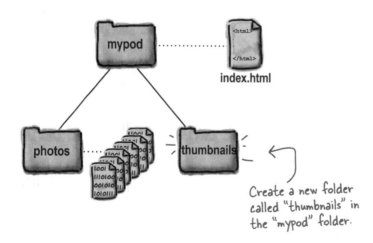

Create a new folder called "thumbnails" in the "mypod" folder.

Create the thumbnails

You've got a place to put your thumbnails, so let's create them. Start by opening "seattle_med.jpg" with your photo editing application. You're going to resize it to 150x100 pixels using the same method you used to create the 600x400 version:

In Photoshop Elements, choose the "Save for Web" menu option.

Then change the width to 150 and the height to 100 and click "Apply".

Don't forget to change the format to JPEG, Medium quality.

Finally, click OK.

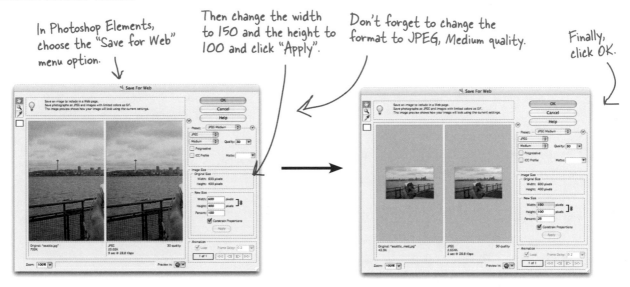

With the image resized, choose "OK" and save it as the same name but *in the thumbnail folder*. **Be careful**: if you save it to the "photos" folder you'll be replacing the larger image.

Now, repeat this for each photo in your "photos" folder.

If you're working with the example files, you'll find the thumbnails already in the "thumbnails" folder so you don't have to do every one (after all, you're learning HTML, not batch photo processing).

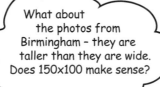

> What about the photos from Birmingham – they are taller than they are wide. Does 150x100 make sense?

Good catch. Because these images are taller than they are wide, we have two choices: we can switch the dimensions and make them 100x150 or we can crop each image and make a 150x100 pixel thumbnail from it. We're going to make ours 100x150; feel free to crop them and create 150x100 pixel images if you'd like to explore how to do that in your photo editing application.

Rework the HTML to use the thumbnails

Now you just need to change the HTML so that the **<img>** elements get their images from the "thumbnails" folder rather than the "photos" folder. And, because you're currently using relative paths like "photos/seattle_med.jpg", that's going to be simple: for each **<img>** element, all you need to do is change the folder from "photos" to "thumbnails".

```html
<html>
    <head>
        <title>myPod</title>
        <style type="text/css">
            body { background-color: #eaf3da; }
        </style>
    </head>
    <body>

        <h1>Welcome to myPod</h1>
        <p>
            Welcome to the place to show off your iPod, wherever you might be.
            Wanna join the fun? All you need is any iPod, from the early classic
            iPod to the latest iPod Nano, the smallest iPod Shuffle to the largest
            iPod Photo, and a digital camera.  Just take a snapshot of your iPod in
            your favorite location and we'll be glad to post it on myPod. So, what
            are you waiting for?
        </p>

        <h2>Seattle, Washington</h2>
        <p>
            Me and my iPod in Seattle!  You can see rain clouds and the
            Space Needle.  You can't see the 628 coffee shops.
        </p>

        <p>
          <img src="thumbnails/seattle_med.jpg" alt="My iPod in Seattle, WA">
          <img src="thumbnails/seattle_shuffle.jpg" alt="A iPod Shuffle in Seattle, WA">
          <img src="thumbnails/seattle_downtown.jpg" alt="An iPod in downtown Seattle, WA">
        </p>

        <h2>Birmingham, England</h2>
        <p>
            Here are some iPod photos around Birmingham. We've obviously got some
            passionate folks over here who love their iPods. Check out the classic
            red British telephone box!
        </p>

        <p>
          <img src="thumbnails/britain.jpg" alt="An iPod in Birmingham at a telephone box">
          <img src="thumbnails/applestore.jpg" alt="An iPod at the Birmingham Apple store">
        </p>
    </body>
</html>
```

All you need to do is change the folder from "photos" to "thumbnails".

Take myPod for another test drive

Ahhh... much better. Visitors can see all the available pictures at a glance. They can also tell which photos go with each city more easily. Now we need to find a way to link from each thumbnail to the corresponding large image.

Welcome to myPod

Welcome to the place to show off your iPod, wherever you might be. Wanna join the fun? All you need is any iPod from, the early classic iPod to the latest iPod Nano, the smallest iPod Shuffle to the largest iPod Photo, and a digital camera. Just take a snapshot of your iPod in your favorite location and we'll be glad to post it on myPod. So, what are you waiting for?

Seattle, Washington

Me and my iPod in Seattle! You can see rain clouds and the Space Needle. You can't see the 628 coffee shops.

Birmingham, England

Here's some iPod photos around Birmingham. We've obviously got some passionate folks over here who love their iPods. Check out the classic red British telephone box!

> Wait a sec, don't you think you're pulling a fast one? The images used to be on top of each other; now they're side by side.

Right; but remember the <img> element is an <u>inline</u> element.

In other words, we didn't "pull anything." Because **<img>** is an inline element, it doesn't cause linebreaks to be inserted before and after the element is displayed. So, if there are several images together in your HTML, the browser will fit them side by side if the browser window is wide enough.

The reason the larger photos weren't side by side is because the browser didn't have room to display them next to each other. Instead, it displayed them on top of each other. A browser always displays vertical space before and after a block element, and if you look back at the screenshots, you'll see the images are right on top of each other with no space in between. That's another sign **<img>** is an inline element.

Turning the thumbnails into links

You're almost there. Now you just need to create a link from each thumbnail image to its larger version. Here's how this is going to work:

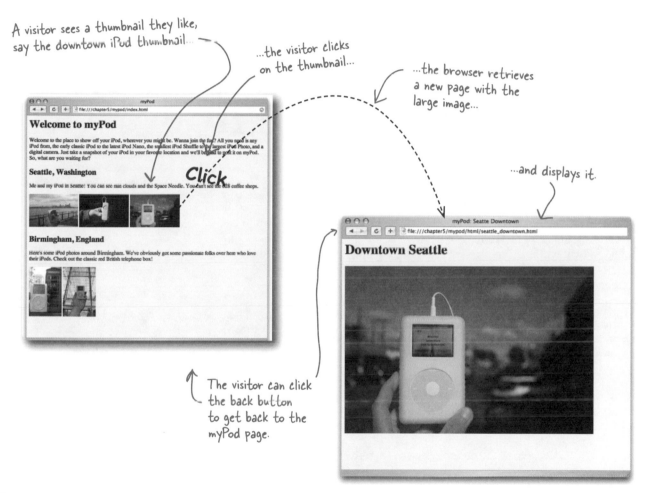

A visitor sees a thumbnail they like, say the downtown iPod thumbnail...

...the visitor clicks on the thumbnail...

...the browser retrieves a new page with the large image...

...and displays it.

Click

The visitor can click the back button to get back to the myPod page.

To do this you need two things:

① **A page to display each photo along with a heading that describes its content.**

② **A link from each thumbnail in "index.html" to its corresponding photo page.**

Let's create the pages first, and then we'll come back and finish off the links.

Create individual pages for the photos

First, create a new folder called "html" to hold these individual pages, just below the "mypod" folder:

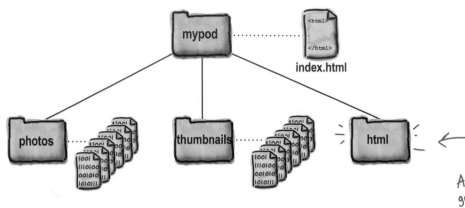

As you've probably guessed, we've already created this folder for you in the book examples.

Now we're going to create one HTML file for each photo. If the photo is called "seattle_med.jpg", then let's call the HTML file "seattle_med.html" just to be consistent. In each HTML file, we'll have a heading that describes the photo, followed by the photo. Here's the HTML for the first Seattle photo. All the other pages will follow this same format:

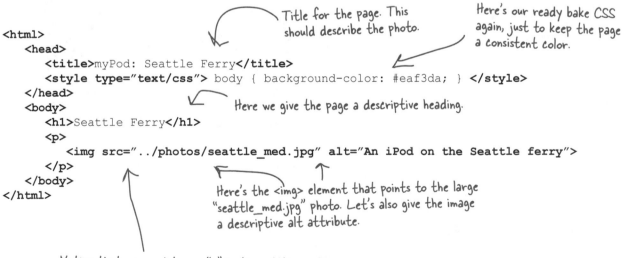

```
<html>
    <head>
        <title>myPod: Seattle Ferry</title>
        <style type="text/css"> body { background-color: #eaf3da; } </style>
    </head>
    <body>
        <h1>Seattle Ferry</h1>
        <p>
            <img src="../photos/seattle_med.jpg" alt="An iPod on the Seattle ferry">
        </p>
    </body>
</html>
```

Title for the page. This should describe the photo.

Here's our ready bake CSS again, just to keep the page a consistent color.

Here we give the page a descriptive heading.

Here's the <img> element that points to the large "seattle_med.jpg" photo. Let's also give the image a descriptive alt attribute.

Notice that we need to use ".." in the relative path because the "html" folder is a sibling of the "photos" folder, so we have to go up one folder and then down into "photos" when using relative links.

Exercise

If you look in the "html" folder in the chapter example files, you'll find all of the single photo pages already there, except one – the page for "seattle_downtown.jpg". Create a page called "seattle_downtown.html" in the "html" folder, and test it out. Get this working before you move on. You'll find the answer in the back of the chapter if you have any problems.

So, how do I make links out of images?

You've got your large photos, your smaller thumbnails, and even a set of HTML pages for displaying individual photos. Now you need to put it all together and get those thumbnails in "index.html" linked to the pages in the "html" folder. But how?

To link an image, you put the **<img>** element inside an **<a>** element, like this:

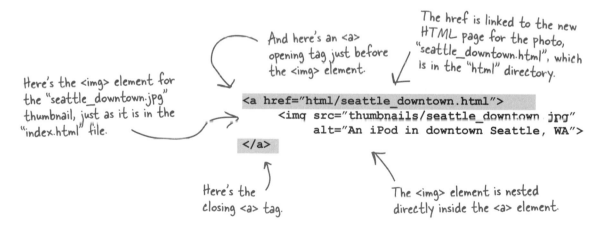

And here's an <a> opening tag just before the <img> element.

The href is linked to the new HTML page for the photo, "seattle_downtown.html", which is in the "html" directory.

Here's the <img> element for the "seattle_downtown.jpg" thumbnail, just as it is in the "index.html" file.

```
<a href="html/seattle_downtown.html">
    <img src="thumbnails/seattle_downtown.jpg"
         alt="An iPod in downtown Seattle, WA">
</a>
```

Here's the closing <a> tag.

The <img> element is nested directly inside the <a> element.

Once you've placed the **<img>** element into an **<a>** element, the browser treats the image as a clickable link. When you click the image, the browser will retrieve the page in the **href**.

Add the image links to "index.html"

This is the last step. You just need to wrap **<a>** elements around each thumbnail's **<img>** element in your "index.html" file. Remember, the **href** of each **<a>** element should link to the page containing the large version of the image in the "html" folder. Make sure that your links, thumbnails, and pages all match up correctly.

Here's the complete "index.html" file. All you need to do is add the HTML marked in gray.

```
<html>
    <head>
        <title>myPod</title>
        <style type="text/css">
            body { background-color: #eaf3da;}
        </style>
    </head>
    <body>

        <h1>Welcome to myPod</h1>
        <p>
            Welcome to the place to show off your iPod, wherever you might be.
            Wanna join the fun? All you need is any iPod, from the early classic
            iPod to the latest iPod Nano, the smallest iPod Shuffle to the largest
            iPod Photo, and a digital camera.  Just take a snapshot of your iPod in
            your favorite location and we'll be glad to post it on myPod. So, what
            are you waiting for?
        </p>

        <h2>Seattle, Washington</h2>
        <p>
            Me and my iPod in Seattle!  You can see rain clouds and the
            Space Needle.  You can't see the 628 coffee shops.
        </p>

        <p>
        <a href="html/seattle_med.html">
            <img src="thumbnails/seattle_med.jpg" alt="My iPod in Seattle, WA">
        </a>
        <a href="html/seattle_shuffle.html">
            <img src="thumbnails/seattle_shuffle.jpg" alt="A iPod Shuffle in Seattle, WA">
        </a>
        <a href="html/seattle_downtown.html">
            <img src="thumbnails/seattle_downtown.jpg" alt="An iPod in downtown Seattle, WA">
        </a>
        </p>

        <h2>Birmingham, England</h2>
        <p>
            Here are some iPod photos around Birmingham. We've obviously got some
```

```
        passionate folks over here who love their iPods. Check out the classic
        red British telephone box!
    </p>

    <p>
    <a href="html/britain.html">
        <img src="thumbnails/britain.jpg" alt="An iPod in Birmingham at a telephone box">
    </a>
    <a href="html/applestore.html">
        <img src="thumbnails/applestore.jpg" alt="An iPod at the Birmingham Apple store">
    </a>
    </p>
    </body>
</html>
```

For each thumbnail image, wrap an <a> element around it. Just be careful to get the right href in each link!

Add these **<a>** elements to your "index.html" file.
Save, load into your browser and check out myPod!

---

there are no
Dumb Questions

Q: When we put an <a> element around text we get an underline. Why don't we get something equivalent with images?

A: Actually, most browsers DO put a border around an image to show it is linked. (Our browser, Safari, is one of the few that don't.) If your browser puts a border around your linked images, and you don't like it, hold on a few more chapters and you'll learn how to take that border off with CSS. Also notice that when you pass your mouse over an image, your cursor will change to indicate you can click on the linked image. In most cases your users will know an image is linked by context and by the mouse cursor, even if there's no border.

Q: Can't we just link to the JPEG image directly without all those HTML pages? I thought the browser was smart enough to display images by themselves.

A: You're right, you could link directly to the image, like this: <a href="photos/seattle_downtown.jpg"> ... </a>. If you did that and clicked on the link, the browser would display the image by itself on a blank page. In general though, linking directly to an image is considered bad form, because you usually want to provide some context for the images you are displaying.

The myPod Web page is looking awesome! I think you should add a logo to the page - that would add a great finishing touch.

Great idea. In fact, we've got a myPod logo all ready to go.

Take another look in the folder "chapter5/mypod", and you'll find a folder called "logo". In that folder you'll find a file called "mypod.psd". The ".psd" means that the file has been saved in the Photoshop format, a common format for digital images. But Photoshop format files are meant for processing digital images, not for Web pages, so we'll have to do some work to get a "Web ready" image from it.

Many photo editing applications understand .psd files, so even if you don't have Photoshop Elements, follow along for the next few pages. If your application can't open the ".psd" file, you'll find the images from each step in the "logo" folder.

Open the myPod logo

Let's check out the myPod logo: open up the file "mypod.psd" in the "chapter5/mypod/logo" folder in Photoshop Elements:

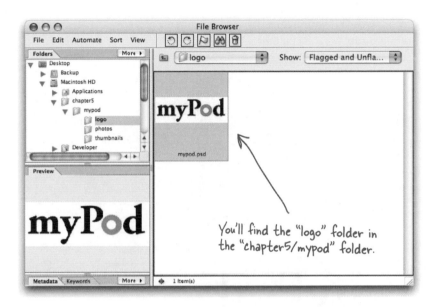

If your photo editing application won't open the file, follow along anyway — the same principles apply for other formats as well.

You'll find the "logo" folder in the "chapter5/mypod" folder.

A closer look...

Nice logo, it's got some typography combined with two circles, one gray and one white (obviously inspired by the click-wheel controls on the iPod).

But what is that checkered pattern in the background? That's the way most photo editing applications show you areas that are transparent. Keep all that in mind as we choose a graphic format for the logo...

Whenever you see this checkered pattern, that indicates a transparent area in the image.

What format should we use?

You already know that we have a couple of options in deciding how to save this image: we could use JPEG or GIF. This logo uses only three colors, text, and some geometric shapes. From what you've learned about the two formats, you're probably leaning towards GIF (good choice!).

So, go ahead and choose GIF in the format drop down, and you'll see we have a few more options. Let's take a look...

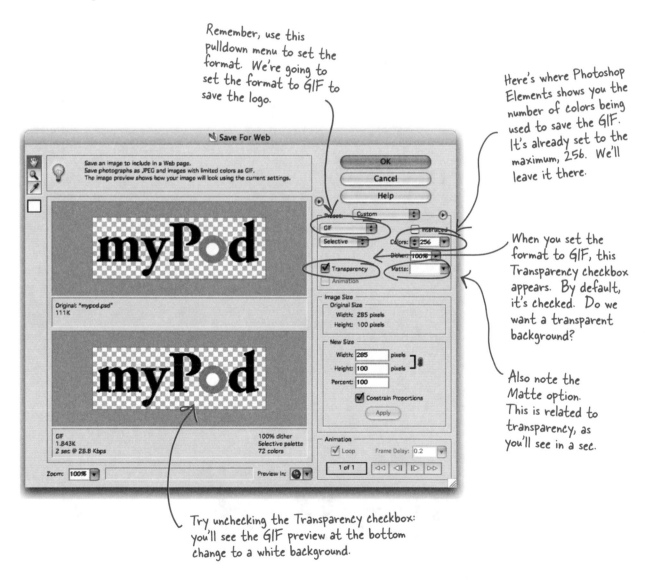

Remember, use this pulldown menu to set the format. We're going to set the format to GIF to save the logo.

Here's where Photoshop Elements shows you the number of colors being used to save the GIF. It's already set to the maximum, 256. We'll leave it there.

When you set the format to GIF, this Transparency checkbox appears. By default, it's checked. Do we want a transparent background?

Also note the Matte option. This is related to transparency, as you'll see in a sec.

Try unchecking the Transparency checkbox: you'll see the GIF preview at the bottom change to a white background.

To be transparent, or not to be transparent? That is the question...

The myPod logo is going to be placed on a light green background, so you might think that transparency is going to be a good thing, right? Well, let's compare how the logo looks using a few options in the "Save for Web" dialog:

Here's the logo saved in three different ways and displayed on a Web page with a green background.

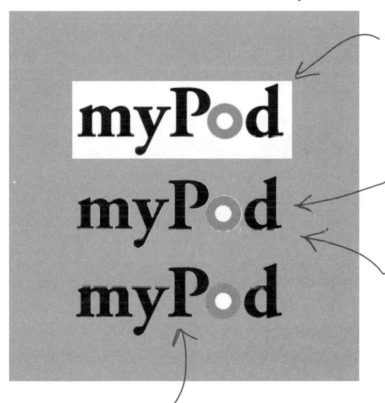

Without transparency things look pretty bad. Clearly, a white background isn't going to work on a green Web page. (It might, however, work just fine on a white Web page).

Here's what we get if we check Transparency and save. Better... but what's that white "halo" around the letters in the logo?

The halos happen because the photo editing application creates a "matte" to soften the text's edges against the background color. When it did that for this logo, however, it assumed it was softening the edges against a <u>white</u> background.

Ah, now we're talking; this looks great. For this version we told Photoshop Elements to create the matte around the text using a <u>green</u> background. How? We'll show you next.

Save the transparent GIF

You know you want a transparent GIF version of the logo,
and you also know we'll need to use a matte to prevent the
halos around the text. Let's check out the GIF panel of the
"Save for Web" dialog.

You know to choose GIF already.

And check Transparency.

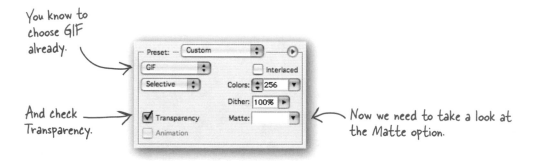

Now we need to take a look at the Matte option.

The Matte option allows you to select the color for the matte
around the text. And we want that to be the color of the Web
page background.

The Matte option supplies the color for softening the edges of the text. Since the Web page is a light green, we want to use the same color for the matte.

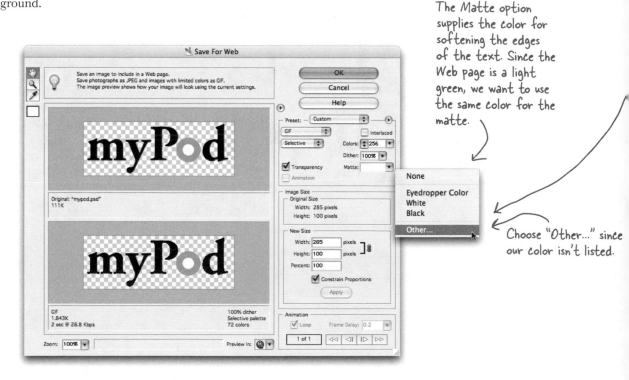

Choose "Other..." since our color isn't listed.

Wait, what *is* the color of the Web page background?

Remember that **Ready Bake CSS** in the myPod "index.html" file? That CSS is what sets the background color of the page to light green. And that's where we can get the color:

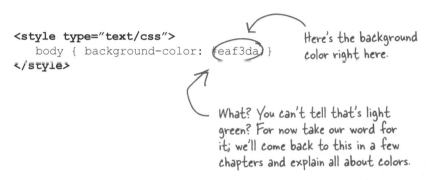

```
<style type="text/css">
    body { background-color: #eaf3da }
</style>
```

Here's the background color right here.

What? You can't tell that's light green? For now take our word for it; we'll come back to this in a few chapters and explain all about colors.

Set the matte color

When you click on the Matte pulldown menu and choose the "Other..." menu option, Photoshop Elements will bring up the Color Picker dialog.

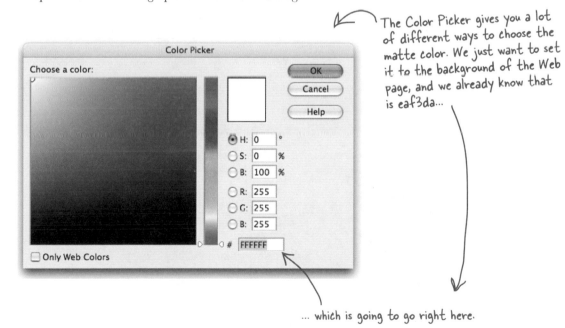

The Color Picker gives you a lot of different ways to choose the matte color. We just want to set it to the background of the Web page, and we already know that is eaf3da...

... which is going to go right here.

Set the matte color, continued

Go ahead and enter the color, "eaf3da", into the "Color Picker" dialog box. You'll see the color change to the background color of the myPod page.

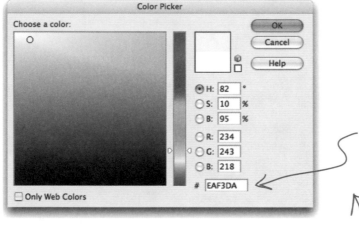

Type these letters in right here. This box is designed specifically for colors written in the Web format. You can type the letters in upper- or lowercase, it doesn't matter.

Once you've typed the color into the Color Picker, click "OK" and it will apply the change to the logo.

Check out the logo with a matte

Now take a close look at the logo again in the preview pane. You'll see Photoshop Elements has added a light green matte around the hard edges, which will give the myPod logo text a softer, more polished look when the logo is in the Web page.

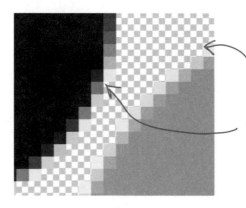

Now, when you look close up at the logo, you'll see the matte matches the green color in the background of the "mypod.html" Web page.

Save the logo

Okay you've made all the adjustments you need to in the "Save for Web" dialog, so go ahead and click "OK" to save the image as "mypod.gif".

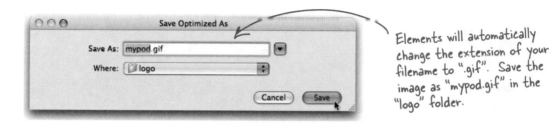

Elements will automatically change the extension of your filename to ".gif". Save the image as "mypod.gif" in the "logo" folder.

Add the logo to the myPod Web page

Now all you need to do is add the logo to the myPod Web page. We'll add it to the top so it appears above the Web site description and iPod images. That way, it's the first thing your visitors see when they come to your myPod page.

```html
<html>
    <head>
        <title>myPod</title>
        <style type="text/css">
            body { background-color: #eaf3da; }
        </style>
    </head>
    <body>
        <p>
            <img src="logo/mypod.gif" alt="myPod Logo">
        </p>

        <h1>Welcome to myPod</h1>
        .
        .
        .
    </body>
</html>
```

Add the logo image at the top of the myPod Web page. Remember to use the correct relative path for the logo, in the "logo" folder, and add an alt attribute that describes the image.

← Rest of "index.html" HTML here...

And now for the final test drive

Let's test this puppy! Reload the Web page in the browser and see how your myPod transparent GIF logo works.

And it works – all that hard work paid off. You have a great looking logo on your myPod Web page.

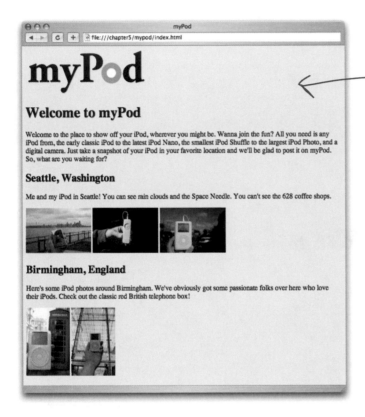

Excellent work. The logo looks great. You've got a kick-ass myPod Web site here!

Q: Do I really need to know all this stuff about image formats to write good Web pages?

A: No. You can build great Web pages without any images. However, images are a big part of the Web, so some knowledge of how images work can really help. Sometimes just an image or two makes the difference between a good page and a great one. There's a lot to know about images, but it's easy to learn as you go.

Q: Why does the text need its edges softened?

A: Check out the two versions of the myPod logo below:

myPod
myPod

You'll see the top version has very hard, jagged edges and is less readable. This is the way text is displayed by default on a computer screen. The second version has had its edges softened using a technique called anti-aliasing. Words that are anti-aliased on a computer screen are more readable and more pleasant to the eye.

Q: So where does the "Matte" come in?

A: The process of anti-aliasing softens the edges relative to the background color. If you put the bottom version of the logo (from the previous Q&A) against a colored background, you'd see it has white edges in it. The Matte option in Photoshop Elements allows you to specify the color of the background that the text will be placed on, so when the text is softened it is done so against that color.

Q: Does this technique just work for text?

A: No, it works for any lines in your graphics that might result in "jaggies". Check out the circle in the myPod logo; it was matted too.

Q: Why can't I just make the logo background color solid and match the color to the Web page?

A: You could do that too, but there is one disadvantage: if there are other things in your Web page that are showing through the transparency, then they won't be seen with the solid color version. You haven't seen any examples of this yet, but when we get into CSS, you will.

Q: What if I change my background color after I make the matted version?

A: A slight variation in your background color probably wouldn't be noticeable; however, if you change the color dramatically, you'll have to recreate the GIF with a new matte color.

BULLET POINTS

- Use the <img> element to place images in your Web page.

- Browsers treat <img> elements a little differently than other HTML elements; after reading the HTML page, the browser retrieves each image from the Web server and displays it.

- If you have more than a couple of large images on a Web page, you can make your Web page more usable and faster to download by creating thumbnails – small images that the user can click on to see the large version of the image.

- The <img> element is an inline element, which means that the browser doesn't put a linebreak before or after an image.

- The src attribute is how you specify the location of the image file. You can include images from your own site using a relative path in the src attribute, or images from other sites using a URL.

- The alt attribute of an <img> element is a meaningful description of the image. It is displayed in some browsers if the image can't be located, and is used by screen readers to describe the image for the visually impaired.

- A width of less than 800 pixels is a good rule of thumb for the size of photo images in a Web page. Most photo images that are created by digital cameras are too large for Web pages, so you'll need to resize them.

- Photoshop Elements is one of many photo editing applications you can use to resize your images.

- Images that are too large for the browser make Web pages difficult to use and slow to download and display.

- A pixel is the smallest dot that can be represented on the screen. Each image is composed of thousands of pixels. Depending on your monitor, there can be anywhere from 72 pixels in an inch to 120 pixels in an inch.

- JPEG and GIF are the two formats for images that are widely supported by Web browsers.

- The JPEG format is best for photographs and other complex images.

- The GIF format is best for logos and other simple graphics with solid colors, lines, or text.

- JPEG images can be compressed at a variety of different qualities, so you can choose the best balance of quality and file size for your needs.

- The GIF image format allows you to make an image with a transparent background. If you put an image with a transparent background in a Web page, what's behind the image, such as the background color of the page, will show through the transparent parts of the image.

- In Photoshop Elements, use the Matte color menu in the "Save for Web" dialog to choose the right color for softening the edges of your transparent GIF image.

- Images can be used as links to other Web pages. To create a link from an image, use the <img> element as the content of an <a> element, and put the link in the href attribute of the <a> element.

HTMLcross

It's time to give your right brain a break and put that left brain to work.
All these words are HTML-related and from this chapter.

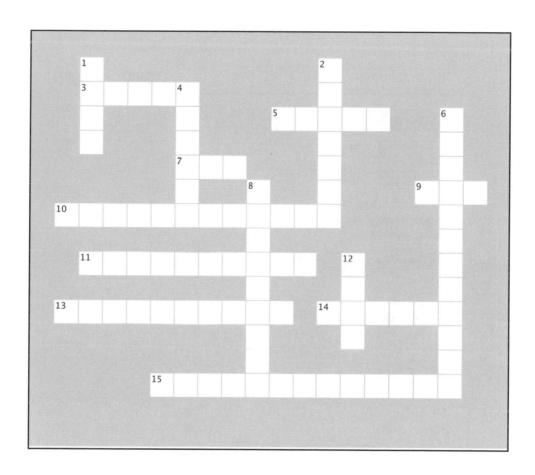

Across

3. Smallest element on a screen.
5. Web server makes a request for each one of these.
7. Better for solid colors, lines, and small text.
9. Newcomer image format.
10. Most Web servers retrieve images this way.
11. Miles you can draw with a pencil.
13. Small images on a page.
14. You used Photoshop Elements to do this to images.
15. The alt attribute improves this.

Down

1. Lovable MP3 player.
2. With JPEG you can control this.
4. The larger the image, the _____ it takes to transfer it.
6. GIF has it, JPEG doesn't.
8. Technique for softening edges of text.
12. Better for photos with continuous tones.

Exercise Solutions

WHICH IMAGE FORMAT?

Congratulations: you've been elected "Grand Image Format Chooser" of the day. For each image below, choose the format that would best represent it on the Web.

JPEG or GIF

A photo with lots of continuous shades of gray. ☑ ☐

Only a couple of colors with some text; definitely a GIF. ☐ ☑

A photo with lots of colors; definitely a JPEG. ☑ ☐

Just a simple black and white icon; a GIF. ☐ ☑

This image is borderline. It has lots of continuous colors (JPEG), but is also slightly geometric (GIF) and you may want to use this in a way that requires transparency (GIF). ☑ ☑

Sharpen your pencil
Solution

Here's a "Sharpen your pencil" that is actually about pencils (oh, and images of course). This exercise involves a bit of trivia: *Given a typical, brand-new pencil, if you drew one continuous line with it, using the entire pencil up, how long would the line be?*

What's that got to do with images? To find the answer you're going to have to write some HTML. The answer is contained in the image that is at the URL: http://www.headfirstlabs.com/trivia/pencil.gif. Your job is to add an image to this HTML and retrieve the answer:

```html
<html>
    <head>
        <title>Sharpen your pencil trivia</title>
    </head>
    <body>
        <p>How long a line can you draw with the typical pencil?</p>
        <p>
            <img src="http://www.headfirstlabs.com/trivia/pencil.gif">
        </p>
    </body>
</html>
```

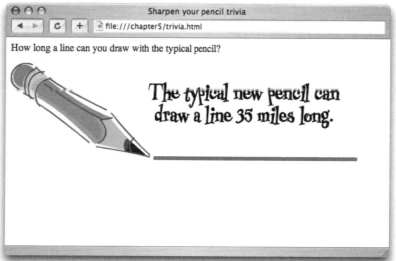

Source: http://www.papermate.com

Exercise Solutions

Here are the results of having a broken image in a few different browsers. In most cases, the browser is able to use the extra `alt` attribute information to improve what is displayed. Why do we care? After all, this is an error in a Web page; we should just fix it, right? Well, in the real world things are often not ideal; sometimes things break, Internet connections go bad in the middle of a page load, or visually impaired users need to *hear* what is in the image, because they can't see it.

↑ PC

The Firefox browser just displays the alt attribute, as if it were text, if the image can't be retrieved.

↓ Mac

Internet Explorer displays a broken image icon and the alt attribute text next to it.

Safari on the Mac doesn't make good use of the alt attribute from broken images.

On the Mac, Internet Explorer also displays a broken image icon and the alt attribute text next to it.

Exercise
Solutions

WHICH IMAGE FORMAT?²

Did you notice how the image quality degrades?

Format	Quality	Size	Time	Winner
			Note that your numbers may differ depending on the version of software you are using.	
JPEG	Maximum	232K	83 Seconds	☐
JPEG	Very High	112K	41 Seconds	☐
JPEG	High	64K	24 Seconds	☐
JPEG	Medium	30K	12 Seconds	☑
JPEG	Low	18K	7 Seconds	☐
GIF	N/A	221K	80 Seconds	☐

Is the winner really *Medium*? Not necessarily. It all depends on what your needs are. If you want a really high quality image, then you might want Very High. If you want the fastest possible site, then try Low. We've chosen Medium because it is a nice trade off in size versus the quality of the image. You may think Low is good enough, or that it's worth bumping the quality up to High. So, it's all very subjective. One thing is for sure however, GIF doesn't work very well for this image (which should not be a surprise).

Exercise Solutions

If you look in the "html" folder with the chapter examples, you'll find all of the single photo pages already there, except one: the page for "seattle_downtown.jpg". Create a page called "seattle_downtown.html" in the "html" folder, and test it out. Get this working before you move on.

Here's the answer:

Here's the HTML; this file should be called "seattle_downtown.html".

```html
<html>
   <head>
      <title>myPod: Seattle Downtown</title>
      <style type="text/css"> body { background-color: #eaf3da; } </style>
   </head>
   <body>
      <h1>Downtown Seattle</h1>
      <p>
      <img src="../photos/seattle_downtown.jpg" alt="An iPod in downtown Seattle, WA">
      </p>
   </body>
</html>
```

This file should go in the "html" folder under "mypod".

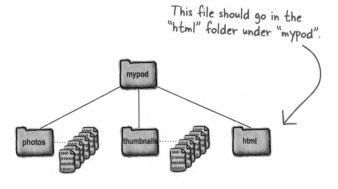

Here's the test drive.

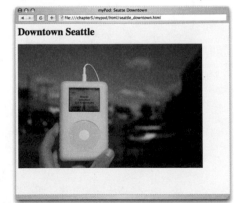

Exercise Solutions

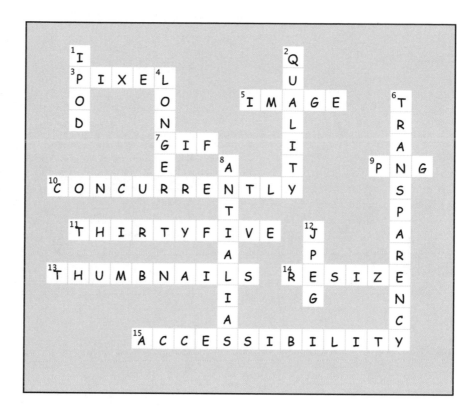

The crossword puzzle solution:

Across:
3. PIXEL
5. IMAGE
7. GIF
9. PNG
10. CONCURRENTLY
11. THIRTYFIVE
13. THUMBNAILS
14. RESIZE
15. ACCESSIBILITY

Down:
1. IPOD
2. QUALITY
4. LONGEST
6. TRANSPARENCY
8. ATTRIBUTE
12. JPG

Sharpen your pencil

Here's how you add the image "seattle.jpg" to the file "index.html".

```
<h2>Seattle, Washington</h2>
<p>
    Me and my iPod in Seattle!  You can see rain clouds and the
    Space Needle.   You can't see the 628 coffee shops.
</p>

<p>
    <img src="photos/seattle.jpg" alt="My iPod in Seattle, WA">
</p>
```

Serious HTML

What else is there to know about HTML?

You're well on your way to mastering HTML. In fact, isn't it about time we move on to CSS and learn how to make all this bland markup look fabulous? Before we do, we need to make sure your HTML is really tight (you know... buttoned up, ship shape, nailed down) and we're going to do that by getting serious about the way we write our HTML. Don't get us wrong, you've been writing first-class HTML all along, but there's a few things you can do to help the browser faithfully display your pages and to make sure that little mistakes don't creep into your markup. What's in it for you? Pages that display more uniformly across browsers (and even display well on mobile devices and screen readers for the visually impaired), pages that load faster, and pages that are guaranteed to play well with CSS. Get ready, this is the chapter where you move from Web tinkerer to Web professional.

Jim

Frank

Joe

Hey guys, the boss just sent an email. Before we move Head First Lounge to CSS, he wants us to button up our HTML.

Jim: Button up?

Frank: You know, make sure it meets the HTML "standards."

Jim: Our HTML is just fine... here, look at it in the browser. It looks beautiful. We're a careful bunch. We know how to correctly form our elements.

Joe: Yeah, that's what I think... they're just trying to give us another thing to worry about. Standards, schmandards. We know what we're doing.

Frank: Actually guys, I hate to admit it but I think the boss is right on this one.

Jim, Joe: Huh?!

Joe: Come on, this is just going to mean even *more* work. We've already got enough to do.

Frank: Guys, what I'm saying is that I think this will help us do *less* work in the future.

Joe: Ha! This should be good...

Frank: Okay, here goes: the browser reads our HTML and then does its best to display it, right? In fact, browsers are pretty forgiving... you can have a few mistakes here and there, or use HTML incorrectly – like putting a block element accidentally inside an inline element – and the browser tries to do the right thing.

Jim: Yeah, and?

Frank: But different browsers (say Internet Explorer versus Firefox versus Safari) have different ways of handling imperfect HTML. In other words, if you have mistakes in your HTML, then all bets are off in terms of how your pages will look in different browsers. It's only when you *don't have* mistakes that most browsers display things consistently. And when we start adding presentation to our HTML with CSS, the differences will get even more dramatic if our HTML isn't up to snuff.

So, by making sure we're, as they say, "compliant" with the "standards," we'll have a lot fewer problems with our pages displaying incorrectly for our customers.

Jim: If that reduces the number of 3 a.m. calls I get, then that sounds like a good idea to me. After all, our customers use every browser under the sun.

Joe: Wait a sec, I still don't get it. Aren't we compliant now? What's wrong with our HTML?

Frank: Maybe nothing, but there are a few things we can to do to make sure.

Joe: Like what?

Frank: Well, we can start by helping the browser a bit by telling it exactly which version of HTML we're using.

Joe: I'm not even sure I know which version we're using.

Frank: Ah ha! So there is some room for improvement here. Okay, let's begin by figuring out which version of HTML we're using and how we can tell the browser about it. There are a few other things we need to do too, but don't worry, this isn't a big deal. And, when we're done, life will be much easier when we start using CSS.

BRAIN POWER

Browsers all do a pretty good job of consistently displaying your pages when you write correct HTML, but when you make mistakes or do nonstandard things in your HTML, pages are often displayed differently from one browser to another. Why do you think that is the case?

A Brief History of HTML

HTML 1.0-2.0

These were the early days; you could fit everything there was to know about HTML into the back of your car. Pages weren't pretty, but at least they were hypertext enabled. No one cared much about presentation, and just about everyone on the Web had their very own "home page." Even a count of the number of pencils, paperclips, and Post-it notes on your desk was considered "Web content" back then (you think we're kidding).

HTML 3

The long, cold days of the "Browser Wars." Netscape and Microsoft were duking it out for control of the world. After all, he who controls the browser controls the Universe, right?

At the center of the fallout was the Web developer. During the wars, an arms race emerged as each browser company kept adding their own proprietary extensions in order to stay ahead. Who could keep up? And not only that, back in those days, you had to often write *two* separate Web pages: one for the Netscape browser and one for Internet Explorer. Not good.

HTML 4

Ahhh... the end of the Browser Wars and, to our rescue, the World Wide Web Consortium (nickname: W3C). Their plan: to bring order to the Universe by creating the ONE HTML "standard" to rule them all.

The key to their plan? Separate HTML's structure and presentation into two languages – a language for structure (HTML 4.0) and a language for presentation (CSS) – and convince the browser makers it was in their best interest to adopt these standards.

But did their plan work?

Uh, almost... with a few changes (see HTML 4.01).

| 1989 | 1991 | 1995 | 1998 |

Our goal in this chapter is to get ourselves up to HTML 4.01.

Starting in Chapter 7, our goal is to be faithful to XHTML 1.0. As always, the world keeps moving, so we'll also talk later in the book about where things are going.

HTML 4.01

XHTML 1.0

Ah, the good life. HTML 4.01 entered the scene in 1999, and is the most current version of HTML. While everyone hoped 4.0 would be the ONE, it's always the case that a few fixes are needed here and there. No biggies and nothing to worry about.

Compared to the early days of HTML (when we all had to walk barefoot in 6 feet of snow, uphill both ways), we were all cruising along writing HTML 4.01 and sleeping well at night knowing that almost all browsers (at least the ones anyone would care about) are going to display your content just fine.

But, of course, just as we were all getting comfortable, new technologies were created and things changed. HTML and another markup language known as XML got together, and sooner than you can say "arranged marriage," XHTML 1.0 was born. XHTML inherited traits from both parents: popularity and browser-friendliness from HTML, and extensibility and strictness from XML. What does that mean? You'll find out soon enough, because we're going to have you creating XHTML Web pages before you can say "Extensible Hypertext Markup Language." Well, at least in the next chapter.

????

And what will happen in the future? Will we all be going to work in flying cars and swallowing nutrition pills for dinner? Keep reading to find out.

1999

2000

The Browser Exposed

This week's interview:
Why do you care which version
of HTML you're displaying?

Head First: We're glad to have you here, Browser. As you know, "HTML versions" have become a popular issue. What's the deal with that? You're a Web browser after all. I give you HTML and you display it the best you can.

Browser: Being a browser is tough these days... there are a lot of Web pages out there and many are written with old versions of HTML or with mistakes in their markup. Like you said, my job is to try to display every single one of those pages, no matter what.

Head First: So what's the big deal? What does it really matter which version of HTML I use?

Browser: Remember the browser wars? All kinds of elements were added to HTML that we aren't supposed to use anymore. But some people expect us browsers to be able to display them anyway, and we don't always agree on how that should be done.

Head First: Why aren't we supposed to use those elements any more?

Browser: Well, before CSS was invented, HTML had elements that were there for presentation, not structure. Now, with CSS, we don't need those anymore, but there are still plenty of Web pages out there that use them.

Head First: I think I'm starting to see the problem. So how do you manage to display all these pages in all these different versions of HTML? That's quite a tall order.

Browser: Yeah, like I said, it's tough being a browser. What we end up doing is having two sets of rules for displaying Web pages: one for old HTML and one for the newer, standard HTML. When I use the old rules, I call that my "quirks mode" because

there are so many weird things that can happen on those pages.

Head First: That sounds like a pretty good solution to me...

Browser: Well, it can get you into trouble, though. If you're writing new HTML, but you don't *tell me* you're writing new HTML, then I have to *assume* you're writing old HTML, and go into quirks mode just in case. And you don't want that.

Head First: What do you mean?

Browser: Not all browsers agree on how to display the older stuff, but we all do a pretty consistent job with standard HTML. So if you're using standard HTML, tell me and you'll get more consistent results in all browsers.

Head First: Oh, so you can end up using the quirks mode rules on the pages written using new HTML?

Browser: Exactly. If I don't know you're writing new HTML, I go into my quirks mode and do the best I can. But, you don't want that because all those "quirks" mean that your pages might end up looking a bit off, when they could have looked beautiful if I'd only known you were using new HTML.

Head First: Ahh. So, what's the solution to this mess? We definitely want our Web pages to look good.

Browser: Easy. Tell me up front which version of HTML you're using. That way I know which rules to use to display your page.

Head First: Got it. Thank you, Browser!

We can't have your pages putting the browser into Quirks Mode!

We'll all be better off for telling the browser up front: "Hey, we're an HTML page that gets it. We're standards compliant. This is HTML 4.01, baby!"

When you do that, the browser knows exactly how to handle your page and (at least on any browser you'd care about) the page is going to display as you'd expect.

So, how do you tell the browser? Easy, you just add one line to the top of your HTML files. Here's what the line looks like:

```
<!DOCTYPE HTML PUBLIC "-//W3C//DTD HTML 4.01 Transitional//EN" "http://www.w3.org/TR/html4/loose.dtd">
```

Okay, we know that is one butt ugly line, but keep in mind, it is written for your browser, not you. This line is called a *document type definition* because it tells the browser the *type* of the *document*, and in this case, the document is your HTML page. Let's just take a quick peek at this line to get a feel for it. But again, this is browser speak, not something you need to know well or memorize. Just throw it in the top of your HTML and you're ready to go.

Tells the browser this is specifying a document type for this page.

This means that <html> is the root (first) element in your page.

This just means the HTML 4.01 standard is publicly available.

This part says we're using HTML version 4.01 and that HTML markup is written in English.

You can type this all on one line, or if you want, you can add a return where we did. Just make sure you only press return in between the parts in the quotes.

```
<!DOCTYPE html PUBLIC "-//W3C//DTD HTML 4.01 Transitional//EN"
          "http://www.w3.org/TR/html4/loose.dtd">
```

Notice that this is <u>NOT</u> an HTML element. It has a "!" after the "<" at the beginning, which tells you this is something different.

This points to a file that identifies this particular standard.

We'll talk more about the word transitional in a bit....

This is all tricky to type in with all the slashes, quotes, and so on. So instead of typing it in, you can copy and paste this text from the file "doctype.txt". You'll find this file in the "chapter6" folder when you download the files for the book from the headfirstlabs.com Web site.

there are no
Dumb Questions

Q: What exactly do you mean when you say we're "compliant," or that we're writing "standard HTML?"

A: "Standard HTML" just means the version of HTML that everyone has agreed is "the standard," and right now that is HTML 4.01.

Being compliant is just another way of saying your pages meet the standard.

Q: And why should I care about standard HTML, or about making my pages compliant? They look fine to me.

A: Do you really want to go to all the trouble of writing Web pages and then styling them with CSS, only to have them display inconsistently (which is another way of saying "display badly") in some browsers? By making them compliant, you're assuring that your pages are going to display as consistently as possible in a variety of browsers.

Q: How do I make sure my pages are compliant, then?

A: You need to do a couple of things, which we're going to go through, but we're also going to make use of a freely available tool on the Web that checks your pages to make sure they're compliant.

Q: So, we're calling HTML 4.01 the standard?

A: Yes, HTML 4.01 is the HTML standard most widely supported by browsers. The Web keeps moving ahead, though, so we'll talk in the very next chapter about what's new in the standards world.

Q: What happens when there is an HTML 5?

A: Good question. It's likely that there won't be an HTML 5 because the new standard for writing Web pages is XHTML. You're going to learn all about XHTML in the next chapter. The good news is that you're already in great shape to use either HTML 4.01 or

XHTML, so no matter which standard you choose, it will be easy for you to write Web pages based on what you've learned so far.

Q: Let me get this straight: if I throw the document type definition in the top of my HTML file, then the browser sees it and can make certain assumptions about my HTML, which is a good thing?

A: That's right. The document type definition tells your browser, "I'm using HTML 4.01." When the browser sees that, it assumes you know what you're talking about and that you *really are* writing HTML 4.01. That's good because the browser will use the layout and display rules for HTML 4.01, and not use quirks mode.

Q: What if I tell the browser I'm using HTML 4.01, and I'm not?

A: The browser will figure out that you're not really writing HTML 4.01 and go back to quirks mode. And then you're back to the problem of having the various browsers handle your page in different ways. The only way you can get predictable results is to tell the browser you're using "HTML 4.01" and to actually do so.

Q: I really don't have to worry about what's in the document type line? Just throw it on my page?

A: Yup, that's pretty much the case. Although there is one gotcha: there are a few different document types you might want to know about and we're going to talk about another one of those in just a sec. But, in terms of using the document type, just throw it in the top of your file. Once you've got the DOCTYPE in there, no one worries on a daily basis about what it has in it.

Q: The word "transitional" in that document type worries me a bit. I thought this was a standard, but it sounds less than standard if it is "transitional."

A: Good catch, and you've got good instincts. If you'll hold on a few pages we'll get to the bottom of that question.

Okay, I think we've got it now. Let's get that DOCTYPE in the lounge files.

Adding the document type definition

Enough talk, let's get that DOCTYPE in the HTML. You can attempt to type it in yourself (we hope you have really good eyes), or you can copy and paste it from the file "doctype.txt" in the "chapter6" folder.

> Here's the DOCTYPE line. Just add it as the very first thing in the "lounge.html" file.

```
<!DOCTYPE html PUBLIC "-//W3C//DTD HTML 4.01 Transitional//EN"
    "http://www.w3.org/TR/html4/loose.dtd">
<html>
  <head>
    <title>Head First Lounge</title>
  </head>
  <body>
    <h1>Welcome to the New and Improved Head First Lounge</h1>
        <img src="drinks.gif">
    <p>
        Join us any evening for refreshing
        <a href="elixir.html">elixirs</a>,
        conversation and maybe a game or two
        of <em>Dance Dance Revolution</em>.
        Wireless access is always provided;
        BYOWS (Bring Your Own Web Server).
    </p>
    <h2>Directions</h2>
    <p>
        You'll find us right in the center of downtown
        Webville.  If you need help finding us, check out our
        <a href="directions.html">detailed directions</a>.
        Come join us!
    </p>
  </body>
</html>
```

> Remember, you can type it all on one line, or you can hit return between the quoted parts like we've done here.

The DOCTYPE test drive

Make the changes to your "lounge.html" file in the
"chapter6/lounge" folder and then load the page in your browser.

Wow, no difference. Well, we didn't
really expect any because all the
DOCTYPE does is let the browser
know for sure you're using HTML 4.01.

Exercise

Add a DOCTYPE to the "directions.html" and "elixir.html" file as well. Go
ahead and give them a good test. Just like "lounge.html", you won't see
any fireworks (but you might sleep a bit better tonight).

See, piece of cake. The DOCTYPE is in our pages and working fine.

Jim: Yeah, really easy. But here's what I still don't get: we put this DOCTYPE at the top of our file to tell the browser our page is HTML 4.01 but that doesn't ensure that the file *really is* HTML 4.01. We could have made a mistake. So what's the point?

Frank: You're right, because your promise to the browser is only good if you actually have written perfect HTML 4.01. That's what I was going to get to next. What we can do is make use of a free online service that can look at a page and tell us if it's compliant.

Jim: Really? How does that work?

Frank: Well, this service first looks at the document type and then checks all your HTML and makes sure it's actually correct... like checking to make sure you're spelling your tag names right, your elements are nested properly, that your inline elements are inside block elements and so on. It's called a validator.

Jim: Wow, and this is free? Who provides this service?

Frank: The guys who came up with the standards. They're called the World Wide Web Consortium, or W3C for short.

Jim: This sounds like the answer to writing compliant HTML. But how do I know all those things you just mentioned, like what elements go inside what elements?

Frank: Let's check out the validator first and then we'll come back to that...

Meet the W3C validator

Let's give the validator a spin and have it check out the lounge files. To follow along, just point your browser to http://validator.w3.org.

The W3C validator is located at http://validator.w3.org.

The W3C Markup Validation Service

http://validator.w3.org/

W3C **Q**UALITY **A**SSURANCE **Markup Validation Service** v0.7.0

Home   About...   News   Docs   Help & FAQ   Feedback   Link Checker

This is the W3C Markup Validation Service, a free service that checks Web documents in formats like HTML and XHTML for conformance to W3C Recommendations and other standards.

Validate:
by URL
by File Upload
by direct Input

Validate Your Markup

Validate by URL

Address: [   ] (Check)

Enter the URL of the page you want to check. Advanced options are available from the Extended Interface.

Validate by File Upload

Local File: (Choose File) no file selected   (Check)

Select the file you want to upload and check. Advanced options are available from the Extended File Upload Interface.

Note: file upload may not work with Internet Explorer on some versions of Windows XP Service Pack 2, see our information page on the W3C QA Website.

Validate by Direct Input

Input the markup you would like to validate in the text area below:

[   ]

(Check)

Only complete documents (along with a Doctype declaration) will be validated. Advanced options are available from the Extended Direct Input Interface.

There are three ways you can check your HTML:

(1) If your page is on the Web, then you can type in the URL here, click the "Check" button, and the service will retrieve your HTML and check it.

(2) You can click "Choose file" (or "Browse" if you're using Windows) and choose a file on your computer. When you've selected the file, click "Check", and the browser will upload the page for the service to check.

(3) Or, copy and paste your HTML into this form. Then click "Check" and the service will check your HTML.

Validating the Head First Lounge

We're going to use option (3) to validate the "lounge.html"
file. That means we need to copy and paste the HTML from
"lounge.html" into the form at the bottom of the W3C validator
Web page; keep following along and give it a try...

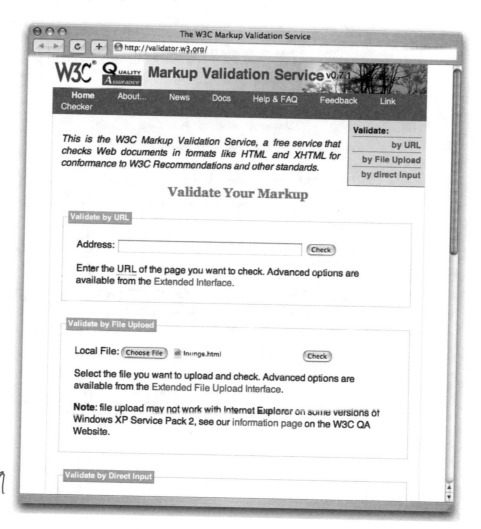

We're using method (2) here. We clicked on the "Choose File" button and browsed to
the file "lounge.html", which now has the DOCTYPE for Transitional HTML 4.01 at
the top. We're ready for the big moment... will the Web page validate? Bets anyone?
Click "Check" (and turn the page) to find out...

Feel free to use method (1) or
(3) if it's more convenient.

Houston, we have a problem...

That red on the page can't be good. It doesn't look
like the page validated. We'd better take a look...

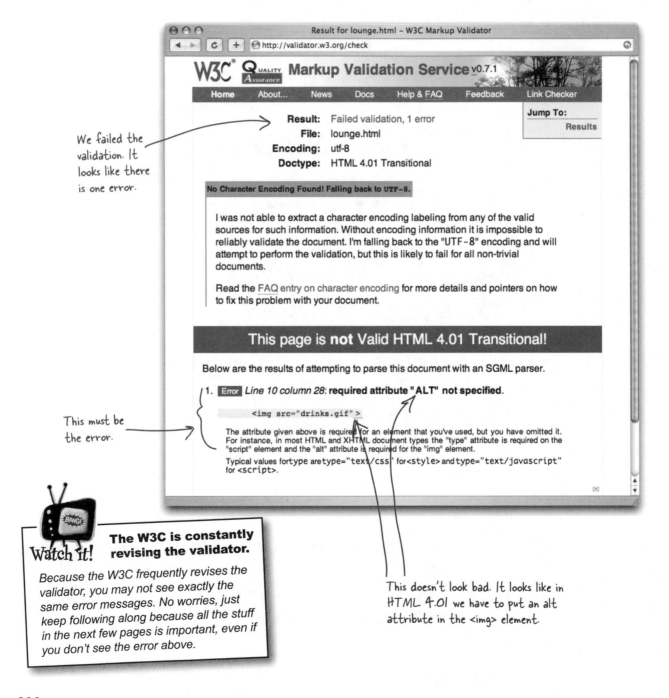

We failed the
validation. It
looks like there
is one error.

This must be
the error.

This doesn't look bad. It looks like in
HTML 4.01 we have to put an alt
attribute in the <img> element.

Watch it!

The W3C is constantly revising the validator.

*Because the W3C frequently revises the
validator, you may not see exactly the
same error messages. No worries, just
keep following along because all the stuff
in the next few pages is important, even if
you don't see the error above.*

Fixing that error

Okay, this looks pretty simple to fix. You just need to add an **alt** attribute to your **<img>** elements in HTML 4.01. Go ahead and open "lounge.html", make the change, save, and then let's try to validate again.

```
<!DOCTYPE html PUBLIC "-//W3C//DTD HTML 4.01 Transitional//EN"
    "http://www.w3.org/TR/html4/loose.dtd">
<html>
  <head>
    <title>Head First Lounge</title>
  </head>
  <body>
    <h1>Welcome to the New and Improved Head First Lounge</h1>
        <img src="drinks.gif" alt="Drinks">
    <p>
        Join us any evening for refreshing
        <a href="elixir.html">elixirs</a>,
        conversation and maybe a game or two
        of <em>Dance Dance Revolution</em>.
        Wireless access is always provided;
        BYOWS (Bring Your Own Web Server).
    </p>
    <h2>Directions</h2>
    <p>
        You'll find us right in the center of downtown
        Webville. If you need help finding us, check out our
        <a href="directions.html">detailed directions</a>.
        Come join us!
    </p>
  </body>
</html>
```

You know the alt attribute; add it into the <img> element.

BRAIN POWER

Why do you think the **alt** attribute is required in HTML 4.01?

We're not there yet...

Hmm; it looks like we're now "tentatively valid HTML 4.01 Transitional." That sounds like "close, but no cigar." Let's take a look:

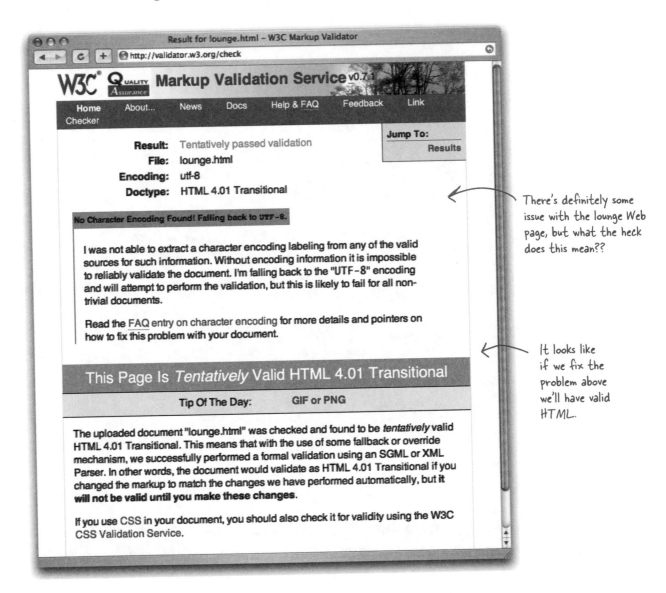

There's definitely some issue with the lounge Web page, but what the heck does this mean??

It looks like if we fix the problem above we'll have valid HTML.

So, we've got a perfectly valid HTML file in terms of how we've written the HTML, but it looks like we have to tell it something about our "Character Encoding". To solve that we're going to have to find out what the heck it means...

See, we're getting this error message that the validator can't find a character encoding.

No Character Encoding Found! Falling back to UTF-8.

I was not able to extract a character encoding labeling from any of the valid sources for such information. Without encoding information it is impossible to reliably validate the document. I'm falling back to the "UTF-8" encoding and will attempt to perform the validation, but this is likely to fail for all non-trivial documents.

Frank: The character encoding tells the browser what kind of characters are being used in the page. For instance, pages can be written using encodings for English, Chinese, Arabic, and lots of other types of characters.

Jim: What's so hard about figuring out how to display a character? If there's an "a" in the file, then the browser should display an "a". Right?

Frank: Well, what if you're using Chinese in your pages? It's an entirely different "alphabet" and it has a heck of a lot more than 26 A-Z characters.

Jim: Oh. Good point.... But shouldn't the browser be able to tell the difference? Those other languages look nothing like English.

Frank: No; the browser is just reading data. It could assume it was getting English-language characters, but what if it's not? The character encoding takes the guesswork out of it.

Jim: We've had the site up for a long time; why is this an issue now?

Frank: Because the validator is saying "Hey, if I'm going to validate your page, you'd better tell me up front what characters you're going to use!" And think about it, we'd want to do that for the browsers out there anyway. Don't stress, we just need to add one more line to our HTML, called a **<meta>** tag. I should have thought of this sooner.

Jim: Got any other surprises for us? I really thought our Web page would validate after we put the document type definition in our file...

Frank: I sure hope there are no more surprises! Let's get the **<meta>** tag in there and find out.

Adding a <meta> tag to specify the content type

Most of you reading this book are probably using English or Western-European languages (the so-called "Latin" languages), so you'll need a **<meta>** tag in your HTML that looks like this:

```
<meta http-equiv="Content-Type" content="text/html; charset=ISO-8859-1">
```

You're going to throw this line in as the first thing inside the **<head>** element of your HTML. This tag tells any browser the content type of your file, and what kinds of characters are used to encode it. Let's look at the **<meta>** tag in a little more detail...

"meta" means we're going to tell the browser something about the page...

And we're going to tell it something more about the content type of the page.

The content attribute is where we specify the content type information.

Here's the new part; this tells the browser that we're using the ISO-8859-1 character encoding.

```
<meta http-equiv="Content-Type" content="text/html; charset=ISO-8859-1">
```

Just like other HTML tags, the <meta> tag has attributes.

First we tell it that this is an HTML file. This is a bit redundant, because the browser already knows that (remember we told it that in the DOCTYPE as well).

Notice that this whole string is the value of the content attribute.

---

there are no Dumb Questions

Q: DOCTYPES, <meta> tags... ugh, do I need to really remember all this to write Web pages?

A: Specifying a DOCTYPE and a **<meta>** content tag are kind of like taxes: you gotta do them to be compliant. Look at it this way: you already understand them more than 99% of the Web page writing population, which is great. But at the end of the day, everyone just puts the DOCTYPE and <meta> tag in their HTML and moves on with life. So make sure you've got the right DOCTYPE and <meta> tag and then go do something much more fun.

Q: ISO-8859-1?

A: Work with us here. It's like WD-40; you don't worry about why it's called that, you just use it.

ISO-8859-1 is the character encoding for "Latin-1" characters, which can represent almost all the European languages. If you're writing in another language, check out the information on character encoding at http://www.w3.org/International/O-charset.html.

Making the validator (and more than a few browsers) happy with a <meta> content tag...

Okay, you know the plan. You just need to type the **<meta>** content type line right into your HTML. Let's first add it to the "lounge.html" file:

> Here's the <meta> tag. We've added it to the <head> element above the <title> element.

```
<!DOCTYPE html PUBLIC "-//W3C//DTD HTML 4.01 Transitional//EN"
    "http://www.w3.org/TR/html4/loose.dtd">
<html>
  <head>
    <meta http-equiv="Content-Type" content="text/html; charset=ISO-8859-1">
    <title>Head First Lounge</title>
  </head>
  <body>
    <h1>Welcome to the New and Improved Head First Lounge</h1>
      <img src="drinks.gif" alt="Drinks">
    <p>
      Join us any evening for refreshing
      <a href="elixir.html">elixirs</a>,
      conversation and maybe a game or two
      of <em>Dance Dance Revolution</em>.
      Wireless access is always provided;
      BYOWS (Bring Your Own Web Server).
    </p>
    <h2>Directions</h2>
    <p>
      You'll find us right in the center of downtown
      Webville. If you need help finding us, check out our
      <a href="directions.html">detailed directions</a>.
      Come join us!
    </p>
  </body>
</html>
```

> Always add this line above any other elements in the <head> element.

Want to place another bet? Is this going to validate? First, make the changes to your "lounge.html" file, save it and reload it into your browser. Once again, *you* won't notice any change, but the *browser* will. Now let's see if it validates...

Third time's the charm?

Just like before, upload your "lounge.html" HTML file to the W3C validator Web page at http://validator.w3.org. Or, you can validate by copying and pasting your HTML into the form, or even transfer the files to your Web site and give the validator your URL, whichever you prefer. Once you've done that, click the "Check" button...

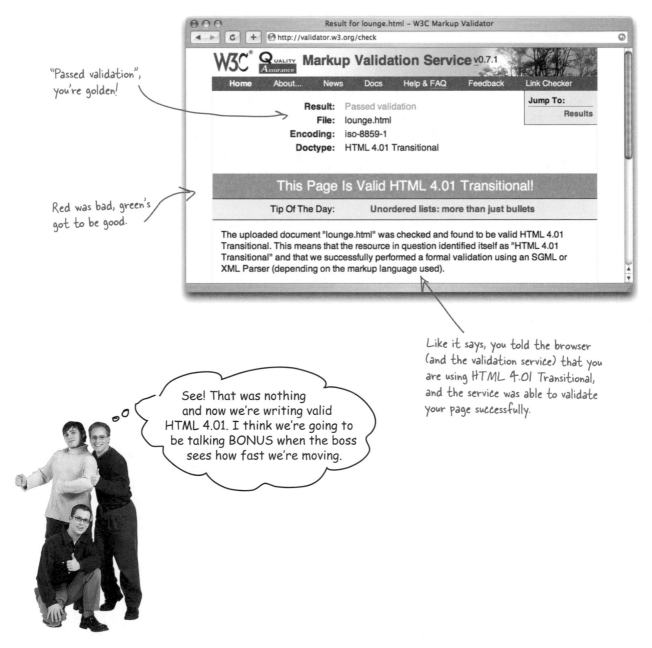

"Passed validation", you're golden!

Red was bad, green's got to be good.

Like it says, you told the browser (and the validation service) that you are using HTML 4.01 Transitional, and the service was able to validate your page successfully.

See! That was nothing and now we're writing valid HTML 4.01. I think we're going to be talking BONUS when the boss sees how fast we're moving.

Okay, it's been more than a "few pages" since you said you were going to talk about what "transitional" means. What's with this transitional stuff? If we're writing "standard" HTML 4.01, why is it transitional?

There are actually two DOCTYPEs, one for those <u>transitioning</u> to HTML 4.01, and a more <u>strict</u> DOCTYPE for those who are already there.

Imagine you've got a Web site with hundreds of Web pages, all written in nonstandard HTML. You'd like to improve the site and get all that HTML up to the 4.01 standard, but you're using lots of old legacy stuff from back in the 2.0 and 3.2 days of HTML.

What do you do? Use the HTML 4.01 Transitional DOCTYPE, which allows you to validate your pages but still permits some of the legacy HTML. That way, you can be sure you don't have any outright mistakes in your markup (like typos, mismatched tags, and so on) but you won't have to rework all your HTML to get it to validate.

Then, after you've removed all the legacy HTML, you're all ready for the strict document type, which ensures you have a fully compliant, standardized Web site.

Okay, so it gives us a transition point between old style HTML and standard HTML 4.01. But why are we using it? Why didn't we just start with strict?

We certainly could have.

That would have been a perfectly valid approach. But, while we've been writing pretty decent HTML in this book, we're just now learning how to write it in a way that is correct and standardized. Right? And, as you can see, it took us a few steps to get there, what with all the DOCTYPEs and **<meta>** tags and the **alt** attribute.

But now that we're there, and we've got validated transitional 4.01 HTML, we're in a good position to start using the strict form of HTML. Let's give strict a try and then we can talk a little more about transitional versus strict.

I think we've been pretty darn strict in our HTML. Let's throw the strict DOCTYPE in and see what happens.

To move from transitional HTML 4.01 to strict, we change the DOCTYPE to the strict version. Once we've done that, the validator (and browsers) will assume we're playing by stricter rules that don't allow some of the legacy HTML. We'll talk about those rules in a sec, but for now let's give the strict DOCTYPE a try. To do that, we'll start by taking a quick look at the DOCTYPE:

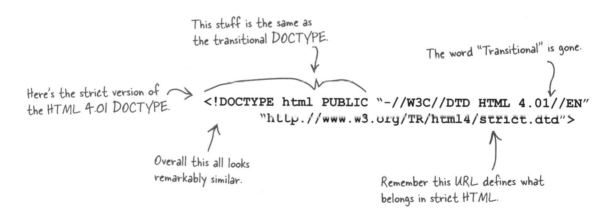

This stuff is the same as the transitional DOCTYPE.

The word "Transitional" is gone.

Here's the strict version of the HTML 4.01 DOCTYPE.

```
<!DOCTYPE html PUBLIC "-//W3C//DTD HTML 4.01//EN"
        "http://www.w3.org/TR/html4/strict.dtd">
```

Overall this all looks remarkably similar.

Remember this URL defines what belongs in strict HTML.

No big differences here. The "transitional" word is gone and we have a different URL that defines the strict version of HTML 4.01. Let's replace the transitional DOCTYPE with the strict and try to validate.

Changing the DOCTYPE to strict

Open your "lounge.html" file again. To change from transitional to
strict, you just need to do two things to the DOCTYPE: delete the word
"Transitional" and, in the URL, change "loose.dtd" to "strict.dtd". Or if
you like, you can delete the old line and type the new one in.

*First, remove the word
"Transitional".*

```
<!DOCTYPE html PUBLIC "-//W3C//DTD HTML 4.01//EN"
    "http://www.w3.org/TR/html4/strict.dtd">
<html>
  <head>
    <meta http-equiv="Content-Type" content="text/html; charset=ISO-8859-1">
    <title>Head First Lounge</title>
  </head>
  <body>
    <h1>Welcome to the New and Improved Head First Lounge</h1>
      <img src="drinks.gif" alt="Drinks">
    <p>
      Join us any evening for refreshing
      <a href="elixir.html">elixirs</a>,
      conversation and maybe a game or two
      of <em>Dance Dance Revolution</em>.
      Wireless access is always provided;
      BYOWS (Bring Your Own Web Server).
    </p>
    <h2>Directions</h2>
    <p>
      You'll find us right in the center of downtown
      Webville. If you need help finding us, check out our
      <a href="directions.html">detailed directions</a>.
      Come join us!
    </p>
  </body>
</html>
```

And then replace "loose.dtd" with "strict.dtd".

That's it. Just make sure your DOCTYPE looks exactly as it does above.

Now all that remains is to ask the validator if our HTML is compliant with
the strict version of HTML 4.01. Use the validator again to check the page,
after making sure your page has the changes above.

Do we have validation?

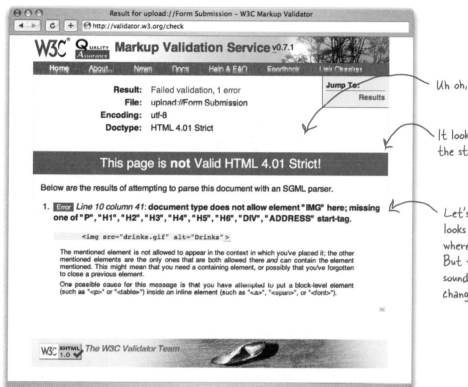

Uh oh, red again. That can't be good.

It looks like we're not valid under the strict rules, but why?

Let's look at the error message: it looks like strict HTML doesn't like where we put the `<img>` element. But transitional was okay with it... sounds like maybe the nesting rules changed in strict HTML?

"I think we've been pretty darn strict..." How's this for strict?

Judy

Joe: We're not?

Judy: No. Look here, you've got an **<img>** element that's nested in the **<body>** element. That was okay in older versions of HTML, and 4.01 transitional lets it slide, but in the current standard, inline elements belong inside block elements.

Joe: Oh right, **<img>** is an inline element.

Judy: Yup. It's easy to fix though; all you have to do is stick your image in a block element like **<p>** and you'll be good to go.

Joe: I guess that's clear if you look at that error message... the elements I recognize are all block elements. Like **<h1>**, **<p>**, etc.

Judy: Exactly.

Joe: But I don't see all the block elements we've used... for instance, **<blockquote>** seems to be missing from the list. That's a block element, right?

Judy: Good point. You can't stick the **<img>** element into just *any* block element in HTML 4.01 strict. **<blockquote>** is an example of a block element that you can't nest inline elements directly inside.

Joe: Well, how are we supposed to know if we're nesting things properly *before* we try to validate – is there a list of "nesting rules" somewhere?

Judy: There is, but you can remember most of them using common sense once you've looked at the rules.

Frank: Judy, are there any other places where we didn't nest things properly?

Judy: I don't see any... the rest of this looks pretty good to me. But that's why we have validators. They never miss a thing. Humans do.

Frank: Okay, well let's fix it and get this page validated. I'm ready to see the green bar of success here, guys.

Judy: Good luck and good work. It looks like you've almost got it.

Fixing the nesting problem

So it looks like strict HTML 4.01 prefers that images, which are inline elements, be nested inside a block element, like a paragraph or a heading. That's a simple change to make. Open your "lounge.html" file and add a **<p>** element around the **<img>** element.

```
<!DOCTYPE html PUBLIC "-//W3C//DTD HTML 4.01//EN"
    "http://www.w3.org/TR/html4/strict.dtd">
<html>
  <head>
    <meta http-equiv="Content-Type" content="text/html; charset=ISO-8859-1">
    <title>Head First Lounge</title>
  </head>
  <body>
    <h1>Welcome to the New and Improved Head First Lounge</h1>
    <p>
        <img src="drinks.gif" alt="Drinks">
    </p>
    <p>
        Join us any evening for refreshing
        <a href="elixir.html">elixirs</a>,
        conversation and maybe a game or two
        of <em>Dance Dance Revolution</em>.
        Wireless access is always provided;
        BYOWS (Bring Your Own Web Server).
    </p>
    <h2>Directions</h2>
    <p>
        You'll find us right in the center of downtown
        Webville. If you need help finding us, check out our
        <a href="directions.html">detailed directions</a>.
        Come join us!
    </p>
  </body>
</html>
```

Now, the image "drinks.gif" is safely nested inside a <p> element.

All our other inline elements, like <a> and <em>, are already inside block elements – these paragraphs.

Once you've done that, save and reload the page in your browser. You'll see it doesn't really affect the look of the page. Why? Because the heading above the image and the paragraph below are already block elements with linebreaks below and above them, respectively. So the **<p>** element around the image doesn't actually add any new linebreaks or spacing.

One more chance to be strict...

You know the game. Ask the validator to give your "lounge.html" file another try. Let's see if we're worthy...

It works! The big green badge of success.

And we're HTML 4.01 Strict.

Q: Okay, I think I get all this, and it was kind of fun having the validator check my HTML, but SO WHAT? Again, what is all this "compliance" really getting me?

A: How does happier customers sound? If you know your HTML is valid, then it's more likely that your Web pages will work consistently in a wide variety of browsers, which is going to give your Web page users a better experience. There are a few other benefits: Web pages with compliant HTML load faster and work better on other devices that are now being used to surf the Web (like TVs and phones). They're also more accessible to the visually impaired who are using aural screen readers.

Q: So can you explain the error in detail? I want to understand exactly what it means.

A: The error was caused by the `<img>` element not being nested inside a block element. Imagine the browser is reading through your HTML, and sees an `<img>` element where it expected

a block element. The first thing it does is say, "Hey, I expected a block element here." It keeps reading, and then gets to the end of the `<img>` element (which, since `<img>` is an empty element, happens as soon as it sees the ">" at the end of the `<img>` tag) and says, "Hey you can't be ending an `<img>` element here because there shouldn't be an `<img>` element here to start with."

Also, you might find that you see multiple error messages from one mistake. Just take it one error message at a time, fix your mistake, and you'll often find you eliminate more than one error message in the process.

Q: Are all the validator's error messages so difficult to understand?

A: Generally, yes, the error messages can be a little difficult to decipher. This is a piece of software telling you what is wrong, not a human or a Head First book. Remember, the validator doesn't know what you *meant* to do and can only attempt to decipher and indicate errors in what you *actually* did. Most of the time, it will point you to the right line in your HTML where your error is occurring, which is half the battle. Then

hopefully you'll spot your mistake.

After reading these error messages for a while you'll start to get the hang of them and often know what they are referring to, even if the validator doesn't tell you specifically.

Q: Why are all the element names listed in that error message in uppercase? I thought element names were written in lowercase.

A: Good question. HTML actually allows element names to be uppercase or lowercase, or even mixed case. You could write <IMG> or even <ImG> if you wanted. However, the W3C is changing the rules, so in the future element names will all be lowercase. So, while technically the validator for Strict HTML 4.01 still allows (and displays) uppercase tags, we're only using lowercase so you'll get into the habit of using only lowercase. This means you won't have to update your tag names down the road (and that means less work for you). And when we say "down the road," we actually mean in the next chapter.

Exercise

Your turn. Add the strict DOCTYPE and the <meta> tag to "directions.html" and "elixir.html". Try validating them – do they validate? If not, fix them so that they do.

Strict HTML 4.01, grab the handbook

You've been in Webville for a few chapters now. Don't you think it's about time you learn the local rules of the road? Luckily, Webville has prepared a handy guide to using strict HTML 4.01. This guide is meant for you – someone who is new to Webville. It isn't an exhaustive reference, but rather focuses on the more important common sense rules of the road. And you'll definitely be adding to the knowledge in this guide as you get to know your way around Webville in coming chapters. But for now, take one – they're FREE.

The HTML 4.01 HANDBOOK
City of Webville

FREE
Take One

Webville Guide to Strict HTML 4.01

Traveling on the information super-highway can be dangerous if you don't know the rules. In this handy guide, we've boiled strict HTML 4.01 down into a common sense set of rules, starting with the major rules first:

The `<html>` element: don't leave home without it.

Always start each page with a DOCTYPE, but following that, the `<html>` element must always be the top, or root, element of your Web page. So, after the DOCTYPE, the `<html>` tag will start your page and the `</html>` tag should end it, with everything else in your page nested inside.

Remember to use both your `<head>` and your `<body>` for better HTML.

Only the `<head>` and `<body>` elements can go directly inside your `<html>` element. This means that every other element must go either inside the `<head>` or the `<body>` element. No exceptions!

What's a `<head>` without a `<title>`?

Always give your `<head>` element a `<title>` element. It's the law. Failure to do so will result in HTML that isn't compliant. The `<head>` element is the only place you should put your `<title>`, `<meta>`, and `<style>` elements.

Feed your `<body>` only wholesome block elements.

You can put only block elements (`<h1>`, `<h2>`, ..., `<h6>`, `<p>`, `<blockquote>`, and so on) directly inside your `<body>` element. All inline elements and text need to be inside another block element before they can go in the `<body>` element.

Keep block elements out of your inline elements.

The only things you can put in an inline element are text and other inline elements. Block elements are not allowed under any circumstances.

Webville Guide to Strict HTML 4.01 Continued

Now that you've got the major rules down, let's look at some of the finer points of the law.

Keep block elements out of your `<p>` element.
Paragraphs are for text, so keep block elements out of your paragraphs. Of course it is perfectly fine to use all the inline elements you want in them (`<em>`, `<a>`, `<strong>`, `<img>`, `<q>`, and so on).

Lists are for list items.
Only the `<li>` element is allowed in the `<ul>` and `<ol>` elements. Why would you want to put anything other than a list item in an unordered or ordered list anyway?

Go ahead, put whatever you want in a list item.
Webville has very liberal laws when it comes to the `<li>` element: you can put text, inline elements, or block elements inside your list items.

Who knew? The `<blockquote>` only likes block elements.
The `<blockquote>` element requires one or more block elements inside it. While it's common to see text directly inside a block quote, that isn't up to code here in Webville. Please always put your text and inline elements inside block elements before adding them to a `<blockquote>`.

Oops! We weren't up to the 4.01 standard when we did Tony's `<blockquote>` in Chapter 3. That text should have been put inside a `<p>` first.

Be careful about nesting an inline element inside another inline element.
While you can nest just about any inline element in another, there are a couple of cases that don't make sense. Never nest an `<a>` element inside another `<a>` element because that would be too confusing for our visitors. Also, empty elements like `<img>` provide no way to nest other inline elements within them.

Q: That wasn't too bad; I was expecting *pages* of rules I had to remember. Can I really write strict HTML 4.01 just following these rules?

A: These rules will get you a long way, but remember, you haven't learned everything about HTML yet, so there are going to be a few new things that you'll need to keep in mind too. That said, there is no reason to memorize all these rules. Your common sense and this guide is a good start, and from there you can also consult an HTML reference or just ask the validator if your HTML is valid (you should anyway!) when you get into some tricky areas.

Q: So whenever possible, always go with strict?

A: It depends. Just throwing up a page that three people in the world will see? Hey, as long as it looks good in all your browsers, who cares. But if you're doing something a fair number of people will visit, you'll be better off keeping your HTML up to standards and validating it. Should that be the transitional or strict standard? Well, the world is moving in the strict direction, so you can pay now or pay later, but eventually, it will be in your best interest to go strict. When you're starting fresh, strict is just as easy. And if you use strict, moving to XHTML will be a lot easier, and we're going to do that in the very next chapter and use XHTML in the rest of the book.

Q: So I get that putting an <a> inside an <a> is confusing and wouldn't work anyway. But I can really put an <em> inside an <em>? What's the point of that?

A: In principle, someone might want to put emphasis on emphasis. That seems silly, but since it doesn't cause problems, like nested <a> elements do, the standard just says, if you want to do it, you can. What about a <q> within a <q>, would that ever make sense? Sure, you might quote someone who

quotes someone else. So, in general you can nest any of the inline elements inside other inline elements. Some of these make more sense than others, but the <a> element is the only one that you can't nest inside itself. Remember too, that the <img> element is empty, so you can't nest anything inside it.

Q: So why can't I put text directly in a <blockquote>? A list item can have text *or* a block element. That seems inconsistent.

A: 'Cause the standard says so. Just kidding. You're right, it does seem inconsistent, but it's all based on the intent of the element. Take the <p> element, for instance. It's for one text paragraph, so of course no other block elements are allowed in it. <blockquote>? It's for quoting large portions of text from another source, which might include headings, paragraphs, whatever. So the point is to "quote blocks." List items? They're like the contortionists of the element world – they have to be able to hold simple text, large bits of text like paragraphs or even other lists, so they can handle everything.

Q: I noticed the validator said the standard requires the "alt" attribute on <img> elements. Are there any other attributes that are required?

A: Wow, good catch. Yes, the **alt** attribute is required on images for accessibility, so that, for instance, the visually impaired can know what the image is, even if they can't see it. The other required attribute is the **src** attribute on an image – what good is an **<img>** element if it doesn't point to an image? There are also some attributes that were okay with HTML 3.2 that you can't use anymore with strict HTML 4.01. Why? Because most of them affected the way Web pages looked, and you're supposed to be using CSS for that kind of styling (more on this topic in just a couple of chapters).

Webville's a friendly place. Forget a rule? Just run it by me, the Validator. I'll get you pointed in the right direction.

Validator

Fireside Chats

Tonight's talk: **Transitional and Strict try to recruit followers.**

Transitional

Hey there, Strict. You here to talk about how much you love frustrating Web page writers?

Oh, you know, all those Web page writers out there who are struggling to get their Web pages to validate with your strict DOCTYPE. You're pretty tough, you know.

Tough love?

Oh, please. Not everyone wants to be strict all the time.

Not everyone can, or wants to, transition their entire Web site to the strict standard overnight, you know. Sheesh, I'm playing an important role here.

How is it future-proofing anything?

Strict

What's that supposed to mean?

It's tough *love*, man.

Yeah. Sooner or later any page of importance really needs to move to strict. You may think I'm tough now, but you'll love me later.

Huh? You encourage people to stay behind the times with all those old tags and attributes. You're just a crutch.

The way I see it, people get to say they're "standard HTML" when in reality, they're still relying on old habits. I say, strict is the way to go. That's the only way to future-proof a Web site.

Hey man, some of your tags have been "deprecated." Do you know what that means? It means they're going away. By going strict now, it'll be a lot easier to update to the next version of HTML.

Transitional

So, you're just going to leave behind all those millions of Web pages out there that still use older versions of HTML? Ignore them completely? I bet you use some nonstrict Web pages yourself. How 'bout I come over and check your history list?

Not everyone wants to be on the cutting edge, you know. Some people like using those old tags. Other people want to take things a bit slower, make sure they understand exactly what the new standard is before jumping in and willy-nilly changing their pages.

You know, you really should be nice to me; I've helped a lot of pages move to strict.

True, they can just start strict and won't need me. Anyway, I'm going back to my kinder and gentler method of moving pages to strict. You can go back to cracking your whip.

Yeah, yeah. Did you bother telling the readers that by the end of the chapter, you'll be obsolete too?

Strict

Oh no, you're not coming near my browser history; keep your grubby paws off it. You're right, there are a lot of useful pages out there that need to be updated, and maybe they never will be, but we're trying to build a better Web. So stop encouraging people to stay behind the times.

Willy-nilly? There's nothing willy-nilly about 4.01. It's actually cleaner and simpler to understand than the older HTML versions. And, if people write their Web pages correctly, they'll be well prepared to have their pages work well in browsers for a long time.

Okay, it *is* helpful for people to be able to mark their pages as transitional until they learn the new stuff. All I'm saying here is transitional shouldn't be used as a crutch. And anyone reading this book who is new to HTML and CSS has no need to be transitional.

Hey! Watch it. Pages will be thanking me down the road for keeping them strict.

Uhhhh....

One more question about this transitional stuff. What is all this old markup that isn't allowed in strict? Have we seen any examples?

No, we've been writing mostly strict HTML all along.

Even though we haven't been including a DOCTYPE or a **<meta>** tag, and we've been a little lazy on the image nesting rules, throughout this book you've been writing HTML that is very close to the standard. So, you haven't had much opportunity to see the phased out elements and attributes.

That's a good thing, because sometimes unlearning a bad habit is the hardest part of a new standard.

Want to see some? Just visit a few Web pages with your browser and choose "View Source" from the "View" menu (your browser's menus may differ). Any tag or attribute that looks like it is used to alter the display of the page is most likely deprecated in HTML 4.01 (because that is now CSS's job). It doesn't hurt to know a little about these legacy elements, because you are quite likely to run into some of them now and then. Let's take a quick look...

HTML Archeology

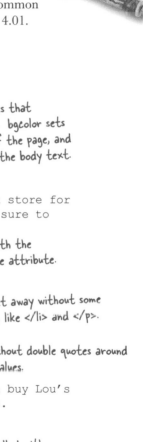

We did some digging and found an HTML 3.2 page that contains some elements and attributes that are no longer part of the standard, as well as a couple of common mistakes that are no longer allowed in strict HTML 4.01.

```
<html>
<head>
    <title>Webville Forecast</title>
</head>

<body bgcolor="tan" text="black">

    <p>
        The weather report says lots of rain and wind in store for
        <font face="arial">Webville</font> today, so be sure to
        stay inside if you can.
    </p>

    <ul>
        <li>Tuesday: Rain and 60 degrees.
        <li>Wednesday: Rain and 62 degrees.
    </ul>

    <p align=right>
        Bring your umbrella!

    <center><font size="small">This page brought to you buy Lou's
        Diner, a Webville institution for over 50 years.
    </font></center>

</body>
</html>
```

Here are some attributes that controlled presentation. bgcolor sets the background color of the page, and text sets the color of the body text.

Font changes were made with the <font> element and its face attribute.

You could get away without some closing tags, like </li> and </p>.

Or even without double quotes around attribute values.

Text size was controlled with the <font> element, using the size attribute.

Here are two ways to align text. Right align a paragraph, or center a piece of text.

BE the Validator

Below, you'll find an HTML file. Your job is to play like you're the validator and locate ALL the errors. After you've done the exercise, look at the end of the chapter to see if you caught them all.

Use the validator to check your work once you've done (or if you need hints).

```html
<!DOCTYPE html PUBLIC "-//W3C//DTD HTML 4.01//EN"
    "http://www.w3.org/TR/html4/strict.dtd">
<html>
<head>
    <meta http-equiv="Content-Type" content="text/html; charset=ISO-8859-1">
</head>
<body>
    <img src="chamberofcommerce.gif">
    <h1>Tips for Enjoying Your Visit in Webville</h1>
    <p>
        Here are a few tips to help you better enjoy your stay in Webville.
        <ul>
            <li>Always dress in layers and keep an html around your
                head and body.</li>
            <li>Get plenty of rest while you're here, sleep helps all
                those rules sink in.</li>
            <li>Don't miss the work of our local artists right downtown
                in the CSS gallery.</li>
        </ul>
    </p>
    <p>
        Having problems? You can always find answers at
        <a href="http://www.headfirstlabs.com"><em>Head First Labs</em></a>.
        Still got problems? Relax, Webville's a friendly place, just ask someone
        for help. And, as a local used to say:
    </p>
    <blockquote>
        Don't worry. As long as you hit that wire with the connecting hook
        at precisely 88mph the instant the lightning strikes the tower...
        everything will be fine.
    </blockquote>
</body>
</html>
```

Doh! We got it wrong – the boss wants us to go to strict XHTML, not HTML. Help! That's a whole different language isn't it?

BULLET POINTS

- HTML 4.01 is the HTML standard that is most widely supported by browsers.

- The World Wide Web Consortium (W3C) is the standards organization that defines what "standard HTML" is.

- Many browsers have two modes for displaying HTML: "quirks" mode for old HTML and standards mode for HTML 4.01.

- If you don't toll the browser which version of HTML you are using, many browsers will use quirks mode, which may cause inconsistent page display in various browsers.

- The document type definition (DOCTYPE) is used to tell the browser which version of HTML your Web page is written in.

- The strict DOCTYPE is used if you are writing fully compliant HTML 4.01.

- Use the transitional DOCTYPE if you are transitioning HTML that still includes display-oriented elements and attributes.

- The <meta> tag in the <head> element tells the browser additional information about a Web page, such as the content type and character encoding.

- A character encoding tells the browser the character set that is used in the Web page.

- Most Western-European languages used on computers today can be represented with the ISO-8859-1 character encoding.

- The W3C validator is a free online service that checks pages for compliance with standards.

- Use the validator to ensure that your HTML is well formed and that your elements and attributes meet the standards.

- By adhering to standards, your pages will display more quickly and with fewer display differences between browsers.

HTMLcross

It's been a heck of a chapter. Go ahead and grab a cup of your favorite beverage, sit back, and strengthen those neural connections by doing this crossword. All the answers come from the chapter.

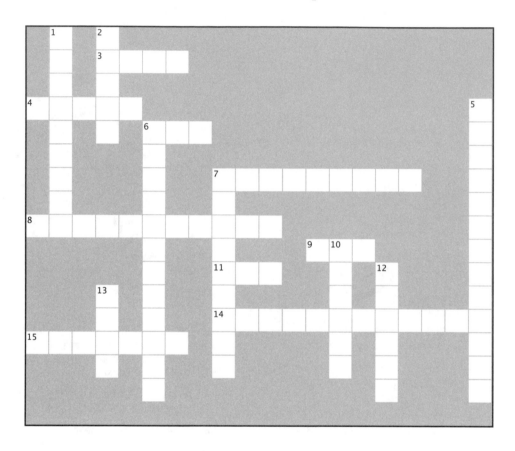

Across

3. True or false: element names should be lowercase.
4. Required in the <head> element.
6. Standards organization that supplies the validator.
7. When your HTML meets the standards, it is this.
8. Microsoft versus Netscape.
9. The boss wanted to standardize before adding this to the HTML.
11. <img> attribute required in standard HTML.
14. DOCTYPE that allows older HTML tags.
15. Definition that tells the browser and validator what kind of HTML you're using.

Down

1. This service will check your HTML for compliance with the standards.
2. In the old days of HTML, this was mixed with HTML structure.
5. Reason alt attribute is required.
6. Victim of the browser wars.
7. The _____ encoding tells the browser which set of characters you're using.
10. DOCTYPE that expects your HTML to be fully compliant with 4.01.
12. If the browser can't tell what version of HTML a page is, it uses this mode.
13. Tag that tells the browser about the page.

Exercise Solutions

BE the Validator

Below, you'll find an HTML file. Your job is to play like you're the validator and locate ALL the errors. Here's the solution.

```
<!DOCTYPE html PUBLIC "-//W3C//DTD HTML 4.01//EN"
    "http://www.w3.org/TR/html4/strict.dtd">
<html>
<head>
    <meta http-equiv="Content-Type" content="text/html; charset=ISO-8859-1">
</head>
<body>
    <img src="chamberofcommerce.gif">
    <h1>Tips for Enjoying Your Visit in Webville</h1>
    <p>
      Here are a few tips to help you better enjoy your stay in Webville.
      <ul>
        <li>Always dress in layers and keep an html around your
            head and body.</li>
        <li>Get plenty of rest while you're here, sleep helps all
            those rules sink in.</li>
        <li>Don't miss the work of our local artists right downtown
            in the CSS gallery.</li>
      </ul>
    </p>
    <p>
      Having problems? You can always find answers at
      <a href="http://www.headfirstlabs.com"><em>Head First Labs</em></a>.
      Still got problems? Relax, Webville's a friendly place, just ask someone
      for help. And, as a local used to say:
    </p>
    <blockquote>
      Don't worry. As long as you hit that wire with the connecting hook
      at precisely 88mph the instant the lightning strikes the tower...
      everything will be fine.
    </blockquote>
</body>
</html>
```

<title> should be in the <head>.

Inline element at top level of <body>.

No alt attribute.

Block element inside a <p>.

<blockquote> only accepts block elements directly in it.

 Solution

```
 1V    2S
 A    3T R U E
 L     Y
4T I T L E                                    5A
 D     E    6W 3 C                             C
 A     E                                       C
 T     B           7C O M P L I A N T          E
 O     D           H                           S
8B R O W S E R W A R S              9C 10S     S
       V         R        11A L T    T         I
       E         R         L        R    12Q   B
      13M        L         C        U    U     I
       E         O       14T R A N S I T I O N A L
15D O C T Y P E  E         E        C    R     I
       A         E         R        T    K     T
       R                            S          Y
```

Exercise Solution

Your turn. Add the strict DOCTYPE and the <meta> tag to "directions.html" and "elixir.html". Try validating them – do they validate? If not, fix them so that they do.

Solution: To validate "elixir.html", you'll have to add the alt attribute to each of your <img> elements.

7 moving to XHTML

Putting an 'X' into HTML

You mean, there's still MORE HTML? Doesn't this EVER end? When do we get to CSS?

We've been keeping a dirty secret from you. We know you *thought* you bought an HTML book, but this is really an XHTML book in disguise. In fact, we've been teaching you mostly XHTML all along. You're probably wondering, just what the heck is XHTML? Well, meet eXtensible HTML – otherwise known as XHTML – the next evolution of HTML. It's leaner, meaner, and even more tuned for compatibility with browsers on a wide range of devices. In this short little chapter we're going to get you from HTML to XHTML in three simple steps. So, turn the page, you're almost there... (and then we're on to CSS).

Frank   Jim   Joe

Joe: I can't believe *our manager* knows what it is.

Frank: Hey guys, XHTML is the new standard for HTML. There's not going to be an HTML 5; the new standard is XHTML 1.0.

Jim: That's great, but do we need to be so cutting edge?

Frank: Actually, XHTML 1.0 has been around since 2000, so it's not as cutting edge as it sounds.

Jim: What's the "X" for? Because it sounds cool... X-Men, X-Games, X-Files, gen-X, and now X-HTML?

Frank: Good one, Jim, but no. The X in XHTML is for "eXtensible," which is another way of saying it's based on something called XML.

Joe: Don't the software guys use that to store some of our data?

Frank: Yup, they sure do. XML stands for eXtensible Markup Language.

Joe: Uh oh, I see some comparison to Hypertext Markup Language coming.

Frank: Yes, exactly, Joe. XML is a markup language like HTML, but you can use it to do all kinds of things beyond "marking up" Web pages. Here, let me show you...

What is XML?

Okay, we're going to take a big step back, for a page or two, and look at XML (not to be confused with XHTML). This is going to be a fast ride, so hang on...

Let's use HTML for comparison. With HTML you're basically told what elements you can and can't use, right? So, if you want to just make up an element, like **<cool>**, to wrap around content, you can't do it, can you? Ah, but with XML, *you can*. If fact, you can invent totally new markup languages using XML. Let's look at an example:

Here's the root element. It's not called <html>, it's called <recipe>, since this is the XML for a recipe. Notice it has some extra attributes in it, which you've never seen on an <html> element in HTML.

```
<recipe xmlns="http://www.foodnetwerk.com/recipe" lang="en" xml:lang="en">
    <name>Head First Lounge Iced Tea</name>
    <description>A brisk iced tea with a bit of a kick. We
                serve this all day long.
    </description>
    <ingredients>
        <ingredient measurement="6 cups">water</ingredient>
        <ingredient measurement="2 bags">black tea</ingredient>
        <ingredient measurement="2 bags">earl grey tea</ingredient>
        <ingredient measurement="6 cups">ice</ingredient>
    </ingredients>
    <preparation>
        <time duration="10 minutes" />
        <step>Boil one cup of water in a pan, remove pan, and
                add tea. Let steep for five minutes.</step>
        <step>Add ice to a pitcher, then add tea,
                then 5 cups cold water.</step>
        <step>Mix well and serve. Give tea a
                quick shake in a shaker for an
                extra touch.</step>
    </preparation>
</recipe>
```

Wow, look at these tags. The <h1>s and <p>s are all gone, and instead we've got <recipe>, <name>, <description>, <ingredient>s, <preparation>, and so on.

Just by looking at the element names you can tell this is a recipe.

This empty element looks a little strange. We'll come back to that in a bit.

Other than the element names, the way the elements look and are used is just like HTML (opening tags, closing tags, and so on).

Think about how you would create a Web page using HTML to represent the recipe. How would that be different from using XML?

What does this have to do with HTML?

If XML is a language that can be used to invent new markup languages, and HTML is a markup language, can we use XML to *recreate* HTML? We sure can. Let's see how this might look before we talk about why in the heck you'd actually want to:

> And here's a DOCTYPE. You've seen these before, but notice that we're now using XHTML 1.0, instead of HTML 4.01.

> The <html> element now has an xmlns attribute, and lang and xml:lang attributes, like the recipe did.

```
<!DOCTYPE html PUBLIC "-//W3C//DTD XHTML 1.0 Strict//EN"
                      "http://www.w3.org/TR/xhtml1/DTD/xhtml1-strict.dtd">
<html xmlns="http://www.w3.org/1999/xhtml" lang="en" xml:lang="en">

  <head>

    <meta http-equiv="Content-Type" content="text/html; charset=UTF-8" />

    <title>Head First Lounge</title>

  </head>

  <body>

    <h1>Welcome to the New and Improved Head First Lounge</h1>

    <p><img src="drinks.gif" alt="The drinks" /></p>

    <p>
        Join us any evening for refreshing
        <a href="elixir.html">elixirs</a>,
        conversation and maybe a game or two
        of <em>Dance Dance Revolution</em>.
        Wireless access is always provided;
        BYOWS (Bring Your Own Web Server).
    </p>

    <h2>Directions</h2>

    <p>
        You'll find us right in the center of downtown
        Webville.   If you need help finding us, check out our
        <a href="directions.html">detailed directions</a>.
        Come join us!
    </p>

  </body>

</html>
```

> Everything here looks normal, except the empty elements have that weird "/>" on the end again.

> But the rest of the HTML is EXACTLY like HTML 4.01 Strict. Wow, XHTML looks a lot like HTML.

So why would you want to use XHTML?

By using HTML 4.01 Strict, you're already reaping some of the benefits of XHTML. However, because XHTML *is XML*, it has some interesting advantages beyond HTML 4.01. Let's take a look at everything XHTML gets you, including some of the benefits you're already getting out of using HTML 4.01 Strict, through the eyes of a few people already using XHTML.

By using XHTML I'm future-proofing my Web pages to take advantage of all the latest and greatest browser advances to come. My pages are also more likely to work on mobile devices and a variety of browsers.

Hobbyist, runs a popular gaming Web site.

XHTML's strict syntax allows aural screen readers and other browsers for the visually impaired to more easily consume Web content.

Visually impaired Web user.

I like keeping up with trends and technologies. XHTML is the future, and since it's almost exactly like HTML, why not go with the better technology?

Maintains her own blog.

Unlike HTML, XHTML can be extended to include new markup. For instance, there are already extensions that add elements for vector graphics and mathematical formulas.

Mathematics researcher, large university.

I don't get it. We changed the DOCTYPE and added a couple of new attributes, but the rest of this example is totally like HTML 4.01. So, what's the big deal?

This is going to sound very anticlimatic, but XHTML is XML while HTML is, well, *just* HTML. The big distinction may be difficult for you to see at first glance, but the reason XML is a good thing (and the reason the W3C and others have gone to all the trouble of creating XHTML, when they already had HTML) is that once your pages are written in XHTML, all sorts of things become possible that aren't possible with HTML. (You'll get a feel for some of those things in just a sec).

There's another way to look at this: the differences between HTML and XHTML can all be seen on the previous page. You've got a new DOCTYPE, and some minor changes to attributes and the way you write empty elements. These small changes are all that is required to turn your HTML into XHTML.

Now that you know that moving to XHTML is so easy, it's time for you to get a better idea of what it gets you.

XHTML is becoming the language of choice for browsers on mobile devices and cell phones. In the future, XHTML is going to let us pick and choose the parts of the language we want to support in each mobile device, as well.

Business development, mobile phone company.

There's already a lot of data and information written in XML, and it's more easily transformed into XHTML than to HTML. So, we'll be able to get all that information on the Web more easily with XHTML.

Database engineer, media company.

XHTML can be read by our existing software applications that already understand how to read XML.

Junior software developer.

XHTML gives us the benefits of XML (which is great for storing large, structured document collections) along with the benefits of HTML, such as CSS for creating presentation.

Librarian at major metropolitan library.

You're much closer to using XHTML than you might think

Even though HTML and XHTML are almost the same, there are a few small differences, as you've seen. Here's a handy checklist for moving from HTML 4.01 Strict to XHTML 1.0 Strict:

The XHTML 1.0 checklist

Here's the list of things you must do to convert from HTML to XHTML.

☐ Change your DOCTYPE to Strict XHTML. Or, you can use Transitional XHTML if you're still using Transitional HTML.

☐ Add the **xmlns**, **lang**, and **xml:lang** attributes to your **<html>** opening tag.

☑ The **<html>** tag must be the first tag after the DOCTYPE and the **</html>** closing tag must be the last tag in the document.

☑ All element names must be written with lowercase letters.

☐ All opening tags must have closing tags. Or, if an element is empty, the tag must end with a space and then **/>**.

☑ All attributes must have values, and those values must be surrounded by double quotes.

☑ Don't use **&** in the content of your HTML. **&** is for starting entities, so use **&** instead. Also convert any other special characters to entities.

We've checked off the requirements that you're already on top of. So, that doesn't leave you with much to do to move to XHTML 1.0.

We're going to talk about what this means.

If you started from scratch reading this book and you've been diligent in using strict HTML 4.01, then moving to XHTML 1.0 is going to be fast for you. You really only have a few things you need to take care of, and we'll talk about those next.

On the other hand, if you have a lot of legacy HTML you need to convert, then you may have a big job on your hands. But, even in that case, there are some tools that can help get you there. We'll talk about those too.

If my HTML is transitional 4.01, and I want to switch to XHTML strict, then I have a little more work to do, right?

Right. The checklist assumes you're already writing strict HTML.

HTML 4.01 Strict and XHTML 1.0 Strict are basically the same. So, going from transitional HTML 4.01 to HTML Strict or XHTML Strict is about the same amount of work. To change your transitional HTML to either, you'll first need to do all the things we mentioned in Chapter 6 to remove presentation tags and clean up your HTML.

There is also a transitional XHTML 1.0 version, which is essentially the same as transitional HTML 4.01. They both allow deprecated presentational elements, and inline elements directly in the body of your page. So, if you want to use that instead, remember to use the transitional XHTML 1.0 DOCTYPE instead of the strict DOCTYPE.

Going from strict HTML to XHTML 1.0 in three steps

1 Change your DOCTYPE to XHTML 1.0 Strict.

You already know all about DOCTYPEs and you're used to seeing the HTML 4.01 Strict document type. Well, there's also a document type for XHTML 1.0 Strict, and you need to change your DOCTYPE to use it instead. Here's what it looks like:

Just like the HTML DOCTYPE, this is a public document type.

It's for the XHTML 1.0 Strict version of XHTML.

```
<!DOCTYPE html
    PUBLIC "-//W3C//DTD XHTML 1.0 Strict//EN"
    "http://www.w3.org/TR/xhtml1/DTD/xhtml1-strict.dtd">
```

And it has a URL pointing to the definition of XHTML 1.0 Strict.

2 Add the xmlns, lang and xml:lang attributes to your <html> element.

Remember that XML can be used to define many markup languages other than XHTML. To keep all those languages straight, XML needs to know *which* language you're talking about when you use the element **<html>** (after all, someone could come along and make up their own language with XML and call it the "Hippo Tipping Markup Language," which would cause mass confusion). So, to keep things straight, the **xmlns** attribute specifies *which* language the **<html>** element belongs to. And what about all the rest of the elements inside the **<html>** element? By default, they inherit the **xmlns** attribute of their parent.

The **<html>** element also needs **lang** and **xml:lang** attributes, which specify the language being used in the XML document. Here's what your **<html>** opening tag should look like in XHTML:

```
<html xmlns="http://www.w3.org/1999/xhtml" lang="en" xml:lang="en">
```

The xmlns attribute is used to identify which XML language "html" belongs to.

XML uses a URL as a unique identifier for a language. If someone has written a "Hippo Tipping Markup Language" they might have used "http://www.hippotipping.com/html" as their identifier. It doesn't matter what is at the URL — the URL alone is enough to make it unique.

And we just need to specify that we're using English. Depending on the way your XHTML is interpreted by the browser, you may need either one of these, so it's best practice to use both.

③ All empty tags should end in " />", not ">".

This is the final, and most bizarre step of the HTML to XHTML 1.0 transformation. But it's not so mysterious if you know the background.

We've told you XHTML is stricter than HTML, and one area where it is stricter is with closing tags. In HTML, you can have an empty element without a closing tag. But in XHTML, if you aren't going to have a closing tag, you have to tell the browser about it by putting a slash before the final ">". So, take the **\
** element as an example. In HTML we just write **\
**. But in XHTML, we write **\
**. That little slash on the end tells the browser it shouldn't expect a closing tag, because the **\
** is all there is.

Now you might have noticed we didn't include a space before the "/>". That's because XHTML doesn't require it. However, some older browsers can't recognize "/>" without a space before the slash, so, to be backwards compatible, just put a space before your slash in " />".

Let's look at a couple of examples so you know how to transform HTML empty elements into XHTML empty elements:

Old school HTML 4.01 Strict

```
<br>
```

```
<img src="drinks.gif" alt="Drinks">
```

No closing tags? No problem in HTML.

New and improved XHTML 1.0

```
<br />
```

```
<img src="drinks.gif" alt="Drinks" />
```

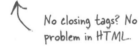

But with XHTML we gotta declare our intentions. If your element is empty, let the browser know by putting a "/" before the ending ">".

And, give those older browsers a break by inserting a space before the forward slash.

Exercise

You're going to take Tony's journal (remember him from Chapter 3?) and convert it to XHTML. We already cleaned up his code and changed it to HTML 4.01 Strict for you – we nested his <img> elements inside <p> elements and added alt attributes, put his Burma Shave slogan in a <p> element, and added a <meta> tag. You'll find this HTML 4.01 Strict version of "journal.html" in the "chapter7/journal" folder.

Here's what you need to do:

1 Change your DOCTYPE from HTML 4.01 Strict to XHTML 1.0 Strict.

2 Add the xmlns, lang and xml:lang attributes to your <html> opening tag.

3 Change the ending ">" characters on your empty elements to " />".

4 Save, and reload the page in your browser.

Be sure to check your work at the end of the chapter.

there are no Dumb Questions

Q: **Can you explain the xmlns attribute a bit more; I feel like I missed something.**

A: You're not the only one. This is one of the most confusing parts of XML. Okay, it works like this: lots of people can create XML languages (personally, we say get out and see the world, but some people seem to be into this sort of thing). Let's say two people call their elements the same thing. Take the name <table>, for instance. For some people this is an element in HTML; for others, it's part of an XML language for furniture. So, if you use <table> in your XML, how do we know which one you mean? That's where the xmlns attribute comes in. The xmlns attribute holds a unique identifier that determines which language you mean. In the case of XHTML, that identifier is `http://www.w3.org/1999/xhtml`

Q: **But wait, that's a URL, not an identifier.**

A: Yeah, XML people are weird that way. It may look like a URL to you, but just think of it as something that is supposed to be unique. The idea is that you could visit that URL and find out something about the language, although there is no requirement that anything actually exist at the URL.

Q: **If this is XHTML, how come the root element isn't <xhtml> rather than <html>?**

A: Because XHTML is meant to be backwards compatible with HTML. If they changed the root element to <xhtml> then older browsers wouldn't know how to display your pages.

Q: **You mentioned some tools earlier that could help convert my HTML to XHTML.**

A: Yes, there's a great little tool called Tidy that can do much of the work to get your HTML documents validating and ready for XHTML. Tidy has a number of options and can take nonvalidating HTML and perform many of the tasks needed to make HTML validate. It can also remove a fair amount of legacy presentational HTML and replace it with CSS. You can find Tidy at http://tidy.sourceforge.net.

Q: **So if I have strict HTML, this is really all I have to do to move to XHTML?**

A: That's right. In fact, let's give it a try...

Validation: it's not just for HTML

After Chapter 6, you're an expert at using the W3C validator, and you'll find the validator is up to date and ready to validate your XHTML. You do that in exactly the same way that you validated HTML.

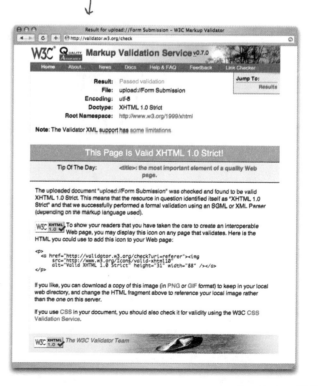

We're totally up on the new XHTML standards and ready to enforce them.

Validator

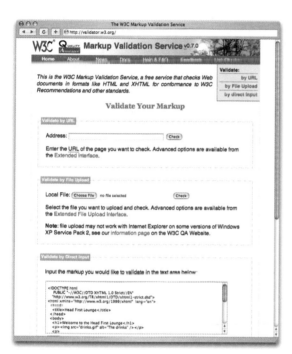

Go to validator.w3.org and either paste in your XHTML, upload it, or point the validator to your URL.

The validator will check your XHTML and report that it's valid, or report any errors to you.

there are no Dumb Questions

Q: How does the validator know whether I'm validating HTML or XHTML? After all, this is the same page I used for HTML.

A: The validator looks at your DOCTYPE declaration, which states that the document is either XHTML Transitional or XHTML Strict, and that's what it bases its validation on.

Exercise

You didn't think we'd let you off the hook without validating your XHTML did you? Validate the "lounge.html" file in the "chapter7/lounge" folder, and the "journal.html" file in the "chapter7/journal/" folder (the one you turned into XHTML a couple of pages ago) at the W3C. If you see any errors, check your typing, get them fixed, and try again.

Congratulations, you've just written your first XHTML!

You've done it: you've transitioned your HTML over to XHTML. While your markup doesn't look much different, there's a whole new set of possibilities coming down the road for XHTML documents. And, even better, you've adopted a whole technology that isn't that much different from what you already know. Now's the time you can go tell all your friends you're *already using* XHTML (we won't tell them there isn't much of a difference between HTML and XHTML if you don't).

Oh, and if we haven't said so already, XHTML is just as compatible with CSS for styling, and you're just a few pages from adding your first style to an XHTML page.

XHTML sounds like a good thing. Is it really ready for prime time?

XHTML does seem like a good thing, and moving from HTML 4.01 Strict is almost trivial, so, why not just go for it? But, before you do, you should know that XHTML is still a little ahead of the curve in terms of browser support. So, while you *can* use XHTML today, there are a few issues you need to keep in mind.

Right now the biggest problem you're going to encounter is that while you might be using XHTML, some browsers are still going to treat your pages as HTML. In most cases, this is fine, because XHTML is designed to be backwards compatible with HTML. However, in the worst case, a browser may display your XHTML in the dreaded quirks mode (look back at Chapter 6 if you've forgotten about quirks mode), so you could get some inconsistent display of your XHTML. What to do? Well, the best you can do right now is test your XHTML in a variety of browsers to make sure things are working as you expect.

If browsers are just going to treat my XHTML like HTML, then why should I bother writing XHTML? Seems like a waste of time to me.

It really comes down to whether or not the XML benefits of XHTML are meaningful to you. If they are, you can start using XHTML today – just be diligent about validating so that in the future, when real, strict XHTML browsers emerge, your pages will play well with them. (Because XHTML browsers are strict, they won't accept invalid XHTML.)

HTML has a long life ahead of it, so if you don't have a good reason to switch, you can stick with HTML for a while. And, if you use HTML 4.01 Strict and validate your pages, you'll be ready to switch to XHTML at a moment's notice.

Fireside Chats

Tonight's talk: **HTML and XHTML ask for your support.**

HTML

I'm certainly glad to have the opportunity to persuade you to stick with me: HTML 4.01. I'm going to be around a long time, have no worries there.

There's really just not enough difference between you and me for people to really care. I mean, 4.01 is exactly the same as XHTML 1.0.

And right now, that and a quarter won't even get you a cup of coffee.

That's the problem: you think everyone *wants* to have applications using XHTML, or that everyone is creating Web sites for mobile devices. Some people just wanna make good Web sites. Why are you asking them to go through all this pain?

XHTML

HTML, face it, you're yesterday's news. The standards guys have already moved on. I'm the future. Anyone with their head on straight should be moving to XHTML.

How can you say we're the same? You're HTML; I'm XML.

Ah, but just wait. The number of devices that read XHTML is increasing every day. And there are a lot of applications out there that are gearing up to use XHTML.

Well that's just it – there really is no pain. If you're already using HTML 4.01, then XHTML is just a hop, skip, and jump away. All you have to do is change your DOCTYPE, and add a couple of attributes to your **<html>** element. So, what's the big deal? Why not have the latest and greatest with just a few minutes work?

HTML

You're forgetting a few of the downsides. A lot of browsers don't handle XHTML very well. In fact, they just see it as HTML. So you do all that work and then you're just fooling yourself that your XHTML is somehow different.

But what's the point? If your XHTML is just considered HTML by a browser, then it's just HTML!

This is all great, but I keep saying people just don't care. I'm already good enough for them. Lots of people have no need for XML.

Okay; let's say you're right, and XHTML is going to be the way of the future. Fine. But as you also said, XHTML is just a hop, skip, and a jump away. So, my users can just wait until XHTML gets here, and they can hop, skip, and jump then.

I think you mean "You can lead a horse to water..."

XHTML

Hey, that's a *good thing*. The designers of XHTML *knew* that not all browsers would support XHTML, so they made it backwards compatible. In other words, you can move to XHTML today, and still have it all work even on older browsers.

Ah, but that's changing; more and more support for XHTML is arriving every day. So, I say, go ahead and change over. It's easy, and when the new browsers and devices get here, you'll be ready without even trying.

You can't envision all the ways XHTML is going to be used in the future. XHTML is the way, and by moving to XHTML now, you'll be ready.

What's that saying? "You can't teach an old dog a new trick?"

HTML or XHTML? The choice is yours...

Do any of the advantages of XHTML matter to you? Are you translating existing XML into HTML for the Web? Are you working on pages that you need to display well on mobile devices? Are some of the newer XHTML technologies going to be important to you in the near future? Or, do you just want to be on the cutting edge? Well, we have good news: you can move to XHTML today. All it will cost you is a new DOCTYPE and some minor changes to a couple of tags.

Now, not every browser will give you credit for moving to XHTML, but sooner or later they will have to, and, until they do, your pages will display just fine because the browser will treat them as HTML (although, don't forget the caveat we already mentioned). So, bon voyage, and enjoy your journey to XHTML.

None of that is important to you? You're mainly concerned with making great Web pages? We have good news for you, too: you can easily stick with HTML 4.01 Strict and reap all the rewards of using the browser's current choice of languages. And, should you ever feel the need to upgrade to XHTML, then you can follow the three-step program outlined in this chapter to get you there.

So, no matter what your choice is, you've made an excellent one, and we wish you the best. That said, the differences between HTML and XHTML are really minimal, so why not go ahead and move to XHTML? We have, and in the rest of this book we'll be using XHTML 1.0. If, for some reason, you need to stick with HTML 4.01, that's fine. And in fact, since they really are basically the same, you'll have no problems with the rest of the book. Just make sure you're using the right DOCTYPE for whichever version you're using.

Micro XHTMLcross

It's been a small chapter (aren't you glad!). Here's a Micro XHTMLcross for you.

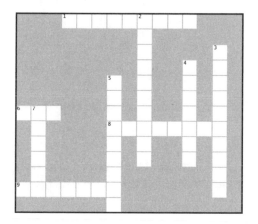

Across

1. Used to double check your XHTML.
6. XHTML is this type of markup.
8. Use these for special characters.
9. We invented an XML language for these.

Down

2. XHTML requires additional _____ in the <html> element.
3. The X in XHTML is for _____.
4. In XHTML you have to explicitly have _____ tags.
5. In XHTML all element names must be this.
7. These kinds of devices are adopting XHTML.

Micro XHTMLcross Solution

It's been a small chapter (aren't you glad!). Here's a Micro XHTMLCross for you.

```
       ¹V A L I D A²T O R
               T        ³E
               T    ⁴C   X
             ⁵L  R    L   T
              O  I    O   E
 ⁶X ⁷M L     W  B    S   N
    O        ⁸E N T I T I E S
    B        R  U    N   I
    I        C  E    G   B
    L        A        L
 ⁹R E C I P E S        E
              E
```

Exercise Solutions

You're going to take Tony's journal (remember him from chapter 3?) and convert it to XHTML. We've put the most recent version of the journal in the "chapter7/journal" folder, where you'll find an HTML 4.01 strict version of "journal.html".

Here's the solution:

Change the DOCTYPE to XHTML 1.0 Strict.

Add the three attributes to the `<html>` opening tag.

```
<!DOCTYPE html
    PUBLIC "-//W3C//DTD XHTML 1.0 Strict//EN"
    "http://www.w3.org/TR/xhtml1/DTD/xhtml1-strict.dtd">
<html xmlns="http://www.w3.org/1999/xhtml" lang="en" xml:lang="en">
  <head>
  <meta http-equiv="Content-Type" content="text/html; charset=ISO-8859-1" />
     <title>My Trip Around the USA on a Segway</title>
    .
    .
    .
  </body>
</html>
```

The `<meta>` tag needs a " />", too.

Don't forget to put " />" in your empty elements.

8 getting started with CSS

Adding a Little Style

Don't get me wrong, the hair, the hat, it all looks great. But don't you think he'd like it if you spent a little more time adding some style to your XHTML?

I was told there'd be CSS in this book. So far you've been concentrating on learning XHTML to create the structure of your Web pages. But as you can see, the browser's idea of style leaves a lot to be desired. Sure, we could call the fashion police, but we don't need to. With CSS, you're going to completely control the presentation of your pages, often without even changing your XHTML. Could it really be so easy? Well, you *are* going to have to learn a new language; after all, Webville is a bilingual town. After reading this chapter's guide to learning the language of CSS, you're going to be able to stand on *either* side of Main Street and hold a conversation.

Remember the Wizard of Oz? Well, this is the part of the book where things go from black & white to color.

You're not in Kansas anymore

You've been a good sport learning about markup and structure and validation and proper syntax and nesting and compliance, but now you get to really start *having some fun* by styling your pages. But no worries, all those XHTML pushups you've been doing aren't going to waste. In fact, you're going to see that a solid understanding of XHTML is crucial to learning (and using) CSS. And, learning CSS is just what we're going to do over the next several chapters.

Just to tease you a bit, on these two pages we've sprinkled a few of the designs you're going to work with in the rest of the book. Quite a difference from the pages you've been creating so far, isn't it? So, what do you need to do to create them? Learn the language of CSS of course.

Let's get started...

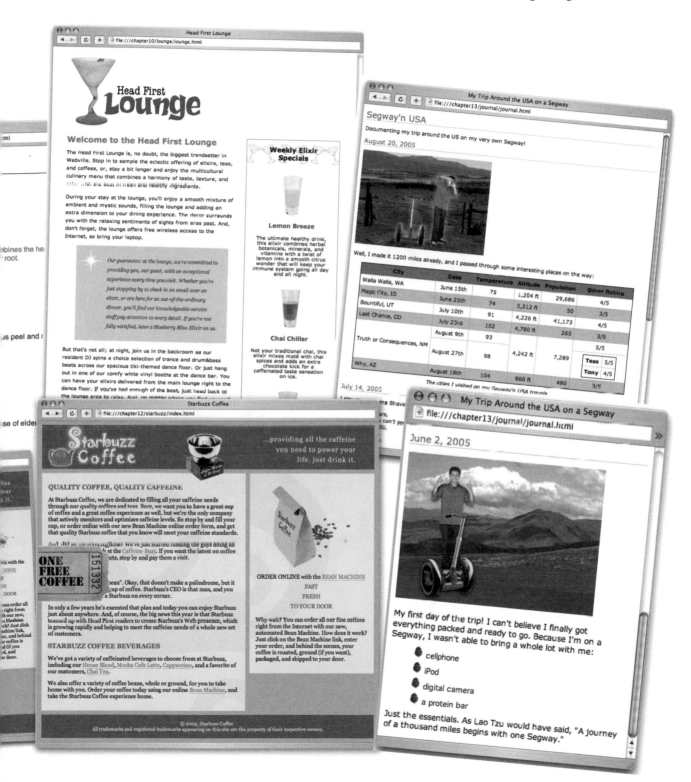

Overheard on Webville's "Trading Spaces"

Not up on the latest reality TV? No problem, here's a recap: take two neighbors, two homes, and $1,000. The two neighbors switch homes, and using the $1,000, totally redesign a room or two in 48 hours. Let's listen in...

Of course, in the Webville edition of the show, everyone talks about design in CSS. If you're having trouble understanding them, here's a little translation tip: each statement in CSS consists of a location (like bedroom), a property in that location (like drapes, or carpet), and a style to apply to that property (like the color blue, or 1 inch tiles).

Using CSS with XHTML

We're sure CSS has a bright future in the home design category, but let's get back to XHTML. XHTML doesn't have rooms, but it does have elements and those elements are going to be the locations that we're styling. Want to paint the walls of your **\<p\>** elements red? No problem; only paragraphs don't have walls, so you're going to have to settle for the paragraph's **background-color** property instead. Here's how you do that:

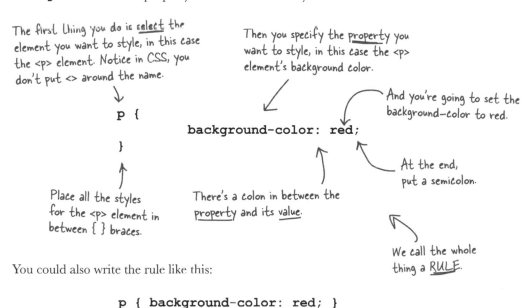

The first thing you do is __select__ the element you want to style, in this case the \<p\> element. Notice in CSS, you don't put \<\> around the name.

Then you specify the __property__ you want to style, in this case the \<p\> element's background color.

And you're going to set the background-color to red.

```
p {

}
```

```
background-color: red;
```

At the end, put a semicolon.

Place all the styles for the \<p\> element in between { } braces.

There's a colon in between the __property__ and its __value__.

We call the whole thing a __RULE__.

You could also write the rule like this:

```
p { background-color: red; }
```

Here, all we've done is remove the linebreaks. Like XHTML, you can format your CSS pretty much as you like. For longer rules you'll usually want to add some linebreaks and indenting to make the CSS more readable (for you).

Wanna add more style?

You can add as many properties and values as you like in each CSS rule. Say you wanted to put a border around your paragraphs, too. Here's how you do that:

```
p {
        background-color: red;
        border: 1px solid gray;
}
```

All you have to do is add another property and value.

The \<p\> element will have a border...

...that is 1 pixel thick, solid, and gray.

there are no
Dumb Questions

Q: **Does every <p> element have the same style? Or can I, say, make two paragraphs different colors?**

A: The CSS rules we've used so far define the style for *all* paragraphs, but CSS is very expressive: it can be used to specify styles in lots of different ways, for lots of different elements – even subsets of elements. You'll see how to make paragraphs two different colors later in this chapter.

Q: **How do I know what properties I can set on an element?**

A: Well, there are *lots* of properties that can be set on elements, certainly more than you'd want to memorize, in any case. You're going to get quite familiar with the more common properties in the next few chapters. You'll probably also want to find a good CSS reference. There are plenty of references online, and O'Reilly's *CSS Pocket Reference* is a great little book.

Q: **Remind me why I'm defining all this style in a separate language, rather than in XHTML. Since the elements are written in XHTML, wouldn't it be easier just to write style in XHTML, too?**

A: You're going to start to see some big advantages to using CSS in the next few chapters. But, here's a quick answer: CSS really is better suited for specifying style information than XHTML. Using just a small bit of CSS, you can create fairly large effects on the style of your XHTML. You're also going to see that CSS is a much better way to handle styles for multiple pages. You'll see how that works later in this chapter.

Say you have an <em> element inside a paragraph. If you change the background color of the paragraph, do you think you also have to change the background of the <em> element so it matches the background color of the paragraph?

Getting CSS into your XHTML

Okay, you know a little about CSS syntax now. You know how to select an element and then write a rule with properties and values inside it. But you still need to get this CSS into some XHTML. First, we need some XHTML to put it in. In the next few chapters, we're going to revisit our old friends – Starbuzz, and Tony and his Segway journal – and make things a little more stylish. But, who do you think is dying to have their site styled first? Of course, the Head First Lounge guys. So, here's the XHTML for the Head First Lounge main page. Remember, in the last chapter we fixed things up a little and made it strict XHTML (would you have expected any less of us?). Now, we're adding some style tags, the easiest way to get style into your pages.

> But not necessarily the best way. We'll come back to this later in the chapter and see another way.

```
<!DOCTYPE html PUBLIC "-//W3C//DTD XHTML 1.0 Strict//EN"
    "http://www.w3.org/TR/xhtml1/DTD/xhtml1-strict.dtd">
<html xmlns="http://www.w3.org/1999/xhtml" lang="en" xml:lang="en" >
  <head>
    <meta http-equiv="Content-Type" content="text/html; charset=ISO-8859-1" />
    <title>Head First Lounge</title>

    <style type="text/css">


    </style>

  </head>
  <body>
    <h1>Welcome to the Head First Lounge</h1>
    <p>
        <img src="images/drinks.gif" alt="Drinks" />
    </p>
    <p>
        Join us any evening for refreshing
        <a href="beverages/elixir.html">elixirs</a>,
        conversation and maybe a game or two
        of <em>Dance Dance Revolution</em>.
        Wireless access is always provided;
        BYOWS (Bring your own web server).
    </p>
    <h2>Directions</h2>
    <p>
        You'll find us right in the center of downtown
        Webville. If you need help finding us, check out our
        <a href="about/directions.html">detailed directions</a>.
        Come join us!
    </p>
  </body>
</html>
```

Here's what we're interested in: the <style> element.

To add CSS style directly to your XHTML, add opening and closing style tags in the <head> element.

And a style type of "text/css".

And your CSS rules are going to go right in here.

Adding style to the lounge

Now that you've got the **\<style\>** element in your XHTML, you're going to add some style to the Lounge to get a feel for writing CSS. This design probably won't win you any "design awards," but you gotta start somewhere.

The first thing we're going to do is change the color (something to match those red lounge couches) of the text in the paragraphs. To do that, we'll use the CSS **color** property like this:

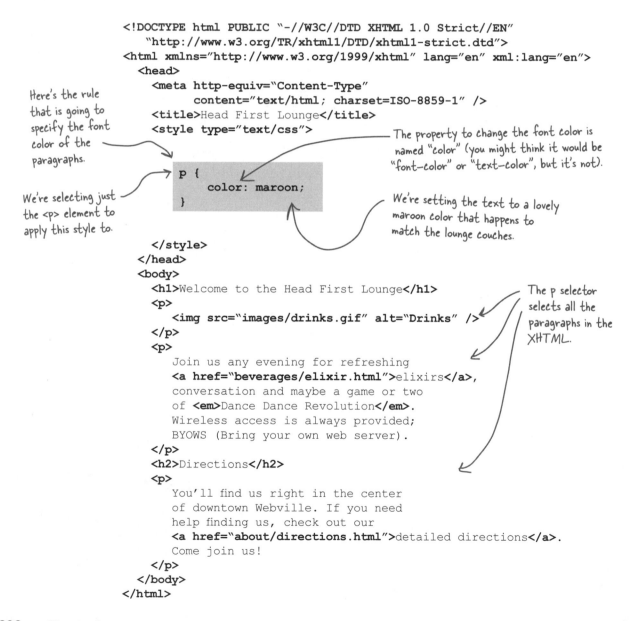

```
<!DOCTYPE html PUBLIC "-//W3C//DTD XHTML 1.0 Strict//EN"
    "http://www.w3.org/TR/xhtml1/DTD/xhtml1-strict.dtd">
<html xmlns="http://www.w3.org/1999/xhtml" lang="en" xml:lang="en">
    <head>
        <meta http-equiv="Content-Type"
            content="text/html; charset=ISO-8859-1" />
        <title>Head First Lounge</title>
        <style type="text/css">

            p {
                color: maroon;
            }

        </style>
    </head>
    <body>
        <h1>Welcome to the Head First Lounge</h1>
        <p>
            <img src="images/drinks.gif" alt="Drinks" />
        </p>
        <p>
            Join us any evening for refreshing
            <a href="beverages/elixir.html">elixirs</a>,
            conversation and maybe a game or two
            of <em>Dance Dance Revolution</em>.
            Wireless access is always provided;
            BYOWS (Bring your own web server).
        </p>
        <h2>Directions</h2>
        <p>
            You'll find us right in the center
            of downtown Webville. If you need
            help finding us, check out our
            <a href="about/directions.html">detailed directions</a>.
            Come join us!
        </p>
    </body>
</html>
```

Here's the rule that is going to specify the font color of the paragraphs.

We're selecting just the \<p\> element to apply this style to.

The property to change the font color is named "color" (you might think it would be "font-color" or "text-color", but it's not).

We're setting the text to a lovely maroon color that happens to match the lounge couches.

The p selector selects all the paragraphs in the XHTML.

Cruising with style: the test drive

Go ahead and make all the changes from the last couple of pages to your "lounge.html" file in the "chapter8/lounge" folder, save, and reload the page in your browser. You'll see that the paragraph text color has changed to maroon:

Everything else is as it should be: the headings are still black, because all we selected to style were the <p> elements.

Here's our new maroon paragraph text.

Notice that the color of the links didn't change. Keep that in the back of your mind...

Instead of setting the **color**, what if you set **background-color** of the **<p>** elements to **maroon** instead? How would it change the way the browser displays the page?

Style the heading

Now let's give those headings some style. How about changing the font a bit? Let's change both the type of font, and also the color of the heading fonts:

> How about a different font for the Lounge headings? Make them *really* stand out. I'm seeing big, clean, gray...

```
h1 {
    font-family: sans-serif;
    color:       gray;
}

h2 {
    font-family: sans-serif;
    color:       gray;
}

p {
    color: maroon;
}
```

Here's the rule to select <h1> elements and change the font-family to sans-serif and the font color to gray. We'll talk a lot more about fonts later.

And here's another rule to do the exact same thing to the <h2> element.

Actually, since these rules are *exactly* the same, we can combine them, like this:

```
h1, h2 {
    font-family: sans-serif;
    color:       gray;
}

p {
    color: maroon;
}
```

To write a rule for more than one element, just put commas between the selectors, like "h1, h2".

Test drive...

Add this new CSS to your "lounge.html" file and reload. You'll see that with one rule, you've selected both the **<h1>** and **<h2>** headings.

Both of the headings on the page are now styled with a sans-serif font and colored gray.

Let's put a line under the welcome message too

Let's touch up the welcome heading a bit more. How about a line under it? That should set the main heading apart visually and add a nice touch. Here's the property we'll use to do that:

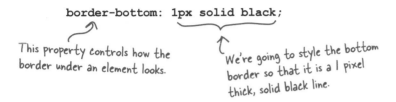

`border-bottom: 1px solid black;`

This property controls how the border under an element looks.

We're going to style the bottom border so that it is a 1 pixel thick, solid black line.

The trouble is, if we add this property and value to the combined "h1, h2" rule in our CSS, we'll end up with borders on both our headings:

```
h1, h2 {
    font-family:    sans-serif;
    color:          gray;
    border-bottom: 1px solid black;
}

p {
    color: maroon;
}
```

Here we're adding a property to change the bottom border for both the <h1> and <h2> elements.

If we do this...

we get bottom borders on both our headings. Not what we want.

So, how can we set the bottom border on *just* the **<h1>** element, without affecting the **<h2>** element? Do we have to split up the rules again? Turn the page to find out...

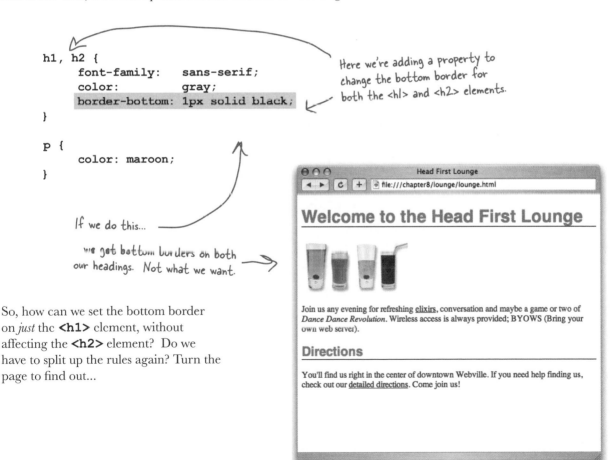

Head First Lounge

file:///chapter8/lounge/lounge.html

Welcome to the Head First Lounge

Join us any evening for refreshing elixirs, conversation and maybe a game or two of *Dance Dance Revolution*. Wireless access is always provided; BYOWS (Bring your own web server).

Directions

You'll find us right in the center of downtown Webville. If you need help finding us, check out our detailed directions. Come join us!

We have the technology: specifying a second rule, just for the <h1>

We don't have to split the "h1, h2" rule up, we just need to add another rule that is only for "h1" and add the border style to it.

```
h1, h2 {
    font-family:      sans-serif;
    color:            gray;
}

h1 {
    border-bottom:  1px solid black;
}

p {
    color: maroon;
}
```

The first rule stays the same. We're still going to use a combined rule for the font-family and color for both <h1> and <h2>.

But now we're adding a second rule that adds another property just to <h1>: the border-bottom property.

Another test drive...

Change your CSS and reload the page. You'll see that the new rule added a black border to the bottom of the main heading, which gives us a nice underline on the heading and really makes it stand out.

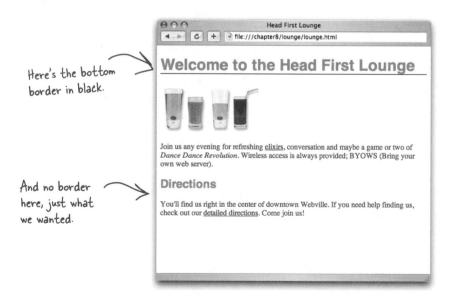

Here's the bottom border in black.

And no border here, just what we wanted.

Q: So how does that work when you have more than one rule for an element?

A: You can have as many rules as you want for an element. Each rule adds to the style information of the rule before it. In general, you try to group together all the common styles between elements, like we did with <h1> and <h2>, and then any style that is specific to an element, you write in another rule, like we did with the border-bottom style for the main heading.

Q: What's the advantage of that approach? Isn't it better to organize each element separately, so you know exactly what styles it has?

A: Not at all. If you combine common styles together, then if they change, you only have to change them in one rule. If you break them up, then there are many rules you have to change, which is error-prone.

Q: Why do we use a bottom border to underline text? Isn't there an underline style for text?

A: Good question. There is an underline style for text and we could use that instead. However, the two styles have slightly different effects on the page: if you use border-bottom then the line will extend to the edge of the page. An underline is only shown under the text itself. The property to set text underline is called text-decoration and has a value of "underline" for underlined text. Give it a try and check out the differences.

So, how do selections really work?

You've seen how to select an element to style it, like this:

We call this the <u>selector</u>.

```
h1 {
        color: gray;
}
```

The style is applied to the elements described by the selector – in this case, <h1> elements.

Or, how to select more than one element, like this:

Another selector. The style is applied to <h1> and <h2> elements.

```
h1, h2 {
        color: gray;
}
```

You're going to see that CSS allows you to specify all kinds of selectors that determine which elements your styles are applied to. Knowing how to use these selectors is the first step in mastering CSS, and to do that you need to understand the organization of the XHTML that you're styling. After all, how can you select elements for styling if you don't have a good mental picture of what elements are in the XHTML, and how they relate to one another?

So, let's get that picture of the Lounge XHTML in your head, and then we'll dive back into selectors.

Markup Magnets

Remember drawing the diagram of HTML elements in Chapter 3? You're going to do that again for the Lounge's main page. Below, you'll find all the element magnets you need to complete the diagram. Using the Lounge's XHTML (on the right), complete the tree below. We've done a couple for you already. You'll find the answer in the back of the chapter.

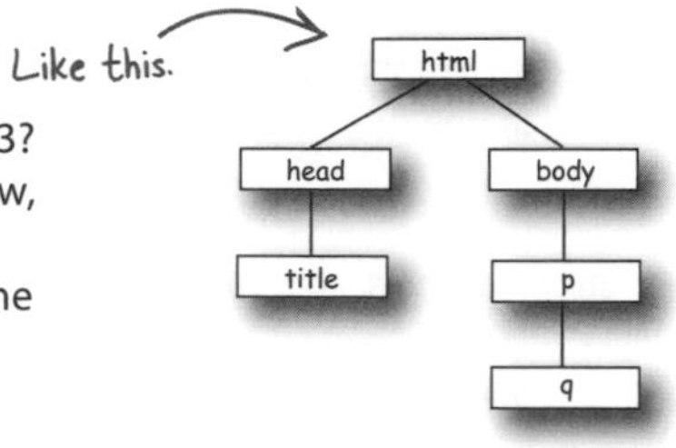

Like this.

```
        html
       /    \
    head    body
     |        |
   title      p
              |
              q
```

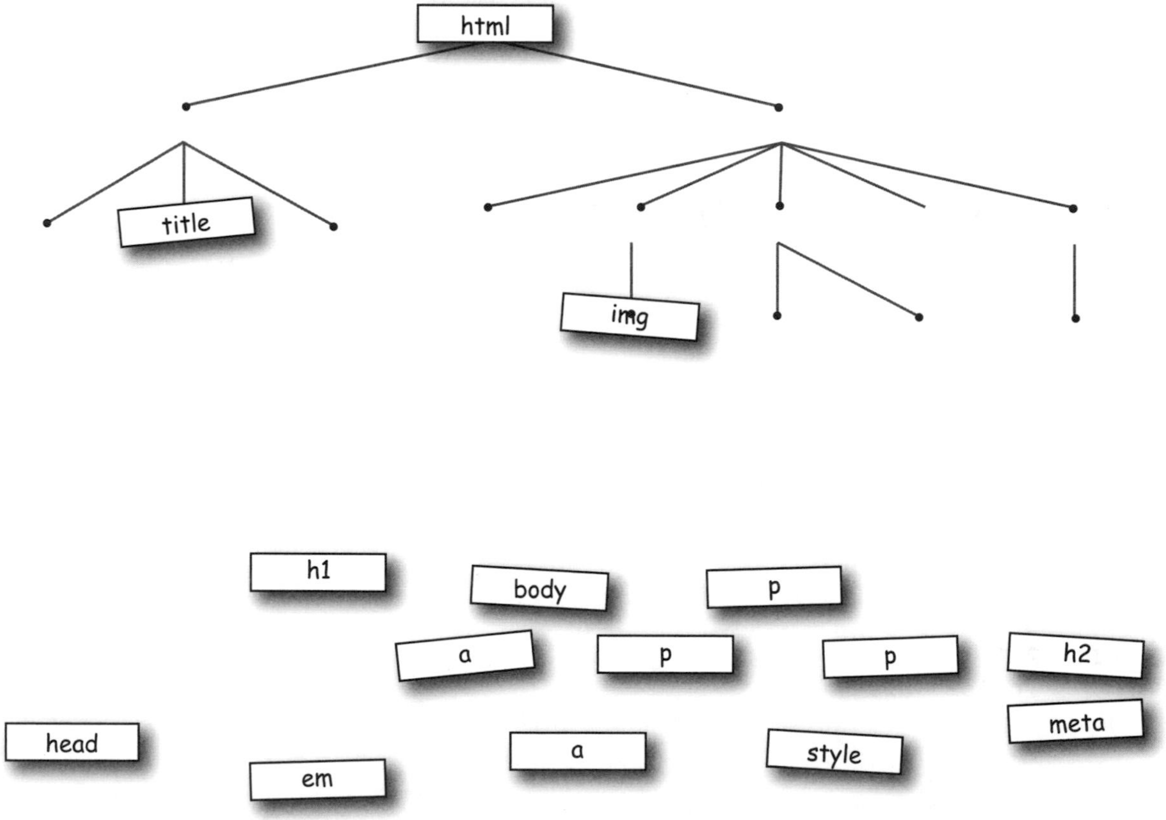

```
                    html
                  /      \
            title          ●
           /     \        /|  |  |  \
                      img  |  |  |   |
                           | /\     |
```

h1

body

p

a

p

p

h2

head

em

a

style

meta

```
<!DOCTYPE html PUBLIC "-//W3C//DTD XHTML 1.0 Strict//EN"
    "http://www.w3.org/TR/xhtml1/DTD/xhtml1-strict.dtd">
<html xmlns="http://www.w3.org/1999/xhtml" lang="en" xml:lang="en">
  <head>
    <meta http-equiv="Content-Type" content="text/html; charset=ISO-8859-1" />
    <title>Head First Lounge</title>

    <style type="text/css">
      h1, h2 {
              font-family:    sans-serif;
              color:          gray;
      }

      h1 {
              border-bottom: 1px solid black;
      }

      p {
              color: maroon;
      }
    </style>

  </head>
  <body>
    <h1>Welcome to the Head First Lounge</h1>
    <p>
        <img src="images/drinks.gif" alt="Drinks" />
    </p>
    <p>
       Join us any evening for refreshing
       <a href="beverages/elixir.html">elixirs</a>,
       conversation and maybe a game or two
       of <em>Dance Dance Revolution</em>.
       Wireless access is always provided;
       BYOWS (Bring your own web server).
    </p>
    <h2>Directions</h2>
    <p>
       You'll find us right in the center of downtown
       Webville. If you need help finding us, check out our
       <a href="about/directions.html">detailed directions</a>.
       Come join us!
    </p>
  </body>
</html>
```

The Head First Lounge XHTML.

Seeing selectors visually

Let's take some selectors and see how they map to the tree you just created. Here's how this "h1" selector maps to the graph:

```
h1 {
    font-family: sans-serif;
}
```

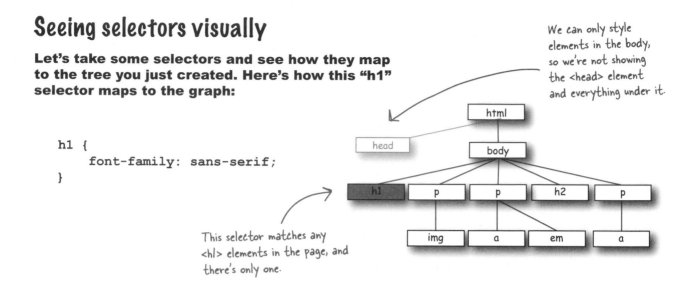

We can only style elements in the body, so we're not showing the <head> element and everything under it.

This selector matches any <h1> elements in the page, and there's only one.

And here's how the "h1, h2" selector looks:

```
h1, h2 {
    font-family: sans-serif;
}
```

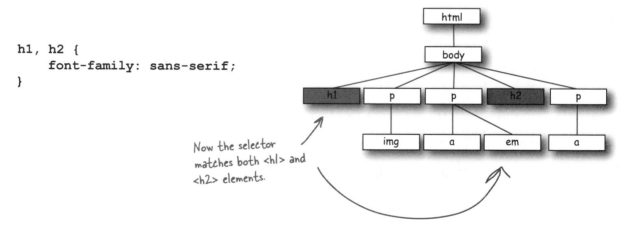

Now the selector matches both <h1> and <h2> elements.

If we use a "p" selector, here's how that looks:

```
p {
    font-family: sans-serif;
}
```

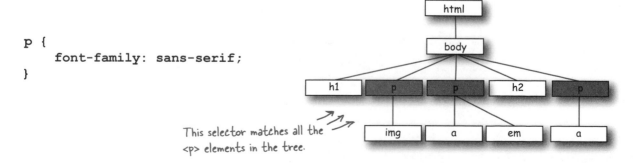

This selector matches all the <p> elements in the tree.

Sharpen your pencil

Color in the elements that are **selected** by these selectors:

```
p, h2 {
    font-family: sans-serif;
}
```

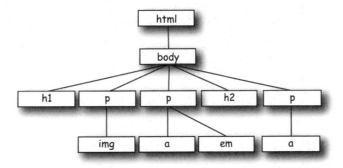

```
p, em {
    font-family: sans-serif;
}
```

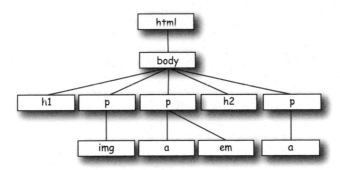

The Case of Brute Force versus Style

When we last left RadWebDesign in Chapter 4, they had just blown the corporate demo and lost RobotsRUs' business. CorrectWebDesign was put in charge of the entire RobotsRUs site and got to work getting everything nailed down before the site launch later in the month. But, you'll also remember that RadWebDesign decided to bone up on their XHTML & CSS. They decided to rework the RobotsRUs site on their own, using strict XHTML and style sheets, just to get some experience under their belt before they took on another consulting job.

Five-Minute Mystery

As fate would have it, just before RobotsRUs' big site launch, it happened again: RobotsRUs called CorrectWebDesign with an urgent message. "We're changing our corporate look and we need all the colors, backgrounds, and fonts changed on our site." At this point, the site consisted of almost a hundred pages, so CorrectWebDesign responded that it would take them a few days to rework the site. "We don't have a few days!" the CEO said. Desperate, the CEO decided to call in RadWebDesign for help. "You flubbed up the demo last month, but we really need your help. Can you help the CorrectWebDesign guys convert the site over to the new look and feel?" RadWebDesign said they could do better than that; in fact they could deliver the entire site to them in less than an hour.

How did RadWebDesign go from disgrace to Web page superheroes? What allowed them to change the look and feel of a hundred pages faster than a speeding bullet?

Uh, I think you forgot to style the elixirs and directions pages?

Getting the Lounge style into the elixirs and directions pages

It's great that we've added all this style to "lounge.html", but what about "elixir.html" and "directions.html"? They need to have a look that is consistent with the main page. Easy enough... just copy the style element and all the rules into each file, right? **Not so fast.** If you did that, then whenever you needed to change the style of the site, you'd have to change *every single file* – not what you want. But, luckily, there is a better way. Here's what you're going to do:

1 Take the rules in "lounge.html" and place them in a file called "lounge.css".

2 Create an *external link* to this file from your "lounge.html" file.

3 Create the same external links in "elixir.html" and "directions.html".

4 Give all three files a good test drive.

Creating the "lounge.css" file

You're going to create a file called "lounge.css" to contain the style rules for all your Head First Lounge pages. To do that, create a new text file named "lounge.css" in your text editor.

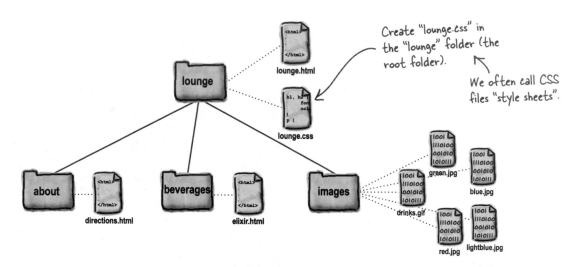

Create "lounge.css" in the "lounge" folder (the root folder).

We often call CSS files "style sheets".

Now type, or copy and paste from your "lounge.html" file, the CSS rules into the "lounge.css" file. Delete the rules from your "lounge.html" file while you're at it.

Note that you should *not* copy the **<style>** and **</style>** tags because the "lounge.css" file contains only CSS, not XHTML.

```
h1, h2 {
    font-family: sans-serif;
    color: gray;
}

h1 {
    border-bottom: 1px solid black;
}

p {
    color: maroon;
}
```

Your "lounge.css" file should look like this. Remember, no <style> tags!

Linking from "lounge.html" to the external style sheet

Now we need a way to tell the browser that it should style this page with the styles in the external style sheet. We can do that with an XHTML element called **<link>**. Here's how you use the **<link>** element in your XHTML:

```
<!DOCTYPE html PUBLIC "-//W3C//DTD XHTML 1.0 Strict//EN"
    "http://www.w3.org/TR/xhtml1/DTD/xhtml1-strict.dtd">
<html xmlns="http://www.w3.org/1999/xhtml" lang="en" xml:lang="en">
  <head>
    <meta http-equiv="Content-Type"
          content="text/html; charset=ISO-8859-1" />
    <title>Head First Lounge</title>
    <link type="text/css" rel="stylesheet" href="lounge.css" />
    <style type="text/css">
    </style>

  </head>
  <body>
    <h1>Welcome to the Head First Lounge</h1>
    <p>
      <img src="drinks.gif" alt="Drinks" />
    </p>
    .
    .
    .
    </p>
  </body>
</html>
```

Here's the XHTML that links to the external style sheet.

You don't need the <style> element any more — just delete it.

The rest of the XHTML is the same.

 ## XHTML Up Close

Let's take a closer look at the **<link>** element since you haven't seen it before:

Use the link element to "link in" external information.

The type of this information is "text/css". In other words, a CSS style sheet.

And the style sheet is located at this href (in this case we're using a relative link, but it could be a full-blown URL).

```
<link type="text/css" rel="stylesheet" href="lounge.css" />
```

The rel attribute specifies the relationship between the XHTML file and the thing you're linking to. We're linking to a style sheet, so we use the value "stylesheet".

<link> is an empty element.

Linking from "elixir.html" and "directions.html" to the external style sheet

Now you're going to link the "elixir.html" and "directions.html" files just as you did with "lounge.html". The only thing you need to remember is that "elixir.html" is in the "beverages" folder, and "directions.html" is in the "about" folder, so they both need to use the relative path "../lounge.css".

So, all you need to do is add the following **<link>** element to both files:

```
<!DOCTYPE html PUBLIC "-//W3C//DTD XHTML 1.0 Strict//EN"
                     "http://www.w3.org/TR/xhtml1/DTD/xhtml1-strict.dtd">
<html xmlns="http://www.w3.org/1999/xhtml" lang="en" xml:lang="en">
  <head>
    <meta http-equiv="Content-Type" content="text/html; charset=ISO-8859-1" />
    <title>Head First Lounge Elixirs</title>
    <link type="text/css" rel="stylesheet" href="../lounge.css" />
  </head>
  <body>
  .
  .
  .
  </body>
</html>
```

This is "elixir.html". Just add the <link> line.

```
<!DOCTYPE html PUBLIC "-//W3C//DTD XHTML 1.0 Strict//EN"
                     "http://www.w3.org/TR/xhtml1/DTD/xhtml1-strict.dtd">
<html xmlns="http://www.w3.org/1999/xhtml" lang="en" xml:lang="en">
  <head>
    <meta http-equiv="Content-Type" content="text/html; charset=ISO-8859-1" />
    <title>Head First Lounge Directions</title>
    <link type="text/css" rel="stylesheet" href="../lounge.css" />
  </head>
  <body>
  .
  .
  .
  </body>
</html>
```

Same for "directions.html". Add the <link> line here.

Test driving the entire lounge...

Save each of these files and then open "lounge.html" with the browser. You should see no changes in its style, even though the styles are now coming from an external file. Now click on the "elixirs" and "detailed directions" links.

Wow! We have a whole new style for the Elixirs and Directions pages with only a *one line change* to the HTML in each file! Now you can really see the power of CSS.

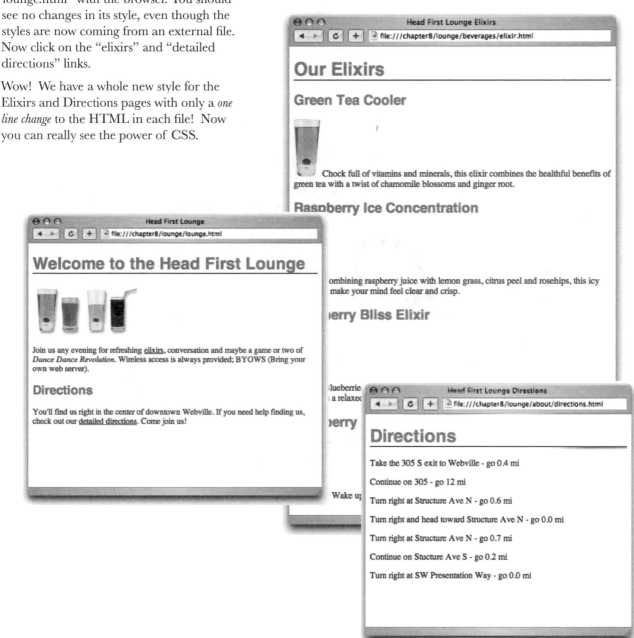

The Case of Brute Force versus Style

So, how did RadWebDesign become Web page superheroes? Or, maybe we should first ask how the "do no wrong" CorrectWebDesign firm flubbed things up this time? The root of the problem was that CorrectWebDesign was creating the RobotsRUs pages using circa 1998 techniques. They were putting their style rules right in with their HTML (copying and pasting them each time), and, even worse, they were using a lot of old HTML elements like **<font>** and **<center>** that have now been deprecated. So, when the call came to change the look and feel, that meant going into *every* Web page and making changes to the CSS. Worse, it meant going through the HTML to change elements as well.

Compare that with what RadWebDesign did: they used strict XHTML 1.0, so they had no old presentation HTML in their pages, and they used an external style sheet. The result? To change the style of the entire site, all they had to do was go into their external style sheet and make a few changes to the CSS, which they easily did in minutes, not days. They even had time to try out multiple designs and have three different versions of the CSS ready for review before the site launch. Amazed, the RobotsRUs CEO not only promised RadWebDesign more business, but he also promised them the first robot that comes off the assembly line.

Five-Minute Mystery

Solved

Sharpen your pencil

Now that you've got one external style file (or "style sheet"), use it to change all the paragraph fonts to "sans-serif" to match the headings. Remember, the property to change the font style is "font-family", and the value for sans-serif font is "sans-serif". You'll find the answer on the next page.

The headings use sans-serif fonts, which don't have "serifs" and have a very clean look.

The paragraphs still use the default serif fonts, which have "serifs", and are often considered more difficult to read on a computer screen.

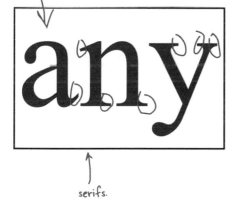

serifs.

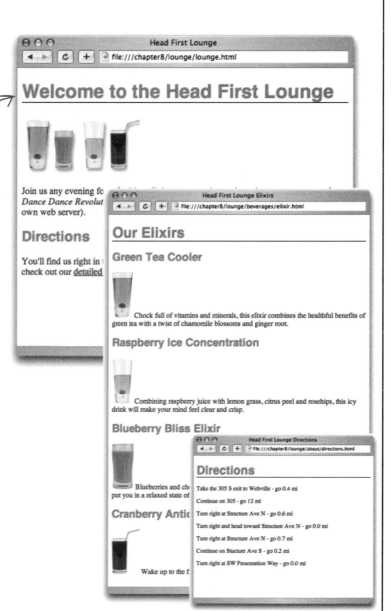

Sharpen your pencil
Solution

```
h1, h2 {
        font-family:   sans-serif;
        color:         gray;
}

h1 {
        border-bottom: 1px solid black;
}

p {
        font-family:   sans-serif;
        color:         maroon;
}
```

Just add a font–family property to your paragraph rule in the "lounge.css" file.

I'm wondering if that is really the best solution. Why are we specifying the font-family for EACH element? What if someone added a <blockquote> to the page - would we have to then add a rule for that too? Can't we just tell the *whole* page to be sans-serif?

It's time to talk about your inheritance...

Did you notice when you added the **font-family** property to your "p" selector that it also affected the font family of the elements inside the **<p>** element? Let's take a closer look:

> When you added the font-family property to your CSS p selector, it changed the font family of your <p> elements. But it also changed the font family of the two links and the emphasized text.

The elements inside the <p> element <u>inherit</u> the font-family style from <p>

Just like you can inherit your blue eyes or brown hair from your parents, elements can inherit styles from their parents. In this case, the **<a>** and **<em>** elements inherited the **font-family** style from the **<p>** element, which is their parent element. It makes sense that changing your paragraph style would change the style of the elements in the paragraph, doesn't it? After all, if it didn't, you'd have to go in and add CSS rules for every inline element in every paragraph in your whole site... which would definitely be so NOT fun.

> Not every style is inherited. Just some are, like font-family.

> Not to mention, error-prone, tedious, and time-consuming.

Let's take a look at our XHTML tree to see how inheritance works:

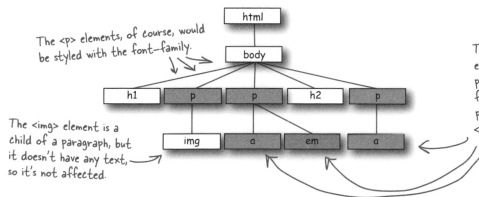

> If we set the font-family of all the <p> elements, here are all the elements that would be affected.

> The <p> elements, of course, would be styled with the font-family.

> The <a>, <em>, and <a> elements in the two paragraphs inherit the font-family from their parent elements, the <p> elements.

> The <img> element is a child of a paragraph, but it doesn't have any text, so it's not affected.

What if we move the font up the family tree?

If most elements inherit the **font-family** property, what if we move it up to the **<body>** element? That should have the effect of changing the font for all the **<body>** element's children, and children's children.

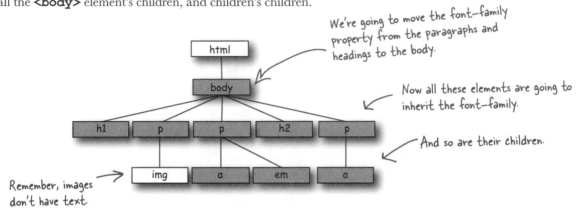

We're going to move the font-family property from the paragraphs and headings to the body.

Now all these elements are going to inherit the font-family.

And so are their children.

Remember, images don't have text.

Wow, this is powerful. Simply by changing the font-family property in the body rule, we could change the font for an entire site.

What are you waiting for... give it a try

Open your "lounge.css" file and add a new rule that selects the **<body>** element. Then remove the **font-family** properties from the headings and paragraph rules, because you're not going to need them anymore.

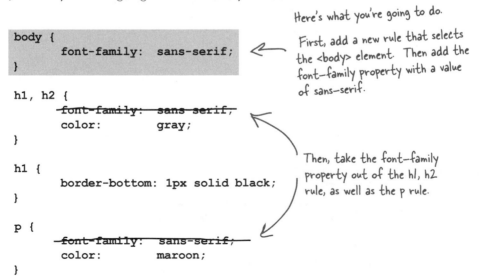

Here's what you're going to do.

First, add a new rule that selects the <body> element. Then add the font-family property with a value of sans-serif.

```
body {
        font-family:  sans-serif;
}

h1, h2 {
        font-family:  sans-serif;
        color:        gray;
}

h1 {
        border-bottom: 1px solid black;
}

p {
        font-family:  sans-serif;
        color:        maroon;
}
```

Then, take the font-family property out of the h1, h2 rule, as well as the p rule.

Test drive your new CSS

As usual, go ahead and make these changes in the "lounge.css" style sheet, save, and reload the "lounge.html" page. You shouldn't expect any changes, because the style is the same. It's just coming from a different rule. But you should feel better about your CSS because now you can add new elements to your pages and they'll automatically inherit the sans-serif font.

Surprise, surprise. This doesn't look any different at all, but that is exactly what we were expecting, isn't it? All you've done is move the sans-serif font up into the body rule and let all the other elements inherit that.

Okay, so now that the whole site is set to sans-serif with the body selector, what if I want *one* element to be a different font? Do I have to take the font-family out of the body and add rules for every element separately again?

Overriding inheritance

By moving the **font-family** property up into the body, you've set that
font style for the entire page. But what if you don't want the sans-serif
font on every element? For instance, you could decide that you want
<em> elements to use the serif font instead.

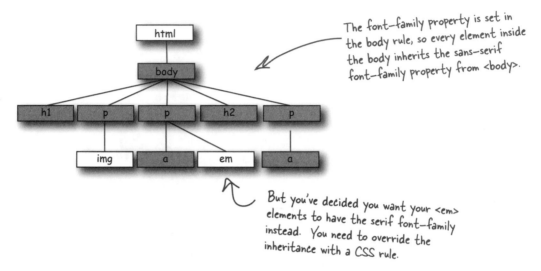

The font-family property is set in the body rule, so every element inside the body inherits the sans-serif font-family property from <body>.

But you've decided you want your <em> elements to have the serif font-family instead. You need to override the inheritance with a CSS rule.

Well, then you can override the inheritance by supplying a
specific rule just for **<em>**. Here's how you add a rule for **<em>**
to override the font-family specified in the body:

```
body {
        font-family:  sans-serif;
}

h1, h2 {
        color:        gray;
}

h1 {
        border-bottom: 1px solid black;
}

p {
        color:        maroon;
}

em {
        font-family:  serif;
}
```

To override the font-family property inherited from body, add a new rule selecting em with the font-family property value set to serif.

Test drive

Add a rule for the **<em>** element to your CSS with a
font-family property value of **serif**, and reload
your "lounge.html" page:

*Notice that the "Dance Dance
Revolution" text, which is the text in
the <em> element, is now a serif font.*

*As a general rule, it's not a good idea to change fonts
in the middle of a paragraph like this, so go ahead and
change your CSS back to the way it was (without the em
rule) when you're done testing.*

there are no
Dumb Questions

Q: How does the browser know
which rule to apply to <em> when I'm
overriding the inherited value?

A: With CSS, the most specific rule
is always used. So, if you have a rule for
<body>, and a more specific rule for <em>
elements, it is going to use the more specific
rule. We'll talk more later about how you
know which rules are most specific.

Q: How do I know which CSS
properties are inherited and which are
not?

A: This is where a good reference
really comes in handy, like O'Reilly's *CSS
Pocket Reference*. In general, all of the
styles that affect the way your text looks,
such as font color (the color property), the

font-family, as you've just seen, and other
font related properties such as font-size,
font-weight (for bold text), and font-style
(for italics) are inherited. Other properties,
such as border, are not inherited, which
makes sense, right? Just because you want
a border on your <body> element doesn't
mean you want it on *all* your elements. A
lot of the time you can follow your common
sense (or just try it and see), and you'll get
the hang of it as you become more familiar
with the various properties and what they do.

Q: Can I always override a property
that is being inherited when I don't want
it?

A: Yes. You can always use a more
specific selector to override a property from
a parent.

Q: This stuff gets complicated. Is
there any way I can add comments to
remind myself what the rules do?

A: Yes. To write a comment in your
CSS just enclose it between /* and */. For
instance:

```
/*  this rule selects all para-
graphs and colors them blue */
```

Notice that a comment can span multiple
lines. You can also put comments around
CSS and browsers will ignore it, like:

```
/* this rule will have no effect
because it's in a comment

p { color: blue; }   */
```

> I was thinking it would be cool to have the text below each elixir match the color of the elixir. Can you do that?

We're not sure we agree with the aesthetics of that suggestion, but, hey, you're the customer.

Can you style each of these paragraphs separately so that the color of the text matches the drink? The problem is that using a rule with a "p" selector applies the style to *all* **<p>** elements. So, how can you select these paragraphs individually?

That's where *classes* come in. Using both XHTML and CSS, we can define a class of elements, and then apply styles to any element that belongs to that class. So, what exactly is a class? Think of it like a club – someone starts a "greentea" club, and by joining you agree to all the rights and responsibilities of the club, like adhering to their style standards. Anyway, let's just create the class and you'll see how it works.

Green text. →

Blue text. →

Purple text. →

Red text... oh, we don't need to change this one. →

Our Elixirs

Green Tea Cooler

Chock full of vitamins and minerals, this elixir combines the healthful benefits of green tea with a twist of chamomile blossoms and ginger root.

Raspberry Ice Concentration

Combining raspberry juice with lemon grass, citrus peel and rosehips, this icy drink will make your mind feel clear and crisp.

Blueberry Bliss Elixir

Blueberries and cherry essence mixed into a base of elderflower herb tea will put you in a relaxed state of bliss in no time.

Cranberry Antioxidant Blast

Wake up to the flavors of cranberry and hibiscus in this vitamin C rich elixir.

Adding a class to "elixir.html"

Open up the "elixir.html" file and locate the "Green Tea Cooler" paragraph.
This is the text we want to change to green. All you're going to do is add the **<p>**
element to a class called **greentea**. Here's how you do that:

```
<!DOCTYPE html PUBLIC "-//W3C//DTD XHTML 1.0 Strict//EN"
    "http://www.w3.org/TR/xhtml1/DTD/xhtml1-strict.dtd">
<html xmlns="http://www.w3.org/1999/xhtml" lang="en" xml:lang="en">
  <head>
    <meta http-equiv="Content-Type" content="text/html; charset=ISO-8859-1" />
    <title>Head First Lounge Elixirs</title>
    <link type="text/css" rel="stylesheet" href="../lounge.css" />
  </head>
  <body>
    <h1>Our Elixirs</h1>
    <h2>Green Tea Cooler</h2>
    <p class="greentea">
            <img src="../images/green.jpg" />
            Chock full of vitamins and minerals, this elixir
            combines the healthful benefits of green tea with
            a twist of chamomile blossoms and ginger root.
    </p>
    <h2>Raspberry Ice Concentration</h2>
    <p>
            <img src="../images/lightblue.jpg" />
            Combining raspberry juice with lemon grass,
            citrus peel and rosehips, this icy drink
            will make your mind feel clear and crisp.
    </p>
    <h2>Blueberry Bliss Elixir</h2>
    <p>
            <img src="../images/blue.jpg" />
            Blueberries and cherry essence mixed into a base
            of elderflower herb tea will put you in a relaxed
            state of bliss in no time.
    </p>
    <h2>Cranberry Antioxidant Blast</h2>
    <p>
            <img src="../images/red.jpg" />
            Wake up to the flavors of cranberry and hibiscus
            in this vitamin C rich elixir.
    </p>
  </body>
</html>
```

To add an element to a class, just add
the attribute "class" along with the name
of the class, like "greentea".

And, now that the green tea paragraph belongs to the **greentea** class, you just
need to provide some rules to style that class of elements.

Creating a selector for the class

To select a class, you write the selector like this:

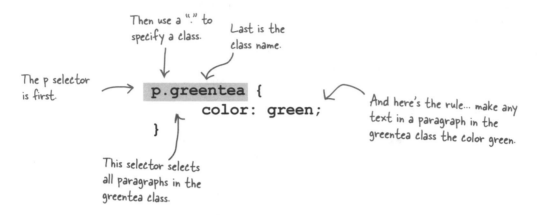

Then use a "." to specify a class.

Last is the class name.

The p selector is first.

p.greentea {
    color: green;
}

This selector selects all paragraphs in the greentea class.

And here's the rule... make any text in a paragraph in the greentea class the color green.

So now you have a way of selecting **<p>** elements that belong to a certain class. All you need to do is add the **class** attribute to any **<p>** elements you want to be green, and this rule will be applied. Give it a try: open your "lounge.css" file and add the **p.greentea** class selector to it.

```
body {
    font-family: sans-serif;
}

h1, h2 {
    color: gray;
}

h1 {
    border-bottom: 1px solid black;
}

p {
    color: maroon;
}

p.greentea {
    color: green;
}
```

A greentea test drive

Save, and then reload to give your new class a test drive.

Here's the new greentea class applied to the paragraph. Now the font is green and matches the Green Tea Cooler. Maybe this styling wasn't such a bad idea after all.

Sharpen your pencil

Your turn: add two classes, "raspberry" and "blueberry", to the correct paragraphs in "elixir.html", and then write the styles to color the text blue and purple, respectively. The property value for raspberry Is "blue" and for blueberry is "purple". Put these at the bottom of your CSS file, under the greentea rule: raspberry first, and then blueberry.

Yeah, we know you're probably thinking, how can a raspberry be blue? Well, if Raspberry Kool-aid is blue, that's good enough for us. And seriously, when you blend up a bunch of blueberries, they really are more purple than blue. Work with us here.

Taking classes further...

You've already written one rule that uses the **greentea** class to change any paragraph in the class to the color "green":

```
p.greentea {
        color: green;
}
```

But what if you wanted to do the same to all **<blockquote>**s?
Then you could do this:

```
blockquote.greentea, p.greentea {
        color: green;
}
```

Just add another selector to handle <blockquote>s that are in the greentea class. Now this rule will apply to <p> and <blockquote> elements in the greentea class.

And in your XHTML you'd write:

```
<blockquote class="greentea">
```

So what if I want to add <h1>, <h2>, <h3>, <p>, and <blockquote> to the green tea class? Do I have to write one *huge* selector?

No, there's a better way. If you want all elements that are in the **greentea** class to have a style, then you can just write your rule like this:

```
.greentea {
        color: green;
}
```

If you leave out all the element names, and just use a period followed by a class name, then the rule will apply to all members of the class.

Cool! Yes, that works. One more question... you said being in a class is like being in a club. Well, I can join many clubs. So, can an element be in more than one class?

Yes, elements can be in more than one class.

It's easy to put an element into more than one class. Say you want to specify a **<p>** element that is in the **greentea**, **raspberry**, and **blueberry** classes. Here's how you would do that in the opening tag:

```
<p class="greentea raspberry blueberry">
```

Place each class name into the value of the class attribute, with a space in between each. The ordering doesn't matter.

So, for example, I could put an <h1> into my "products" class that defines a font size and weight, and also a "specials" class to change its color to red when something's on sale?

Exactly. Use multiple classes when you want an element to have styles you've defined in different classes. In this case, all your **<h1>** elements associated with products have a certain style, but not all your products are on sale at the same time. By putting your "specials" color in a separate class, you can simply add only those elements associated with products on sale to the "specials" class to add the red color you want.

Now you may be wondering what happens when an element belongs to multiple classes, all of which define the *same* property – like our **<p>** element up there. How do you know which style gets applied? You know each of these classes has a definition for the **color** property. So, will the paragraph be green, blue (raspberry), or purple?

We're going to talk about this in great detail after you've learned a bit more CSS, but on the next page you'll find a quick guide to hold you over.

The world's smallest & fastest guide to how styles are applied

Elements and document trees and style rules and classes... it can get downright confusing. How does all this stuff come together so that you know which styles are being applied to which elements? As we said, *to fully answer that* you're going to have to know a little more about CSS, and you'll be learning that in the next few chapters. But before you get there, let's just walk through some common sense rules-of-thumb about how styles are applied.

First, do <u>any</u> selectors select your element?

Let's say you want to know the **font-family** property value for an element. The first thing to check is: is there a selector in your CSS file that selects your element? If there is, and it has a **font-family** property and value, then that's the value for your element.

What about inheritance?

If there are no selectors that match your element, then you rely on inheritance. So, look at the element's parents, and parents' parents, and so on, until you find the property defined. When and if you find it, that's the value.

Struck out again? Then use the default

If your element doesn't inherit the value from any of its ancestors, then you use the default value defined by the browser. In reality, this is a little more complicated than we're describing here, but we'll get to some of those details later in the book.

What if multiple selectors select an element?

Ah, this is the case we have with the paragraph that belongs to all three classes:

```
<p class="greentea raspberry blueberry">
```

There are multiple selectors that match this element and define the same **color** property. That's what we call a "conflict". Which rule breaks the tie? Well, if one rule is more *specific* than the others, then it wins. But what does more specific mean? We'll come back in a later chapter and see *exactly* how to determine how specific a selector is, but for now, let's look at some rules and get a feel for it:

```
p { color: black;}
```
Here's a rule that selects any old paragraph element.

```
.greentea { color: green; }
```
This rule selects members of the greentea class. That's a little more specific.

```
p.greentea { color: green; }
```
And this rule selects only paragraphs that are in the greentea class, so that's even more specific.

```
p.raspberry { color: blue; }

p.blueberry { color: purple; }
```
These rules also select only paragraphs in a particular class. So they are about the same in specificity as the p.greentea rule.

And if we still don't have a clear winner?

So, if you had an element that belonged only to the **greentea** class there would be an obvious winner: the **p.greentea** selector is the most specific, so the text would be green. But you have an element that belongs to *all three* classes: **greentea**, **raspberry**, and **blueberry**. So, **p.greentea**, **p.raspberry**, and **p.blueberry** all select the element, and are of equal specificity. What do you do now? You choose the one that is listed *last* in the CSS file. If you can't resolve a conflict because two selectors are equally specific, you use the ordering of the rules in your style sheet file. That is, you use the rule listed last in the CSS file (nearest the bottom). And in this case, that would be the **p.blueberry** rule.

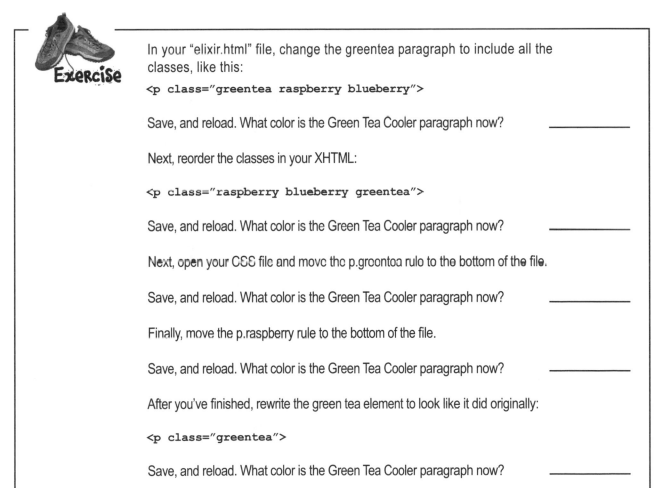

Exercise

In your "elixir.html" file, change the greentea paragraph to include all the classes, like this:

```
<p class="greentea raspberry blueberry">
```

Save, and reload. What color is the Green Tea Cooler paragraph now? _____

Next, reorder the classes in your XHTML:

```
<p class="raspberry blueberry greentea">
```

Save, and reload. What color is the Green Tea Cooler paragraph now? _____

Next, open your CSS file and move the p.greentea rule to the bottom of the file.

Save, and reload. What color is the Green Tea Cooler paragraph now? _____

Finally, move the p.raspberry rule to the bottom of the file.

Save, and reload. What color is the Green Tea Cooler paragraph now? _____

After you've finished, rewrite the green tea element to look like it did originally:

```
<p class="greentea">
```

Save, and reload. What color is the Green Tea Cooler paragraph now? _____

Fireside Chats

Tonight's talk: **CSS & XHTML compare languages**

CSS	**XHTML**

CSS

Did you see that? I'm like Houdini! I broke right out of your **<style>** element and into my own file. And you said in Chapter 1 that I'd never escape.

XHTML

Don't get all excited; I still have to link you in for you to be at all useful.

Have to link me in? Come on; you know your pages wouldn't cut it without my styling.

Here we go again... while me and all my elements are trying to keep things structured, you're talking about hair highlights and nail color.

If you were paying attention in this chapter, you would have seen I'm downright powerful in what I can do.

Okay, okay, I admit it; using CSS sure makes my job easier. All those old deprecated styling elements were a pain in my side. I do like the fact that my elements can be styled without inserting a bunch of stuff in the XHTML, other than maybe an occasional class attribute.

Well now, that's a little better. I like the new attitude.

But I still haven't forgotten how you mocked my syntax... <remember>?

CSS

You have to admit XHTML is kinda clunky, but that's what you get when you're related to an early '90s technology.

Are you kidding? I'm very expressive. I can select just the elements I want, and then describe exactly how I want them styled. And you've only just begun to see all the cool styling I can do.

Yup; just wait and see. I can style fonts and text in all kinds of interesting ways. I can even control how each element manages the space around it on the page.

Bwahahahaa. And you thought you had me controlled between your **<style>** tags. You're going to see I can make your elements sit, bark, and rollover if I want to.

XHTML

I call it standing the test of time. And you think CSS is elegant? I mean, you're just a bunch of rules. How's that a language?

Oh yeah?

Hmmm... sounds as if you have a little too much power; I'm not sure I like the sound of that. After all, my elements want to have some control over their own lives.

Whoa now! Security... security?!

Who gets the inheritance?

Sniff, sniff; the **\<body\>** element has gone to that great browser in the sky. But he left behind a lot of descendants and a big inheritance of **color** "green". Below you'll find his family tree. Mark all the descendants that inherit the **\<body\>** element's color green. Don't forget to look at the CSS below first.

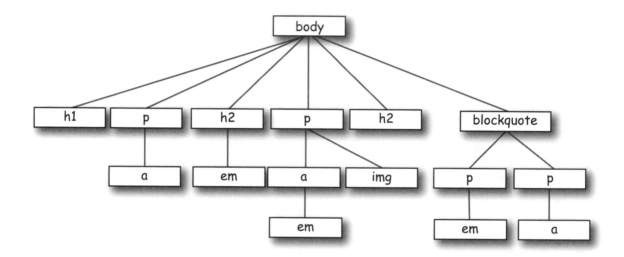

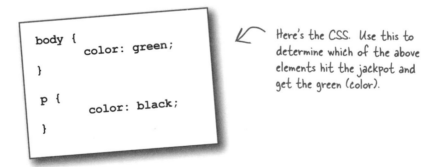

```
body {
        color: green;
}

p {
        color: black;
}
```

Here's the CSS. Use this to determine which of the above elements hit the jackpot and get the green (color).

BE the Browser

Below, you'll find the CSS file "style.css", with some errors in it. Your job is to play like you're the browser and locate all the errors. After you've done the exercise look at the end of the chapter to see if you caught all the errors.

If you have errors in your CSS, usually what happens is all the rules below the error are ignored. So, get in the habit of looking for errors now, by doing this exercise.

The file "style.css"

```
<style>

body {
    background-color: white

h1, {
    gray;
    font-family: sans-serif;
}

h2, p {
    color:
}

<em> {
    font-style: italic;
}

</style>
```

The exercise got me thinking... is there a way to validate CSS like there is with HTML and XHTML?

Of course!

Those W3C boys and girls aren't just sitting around on their butts, they've been working hard. You can find their CSS validator at:

`http://jigsaw.w3.org/css-validator/`

Type that URL in your browser and we think you'll feel quite at home when you get there. You're going to find a validator that works almost exactly like the HTML and XHTML validators. To use the CSS version, just point the validator to your CSS URL, upload a file with your CSS in it, or just paste it into the form and submit.

You shouldn't encounter any big surprises, like needing DOCTYPEs or character encodings with CSS. Go ahead, give it a try (like we're not going to make you do it on the next page, anyway).

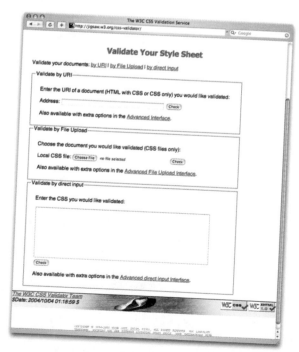

Making sure the Lounge CSS validates

Before you wrap up this chapter, wouldn't you feel a lot better if all that Head First Lounge CSS validated? Sure you would. Use whichever method you want to get your CSS to the W3C. If you have your CSS on a server, type your URL into the form; otherwise, either upload your CSS file or just copy and paste the CSS into the form. (If you upload, make sure you're directing the form to your CSS file, not your XHTML file.) Once you've done that, click on "Check".

If your CSS didn't validate, check it with the CSS a few pages back and find any small mistakes you've made, then resubmit.

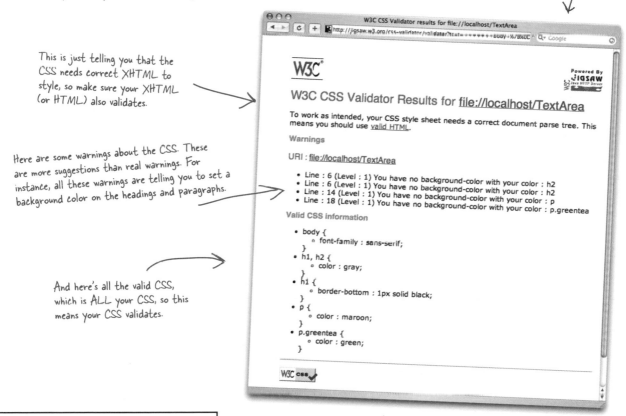

This is just telling you that the CSS needs correct XHTML to style, so make sure your XHTML (or HTML) also validates.

Here are some warnings about the CSS. These are more suggestions than real warnings. For instance, all these warnings are telling you to set a background color on the headings and paragraphs.

And here's all the valid CSS, which is ALL your CSS, so this means your CSS validates.

There's no "green badge of success" when you pass validation like there is when you validate XHTML. So check the top of the page for "Errors". If you don't see that, your CSS validated!

---

there are no Dumb Questions

Q: Do I need to worry about those warnings? Or do what they say?

A: It's good to look them over, but you'll find some are more in the category of suggestions than "must do's". The validator can err on the side of being a little anal, so just keep that in mind.

Property Soup

top

Controls the position of the top of the element.

text-align

Use this property to align your text to the left, center, or right.

letter-spacing

This lets you set the spacing between letters. L i k e t h i s.

Use color to set the font color of text elements.

color

background-color

This property controls the background color of an element.

Use this property for italic or oblique text.

font-style

This property controls the weight of text. Use it to make text bold.

font-weight

border

This property puts a border around an element. You can have a solid border, a ridged border, a dotted border...

This property lets you change how list items look in a list.

list-style

left

This is how you tell an element how to position its left side.

margin

If you need space between the edge of an element and its content, use margin.

This property sets the space between lines in a text element.

Makes text bigger or smaller.

Use this property to put an image behind an element.

line-height

font-size

background-image

CSS has a *lot* of style properties. You'll see quite a few of these in the rest of this book, but have a quick look now to get an idea of all the aspects of style you can control with CSS.

It looks like you're getting the hang of this style stuff. We're looking forward to seeing what you come up with in the next couple of chapters.

BULLET POINTS

- CSS contains simple statements, called rules.

- Each rule provides the style for a selection of XHTML elements.

- A typical rule consists of a selector along with one or more properties and values.

- The selector specifies which elements the rule applies to.

- Each property declaration ends with a semicolon.

- All properties and values in a rule go between { } braces.

- You can select any element using its name as the selector.

- By separating element names with commas, you can select multiple elements at once.

- One of the easiest ways to include a style in HTML is the <style> tag.

- For XHTML and for sites of any complexity, you should link to an external style sheet.

- The <link> element is used to include an external style sheet.

- Many properties are inherited. For instance, if a property that is inherited is set for the <body> element, all the <body>'s child elements will inherit it

- You can always override properties that are inherited by creating a more specific rule for the element you'd like to change.

- Use the `class` attribute to add elements to a class.

- Use a "." between the element name and the class name to select a specific element in that class.

- Use ".classname" to select any elements that belong to the class.

- An element can belong to more than one class by placing multiple class names in the class attribute with spaces between the names.

- You can validate your CSS using the W3C validator, at http://jigsaw.w3.org/css-validator.

XHTMLcross

Here are some clues with mental twist and turns that will help you burn alternative routes to CSS right into your brain!

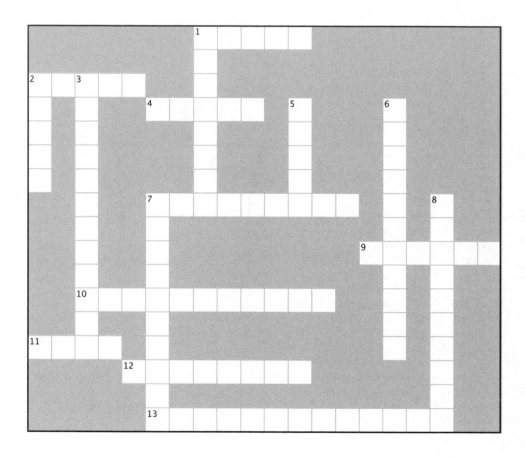

Across

1. Defines a group of elements.
2. Ornamental part of some fonts.
4. Styles are defined in these.
7. Fonts without serifs.
9. Each rule defines a set of properties and?
10. How elements get properties from their parents.
11. Use this element to include an external style sheet.
12. Selects an element.
13. Reality show.

Down

1. With inheritance, a property set on one element is also passed down to its _____.
2. You can place your CSS inside these tags in an HTML file.
3. Won this time because they used external style sheets.
5. Property that represents font color.
6. Property for font type.
7. An external style file is called this.
8. They really wanted some style.

Markup Magnets Solution

Remember drawing the diagram of XHTML elements in
Chapter 3? You did that again for the Lounge's main page.
Here's the answer:

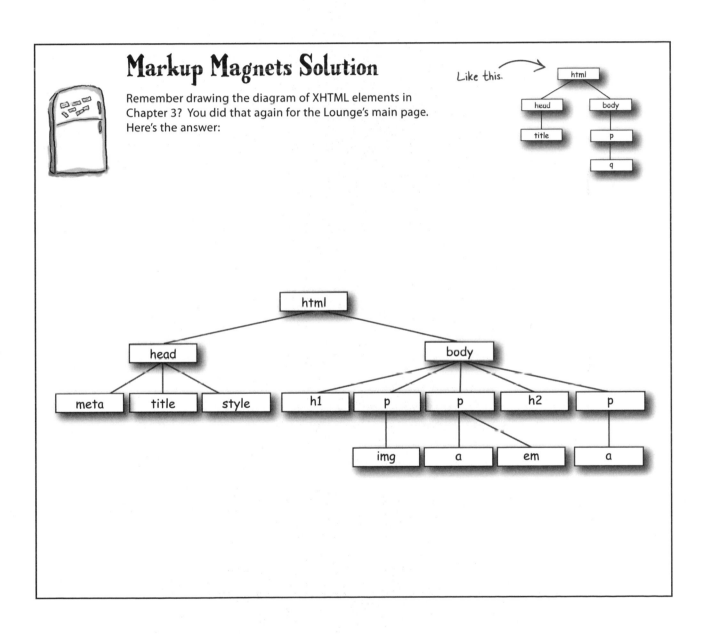

Solution

The selected elements are colored:

```
p, h2 {
    font-family: sans-serif;
}
```

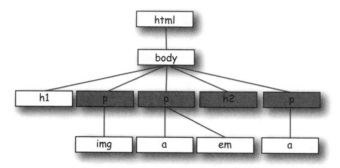

```
p, em {
    font-family: sans-serif;
}
```

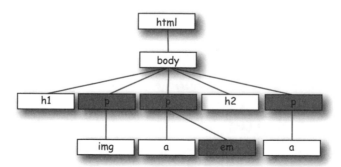

Sharpen your pencil
Solution

Your turn: add two classes, "raspberry" and "blueberry" to the correct paragraphs in "elixir.html" and then write the styles to color the text blue and purple respectively. The property value for raspberry is "blue" and for blueberry is "purple".

```css
body {
        font-family: sans-serif;
}

h1, h2 {
        color: gray;
}

h1 {
        border-bottom: 1px solid black;
}

p {
        color: maroon;
}

p.greentea {
        color: green;
}

p.raspberry {
        color: blue;
}

p.blueberry {
        color: purple;
}
```

Sharpen your pencil
Solution

```
<!DOCTYPE html PUBLIC "-//W3C//DTD XHTML 1.0 Strict//EN"
    "http://www.w3.org/TR/xhtml1/DTD/xhtml1-strict.dtd">
<html xmlns="http://www.w3.org/1999/xhtml" lang="en" xml:lang="en">
  <head>
    <meta http-equiv="Content-Type" content="text/html; charset=ISO-8859-1" />
    <title>Head First Lounge Elixirs</title>
    <link type="text/css" rel="stylesheet" href="../lounge.css" />
  </head>
  <body>
    <h1>Our Elixirs</h1>
    <h2>Green Tea Cooler</h2>
    <p class="greentea">
            <img src="../images/green.jpg" />
            Chock full of vitamins and minerals, this elixir
            combines the healthful benefits of green tea with
            a twist of chamomile blossoms and ginger root.
    </p>
    <h2>Raspberry Ice Concentration</h2>
    <p class="raspberry" >
            <img src="../images/lightblue.jpg" />
            Combining raspberry juice with lemon grass,
            citrus peel and rosehips, this icy drink
            will make your mind feel clear and crisp.
    </p>
    <h2>Blueberry Bliss Elixir</h2>
    <p class="blueberry" >
            <img src="../images/blue.jpg" />
            Blueberries and cherry essence mixed into a base
            of elderflower herb tea will put you in a relaxed
            state of bliss in no time.
    </p>
    <h2>Cranberry Antioxidant Blast</h2>
    <p>
            <img src="../images/red.jpg" />
            Wake up to the flavors of cranberry and hibiscus
            in this vitamin C rich elixir.
    </p>
  </body>
</html>
```

Exercise solutions

Who gets the inheritance?

```
body {
        color: green;
}

p {
        color: black;
}
```

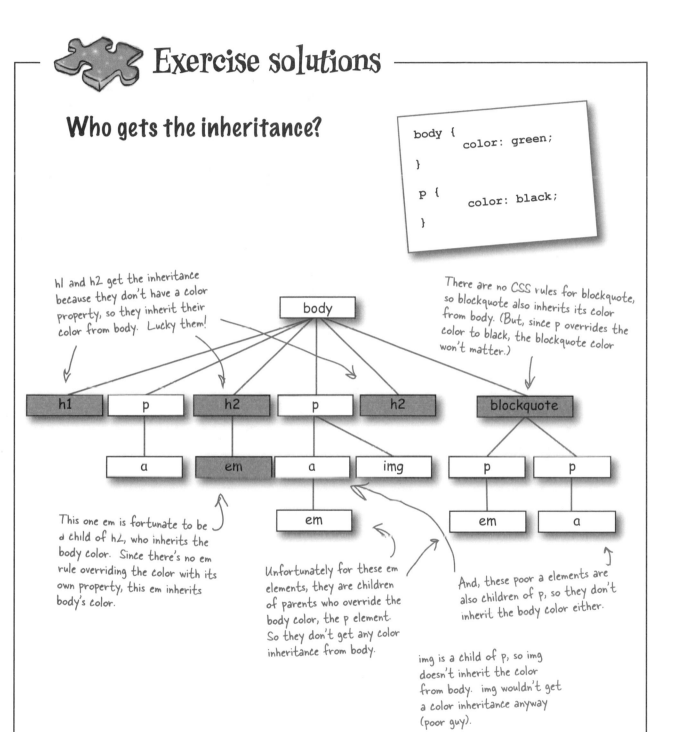

h1 and h2 get the inheritance because they don't have a color property, so they inherit their color from body. Lucky them!

There are no CSS rules for blockquote, so blockquote also inherits its color from body. (But, since p overrides the color to black, the blockquote color won't matter.)

This one em is fortunate to be a child of h2, who inherits the body color. Since there's no em rule overriding the color with its own property, this em inherits body's color.

Unfortunately for these em elements, they are children of parents who override the body color, the p element. So they don't get any color inheritance from body.

And, these poor a elements are also children of p, so they don't inherit the body color either.

img is a child of p, so img doesn't inherit the color from body. img wouldn't get a color inheritance anyway (poor guy).

Exercise solutions

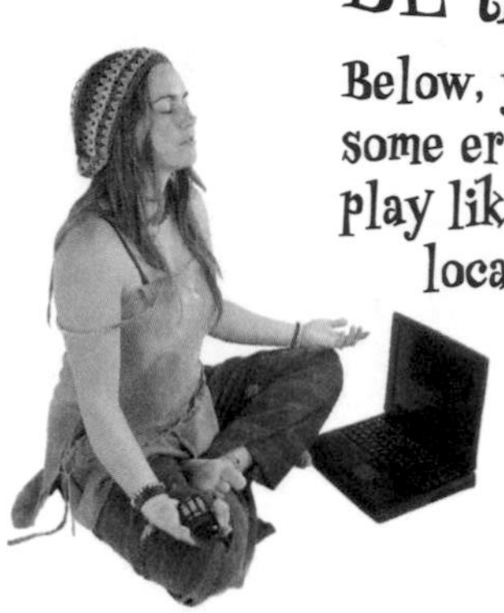

BE the Browser

Below, you'll find a CSS file with some errors in it. Your job is to play like you're the browser and locate all the errors. Did you find them all?

```
<style>
```
← No XHTML in your CSS! The <style> tags are XHTML and don't work in a CSS style sheet.

```
body {
    background-color: white
```
← Missing semicolon.

← Missing }

```
h1, {
```
↖ Extra comma.

← Missing property name.

```
    gray;
    font-family: sans-serif;
}

h2, p {
    color:
```
↖ Missing property value and semicolon.

```
}

<em> {
```
← Using the XHTML tag instead of just the element name. This should be em.

```
    font-style: italic;
}

</style>
```
← No </style> tags needed in the CSS stylesheet.

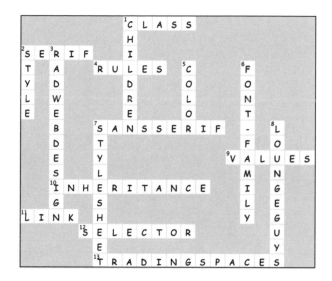

Exercise Solutions

In your "lounge.html" file, change the greentea paragraph to include all the classes, like this:

```
<p class="greentea raspberry blueberry">
```

Save, and reload. What color is the Green Tea Cooler paragraph now?   <u>purple</u>

It's purple because the blueberry rule is last in the CSS file.

Next reorder the classes in your XHTML:

```
<p class="raspberry blueberry greentea">
```

Save, and reload. What color is the Green Tea Cooler paragraph now?   <u>purple</u>

It's still purple because the ordering of the names in the class attribute doesn't matter.

Next open your CSS file and move the p.greentea rule to the bottom of the file.

Save, and reload. What color is the Green Tea Cooler paragraph now?   <u>green</u>

Now, it's green, because the greentea rule comes last in the CSS file.

Finally, move the p.raspberry rule to the bottom of the file.

Save, and reload. What color is the Green Tea Cooler paragraph now?   <u>blue</u>

Now, it's blue, because the raspberry rule comes last in the CSS file.

After you've finished, rewrite the green tea element to look like it did originally:

```
<p class="greentea">
```

Save, and reload. What color is the Green Tea Cooler paragraph now?   <u>green</u>

Okay, now the <p> element only belongs to one class, so we use the most specific rule, which is p.greentea.

9 styling with fonts and colors

Expanding your Vocabulary

Your CSS language lessons are coming along nicely. You already have the basics of CSS down and you know how to create CSS rules to select and specify the style of an element. Now it's time to build your vocabulary, and that means picking up some new properties and learning what they can do for you. In this chapter we're going to work through some of the most common properties that affect the display of text. To do that, you'll need to learn a few things about fonts and color. You're going to see you don't have to be stuck with the fonts everyone else uses, or the clunky sizes and styles the browser uses as the defaults for paragraphs and headings. You're also going to see there is a lot more to color than meets the eye.

Text and fonts from 30,000 feet

A lot of the CSS properties are dedicated to helping you style your text. Using CSS, you can control typeface, style, color, and even the decorations that are put on your text, and we're going to cover all these in this chapter. We'll start by exploring the actual fonts that are used to display your pages. You've already seen the **font-family** property and in this chapter you're going to learn a lot more about specifying fonts.

Before we dive in, let's get the 30,000 foot view of some properties you can use to specify and change the look of your fonts. After that, we'll take the fonts one by one and learn the ins and outs of using each.

Customize the fonts in your pages with the font-family property.

Fonts can have a dramatic effect on your page designs. In CSS, fonts are divided into "font families" from which you can specify the fonts you'd like used in each element of your page. Only certain fonts are commonly installed on most computers, so you need to be careful in your font choices. In this chapter we'll take you through everything you need to know to specify and make the best use of fonts.

Andale Mono

Arial

Arial Black

Comic Sans

Courier New

Georgia

Impact

Times New Roman

Trebuchet MS

Verdana

```
body {
        font-family: Verdana, Geneva, Arial, sans-serif;
}
```

Control the size of your fonts with the font-size property.

Font size also has a big impact on the design and the readability of your Web pages. There are several ways to specify font sizes with CSS, and in this chapter we'll cover each one, but we'll also teach you how to specify your fonts in a way that allows your users to increase the font size without affecting your designs.

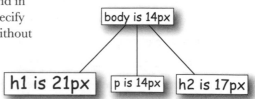

```
body {
        font-size: 14px;
}
```

Add color to your text with the color property.

You can change your text color with the color property. To do that, it helps to know a little about Web colors, and we'll take you through all the ins and outs of color, including the mysterious color "hex codes."

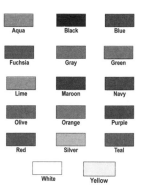

```
body {
        color: silver;
}
```

Affect the weight of your fonts with the font-weight property.

Why settle for boring, average fonts when you can give them some extra weight when needed? Or, are your fonts looking too heavy? Slim them down to a normal weight. All this is easily done with the **font-weight** property.

```
body {
        font-weight: bold;
}
```

lighter

normal

bold

bolder

Add even more style to your text with the text-decoration property.

Using the **text-decoration** property you can decorate your text with decorations including overlines, underlines, and line-throughs. And if you didn't get enough of blinking text on the Web in the 1990s, the designers of CSS have even included a blink value for **text-decoration** (although thankfully they don't require browsers to implement it).

```
body {
        text-decoration: underline;
}
```

<u>underline</u>

o̅v̅e̅r̅l̅i̅n̅e̅

~~line-through~~

blink

What is a font family anyway?

You've already come across the `font-family` property, and so far you've always specified a value of "sans-serif". You can get a lot more creative than that with the `font-family` property, but it helps to know what a font family is first. Here's a quick rundown...

Each font-family contains a set of fonts that share common characteristics. There are five font families: sans-serif, serif, monospace, cursive, and fantasy. Each family includes a large set of fonts, so on this page you'll see only a few examples of each.

Sans-serif Family

Verdana

Arial Black

Trebuchet MS

Arial

Geneva

The serif family includes fonts with serifs. A lot of people associate the look of these fonts with newspaper print.

Serifs are the decorative barbs and hooks on the ends of the letters.

The sans-serif family includes fonts without serifs. These fonts are usually considered more readable on computer screens than serif fonts.

Sans-serif means "without serifs".

Serif Family

Times

Times New Roman

Georgia

Fonts aren't consistently available from one computer to another. In fact, the set of available fonts will vary depending on the operating system as well as what fonts and applications a user has installed. So keep in mind that the fonts on your machine may differ from what is available to your users.

Monospace Family

Courier

Courier New

Andale Mono

← The Monospace family is made up of fonts that have constant width characters. For instance, the horizontal space an "i" takes up will be the same width that an "m" takes up. These fonts are primarily used to show software code examples.

The Cursive family includes fonts that look handwritten. You'll sometimes see these fonts used in headings. ↓

Cursive Family

Comic Sans

Apple Chancery

Take a good look at the font families: serif fonts have an elegant, traditional look, while sans-serif fonts have a very clean and readable look. Monospace fonts feel like they were typed on a typewriter. Cursive and Fantasy fonts have a playful or stylized feel.

Fantasy Family

LAST NINJA

Impact

← The Fantasy font family contains stylized decorative fonts. These fonts are usually not widely available and are rarely used for serious Web designs.

Font Magnets

Your job is to help the fictional fonts below find their way home to their own font family. Move each fridge magnet on the left into the correct font family on the right. Check your answers before you move on. Review the font family descriptions on the previous pages if you need to.

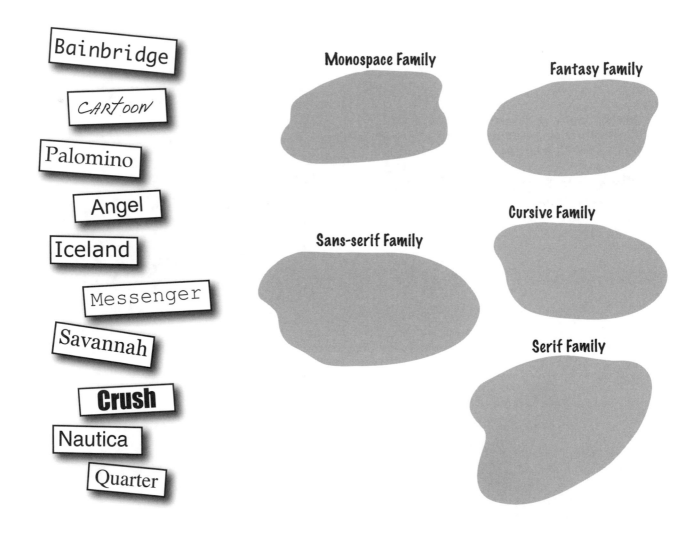

Bainbridge

CARTOON

Palomino

Angel

Iceland

Messenger

Savannah

Crush

Nautica

Quarter

Monospace Family

Fantasy Family

Sans-serif Family

Cursive Family

Serif Family

Specifying font families using CSS

Okay, so there are a lot of good fonts out there from several font families. How do you get them in your pages? Well, you've already had a peek at the **font-family** property in the last chapter, when you specified a **font-family** of "sans-serif" for the lounge. Here's a more interesting example:

Usually your font-family specification contains a list of alternative fonts, all from the same family.

```
body {
      font-family: Verdana, Geneva, Arial, sans-serif;
}
```

You can specify more than one font using the font-family property. Just type the font names separated by commas.

Write font names as they are spelled, including upper- and lower-case letters.

Always put a generic font family name at the end, like "serif", "sans-serif", "cursive", or "monospace". You'll see what this does in a sec.

How font-family specifications work

Here's how the browser interprets the fonts listed in your **font-family** specification:

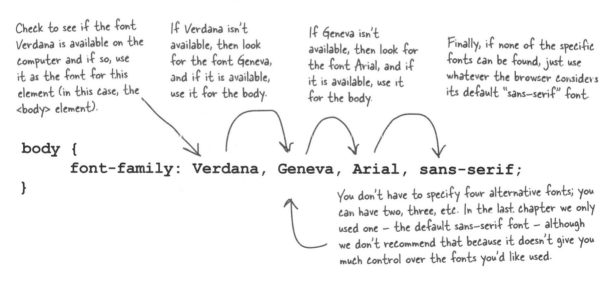

Check to see if the font Verdana is available on the computer and if so, use it as the font for this element (in this case, the <body> element).

If Verdana isn't available, then look for the font Geneva, and if it is available, use it for the body.

If Geneva isn't available, then look for the font Arial, and if it is available, use it for the body.

Finally, if none of the specific fonts can be found, just use whatever the browser considers its default "sans-serif" font.

```
body {
      font-family: Verdana, Geneva, Arial, sans-serif;
}
```

You don't have to specify four alternative fonts; you can have two, three, etc. In the last chapter we only used one – the default sans-serif font – although we don't recommend that because it doesn't give you much control over the fonts you'd like used.

The **font-family** property gives you a way to create a list of preferred fonts. Hopefully most browsers will have one of your first choices, but if not, you can at least be assured that the browser will provide a generic font from the same family.

Let's get some fonts into your pages...

Dusting off Tony's Journal

Now that you know how to specify fonts, let's take another look at Tony's Segway'n USA page and give it a different look. We'll be making some small, incremental changes to the text styles in Tony's page and while no single change is going to look dramatically different, by the end of the chapter we think you'll agree the site has a slick new look. Let's get an idea of where we might make some improvements and then let's give Tony a new **font-family**.

Segway'n USA

Documenting my trip around the US on my very own Segway!

August 20, 2005

Well, I made it 1200 miles already, and I passed through some interesting places on the way:

1. Walla Walla, WA
2. Magic City, ID
3. Bountiful, UT
4. Last Chance, CO
5. Truth or Consequences, NM
6. Why, AZ

July 14, 2005

I saw some Burma Shave style signs on the side of the road today:

> Passing cars,
> When you can't see,
> May get you,
> A glimpse,
> Of eternity.

I definitely won't be passing any cars.

June 2, 2005

My first day of the trip! I can't believe I finally got everything packed and ready to go. Because I'm on a Segway, I wasn't able to bring a whole lot with me:

- cellphone
- iPod
- digital camera
- a protein bar

Just the essentials. As Lao Tzu would have said, "A journey of a thousand miles begins with one Segway."

To do list:

- Charge Segway
- Pack for trip
  - cellphone
  - iPod
  - digital camera
  - a protein bar

Remember that we haven't applied any styles to Tony's site, so his site is using a serif font-family for the entire page.

The default size of the heading fonts is also pretty large and doesn't make for an attractive page.

The quote is just indented. It would be nice to improve its look a bit by adding some font-style.

Except for the photos, this page is rather monochromatic, so we'll also add some font color to make it a little more interesting.

Getting Tony a new font-family

Let's get Tony set up with a **font-family**. We're going to start with some clean sans-serif fonts. First, create a new file, "journal.css" in the "chapter9/journal" folder and add this rule:

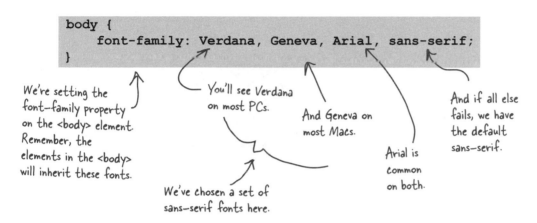

```
body {
        font-family: Verdana, Geneva, Arial, sans-serif;
}
```

We're setting the font-family property on the <body> element. Remember, the elements in the <body> will inherit these fonts.

We've chosen a set of sans-serif fonts here.

You'll see Verdana on most PCs.

And Geneva on most Macs.

Arial is common on both.

And if all else fails, we have the default sans-serif.

Now you need to link Tony's journal to the new style sheet file. To do that, open the file "journal.html" in the "chapter9/journal" folder. All you need to add is the **<link>** element to link in the style in "journal.css", like we did below.

Remember, you fixed up Tony's journal to be strict XHTML in Chapter 7.

```
<!DOCTYPE html PUBLIC "-//W3C//DTD XHTML 1.0 Strict//EN"
    "http://www.w3.org/TR/xhtml1/DTD/xhtml1-strict.dtd">
<html xmlns="http://www.w3.org/1999/xhtml" lang="en" xml:lang="en">
    <head>
        <meta http-equiv="Content-Type" content="text/html; charset=ISO-8859-1" />
        <link type="text/css" rel="stylesheet" href="journal.css" />
        <title>My Trip Around the USA on a Segway</title>
    </head>
    <body>
        .
        .
        .
    </body>
</html>
```

Here's where we're linking in the new "journal.css" file.

After you've made this change, save the file, fire up your browser and load the page.

Test driving Tony's new fonts

Open the page with the new CSS in the browser and you should see we've now got a nice set of sans-serif fonts. Let's check out the changes...

The font definitely gives Tony's Web page a new look. The headings now have a cleaner look without the serifs on the letters, although they still look a tad large on the page.

The paragraph text is also clean and very readable.

Because font-family is an inherited property, all elements on the page are now using a sans-serif font, even the list elements...

... and the <blockquote>s.

And if the serif fonts were more your cup of tea, don't let us stop you. You can always redo the font-family declaration to use serif fonts.

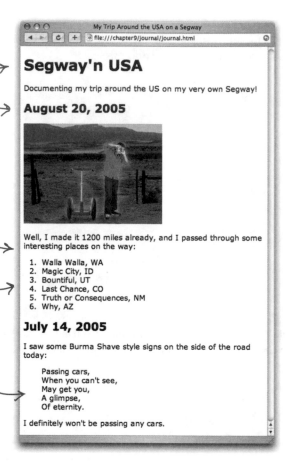

Segway'n USA

Documenting my trip around the US on my very own Segway!

August 20, 2005

Well, I made it 1200 miles already, and I passed through some interesting places on the way:

1. Walla Walla, WA
2. Magic City, ID
3. Bountiful, UT
4. Last Chance, CO
5. Truth or Consequences, NM
6. Why, AZ

July 14, 2005

I saw some Burma Shave style signs on the side of the road today:

> Passing cars,
> When you can't see,
> May get you,
> A glimpse,
> Of eternity.

I definitely won't be passing any cars.

there are no Dumb Questions

Q: How do I specify a font with multiple words in the name, like Courier New?

A: Just put double quotes around the name in your font-family declaration, like this: font-family: "Courier New", Courier;

Q: So the font-family property is really a set of alternative fonts?

A: Yes. It's basically a priority list of fonts. The first is the font you'd like used, followed by a good substitute, followed by more substitutes, and so on. For the last font, you should specify the catch-all generic "sans-serif" or "serif", which should be in the same family as all the fonts in your list.

Q: Are "serif" and "sans-serif" real fonts?

A: "serif" and "sans-serif" are not the names of actual fonts. However, your browser will substitute a real font in place of "serif" or "sans-serif" if the other fonts before it in the font-family declaration can't be found. The font used in its place will be whatever the browser has defined as the default font in that family.

Q: How do I know which to use? Serif or sans-serif?

A: There are no rules. However, on a computer display, many people consider sans-serif the best for body text. You'll find plenty of designs that use serif for body text, or mix serif fonts with sans-serif fonts. So, it really is up to you and what kind of look you want your page to have.

How do I deal with everyone having different fonts?

The unfortunate thing about fonts is that you can't control what fonts are on your users' computers. The best you can do is to create a list of fonts that are most appropriate for your pages and then hope the user has one of those fonts installed. If they don't, well, at least we can count on the browser to supply a generic font in the same font family.

At least, that's the basic strategy for ensuring your page is displayed using appropriate fonts. But it turns out, given the differences in fonts between operating systems (especially Windows versus Mac), you do have to take this a little further to really do your job well. What you need to do is ensure that your **font-family** declaration includes fonts that are likely to occur on both Windows and the Mac (as well as any other platforms your users might be using, like Linux or perhaps mobile devices).

Here's a quick guide to some of the common fonts on each operating system, but we encourage you to explore this area more if you need to closely control the fonts on your pages.

These fonts are likely to be available on both Windows and Macintosh computers.

Andale Mono

Arial

Arial Black

Comic Sans

Courier New

Georgia

Impact

Times New Roman

Trebuchet MS

Verdana

These fonts are most likely to be found on Macintosh computers.

Geneva

Courier

Helvetica

Times

Let's take a look at our definition for Tony's pages again...

(1) We'd like for Verdana to be used, but...

(3) That's okay, because we can probably count on Arial to be on either Windows or Macs, but if it's not...

font-family: Verdana, Geneva, Arial, sans-serif;

(2) If it's not, Geneva would be nice, but this will probably only happen on Macs. But if it's not...

(4) Then that's still okay, we'll just let the browser choose a sans-serif font for us.

Adjusting font sizes

Now that Tony has a new set of fonts, we need to work on those font sizes, as most people find the default sizes of the headings a bit large, at least aesthetically. To do that, you need to know how to specify font sizes, and there are actually a few ways to do this. Let's take a look at some ways to specify **font-size** and then we'll talk about how *best* to specify font size so they are consistent and user friendly.

If you do things right, any user will be able to increase the font sizes on your Web page for readability. You'll see how in a couple of pages.

You can specify your font size in pixels, just like the pixel dimensions you used for images in Chapter 5. When you specify font size in pixels, you're telling the browser how many pixels tall the letters should be.

```
font-size: 14px;
```

The px must come right after the number of pixels. You can't have a space in between.

In CSS you specify pixels with a number followed by "px". This says that the font-size should be 14 pixels high.

 14 pixels

Here's how you'd specify font-size within a body rule.

```
body {
        font-size: 14px;
}
```

Setting a font to 14 pixels high means that there will be 14 pixels between the lowest part of the letters and the highest.

%

Unlike pixels, which tell the font exactly how big it should be in pixels, a font size specified as a percentage tells the font how big it should be *relative* to another font size. So,

```
font-size: 150%;
```

says that the font size should be 150% of another font size. But, *which* other font size? Well, since **font-size** is a property that is inherited from the parent element, when you specify a % font size, it is relative to the parent element. Let's check out how that works...

Here we've specified a body font size in pixels, and a level one heading as 150%.

```
body {
        font-size: 14px;
}
h1 {
        font-size: 150%;
}
```

You can also specify font sizes using "em", which, like percentage, is another relative unit of measure. With em you don't specify a percentage; instead you specify a scaling factor. Here's how you use em:

Don't mix this up with the <em> element!

font-size: 1.2em;

This says that the font size should be scaled by 1.2.

Say you use this measurement to specify the size of an **<h2>** heading. Your **<h2>** headings will be 1.2 times the font size of the parent element, which in this case is 1.2 times 14px, which is about 17px.

It's actually 16.8, but most browsers will round it up to 17.

```
body {
        font-size: 14px;
}
h1 {
        font-size: 150%;
}
h2 {
        font-size: 1.2em;
}
```

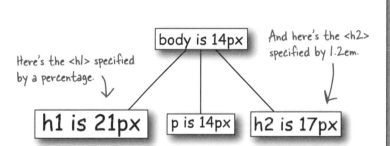

Here's the <h1> specified by a percentage.

And here's the <h2> specified by 1.2em.

If we draw a little document tree, you can see that <h1> inherits from <body>, so its font is going to be 150% of the body's font size.

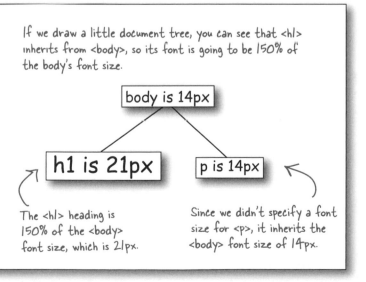

The <h1> heading is 150% of the <body> font size, which is 21px.

Since we didn't specify a font size for <p>, it inherits the <body> font size of 14px.

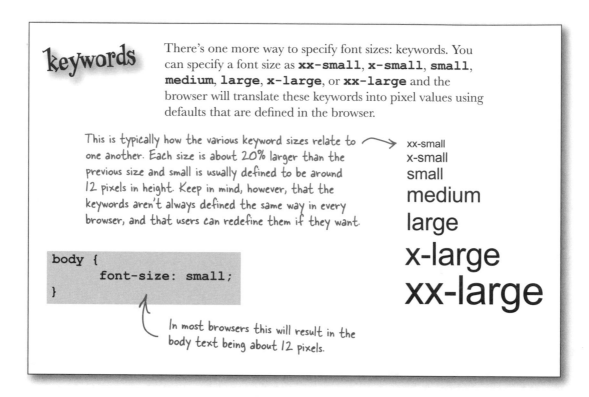

keywords

There's one more way to specify font sizes: keywords. You can specify a font size as **xx-small**, **x-small**, **small**, **medium**, **large**, **x-large**, or **xx-large** and the browser will translate these keywords into pixel values using defaults that are defined in the browser.

This is typically how the various keyword sizes relate to one another. Each size is about 20% larger than the previous size and small is usually defined to be around 12 pixels in height. Keep in mind, however, that the keywords aren't always defined the same way in every browser, and that users can redefine them if they want.

xx-small
x-small
small
medium
large
x-large
xx-large

```
body {
        font-size: small;
}
```

In most browsers this will result in the body text being about 12 pixels.

So, how should I specify my font sizes?

You've got quite a few choices for specifying font sizes: px, em, percentages, and keywords. So, which do you use? Here's a recipe for specifying font sizes that will give you consistent results for most browsers.

① Choose a keyword (we recommend small or medium) and specify it as the font size in your body rule. This acts as the default size for your page.

② Specify the font sizes of your other elements relative to your body font size using either em or percentages (the choice between em and percentages is yours, as they are essentially two ways to do the same thing).

Nice recipe, but what's good about it? By defining your fonts relative to the body font size, it's really easy to change the font sizes in your Web page simply by changing the body font size. Want to redesign the page to make the fonts larger? If your body font size value is **small**, simply change it to **medium** and, voilà – every other element will automatically get larger in proportion because you specified their font sizes relative to the body's font size. Better yet, say your users want to resize the fonts on the page. Again, no problem; using this recipe, all the fonts on the page will automatically readjust.

Let's look at how this all works. First, you set a size for your
<body> element. Then, you set all the other font sizes relative to
that size, like this:

```
body { font-size: small; }
h1 { font-size: 150%; }
h2 { font-size: 120%; }
```

That gives you a document tree that looks like this:

Watch it! **Internet Explorer does NOT support text scaling when the font size is specified using pixels.**

Unfortunately, Internet Explorer users cannot resize fonts if your font sizes are specified using pixels. So, that's one reason to stay away from pixel sizes. If you use pixels, you'll be reducing the accessibility of your pages for many of your users.

Fortunately, if you follow the recipe of supplying a keyword to define your body's font size, and use relative sizes for your other elements using em or %, then IE will properly scale your fonts if the browser is asked to make the text bigger or smaller.

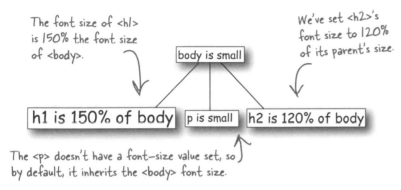

The font size of <h1> is 150% the font size of <body>.

We've set <h2>'s font size to 120% of its parent's size.

body is small

h1 is 150% of body   p is small   h2 is 120% of body

The <p> doesn't have a font-size value set, so by default, it inherits the <body> font size.

Now, let's say you want to increase the size of the fonts on the page,
or perhaps the user does. Then you get a tree that looks like this:

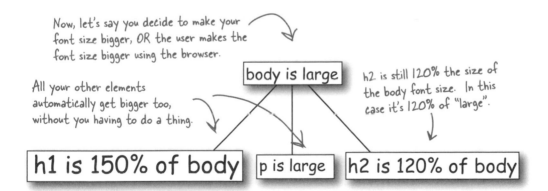

Now, let's say you decide to make your font size bigger, OR the user makes the font size bigger using the browser.

All your other elements automatically get bigger too, without you having to do a thing.

body is large

h2 is still 120% the size of the body font size. In this case it's 120% of "large".

h1 is 150% of body   p is large   h2 is 120% of body

Now the body font size has changed to large, and everything else has
changed too, in relation to the body font size. That's great, because
you didn't have to go through and change all your other font sizes;
all you had to do was change the body font size. And if you're a user,
everything happened behind the scenes. When you increased the text
size, *all* the text got bigger because all the elements are sized relative to
one another, so the page still looks good at a larger font size.

Let's make these changes to the font sizes in Tony's Web page

It's time to try these font sizes in Tony's Web page. Add the new properties to the "journal.css" file in the "chapter9/journal" folder. Once you've made the changes, reload the page in the browser and check out the differences in the font size. If you don't see a difference, check your CSS carefully for errors.

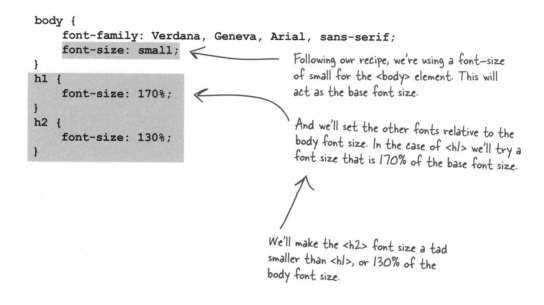

```
body {
    font-family: Verdana, Geneva, Arial, sans-serif;
    font-size: small;
}
h1 {
    font-size: 170%;
}
h2 {
    font-size: 130%;
}
```

Following our recipe, we're using a font-size of small for the <body> element. This will act as the base font size.

And we'll set the other fonts relative to the body font size. In the case of <h1> we'll try a font size that is 170% of the base font size.

We'll make the <h2> font size a tad smaller than <h1>, or 130% of the body font size.

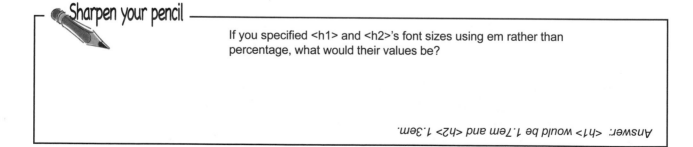

Sharpen your pencil

If you specified <h1> and <h2>'s font sizes using em rather than percentage, what would their values be?

Answer: <h1> would be 1.7em and <h2> 1.3em.

Test driving the font sizes

Here's the evolving journal, complete with new smaller fonts. Check out the differences...

Here's the new version with smaller fonts. The design is starting to look a little less clunky!

Here's the previous version before the change in font sizes.

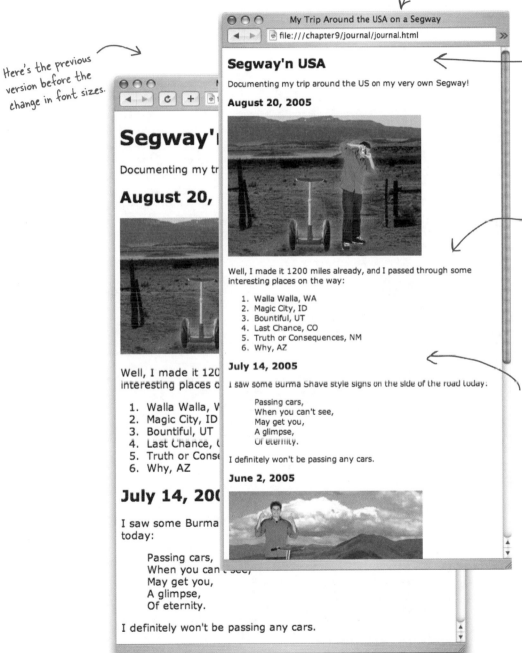

This <h1> heading looks much better now. It doesn't overwhelm the body text and the page in size.

The body text is a tad smaller. The default body text font size is usually 16px, although it does depend on the browser. But it's still easily readable at the "small" size, which is probably about 12px.

The <h2> heading is a bit smaller too, and is a good size compared to the <h1> heading.

there are no Dumb Questions

Q: So, by defining a font size in the `<body>` element, I'm somehow defining a default size for the page? How does that work?

A: Yes, that's right. By setting a font size in your `<body>` element, you can then define the other font sizes of your elements in relation to their parent. What's so great about that? Well, if you need to change the font size, then all you need to do is change the body font size, and everything else will change in proportion.

Q: Do we really need to worry about users resizing their browser fonts? I never do that.

A: Yes. Almost all browsers allow their user to make the text of a page bigger or smaller, and many users take advantage of this feature. If you define your fonts in a relative manner, then your users will have no trouble doing this. Just be careful not to use pixel sizes, because some browsers have problems resizing those.

Q: I like the idea of using pixels because then my page will look exactly like I specify it.

A: There is some truth to that – by using pixels for every element's font size, you are choosing the precise font size you want for each element. But you do that at the cost of giving some of your users (the ones using certain versions of Internet Explorer) the flexibility to pick a font size that is appropriate for their display and eyesight.

You also are creating pages that are a little harder to maintain because if you suddenly want to increase the font sizes of all the elements in a page, you have a lot of changes to make.

Q: What's the difference between em and %? They seem like the same thing.

A: They are basically two different ways to achieve the same thing. Both give you a way to specify a size relative to the parent font size. A lot of people find percent easier to think about than em, and also easier to read in your CSS. But you should use whichever you want.

Q: If I don't specify any font sizes, do I just get the default font sizes?

A: Yes, and what those sizes are depends on your browser, and even the version of the browser you are running. But in most cases the default body font size will be 16 pixels.

Q: And what are the default sizes for the headings?

A: Again, it depends on the browser, but in general, `<h1>` is 200% of the default body text font size, `<h2>` is 150%, `<h3>` is 120%, `<h4>` is 100%, `<h5>` is 90%, and `<h6>` is 60%. Notice that by default `<h4>` is the same font size as the body font size, and `<h5>` and `<h6>` are smaller.

Q: So rather than using the size keywords, can I use em or % in the body rule? If I use 90% for the font-size of the body, what does that mean exactly? It's 90% of what?

A: Yes, you can do that. If you specify a font size of 90% in your body rule, then that would be 90% of the default font size, which we just said is usually 16 pixels, so 90% would be about 14 pixels. If you'd like a font size slightly different than the keywords provide, go ahead and use % or em.

Q: There seems to be so many differences between browsers: font-family, font-size, various default settings, and so on. How will I ever know if my design looks good on other browsers?

A: Great question. The easy answer is that if you follow the guidelines in this chapter then most of your designs are going to look just fine in other browsers. However, you should know that they may look slightly different in different browsers – the fonts may be slightly bigger or smaller, spacing here and there may be different, etc. But, all the differences should be very minor and should not affect the readability of your pages.

However, if you really care about having your pages looking almost identical in many browsers, then you really need to test them in lots of browsers. And, to really take this to the extreme, you'll find a variety of CSS "hacks" to try to make different browsers behave the same. If you want to take it this far, there's nothing wrong with that, but just keep in mind a lot of these activities take time and have diminishing returns.

Changing a font's weight

The **font-weight** property allows you to control how bold the text looks. As you know, bold text looks darker than normal text and tends to be a bit fatter too. You can make any element use bold text by setting the **font-weight** property to **bold**, like this:

```
font-weight: bold;
```

You can also go the other way. If you have an element that is set to bold by default, or is inheriting bold from a parent, then you can remove the bold style like this:

```
font-weight: normal;
```

There are also two relative font-weight properties: **bolder** and **lighter**. These will make your text style a little bolder or a little lighter relative to its inherited value. These values are seldom used and because not many fonts allow for slight differences in the amount of boldness, in practice these two values often have no effect.

You can also set your **font-weight** property to a number between 100 and 900, but again, this is not well supported across fonts and browsers and so is not often used.

font-weight: normal;

font-weight: bold;

Sharpen your pencil

Write the CSS to change the headings in Tony's page from their default bold value to normal weight. Then, add the rule to your CSS and give it a test drive. You'll find the answer to this one on the next page.

Test drive the normal weight headings

Here's what your CSS should look like after you make the change to use a normal **font-weight** for both the <h1> and <h2> headings:

```
body {
       font-family: Verdana, Geneva, Arial, sans-serif;
       font-size: small;
}
h1, h2 {
       font-weight: normal;
}
h1 {
       font-size: 170%;
}
h2 {
       font-size: 130%;
}
```

Here we're changing the font-weight of both headings to normal in the same CSS rule. It's a good idea to combine common properties into one rule like this to avoid duplication.

And here are the results. The headings are now lighter looking.

My Trip Around the USA on a Segway

file:///chapter9/journal/journal.html

Segway'n USA

Documenting my trip around the US on my very own Segway!

August 20, 2005

Well, I made it 1200 miles already, and I passed through some interesting places on the way:

1. Walla Walla, WA
2. Magic City, ID
3. Bountiful, UT
4. Last Chance, CO
5. Truth or Consequences, NM
6. Why, AZ

July 14, 2005

I saw some Burma Shave style signs on the side of the road today:

    Passing cars,
    When you can't see,
    May get you,
    A glimpse,
    Of eternity.

I definitely won't be passing any cars.

June 2, 2005

Adding style to your fonts

You're familiar with *italic* text, right? Italic text is slanted, and sometimes has extra curly serifs. For example, compare these two styles:

not italic
italic

The italic text is slanted to the right and has extra curls on the serifs.

You can add an italic style to your text in CSS using the **font-style** property:

```
font-style: italic;
```

A common mistake is to write "italic" as "italics". If you do, you won't see italic text. So remember to check your spelling.

However, not all fonts support the italic style, so what you get instead is called *oblique text*. Oblique text is also slanted text, but rather than using a specially designed slanted set of characters in the font, the browser just applies a slant to the normal letters. Compare these non oblique and oblique styles:

not oblique
oblique

The regular letters are slanted to the right in the oblique style.

You can use the **font-style** property to get oblique text too, like this:

```
font-style: oblique;
```

In practice, you're going to find that, depending on your choice of font and browser, sometimes the two styles will look identical, and sometimes they won't. So, unless italic versus oblique is very important to you, choose one and move on. If, on the other hand, it is important, you'll need to test your font and browser combination for the best effect.

Italic and oblique styles are two styles that give fonts a slanted appearance.

Unless you can control the fonts and browsers your visitors are using, you'll find that sometimes you get italic, and sometimes oblique, no matter which style you specify.

So just go with italic and don't worry about the differences (you probably can't control them anyway).

Styling Tony's quotes with a little italic

Now we're going to use the **font-style** property to add a little pizazz to Tony's quotes. Remember the Burma Shave slogan in the **<blockquote>** element? We're going to change the slogan to italic style to set it off from the rest of the text. To do that we just need to style the **<blockquote>** with a **font-style** of italic, like this:

```
blockquote {
        font-style: italic;
}
```

Add this new CSS rule to the CSS in your "journal.css" file, save it, and give the page a test drive. You should see the Burma Shave slogan change to italic; here's our test drive.

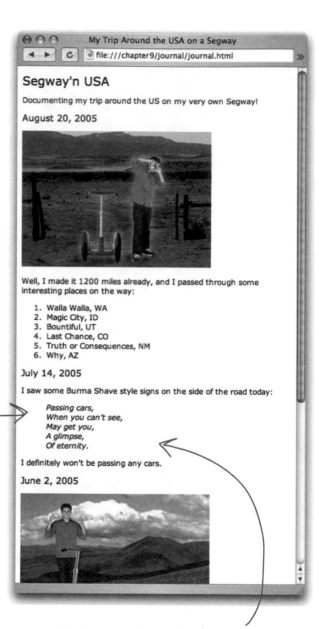

Here's the new style on the Burma Shave slogan in Tony's page. We got slanted text, just like we wanted.

there are no Dumb Questions

Q: The text for the <blockquote> is actually inside a <p> that's inside the <blockquote>. So, how did this change the paragraph to italic?

A: Remember, by default most elements get their font styles from their parents, and the parent of this paragraph is the <blockquote> element. So the paragraph within the <blockquote> inherits the italic style.

Q: Why didn't we just put the text into an <em> element inside the <blockquote>? Wouldn't that do the same thing and make the <blockquote> italic?

A: Remember that <em> is for specifying structure. <em> says that a set of words should be emphasized. What we're doing is styling a <blockquote>, we are not indicating that the text in the <blockquote> should be emphasized. So, while you're right, on most browsers <em> is styled with italic, it's not the right way to style the text in the <blockquote>. Also, keep in mind that the style of <em> could change, so you shouldn't count on <em> always being italic.

Cool. Love the new look. Hey, how about a little color in those fonts? Say, ummm... the color of my shirt? I love orange!

You'd think we could just tell you there was a **color** property and send you on your way to use it. But, unlike font sizes or weights or text styles, you've got to understand a fair bit about color to be able to work with it and specify it in CSS.

So, over the next few pages, you're going to dive into color and learn everything you need to know to use it on your pages: how colors on the screen work, the various ways of describing color in CSS, what those mysterious hex codes are all about, whether you should be worried about "Web safe colors," and what's the easiest way to find and specify colors.

How do Web colors work?

You're starting to see that there are lots of places you can add color to your pages: background colors, border colors, and soon, font colors as well. But, how do colors on a computer actually work? Let's take a look.

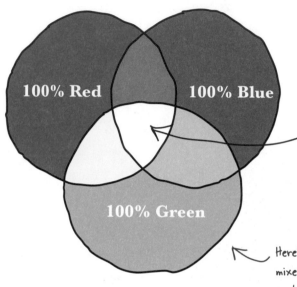

Web colors are specified in terms of how much red, green, and blue make up the color. You specify the amount of each color from 0 to 100% and then add them all together to arrive at a final color. For instance if you add 100% red, 100% green, and 100% blue together, you get white. Notice that on a computer screen, mixing together colors results in a lighter color. After all, this is light we're mixing!

Here's red, green and blue being mixed together. If you look at the center you'll see how they all add up.

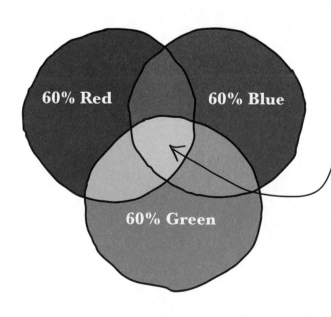

But, if you add, say, only 60% of each component (red, green, and blue) then what would you expect? Less white, right? In other words, you get a gray color, because we're sending equal amount of the three colors, but not as much light to the screen.

On a computer screen, if 0% blue is added, then blue doesn't add anything to the color.

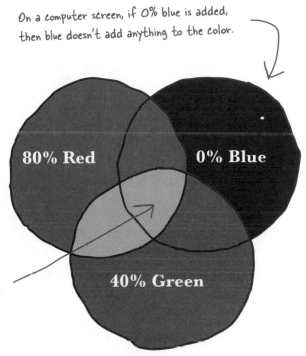

80% Red

0% Blue

40% Green

Or, say you mix together 80% red and 40% green. You'd expect an orange color, right? Well, that's exactly what you'll get. Notice that if a color is contributing zero, then it doesn't affect the other two colors. Again, this is because there is no blue light being mixed with red and green.

Mixing 80% red and 40% green we get a nice orange color.

And what if you mix 0% of red, green, and blue, then what do you get? That means you're sending no light of any kind to the screen, so you get black.

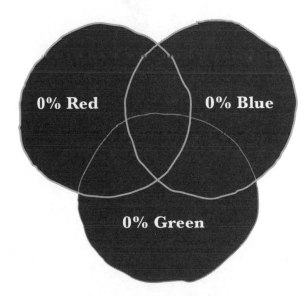

0% Red

0% Blue

0% Green

Why do I need to know all this "color theory"? Can't I just specify my colors by name? Like "red", "green", or "blue"? That's what we've been doing so far.

You certainly can use color names all you like, but CSS defines the names of only 17 colors.

Having seventeen colors in your palette gets old pretty quickly and really limits the expressiveness of your pages. We're going to show you how to specify colors in a way that will allow you to name a lot more than seventeen colors; in fact, you'll be able to work from a palette of *sixteen million* colors.

Now, you've already seen a few examples of colors in XHTML, and yes, they do look a little funky, like **#fc1257**. So, let's first figure out how to specify colors and then you'll see how you can easily use color charts or your photo-editing application to pick your colors.

How do I specify Web colors?
Let me count the ways...

CSS gives you a few ways to specify colors. You can specify the *name* of a color, specify a color in terms of its *relative percentages* in red, green and blue, or you can specify your color using a *hex code*, which is shorthand for describing the red, green, and blue components of the color.

While you might think that the Web would have decided on one format by now, all these formats are commonly used, so it's good to know about them all. However, hex codes are by far the most common way of specifying Web colors. But, remember that all these ways of specifying color ultimately just tell the browser the amount of red, green, and blue that goes into a color.

Let's work through each method of specifying colors in CSS.

Specify color by name

The most straightforward way to describe a color in CSS is just to use its name. But, as you know, there are only seventeen colors that can be specified this way. Let's say you want to specify the color "silver" as the background color of a **body** element; here's how you write that in CSS:

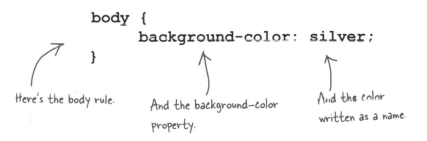

```
body {
        background-color: silver;
}
```

Here's the body rule.

And the background-color property.

And the color written as a name.

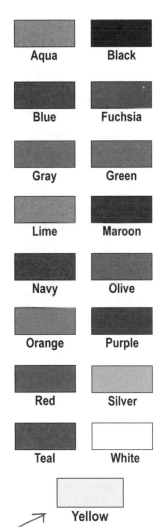

Aqua | Black
Blue | Fuchsia
Gray | Green
Lime | Maroon
Navy | Olive
Orange | Purple
Red | Silver
Teal | White
Yellow

So, to specify a color by name, just type the color name as the value of the property. CSS color names are case-insensitive, so you can type silver, Silver, or SILVER and all will work. Here are the seventeen predefined colors in CSS. Remember these are just names for predefined amounts of red, green, and blue.

Color in a book happens by light bouncing off the printed page. On a computer, the light is emitted by the screen, so these colors will look slightly different in your Web pages.

Specify color in red, green and blue values

You can also specify a color as the amount of red, green, and blue. So, say you wanted to specify the orange color we looked at a couple of pages back, which consisted of 80% red, 40% green, and 0% blue. Here's how you do that:

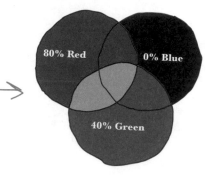

80% Red   0% Blue   40% Green

```
body {
    background-color: rgb(80%, 40%, 0%);
}
```

Begin with "rgb", short for red, green, blue.

And then specify the percentages for red, green, and blue within parentheses, and with a % sign after each one.

You can also specify the red, green, and blue values as a numeric value between 0 and 255. So, instead of 80% red, 40% green, and 0% blue, you can use 204 red, 102 green, and 0 blue.

Where did these numbers come from?

80% of 255 is 204,

40% of 255 is 102, and

0% of 255 is 0.

Here's how you use straight numeric values to specify your color:

```
body {
    background-color: rgb(204, 102, 0);
}
```

We still start with "rgb".

To specify numeric values and not percentages, just type in the value and don't use a "%".

there are no Dumb Questions

Q: **Why are there two different ways to specify rgb values? Don't percentages seem more straightforward?**

A: Sometimes they are more straightforward, but there is some sanity to using numbers between 0 and 255. This number is related to the number of values that can be held in one byte of information. So, for historical and technical reasons, 255 is often used as a unit of measurement for specifying red, green, and blue values in a color. In fact, you might have noticed that

photo-editing applications often allow you to specify color values from 0 to 255 (if not, you'll see how to do that shortly).

Q: **I never see anyone use rgb or actual color names in their CSS. It seems everyone uses the #00fc9a type of color codes.**

A: Using rgb percents or numeric values are becoming more common, but you are right, "hex codes" are still the most

widely used because people consider them a convenient way to specify color.

Q: **Is it important that I look at something like rgb(100, 50, 200) and know what color it is?**

A: Not at all. The best way to know what rgb(100, 50, 200) looks like is to load it in your browser or use a photo-editing application to see it.

Specify color using hex codes

Now let's tackle those funky looking hex codes. Here's the secret to them: each set of two digits of a hex code just represents the red, green, and blue component of the color. So the first two digits represent the red, the next two the green, and the last two represent the blue. Like this:

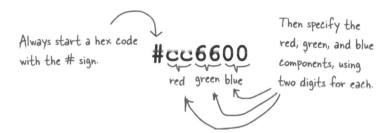

Always start a hex code with the # sign.

#cc6600

red green blue

Then specify the red, green, and blue components, using two digits for each.

Wait a sec, how is "f" or "c" a digit? Those are letters!

Believe it or not, they <u>are</u> digits, but they're written using a notation only a computer scientist could love.

Okay, here's the second secret to reading hex codes: each set of two digits represents a number from 0 to 255. (Sound familiar?) The problem is that if we used numbers, we'd only be able to represent up to 99 in two digits, right? Well, not wanting to be constrained by something as simple as the digits 0-9, computer scientists decided they could represent all 255 values with the help of some letters too (A through F).

Let's take a quick look at how hex codes really work and then we'll show you how to get them from color charts or your photo editing application.

The two minute guide to hex codes

The first thing you need to know about hex codes is that they aren't based on ten
digits (0 to 9) – they're based on 16 digits (0 to F). Here's how hex digits work:

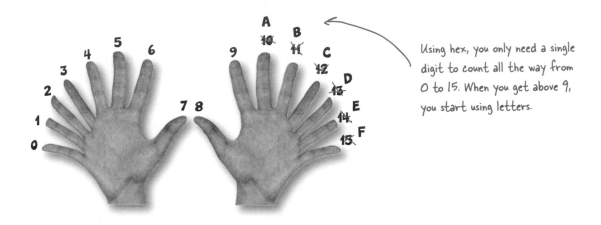

Using hex, you only need a single
digit to count all the way from
0 to 15. When you get above 9,
you start using letters.

So if you see a hex number like B, you know that just means 11. But, what does BB,
or E1, or FF mean? Let's disassemble a hex color and see what it actually represents.
In fact, here's how you can do that for any hex color you might encounter.

Step one:

Separate the hex color into its three components.

Remember that each hex color is made up of a red, green and blue component.
The first thing you want to do is separate those.

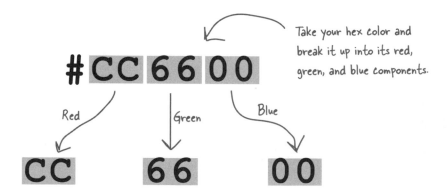

Take your hex color and
break it up into its red,
green, and blue components.

Step two:

Convert each hex number into its decimal equivalent.

Now that you have the components separated you can compute the value for each from 0 to 255. Let's start with the hex number for the red component:

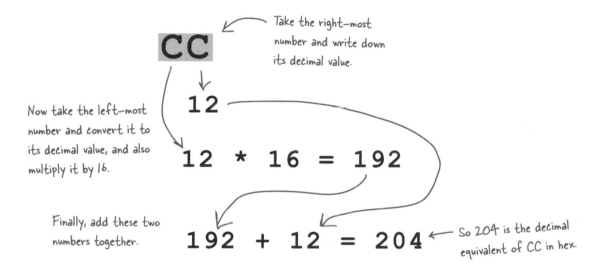

CC

Take the right-most number and write down its decimal value.

12

Now take the left-most number and convert it to its decimal value, and also multiply it by 16.

12 * 16 = 192

Finally, add these two numbers together.

192 + 12 = 204 ← So 204 is the decimal equivalent of CC in hex.

Step three:

Now do this for the other two values.

Repeat the same method on the other two values. Here's what you should get:

CC	66	00
↓	↓	↓
204	102	0

To calculate 66, you have
(6 * 16) + 6 = 102

To calculate 00, you have
(0 * 16) + 0 = 0

Step four:

There is no step four, you're done!

That's it. Now you've got the numbers for each component and you know exactly how much red, green, and blue go into the color. You can disassemble any hex color in exactly the same way. Now let's see how you'll usually determine Web colors.

Putting it all together

You've now got a few different ways to specify colors. Take our orange color that is made up of 80% red, 40% green, and 0% blue. In CSS we could specify this color in any of these ways:

```
body {
        background-color: rgb(80%, 40%, 0%);
}
```
← Specify by the percentage of red, green and blue.

```
body {
        background-color: rgb(204, 102, 0);
}
```
← Specify the amount of red, green and blue on the scale 0–255.

```
body {
        background-color: #cc6600;
}
```
← Specify using a compact hex code.

80% Red   *0% Blue*   *40% Green*

How to find Web colors

The two most common ways to find Web colors are to use a color chart or an application like Photoshop Elements. You'll also find a number of Web pages that allow you to choose Web colors and translate between rgb and hex codes. Let's check out Photoshop Elements (most photo-editing applications offer the same functionality).

Most photo-editing applications provide a Color Picker that allows you to visually choose your color by using one or more color spectrums.

Color Pickers also allow you to select only "Web safe" colors. We'll talk about this in a sec.

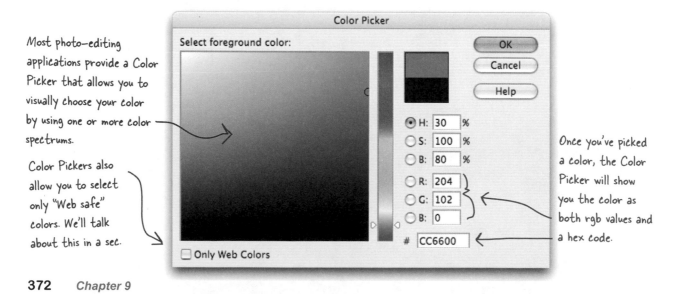

Once you've picked a color, the Color Picker will show you the color as both rgb values and a hex code.

Using an online color chart

You'll also find some useful color charts on the Web. These charts typically display Web colors that are arranged according to a number of different criteria with their corresponding hex code. Using these colors is as easy as choosing the colors you want in your page and copying the hex codes into your CSS.

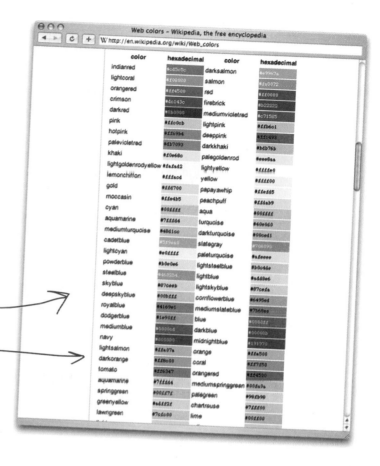

This chart is maintained by the wikipedia at http://en.wikipedia.org/wiki/Web_colors You'll also find many others by searching for "HTML color charts".

Make sure you use the hex code for your colors, not the decorative name, which isn't likely to be supported across browsers.

there are no Dumb Questions

Q: I heard that if I don't use Web-safe colors, my pages will never look right on other browsers. Why haven't we talked about Web-safe colors?

A: Back in the early days of Web browsers, few people had computer screens that supported a lot of colors, so the Web-safe palette of colors was created to ensure that pages looked consistent on most displays.

Today the picture has changed drastically and most Web users have computer displays that support millions of colors. So, unless you have a special set of users that you know have limited color displays, you can pretty much count "Web-safe colors" as a thing of the past.

Q: I know how to specify colors now, but how do I choose font colors that work well together?

A: It would take an entire book to answer that question properly, but there are some basic guidelines to selecting font colors. The most important is to use colors with high contrast for the text and the background to aid readability. For instance, black text on a white background has the highest contrast. You don't always have to stick with black and white, but do try to use a dark hue for the text, and a light hue for the background. Some colors, when used together, can create strange visual effects (like blue and orange, or red and green), so try your color combinations out on some friends before launching them on the world.

Q: I've seen hex codes like #cb0; what does that mean?

A: You're allowed to use shorthand if each two-digit pair shares the same numbers. So, for instance, #ccbb00 can be abbreviated #cb0, or #11eeaa as #1ea. However, if your hex code is something like #ccbb10, then you can't abbreviate it.

Crack the Safe Challenge

Dr. Evel's master plans have been locked away inside his personal safe and you've just received a tip that he encodes the combination in hex code. In fact, so he won't forget the combination, he makes the hex code the background color of his home page. Your job is to crack his hex code and discover the combination to the safe. To do that, simply convert his Web color into its red, green, and blue decimal values and you'll have the right-left-right numbers of his combination. Here's the background Web color from his home page:

```
body {
        background-color: #b817e0;
}
```

Crack the code, and then write the combination here:

RIGHT _____   LEFT _____   RIGHT _____

Back to Tony's page... We're going to make the headings orange, and add an underline too

Now that you know all about color, it's time to add some color to Tony's Web page. He wanted orange and he's going to get orange. But, rather than making all his text orange – which would probably be unattractive and hard to read against a white background – we're going to add a subtle splash of color in his headings. The orange is dark enough that there is good contrast between the text and the background, and by color-coordinating with the orange in the photos (Tony's shirt), we're creating a color relationship between the headings and the photos that should tie the images and text together. And just to make sure the headings stand out and create separation between the journal entries, we'll also add an underline to each heading. You haven't seen how to add an underline yet, but let's do it, and then we'll look at more about text decorations.

Here are all the changes in the CSS. Make these changes in your "journal.css" file.

```css
body {
        font-family: Verdana, Geneva, Arial, sans-serif;
        font-size: small;
}

h1, h2 {
        font-weight: normal;
        color: #cc6600;
        text-decoration: underline;
}

h1 {
        font-size: 170%;
}

h2 {
        font-size: 130%;
}

blockquote {
        font-style: italic;
}
```

We're going to make both <h1> and <h2> orange, so we're putting the color property in the shared rule.

Here's the hex code for the orange color Tony wants, otherwise known as rgb(80%, 40%, 0%).

And here's the way we create an underline. We use the text-decoration property and set it to underline.

Test drive Tony's orange headings

Once you've made the changes to your "journal.css" file to add the color property to the "h1, h2" rule, reload the Web page and check out the results.

Now both <h1> and <h2> headings are orange. This ties in nicely with Tony's orange theme and shirt.

The headings are also set off further with underlines. Hmmm... we thought this would be a good way to distinguish the headings, but actually they seem to look a little too much like clickable links, since people tend to think anything underlined in a Web page is clickable.

So, underlines may have been a bad choice. Let's quickly look at some other text decorations, then we'll reconsider these underlines in the Web page.

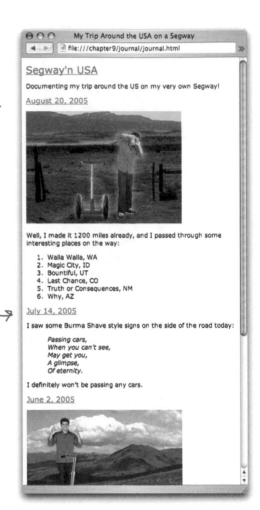

Sharpen your pencil

What do all these colors have in common? Try each one in a Web page, say as a font color, or use your photo-editing application's color picker to determine what colors they are by entering the hex code into the dialog box directly.

```
#111111    #444444    #777777    #aaaaaa    #dddddd
#222222    #555555    #888888    #bbbbbb    #eeeeee
#333333    #666666    #999999    #cccccc
```

Everything you ever wanted to know about text-decorations in less than one page

Text decorations allow you to add decorative effects to your text like underlines, overlines, line-throughs (also known as a strike-through) and, on some browsers, blinking text. To add a text decoration, just set the text-decoration property on an element, like this:

```
em {
        text-decoration: line-through;
}
```

This rule will cause the <em> element to have a line through the middle of the text.

You can set more than one decoration at a time. Say you want underline and overline at the same time, then you specify your text decoration like this:

```
em {
        text-decoration: underline overline;
}
```

This rule results in the <em> element having an underline AND overline.

And if you have text that is inheriting text decoration you don't want, just use the value "none":

```
em {
        text-decoration: none;
}
```

With this rule, <em> elements will have no decoration.

---

there are no Dumb Questions

Q: **So if I have two different rules for an <em>, and one specifies overline and the other underline, will they be added together so I get both?**

A: No. You need to combine the two values into one rule to get both text decorations. Only one rule is chosen for the text-decoration, and decorations in separate rules are not added together. Only the rule that is chosen for the text-decoration styling will determine the decoration used, so the only way to get two decorations is to specify them both in the same text-decoration declaration.

Q: **I've been meaning to ask why the color property isn't called text-color?**

A: The color property really controls the foreground color of an element, so it controls the text and the border color, although you can give the border its own color with the border-color property.

Q: **I like the line-through decoration. Can I use it on text I'm editing to indicate things that need to be deleted?**

A: You could, but there's a better way. XHTML has an element we haven't talked about called <del> that marks content in your XHTML as content that should be deleted. There is a similar element called <ins> that marks content that should be inserted. Typically browsers will style these elements with a strike-through and underline respectively. And with CSS you can style them any way you like. By using <del> and <ins>, you are marking the meaning of your content in addition to styling it.

Q: **When would you use the blink decoration?**

A: Blink is a holdover from an old Netscape style. Browsers aren't required to implement it, and most people consider using blink to be in bad Web taste. So we recommend forgetting we ever mentioned it.

Removing the underline...

Let's get rid of that confusing underline and instead add
a nice bottom border like we did in the Lounge. To do
that, open your "journal.css" file and make these changes
to the combined "h1, h2" rule:

Add a border on the bottom of the <h1> and
<h2> elements. You can almost read this like
English: "add a thin, dotted line with the
color #888888 on the bottom border"...

```
h1, h2 {
     font-weight: normal;
     color: #cc6600;
     border-bottom: thin dotted #888888;
     text-decoration: underline;
}
```

... In the next chapter we are going to go into
borders in detail. Hang on, we're almost there!

Delete the text decoration.

And here's how our new "underline" looks.
Definitely more stylish and less confusing
than a text decoration underline.

Now we've got borders under the <h1>
and <h2> element, not underlines.

Notice that borders extend all the way
to the end of the page, rather than
just under the text. Why? You'll find
out in the next chapter.

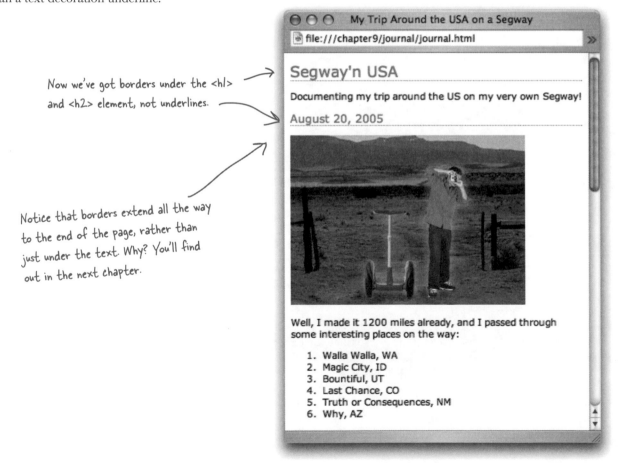

BULLET POINTS

- CSS gives you lots of control over the look of your fonts, including properties like font-family, font-weight, font-size, and font-style.

- A font-family is a set of fonts that share common characteristics.

- The font families for the Web are serif, sans-serif, monospace, cursive, and fantasy. Serif and sans-serif fonts are most common.

- The fonts that your visitors will see in your Web page depend on the fonts they have installed on their own computers.

- It's a good idea to specify font alternatives in your font-family CSS property in case your users don't have your preferred font installed.

- Always make the last font a generic font like serif or sans-serif, so that the browser can make an appropriate substitution if no other fonts are found.

- Font-sizes are usually specified using px, em, %, or keywords.

- If you use pixels ("px") to specify your font size, you are telling the browser how many pixels tall to make your letters.

- em and % are relative font sizes, so specifying your font size using em and % means the size of the letters will be relative to the font size of the parent element.

- Using relative sizes for your fonts can make your pages more maintainable.

- Use the font size keywords to set the base font size in your body rule, so that all browsers can scale

- the font sizes if users want the text to be bigger or smaller.

- You can make your text bold using the font-weight CSS property.

- The font-style property is used to create italic or oblique text. Italic and oblique text is slanted.

- Web colors are created by mixing different amounts of red, green, and blue.

- If you mix 100% red, 100% green, and 100% blue, you will get white.

- If you mix 0% red, 0% green, and 0% blue, you will get black.

- CSS has 17 predefined colors, including black, white, red, blue, and green.

- You can specify which color you want using percentages of red, green, and blue, using numerical values of 0-255 for red, green, and blue, or using a color's hex code.

- An easy way to find the hex code of a color you want is to use a photo-editing application's color picker or one of many online Web tools.

- Hex codes have 6 digits, and each digit can be from 0-F. The first two digits represent the amount of red, the second two the amount of green, and the last two the amount of blue.

- You can use the text-underline property to create an underline for text. Underlined text is often confused as linked text by users, so use this property carefully.

XHTMLcross

You've absorbed a lot in this chapter: fonts, color, weights, and styles. It's time to do another crossword and let it all sink in.

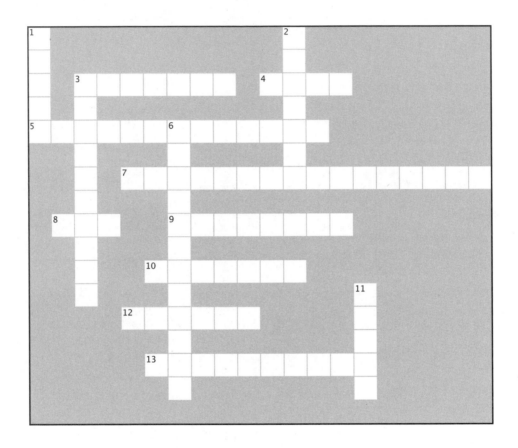

Across

3. Hex codes use this many different digits.
4. Colors like #111111 through #EEEEEE, are all shades of _____.
5. Similar fonts are grouped into _____.
7. Browser that doesn't handle pixel font sizes well.
8. Element that can be used to mark text for deletion.
9. em and % are both this kind of size.
10. Font family almost never used in Web pages.
12. Controls how bold a font looks.
13. Underline and line-through are examples of text _____.

Down

1. Fonts with little barbs on them.
2. You can specify fonts in terms of pixels, em, or _____.
3. Considered cleaner and easier to read on a computer display.
6. When you specify fonts in the font-family property, you are specifying _____.
11. A text decoration you would never use.

Markup Magnets Solutions

Your job is to help the fictional fonts below find their way home to their own font family. Move each fridge magnet on the left into the correct font family on the right. Check your answers before you move on. Here's the solution.

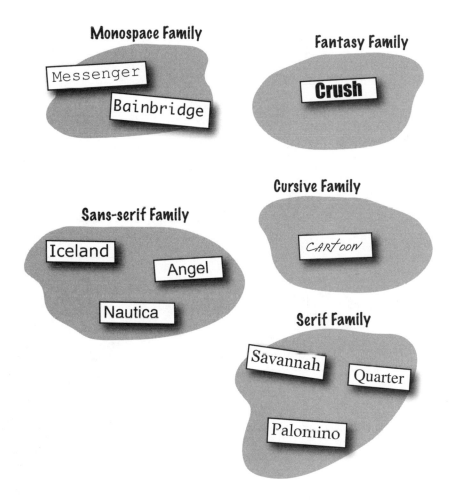

Monospace Family

Messenger

Bainbridge

Fantasy Family

Crush

Sans-serif Family

Iceland

Angel

Nautica

Cursive Family

CARtoon

Serif Family

Savannah

Quarter

Palomino

Crack the Safe Solution

Dr. Evel's master plans have been locked away inside his personal safe and you've just received a tip that he encodes the combination in hex code. In fact, so he won't forget the combination, he makes the hex code the background color of his home page. Your job is to crack his hex code and discover the combination to the safe. To do that, simply convert his Web color into its red, green, and blue decimal values and you'll have the right-left-right numbers of his combination. Here's the background Web color from his home page:

```
body {
        background-color: #b817e0;
}
```

Crack the code, and then write the combination here:

$(11 * 16) + 8 =$ $(1 * 16) + 7 =$ $(14 * 16) + 0 =$

RIGHT ___184___   **LEFT** ___23___   **RIGHT** ___224___

Sharpen your pencil
Solution

What do all these colors have in common? You can try each one in a Web page, or use the color picker to determine what colors they are, by entering the hex code into the dialog box directly.

#111111
#222222
#333333
#444444
#555555
#666666
#777777
#888888
#999999
#aaaaaa
#bbbbbb
#cccccc
#dddddd
#eeeeee

All colors that use just one digit in their hex codes are grays, from very dark (almost black) to very light (almost white).

XHTMLcross
Solution

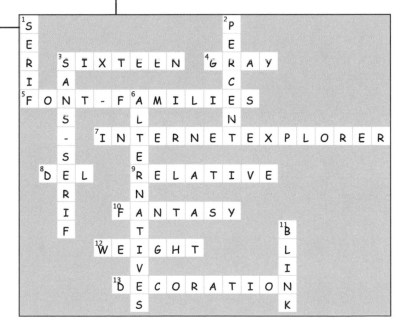

10 the box model

Getting Intimate with Elements

I think we'd be a little closer if it weren't for all the padding, margins, and this damn table.

To do advanced Web construction you really need to know your building materials. In this chapter we're going to take a close look at our building materials: the XHTML elements. We're going to put block and inline elements right under the microscope and see what they're made of. You'll see how you can control just about every aspect of how an element is constructed with CSS. But we don't stop there – you'll also see how you can give elements unique identities. And, if that weren't enough, you're going to learn when and why you might want to use multiple style sheets. So, turn the page and start getting intimate with elements.

The lounge gets an upgrade

You've come a long way in nine chapters, and so has the Head First Lounge. In fact, over the next two chapters, we're giving it a total upgrade with all new content for the main page and restyling it from scratch. And, just to entice you, we're going to give you a little sneak peek before we even get started. Check this out – on this page you'll find the new unstyled lounge page with all the new content. On the next page you'll find the stylized version that we're going to create by the end of the next chapter.

← There's a new graphic for the header of the page.

Welcome to the Head First Lounge

The Head First Lounge is, no doubt, the biggest trendsetter in Webville. Stop in to sample the eclectic offering of elixirs, teas, and coffees, or, stay a bit longer and enjoy the multicultural culinary menu that combines a harmony of taste, texture, and color with the best in fresh and healthy ingredients.

During your stay at the lounge, you'll enjoy a smooth mixture of ambient and mystic sounds, filling the lounge and adding an extra dimension to your dining experience. The decor surrounds you with the relaxing sentiments of sights from eras past. And, don't forget, the lounge offers free wireless access to the Internet, so bring your laptop.

Our guarantee: at the lounge, we're committed to providing you, our guest, with an exceptional experience every time you visit. Whether you're just stopping by to check in on email over an elixir, or are here for an out-of-the-ordinary dinner, you'll find our knowledgeable service staff pay attention to every detail. If you're not fully satisfied, have a Blueberry Bliss Elixir on us.

But that's not all; at night, join us in the backroom as our resident DJ spins a choice selection of trance and drum&bass beats across our spacious tiki-themed dance floor. Or just hang out in one of our comfy white vinyl booths at the dance bar. You can have your elixirs delivered from the main lounge right to the dance floor. If you've had enough of the beat, just head back to the lounge area to relax. And, no matter where you find yourself in the lounge, you'll always be connected with our wireless Internet access.

Now that you've experienced the lounge *virtually*, isn't it time to check us out *for real?* We're located right in the heart of Webville, and we've created some detailed directions to get you here in record time. No reservations necessary; come and join us anytime.

The lounge guys have supplied a lot of new text describing the lounge and what it offers.

Weekly Elixir Specials

Lemon Breeze

The ultimate healthy drink, this elixir combines herbal botanicals, minerals, and vitamins with a twist of lemon into a smooth citrus wonder that will keep your immune system going all day and all night.

They've included a set of elixir specials for the week.

Chai Chiller

Not your traditional chai, this elixir mixes maté with chai spices and adds an extra chocolate kick for a caffeinated taste sensation on ice.

Black Brain Brew

Want to boost your memory? Try our Black Brain Brew elixir, made with black oolong tea and just a touch of espresso. Your brain will thank you for the boost.

Join us any evening for these and all our other wonderful elixirs.

And they even let visitors sample some of the music that is played in the lounge each week, a common request of customers.

What's playing at the Lounge

We're frequently asked about the music we play at the lounge, and no wonder, it's great stuff. Just for you, we keep a list here on the site, updated weekly. Enjoy.

- Buddha Bar, Claude Challe
- When It Falls, Zero 7
- Earth 7, L.T.J. Bukem
- Le Roi Est Mort, Vive Le Roi!, Enigma
- Music for Airports, Brian Eno

Finally, they've got some legalese in the footer of the page with a copyright.

© 2005, Head First Lounge
All trademarks and registered trademarks appearing on this site are the property of their respective owners.

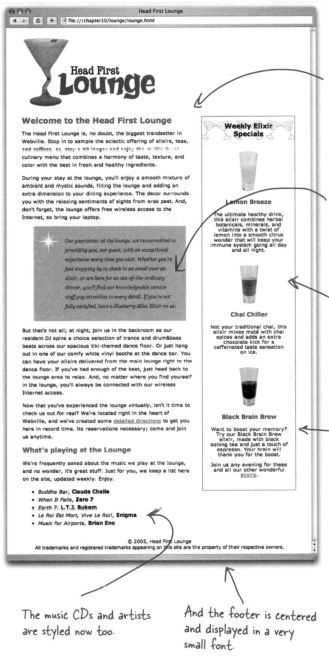

We've got headings that match the site's color theme, an aquamarine. The fonts are also a very readable sans-serif.

This paragraph has been highly stylized, which helps set it off from the text and gives the page an attractive look. It also looks like the font is a serif font, which is different from the main text.

The elixirs have been dramatically restyled into an appetizing display of drinks.

The elixirs have also been moved over to the side. How did that happen?

The music CDs and artists are styled now too.

And the footer is centered and displayed in a very small font.

The new and improved, ultra-stylish lounge

Not too shabby. Now the Lounge design might be a tad on the, well, "ultra-stylish" side for you, but hey, it *is* a lounge. And we're sure that you can see this design is starting to look downright sophisticated – just think what the same techniques could do for your pages. Well, after this chapter and the next, designs like this are going to be easily within your reach.

Setting up the new lounge

Before we start the major construction, let's get familiar with the new lounge.
Here's what you need to do:

1 Take a look at the "chapter10/lounge" folder and you'll find the file "lounge.html",
with all new content. Open the file in your editor and have a look around. Everything
should look familiar: head, paragraphs, a few images, and a list.

2 You're going to spend most of this chapter adding style to this XHTML, so you need a
place for your CSS. You're going to create all new styles for the lounge in the style sheet
file "lounge.css", so you'll find your **<link>** element in the **<head>** of "lounge.html" is
still there, but the previous version of "lounge.css" style sheet is gone.

```
<link type="text/css" rel="stylesheet" href="lounge.css" />
```

Remember, this **<link>** element tells the browser to look for an external style sheet called
"lounge.css".

3 Next, you need to create the new "lounge.css" in the "chapter10/lounge" folder. This file
is going to hold all the new CSS for the new lounge.

Starting with a few simple upgrades

Now you're all ready to start styling the lounge. Let's add a few
rules to your CSS just to get some basics out of the way – like the
font family, size, and some color – that will immediately improve
the lounge (and give you a good review from the last chapter). So,
open your "lounge.css" and add the following rules.

Here's the default font size for the page.

```
body {
        font-size:    small;
        font-family: Verdana, Helvetica, Arial, sans-serif;
}

h1, h2 {
        color: #007e7e;
}

h1 {
        font-size: 150%;
}

h2 {
        font-size: 130%;
}
```

We're going to go with a sans-serif font-family for the lounge. We've picked a few font alternatives, and ended the declaration with the generic sans-serif font.

We're going to set the color of the <h1> and <h2> elements to an aquamarine to match the glass in the logo.

Now let's get some reasonable heading sizes for <h1> and <h2>. Since we're setting two different sizes for these, we need separate rules and can't add them to the combined rule for <h1> and <h2>.

A very quick test drive

Let's do a quick test drive just to see how these styles affect the page. Make sure you've made all the changes; then save, and test.

Headings are now sans-serif and a color that matches the logo, creating a theme for the page.

Paragraph text is also sans-serif since every element inherits the <body>'s font-family property.

The <h2> heading is also styled with a new color and sans-serif, but a tad smaller.

We haven't applied any styles to the <h3> so it just inherits the font-family property from <body>.

This link looks oddly out of place with its default blue color. We'll have to fix that. (later).

One more adjustment

We're going to make one more adjustment to the lounge before we move on to start making some bigger changes. This adjustment involves a new property you haven't seen before, but, at this point, you've got enough experience under your belt that we're not going to treat you with kid gloves every time a new property comes along. So, just jump in and give it a try.

Here's what we're going to do: we're going to adjust the line height of the text on the entire page so that there's more vertical space between each line. To do that we add a **line-height** property in the **body** rule:

Increasing the line height of your text can improve readability. It also gives you another way to provide contrast between different parts of your page (you'll see how that works in a bit).

Here we're changing the space between each line to 1.6em, in other words, 1.6 times the font size.

```
body {
    font-size:    small;
    font-family: Verdana, Helvetica, Arial, sans-serif;
    line-height: 1.6em;
}
```

Checking out the new line height

As you might have guessed, the **line-height** property allows you to specify the amount of vertical space between each line of your text. Like other font-related properties, you can specify the line height in pixels, or using an em or percent value that's relative to the font size.

Let's see what the effect of the **line-height** property is on the lounge. Make sure you add the **line-height** property to your CSS file and then save. You should see the line height increase when you refresh.

Using the line-height property we've increased the space between each line of text from the default to 1.6em.

Before

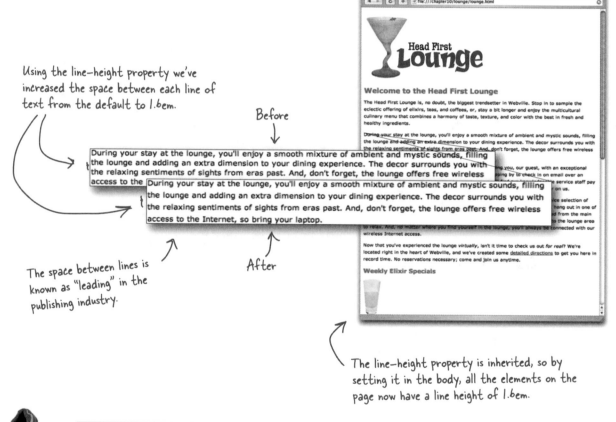

During your stay at the lounge, you'll enjoy a smooth mixture of ambient and mystic sounds, filling the lounge and adding an extra dimension to your dining experience. The decor surrounds you with the relaxing sentiments of sights from eras past. And, don't forget, the lounge offers free wireless access to the

During your stay at the lounge, you'll enjoy a smooth mixture of ambient and mystic sounds, filling the lounge and adding an extra dimension to your dining experience. The decor surrounds you with the relaxing sentiments of sights from eras past. And, don't forget, the lounge offers free wireless access to the Internet, so bring your laptop.

The space between lines is known as "leading" in the publishing industry.

After

The line-height property is inherited, so by setting it in the body, all the elements on the page now have a line height of 1.6em.

Exercise

Try a few different values for line-height, like 200%, .5em, and 20px to see the effect. Which looks the best? The worst? Which is most readable? When you're done, make sure you change the line-height back to 1.6em.

Getting ready for some major renovations

After only a few pages of this chapter, you already have a ton of text style on the new lounge. Congrats!

Now things are going to get really interesting. We're going to move from changing simple properties of elements, like size, color, and decorations, to really tweaking some fundamental aspects of how elements are displayed. This is where you move up to the big leagues.

But to move up to the big leagues, you've got to know *the box model*. What's that? It's how CSS sees elements. CSS treats every single element as if it were represented by a box. Let's see what that means.

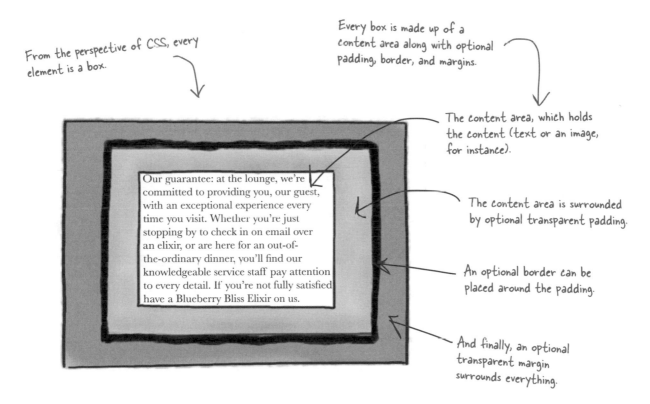

From the perspective of CSS, every element is a box.

Every box is made up of a content area along with optional padding, border, and margins.

The content area, which holds the content (text or an image, for instance).

Our guarantee: at the lounge, we're committed to providing you, our guest, with an exceptional experience every time you visit. Whether you're just stopping by to check in on email over an elixir, or are here for an out-of-the-ordinary dinner, you'll find our knowledgeable service staff pay attention to every detail. If you're not fully satisfied have a Blueberry Bliss Elixir on us.

The content area is surrounded by optional transparent padding.

An optional border can be placed around the padding.

And finally, an optional transparent margin surrounds everything.

All elements are treated as boxes: paragraphs, headings, block quotes, lists, list items, and so on. Even inline elements like <em> and links are treated by CSS as boxes.

A closer look at the box model

You're going to be able to control every aspect of the box with CSS: the size of the padding around the content, whether or not the element has a border (as well as what kind and how large), and how much margin there is between your element and other elements. Let's check out each part of the box and its role:

The content area holds the element's content. It's typically just big enough to hold the content.

What is the content area?

Every element starts with some content, like text or an image, and this content is placed inside a box that is just big enough to contain it. Notice that the content area has no whitespace between the content and the edge of this box.

We've drawn an edge around the content area just so you know how big it is. But in a browser there is never a visible edge around the content area.

> Our guarantee: at the lounge, we're committed to providing you, our guest, with an exceptional experience every time you visit. Whether you're just stopping by to check in on email over an elixir, or are here for an out-of-the-ordinary dinner, you'll find our knowledgeable service staff pay attention to every detail. If you're not fully satisfied have a Blueberry Bliss Elixir on us.

The browser adds optional padding around the content area.

What is the padding?

Any box can have a layer of padding around the content area. Padding is optional, so you don't have to have it, but you can use padding to create visual whitespace between the content and the border of the box. The padding is transparent and has no color or decoration of its own.

> Our guarantee: at the lounge, we're committed to providing you, our guest, with an exceptional experience every time you visit. Whether you're just stopping by to check in on email over an elixir, or are here for an out-of-the-ordinary dinner, you'll find our knowledgeable service staff pay attention to every detail. If you're not fully satisfied have a Blueberry Bliss Elixir on us.

Using CSS, you're going to be able to control the width of the padding around the entire content area, or even control the padding on any one side (top, right, bottom, or left).

Notice that the padding separates the content area from the border.

Using CSS, you're going to be able to control the width, color, and style of the border.

What is the border?

Elements can have an optional border around them. The border surrounds the padding and, because it takes the form of a line around your content, borders provide visual separation between your content and other elements on the same page. Borders can be various widths, colors, and styles.

Border.

Padding.

Content.

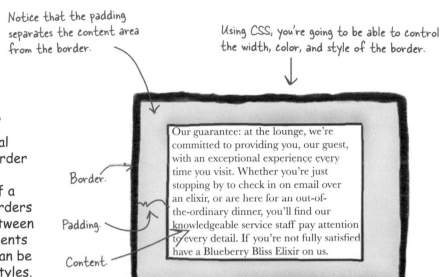

Our guarantee: at the lounge, we're committed to providing you, our guest, with an exceptional experience every time you visit. Whether you're just stopping by to check in on email over an elixir, or are here for an out-of-the-ordinary dinner, you'll find our knowledgeable service staff pay attention to every detail. If you're not fully satisfied have a Blueberry Bliss Elixir on us.

Using CSS, you're going to be able to control the width of the entire margin, or of any particular side (top, right, bottom, or left).

What is the margin?

The margin is also optional and surrounds the border. The margin gives you a way to add space between your element and other elements on the same page. If two boxes are next to each other, the margins act as the space in between them. Like padding, margins are transparent and have no color or decoration of their own.

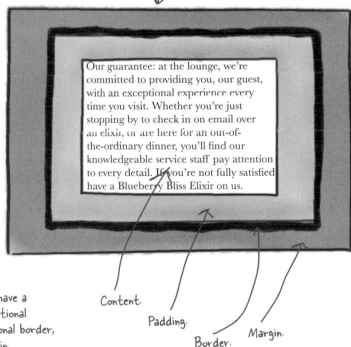

Our guarantee: at the lounge, we're committed to providing you, our guest, with an exceptional experience every time you visit. Whether you're just stopping by to check in on email over an elixir, or are here for an out-of-the-ordinary dinner, you'll find our knowledgeable service staff pay attention to every detail. If you're not fully satisfied have a Blueberry Bliss Elixir on us.

This is the entire element. We have a content area, surrounded by optional padding, surrounded by an optional border, surrounded by an optional margin.

Content.

Padding.

Border.

Margin.

What you can do to boxes

The box model may look simple with just the content, some padding, a border, and margins. But when you combine these all together there are endless ways you can determine the layout of an element with its internal spacing (padding) and the spacing around it (margins). Take a look at just a few examples of how you can vary your elements.

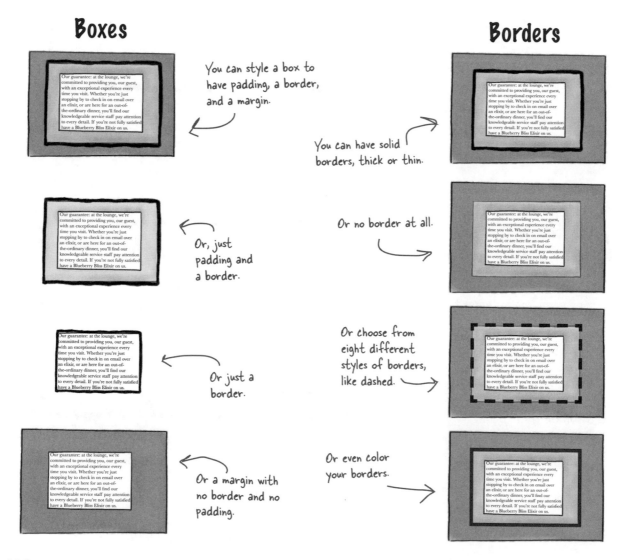

Boxes

You can style a box to have padding, a border, and a margin.

Or, just padding and a border.

Or just a border.

Or a margin with no border and no padding.

Borders

You can have solid borders, thick or thin.

Or no border at all.

Or choose from eight different styles of borders, like dashed.

Or even color your borders.

Padding

With CSS you can control padding on any side of the content area. Here we've got a lot of left and right padding.

And here a lot of top and bottom padding.

And here the content is offset to the bottom right with padding on the top and left.

Margins

You have the same level of control over the margins. Here there's a lot of top and bottom margin.

And here's a lot of left and right margin.

And like padding, you can specify all sides independently to create margins like this.

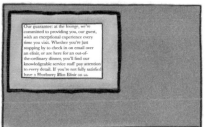

Content Area

You can even control width and height in a variety of ways. Here, the content area has been made wide.

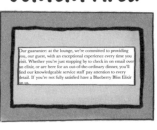

And here the content area is tall but thin.

there are no Dumb Questions

Q: It seems like knowing this box stuff would be important if I were someone creating the software for a Web browser, but how is this going to help me make better Web pages?

A: To go beyond simple Web pages that use the browser's default layout, you need to be able to control how elements sit on the page, as well as the relative position of other elements. To do that, you alter various aspects of each element's padding and margins. So to create interesting Web page designs, you definitely need to know something about the box model.

Q: What's the difference between padding and margin? They seem like the same thing.

A: The margin provides space between your element and other elements, while padding gives you extra space around your content. If you have a visual border, the padding is on the inside of the border and the margin on the outside. Think of padding as part of the element, while the margin surrounds your element and buffers it from the things around it.

Q: I know they are all optional, but do you need to have padding to have a border or a margin?

A: No, they are all totally optional and don't rely on each other. So you can have a border and no padding, or a margin and no border, and so on.

Q: I'm not sure I get how elements get laid out and how margins fit into that.

A: Hold that thought. While you're going to see a little of how margins interact with other elements in this chapter, we'll get way into this topic in Chapter 11 when we talk about positioning.

Q: So other than size, it sounds like I can't really style padding and margins?

A: That's basically right. Both are used to provide more visual space, and you can't give the padding or margin a direct color or any kind of decoration. But, because they are transparent, they will take on the color of any background colors or background images. One difference between padding and margins is that the element's background color (or background image) will extend under the padding, but not the margin. You'll see how this works in a bit.

Q: Is the size of the content area determined solely by the size of the content in it?

A: Browsers use a lot of different rules to determine the width and height of the content area, and we'll be looking at that more in-depth later. The short answer is that you can set the width and height yourself if you need control over the size of the element.

Hey guys, love the shop talk, really do. But did you forget you were in the middle of renovating the lounge?

Meanwhile back at the lounge...

We do have our work cut out for us on the lounge page, so let's get back to it. Did you notice the blue, stylized paragraph when you looked at the final version of the lounge page in the beginning of the chapter? This paragraph contains text with the lounge's guarantee to their customers, and obviously they want to really highlight their promise. Let's take a close look at this paragraph, and then we'll build it.

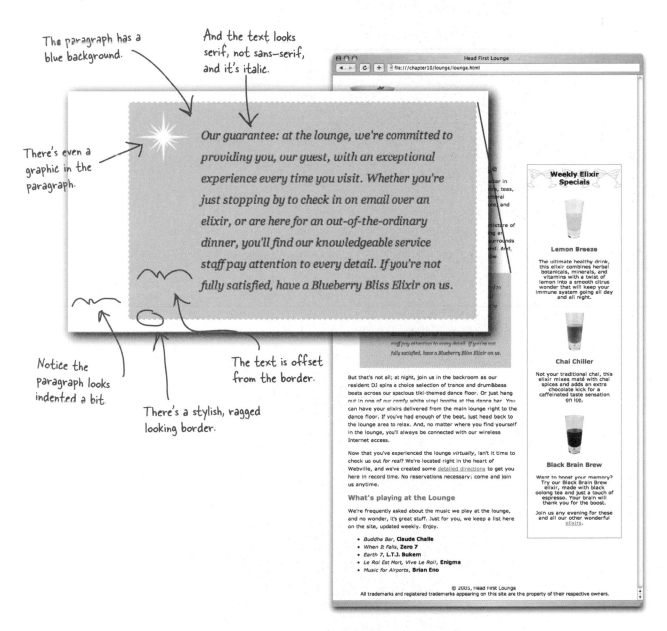

The paragraph has a blue background.

And the text looks serif, not sans-serif, and it's italic.

There's even a graphic in the paragraph.

Notice the paragraph looks indented a bit.

There's a stylish, ragged looking border.

The text is offset from the border.

 Sharpen your pencil

See if you can identify the padding, border and margins of this paragraph. Mark all the padding and margins (left, right, top, and bottom):

don't forget, the lounge offers free wireless access to the Internet, so bring your laptop.

 Our guarantee: at the lounge, we're committed to providing you, our guest, with an exceptional experience every time you visit. Whether you're just stopping by to check in on email over an elixir, or are here for an out-of-the-ordinary dinner, you'll find our knowledgeable service staff pay attention to every detail. If you're not fully satisfied, have a Blueberry Bliss Elixir on us.

But that's not all; at night, join us in the backroom as our resident DJ spins a choice selection of trance and drum&bass beats across our spacious tiki-themed dance floor. Or just hang

BRAIN POWER

Before going on to the next page, think about how you might use padding, borders, and margins to transform an ordinary paragraph into the "guarantee paragraph."

Creating the guarantee style

Let's get started by making a few small changes to the style of the
guarantee paragraph just to get a feel for how the paragraph's box is set up.
To do that you're going to add the paragraph to a class called "guarantee"
so that you can create some custom styles for just this paragraph. You're
then going to add a border along with a little background color, which will
let you see exactly how the paragraph is a box. Then we'll get to work on
the rest of the style. Here's what you need to do:

1 Open your "lounge.html" file and locate the paragraph that starts "Our
guarantee". Add a class called "guarantee" to the element like this:

*Add the class attribute along with a value of "guarantee".
Remember, a class will allow you to style this paragraph
independently of the other paragraphs.*

```
<p class="guarantee">
    Our guarantee: at the lounge, we're committed to providing
    you, our guest, with an exceptional experience every time you
    visit. Whether you're just stopping by to check in on email
    over an elixir, or are here for an out-of-the-ordinary dinner,
    you'll find our knowledgeable service staff pay attention to every
    detail. If you're not fully satisfied have a Blueberry Bliss Elixir
    on us.
</p>
```

2 Save your "lounge.html" file and open the "lounge.css" file. You're going
to add a border and background color to the guarantee paragraph. Add
the following CSS to the bottom of your style sheet and then save.

*The first three properties add a border to any
element that is in the guarantee class. So far
that's just this paragraph.*

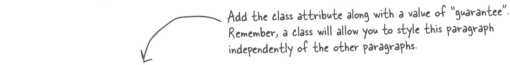

```
.guarantee {
    border-color:       black;
    border-width:       1px;
    border-style:       solid;
    background-color:   #a7cece;
}
```

We're making the color of the border black...

... and one pixel thick...

... and solid.

*We're also giving the element a background color, which
will help you see the difference between padding and
margins, and make the guarantee look good.*

A test drive of the paragraph border

Reload the page in your browser and you'll now see the guarantee paragraph with an aquamarine background and a thin black border around it. Let's examine this a little more closely...

It doesn't look like the paragraph has any padding around the content – there is no space between the text and the border.

the lounge and adding an extra dimension to your dining experience. The decor surrounds you with the relaxing sentiments of sights from eras past. And, don't forget, the lounge offers free wireless access to the Internet, so bring your laptop.

Our guarantee: at the lounge, we're committed to providing you, our guest, with an exceptional experience every time you visit. Whether you're just stopping by to check in on email over an elixir, or are here for an out-of-the-ordinary dinner, you'll find our knowledgeable service staff pay attention to every detail. If you're not fully satisfied, have a Blueberry Bliss Elixir on us.

But that's not all; at night, join us in the backroom as our resident DJ spins a choice selection of trance and drum&bass beats across our spacious tiki-themed dance floor. Or just hang out in one of our comfy white vinyl booths at the dance bar. You can have your elixirs delivered from the main

But there does seem to be a margin on the top and bottom of the paragraph element.

There isn't a noticeable margin between the left and right edges of the paragraph and the browser window edges.

Here's what the paragraph would look like if we drew it as a box model diagram:

We've got a top and bottom margin.

Our guarantee: at the lounge, we're committed to providing you, our guest, with an exceptional experience every time you visit. Whether you're just stopping by to check in on email over an elixir, or are here for an out-of-the-ordinary dinner, you'll find our knowledgeable service staff pay attention to every detail. If you're not fully satisfied have a Blueberry Bliss Elixir on us.

But the left and right margins are very small.

And we have a border, but it's right up against the content, which means the padding is set very small, or there's no padding at all.

Padding, border, and margins for the guarantee

Now that you've seen how the padding, border, and margins are currently set on the guarantee paragraph, let's think more about how we'd actually like them to look.

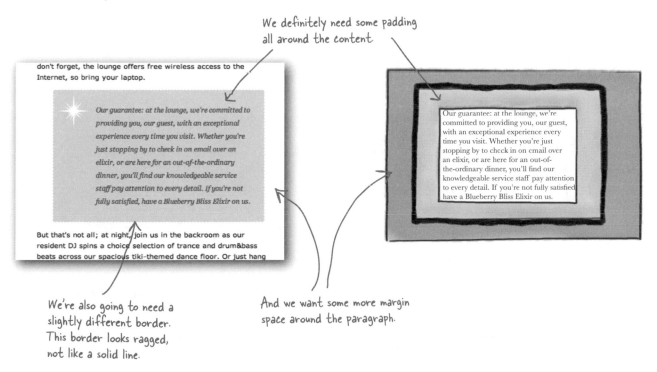

We definitely need some padding all around the content.

We're also going to need a slightly different border. This border looks ragged, not like a solid line.

And we want some more margin space around the paragraph.

Adding some padding

Let's start with the padding. CSS has a **padding** property that you can use to set the same padding for all four sides of the content. You can set this property either to a number of pixels or a percentage of area inside the border. We'll use pixels and set the padding to 25 pixels.

```
.guarantee {
    border-color:       black;
    border-width:       1px;
    border-style:       solid;
    background-color: #a7cece;
    padding:            25px;
}
```

We're adding 25 pixels of padding to all sides of the content (top, right, bottom, and left).

A test drive with some padding

When you reload the page in your browser, you'll notice the text in the guarantee paragraph has a little more breathing room on the sides now. There's some space between the text and the border, and it's much easier to read.

Now you can see 25 pixels of space between the edge of the text content and the border.

Notice that the background color is under both the content and the padding. But it doesn't extend into the margin.

the relaxing sentiments of sights from eras past. And, don't forget, the lounge offers free wireless access to the Internet, so bring your laptop.

Our guarantee: at the lounge, we're committed to providing you, our guest, with an exceptional experience every time you visit. Whether you're just stopping by to check in on email over an elixir, or are here for an out-of-the-ordinary dinner, you'll find our knowledgeable service staff pay attention to every detail. If you're not fully satisfied, have a Blueberry Bliss Elixir on us.

But that's not all; at night, join us in the backroom as our resident DJ spins a choice selection of trance and drum&bass beats across our spacious tiki-themed dance floor. Or just hang out in one of

Now let's add some margin

Margins are easy to add using CSS. Like padding, you can specify the margin as a percentage or in pixels. You're going to add a 30-pixel margin around the entire guarantee paragraph. Here's how you do that:

```
.guarantee {
        border-color:      black;
        border-width:      1px;
        border-style:      solid;
        background-color:  #a7cece;
        padding:           25px;
        margin:            30px;

}
```

We're adding 30 pixels of margin to all sides of the content (top, right, bottom, and left).

A test drive with the margin

When you reload the lounge page, you'll see the paragraph is really beginning to stand out on the page. With the margins in place, the paragraph looks inset from the rest of the text, and that, combined with the background color, makes it look more like a "call out" than an ordinary paragraph. As you can see, with only a few lines of CSS, you're doing some powerful things.

Now we have 30 pixels of margin on all sides.

the relaxing sentiments of sights from eras past. And, don't forget, the lounge offers free wireless access to the Internet, so bring your laptop.

Our guarantee: at the lounge, we're committed to providing you, our guest, with an exceptional experience every time you visit. Whether you're just stopping by to check in on email over an elixir, or are here for an out-of-the-ordinary dinner, you'll find our knowledgeable service staff pay attention to every detail. If you're not fully satisfied, have a Blueberry Bliss Elixir on us.

But that's not all; at night, join us in the backroom as our resident DJ spins a choice selection of trance and drum&bass beats across our spacious tiki-themed dance floor. Or just hang out in one of

Exercise

If you look at the guarantee paragraph as it's supposed to look in its final form, it has an italic, serif font, a line height greater than the rest of the page, and if you're looking really close, gray text. Write the CSS below to set the line height to 1.9em, the font style to italic, the color to #444444, and the font family to Georgia, "Times New Roman", Times, serif. Check your CSS with the answers in the back of the chapter, then type it in and test.

Adding a background image

You're almost there. What's left? We still need to get the white "guarantee star" graphic into the paragraph and work on the border, which is a solid, black line. Let's tackle the image first.

If you look in the "chapter10/lounge/images" folder, you'll find a GIF image called "background.gif" that looks like this:

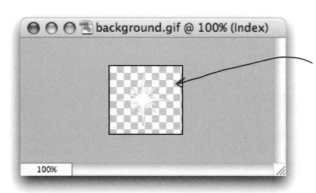

This image is a simple star–like pattern in white against a transparent background. Notice that it also has a matte around it that matches the color of the background.

Now, you just need to get that image into your paragraph element, so you'll be using an **\<img\>** element, right? *Not so fast.* If you're adding an image to the background of an element, there is another way. Using CSS, you can add a background image to any element using the **background-image** property. Let's give it a try and see how it works:

Here are the properties you added in the exercise on the previous page.

```
.guarantee {
        line-height:       1.9em;
        font-style:        italic;
        font-family:       Georgia, "Times New Roman", Times, serif;
        color:             #444444;
        border-color:      black;
        border-width:      1px;
        border-style:      solid;
        background-color:  #a7cece;
        padding:           25px;
        margin:            30px;
        background-image:  url(images/background.gif);
}
```

Add this to your CSS, save, and reload your page.

Wait a sec, it seems like we have two ways to put images on a page. Is background-image a replacement for the <img> element?

No, the **background-image** property has a very specific purpose, which is to set the background image of an element. It isn't for placing images in a page – for that you definitely want to use the **<img>** element.

Think about it this way: a background image is pure presentation, and the only reason you would use a **background-image** is to improve the attractiveness of your element. An **<img>** element, on the other hand, is used to include an image that has a more substantial role in the page, like a photo or a logo.

Now, we could have just placed the image inside the paragraph, and we could probably get the same look and feel, but the guarantee star is pure decoration – it has no real meaning on the page and it's only meant to make the element look better. So, **background-image** makes more sense.

Test driving the background image

Well, this is certainly an interesting test drive – we have a background image, but it appears to be repeated many times. Let's take a closer look at how to use CSS background images, and then you'll be able to fix this.

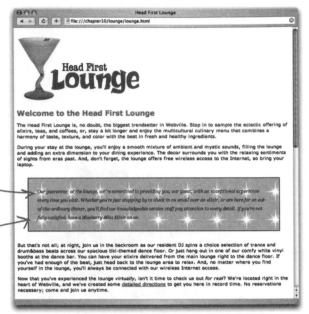

Here's the guarantee star image in the background. Notice that it sits on top of the background color, and because it has a transparent background, it lets the color show through.

Also notice that background images, like the background color, only show under the content area and padding, and not outside the border in the margin.

 CSS Up Close

The <u>background-image</u> property places an image in the background of an element. Two other properties also affect the background image: background-position and background-repeat.

```
background-image: url(images/background.gif);
```

The background-image property is set to a URL, which can be a relative path or a full blown URL (http://...).

Notice that no quotes are required around the URL.

Fixing the background image

By default, background images are repeated. Luckily there is a **no-repeat** value
for the **background-repeat** property. Also, by default, browsers position a
background image in the top, left of the element, which is where we want it, but
let's also add a **background-position** property just to give it a try.

```
.guarantee {
        line-height:         1.9em;
        font-style:          italic;
        font-family:         Georgia, "Times New Roman", Times, serif;
        color:               #444444;
        border-color:        black;
        border-width:        1px;
        border-style:        solid;
        background-color:    #a7cece;
        padding:             25px;
        margin:              30px;
        background-image:    url(images/background.gif);
        background-repeat:   no-repeat;
        background-position: top left;
}
```

← You've got two new
   properties to add.

We want the
background image
to not repeat.

And we want it in
the top left corner.

The <u>background-position</u> property sets the position of the image and can be specified in pixels, or
as a percentage, or by using keywords like top, left, right, bottom, and center.

Places the image in the top, left of the element.

```
background-position: top left;
```

There are many different ways to position things in CSS and
we'll be talking more about that in two chapters.

By default, a background image is "tiled", or repeated over and over to fill the background space.
The <u>background-repeat</u> property controls how this tiling behaves.

Here are the other background-repeat values you can use.

```
background-repeat: repeat;
```

Sets the image to repeat both
horizontally and vertically. This is the
default behavior.

no-repeat ← Display the image once, don't
repeat the image at all.

repeat-x ← Repeat the image only horizontally.

repeat-y ← Repeat the image only vertically.

inherit ← Just do whatever the parent element does.

Another test drive of the background image

Here we go again. This time, it looks like we're much closer to what we want. But, since this is a background image, the text can sit on top of it. How do we fix this? That's exactly what padding is for! Padding allows you to add visual space around the content area. Let's increase the padding on the left and see if we can nail this down once and for all.

This is much better. Now the image isn't repeated.

But we'd really like for the text not to run over the top of the image.

How do you add padding only on the left?

For padding, margins, and even borders, CSS has a property for every direction: top, right, bottom, and left. To add padding on the left side, use the **padding-left** property, like this:

```
.guarantee {
        line-height:         1.9em;
        font-style:          italic;
        font-family:         Georgia, "Times New Roman", Times, serif;
        color:               #444444;
        border-color:        black;
        border-width:        1px;
        border-style:        solid;
        background-color:    #a7cece;
        padding:             25px;
        padding-left:        80px;
        margin:              30px;
        background-image:    url(images/background.gif);
        background-repeat:   no-repeat;
        background-position: top left;
}
```

We're using the padding-left property to increase the padding on the left.

Notice that we first set the padding on all sides to 25 pixels, and then we specify a property for the left side.

Order matters here — if you switch the order, then you'll set the padding for the left side first, and then the general padding property will set all sides back to 25 pixels, including the left side!

Are we there yet?

Make sure you save your changes and reload the page. You should see more padding on the left side of the paragraph, and the text is now positioned well with respect to the guarantee star. This is a great example of where you use padding instead of margins. If you need more visual space around the content area itself, use padding, as opposed to if you want space between elements or the sides of the page, in which case, use margin. In fact, we could actually use a little more margin on the right side to set the paragraph off even more. Let's do that, and then all we need to do is fix the border.

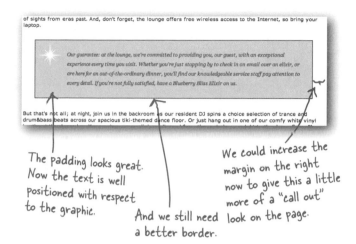

The padding looks great. Now the text is well positioned with respect to the graphic.

And we still need a better border.

We could increase the margin on the right now to give this a little more of a "call out" look on the page.

How do you increase the margin just on the right?

You do this just like you did with the padding: add another property, **margin-right**, to increase the right margin.

See the pattern? There's a property to control all sides together, and properties for each side if you want to set them individually.

```
.guarantee {
        line-height:        1.9em;
        font-style:         italic;
        font-family:        Georgia, "Times New Roman", Times, serif;
        color:              #444444;
        border-color:       black;
        border-width:       1px;
        border-style:       solid;
        background-color:   #a7cece;
        padding:            25px;
        padding-left:       80px;
        margin:             30px;
        margin-right:       250px;
        background-image:   url(images/background.gif);
        background-repeat:  no-repeat;
        background-position: top left;
}
```

Remember we're already setting the margins to be 30 pixels.

And now we're going to override that setting for the right side, and set it to 250 pixels.

Add the new **margin-right** property and reload. Now the paragraph should have 250 pixels of margin on the right side.

250 pixels

A two-minute guide to borders

There's only one thing left to do to perfect the guarantee paragraph:
add a better border. Before you do, take a look at all the different ways
you can control the border of an element.

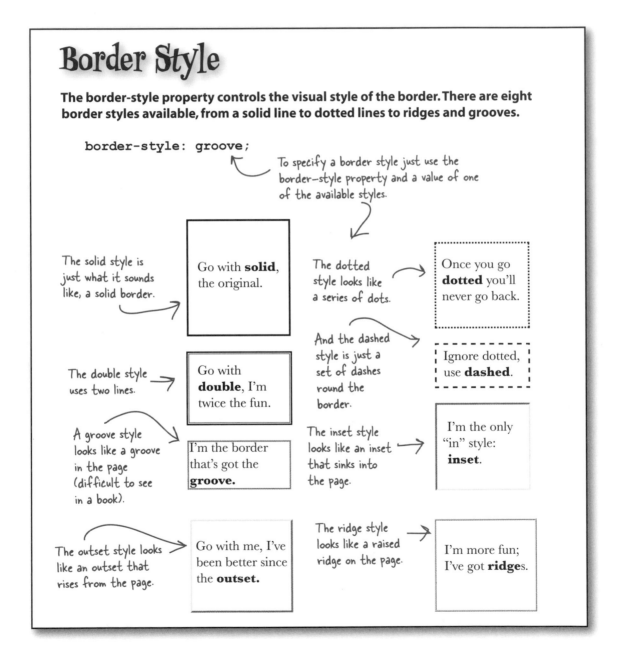

Border Width

The border-width property controls the width of the border. You can use keywords or pixels to specify the width.

```
border-width: thin;
border-width: 5px;
```

You can specify widths using the keywords thin, medium, or thick, or by the number of pixels.

	1px
	2px
	3px
thin	4px
medium	5px
thick	6px

Border Color

The border-color property sets the color of the border. This works just like setting font colors; you can use color names, rgb values, or hex codes to specify color.

```
border-color: red;
border-color: rgb(100%, 0%, 0%);
border-color: #ff0000;
```

Use border-color to specify the color of a border. You can use any of the common ways to specify color.

Specifying Border Sides

```
border-top-color
border-top-style
border-top-width
```

```
border-right-color
border-right-style
border-right-width
```

```
border-bottom-color
border-bottom-style
border-bottom-width
```

```
border-left-color
border-left-style
border-left-width
```

Just like margins and padding you can specify border style, width, or color on any side (top, right, bottom, or left):

```
border-top-color: black;
border-top-style: dashed;
border-top-width: thick;
```

These properties are for the top border only. You can specify each side of the border independently.

Border fit and finish

It's time to finish off the guarantee paragraph. All we need to do is give it a ragged-looking border. But which style is that? The available styles are solid, double, dotted, dashed, groove, ridge, inset, and outset. So how do we make it look ragged? It's actually just a trick: we're using a dashed border that has its color set to white (matching the background color of the page). Here's how you do it. Begin by just making the border dashed. Find the **border-style** property in your "lounge.css" and change it, like this:

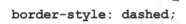
border-style: dashed;

Here we've changed the border from solid to dashed.

Go ahead and save the file and reload. You should see a border like this:

Now, to get a ragged-looking border, just set the color of the border to white. This makes the border look like it is cutting into the background color. Give it a try: find the **border-color** property and set it to **white**.

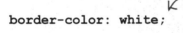
border-color: white;

And here we've changed the border color from black to white.

Save the file and reload again. Now you should see the ragged border:

Watch it!

Browsers don't always agree on the size of thin, medium, and thick.

Browsers can have different default sizes for the keywords thin, medium, and thick, so if the size of your border is really important to you, consider using pixel sizes instead.

Nice! I can't wait to see the entire page remodeled. Take a break and have an iced chai on me!

Congratulations!

Bravo! You've taken an ordinary HTML paragraph and transformed it into something a lot more appealing and stylish using only fifteen lines of CSS.

It was a long trip getting here, so at this point we encourage you to take a little break. Grab yourself an iced chai and take a little time to let things sink in – when you come back, we'll nail down a few more of the fine points of CSS.

Welcome back, and good timing. We're just about to listen in on an interview with an XHTML class...

The Class Exposed
This week's interview: are classes always right?

Head First: Hey, Class; you know we've been making good use of you, but we still don't know a lot about you.

Class: Well, there's not all that much to know. If you want to create a "group, " so to speak, that you can style, just come up with a class, put your elements in it, and then you can style all the elements in that class together.

Head First: So the class lets you take sets of elements and apply one or more style properties to them?

Class: Exactly. Say you have some holiday-themed areas in your page; one Halloween, one Christmas. You could add all Halloween elements to the "halloween" class and all Christmas elements to the "christmas" class. Then you can style those elements independently, say orange for Halloween and red for Christmas, by writing rules that apply to each class.

Head First: That makes a lot of sense. We just saw a good example of that in this chapter, didn't we?

Class: I'm not sure, I was off working. You'll have to catch me up.

Head First: Well, we have a paragraph on the Head First Lounge page that contains a written guarantee from the owners, and they want this paragraph to stand out independently of the other paragraphs.

Class: So far, so good... but let me ask you this: are there a few of these paragraphs, or just the one?

Head First: Well, I don't think there is any reason to have multiple guarantee paragraphs and I don't see the same style being applied anywhere else in the page, so just the one.

Class: Hmmm, I don't like the sound of that. You see, classes are meant to be used for styles that you want to reuse with multiple elements. If you've got one unique element that you need styled, that's not really what classes are for.

Head First: Wait a second – a class seemed to work perfectly... how can this be wrong?

Class: Whoa, now, don't freak out. All you need to do is switch your **class** attribute to an **id** attribute. It will only take you a minute.

Head First: An **id** attribute? I thought those were for those destination anchors, like in Chapter 4?

Class: **id**s have lots of uses. They're really just unique identifiers for elements.

Head First: Can you tell us a little more about **id** attributes? This is all news to me. I mean, I just went through an entire chapter using **class** incorrectly!

Class: Hey, no worries; it's a common mistake. Basically all you need to know is that you use a **class** when you might want to use a style with more than one element. And, if what you need to style is unique and there's only one on your page, then use an **id**. The **id** attribute is strictly for naming unique elements.

Head First: Okay, I think I've got it, but why does it really matter? I mean, **class** worked just fine for us.

Class: Because there are some things you really want *only one* of on your page. The guarantee paragraph you mentioned is one example; but there are better examples, like the header or footer on your page, or a navigation bar. You're not going to have two of those on a page. Of course, you *can* use a class for just one element, but someone else could come along and add another element to the class, and then your element won't have a unique style anymore. It also becomes important when you are positioning HTML elements, which is something you haven't gotten to yet.

Head First: Well, okay, Class. This conversation has certainly been educational for us. It sounds like we definitely need to convert that paragraph from a **class** to an **id**. Thanks again for joining us.

Class: Anytime, Head First!

BRAIN POWER

Choose whether you'd use class or id for the following elements:

id   class

- ❏ ❏ A paragraph containing the footer of a page.
- ❏ ❏ A set of headings and paragraphs that contain company biographies.
- ❏ ❏ An **<img>** element containing a "picture of the day."

id   class

- ❏ ❏ A set of **<p>** elements containing movie reviews.
- ❏ ❏ An **<ol>** element containing your to do list.
- ❏ ❏ **<q>** elements containing Buckaroo Bonzai quotes.

Answer: The footer, the picture of the day, and the to do list are great candidates for using id.

The id attribute

Because you've already used **id**s on **\<a>** elements, and because you already know how to use a **class** attribute, you're not going to have to learn much to use the **id** attribute. Say you have a footer on your page. There's usually only one footer on any page, so that sounds like the perfect candidate for an id. Here's how you'd add the identifier "footer" to a paragraph that contains the footer text:

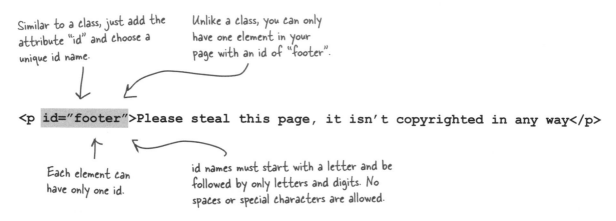

Similar to a class, just add the attribute "id" and choose a unique id name.

Unlike a class, you can only have one element in your page with an id of "footer".

```
<p id="footer">Please steal this page, it isn't copyrighted in any way</p>
```

Each element can have only one id.

id names must start with a letter and be followed by only letters and digits. No spaces or special characters are allowed.

Giving an element an id is similar to adding an element to a class. The only differences are that the attribute is called "id", not "class", an element can't have multiple ids, and you can't have more than one element on a page with the same id.

---

there are no
Dumb Questions

Q: **What's the big deal? Why do I need an id just to prove something is unique on the page? I could use a class exactly the same way, right?**

A: Well, you can always "simulate" a unique id with a class, but there are many reasons not to. Say you're working on a Web project with a team of people. One of your teammates is going to look at a class and think it can be reused with other elements. If, on the other hand, she sees an id, then she's going to know that's for a unique element. There are a couple of other reasons ids are important that you won't see for a few chapters. For

instance, when you start positioning elements on a page, you'll need each element you want to position to have a unique id.

Q: **Can an element have an id and also belong to a class?**

A: Yes, it can. Think about it this way: an id is just a unique identifier for an element, but that doesn't prevent it from belonging to one or more classes (just like having a unique name doesn't prevent you from joining one or more clubs).

But how do I use id in CSS?

You select an element with an id almost exactly like you select an element with a class. To quickly review: if you have a class called "specials", there are a couple of ways you can select elements using this class. You could select just certain elements in the class, like this:

```
p.specials {
        color: red;
}
```

This selects <u>only paragraphs</u> that are in the specials class.

Or, you can select all the elements that belong to the "specials" class, like this:

```
.specials {
        color: red;
}
```

This selects <u>all elements</u> in the specials class.

Using an id selector is very similar. To select an element by its id, you use a "#" character in front of the id (compare this to class, where you use a "." in front of the class name). Say you want to select any element with the id "footer":

```
#footer {
        color: red;
}
```

This selects <u>any element</u> that has the id "footer".

Or, you could select only a **<p>** element with the id "footer", like this:

```
p#footer {
        color: red;
}
```

This selects <u>a <p> element</u> if it has the id "footer".

The only other difference between class and id is that an id selector should match <u>only one</u> element in a page.

Using an id in the lounge

Our "guarantee paragraph" really should have an id since it's
intended to be used just once in the page. While we should have
designed it that way from the beginning, making the change is
going to be quite simple.

Step One: change the class attribute to an id in your "lounge.html":

Just change the class attribute to an id.

```
<p id="guarantee">
        Our guarantee: at the lounge, we're committed to providing
        you, our guest, with an exceptional experience every time you
        visit. Whether you're just stopping by to check in on email
        over an elixir, or are here for an out-of-the-ordinary dinner,
        you'll find our knowledgeable service staff pay attention to every
        detail. If you're not fully satisfied have a Blueberry Bliss Elixir
        on us.
</p>
```

Step Two: change the ".guarantee" class selector in "lounge.css" to an id selector:

Just change the "." to a "#" in the selector.

```
#guarantee {
        line-height:           1.9em;
        font-style:            italic;
        font-family:           Georgia, "Times New Roman", Times, serif;
        color:                 #444444;
        border-color:          white;
        border-width:          1px;
        border-style:          dashed;
        background-color:      #a7cece;
        padding:               25px;
        padding-left:          80px;
        margin:                30px;
        margin-right:          250px;
        background-image:      url(images/background.gif);
        background-repeat:     no-repeat;
        background-position:   top left;
}
```

Step Three: save your changes and reload the page.

Well, everything should look EXACTLY the same. But, don't you feel much better now that everything is as it should be?

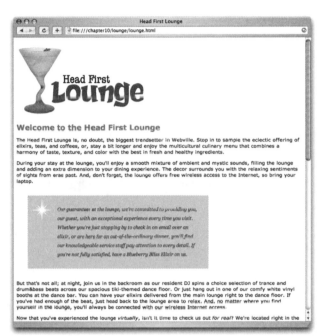

<hr />

there are no
Dumb Questions

Q: So why did you make the selector #guarantee rather than p#guarantee?

A: We could have done either and they both would select the same thing. On this page we know that we will always have a paragraph assigned to the id, so it doesn't really matter (and #guarantee is simpler). However, on a more complex set of pages you might have some pages where the unique id is assigned to, say, a paragraph, and on others it's assigned to a list or block quote. So you might want several rules for the id, like p#someid, and blockquote#someid, depending on which kind of element is on the page.

Q: Should I always start with a class, and then change it to an id when I know it's going to be unique?

A: No. You'll often know when you design your pages if an element is going to be unique or not. We only did things this way in the chapter because, well, you didn't know about id when we started. But don't you think we tied id into the story rather nicely?

☺

Q: In Chapter 4 we used the id attribute with the `<a>` element to create a destination anchor. When I put an id on other types of elements, do they become destinations too?

A: That's the idea, and most modern browsers support this, but older browsers don't.

Remixing style sheets

Before we wind this chapter down, let's have a little fun remixing some style sheets. So far you've been using only one style sheet. Well, who ever said you can't use more than one style sheet? You can specify a whole set of style sheets to be used with any XHTML. But you may be wondering why anyone would want to? There are a couple of good reasons. Here's the first one...

Imagine that the Head First Lounge takes off, gets franchised, does the IPO, and so on (all thanks to you and your terrific Web work, of course). Then there would be a whole corporate Web site with hundreds of pages, and obviously you'd want to style those pages with external CSS style sheets. There would be various company divisions and they might want to tweak the styles in individual ways. And the lounge franchises also might want some control over style. Here's how that might look:

We use all the corporate colors and fonts, but we add in a few special touches of our own, like a different line height.

We've set up all the main styles to be used by the company Web sites. Fonts, colors, and so on.

We've got a young, hip clientele. We tweak the colors a bit and add a little edge, but overall we use the division's main styles.

Corporate

Beverage Division

Seattle Lounge
(part of the Beverage Division)

Using multiple style sheets

So how do you start with a corporate style and then allow the division and the lounge franchises to override and make changes to the styles? You use several style sheets, like this:

In your XHTML you can specify more than one style sheet. Here, we've got three.

One style sheet for the entire corporation.

```
<!DOCTYPE html PUBLIC "-//W3C//DTD XHTML 1.0 Strict//EN"
    "http://www.w3.org/TR/xhtml1/DTD/xhtml1-strict.dtd">
<html xmlns="http://www.w3.org/1999/xhtml" lang="en" xml:lang="en" >
  <head>
    <meta http-equiv="Content-Type" content="text/html; charset=ISO-8859-1" />
    <title>Head First Lounge</title>
      <link type="text/css" href="corporate.css" rel="stylesheet" />
      <link type="text/css" href="beverage-division.css" rel="stylesheet" />
      <link type="text/css" href="lounge-seattle.css" rel="stylesheet"  />
  </head>
  <body>
    .
    .
    .
  </body>
</html>
```

And the lounge in Seattle has its own tweaks in their style sheet.

The beverage division can add to the corporate style a little, or even override some of the corporate styles.

Order matters! A style sheet can override the styles in the style sheets linked above it.

there are no Dumb Questions

Q: **So the order of the style sheets matters?**

A: Yes, they go top to bottom, with the style sheets on the bottom taking precedence. So if you have, say, a font-family property on the <body> element in both the corporate and the division style sheets, the division's takes precedence, since it's the last one linked in the XHTML.

Q: **Do I ever need this for a simple site?**

A: You'd be surprised. Sometimes there's a style sheet you want to base your page on, and rather than changing that style sheet, you just link to it, and then supply your own style sheet below that to specify what you want to change.

Q: **Can you say more about how the style for a specific element is decided?**

A: We talked a little about that in Chapter 8. And for now, just add to that knowledge that the ordering of the style sheets linked into your file matters. Then in the next chapter, after you've learned a few other CSS details, we're going to go through exactly how the browser knows which style goes with which element.

Style sheets - they're not just for desktop browsers anymore...

And now for the second reason you might want to have multiple style files. Let's say you want to have slightly different styles for computer screens, PDAs, or mobile devices, and printed versions of your pages. There is an optional attribute for the **`<link>`** element called **media**, that you can use to specify the kinds of devices your style files are intended for.

If you're interested in more information on print styles and styles for mobile devices, check out the appendix for some pointers.

The media attribute allows you to specify the type of device this style sheet is for.

```
<link type="text/css" rel="stylesheet" href="lounge-screen.css" media="screen" />
```

Here we're specifying that this style sheet is appropriate for computer screens.

You can specify multiple **`<link>`** elements with different media types in one XHTML file, like this:

If you don't supply a media type then the style file should be suitable for all devices.

```
<link type="text/css" href="lounge.css" rel="stylesheet" />
<link type="text/css" href="lounge-print.css" rel="stylesheet" media="print" />
<link type="text/css" href="lounge-mobile.css" rel="stylesheet" media="handheld" />
```

Now we have two other <link> elements, one that specifies print and one for small devices with small screens and limited communication speeds.

Q: That's pretty cool. So I can set up different style sheets for different devices?

A: Yes, you can set up several style sheets and then link to them all in your XHTML. It's the browser's job to grab the right style sheet based on the media type.

Q: Say you have a "handheld" link and a link that applies to all browsers; which one gets applied?

A: The handheld browser will grab both of them. But, assuming the "handheld" link is below the "all" link, the handheld rules take precedence, just like we talked about before with the corporate, division, and lounge CSS files.

Q: So we have screen (computers), print (print-like media), handheld (mobile devices and cell phones). What else is there?

A: Here are a few more: aural (for speech browsers), Braille (for people who need tactile readers), projection (for projected presentations or slides), tty (for teletypes and terminals), and tv (for televisions, of course).

Exercise

In your "chapter10/lounge/print" folder, you'll find "print.css". Open up "lounge.html" in the "chapter10/lounge" folder and add a new link to this style sheet for the media type "print". Make sure you also add the attribute media="screen" to the <link> element that links to "lounge.css", so you have one style sheet for the screen, and one for the printer. Then save, reload the page, and choose your browser's "Print" option. Run to the printer to see the result!

```
<link type="text/css" href="print/print.css"
     rel="stylesheet" media="print" />
```

Here's the new link you need to add to your "lounge.html" file.

Here's the printed version. You've *totally* changed how the page looks when it's printed, using CSS. That structure versus presentation thing is really paying off.

Unfortunately, not all browsers support the media attribute, so if you didn't get this result, try a newer browser.

OPTIONAL PRINTER REQUIRED, NOT INCLUDED WITH BOOK.

BULLET POINTS

- CSS uses a box model to control how elements are displayed.

- Boxes consist of the content area and optional padding, border, and margin.

- The content area contains the content of the element.

- The padding is used to create visual space around the content area.

- The border surrounds the padding and content and provides a way to visually separate the content.

- The margin surrounds the border, padding, and content, and allows space to be added between the element and other elements.

- Padding, border, and margin are all optional.

- An element's background will show under the content and the padding, but not under the margin.

- Padding and margin size can be set in pixels or percentages.

- Border width can be set in pixels or by using the keywords thin, medium, and thick.

- There are eight different styles for borders, including solid, dashed, dotted, and ridge.

- When setting margins, padding, or the border, CSS provides properties for setting all the sides (top, right, bottom, left) at once, or it allows them to be set independently.

- Use the line-height property to add space between lines of text.

- You can place an image in the background of an element with the background-image property.

- Use the background-position and background-repeat properties to set the position and tiling behavior of the background image.

- Use the class attribute for elements that you want to style together, as a group.

- Use the id attribute to give an element a unique name. You can also use the id attribute to provide a unique style for an element.

- There should only be one element in a page with a given id.

- You can select elements by their id using the id # selector; for example #myfavoriteid.

- An element can have only one id, but it can belong to many classes.

- You can use more than one style sheet in your XHTML.

- If two style sheets have conflicting property definitions, the style sheet that is last in the XHTML file will receive preference.

- You can target media devices such as "print" or "handheld" by using the media attribute in your <link> element.

XHTMLcross

You're really expanding your HTML & CSS skills. Strengthen those neural connections by doing a crossword. All the answers come from this chapter.

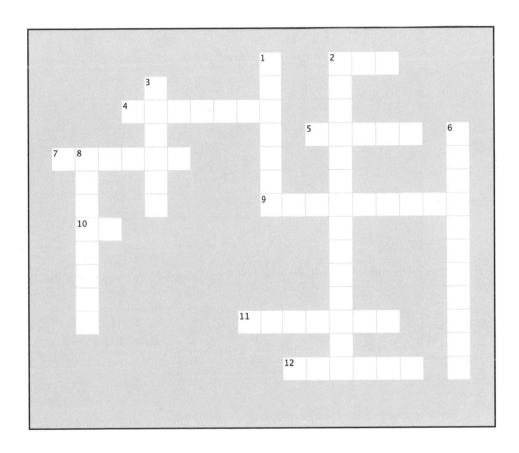

Across

2. CSS sees every element as a _____.
4. The preferred font-family used in the guarantee paragraph.
5. Optional ‹link› attribute for other kinds of _____.
7. Between padding and margin.
9. We changed the _____ class to an id.
10. If you want your element to have a unique style, use this kind of selector.
11. The space between the content and the border.
12. Style of border we used on the guarantee paragraph.

Down

1. Publishing term for the space between lines.
2. Which kind of elixir do you get if you're not fully satisfed?
3. By default, background images do this.
6. Property used to increase the space between lines of text.
8. Padding, borders and margins are all _____.

XHTMLcross Solution

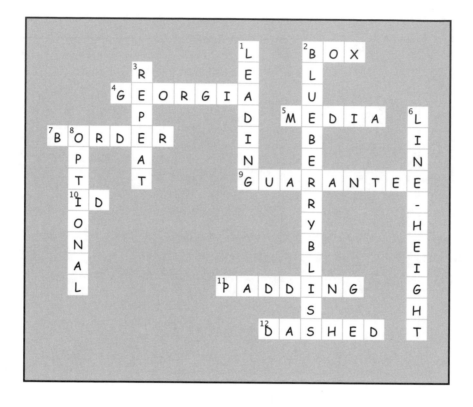

Sharpen your pencil

Solution

See if you can identify the padding, border and margins of this paragraph.
Mark all the padding and margins (left, right, top, and bottom):

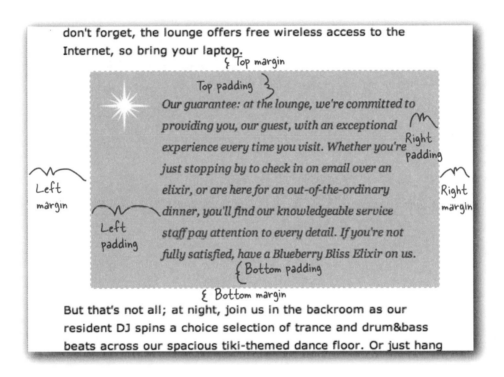

don't forget, the lounge offers free wireless access to the Internet, so bring your laptop.

ʒ Top margin

Top padding ʒ

Our guarantee: at the lounge, we're committed to providing you, our guest, with an exceptional experience every time you visit. Whether you're just stopping by to check in on email over an elixir, or are here for an out-of-the-ordinary dinner, you'll find our knowledgeable service staff pay attention to every detail. If you're not fully satisfied, have a Blueberry Bliss Elixir on us.

Right padding

Left margin

Left padding

Right margin

{ Bottom padding

ʒ Bottom margin

But that's not all; at night, join us in the backroom as our resident DJ spins a choice selection of trance and drum&bass beats across our spacious tiki-themed dance floor. Or just hang

Exercise Solutions

If you look at the guarantee paragraph as it's supposed to look in its final form, it has a italic, serif font, a greater line height than the rest of the page, and if you're looking really close, gray text. Write the CSS below to set the line height to 1.9em, the font style to italic, the color to #444444, and the font family to Georgia, 'Times New Roman', Times, serif. Here's the solution... did you test it?

You can add the new properties anywhere in the rule. We added them at the top.

```
.guarantee {
        line-height:        1.9em;
        font-style:         italic;
        font-family:        Georgia, "Times New Roman", Times, serif;
        color:              #444444;
        border-color:       black;
        border-width:       1px;
        border-style:       solid;
        background-color:   #a7cece;
        padding:            25px;
        margin:             30px;
}
```

Notice that if a font name has spaces in it you should surround it with quotes.

of sights from eras past. And, don't forget, the lounge offers free wireless access to the Internet, so bring your laptop.

Increased line height.

An italic, serif font.

Our guarantee: at the lounge, we're committed to providing you, our guest, with an exceptional experience every time you visit. Whether you're just stopping by to check in on email over an elixir, or are here for an out-of-the-ordinary dinner, you'll find our knowledgeable service staff pay attention to every detail. If you're not fully satisfied, have a Blueberry Bliss Elixir on us.

Gray color gives the text a softer look.

But that's not all; at night, join us in the backroom as our resident DJ spins a choice selection of trance and drum&bass beats across our spacious tiki-themed dance floor. Or just hang out in one of our comfy white vinyl

11 divs and spans

Advanced Web Construction

> Some builders say
> "measure twice, cut once."
> I say "plan, div, and span."

It's time to get ready for heavy construction. In this chapter
we're going to roll out two new XHTML elements, called <div> and <span>. These
are no simple "two by fours," these are full blown steel beams. With <div> and
<span>, you're going to build some serious supporting structures, and once you've
got those structures in place, you're going to be able to style them all in new and
powerful ways. Now, we couldn't help but notice that your CSS toolbelt is really
starting to fill up, so it's time to show you a few shortcuts that will make specifying all
these properties a lot easier. And, we've also got some special guests in this chapter,
the *pseudo-classes*, which are going to allow you to create some very interesting
selectors. (If you're thinking that "pseudo-classes" would make a great name for your
next band, too late, we beat you to it.)

You know, we'd love it if you could make the elixir specials a little more attractive on the Web page. Could you make it look just like our handout menu?

The elixir mixer, Alice

Here's the handout menu with the elixir specials. Wow, the design is a lot different than the rest of the page: it's thin, the text is centered, there are red headings, an aquamarine border around the whole thing, and even some cocktail graphics at the top.

Weekly Elixir Specials

Lemon Breeze

The ultimate healthy drink, this elixir combines herbal botanicals, minerals, and vitamins with a twist of lemon into a smooth citrus wonder that will keep your immune system going all day and all night.

Chai Chiller

Not your traditional chai, this elixir mixes maté with chai spices and adds an extra chocolate kick for a caffeinated taste sensation on ice.

Black Brain Brew

Want to boost your memory? Try our Black Brain Brew elixir, made with black oolong tea and just a touch of espresso. Your brain will thank you for the boost.

Join us any evening for these and all our wonderful elixirs.

A close look at the elixirs XHTML

Alice sure has asked for a tall order, hasn't she? She wants us to take the existing lounge XHTML and make it look like the handout menu. Hmmm... that looks challenging, but *we do* have CSS on our side, so let's give it a try. But, before we jump right into styling, let's get an overview of the existing XHTML. Here's just the XHTML snippet for the elixir specials; you'll find it in "lounge.html" in the "chapter11/lounge" folder:

We have three elixirs, each with the same structure.

The elixir specials section begins with an <h2> heading.

```
<h2>Weekly Elixir Specials</h2>

<p>
        <img src="images/yellow.gif" alt="Lemon Breeze Elixir" />
</p>
<h3>Lemon Breeze</h3>
<p>
        The ultimate healthy drink, this elixir combines
        herbal botanicals, minerals, and vitamins with
        a twist of lemon into a smooth citrus wonder
        that will keep your immune system going all
        day and all night.
</p>

<p>
        <img src="images/chai.gif" alt="Chai Chiller Elixir" />
</p>
<h3>Chai Chiller</h3>
<p>
        Not your traditional chai, this elixir mixes mat&eacute;
        with chai spices and adds an extra chocolate kick for
        a caffeinated taste sensation on ice.
</p>

<p>
        <img src="images/black.gif" alt="Black Brain Brew Elixir" />
</p>
<h3>Black Brain Brew</h3>
<p>
        Want to boost your memory? Try our Black Brain Brew
        elixir, made with black oolong tea and just a touch
        of espresso. Your brain will thank you for the boost.
</p>
<p>
        Join us any evening for these and all our
        other wonderful
        <a href="beverages/elixir.html"
           title="Head First Lounge Elixirs">elixirs</a>.
</p>
```

Each elixir has an image in a <p> element.

...a name, in an <h3> heading...

...and a description, also in a paragraph.

And this structure is repeated for each elixir.

And, finally, at the bottom, there is another paragraph, with some text and a link to the real elixirs page.

This looks tough, guys. There are a lot of style changes we've got to make, and the elixirs style doesn't really match the rest of the page.

Jim   Frank   Joe

Jim: Come on, Frank, you know we can just create a class or two and then style all the elixir elements separately from the rest of the page.

Frank: That's true. Maybe this isn't so bad. I'm sure there is a simple property to make text align to the center And we know how to handle the colored text.

Jim: Wait a sec, what about that border around everything?

Frank: Piece of cake. We just learned how to make borders. Remember, every element can have one.

Joe: Hmm, I don't think so. If you look at the XHTML, this is a bunch of **<h2>**, **<h3>**, and **<p>** elements. If we put separate borders on every element, they'll just look like separate boxes.

Frank: You're right, Joe. What we need is an element to nest all these other elements inside, so we can put a border on that. Then we'll have one border around everything in the elixirs section of the page.

Jim: Well, I see why you get paid the big bucks, Frank. Could we nest the elixir stuff inside a **<p>** element, or a **<blockquote>**?

Frank: We can't use **<p>** because **<p>** can't contain other block elements, and the headings and paragraphs are obviously block elements. I don't think we'd want to do that anyway; paragraphs are for text.

Joe: And **<blockquote>**'s not right either, because this is an elixir menu, not a quote.

Frank: Actually, I think we're on the right track. I've been reading a *certain book* on HTML & CSS and I'm just up to a section on a new element called **<div>**. I think it might be the tool we need.

Joe: **<div>** – what's that? It sounds like it's for math.

Frank: That's not far off, because a **<div>** lets you *divide* your page into logical sections or groupings.

Jim: Hey, that sounds like exactly what we need!

Frank: Yup. Let me show you guys how to divide a page into logical sections, and then I'll show you what I know about **<div>**...

Let's explore how we can divide a page into logical sections

Take a look at the Web page to the right: it's a Web page for PetStorz.com and we're going to spend a few pages looking at how we might add some additional structure to it by identifying some logical sections and then enclosing those inside a **`<div>`** element.

We've drawn an outline of the PetStorz page.

This is a pretty normal looking page: lots of headings, paragraphs, and an image in there.

But by just focussing on the <u>structure</u> of the page, you can't really tell a whole lot about the page. What elements make up the header? Is there a footer on the page? What are the content areas?

Identifying your logical sections

Okay, so our job is to locate "logical sections" in this page. What's a logical section? It's just a group of elements that are all related on the page. For instance, in the PetStorz.com Web page, there are some elements that are used for the cats area on the page, and some that are used for dogs. Let's check it out.

The PetStorz page has two main content areas, one for cats, and one for dogs. It has some other areas too, but we'll come back to those.

In this case, both the cats and dogs sections consist of two elements, a heading and a paragraph. But often these groupings can contain many more elements.

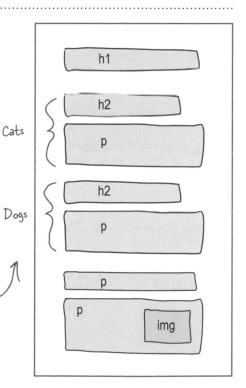

Using <div>s to mark sections

Now that you know which elements belong in each section, you can add some XHTML to mark up this structure. The common way to do this is to place **<div>** opening and closing tags around the elements that belong to a logical section. Let's first do this pictorially, and then we'll come back to the real markup in a couple of pages.

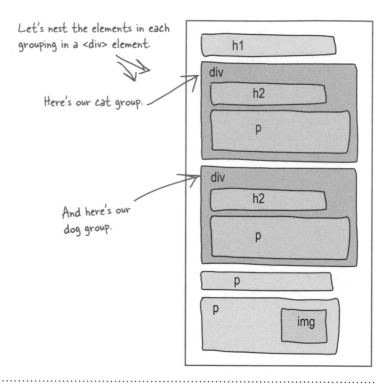

Let's nest the elements in each grouping in a <div> element.

Here's our cat group.

And here's our dog group.

Labelling the <div>s

Just by nesting your elements in **<div>**s, you've indicated that all those elements belong to the same group. But you haven't given them any kind of label that says what the grouping means, right?

A good way to do that is to use an **id** attribute to provide a unique label for the **<div>**. For instance, let's give the cats **<div>** an id of "cats" and the dogs **<div>** an id of "dogs".

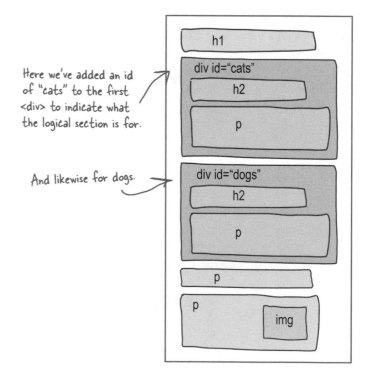

Here we've added an id of "cats" to the first <div> to indicate what the logical section is for.

And likewise for dogs.

BRAIN POWER

On a referral from the Starbuzz CEO, you've been asked to come in and consult on style changes to PetStorz main page. How quickly would you understand the PetStorz Web page if you were shown Page One?

What about Page Two?

Page One

h1
h2
p
h2
p
p
p   Img

Page Two

h1
div id="cats"
h2
p
div id="dogs"
h2
p
p
p   img

Adding some style

Okay, so you've added some logical structure to the PetStorz page, and you've also labeled that structure by giving each **\<div\>** a unique id. That's all you need to start styling the group of elements contained in the **\<div\>**.

Here we have two rules, one for each \<div\>. Each \<div\> is selected by an id selector.

Now the \<div\>s have a little style.

By setting the background on the \<div\>, it also shows through the elements contained in the \<div\>.

The elements in the \<div\> will also inherit some properties from the \<div\>, just as any child element does (like font-size, color, etc).

Each rule sets the background-image property. For cats we have a leopard image, and for dogs we have a mutt image.

```
#cats {
    background-image: url(leopard.jpg);
}

#dogs {
    background-image: url(mutt.jpg);
}
```

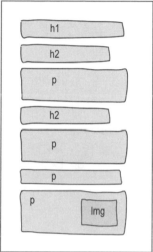
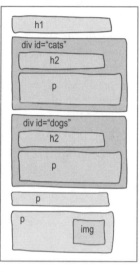
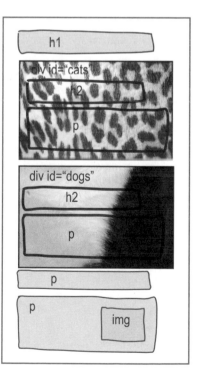

Exposing even more structure

There are a couple of reasons you might want to add more structure to your pages with **<div>**s. First, you may want to further expose the underlying logical structure of your pages, which can help others understand them, and also help in maintaining them. Second, there are times when you need the structure so that you have a way to apply style to a section. Often, you'll want to add the structure for both reasons.

So, in the case of PetStorz, we could take this to the next level and add a few more **<div>**s...

Now we've added another <div> with an id indicating this is the header of the page.

And another indicating the footer of the page.

Adding this structure through <div>s can even help you think through your page design. For instance, does this lone <p> really need to be here?

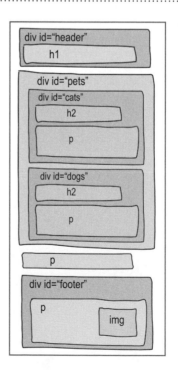

Adding structure on structure

And you don't have to stop there. It is common to nest structure, too. For instance, in the PetStorz page, we have a cat section and a dog section, and the two together are logically the "pets" section of the page. So, we could place both the "cat" and "dog" **<div>**s into a "pets" **<div>**.

Now we've marked up this XHTML so that we know there is a logical section in the page with "pets" content in it. Further, that "pets" section has two logical subsections, one for "cats" and one for "dogs".

there are no
Dumb Questions

Q: So, a <div> acts like a container that you can put elements into to keep them all together?

A: It sure does. In fact, we often describe <div>s as "containers". Not only do they act as logical containers that you can use to hold a bunch of related elements (like the "cat" elements) together, but when we start styling <div>s and using them for positioning in the next chapter, you'll see they act as graphical containers, too.

Q: Beyond the structure I'm already putting into my pages with headings and paragraphs and so on, should I also be adding a higher level of structure with <div>s?

A: Yes and no. You want to add structure where it has a real purpose, but don't add structure for structure's sake. Always keep your structure as simple as possible to get the job done. For instance,

if it is helpful to add a "pets" section that contains both "cats" and "dogs" to the PetStorz page, by all means add it. However, if it provides no real benefit, then it just complicates your page. After working with <div>s for a while, you'll start to get a feel for when and how much to use them.

Q: Do you ever put <div>s in a class instead of giving it an id?

A: Well, remember that an element can have an id *and* be in one or more classes at the same time, so the choice isn't mutually exclusive. And, yes, there are many times you create <div>s and place them into classes. Say you have a bunch of album sections in a page of music playlists; you might put all the elements that make up the album into a <div> and then put them all in a class called "albums". That identifies where the albums are, and they can all be styled together with the class. At the same time you might give each album an id so that it can have additional style applied separately.

Q: I was having a little trouble following the <div> within <div> stuff, with the "pets" and "cats" and "dogs". Could you explain that a little more?

A: Sure. You're used to elements being nested in other elements, right? Like a <p> nested in a <body> nested in an <html> element. You've even seen lists nested within lists. The <div> is really no different; you're just nesting an element inside another element, and, in the case of PetStorz, we're using it to show larger chunks of structure (a "cats" and "dogs" nested in a "pets" section). Or, you might use <div>s to have a beer section nested in a beverages section nested in a menu section.

But, the best way to understand why you'd want something like a <div> within a <div> is by using them and encountering a situation where they mean something to you. Put this in the back of your mind and you'll see an example soon enough where we need one.

Use, don't abuse, <div>s in your pages. Add additional structure where it helps you separate a page into logical sections for clarity and styling. Adding <div>s just for the sake of creating a lot of structure in your pages complicates them with no real benefit.

Meanwhile, back at the lounge...

Okay, enough "theory" about **<div>**s – let's get one into the lounge page. Remember, we're trying to get all the elixir elements into a group and then we're going to style it to make it look like the elixir handout. So, open up your "lounge.html" file in the "chapter11/lounge" folder, locate the elixirs elements, and then insert opening and closing **<div>** tags around them.

```
<div id="elixirs">
    <h2>Weekly Elixir Specials</h2>

    <p>
        <img src="images/yellow.gif" alt="Lemon Breeze Elixir" />
    </p>
    <h3>Lemon Breeze</h3>
    <p>
        The ultimate healthy drink, this elixir combines
        herbal botanicals, minerals, and vitamins with
        a twist of lemon into a smooth citrus wonder
        that will keep your immune system going all
        day and all night.
    </p>

    <p>
        <img src="images/chai.gif" alt="Chai Chiller Elixir" />
    </p>

    <h3>Chai Chiller</h3>
    <p>
        Not your traditional chai, this elixir mixes mat&eacute;
        with chai spices and adds an extra chocolate kick for
        a caffeinated taste sensation on ice.
    </p>

    <p>
        <img src="images/black.gif" alt="Black Brain Brew Elixir" />
    </p>

    <h3>Black Brain Brew</h3>
    <p>
        Want to boost your memory? Try our Black Brain Brew
        elixir, made with black oolong tea and just a touch
        of espresso. Your brain will thank you for the boost.
    </p>

    <p>
        Join us any evening for these and all our
        other wonderful
        <a href="beverages/elixir.html"
           title="Head First Lounge Elixirs">elixirs</a>.
    </p>
</div>
```

Here's the opening tag, and we've given it an id of "elixirs" to identify it.

Remember we're just showing a snippet of XHTML from the entire file. When you open "lounge.html", you'll see all the markup for the page.

And, here's the closing tag.

Taking the <div> for a test drive

That was easy, wasn't it? Now that we've got a more structured page, let's fire up the browser and see how it looks...

Hmmm... no change at all! But that's okay: the <div> is pure structure, and it doesn't have any "look" or default style in the page.

That said, a <div> is just a block element, and you can apply any styles you want to it. So, once you know how to style a block element (and you do), you know how to style a <div>.

Remember, the goal here is to restyle the elixir content on the page so it looks like the handout.

Before we took a detour to learn about <div>s, we were trying to figure out how to get a border around the entire set of elixirs. Now that you've got a <div> in "lounge.html", how would you go about adding a border?

Adding a border

Okay, now that you have a **\<div>** around all the elements in the elixirs section, the fun begins: *you can style it.*

The first thing we want to reproduce in the elixirs handout is a border that wraps around *all* the elements in the elixirs section, right? Well, now that you actually have a **\<div>** element that wraps around the elixirs section, you can style it and add a border. Let's try that now.

You'll need a new rule in the lounge's CSS to select the **\<div>** element using its id. Open up your "lounge.css" file in the "chapter11/lounge" folder, and add this rule at the end:

```
#elixirs {
        border-width: thin;
        border-style: solid;
        border-color: #007e7e;
}
```

Add this at the end of your CSS file. It selects the elixirs \<div> element using its id, and adds a thin, solid border in our favorite aquamarine color.

An over-the-border test drive

After you've added the CSS, save it and then reload your "lounge.html" file.

Here's the border that you just added to the elixirs \<div> element.

You added a visible border to this \<div>, but it still has no padding and no margin. We'll need to add that too.

Notice that the border goes around all the elements inside the \<div> element. The \<div> is a box like every other element, so, when you add a border, the border goes around the content, which is all the elements in the \<div>.

Adding some real style to the elixirs section

So far, so good. We've found a way to get that border around the entire section. Now you're going to see how to use the **<div>** to customize the styling of the entire elixirs section independent of the rest of the page.

We obviously have some padding issues to deal with, because the border is right up against the content. But there's a lot of other style we need to work out, too. Let's take a look at everything we need to take care of...

The *width* of the elixirs handout is narrower than the rest of the page.

There's a *background* image at the top.

The main heading and the paragraph text are *black*, while the drink names are a *red* color that matches the red in the logo.

Weekly Elixir Specials

Lemon Breeze

The ultimate healthy drink, this elixir combines herbal botanicals, minerals, and vitamins with a twist of lemon into a smooth citrus wonder that will keep your immune system going all day and all night.

The text and images are *centered*, and there's *padding* on the sides to add space between the text and the border.

Chai Chiller

Not your traditional chai, this elixir mixes mate with chai spices and adds an extra chocolate kick for a caffeinated taste sensation on ice.

The *line-height* of the paragraphs looks a lot more like the default line height for the page (before we changed it in the last chapter).

The font family is a sans-serif font, just like the body font, so we don't have to change that. Remember that the <div> element and all the elements nested in it inherit the font family from the body.

Black Brain Brew

Want to boost your memory? Try our Black Brain Brew elixir, made with black oolong tea and just a touch of espresso. Your brain will thank you for the boost.

This link is aquamarine.

Join us any evening for these and all our other wonderful elixirs.

The game plan

That's a lot of new style, so let's get a game plan together before attacking it. Here's what we need to do:

❏ First, we're going to change the width of the elixirs **<div>** to make it narrower.

❏ Next, we'll knock out some of the styles you're already familiar with, like padding and the background image. We'll also play with the text alignment, which you haven't seen before.

❏ Then all we've got left are the text line heights and the heading colors. You're going to see that you need to upgrade your CSS selector skills just a bit to get those changed.

That's a lot to do, so let's get started.

Working on the elixir width

We'd like the elixirs to be quite narrow, so it looks like the narrow handout menu at the lounge; about 1/4 the width of a typical browser window should be about right. So, if most people set their browser windows to 800 pixels wide, that would be about 200 pixels. You've set the widths of padding, borders, and margins, but you've never set the width of an element before. To do that you use the **width** property, like this:

```
#elixirs {
        border-width: thin;
        border-style: solid;
        border-color: #007e7e;
        width: 200px;
}
```

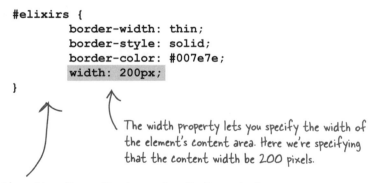

The width property lets you specify the width of the element's content area. Here we're specifying that the content width be 200 pixels.

We're setting this on the elixirs <div>. So the content in the elixirs <div> will be 200 pixels wide, and the browser's layout rules will work to fit all the elements nested in the <div> within that width.

Give this a try. Open your "lounge.css" and add this rule to the bottom.

Test driving the width

Next, save the CSS and then reload the "lounge.html" file. You'll see the elixirs section get much skinnier, thanks to the width you gave it. The width of the content in the **<div>** is now exactly 200 pixels. There's also some interesting behavior you should check out...

Now all the content in the elixirs <div> fits into a space that is 200 pixels wide. It doesn't change, even if you make your browser window really wide, or really narrow. Try it!

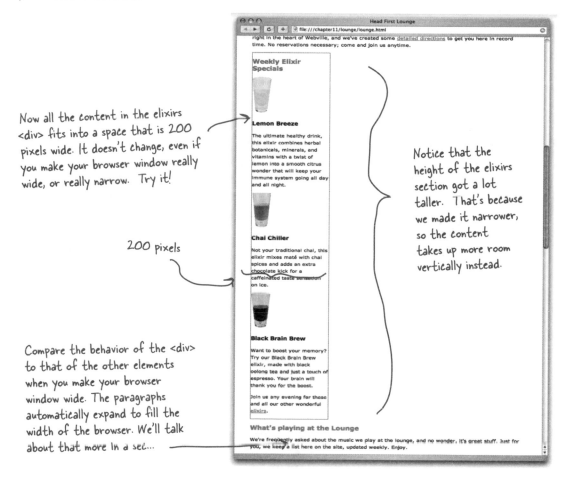

200 pixels

Notice that the height of the elixirs section got a lot taller. That's because we made it narrower, so the content takes up more room vertically instead.

Compare the behavior of the <div> to that of the other elements when you make your browser window wide. The paragraphs automatically expand to fill the width of the browser. We'll talk about that more in a sec...

Can you resize your browser window to less than the width of the elixirs <div>? Some browsers won't let you go that narrow; others will. If you can go narrower, compare the text in the elixirs <div> with the rest of the text on the page. The other paragraphs resize themselves no matter how wide or narrow you go, but the elixirs <div> never gets narrower or wider than 200 pixels.

I was wondering how the width property relates to padding and margins. Is this the width of the content itself? Or the entire box including the padding and margin?

The width property specifies the width for the content area only.

To figure out the width of the entire box, you need to add the width of the content area to the width of the left and right margins, the left and right padding, and the border width. Don't forget that you have to include *twice* the border width, because there is a border on the left and the right.

total width

left margin width
border width
left padding width

width (specified in width property)

right padding width
border width
right margin width

Our guarantee: at the lounge, we're committed to providing you, our guest, with an exceptional experience every time you visit. Whether you're just stopping by to check in on email over an elixir, or are here for an out-of-the-ordinary dinner, you'll find our knowledgeable service staff pay attention to every detail. If you're not fully satisfied have a Blueberry Bliss Elixir on us.

Well then how do we specify the width of the entire element?

You don't. You specify the width of the content area, the padding, the border, and the margin. All of that added together is the width of the entire element.

Say you set the content area width to be 300 pixels using the `width` property in a CSS rule.

And let's say you've set the margins to 20 pixels, the padding to 10 pixels, and you have a 1 pixel border. What's the width of your element's box? Well, it's the width of the content area added to the width of the left and right margins, the left and right padding, and the left and right border width. Let' see how to calculate that...

(1) The content area is 300 pixels.

300 pixels

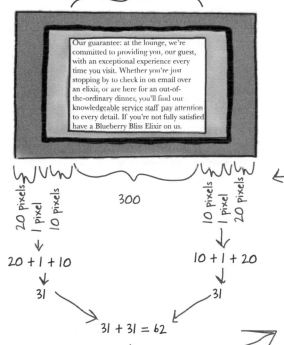

(2) Figure out how much is taken up by the margins, padding, and border.

20 pixels
1 pixel
10 pixels

300

10 pixels
1 pixel
20 pixels

20 + 1 + 10

31

10 + 1 + 20

31

31 + 31 = 62

(3) It looks like 62 pixels are taken up, so add that to the content area's width of 300 pixels, and we have 300 + 62 = 362 pixels for the entire box.

there are no Dumb Questions

Q: If I don't set the width of an element, then where does the width come from?

A: The default width for a block element is "auto", which means that it will expand to fill whatever space is available. If you think about any of the Web pages we've been building, each block element can expand to the entire width of the browser, and that's exactly what it does. Now, hold this thought, because we're going to go into this in detail in the next chapter. Just remember that "auto" allows the content to fill whatever space is available (after taking padding, border, and margin into account).

Q: What if I don't have any margin, padding, or borders?

A: Then your content gets to use the *entire* width of the box. If the width of content area is 300 pixels, and you have no padding, border, or margin, then the width of the entire box would also be 300 pixels.

Q: What are the different ways I can specify widths?

A: You can specify an actual size – usually in pixels – or you can specify a percentage. If you use a percentage, then the width is calculated as a percentage of the width of container the element is in (which could be the <body>, a <div>, etc.).

Q: What about the height?

A: In general, the height of an element is left at the default, which is auto, and the browser expands the content area vertically so all of the content is visible. Take a look at the elixirs section after we set the width to 200 pixels and you'll see the <div> got a lot taller.

You can explicitly set a height, but you risk cutting off the bottom of your content if your height isn't big enough to contain it. In general, leave your element heights unspecified so they default to auto. We're going to talk about this more in the next chapter as well.

Sharpen your pencil

Here's a box that has all the widths labelled. What is the width of the entire box?

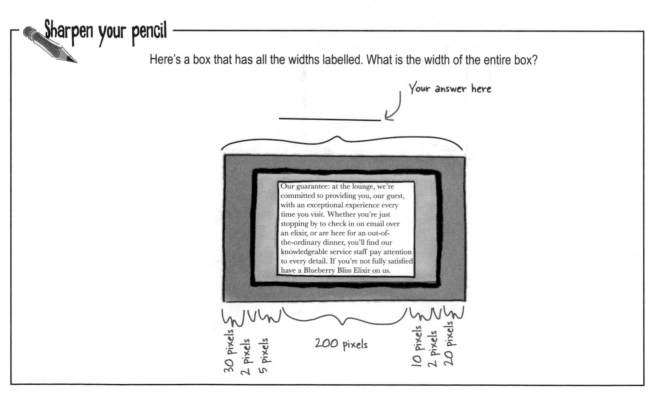

Your answer here

Our guarantee: at the lounge, we're committed to providing you, our guest, with an exceptional experience every time you visit. Whether you're just stopping by to check in on email over an elixir, or are here for an out-of-the-ordinary dinner, you'll find our knowledgeable service staff pay attention to every detail. If you're not fully satisfied have a Blueberry Bliss Elixir on us.

30 pixels 2 pixels 5 pixels   200 pixels   10 pixels 2 pixels 20 pixels

Adding the basic styles to the elixirs

We've got the width out of the way. What's left to do?

☑ First, we're going to change the width of the elixirs **<div>** to make it narrower.

☐ Next, we'll knock out some of the styles you're already familiar with, like padding, text alignment, and the background image.

We're doing this step next.

☐ Then all we've got left are the font line heights and the heading colors. You're going to see that you need to upgrade your CSS selector skills just a bit to get those changed.

Now we're going to concentrate on some of the basic styles, like the padding, the text alignment, and also getting that background image of the cocktail glasses in the elixirs **<div>**. You're already familiar with how most of this works, so let's take a quick look at the CSS:

Remember we're going to apply all this style to the elixirs <div> so that it only affects the <div> and the elements it contains, not the entire page.

The default padding on a <div> is 0 pixels, so we're going to add some padding to provide a bit of space for the content. Notice that we're not adding any padding at the top because there's already plenty of room there thanks to the default margin on the <h2> heading (look back at the last test drive and you'll see there's plenty of room above the <h2>). But we do need it on the right, bottom, and left.

```
#elixirs {
    border-width:       thin;
    border-style:       solid;
    border-color:       #007e7e;
    width:              200px;

    padding-right:      20px;
    padding-bottom:     20px;
    padding-left:       20px;

    margin-left:        20px;

    text-align:         center;

    background-image:   url(images/cocktail.gif);
    background-repeat:  repeat-x;
}
```

We're adding some margin on the left to indent the elixirs from the rest of the page a bit. This is going to come in handy later...

Use text-align on block elements to align the text they contain. Here we're going to center-align the text.

And finally we're specifying an image to use in the background, in this case the cocktail image. We're setting the background-repeat property to repeat-x, which will tile the image only in the horizontal direction.

Test driving the new styles

Now it's time to add those new properties to your "lounge.css" file and reload the page. Let's check out the changes: the headings, the images, and the text are all centered in the **<div>** and have a little more breathing room now that there's some padding in place. We've also got a little decoration at the top with the tiled cocktail image.

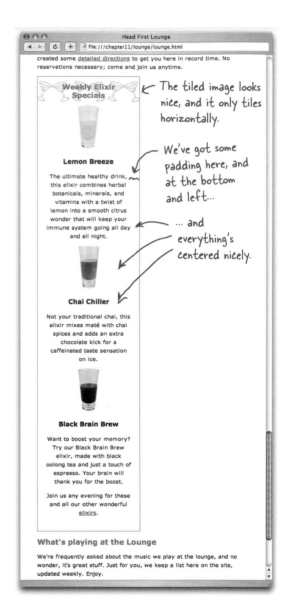

The tiled image looks nice, and it only tiles horizontally.

We've got some padding here, and at the bottom and left...

... and everything's centered nicely.

Wait just a sec... why does the *text*-align property affect the alignment of the images? Shouldn't it align only *text*? Seems like it should be called something else if it aligns images too.

Good point... it doesn't seem right, does it? But the truth is that text-align will align *all inline content* in a block element. So in this case, we're setting the property on the **<div>** block element and all its inline content is nicely centered as a result. Just remember that **text-align**, despite its name, works on any kind of inline element. One other thing to keep in mind: the **text-align** property should be set on block elements only. It has no effect if it's used directly on inline elements (like **<img>**).

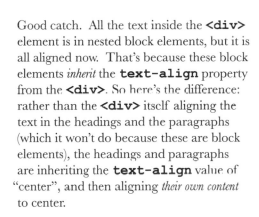

That's interesting because I noticed the text inside the <div> is all inside other block elements, like <h2>, <h3>, and <p>. So, if text-align is aligning *inline elements* in the <div> block element, how is the text in these nested block elements getting aligned?

Good catch. All the text inside the **<div>** element is in nested block elements, but it is all aligned now. That's because these block elements *inherit* the **text-align** property from the **<div>**. So here's the difference: rather than the **<div>** itself aligning the text in the headings and the paragraphs (which it won't do because these are block elements), the headings and paragraphs are inheriting the **text-align** value of "center", and then aligning *their own content* to center.

So what? Well, if you think about it, this gives you a lot of leverage when you use a **<div>**, because you can wrap a section of content in a **<div>** and then apply styles to the **<div>** rather than each individual element. Of course, keep in mind that not all properties are inherited by default, so this won't work for all properties.

Sharpen your pencil

So now that you understand widths, what's the total width of the elixirs box? To start with, we know the content area is 200 pixels. We've also set some left and right padding that affects the width, as well as a border that's set to "thin". Just assume a thin border is 1 pixel thick, like it is on most browsers. And what about margins? We set a left margin value, but no right margin value, so the right margin is 0 pixels by default.

Here are all the properties that relate to width. Your job is to figure out the total width of the elixirs <div>.

```
border-width:    thin;

width:           200px;

padding-right:   20px;
padding-bottom:  20px;
padding-left:    20px;

margin-left:     20px;
```

Weekly Elixir Specials

Lemon Breeze

The ultimate healthy drink, this elixir combines herbal botanicals, minerals, and vitamins with a twist of lemon into a smooth citrus wonder that will keep your immune system going all day and all night.

Chai Chiller

Not your traditional chai, this elixir mixes maté with chai spices and adds an extra chocolate kick for a caffeinated taste sensation on ice.

Black Brain Brew

Want to boost your memory? Try our Black Brain Brew elixir, made with black oolong tea and just a touch of espresso. Your brain will thank you for the boost.

Join us any evening for these and all our wonderful elixirs.

We're almost there...

We're close to having the elixirs done. What's left?

 First, we're going to change the width of the elixirs **<div>** to make it narrower.

 Next, we'll knock out some of the styles you're already familiar with, like padding, text alignment, and the background image.

☐ Then all we've got left are the text line heights and the heading ⟵ *We're on the last step.*
colors. You're going to see that you need to upgrade your CSS
selector skills just a bit to get those changed.

Sounds pretty easy, right? After all, you've done
all this before. In fact, given that you know
you can just set styles on the **<div>** and
they will be inherited, you can take care of
this real fast.

We've almost got this done, we just need to change the header colors and also the line height.

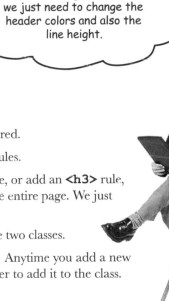

Frank: Yeah, this is interesting.
The main elixirs heading, which is
an **<h2>**, has the aquamarine color
because there is already an **<h2>** rule in
the CSS. But we need for that to be black. Then
we've got the **<h3>**s in the elixirs, which need to be red.

Jim: Yeah, no problem, we'll just add a few more rules.

Frank: But wait a sec... if we change the **<h2>** rule, or add an **<h3>** rule,
then we're going to change the heading colors on the entire page. We just
want these colors in the elixirs section.

Jim: Oh, good point. Hmmm... Well, we could use two classes.

Frank: That would work, although it's a bit messy. Anytime you add a new
heading to the elixirs **<div>** you'll have to remember to add it to the class.

Jim: Yeah, well, c'est la vie.

Frank: Actually Jim, before you use classes, go check out descendant
selectors. I think they'll work better here.

Jim: Descendant selectors?

Frank: Right, they're just a way of specifying a selector like "select an
<h2> element, but only if it's inside an elixirs **<div>**".

Joe: I'm not following.

Frank: Okay, let's step through this...

Frank *Jim*

What are we trying to do?

Let's take a quick look at what we're trying to do
to the heading colors.

What we have now

Here's just the main
heading elements in the
lounge XHTML.

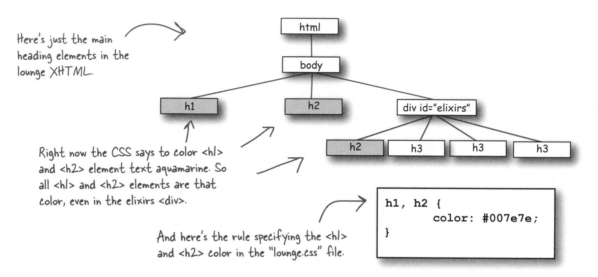

Right now the CSS says to color <h1>
and <h2> element text aquamarine. So
all <h1> and <h2> elements are that
color, even in the elixirs <div>.

And here's the rule specifying the <h1>
and <h2> color in the "lounge.css" file.

```
h1, h2 {
        color: #007e7e;
}
```

What we want

We want the <h1> and <h2> in
the main page to stay aquamarine.

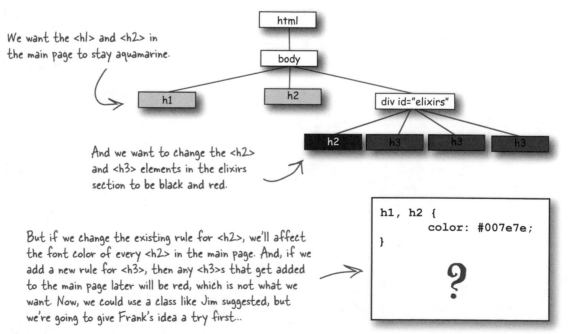

And we want to change the <h2>
and <h3> elements in the elixirs
section to be black and red.

But if we change the existing rule for <h2>, we'll affect
the font color of every <h2> in the main page. And, if we
add a new rule for <h3>, then any <h3>s that get added
to the main page later will be red, which is not what we
want. Now, we could use a class like Jim suggested, but
we're going to give Frank's idea a try first...

```
h1, h2 {
        color: #007e7e;
}

        ?
```

What we need is a way to select <u>descendants</u>

What we're really missing is a way to tell CSS that we want to only select elements that *descend* from certain elements, which is kinda like specifying that you only want your inheritance to go to the children of one daughter or son. Here's how you write a descendant selector.

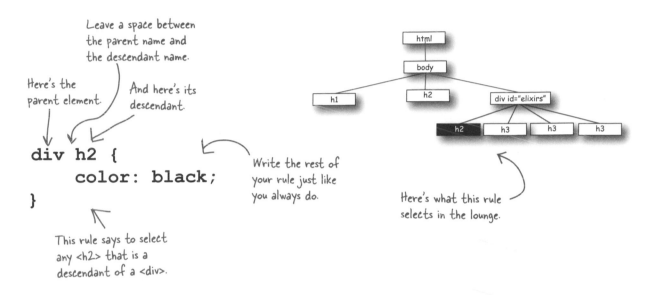

Leave a space between the parent name and the descendant name.

Here's the parent element.

And here's its descendant.

```
div h2 {
     color: black;
}
```

Write the rest of your rule just like you always do.

This rule says to select any <h2> that is a descendant of a <div>.

Here's what this rule selects in the lounge.

Now the only problem with this rule is that if someone created another **<div>** in the "lounge.html" file, they'd get black **<h2>** text, even if they didn't want it. But we've got an **id** on the elixirs **<div>**, so let's use it to be more specific about which descendants we want:

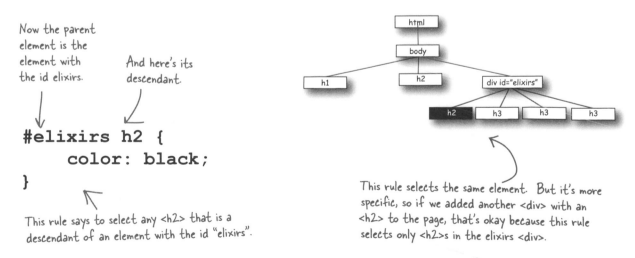

Now the parent element is the element with the id elixirs.

And here's its descendant.

```
#elixirs h2 {
     color: black;
}
```

This rule says to select any <h2> that is a descendant of an element with the id "elixirs".

This rule selects the same element. But it's more specific, so if we added another <div> with an <h2> to the page, that's okay because this rule selects only <h2>s in the elixirs <div>.

Sharpen your pencil

Your turn. Write the selector that selects only <h3> elements inside the elixirs <div>. In your rule, set the color property to #d12c47. Also label the elements in the graph below that are selected.

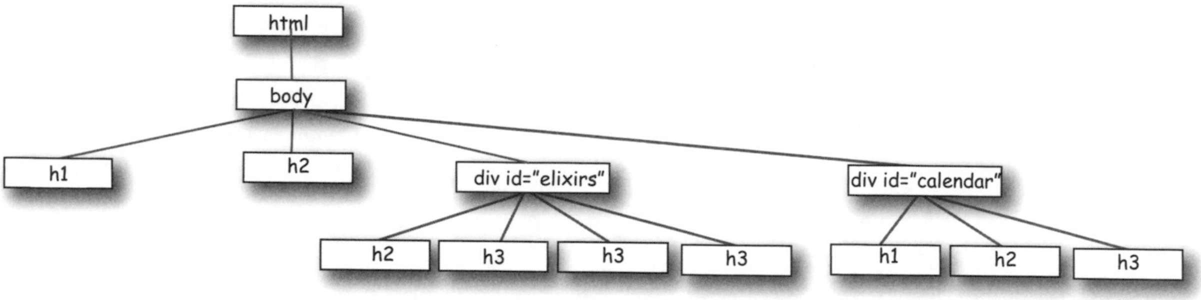

```
                        html

                        body

   h1          h2         div id="elixirs"                    div id="calendar"

                  h2     h3     h3      h3          h1     h2      h3
```

---

there are no
Dumb Questions

Q: **Descendant usually means child, grandchild, great-grandchild. Here, we're just selecting the child descendants, right?**

A: That's a really good point. The selector "#elixirs h2" means ANY descendant of elixirs, so the <h2> could be a direct child of the <div> or nested down inside a <blockquote> or another nested <div> (making it a grandchild) and so on. So a descendant selector selects any <h2> nested inside an element, no matter how deeply it is nested.

Q: **Well, is there a way to select a direct child?**

A: Yes. For example, you could use "#elixirs > h2", to select <h2> only if it is the direct child of an element with an id of "elixirs".

Q: **What if I need something more complex, like an <h2> that is the child of a <blockquote> that is in elixirs?**

A: It works the same way. Just use more descendants, like this:

```
#elixirs blockquote h2 {
    color: blue;
}
```

This selects any <h2> elements that descend from <blockquote>s that descend from an element with an id of "elixirs".

Changing the color of the elixir headings

Now that you know about descendant selectors, let's set the **<h2>** heading to
black and the **<h3>** headings to red in the elixirs. Here's how you do that:

```
#elixirs h2 {
    color: black;
}

#elixirs h3 {
    color: #d12c47;
}
```

↖ Here we're using the descendant
selectors to target just the <h2>
and <h3> elements in the elixirs <div>.
We're setting <h2> to black, and
<h3> to a red color, using a hex code.

A quick test drive...

Go ahead and add these new properties to the bottom of your
"lounge.css" file, save, and reload "lounge.html".

We've got black and red headings
in the elixirs section, and we
haven't affected the aquamarine
color being used for <h2>
headings in the main page.

Now all we need to do is
fix the line height.

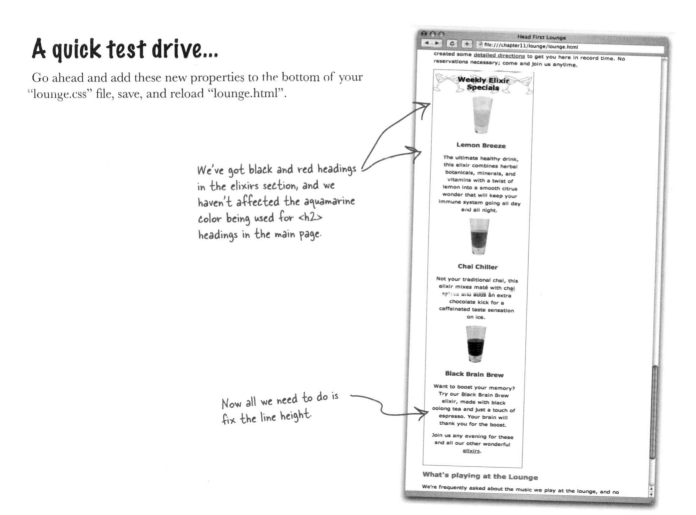

Fixing the line height

Recall that in the last chapter we made the line height of the text in the lounge a little taller than normal. This looks great, but in the elixirs we want our text to be a normal, single-spaced, line height to match the handout. Sounds easy enough, right? Just set the line-height property on the **<div>** and everything will be fine, because line-height is inherited. The only problem is that the headings will also inherit the line-height, and we'll end up with something like this.

```
#elixirs {
    line-height: 1em;
}
```

If you set the line-height property on the entire <div> then it will be inherited by all elements in the <div>, including the headings. Notice that the line height in the heading is too small and the two lines are starting to run together.

The reason that the line-height for the elixirs heading is too small is because every element in the elixirs **<div>** inherits the line-height of 1em, or "1 times the font size of the elixirs element", which in this case is "small", or about 12 pixels (depending on your browser). Remember, the elixirs **<div>** is inheriting its font-size from the **<body>** element, which we set to "small."

Here are the font sizes of the elements. We set body to "small", so that's inherited by elixirs.

The line-height of <h2> is set to 1 times the font size of elixirs, which is "small", or about 12 pixels.

body size is "small"
div id="elixirs" size is "small"
h2 is 120% of "small"

What we really want is for all the elements in the elixirs **<div>** to have a line-height that's based not on the font-size of the elixirs **<div>**, but rather the font-size of each element itself. We want the **<h2>** heading to have a line-height that is 1 times its font-size (which is 120% of "small"), and the **<p>** should also have a line-height of 1 times its font-size (which is "small"). How can you do this? Well, line-height is a bit special because you can use *just a number* instead of a relative measure – like em or % – for line-height. When you use just a number, you're telling each element in the elixirs **<div>** to have a line-height of 1 times its *own* font-size, rather than the font-size of the elixirs **<div>**. Give it a try; set the line-height of the elixirs **<div>** to 1, and you'll see that it fixes the heading.

We want <h2> to have a line-height that is 1 times its own font size, that is, 14 pixels (120% of small).

body line-height is 1.6 times "small"
div id="elixirs" line-height is 1 times "small", or about 12 pixels
h2 is 120% of "small" line-height is 1 times 120% of small, or about 14 pixels

```
#elixirs {
    line-height: 1;
}
```

Add a line-height of 1 to the elixirs <div> to change the line-height of each element in it.

The font-size of the p element is "small" (p inherits its font-size from the elixirs <div>) so it will have a line-height of 12 pixels, which is what we want.

Look what you've accomplished...

Take a look at the elixirs section now. You've completely transformed it, and now it looks just like the handout. And, other than adding a **<div>** and an **id** attribute to your XHTML, you were able to do this with just a few CSS rules and properties.

By now, you should be realizing just how powerful CSS is, and how flexible your Web pages are when you separate your structure (XHTML) from your presentation (CSS). You can give your XHTML a whole new look, simply by changing the CSS.

Remember, this is how the elixirs section looked when we started...

... and here's what it looks like now.

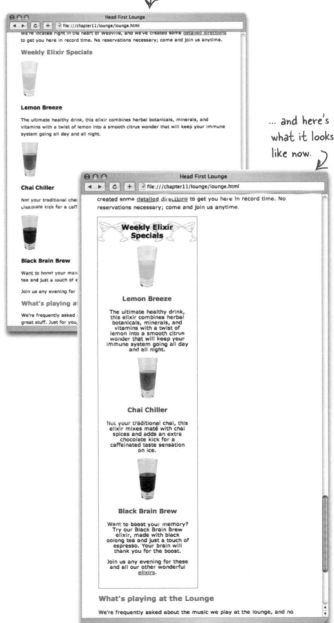

> Wow, that's fantastic! You were able to make the elixirs section on the Web site look like the handout, with just a little CSS.

It's time to take a little shortcut

You've probably noticed that there are quite a few CSS properties that seem to go together. For instance, **padding-left**, **padding-right**, **padding-bottom**, and **padding-top**. Margin properties are the same way. How about **background-image**, **background-color**, and **background-repeat**? Those all set different property values on the background of an element. Have you also noticed it gets a little tedious typing all those in? There are better things to spend your time on than typing all this, right?

```
padding-top:     0px;
padding-right:   20px;
padding-bottom:  30px;
padding-left:    10px;
```

That's a lot of typing just to specify four numbers.

Well, here's a special bonus for this chapter. You're going to learn how to specify all those values without risking carpal tunnel. Here's how:

Here's the old school way of specifying your padding.

```
padding-top:     0px;
padding-right:   20px;
padding-bottom:  30px;
padding-left:    10px;
```

And here's the new and improved way to write them as a <u>shorthand</u>.

```
padding: 0px 20px 30px 10px;
```
top   right   bottom   left

You can use the same sort of shorthand with margins:

```
margin-top:     0px;
margin-right:   20px;
margin-bottom:  30px;
margin-left:    10px;
```

```
margin: 0px 20px 30px 10px;
```
top   right   bottom   left

Just like padding, you can use a shorthand to specify all your margin values with one property.

If your padding or margins are the same value on all sides, you can make the shorthand *really* short:

```
padding-top:     20px;
padding-right:   20px;
padding-bottom:  20px;
padding-left:    20px;
```

```
padding: 20px;
```

This says that the padding should be 20 pixels on every side of the box.

If all your padding values are the same, then you can write it like this.

But there's more...

Here's another common way to abbreviate margins (or padding):

Shortcut Ahead

```
margin-top:      0px;
margin-right:    20px;
margin-bottom:   0px;
margin-left:     20px;
```

top and bottom are the same.

right and left are the same.

If the top and bottom, as well as the right and left margins are the same, then you can use a shorthand.

```
margin: 0px 20px;
```

top and bottom

right and left

And what about the border properties we mentioned?
You can use a shorthand for those too.

```
border-width:    thin;
border-style:    solid;
border-color:    #007e7e;
```

Rewrite border properties as one property. These can be in any order you like.

```
border: thin solid #007e7e;
```

The border shorthand is even more flexible than margins or padding because you can specify them in any order you like.

These are all perfectly valid border shorthands.

```
                              border: solid thin;

border: solid thin #007e7e;   border: #007e7e solid;

border: #007e7e solid thin;   border: solid;
```

...and don't forget the shorthand for backgrounds

You can also use shorthand for backgrounds:

```
background-color:  white;
background-image:  url(images/cocktail.gif);
background-repeat: repeat-x;
```

Like border, values can go in any order in this shorthand. There are also a few other values you can specify in the shorthand, like background-position.

```
background: white url(images/cocktail.gif) repeat-x;
```

And even more shorthands

No description of shorthands would be complete without mentioning font shorthands. Check out all the properties we need for fonts: **font-family**, **font-style**, **font-weight**, **font-size**, **font-variant**, and don't forget **line-height**. Well, there's a shorthand that wraps all these into one. Here's how it works:

Here are the properties that go into the font shorthand. Ordering matters here unless we say otherwise...

You must specify font size.

Finally you need to add your font families. You only need to specify one font, but alternatives are highly encouraged.

```
font:  font-style font-variant font-weight font-size/line-height font-family
```

These values are all optional. You can specify any combination of them, but they need to come before font-size.

The line-height is optional. If you want to specify one, just put a / right after the font-size and add your line height.

Use commas between your font family names.

So let's give this a try. Here are the font properties for the lounge body:

```
font-size: small;
font-family: Verdana, Helvetica, Arial, sans-serif;
line-height: 1.6em;
```

Now let's map those to the shorthand:

We're not using any of these, but that's okay, they're all optional.

```
font:  font-style font-variant font-weight font-size/line-height font-family
```

And now let's write the shorthand:

```
font: small/1.6em Verdana, Helvetica, Arial, sans-serif;
```

And here's the shorthand version. Wow, that's quite a shorthand, huh? You're going to be able to double your time at the slopes (or on the beach) now.

there are no Dumb Questions

Q: Should I always use shorthand?

A: Not necessarily. Some people find the long form more readable. Shorthands do have the advantage of reducing the size of your CSS files, and certainly they are more quickly entered because they require less typing. However, when there is a problem, they are a little more difficult to "debug" if you have incorrect values or the wrong order. So, you should use whichever form is more comfortable because they are both perfectly valid.

Q: Shorthands are more complex because I have to remember the ordering and what is and isn't optional. How do I memorize it all?

A: Well, you'll be surprised how quickly it becomes second nature, but those of us in the "biz" have a little secret we like to call a "reference manual." Just pick one up, and should you need to quickly look up property names or the syntax of a property, just grab your handy reference manual and look it up. We're particularly fond of the *CSS Pocket Reference* by Eric Meyer. It's tiny and makes a great reference.

Make it Stick

To remember the ordering of the padding and margin shorthand values, think of a clock labelled with top, right, bottom, and left. Then, always go in a clockwise direction: top to right to bottom to left.

```
margin: 0px 20px 30px 10px;
```
top   right   bottom   left

Exercise

It's time to put all your new knowledge to work. You'll notice that at the bottom of the lounge, there's a small section with copyright information that acts as a footer for the page. Add a <div> to make this into its own logical section. After you've done that style it with these properties:

```
font-size: 50%;
text-align: center;
line-height: normal;
margin-top: 30px;
```

Let's make the text really small. You know, FINE PRINT.

And let's center the text.

We're also setting the line-height to be "normal", which is a keyword you haven't seen yet. "Normal" allows the browser to pick an appropriate size for the line-height, which is typically based on the font.

And let's add some top margin to give the footer a little breathing room.

And while you're at it, have a look over the entire "lounge.css" file. Is there anywhere you might want to simplify things with shorthands? If so, go ahead and make those changes.

I saw the nice job you did on the elixirs. Can you give us a hand with the music recommendations on the site? We don't need much, just some simple styling.

The lounge's resident DJ.

What's playing at the Lounge

We're frequently asked about the music we play at the lounge, and no wonder, it's great stuff. Just for you, we keep a list here on the site, updated weekly. Enjoy.

- *Buddha Bar*, **Claude Challe**
- *When It Falls*, **Zero 7**
- *Earth 7*, **L.T.J. Bukem**
- *Le Roi Est Mort, Vive Le Roi!*, **Enigma**
- *Music for Airports*, **Brian Eno**

All the CD titles are in an italic font style.

And all the artists are in bold.

BRAIN POWER

What do you think is the best way to style the CD and artists in the "What's playing at the Lounge" section?

I was thinking we could just wrap <em> and <strong> elements around the CDs and artists. On most browsers that's going to give us italic and bold.

Jim

Frank

Frank: Yeah, but that's kind of like using a **<blockquote>** just to indent text. What I mean is that we don't really want to emphasize and strongly emphasize the CD and artists. We just want italic and bold. Plus, what if someone changes the style for **<em>** and **<strong>**? That would show up on the CDs and artists too.

Jim: Well, I actually thought about that, but I couldn't think of any other way to do it. I mean this is just text in the same list item. It's not like we have any way to style it.

Frank: What do you mean?

Jim: We can only style elements, and here we just have a bit of text, like, "Music for Airports, Brian Eno". We'd need an element around each piece of text to be able to style them differently.

Frank: Oh, right, right. I see what you mean.

Jim: I suppose we could use something like

```
<div class="cd">Music for Airports</div>

<div class="artist">Brian Eno</div>.
```

But that's a block element, so that is going to cause linebreaks.

Frank: Ahhh, I think you're on to something, Jim. There's another element like **<div>** that is for inline elements. It's called a **<span>**. That could work out perfectly.

Jim: I'm game. How does it work?

Frank: Well, a **<span>** gives you a way to create a grouping of inline characters and elements. Here, let's just give it a try...

Adding <span>s in three easy steps

<span> elements give you a way to logically separate inline content in the same way that **<div>**s allow you to create logical separation for block level content. To see how this works, we're going to style the music recommendations by first adding **<span>** elements around the CDs and artists, and then we'll write two CSS rules to style the **<span>**s. Here's exactly what you're going to do:

1 You're going to nest the CDs and artists in separate **<span>** elements.

2 You're going to add one **<span>** to the "cd" class and the other to the "artist" class.

3 You're going to create a rule to style the "cd" class with italic, and the "artist" class with bold.

Steps one and two: adding the <span>s

Open your "lounge.html" file and locate the "Who's playing at the Lounge" heading. Just below that you'll see the unordered list of recommendations. Here's what it looks like:

Each list item consists of a CD title, a comma, and then the music artist.

```
<ul>
<li>Buddha Bar, Claude Challe</li>
<li>When It Falls, Zero 7</li>
<li>Earth 7, L.T.J. Bukem</li>
<li>Le Roi Est Mort, Vive Le Roi!, Enigma</li>
<li>Music for Airports, Brian Eno</li>
</ul>
```

Let's try adding **<span>**s to the first CD and artist:

Just add a <span> opening tag along with the class attribute and a value of "cd".

Next, add a closing tag after the CD title.

Do the same for the artist. Nest it in a <span> element, only this time put the <span> in the "artist" class.

```
<ul>
<li><span class="cd">Buddha Bar</span>, <span class="artist">Claude Challe</span></li>
<li>When It Falls, Zero 7</li>
<li>Earth 7, L.T.J. Bukem</li>
<li>Le Roi Est Mort, Vive Le Roi!, Enigma</li>
<li>Music for Airports, Brian Eno</li>
</ul>
```

Step three: styling the <span>s

Before we move on, save the file and reload it in your browser. Like a **<div>**, by default a **<span>** has no effect on style, so you should see no changes.

Now let's add some style. Add these two rules to the bottom of your "lounge.css" file:

> We're going to add a rule for each of the new classes, cd and artist.

> For CDs we'll make the font style italic.

```
.cd {
        font-style: italic;
}

.artist {
        font-weight: bold;
}
```

> And for artists we'll set the font-weight to bold.

Test driving the spans

That's it. Save and reload. Here's what you'll see:

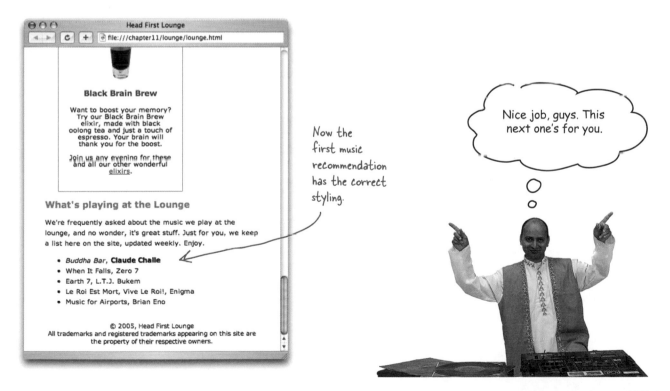

> Now the first music recommendation has the correct styling.

> Nice job, guys. This next one's for you.

Sharpen your pencil

You need to finish the job. Add <span> elements to the rest of the music recommendations and test your page. You'll find the solution in the back of the chapter.

```
<ul>
<li><span class="cd">Buddha Bar</span>, <span class="artist">Claude Challe</span></li>
<li>When It Falls, Zero 7</li>
<li>Earth 7, L.T.J. Bukem</li>
<li>Le Roi Est Mort, Vive Le Roi!, Enigma</li>
<li>Music for Airports, Brian Eno</li>
</ul>
```

there are no Dumb Questions

Q: When do I use a <span> rather than another inline element like <em> or <strong>?

A: As always, you want to mark up your content with the element that most closely matches the meaning of your content. So, if you are emphasizing words, use <em>; if you're trying to make a big point, use <strong>. But, if what you really want is to change the style of certain words, say, the names of albums or music artists on a fan site Web page, then you should use a <span> and put your <span> elements into appropriate classes to group them and style them.

Q: Can I set properties like width on <span> elements? Actually, what about inline elements in general?

A: You can set the width of inline elements like <span>, <em> and <strong>, but you won't notice any effect until you position them (which you'll learn how to do in the next chapter). You can also add margin and padding to these elements, as well as a border. Margins and padding on inline elements work a little differently from block elements – if you add a margin on all sides of an inline element, you'll only see space added to the left and right. You can add padding to the top and bottom of an inline element, but the padding doesn't affect the spacing of the other inline elements around

it, so the padding will overlap other inline elements.

Images are a little different from other inline elements. The width, padding, and margin properties all behave more like they do for a block element. Remember from Chapter 5: if you set the width of an image using either the width attribute in the <img> element or the width property in CSS, the browser scales the image to fit the width you specify. This can sometimes be handy if you can't edit the image yourself to change the dimensions, and you want the image to appear bigger or smaller on the page. But remember, if you rely on the browser to scale your image, you may be downloading more data than you need (if the image is larger than you need).

Hey guys, I know you think you're about done, but you forgot to style the links. They're still that default blue color, which kinda clashes with our site.

Think about the <a> element. Is there something about its style that seems different from other elements?

The <a> element and its multiple personalities

Have you noticed that links act a little differently when it comes to style? Links are chameleons of the element world because, depending on the circumstance, they can change their style at a moment's notice. Let's take a closer look:

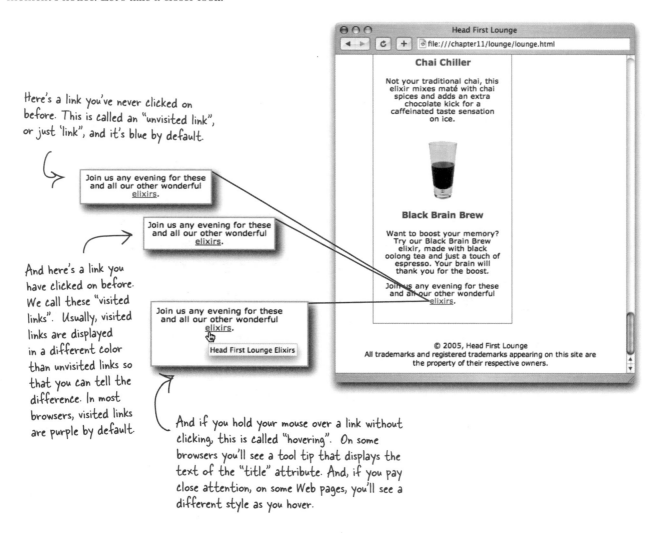

Here's a link you've never clicked on before. This is called an "unvisited link", or just 'link', and it's blue by default.

And here's a link you have clicked on before. We call these "visited links". Usually, visited links are displayed in a different color than unvisited links so that you can tell the difference. In most browsers, visited links are purple by default.

And if you hold your mouse over a link without clicking, this is called "hovering". On some browsers you'll see a tool tip that displays the text of the "title" attribute. And, if you pay close attention, on some Web pages, you'll see a different style as you hover.

Unlike other elements, the style of an **<a>** element changes depending on its *state*. If the link has never been clicked on, it has one style, and if it has been clicked on, another. And if you hover over a link, it can have yet another style. Perhaps there's more to styling **<a>** elements than meets the eye? You betcha... let's take a look.

How can you style elements based on their state?

A link can be in a few states: it can be unvisited, visited, or in the "hover" state (and a couple of other states too). So, how do you take advantage of all those states? For instance, it would be nice to be able to specify what the visited and unvisited colors are. Or maybe highlight the link when the user is hovering over it. If only there were a way...

Well, of course there is, but if we told you it involves using *pseudo-classes* you'd probably just decide you've read enough for the night, and close the book. Right? But hold on! Pretend we never said the word *pseudo-class* and let's just look at how you can style your links:

Notice we have the element <a>, followed by a ":", followed by the state we want to select.

```
a:link {
    color: green;
}
```
This selector is applied to links when they are in an unvisited state.

```
a:visited {
    color: red;
}
```
And this selector is applied to links when they are visited.

```
a:hover {
    color: yellow;
}
```
And this selector is applied when you hover over a link.

Exercise

Add these rules to the bottom of your "lounge.css" file and then save and reload "lounge.html". Play around with the links to see them in each state. Note that you might have to clear your browser history to see the unvisited color (green). *Once you're done, make sure you take these rules out of your "lounge.css" file before you continue.*

The Pseudo-class Exposed

This week's interview: getting to know the pseudo-class.

Head First: Welcome, Pseudo-class. It's a pleasure to have you here. I must confess that when they first asked me to do this interview, I drew a blank. Pseudo-class? The only thing that came to mind was that '80s Phil Collins song.

Pseudo-class: Uh, that would be *Sussudio*. My name is *Pseudo*.

Head First: Oops. Honest mistake. Maybe we could start there. Can you tell us a little about where Pseudo came from?

Pseudo-class: Pseudo usually means something that looks like the real thing, but isn't.

Head First: And the last name? Class?

Pseudo-class: Everyone knows what a CSS class is. It's a grouping you create to place elements in so you can style them together. Put "pseudo" and "class" together and you have a pseudo-class: it acts like a class, but it isn't a real class.

Head First: What's not real about it if it acts like a class?

Pseudo-class: Okay, open up an XHTML file and look for the class :visited, or :link, or :hover. Let me know when you find one.

Head First: I don't see any.

Pseudo-class: And yet, a:link, a:visited, and even a:hover all allow you to specify style, just like they were classes. So, those are pseudo-classes. In other words, you can style pseudo-classes, but no one ever types them into their XHTML.

Head First: Well then, how do they work?

Pseudo-class: You can thank your browser for that. The browser goes through and adds all your **<a>** elements to the right pseudo-classes. If a link's been visited, no problem; it goes into the "visited" class. Is the user hovering over a link? No problem, the browser throws it in the "hover" class. Oh, now the user isn't hovering? The browser yanks it out of the "hover" class.

Head First: Wow, I never knew. So there are all these classes out there that the browser is adding and removing elements from behind the scenes.

Pseudo-class: That's right, and it's damned important to know about, otherwise how would you give your links style that adapted to what state the link was in?

Head First: So, Pseudo, do you just do links?

Pseudo-class: No, I do other elements too. Some browsers already support pseudo-classes like active and hover on other types of elements. And there are some other pseudo-classes, too. For instance, the pseudo-class :first-child is assigned to the first child of any element, like the first paragraph in a **<blockquote>**. But be careful on everything other than :link, :visited, and :hover because browser support isn't fully there yet.

Head First: Well, I've certainly learned something in this interview. Who knew that song was actually called "Sussudio"?! Thanks for being here Pseudo-class.

Putting those pseudo-classes to work

Okay, let's be honest. You've probably just learned the most important thing in this book: pseudo-classes. Why? No, no, not because it allows you to style elements based on various "classes" your browser decides they belong to, like `:link` or `:first-child`. And, no, not because they give you really powerful ways to style elements based on things that happen while your visitors are using your page, like `:hover`. It's because the next time you're in that design meeting and you start talking about pseudo-classes with a real understanding, you're going to move to the *head of the class*. We're talking promotions and bonuses... at a minimum, the awe and respect of your fellow Web buddies.

So, let's put those pseudo-classes to good use. You've already added some pseudo-class rules to your "lounge.css" and they had a dramatic impact on the look of the links, but they're probably not quite right for the lounge. So let's rework the style a little:

Okay, big change here. We're using a descendant selector combined with a pseudo-class. The first selector says to select any unvisited <a> element that is nested in an element with the id "elixirs". So we're JUST styling the links inside elixirs.

```
#elixirs a:link {
    color: #007e7e;
}
```
On these two we're setting the color. For unvisited links, a nice aquamarine...

```
#elixirs a:visited {
    color: #333333;
}
```
...and for visited links we're using a dark gray.

```
#elixirs a:hover {
    background: #f88396;
    color: #0d5353;
}
```
Now for the really interesting rule. When the user is hovering over the link, we're changing the background to red. This makes the link look highlighted when you pass the mouse over it. Give it a try!

Exercise

Open up your "lounge.css" and rework your a:link, a:visited, and a:hover rules to use the new descendant selector and the new style definitions. Save, reload, and turn the page.

Test drive the links

When you reload you should see some new style in the elixirs section. Keep in mind, to see the unvisited links you may have to clear your browser's history, otherwise the browser will know you've visited these links before.

Now we've got green unvisited links, gray visited links, and a very cool red highlight when you hover over the link.

Sharpen your pencil

Your job is to give the "detailed directions" link in the lounge some style. Just like the elixirs link, we want all unvisited links to be aquamarine, and all visited links to be gray. However, we don't want the other links in the lounge to have any hover style... that's unique to the elixirs. So, how would you do it? Fill in the blanks to give the "detailed directions" link, and any other links you might add to the lounge later, this style. Check your answer in the back of the chapter and then make the changes in your lounge files.

_____ { _____ : #007e7e;   }

_____ { _____ : #333333;   }

Isn't it about time we talk about the "cascade"?

Well, well, we're quite far into this book (473 pages to be exact) and we still haven't told you what the "Cascade" in *Cascading* Style Sheets is all about. Truth be told, you have to know a lot about CSS to fully understand the cascade. But guess what, you're almost there, so wait no more.

Here's just one last piece of information you need to understand the cascade. You already know about using multiple style sheets to either better organize your styles or to support different types of devices. But there are actually some other style sheets hanging around when your users visit your pages. Let's take a look:

First, there are all the style sheets you've written for your page.

The Author (that's you!)

Note that there is a way for a reader to actually override your styles. To do that they put "!important" at the end of a property declaration.

But some browsers also allow users to create their own styles for XHTML elements. If your style sheet doesn't define these styles, the user's style sheet is used instead.

The Reader (your users)

And finally, you already know that the browser itself maintains a set of default styles that are used if you don't define the styles for an element. These are also the styles that are used if you don't have any author or reader style sheets.

When the browser needs to determine which style to apply to an element, it uses all these style sheets. Priority is given first to the author's styles (that is, your styles), then to the reader's styles, and then finally to the browser's default styles.

The Browser

So, to review, as the page authors, we can use multiple style sheets with our XHTML. And, the user might also supply their own styles, and then the browser has its default styles, too. And on top of all that we might have multiple selectors that apply to the same element. How do we figure out which styles an element gets?

That's actually another way of asking what cascade does. The cascade is the way the browser decides, given a bunch of styles in a bunch of style sheets, which style is going to be used. To answer that question we need to bring everything together – all the various style sheets hanging around, the rules, and the individual property declarations in those rules.

In the next two pages we're going to step through the nitty gritty details of how all this works. The details involve a lot of sorting and various details of determining which rules are the most specific with respect to an element. But here's the payoff: after going through the next two pages, you'll be able to get to the bottom of any styles that don't seem to be applied in the way you expect, and further, you're going to understand more about the cascade than 99% of Web page developers out there (we're not kidding).

The cascade

For this exercise, you need to "be the browser". Let's say you've got an **\<h1\>** element on a page and you want to know the **font-size** property for it. Here's how you do it:

Step one:

Gather all your style sheets together.

For this step you need ALL the styles sheets: the style sheets the Web page author has written, any style sheets that the reader has added to the mix, and the browser's default styles. (Remember, *you're* the browser now, so you have access to all this stuff!)

Step two:

Find all the declarations that match.

We're looking specifically for the **font-size** property, so look at all the declarations for **font-size** that have a selector which could possibly select the **\<h1\>** element. Go through all the style sheets and pull out any rules that match **\<h1\>** and also have a **font-size** property.

Step three:

Now take all your matches, and sort them.

Now that you've got all the matching rules together, sort them in the order of author, reader, browser. In other words, if you wrote them as the author of the page, then they are more important than if the reader wrote them. And, in turn, the reader's styles are more important than the browser's default styles.

Remember we mentioned that the reader could put !important on their CSS properties, and if they do that, those properties come first when you sort.

Step four:

Now sort all the declarations by how specific they are.

Remember, we talked about this a little, way back in Chapter 8. You can intuitively think about a rule being more specific if it more accurately selects an element; for instance, the descendant selector "blockquote h1" is more specific than just the "h1" selector because it only selects **\<h1\>**s inside of **\<blockquote\>**s. But there is a little recipe you can follow to calculate exactly how specific a selector is, and we'll do that on the next page.

Step five:

Finally, sort any conflicting rules in the order they appear in their individual style sheets.

Now you just need to take the list, and order any conflicting rules so that the ones appearing later (closer to the bottom) of their respective style sheets are more important. That way, if you put a new rule in your style sheet, it can override any rules before it.

That's it! The first rule in the sorted list is the winner, and its **font-size** property is the one to use. Now let's see how you determine how specific a selector is.

Welcome to the "What's my specificity game"

In the old days we used four numbers, but that was before XHTML... aren't you glad you're learning this now?

To calculate the specificity you start with a set of three numbers, like this:

0 0 0

And then we just tally up various things from the selector, like this:

Does the selector have any ids? One point each.

Does the selector have any classes or pseudo-classes? One point each.

Does the selector have any element names? One point for each.

0 0 0

For instance, the selector "h1" has one element in it, so you get:

Read this as the number one. → **0 0 1**

Both "h1" and "h1.blue" have one element, so they both get a "1" in the right most number column.

As another example, the selector "h1.blue" has one element and one class, so you'd get:

Read this as the number eleven. → **0 1 1**

"h1.blue" also has one class, so it gets a "1" in the middle number column.

Neither have ids in their selectors, so they both get a "0" in the left number column

After you've tallied up all the ids, classes, and elements, the bigger the specificity number, the more specific the rule. So, since "h1.blue" has a specificity of 11, it is more specific than "h1", which has a specificity number of 1.

✏ Sharpen your pencil

Try your hand at calculating the specificity of these selectors using the rules above:

h1.greentea _____	ol li p _____	em _____
p img _____	.green _____	span.cd _____
a:link _____	#elixirs h1 _____	#sidebar _____

there are no
Dumb Questions

Q: What makes a specificity number bigger than another?

A: Just read them like real numbers: 100 (one hundred) is bigger than 010 (ten) which is bigger than 001 (one), and so on.

Q: What about a rule like "h1, h2"; what is its specificity?

A: Think of that as two separate rules: an "h1" rule, which has a specificity of "001" and an "h2" rule that also has a specificity of "001".

Q: Can you say more about the !important thing?

A: The reader can override a style by putting an "!important" on the end of their property declarations like this:

```
h1 {
    font-size: 200%
!important;
}
```

and this will override any author styles.

Q: I can't get the reader's style sheet, so how can I ever figure out the way the cascade works?

A: You can't, but look at it this way: if the reader overrides your styles, then that is really beyond your control. So just make your pages look like you want them to using your styles. If the reader chooses to override them, then they'll get what they ask for (for better or for worse).

Putting it all together

Woo hoo! It's time for an example. Say you want to know the **color** property for this **<h1>** element:

```
<h1 class="blueberry">Blueberry Bliss Elixir</h1>
```

Let's take this through all the cascade steps:

Remember, you're the browser, because you're trying to figure out how to display this <h1> element.

Step one:

Gather all your style sheets together.

```
h1 {
    color: black;
}
```

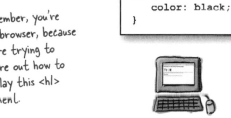

The Browser

That's you (for now).

```
h1 {
    color: #efefef;
}

h1.blueberry {
    color: blue;
}
```

```
body h1 {
    color: #cccccc;
}
```

The Author

Usually, you're the author (the person writing the CSS). But right now, you're the browser.

The Reader

The person using the browser.

Step two:

Find all the declarations that match.

Here are all the rules that could possibly match the <h1> element and that contain the color property.

Reader
```
body h1 {
    color: #cccccc;
}
```

Browser
```
h1 {
    color: black;
}
```

Author
```
h1 {
    color: #efefef;
}
```
```
h1.blueberry {
    color: blue;
}
```

Step three:

Now take all your matches, and sort them by author, reader, browser.

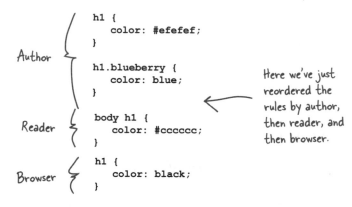

Author
```
h1 {
    color: #efefef;
}
```
```
h1.blueberry {
    color: blue;
}
```

Reader
```
body h1 {
    color: #cccccc;
}
```

Browser
```
h1 {
    color: black;
}
```

Here we've just reordered the rules by author, then reader, and then browser.

Step four:

Now sort the declarations by how specific they are. To do that we need to first calculate each specificity score, and then reorder the rules.

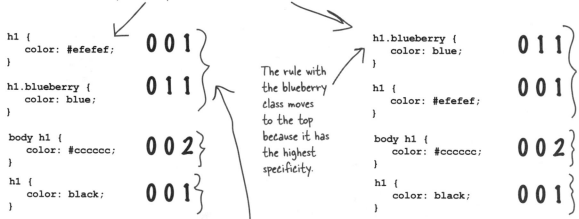

```
h1 {
    color: #efefef;
}
```
0 0 1

```
h1.blueberry {
    color: blue;
}
```
0 1 1

```
body h1 {
    color: #cccccc;
}
```
0 0 2

```
h1 {
    color: black;
}
```
0 0 1

The rule with the blueberry class moves to the top because it has the highest specificity.

```
h1.blueberry {
    color: blue;
}
```
0 1 1

```
h1 {
    color: #efefef;
}
```
0 0 1

```
body h1 {
    color: #cccccc;
}
```
0 0 2

```
h1 {
    color: black;
}
```
0 0 1

Notice that we only sort <u>within</u> the author, reader, and browser categories. We don't re-sort the entire list, or else the "body h1" rule would move above the "h1" rule set by the author.

Step five:

Finally, sort any conflicting rules in the order that they appear in their individual style sheets.

We're okay here, because we don't have any conflicting rules at this point. The blueberry, with a score of 11, is the clear winner. If there had been two rules with a score of 011, then the rule appearing latest would be the winner.

```
h1.blueberry {
    color: blue;
}

h1 {
    color: #efefef;
}
```
Author

```
body h1 {
    color: #cccccc;
}
```
Reader

```
h1 {
    color: black;
}
```
Browser

We have a winner...

After sweating through the first choice of elements, the sorting, more sorting, and being judged on specificity, the "h1.blueberry" rule has risen to the top. So the color property in the <h1> element will be blue.

there are no Dumb Questions

Q: So, one more time: I get that the lower in the CSS file the higher the precedence, but how does having multiple links to style sheets in my XHTML work?

A: It's always top to bottom, whether it is in the same CSS file or not. Just pretend that you inserted the CSS all together right into your file in the order the files are linked. That's the order that counts.

Q: So when you sort for specificity, you don't re-sort everything?

A: No. Think of each time you sort as refining what you've done before. So first you sort for author, reader, browser. Then, within each of those sortings, you sort for specificity. And then, for any elements that have the same specificity, you sort again based on the ordering in the style sheets.

Q: Do readers really make their own style sheets?

A: By and large, no. But there are cases where people with visual impairments do, and of course you've always got the crowd that just has to tinker with everything. But, since each reader is controlling only how they see things, it really shouldn't factor into your designs.

Q: How much of this do I really need to remember?

A: You're going to develop some intuition for how all these style sheets fit together, and on a day to day basis that intuition will get you a long way. Every once in a while, though, you'll see a style popping up in your pages that just boggles your mind, and that's when you fall back on your training. You'll be able to work through the cascade and before you know it, you'll know exactly what's happening in your page.

> So, what happens if, after all this, I still don't have any rules with a property declaration for the property value I'm trying to figure out?

Ah, good question. We actually talked about this a little in Chapter 8. If you don't find a match for the property in any rules in the cascade, then you try to use inheritance. Remember that not all properties are inherited, like border properties for instance. But for the properties that *are* inherited (like color, font-family, line-height, and so on), the browser looks at the ancestors of the element, starting with its parent, and tries to find a value for the property. If it does, there's your property value.

> Got it. Hey, but what if the property isn't inherited or I can't find a value in the ancestor's rules? Then what?

Then the only thing left to do is fall back on the default values that are set in the browser's style sheets, and all browsers should have default styles for every element.

> Oh, and why is this called the "cascade" anyway?

The name "cascade" was chosen because of the way that styles coming from multiple style sheets can all "cascade" down into the page, with the most specific styling being applied to each element. (If that doesn't clear things right up for you about why it's called cascade, don't feel bad. It didn't make it any clearer for us, either. Just call it "CSS" and move on.)

STOP! Do this exercise before
going on to the next chapter!

This is a special brain power; so special that we're going to let
you think about it between chapters. Here's what you need to do:

1 Open the file "lounge.html" and locate the elixirs **<div>**.

2 Move the entire elixirs **<div>** section to the top of the
file so it's just below the paragraph that contains the
lounge logo.

3 Save and reload your page. What changed?

4 Open the file "lounge.css".

5 Locate the "#elixirs" rule.

6 Add this declaration at the bottom of the rule:

```
float: right;
```

7 Save your file, and reload the page in your browser.

What changed? What do you think this declaration does?

BULLET POINTS

- <div> elements are used to group related elements together into logical sections.

- Creating logical sections can help you identify the main content areas, header, and footer of your page.

- You can use <div> elements to group elements together that need a common style.

- Use nested <div> elements to add further structure to your files for clarity or styling. But don't add structure unless you really need it.

- Once you have grouped together sections of content with <div> elements, you can style the <div>s just like you would any other block element. For example, you can add a border around a group of elements using the border property on the <div> they are nested in.

- The width property sets the width of the content area of an element.

- The total width of an element is the width of the content area, plus the width of any padding, border, and margins you add.

- Once you set the width of an element, it no longer expands to fit the entire width of the browser window.

- Text-align is a property for block elements that centers all inline content in the block element. It is inherited by any nested block elements.

- You can use descendant selectors to select elements nested within other elements. For instance, the descendant selector
  ```
  div h2 { ... }
  ```
  selects all <h2>s nested in <div> elements (including children, grandchildren, etc.).

- You can use shortcuts for related properties. For instance, padding-top, padding-right, padding-bottom, and padding-left are all related to padding, and can be specified with one shortcut rule, padding.

- Padding, margin, border, background, and font properties can all be specified with shortcuts.

- The <span> inline element is similar to the <div> element: it is used to group together related inline elements and text.

- Just like with <div>, you can add <span> elements to classes (or give <span> elements unique ids) to style them.

- The <a> element is an example of an element with different states. The main <a> element states are unvisited, visited, and hover.

- You can style each of these states separately with pseudo-classes. The pseudo-classes used most often with the <a> element are :link, for unvisited links, :visited, for visited links, and :hover, for the hover state.

- Other elements support the :hover pseudo-class, and some browsers also support the :first-child, :active, and :focus pseudo-classes for other elements.

XHTMLcross on Vacation

Since you've got a Super Brain Power to work on, we gave the XHTMLcross a vacation in this chapter. Don't worry, he'll be back in the next one.

Sharpen your pencil
Solution

Here's a box that has all the widths labelled. Your job was to figure out the width of an entire box. Here's the solution.

$$30 + 2 + 5 + 200 + 10 + 2 + 20 = \underline{269}$$

Sharpen your pencil
Solution

So now that you understand widths, what's the total width of the elixirs box? To start with, we know the content area is 200 pixels. We've also set some left and right padding that affects the width, as well as a border that's set to "thin". Just assume a thin border is 1 pixel thick, like it is on most browsers. And what about margins? We set a left margin, but no right margin, so the right margin is 0 pixels by default.

Your job was to figure out the total width of the elixirs <div>. Here's the solution.

$$20 + 20 + 200 + 1 + 1 + 0 + 20 = 262$$

left padding right padding content area left border right border right margin left margin

Sharpen your pencil
Solution

Your turn. Write the selector that selects only <h3> elements inside the elixirs <div>. In your rule, set the color property to #d12c47. Also label the elements in the graph below that are selected. Here's the solution.

```
#elixirs h3 {
    color: #d12c47;
}
```

Here's the rule. We select any <h3> descendant of an element with the id elixirs. And here's what the graph looks like.

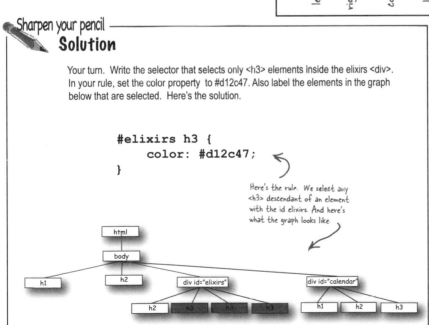

Exercise Solutions

It's time to put all your new knowledge to work. You'll notice at the bottom of the lounge there's a small section with copyright information that acts as a footer for the page. Add a <div> to make this into its own logical section. After you've done that style it with these properties:

```
font-size: 50%;
text-align: center;
line-height: normal;
margin-top: 30px;
```

Let's make the text really small. You know, FINE PRINT.

And let's center the text.

We're also setting the line-height to be "normal".

And let's add some top margin to give the footer a little breathing room.

Place <div> tags around the copyright information.

And give it an id named "footer".

```
<div id="footer">
  <p>
    &copy; 2005, Head First Lounge<br />
    All trademarks and registered trademarks appearing on
    this site are the property of their respective owners.
  </p>
</div>
```

And here's the CSS for the footer.

```
#footer {
    font-size: 50%;
    text-align: center;
    line-height: normal;
    margin-top: 30px;
}
```

Solution

Your job was to finish adding the <span> elements to the rest of the music recommendations and test your page. Here's the solution:

```
<ul>
<li><span class="cd">Buddha Bar</span>,
    <span class="artist">Claude Challe</span></li>
<li><span class="cd">When It Falls</span>,
    <span class="artist">Zero 7</span></li>
<li><span class="cd">Earth 7</span>,
    <span class="artist">L.T.J. Bukem</span></li>
<li><span class="cd">Le Roi Est Mort, Vive Le Roi!</span>,
    <span class="artist">Enigma</span></li>
<li><span class="cd">Music for Airports</span>,
    <span class="artist">Brian Eno</span></li>
</ul>
```

What's playing at the Lounge

We're frequently asked about the music we play at the lounge, and no wonder, It's great stuff. Just for you, we keep a list here on the site, updated weekly. Enjoy.

- *Buddha Bar*, **Claude Challe**
- *When It Falls*, **Zero 7**
- *Earth 7*, **L.T.J. Bukem**
- *Le Roi Est Mort, Vive Le Roi!*, **Enigma**
- *Music for Airports*, **Brian Eno**

Sharpen your pencil

Solution

Your job is to give the "detailed directions" link in the lounge some style. Just like the elixirs link, we want all unvisited links to be aquamarine, and all visited links to be gray. However, we don't want the other links in the lounge to have any hover style... that's unique to the elixirs. So, how would you do it? Fill in the blanks to give the "detailed directions" link, and any other links you might add to the lounge later, this style. Here's the solution.

<u>a:link</u> { <u>color</u> : #007e7e; }

<u>a:visited</u> { <u>color</u> : #333333; }

Sharpen your pencil

Solution

Try your hand at caclulating the specificity of these selectors using the cascade rules. Here's the solution.

Selector	Specificity	Selector	Specificity	Selector	Specificity
h1.greentea	0 1 1	ol li p	0 0 3	em	0 0 1
p img	0 0 2	.green	0 1 0	span.cd	0 1 1
a:link	0 1 1	#elixirs h1	1 0 1	#sidebar	1 0 0

12 layout and positioning

Arranging Elements

You can bet all *my* divs and spans are in the right place.

It's time to teach your XHTML elements new tricks. We're not going to let those XHTML elements just sit there anymore – it's about time they get up and help us create some pages with real *layouts*. How? Well, you've got a good feel for the <div> and <span> structural elements and you know all about how the box model works, right? So, now it's time to use all that knowledge to craft some real designs. No, we're not just talking about more background and font colors, we're talking about full blown professional designs using multi-column layouts. This is the chapter where everything you've learned comes together.

Did you do the Super Brain Power?

If you didn't do the SUPER BRAIN POWER at the end of the last chapter, then march right back there and do it. It's required.

Okay, now that we have that out of the way, at the end of the last chapter, we left you with a bit of a cliffhanger. We asked you to move the elixirs **<div>** up under the logo, and then add one little property to the elixirs rule in your CSS, like this:

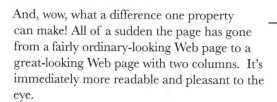

And, wow, what a difference one property can make! All of a sudden the page has gone from a fairly ordinary-looking Web page to a great-looking Web page with two columns. It's immediately more readable and pleasant to the eye.

So what's the magic? How did this seemingly innocent little property produce such big effects? And, can we use this property to do even more interesting things with our pages? Well, of course, this is Head First, after all. But first, you're going to need to learn how a browser lays out elements on a page. Once you know that, we can talk about all kinds of ways you can alter how it does that layout, and also how you can start to position your elements on the page.

Here's the good news: you already know all about block elements and inline elements, and you even know about the box model. These are the real foundations of how the browser puts a page together. Now all you need to know is exactly how the browser takes all the elements in a page, and decides where they go.

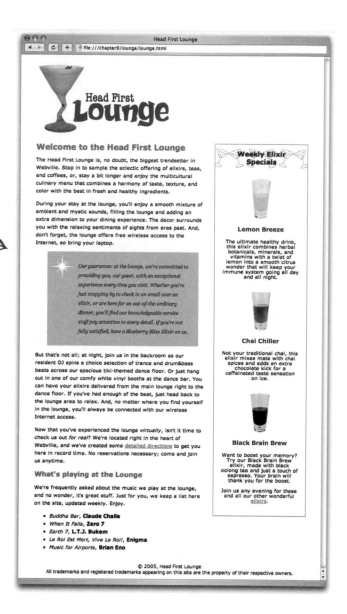

Use the flow, Luke

The Flow is what gives a CSS master his power. It's an energy field created by all living things. It surrounds us and penetrates us. It binds the galaxy together....
Oh, sorry.

Flow is what the browser uses to lay out a page of XHTML elements. The browser starts at the top of any XHTML file and follows the flow of elements from top to bottom, displaying each element it encounters. And, just considering the block elements for a moment, it puts a linebreak between each one. So the first element in a file is displayed first, then a linebreak, followed by the second element, then a linebreak, and so on, from the top of your file to the bottom. That's flow.

Here's a little "abbreviated" XHTML.

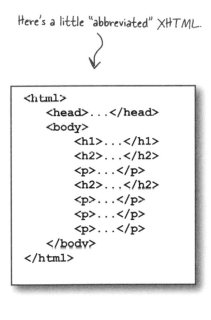

And here's the XHTML flowed onto a page.

Each block element is taken in the order it appears in the markup, and placed on the page.

Each new block element causes a linebreak.

Notice that elements take up the full width of the page.

Here's your page. Flow the block elements in "lounge.html" here.

BE the Browser

Open your "lounge.html" file and locate all the block elements. Flow each one on to the page to the left. Just concentrate on the block elements nested directly inside the body element. You can also ignore the "float" property in your CSS because you don't know what it does yet. Check your answer before moving on.

Here are all the block elements you'll need to complete the job.

h1

h2

p

div

ul

What about inline elements?

So you know that block elements flow top to bottom, with a linebreak in between each element. Easy enough. What about the inline elements?

Inline elements are flowed next to each other, horizontally, from top left to bottom right. Here's how that works.

Here's another little snippet of XHTML.

```
<p>
Join us <em>any evening</em> for
these and all our other wonderful <a
href="beverages/elixir.html" title="Head
First Lounge Elixirs">elixirs</a>.
</p>
```

If we take the inline content of this <p> element and flow it onto the page, we start at the top left.

The inline elements are laid next to one another horizontally, as long as there is room on the right to place them.

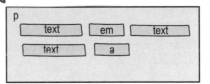

Here, there's room to fit all the inline elements horizontally. Notice that text is a special case of an inline element. The browser breaks it into inline elements that are the right size to fit the space.

So what if we make the browser window a little thinner, or we reduce the size of the content area with the width property? Then there's less room to place the inline elements in. Let's see how this works.

Now the content has been flowed left to right until there's no more room, and then the content is placed on the next line. Notice the browser had to break the text up a little differently to make it fit nicely.

And if we make the content area even thinner, look what happens. The browser uses as many lines as necessary to flow the content into the space.

How it all works together

Now that you know how block and inline elements are flowed, let's put them together. We'll use a typical page with headings, paragraphs, and a few inline elements like spans, some emphasis elements, and even images. And, we can't forget inline text.

We're starting with a browser window that's been resized to a fairly wide width.

Each block element is flowed top to bottom as you'd expect, with a linebreak in between each.

Here, we've resized the browser window, squeezing all the content into a smaller horizontal size.

Things flow the same way, although in some places, the inline elements take up more vertical lines to fit.

And the inline elements are flowed from the top left to the bottom right of the element's content area.

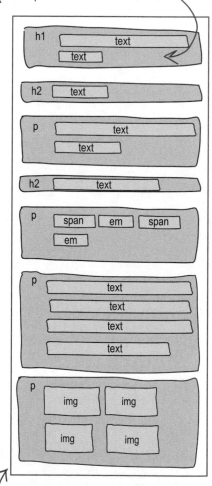

If the inline content of each block fits the width of the content area, then it's placed there; otherwise, more vertical room is made for the content and it's continued on the next line.

Now the block elements take up more vertical room because the inline content has to fit into a smaller horizontal space.

One more thing you should know about flow and boxes

Let's zoom in just a bit and look at one more aspect of how the browser lays out block and inline elements. It turns out that the browser treats margins differently depending on which type of element is being placed on the page.

When the browser is placing two inline elements next to each other...

When the browser has the task of placing two inline elements side by side, and those elements have margins, then the browser does what you might expect. It creates enough space between the elements to account for both margins. So, if the left element has a margin of 10 pixels and the right has a margin of 20 pixels, then there will be 30 pixels of space between the two elements.

margin   margin

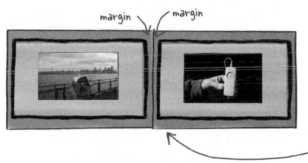

Here we've got two images side by side. Images are inline elements, right? So, the browser uses both of their margins to calculate the space that goes between them.

When the browser is placing two block elements on top of each other...

Here's where things get more interesting. When the browser places two block elements on top of each other, it collapses their shared margins together. The height of the collapsed margin is the height of the largest margin.

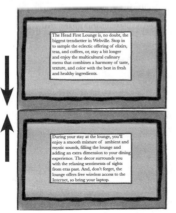

When the browser places two block elements on top of each other, it collapses their margins.

Their shared margin is the size of the larger of the two margins. Say the top element's bottom margin is 10 pixels, and the bottom element's top margin is 20 pixels. Then the collapsed margin will be 20 pixels.

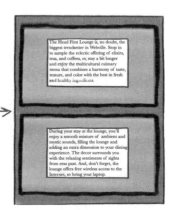

there are no Dumb Questions

Q: So if I have a block element with a zero margin, and a block element below it with a top margin of 20, the margin between them would end up being 20?

A: Right. If one of the margins is bigger, then the margin becomes the larger of the two, even if one margin is zero. But if the margins are the same, say, 10 pixels, then they just get collapsed together to 10 pixels total.

Q: Can inline elements really have margins?

A: They sure can, although you won't find that you set the margins of inline elements often. The one exception is images. It is very common to not only set margins but also borders and padding on images. And while we aren't going to be setting any inline element margins in this chapter, we will be setting the border on one a little later.

Q: What if I have one element nested inside another and they both have margins? Can they collapse?

A: Yes, that can happen. Here's how to figure out when they will: whenever you have two vertical margins touching, they will collapse, even if one element is nested inside the other. Notice that if the outer element has a border, the margins will never touch, so they won't collapse. But if you remove the border, they will. This is sometimes puzzling when you first see it happen, so put it in the back of your mind for when it occurs.

Q: So how exactly does text work as an inline element since its content is not an element?

A: Even if text is content, the browser needs to flow it onto the page, right? So the browser figures out how much text fits on a given line, and then treats that line of text as if it were an inline element. The browser even creates a little box around it. As you've seen, if you resize the page, then all those blocks may change as the text is refit within the content area.

We've been through seven pages of "flow." When are you going to explain that one little property we put into our CSS file? You know, the

float: right;

To understand float, you have to understand flow.

It might be one little property, but the way it works is closely tied to how the browser flows elements and content onto the page. But hey, you know that now, so we can explain float.

Here's the short answer: the float property first takes an element and *floats* it as far left or right as it can (based on the value of float). It then flows all the content below it around the element. Of course there's a few more details, so let's take a look...

How to float an element

Let's step through an example of how you get an element to float, and then we'll look at what it does to the flow of the page when you do.

First, give it an identity

Let's take one of these paragraphs and give it an id. We'd like to call it the "amazing floating paragraph", but we'll just call it "amazing" for short.

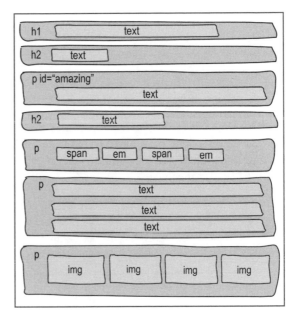

Now give it a width

A requirement for any floating element is that it have a width. We'll make this paragraph 200 pixels wide. Here's the rule:

```
#amazing {
    width: 200px;
}
```

Now the paragraph is 200 pixels wide, and the inline content contained in it has adjusted to that width. Keep in mind, the paragraph is a block element, so no elements are going to move up beside it because all block elements have linebreaks before and after them.

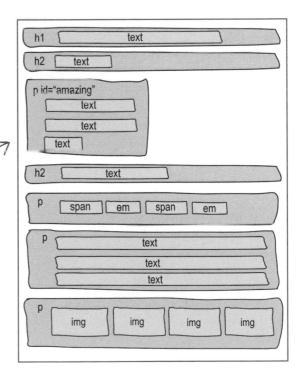

Now float it

Now let's add the **float** property. The **float** property can be set to either left or right. Let's stick with right:

```
#amazing {
    width: 200px;
    float: right;
}
```

Now that we've floated the "amazing" paragraph, let's step through how the browser flows it and everything else on the page.

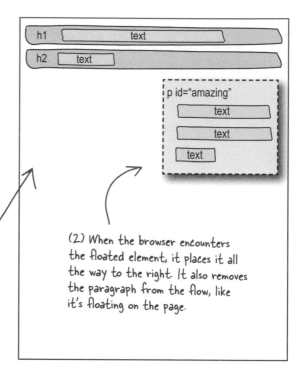

(1) First the browser flows the elements on the page as usual, starting at the top of the file and moving towards the bottom.

(2) When the browser encounters the floated element, it places it all the way to the right. It also removes the paragraph from the flow, like it's floating on the page.

(3) Because the floated paragraph has been <u>removed from</u> the normal flow, the block elements are filled in, like the paragraph isn't even there.

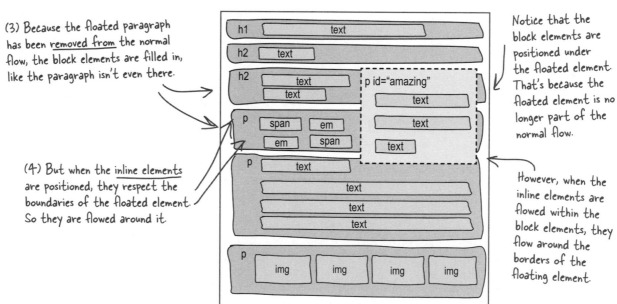

(4) But when the <u>inline elements</u> are positioned, they respect the boundaries of the floated element. So they are flowed around it.

Notice that the block elements are positioned under the floated element. That's because the floated element is no longer part of the normal flow.

However, when the inline elements are flowed within the block elements, they flow around the borders of the floating element.

Behind the scenes at the lounge

Now you know all about flow and how floated elements are placed on the page. Let's look back at the lounge and see how this all fits together.

Remember, in addition to setting the elixirs <div> to float right, we also moved the <div> up just below the logo at the top of the page.

Moving the <div> allowed us to float it to the right and then have the entire page flow around it. If we had left the elixirs <div> below the music recommendations, then the elixirs would have been floated right after most of the page had been placed.

All these elements follow the elixirs in the XHTML, so they are flowed around it.

Remember that the elixirs <div> is floating on top of the page. All the other elements are underneath it, but the inline content respects the elixirs' boundaries when they are flowing into the page.

Also notice that the text wraps around the bottom of the elixirs, because the text is contained in a block element that is the width of the page. If yours doesn't wrap, try narrowing your browser window until the text wraps underneath the elixirs.

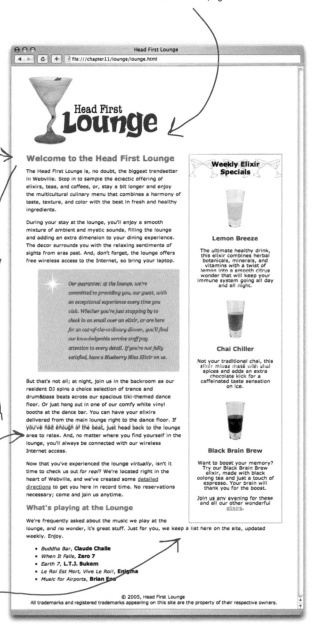

Exercise

Move the elixirs <div> back to its original place below the music recommendations, then save and reload the page. Where does the element float now? Check your answer in the back and then put your elixirs <div> back underneath the header.

> Nice stuff. Do you think I'm going to watch these fantastic lounge designs and not want you to improve Starbuzz? You've got a blank check... take Starbuzz to the next level.

It looks like you've got a new assignment. Starbuzz really could use some improvement. Sure, you've done a great job of creating the typical top to bottom page, but now that you know flow, you should be able to give Starbuzz Coffee a slick new look that is more user-friendly than the last design.

We do have a little secret though... we've been working on this one a bit already. We've created an updated version of the site. Your job is going to be to provide all the layout. Don't worry, we'll bring you up to speed on everything we've done so far – it's nothing you haven't seen before.

The new Starbuzz

Let's take a quick look at what we've got so far, starting with the page as it looks now. Then we'll take a peek at the markup and the CSS that's styling it.

We've got a header now with a new spiffy Starbuzz logo and the company mission statement. This is actually just a GIF image.

We've got four sections: the header, a main content section, a section advertising something new called the "Bean Machine," and a footer.

Each section is a <div> that can be styled independently.

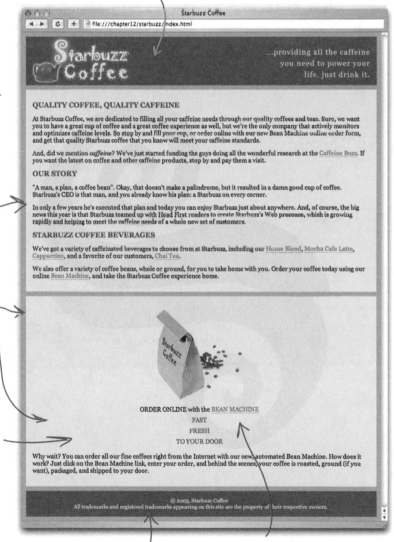

It looks like we've got one background color for the page as a whole, and then each <div> is using an image as a background.

Here's the "Bean Machine" area. This links to a new area of Starbuzz Coffee where you can order your coffee beans online. This link doesn't work just yet because you're going to build the Bean Machine in an upcoming chapter.

Here's the footer. It doesn't use a background image, just a background color.

Notice that we've styled the links in an interesting way, with dotted underlines...

A look at the markup

Now let's take a look at the new Starbuzz markup. We've taken each of the logical sections and placed it into a **<div>**, each with its own **id**. Beyond the **<div>**s and **<span>**s, there's really nothing here that you hadn't already seen by about Chapter 5. So, take a quick look and get familiar with the structure, and then turn the page to check out the CSS style.

```
<!DOCTYPE html PUBLIC "-//W3C//DTD XHTML 1.0 Strict//EN"
    "http://www.w3.org/TR/xhtml1/DTD/xhtml1-strict.dtd">
<html xmlns="http://www.w3.org/1999/xhtml" lang="en" xml:lang="en" >
<head>
        <meta http-equiv="Content-Type" content="text/html; charset=ISO-8859-1" />
        <title>Starbuzz Coffee</title>
        <link type="text/css" rel="stylesheet" href="starbuzz.css" />
</head>
<body>
```

Here's all the usual XHTML administravia.

Followed by a <div> for the header and a <div> for the main content area.

```
<div id="header">
        <img src="images/header.gif" alt="Starbuzz Coffee header image" />
</div>

<div id="main">
        <h1>QUALITY COFFEE, QUALITY CAFFEINE</h1>
        <p>
            At Starbuzz Coffee, we are dedicated to filling all your caffeine needs through our
            quality coffees and teas. Sure, we want you to have a great cup of coffee and a great
            coffee experience as well, but we're the only company that actively monitors and
            optimizes caffeine levels. So stop by and fill your cup, or order online with our new Bean
            Machine online order form, and get that quality Starbuzz coffee that you know will meet
            your caffeine standards.
        </p>
        <p>
            And, did we mention <em>caffeine</em>? We've just started funding the guys doing all
            the wonderful research at the <a href="http://buzz.headfirstlabs.com"
            title="Read all about caffeine on the Buzz">Caffeine Buzz</a>.
            If you want the latest on coffee and other caffeine products,
            stop by and pay them a visit.
        </p>
        <h1>OUR STORY</h1>
        <p>
            "A man, a plan, a coffee bean". Okay, that doesn't make a palindrome, but it resulted
            in a damn good cup of coffee.  Starbuzz's CEO is that man, and you already know his
            plan: a Starbuzz on every corner.
        </p>
        <p>
            In only a few years he's executed that plan and today
            you can enjoy Starbuzz just about anywhere. And, of course, the big news this year
            is that Starbuzz teamed up with Head First readers to create Starbuzz's Web presence,
            which is growing rapidly and helping to meet the caffeine needs of a whole new set of
            customers.
        </p>
        <h1>STARBUZZ COFFEE BEVERAGES</h1>
        <p>
                We've got a variety of caffeinated beverages to choose
```

This is more of the main content area continued over here.

```
                    from at Starbuzz, including our
                    <a href="beverages.html#house" title="House Blend">House Blend</a>,
                    <a href="beverages.html#mocha" title="Mocha Cafe Latte">Mocha Cafe Latte</a>,
                    <a href="beverages.html#cappuccino" title="Cappuccino">Cappuccino</a>,
                    and a favorite of our customers,
                    <a href="beverages.html#chai" title="Chai Tea">Chai Tea</a>.
                </p>
                <p>

                    We also offer a variety of coffee beans, whole or ground, for you to
                    take home with you.  Order your coffee today using our online
                    <a href="form.html" title="The Bean Machine">Bean Machine</a>,
                    and take the Starbuzz Coffee experience home.

                </p>

        </div>
```

```
        <div id="sidebar">
                <p class="beanheading">
                        <img src="images/bag.gif" alt="Bean Machine bag" />
                        <br />
                        ORDER ONLINE
                        with the
                        <a href="form.html">BEAN MACHINE</a>
                        <br />
                        <span class="slogan">
                                FAST <br />
                                FRESH <br />
                                TO YOUR DOOR <br />
                        </span>
                </p>
                <p>
                    Why wait?  You can order all our fine coffees right from the Internet with our new,
                    automated Bean Machine.  How does it work?  Just click on the Bean Machine link,
                    enter your order, and behind the scenes, your coffee is roasted, ground
                    (if you want), packaged, and shipped to your door.
                </p>
        </div>
```

Here's the <div> for the Bean Machine. We've given it an id of "sidebar". Hmm, wonder what that could mean?

```
        <div id="footer">
                &copy; 2005, Starbuzz Coffee
                <br />
                All trademarks and registered trademarks appearing on
                this site are the property of their respective owners.
        </div>
```

And finally, we have the <div> that makes up the footer of the page.

```
</body>
</html>
```

And a look at the style

Let's get a good look at the CSS that styles the new Starbuzz page. Step through the CSS rules carefully. While the new Starbuzz page may look a little advanced, you'll see it's all just simple CSS that you already know.

```css
body {
        background-color: #b5a789;
        font-family:     Georgia, "Times New Roman", Times, serif;
        font-size:       small;
        margin:          0px;
}

#header {
        background-color: #675c47;
        margin:          10px;
        height:          108px;
}

#main {
        background: #efe5d0 url(images/background.gif) top left;
        font-size: 105%;
        padding:   15px;
        margin:    0px 10px 10px 10px;
}

#sidebar {
        background: #efe5d0 url(images/background.gif) bottom right;
        font-size: 105%;
        padding:   15px;
        margin:    0px 10px 10px 10px;
}

#footer {
        background-color: #675c47;
        color:            #efe5d0;
        text-align:       center;
        padding:          15px;
        margin:           10px;
        font-size:        90%;
}

h1 {
        font-size: 120%;
        color:     #954b4b;
}

.slogan { color: #954b4b;}

.beanheading {
        text-align:  center;
        line-height: 1.8em;
}
```

First we just set up some basics in the body: a background color, fonts, and we also set the margin of the body to 0. This makes sure there's no extra room around the edges of the page.

Next we have a rule for each logical section. In each, we're tweaking the font size, adding padding and margins and also — in the case of main and the sidebar — specifying a background image.

Next we set up the fonts and colors on the headings.

And then some colors on the class called slogan, which is used in the sidebar <div>. And likewise with the beanheading class, which is used there as well.

```
a:link {
      color:                        #b76666;
      text-decoration:              none;
      border-bottom:                thin dotted #b76666;
}
a:visited {
      color:                        #675c47;
      text-decoration:              none;
      border-bottom:                thin dotted #675c47;
}
```

And for the last two rules in the Starbuzz CSS we use the a:link and a:visited pseudo-classes to style the links.

Notice that we're getting a nice dotted underline effect on the links by using a dotted bottom border instead of an underline. This is a great example of using the border property on an inline element.

We're setting the border-bottom as a shortcut.

Let's take Starbuzz to the next level

Here's the goal: to turn Starbuzz Coffee into the site on the right. To do that, we need to move the Bean Machine sidebar over to the right so we've got a nice two-column page. Well, you've done this once already with the lounge, right? So, based on that, here's what you need to do:

1 Give the element you're going to float a unique name using an **id**. That's already done.

2 Make sure the element's XHTML is just below the element you want it to float under; in this case, the Starbuzz header.

3 Set a width on the element.

4 Float the element to the left or the right. It looks like you want to float it right.

Let's get started. In a few simple steps, we should have the Starbuzz CEO sending a few Chai Teas over on the house.

We've got a nice two-column look here, with discrete columns.

Move the sidebar just below the header

It's a fact of life that when you float an element, you need to move the XHTML for the element directly below the element that you want it to float below. In this case, the sidebar needs to come under the header. So, go ahead and locate the sidebar **<div>** in your editor and move the entire **<div>** to just below the header **<div>**. You'll find the XHTML in the file "index.html" in the "chapter12/starbuzz" folder. After you've done that and saved, reload the page.

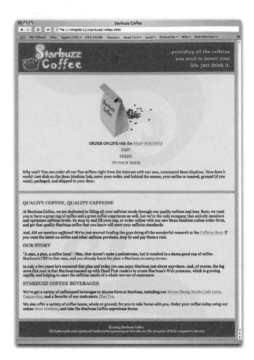

Now the sidebar should be on top of the main content area.

Set the width of the sidebar and float it

Let's set the width of the sidebar to 280 pixels. And to float the sidebar, add a float property, like this:

We're using an id selector to select the element with the id "sidebar", which we know is the <div> for the sidebar.

```
#sidebar {
        background:  #efe5d0 url(images/background.gif) bottom right;
        font-size:   105%;
        padding:     15px;
        margin:      0px 10px 10px 10px;
        width:       280px;
        float:       right;
}
```

We're setting the width of the content area to 280 pixels.

And then we're floating the sidebar to the right. Remember, this moves the sidebar as far right as possible below the header, and it also removes the sidebar from the normal flow. Everything else below the sidebar in the XHTML is going to move up and wrap around it.

I have an idea. In the future, why don't we float the main content to the left, rather than the sidebar to the right. Since the main content is already at the top, we wouldn't have to move things around, and we get the same effect.

That's actually a great idea, but there are a couple of issues.

On paper this looks like a great idea. What we do is set a width on the main content **<div>** and float it to the left, and then let the rest of the page flow around it. That way we get to keep the ordering of the page and we also get two columns.

The only problem is, this doesn't result in a very nice page. Here's why: remember, you have to set a width on the element that you are going to float, and if you set a width on the content area, then its width is going to remain fixed while the rest of the page resizes along with the width of the browser. Typically, sidebars are designed to be narrower than the main content area, and often look terrible when they expand. So, in most designs, you want the main content area to expand, not the sidebar.

But we are going to look at a way to use this idea that works great. So hang on to this idea. We'll also talk a little more about why you'd even care what order your sections are in.

Test driving Starbuzz

Make sure you add the new sidebar properties to the "starbuzz.css" file in the "chapter12/starbuzz" folder, and then reload the Starbuzz page. Let's see what we've got...

Hmm, this looks pretty good, but if you flip back three pages you'll see we're not quite where we want to be.

The main content and the sidebar are on the left and the right, but they don't really look like two columns yet.

Look at how the background images of the two sections just run together. There's no separation between the columns.

And the text wraps around and under the sidebar, which doesn't make this look like two columns either. Hmm, that is actually how the lounge worked too — maybe we should have expected that.

Fixing the two-column problem

Are you sitting there waiting for us to come riding in on a white horse with the magic property that solves all this? Well, that's not going to happen. This is the point in CSS where page layout becomes more an art – or at least a set of techniques – than a set of properties that can solve every problem. So, what we're going to do is solve this using a common technique that is widely used. It's not perfect, as you'll see, but in most cases it gives you good results. And after this, you're going to see a few other ways to approach the same two-column problem. What's important here is that you understand the techniques, and why they work, so you can apply them to your own problems, and even adapt them where necessary.

The first thing to remember is that the sidebar is floating on the page. The main content area extends all the way under it.

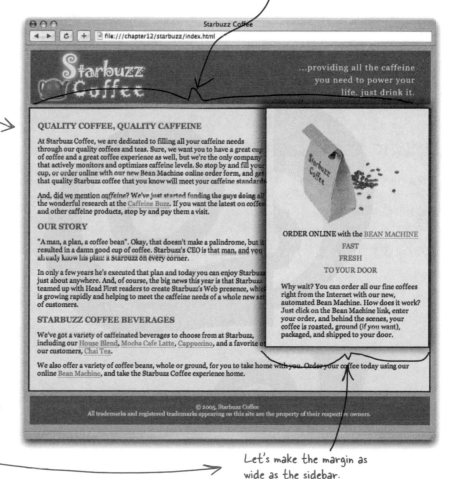

So, what if we give the main content area a right margin that is at least as big as the sidebar? Then its content will extend almost to the sidebar, but not all the way.

Then we'll have separation between the two, and since margins are transparent and don't show the background image, the background color of the page itself should show through. And that's what we're looking for (flip back a few pages and you'll see).

Let's make the margin as wide as the sidebar.

Sharpen your pencil

What we want to do is set a right margin on the main content section so that it's the same width as the sidebar. But how big is the sidebar? Well, we hope you aren't already rusty since the last chapter. Here's all the information you need to compute the width of the sidebar. Check your answer in the back of the chapter.

```
#sidebar {
        background:   #efe5d0 url(images/background.gif) bottom right;
        font-size:    105%;
        padding:      15px;
        margin:       0px 10px 10px 10px;
        width:        280px;
        float:        right;
}
```

You'll find everything you need to compute the width of the sidebar in this rule.

Setting the margin on the main section

The width of the sidebar is 330 pixels, and that includes 10 pixels of left margin on the sidebar, which will provide the separation we need between the two columns (what the publishing world calls a "gutter"). Add the 330 pixel right margin to the **#main** rule in your "starbuzz.css" file, like we've done below:

```
#main {
        background:   #efe5d0 url(images/background.gif) top left;
        font-size:    105%;
        padding:      15px;
        margin:       10px;
        margin:       0px 330px 10px 10px;
}
```

We're changing the right margin to 330 pixels to match the size of the sidebar.

Test drive

As usual, save your "starbuzz.css" file and then reload "index.html". You should now see a nice gutter between the two columns. Let's think through how this is working one more time. The sidebar is floating right, so it's been moved as far to the right as possible, and the whole **<div>** has been removed from the normal flow and is floating on top of the page. Now the main content **<div>** is still taking up the width of the browser (because that's what block elements do), but we've given it a margin as wide as the sidebar to reduce the width of the content area. The result is a nice two column look. You know the box of the main **<div>** still goes under the sidebar, but we won't tell anyone if you don't.

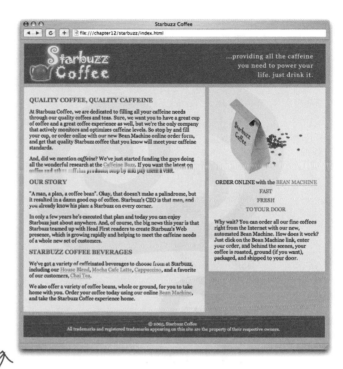

> By expanding the margin of the main <div>, we're creating the illusion of a two column layout, complete with a gutter in between.

> We've got a problem. When you resize your browser to a wide position, the footer and the sidebar start to overlap.

Uh oh, we have another problem

As you were test driving the page you might have noticed a little problem. If you resize the browser to a wide position, the footer comes up underneath the sidebar. Why? Well, remember, the sidebar is not in the flow, so the footer pretty much ignores it, and when the content area is too short, the footer moves right up. We could use the same margin trick on the footer, but then the footer would only be under the content area, not the whole page. So, what now?

> Wait a sec. Before you get way into solving that problem, I have to ask, why did we have to go to all this trouble of using a margin? Why don't we just set the width of the main area? Wouldn't that do the same thing?

This is another solution that sounds good... until you try it.

The problem with setting a width on both the content area and the sidebar is that this doesn't allow the page to expand and contract correctly because both have fixed widths. Check the screenshots below that show how it works (or rather, doesn't work).

But this is good. You're thinking in the right ways, and a little later in the chapter we're going to come back to this idea when we talk about "liquid versus fixed" layouts. There are ways to make your idea work if we lock a few other things down first.

And when the browser window is made small, the two start to overlap.

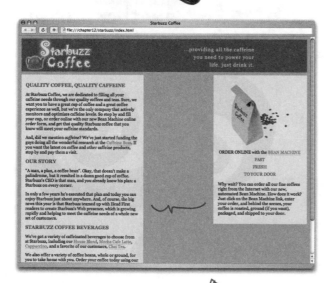

When the browser is wide, the two totally separate.

Back to clearing up the overlap problem

Guess what, this time *we are* going to ride in on a
white horse with a solution, but don't get used to it.
The solution is called the **clear** property, and here's
how it works...

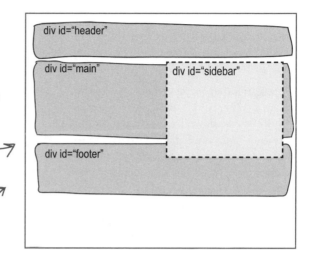

Here's what we've got now. The
"main" <div> is short enough that the
footer <div> is coming right up and
overlapping with the sidebar <div>.

This happens because the sidebar has been pulled out of the flow.
So, the browser just lays out the main and footer <div>s like it
normally would, ignoring the sidebar (although remember that when
the browser flows inline elements, it will respect the borders of
the sidebar and wrap inline elements around it).

We can solve this problem with the CSS **clear** property. You can set this property on an
element to request that as the element is being flowed onto the page, no floating content
is allowed to be on the left, right, or both sides of the element. Let's give it a try...

```
#footer {
        background-color:  #675c47;
        color:             #efe5d0;
        text-align:        center;
        padding:           15px;
        margin:            10px;
        font-size:         90%;
        clear:             right;
}
```

Here we're adding a property to
the footer rule, which says that
no floating content is allowed on
the right of the footer.

Now when the browser places the
elements on the page, it looks to see if
there is a floating element to the right
side of the footer, and if there is, it
moves the footer down until there is
nothing on its right. Now, no matter
how wide you open the browser, the
footer will always be below the sidebar.

Don't even think
about putting a
floating element to the
right of me.

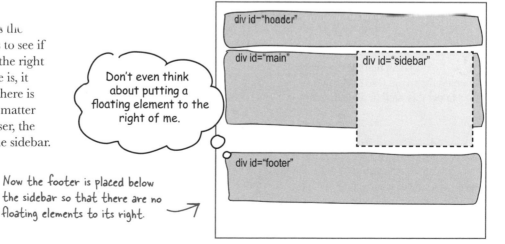

Now the footer is placed below
the sidebar so that there are no
floating elements to its right.

Test drive

Go ahead and add the clear property to your "starbuzz.css" file in the footer rule, and then reload "index.html". You'll see that when the screen is wide, the footer now stays below the sidebar.

There are other improvements we could think about making to this page, like having each column come down to meet the footer. As it is now, there is a gap either between the main content and the footer (if the browser window is set wide), or the sidebar and the footer (if the browser is set to a normal width). Unfortunately, it's not easy to fix this, and we're not going to try to do that in this chapter. Layout in CSS is an art, and no layout solution is perfect. When done right, layout with CSS gives you a better look for your Web page, while still allowing the page to look reasonably good in browsers that don't have as much (or any) support for CSS.

We will take a look at a few more ways to layout your pages using CSS beyond using float. There are many ways to do things in CSS, each with their own strengths and weaknesses.

Now our footer problems are solved. The footer will always be below the sidebar, no matter how narrow or wide the browser.

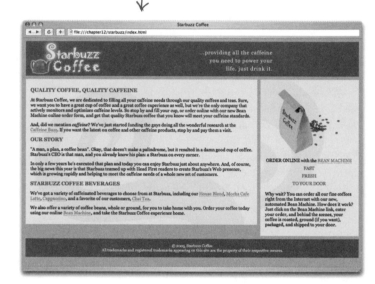

there are no Dumb Questions

Q: So why isn't there just a two-column property in CSS? Why is it so hard to get this stuff to work correctly?

A: Yes, we have a winner! You've asked the $64,000 question. But, more seriously, while it seems like CSS *should* have some way of specifying "give me two columns, dammit!", you have to keep in mind the whole purpose of XHTML and CSS. Remember, XHTML is meant to be a format for structure and content that can be styled by CSS but should be viewable on any device, even if the CSS isn't used. So, it's really no surprise that CSS isn't the end-all-be-all of document presentation, and, if that's what we wanted, we'd probably all just be using Microsoft Word. But CSS does give you some nice tools to create layouts that are attractive and usable, and does a good job of gracefully degrading in less than optimal viewing conditions.

Q: Can I float to the center?

A: No, CSS only allows you to float an element to the left or right. But if you think about it, if you were to float to the center, then the inline content under the floated element would have to be flowed around both sides of your element. While that might be doable, it probably wouldn't be very readable or attractive.

Q: **Do margins collapse on floated elements?**

A: No, they don't, and it's pretty easy to see why. Unlike block elements that are flowed on the page, floated elements are just, well, floating. In other words, the margins of floated elements aren't actually touching the margins of the elements in the normal flow, so they can't be collapsed.

But this raises a good point, and identifies a common error in layouts. If you have a main content area and a sidebar, it is common to set a top margin on each. Then, if you float the sidebar, it still has a margin, and that margin won't be collapsed with whatever is above it anymore. So you can easily end up having different margins on the sidebar and on the main content if you don't remember that floated elements don't collapse margins.

Q: **Can I float an inline element?**

A: Yes, you sure can. The best example – and a common one – is to float images. Give it a try – float an image left or right in a paragraph and you'll see your text flow around it. Don't forget to add padding to give the image a little room, and possibly a border. You can also float any other inline element you like, but it's not commonly done.

Q: **Is it correct to think about floated elements as elements that are ignored by block elements, while inline elements know they are there?**

A: Yes, that's a good way of thinking about it. Inline content nested inside a block element always flows around a floated element, observing the boundaries of the floated element, while block elements are flowed onto the page as normal. The exception is when you set the clear property on a block element, which causes a block element to move down until there are no floating elements next to it on the right, left or both sides, depending on the value of clear.

> The only thing I don't like about this design is that when I view the web page on my PDA, it puts the sidebar content above the main content, so I have to scroll through it.

Right. That happens because of the way we ordered the <div>s.

This is one of the disadvantages of the way we've designed this page – because we need the sidebar to be located just under the header and before the main content, anyone using a browser with limited capabilities (PDAs, mobile phones, screen readers, and so on) will see the page in the order it is written, with the sidebar first. However, most people would rather see your main content before any kind of sidebar or navigation.

So, let's look at another way of doing this, which goes back to your idea of using float "left" on the main content. While we're exploring that, we'll talk about *liquid* versus *frozen* designs as well.

Look Ma, no CSS!

Want to know how your pages are going to look to your users under bad conditions (like on a browser that doesn't support CSS)? Then open your "index.html" file and remove the <link> from the <head>, save, and reload the page in your browser. Now you can see the real order things will be seen in (or heard from a screen reader). Go ahead and give it a try. Just make sure you put it back when you're done (after all, this is a chapter on CSS).

Here's the Starbuzz page without CSS. For the most part we're in good shape. It is still very readable, although the Bean Machine does come before the main content, which probably isn't what we want.

Righty tighty, lefty loosey

Let's get the Starbuzz page switched over so that the main content is floating left. We'll check out how that works, and then move on to make it *really* work. You're going to see the mnemonic righty tighty, lefty loosey holds true in the CSS world too... well, for our sidebar, anyway. Here's how we convert the page over... just a few simple steps.

Step One: start with the sidebar

We're basically swapping the roles of the sidebar and the main content area. The content area is going to have a fixed width and float, while the sidebar is going to wrap around the content. We're also going to use the same margin technique to keep the two visually separate. But before we start changing CSS, go to your "index.html" file and move the "sidebar" **<div>** down below the "main" **<div>**. After you've done that, here are the changes you need to make to the sidebar CSS rule:

```
#sidebar {
         background:   #efe5d0 url(images/background.gif) bottom right;
         font-size.    105%;
         padding:      15px;
         margin:       0px 10px 10px 470px;
         width:        280px;
         float:        right;
}
```

Because the sidebar is now going to flow under the main content, we need to move the large margin to the sidebar. The total width of the main content area is 470 pixels. (Go ahead and compute that yourself in all that free time you have. Compute it in the same way as you did for the sidebar. You should know that we're going to set the width of the main content area to 420 pixels.)

We're setting a fixed width on the main content <div>, so delete the sidebar width property along with the float.

Step Two: take care of the main content

Now we need to float the main **<div>**. Here's how to do it:

```
#main {
         background: #efe5d0 url(images/background.gif) top left;
         font-size:    105%;
         padding:      15px;
         margin:       0px 10px 10px 10px;
         width:        420px;
         float:        left;
}
```

We're changing the right margin from 330 pixels back to 10 pixels.

We need to set an explicit width because we're going to float this element. Let's use 420 pixels.

We're going to float the main <div> to the left.

Step Three: take care of the footer

Now, we just need to adjust the footer to clear everything to the left, rather than the right.

```
#footer {
         background-color: #675c47;
         color:            #efe5d0;
         text-align:       center;
         padding:          15px;
         margin:           10px;
         font-size:        90%;
         clear:            left;
}
```

Change the clear property to have a value of left, rather than right. That way the footer will stay clear of the main content area.

A quick test drive

We've already said there might be a few problems with this method of floating the content to the left. Do a quick test drive before you move on just to see how this is all working. Go ahead and make the changes to your "starbuzz.css" file and then reload "index.html" in your browser. Get a good feel for how the page performs when it is resized to narrow, normal, and wide.

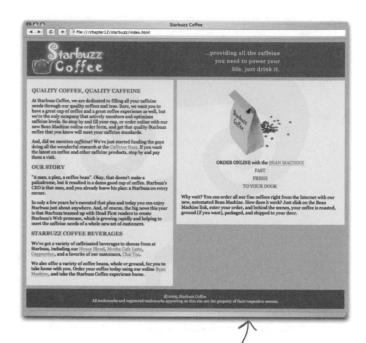

Actually, this looks pretty good, and we have the <div>s in the right order now. But it's not great that the sidebar expands; it looks a lot better fixed. Sidebars are often used for navigation and they don't look very good when expanded.

When we float the sidebar <div> right, then the design stays nice and tight, allowing the content to expand, but if we float the main content to the left, the design feels too loose, allowing the sidebar to expand.

BRAIN POWER

Design-wise, the first design worked better, while information-wise, the second works better (because of the placement of the <div>s). Is there a way we can have the best of both worlds: have the sidebar at a fixed width, but the main <div> still first in the XHTML? What design tradeoffs could we make to get there?

Liquid and Frozen Designs

All the designs we've been playing with so far are called *liquid layouts* because they expand to fill whatever width we resize the browser to. These layouts are useful because, by expanding, they fill the space available and allow users to make good use of their screen space. Sometimes, however, it is more important to have your layout locked down so that when a user resizes the screen, your design still looks as it should. There are a couple of layouts that work like this, but let's start with *frozen layouts*. Frozen layouts lock the elements down, frozen to the page, so they can't move at all, and so we avoid a lot of issues that are caused by the window expanding. Let's give a frozen layout a try.

Going from your current page to a frozen page only requires one addition to your XHTML, and one new rule in your CSS.

XHTML Changes

In your XHTML, you're going to add a new **<div>** element with the id "allcontent". Like its name suggests, this **<div>** is going to go around all the content in your page. So place the opening **<div>** tag before the header **<div>** and the closing tag below the footer **<div>**.

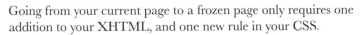

```
<body>
    <div id="allcontent">
        <div id="header">
            ... rest of the XHTML goes here ...
        </div>
    </div>
</body>
```

Add a new <div> with the id of "allcontent" around all the other elements in the <body>.

This <div> closes the footer <div>.

CSS Changes

Now we're going to use this **<div>** to constrain the size of all the elements and content in the "allcontent" **<div>** to a fixed width of 800 pixels. Here's the CSS rule to do that:

We're going to set the width of "allcontent" to 800 pixels. This will have the effect of constraining everything in it to fit within 800 pixels.

```
#allcontent {
    width:              800px;
    padding-top:        5px;
    padding-bottom:     5px;
    background-color:   #675c47;
}
```

While we're at it, since this is the first time we're styling this <div>, let's add some padding and give it its own background color. You'll see this helps to tie the whole page together.

The outer "allcontent" <div> is always 800 pixels, even when the browser is resized, so we've effectively frozen the <div> to the page, along with everything inside it.

A frozen test drive

Go ahead and add this rule to the bottom of
"starbuzz.css", and then reload "index.html". Now
you can see why we call it a frozen layout. It doesn't
move when the browser is resized.

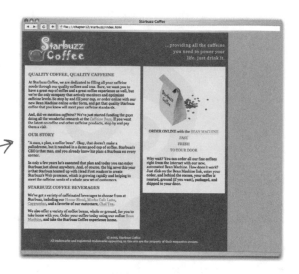

Now the "allcontent" <div> is 800 pixels in width, no matter
how you resize the browser. And, because all the other <div>s
are inside "allcontent", they will also fit into the 800 pixel
space as well. So, the page is basically frozen to 800 pixels.

This certainly solves the problem of the sidebar
expanding and it looks pretty nice. It is a little
strange when the browser is very wide, though,
because of all the empty space on the right side.

But, we're not done yet; we've got a
little room for improvement.

What's the state between liquid and frozen? Jello, of course!

The frozen layout has some benefits, but it also just plain
looks bad when you widen the browser. But we've got a fix,
and it's a common design you'll see on the Web. This design
is between frozen and liquid, and it has a name to match:
Jello. Jello layouts lock down the width of the content area in
the page, but center it in the browser. It's actually easier to
change the layout to a jello layout and let you play with it,
than to explain how it behaves, so let's just do it:

Rather than having fixed left and right
margins on the "allcontent" <div>, we're
setting the margins to "auto".

```
#allcontent {
    width: 800px;
    padding-top:    5px;
    padding-bottom: 5px;
    background-color: #675c47;
    margin-left:  auto;
    margin-right: auto;
}
```

If you remember, when we talked about giving a content area a width of "auto", the
browser expanded the content area as much as it needed to. With "auto" margins,
the browser figures out what the correct margins are, but also makes sure the left
and right margins are the same, so that the content is centered.

Test driving with a tank of jello

Add the two margin properties to your "starbuzz.css" file, and then reload
the page. Now play with the size of the browser. Pretty nice, huh?

Narrow.

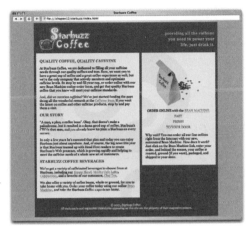

Wide.

> So if we want our content
> in the correct order, we either
> have to live with an expanding
> sidebar or we have to use a jello
> layout? Is there any other way to
> do this?

With CSS, there are typically lots of ways to approach a layout, each with their
own strengths and weaknesses. Actually, we're just about to look at another
common technique for creating a two-column layout that keeps the content in
the correct order, and avoids some of the problems of the liquid layouts. But,
as you'll see, there are some tradeoffs.

With this new technique we're not going to float elements at all. Instead we're
going to use a feature of CSS that allows you to precisely *position* elements on
the page. It's called *absolute positioning*. You can also use absolute positioning
for some nice effects beyond just multi-column layouts, and we'll look at an
example of that, too.

To do all this, we're going to step back to the original XHTML and CSS we
started with in the beginning of this chapter. You can find a fresh copy of these
files in the "chapter12/absolute" folder. Be sure and take another look at these
files so you remember what they originally looked like. Recall that we've got
a bunch of **<div>**s: one for the header, one for main, one for the footer, and
also a sidebar. Also remember that in the original XHTML, the sidebar **<div>**
is below the main content area, where we'd optimally like to have it.

How absolute positioning works

Let's start by getting an idea of what absolute positioning does, and how it works. Here's a little CSS to position the sidebar **<div>** with absolute positioning. Don't type this in just yet; right now we just want you to get a feel for how this works:

The first thing we do is use the position property to specify that the element will be positioned absolutely.

```
#sidebar {
    position: absolute;
    top:    100px;
    right:  200px;
    width:  280px;
}
```

Next we set top and right properties.

And we also give the <div> a width.

What the CSS does

Now let's look at what this CSS does. When an element is absolutely positioned, the first thing the browser does is remove it completely from the flow. The browser then places the element in the position indicated by the **top** and **right** properties (you can use **bottom** and **left** as well). In this case, the sidebar is going to be 100 pixels from the top of the page, and 200 pixels from the right side of the page. We're also setting a width on the **<div>**, just like we did when it was floated.

The sidebar is positioned 200 pixels from the right of the page.

Because sidebar is now absolutely positioned, it is removed from the flow and positioned according to any top, left, right, or bottom properties that are specified.

div id="header"

div id="sidebar"

div id="main"

And, the sidebar is positioned 100 pixels from the top of the page.

Because the sidebar is out of the flow, the other elements don't even know it is there, and they ignore it totally.

div id="footer"

Elements that are in the flow don't even wrap their inline content around an absolutely positioned element. They are totally oblivious to it being on the page.

Another example of absolute positioning

Let's look at another example. Say we have another **\<div\>** with the **id** "annoyingad". We could position it like this:

```
#annoyingad {
    position: absolute;
    top:    150px;
    left:   100px;
    width:  400px;
}
```

The annoying ad is being positioned 100 pixels from the left, and 150 pixels from the top. It's also a bit wider than the sidebar, at 400 pixels.

Just like with the sidebar, we've placed the annoying ad **\<div\>** at a precise position on the page. Any elements underneath that are in the normal flow of the page don't have a clue about the absolutely positioned elements layered overhead. This is a little different from floating an element, because elements that were in the flow adjusted their inline content to respect the boundaries of the floated element. But absolutely positioned elements have no effect whatsoever on the other elements.

Who's on top?

Another interesting thing about absolutely positioned elements is that you can layer them on top of each other. But if you've got a few absolutely positioned elements at the same position in a page, how do you know the layering? In other words, who's on top?

Each positioned element has a property called a **z-index** that specifies its placement. You'll see how to specify a z-index in just a few pages.

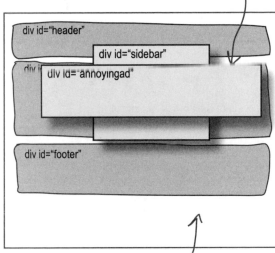

Now we have a second \<div\>, positioned absolutely, about 100 pixels from the left and 150 pixels from the top.

Notice the annoyingad \<div\> is on top of the sidebar \<div\>.

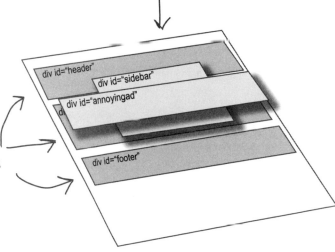

The sidebar and annoyingad \<div\>s are layered on the page, with the annoyingad having a greater z-index than the sidebar, so it's on top.

The header, main, and footer \<div\>s are all in the flow, and flat on the page.

Q: What is the position property set to by default?

A: The default value for positioning is "static". With static positioning the element is placed in the normal document flow and isn't positioned by you – the browser decides where it goes. You can use the float property to take an element out of the flow, and you can say it should float left or right, but the browser is still ultimately deciding where it goes. Compare this to the "absolute" value for the position property. With absolute positioning, you're telling the browser exactly where to position elements.

Q: Can I only position <div>s?

A: You can absolutely position any element, block or inline. Just remember that when an element is absolutely positioned, it is removed from the normal flow of the page.

Q: So, I can position an inline element?

A: Yes, you sure can. For instance, it's common to position the <img> element. You can position <em>s, <span>s, and so on as well, but it isn't common to do so.

Q: Are there position property values other than static and absolute?

A: There are actually four: static, absolute, fixed, and relative. You've already heard about static and absolute. Fixed positioning places an element in a location that is relative to the browser window (rather than the page), so fixed elements never move. You'll see an example of fixed positioning in a few pages. Relative positioning takes an element and flows it on the page just like normal, but then offsets it before displaying it on the page. Relative positioning is commonly used for more advanced positioning and special effects. You're going to see an example of that too.

Q: Do I have to specify a width for an absolutely positioned element just like the floated elements?

A: No, you don't have to specify a width for absolutely positioned elements. But if you don't, by default, the block element will take up the entire width of the browser, minus any offset you specify from the left or right. This might be exactly what you want, or it might not. So set the value of the width property if you want to change this default behavior.

Q: Do I have to use pixels for positioning?

A: No – another common way to position elements is using percentages. If you use percentages, the positions of your elements may appear to change as you change the width of your browser. So, for example, if your browser is 800 pixels wide, and your element's left position is set to 10%, then your element will be 80 pixels from the left of the browser window. But if your browser is resized to 400 pixels wide, then the width will be reduced to 10% of 400 pixels, or 40 pixels from the left of the browser window.

Another common use for percentages is in specifying widths. If you don't need specific widths for your elements or margins, then you can use percentages to make both your main content area and your sidebars flexible in size. You'll see this done a lot in two- and three-column layouts.

Q: Do I have to know how to use z-indexes to use absolute positioning?

A: No, z-indexes tend to be used most often for various advanced uses of CSS, especially when Web page scripting is involved, so they're a little beyond the scope of this book. But they are a part of how absolute positioning works, so it's good to know about z-index (and in fact, you'll see a case where knowing about z-index is important in just a bit).

Using absolute positioning

We're now going to create a two column Starbuzz page using techniques similar to those we used with the float version of the page; however, this time we'll use absolute positioning. Here's what we're going to do:

① First we're going to make the sidebar **<div>** absolutely positioned. In fact, we're going to position it in exactly the same place that we floated it to before.

② Next, we're going to give the main content another big margin so that the sidebar can sit on top of the margin space.

③ Finally, we're going to give this a good testing and see how it compares to the float version.

Changing the Starbuzz CSS

Our XHTML is all ready to go, and the sidebar **<div>** is right where we want it (below the important main content). All we need to do is make a few CSS changes and we'll have a sidebar that is absolutely positioned. Open your "starbuzz.css" file and let's make a few changes to the sidebar:

Remember, we are going back to the original versions of the files, which you can find in the "chapter12/absolute" folder.

You can work out of the "absolute" folder, or copy the files "index.html" and "starbuzz.css" into the "starbuzz" folder and work from there, like we did.

```
#sidebar {
    background:  #efe5d0 url(images/background.gif) bottom right;
    font-size:   105%;
    padding:     15px;
    margin:      0px 10px 10px 10px;
    position:    absolute;
    top:         128px;
    right:       0px;
    width:       280px;
}
```

Okay, now we're going to specify that the sidebar is absolutely positioned 128 pixels from the top, and 0 pixels from the right of the page. We also want the sidebar to have a width, so let's make it the same as the float version: 280 pixels.

You'll see where the "128" came from in a sec...

0 pixels from the right will make sure that the sidebar sticks to the right side of the browser.

Now we just need to rework the main <div>

Actually, there's not much reworking to be done. We're just adding a margin like we did with the float version. So, change the right margin of the main **<div>** to be 330 pixels, like you did last time.

```
#main {
    background:  #efe5d0 url(images/background.gif) top left;
    font-size:   105%;
    padding:     15px;
    margin:      0px 330px 10px 10px;
}
```

We're going to give the sidebar some space to be positioned over by giving the main <div> a big margin. This is really the same technique we used with the float. The only difference is the way the sidebar <div> is being placed over the margin.

Okay, all you need to do is make that change to your margin, and then save. But, before we take this for a test drive, let's think about how this is going to work with the absolutely positioned sidebar.

We're positioning the sidebar to be 128 pixels from the top, and up against the right side of the page. Keep in mind, the sidebar has 10 pixels of margin on the right, so the background color will show through that like before.

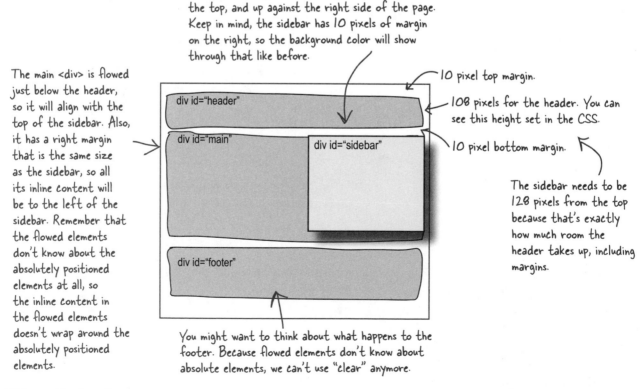

The main <div> is flowed just below the header, so it will align with the top of the sidebar. Also, it has a right margin that is the same size as the sidebar, so all its inline content will be to the left of the sidebar. Remember that the flowed elements don't know about the absolutely positioned elements at all, so the inline content in the flowed elements doesn't wrap around the absolutely positioned elements.

10 pixel top margin.

108 pixels for the header. You can see this height set in the CSS.

10 pixel bottom margin.

The sidebar needs to be 128 pixels from the top because that's exactly how much room the header takes up, including margins.

You might want to think about what happens to the footer. Because flowed elements don't know about absolute elements, we can't use "clear" anymore.

Time for the absolute test drive

Make sure you've saved the new CSS and then reload
"index.html" in your browser. Let's check out the results:

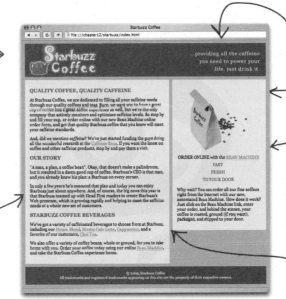

Wow, this looks amazingly like the float version; however, you know that the sidebar is being positioned absolutely.

The main content area has a margin that is exactly the width of the sidebar, and the sidebar sits on top of that space.

As you resize the browser, the sidebar always sits 128 pixels from the top, and sticks to the right of the page.

And the sidebar has a 10 pixel right margin, so it has spacing between it and the edge of the page.

And we've still got a nice gutter between the two columns.

But we are now back to having a problem with the
footer. When the browser gets wide enough, the
absolutely positioned sidebar comes down over the top
of the footer. Unfortunately, we can't fall back on the
clear property this time, because flowed elements
ignore the presence of absolutely positioned elements.

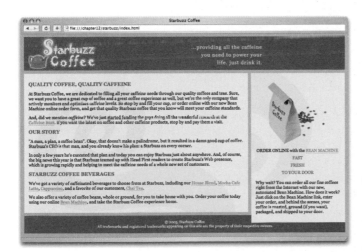

When the browser is wide, the vertical space of the main content area is reduced, and the sidebar can come down over the footer.

What can we do? Or, can't you just tell me how to do a two-column layout that doesn't break?

Okay, you know that one of the big motivations behind CSS was to separate structure from style. Right? And CSS does a great job of allowing you to create XHTML documents that can be used in a lot of different browsers (even screen readers or text-only browsers) without having unnecessary style embedded into the XHTML. But this also means that CSS is not meant to be a full-blown page layout language. Rather, it gives you some interesting tools that you can use to arrange and position elements in XHTML documents. Depending on the environment the page is viewed in, your mileage may vary in terms of what the end result is. If you resize your browser to be ultra wide, well, then the layout may break.

So where does this leave you? In this chapter we've looked at several techniques for creating two-column layouts. None of them were perfect and, in fact, they all had various tradeoffs. Let's quickly review the various examples.

The Floating Layout

Ahh, how cute, remember your first two-column Starbuzz page? You used a **float** property along with a **clear** on the footer and life was good. The only problem is that this solution often results in putting your content in an order your users might not appreciate if they are using another kind of browser, like a screen reader that reads the content aloud to the user.

The Jello Layout

First we created a frozen layout by wrapping a fixed size **<div>** around all the content in the page, and then we made it jello by allowing the margins to expand with the "auto" property value. This makes for a great looking layout, and lots of pages on the Web use this design. This also solved the problem of our content ordering. The disadvantage here is that the content doesn't expand to fill the entire browser window (which many people don't find to be a disadvantage at all).

The Absolute Layout

Finally, we were on a mission to have a liquid layout and yet have the content ordered like we wanted. So, we used absolute positioning and actually achieved our goal. But, there was a downside: since you can't use the **clear** property with absolute elements, the footer creeps up under the sidebar when the browser is wide.

So are we done yet? Maybe. If one of these designs meets your needs, great, go with it. For instance, lots of people are very happy with jello layouts. But there is always more tweaking you can do to perfect your particular layout. For instance, take the absolute design. Can we fix the footer? Not really, but we can make a tradeoff. Your design might be fine if the footer only showed under the main content area. If that's the case, then we *can* fix the footer problem. Let's give that a quick try.

One tradeoff you can make to fix the footer

To try this solution, just give the footer the same right margin size as the main content area, like this:

```
#footer {
        background-color:   #675c47;
        color:              #efe5d0;
        text-align:         center;
        padding:            15px;
        margin:             10px 330px 10px 10px;
        font-size:          90%;
}
```

If you save this and reload your page, you'll see that the footer is now under the main content area only, and never creeps up under the sidebar. Is this optimal? No, but it's also not bad. And, as we've said, doing CSS layout is a bit of an art. To do layout, you need to *experiment*, *explore*, and keep an eye on the layouts others are creating with CSS (you'll find some references for good CSS hang-outs at the end of the chapter).

This solution trades having the footer under just the main content for having a footer under the entire page, to keep it from creeping up under the sidebar.

So this is all great, but what am I supposed to do? Use a liquid or jello design? Use float or absolute positioning?

In terms of whether you want your layout to be liquid or frozen or jello, that really is a matter of deciding what works best for your pages. For some pages, a fixed content area size with expandable margins works great, and in fact can be more readable on wide browsers. For other uses, you might want to use as much of the browser as you can. So, decide what works best for you.

Once you've decided, you still need to figure out which method you're going to use to create your pages (float? absolute? some combination?). You've already learned the basics, so now it is time to start exploring, as there are many other approaches out there, and new ones being created every day. The techniques you've learned in this chapter are often used as the basis for more sophisticated designs.

You should know that, in general, using float is considered the most flexible solution for multi-column layouts. Just keep in mind, you may have to be careful in the order of your content, depending on the design.

Holy beans! Starbuzz just won the Roaster of the Year Award. This is huge. Can we get it on the page front and center? All our customers need to see this. Top priority, make it happen!

The award.

Well, we could just throw this as an image into any old paragraph on the page, but the CEO really wants this to be noticeable on the page. What if we could place the award on the page like this?

Not only does that look great, but it's exactly what the CEO wants. But how? Well, you know all about absolute positioning now, so why not position the image on the page using that? After all, by using absolute positioning you can place it anywhere on the page you want, and since it isn't in the flow it won't affect any other element on the page. Seems like an easy addition to make to the page without disrupting what's already there.

Let's give it a try. Start by adding a new **<div>**, just below the header (the CEO thinks this is pretty important, so it should be up high in the order of content). Here's the **<div>**

```
<div id="award">
    <img src="images/award.gif"
        alt="Roaster of the Year award" />
</div>
```

The <div> contains the image of the award.

Positioning the award

We want the award to sit just about in the middle of the page when the browser's open to 800 pixels (the width of the image in the header, and a typical size for browser widths) and just overlapping the main content **<div>**.

So we're going to use the top and left properties to position the award 30 pixels from the top, and 365 pixels from the left.

```
#award {
    position:  absolute;
    top:       30px;
    left:      365px;
}
```

We're using an absolute position for the award <div> that is 30 pixels from the top and 365 pixels from the left.

Add this CSS to your "starbuzz.css" file, save, and reload the Web page. You'll see the award image appear like magic, right where we want it. Make sure you resize the browser to see how the award displays.

A small glitch

Did you notice a small glitch when you were resizing the browser? Depending on your browser, you may have seen the sidebar **<div>** overlap the awards image. What on earth is going on? Remember how each absolutely positioned element has a z-index that describes the stacking behavior of the elements? Some browsers will give the award element a lower z-index than the sidebar **<div>** by default. All you need to do to fix that is to specify the z-index for the award, and give it a number higher than the sidebar.

On some browsers the sidebar will overlap and occlude the awards image. Oh dear.

```
#award {
    position:  absolute;
    top:       30px;
    left:      365px;
    z-index:   99;
}
```

Let's give the award <div> a really high number to make sure it is always on top.

Go ahead and add the z-index property to your "starbuzz.css" file. When you save and reload, you'll see that now the award **<div>** is on top of the sidebar, and the overlap glitch is gone.

Fireside Chats

Tonight's talk: **Float and Absolute discuss who's more appropriate for layout.**

Float	**Absolute**
Absolute, have you noticed lots of people are going with me to do their layouts?	
	Are you sure? I'm used on a lot of pages too, you know.
Well, everyone knows I'm better for CSS layout. I'm so much easier to use. Didn't you see? All you have to do is add one little float property to your CSS in the right place, and bam! You've got two columns.	
	Hmm, I seem to remember a width property and a margin property to get things just right...
Details, details. My point is that, with me, you don't have to go around counting pixels to figure out where your content's going to go – you can just float it and leave the rest to me.	
	Now, wait a sec. We had to move the *entire* sidebar to a different location in the XHTML to get the float to work the first time. I don't call that "leaving the rest to you." That's a lot of work. At least with me, it doesn't matter what order the content comes in; I'll always do the right thing.
Well, what about that footer issue? You're always going to overlap things in weird ways, aren't you? If readers aren't careful, they'll have big chunks of their Web pages sitting right on top of other content. At least I respect that handy clear property.	
	Hey, you sit on top of elements too.

Float

But the important part, the inline content, flows around me, just like it should.

You're missing the point. I'm more flexible and I give people a great way to lay out their pages. I'm sure I can do any layout you can.

Hmmm...

Well, maybe I can't do *everything* you can do, but I think I'm a lot easier for people doing basic layouts, which is mostly what people want.

I used to have that reputation, but most modern browsers arc just fine with me now. And, now that Web developers are figuring that out, they're going with me, like I said at the beginning.

I never said you didn't. But check out all the designs out there that use float.

Well, that's not really the point, is it? Anyway, I've got a float to clear, gotta run.

Absolute

Sometimes people *want* to position elements right on top of other elements, you know. And with me, you can position elements anywhere you want. None of this right and left crap like with you. You don't give people that many options, really, if you think about it.

Really? There's no way you could have done that cool thing with the award.

Admit it! You're actually not as flexible as I am.

I dunno, I heard you're kind of buggy in older browsers. That would be frustrating for new Web developers.

I don't think you've seen the end of me; I've got a lot of uses on Web pages.

Hey, don't start thinking you're perfect. You might be good for Web layouts, but you're not exactly the state of art in graphic design.

Clear this, Float.

One more thing you should know about absolute positioning

So far, when you've used the **left**, **right**, **top**, and **bottom** properties to specify the position, these numbers have always been with respect to the edge of the page, right? Well, we need to refine that just a bit.

When you position an element, you're specifying the position relative to the closest ancestor element that is also positioned. So, you're probably saying, "What? I haven't positioned anything except for the sidebar. How could there be an ancestor in my XHTML that is already positioned?" Believe it or not there is – the **<html>** element, which the browser positions for you when it creates the page.

But, let's take this one step further. Say you wanted to absolutely position another **<div>** inside the sidebar.

> Here's a new <div> nested inside the sidebar.

```
<div id="sidebar">

    <div id="tv">
        <img src="AsSeenOnTv.gif" alt="As Seen on TV" />
    </div>

    <p class="beanheading">
        ... more XHTML here ...
    </p>
    ...
</div>
```

The "tv" <div> is positioned relative to the sidebar <div>, not to the page.

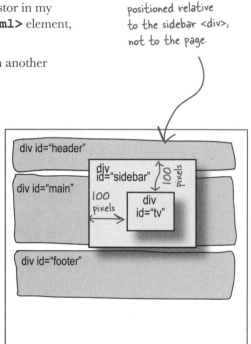

If we absolutely position the "tv" **<div>**, its closest positioned ancestor is the sidebar **<div>**. And so, the positioning will be relative to the edges of the sidebar, not the page.

```
#tv {
    position: absolute;
    top:     100px;
    left:    100px;
    width:   100px;
}
```

Another thing to know... if you get caught in a conversation about "closest ancestors that are positioned" at your next cocktail party, just say the "nearest containing block that is positioned." That's the terminology the experts use.

Watch it

If you're positioning with respect to the <html> element, then the bottom property may not do what you'd expect. You'd think the "bottom" would be the very bottom of the Web page itself, but the <html> element actually defines this as the bottom of the browser window. So, if you want to absolutely position an element from the bottom of the page, rather than the browser window, you need to place your element inside an element that extends to the bottom of your page, and is positioned. One way to do this is to put your element into a relatively positioned element at the bottom of the page. We'll look at relative positioning later in the chapter.

Sharpen your pencil

Time to put all this knowledge about floating and positioning to a test! Take a look at the Web page below. There are four elements with an id. Your job is to correctly match each of these elements with the CSS rules on the right, and fill in the correct id selector for each one. Check your answers at the end of the chapter.

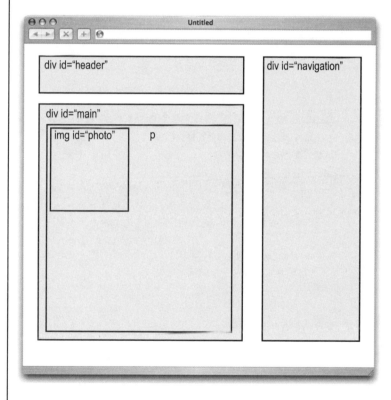

Fill in the selectors to complete the CSS.

```
_____ {
    margin-top:   140px;
    margin-left:  20px;
    width:        500px;
}

_____ {
    position: absolute;
    top:      20px;
    left:     550px;
    width:    200px;
}

_____ {
    float: left;
}

_____ {
    position: absolute;
    top:      20px;
    left:     20px;
    width:    500px;
    height:   100px;
}
```

Hey, can we get a coupon on the site and put it right in customers' faces so they can't miss it? I'd like to offer one free coffee to everyone who clicks on the coupon, for a limited time, of course.

Just the words we've been waiting for: "right in the customer's face"

Why? Because it's going to give us the opportunity to try a little *fixed* positioning. What we're going to do is put a coupon on the page that always stays on the screen, even if you scroll. Is this a great technique to make your users happy? Probably not, but work with us here... it is going to be a fun way to play with fixed positioning.

How does fixed positioning work?

Compared to absolute positioning, fixed positioning is pretty straightforward. With fixed positioning, you specify the position of an element just like you do with absolute positioning, but the position is an offset from the edge of the browser's *window* rather than the *page*. The interesting effect this has is that once you've placed content with fixed positioning, it stays right where you put it, and doesn't move, even if you scroll the page.

Impress friends and coworkers by referring to the browser window as the viewport. Try it, it works, and the W3C will nod approvingly.

So, say you have a **\<div\>** with an **id** of "coupon". You can position the **\<div\>** fixed to a spot 300 pixels from the top of the viewport, and 100 pixels from the left side, like this:

Here's the id selector for the coupon \<div\>.

We're using fixed positioning.

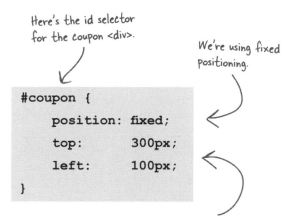

```
#coupon {
    position: fixed;
    top:        300px;
    left:       100px;
}
```

Position the coupon 300 pixels from the top, and 100 pixels from the left. You can also use right and bottom, just like with absolute positioning.

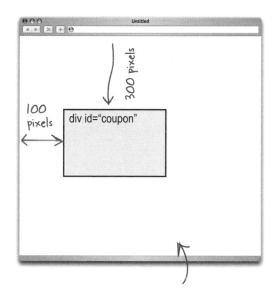

Here's where the element gets positioned within the viewport.

Once you've got an element positioned, then comes the fun: scroll around... it doesn't move. Resize the window... it doesn't move. Pick up your monitor and shake it... it doesn't move. Okay, just kidding on the last one. But, the point is, fixed position elements don't move; they are there for good as long as the page is displayed.

Now, we're sure you're already thinking of fun things to do with fixed positioning, but you've got a job to do. So let's get that coupon on the Starbuzz page.

Watch it

Unfortunately, Internet Explorer version 6 (and earlier) doesn't support fixed positioning. So if you're using Internet Explorer you won't be able to see the coupon properly placed on the Starbuzz Coffee Web page.

Putting the coupon on the page

Now we're going to get the Free Coffee Coupon on the page.
Let's start by creating a **<div>** for the coupon to go into:

Here's the <div> with an id of "coupon".

Inside we've got an image of the coupon, which you'll find in the "chapter12/starbuzz/images" folder.

```
<div id="coupon">

    <a href="freecoffee.html" title="Click here to get your free coffee">
        <img src="images/ticket.gif" alt="Starbuzz coupon ticket" />
    </a>
</div>
```

And we've wrapped the image in an <a> element so that users can click on the image to be taken to a page with a coupon they can print.

Go ahead and add this **<div>** at the bottom of your "index.html" file, just
below the footer. Because we're going to position it, the placement in the
XHTML will only matter to browsers that don't support positioning, and
the coupon isn't important enough to have at the top.

Now let's write the CSS to position the coupon:

```
#coupon {
    position: fixed;
    top: 300px;
    left: 0px;
}

#coupon img {
    border: none;
}

#coupon a:link {
    border: none;
}
#coupon a:visited {
    border: none;
}
```

We're going to set the coupon to fixed positioning, 300
pixels from the top of the viewport, and let's put the
left side right up against the edge of the viewport. So
we need to specify 0 pixels from the left.

We need to style the image and the links, too; otherwise,
we may have borders popping up on the image because it
is clickable. So, let's set the border on the image to none,
and do the same on both links and visited links.

Remember that we have a rule in the CSS that says to turn off text-
decoration, and use a border to underline links, instead. Here, we're
overriding that rule for the link in the coupon <div> and saying we
don't want any border on the link. Go back and look at the original CSS
if you need to remind yourself of the other rules for the links.

Putting the coupon on the page

Add the new coupon rules to your "starbuzz.css" file, save, and then reload the page. You may need to make the browser smaller to be able to see that the coupon stays put even when you scroll. Clicking on the coupon should take you to the "freecoffee.html" page.

You know, this looks great, but it might just be even more snazzy if the coupon was offset to the left, so it looks like it's coming out of the side of the viewport. Now, we *could* get into our photo editing software and cut off the left hand side of the image to create that effect. Or, we could just use a negative offset so that the left side of the image is positioned to the left of the edge of the viewport. That's right, *you can do that*.

Using a negative left property value

Specify a negative property value just like you do a positive one: just put a minus sign in front. Like this:

```
#coupon {
    position: fixed;
    top: 300px;
    left: -90px;
}
```

By specifying -90 pixels, we're telling the browser to position the image 90 pixels to the left of the edge of the viewport.

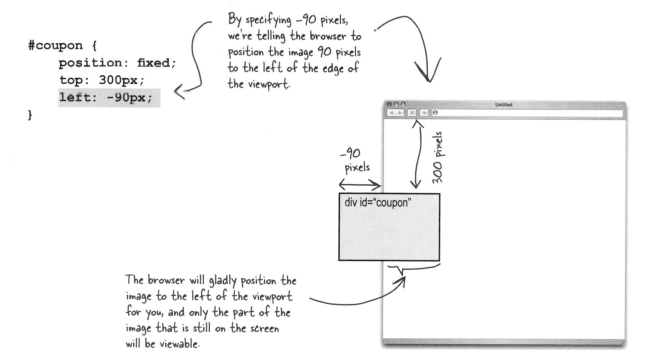

The browser will gladly position the image to the left of the viewport for you, and only the part of the image that is still on the screen will be viewable.

A rather positive, negative test drive

Make sure you've put in the negative left property value, save, and reload the page. Doesn't that look slick? Congrats, you've just achieved your first CSS special effect. Watch out George Lucas!

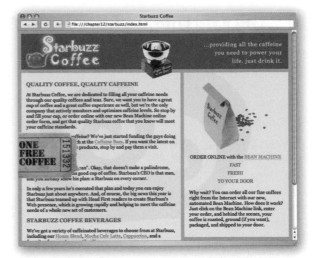

Just remember, using fixed positioning to cover up your content is not the most user-friendly thing to do, but it is FUN.

Can you believe how good this site looks? I mean, look at where it started compared to now. Okay, but we've still got our work cut out for us. We still need to build the Bean Machine, so see you in a couple of chapters.

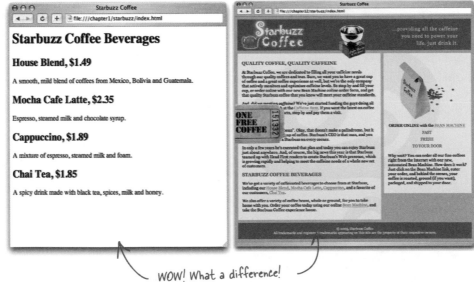

WOW! What a difference!

Getting relative

This is it, the last type of positioning: *relative positioning*. Truth be told, it's also the loneliest of the positions because you just won't find a lot of people using it in their designs. But, new designs come along every day, so when you see relative positioning, you'll want to know how it works and what it does.

Unlike absolute and fixed positioning, an element that is relatively positioned is still part of the flow of the page, but at the last moment, just before the element is displayed, the browser offsets its position. Let's see how this works on the coffee bag in the Starbuzz Page. We're going to take the coffee bag and offset it to the side, so those coffee beans that spilled out of the bag look like they're spilling out of the page, too.

Now we could absolutely position the coffee bag, but if we did, we'd have to find a way for the space it's taking up on the page to get reserved, since absolute positioning takes the document completely out of the flow.

That's where relative positioning comes in. We can *keep* the element in the flow, have its space reserved, and then offset where it actually gets displayed. Let's try it.

We want to take the Starbuzz Coffee bag and move it about 100 pixels to the right.

Here's a new rule that selects the image. We're using a descendant selector here to select only images inside the beanheading.

Notice that images are inline elements, but that's okay. You can use any of the positioning techniques, or even a float, on inline elements too.

```
.beanheading img {
    position: relative;
    left: 120px;
}
```

Then we specify a position of relative, and whatever offsets we want on the image. The offset is from the position where it is placed in the flow.

So here we're specifying that the image should be displayed 120 pixels from the left of where it sits in the flow of the document. You can use right, top, and bottom as well, when specifying offsets.

With absolute positioning, the coffee bag moves, but since it is no longer in the flow, the rest of the page moves up underneath.

Add this rule to your CSS and then save and reload.

The test drive

After reloading the Starbuzz page, you should see the coffee bag over to the right part of the sidebar. What is interesting is that part of the image is actually extending *beyond* the sidebar into the margin and off the edge of the page. How does that work? Well, as you've seen, the browser first flows a relative element onto the page, and only then does it offset where it is displayed. So the element still takes up the same spot on the page, it's just *drawn* in a different location. Relative is a little like static positioning, but with a dash of absolute thrown in. But, unlike absolute, relative positioning is specified just as an offset from the element's real location, not in absolute coordinates from the nearest containing block.

So, does this improve the page? We're not sure, but it *was fun*. (You might want to remove the relative positioning before you show it to the CEO.)

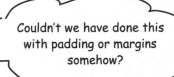

Couldn't we have done this with padding or margins somehow?

Not really.

No matter how you tweaked the padding and margins you still can't get an image to be positioned outside of the box it's in. And why try to do it the hard way? We achieved a better effect with two lines of CSS. You can use relative positioning to display an element well beyond the element's box in the flow, which you just can't do with padding or margins.

To three-columns and beyond...

While we've spent this chapter looking at two-column layouts, the real goal was to learn about the **float** and **clear** properties, along with the various forms of positioning that CSS offers. Now that you've got the basics down, you're in a good position to think about three-column layouts, or any other layout you might desire. So, that's it, the chapter's over.

But, wait! Before we finish it off, let's just think through how a three-column layout might work (and if you want to give it a try, just look in the "chapter12/threecolumn" folder).

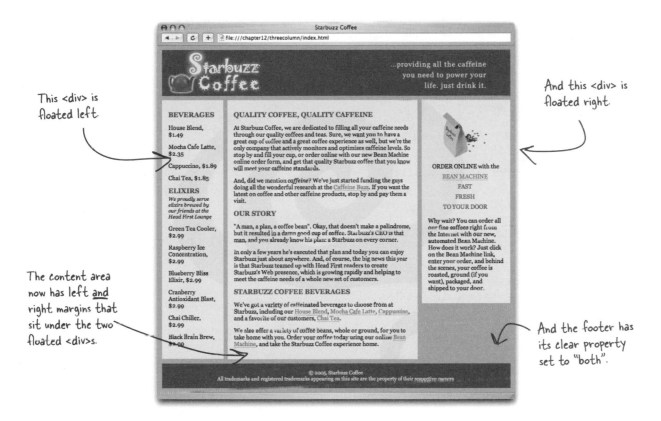

This <div> is floated left.

And this <div> is floated right.

The content area now has left *and* right margins that sit under the two floated <div>s.

And the footer has its clear property set to "both".

This design is built using techniques that you already understand. To explore beyond what you've done here, it really does help to see how others have used CSS to create interesting designs, and we encourage you to get out there and look around. Check out some of our favorite online resources for CSS design at:

http://headfirstlabs.com/books/hfhtml/chapter12/cssdesign.html

BULLET POINTS

- Browsers place elements in a page using flow.

- Block elements flow from the top down, with a linebreak between elements. By default, each block element takes up the entire width of the browser window.

- Inline elements flow inside a block element from the top left to the bottom right. If more than one line is needed, the browser creates a new line, and expands the containing block element vertically to contain the inline elements.

- The top and bottom adjacent margins of two block elements in the normal page flow collapse to the size of the larger margin, or to the size of one margin if they are the same size.

- Floated elements are taken out of the normal flow and placed to the left or right.

- Floated elements sit on top of block elements and don't affect their flow. However, the inline content respects the boundaries of a floated element and flows around it.

- The clear property is used to specify that no floated elements can be on the left or right (or both) of a block element. A block element with clear set will move down until it is free of the block element on its side.

- A floated element must have a specific width set to a value other than auto.

- A liquid layout is one in which the content of the page expands to fit the page when you expand the browser window.

- A frozen layout is one in which the width of the content is fixed and it doesn't expand or shrink with the browser window. This has the advantage of providing more control over your design, but at the cost of not using the browser width as efficiently.

- A jello layout is one in which the content width is fixed, but the margins expand and shrink with the browser window. A jello layout usually places the content in the center of the page. This has the same advantages as the frozen layout, but is often more attractive.

- There are four values the position property can be set to: static, absolute, fixed, and relative.

- Static positioning is the default, and places an element in the normal flow of the page.

- Absolute positioning lets you place elements anywhere in the page. By default, absolutely positioned elements are placed relative to the sides of the page.

- If an absolutely positioned element is nested within another positioned element, then its position is relative to the containing element that is positioned.

- The properties top, right, bottom, and left are used to position elements for absolute, fixed, and relative positioning.

- Absolutely positioned elements can be layered on top of one another using the z-index property. A larger z-index value indicates it is higher in the stack (closer to you on the screen).

- Fixed position elements are always positioned relative to the browser window and do not move when the page is scrolled. Other content in the page scrolls underneath these elements.

- Relatively positioned elements are first flowed into the page as normal, and then offset by the specified amount, leaving empty the space where they would normally sit.

- When using relative positioning, left, right, top, and bottom refer to the amount of offset from the element's position in the normal flow.

- The same design can often be achieved using floating elements or absolutely positioned elements.

- Float provides a flexible solution for multi-column layouts and allows elements to clear floated elements from their sides, something that can't be done with absolute positioning.

XHTMLcross

This has been a turbo-charged chapter, with lots to learn. Help it all sink in by doing this crossword. All the answers come from the chapter.

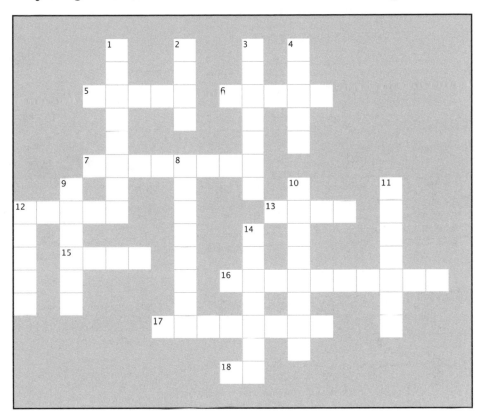

Across

5. State between liquid and frozen.
6. Type of positioning that is relative to the viewport.
7. When you place two inline elements next to each other, their margins don't _____.
12. In general _____ is a better technique for column layouts because you can use clear.
13. Inline elements are flowed from the top _____.
15. Special inline elements that get grouped together into boxes as the page is laid out.
16. Absolute positioning is relative to the positioned _____ block.
17. This kind of margin was used on the coupon for a special effect.
18. Usually used to identify an element that is going to be positioned.

Down

1. Another name for the browser window.
2. Method browser uses to position static elements on the page.
3. Property that describes the layering behavior of positioned elements.
4. Property used to fix footer overlap problems.
8. With this positioning, you specify the position relative to the edges of the containing block.
9. Block elements are flowed top to _____.
10. A positioning type that keeps elements in the flow.
11. When boxes are placed on top of each other, these collapse.
12. Removes element from the flow, and sets it to one side.
14. Inline content flows around _____ elements.

BE the Browser

Open your "lounge.html" file and locate all the block elements. Flow each one on to the page below. Just concentrate on the block elements nested directly inside the body element. You can also ignore the "float" property in your CSS because you still don't know what it does. Here's the solution.

Each block element in your "lounge. html" file is flowed from top to bottom, with a linebreak in between.

These three elements have nested block elements in them.

We didn't ask you to, but if you went the extra mile, here's how they get flowed.

Exercise Solutions

Move the elixirs <div> back to its original place below the music recommendations, then save and reload the page. Where does the element get floated now? You should have seen the elixirs below the music recommendations.

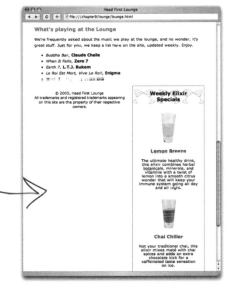

The <div> is floated to the right, just below the music recommendations, and the remainder of the XHTML is floated around it (which is just the footer).

Sharpen your pencil Solution

What we want to do is set a right margin on the main content section so that it's the same width as the sidebar. But how big is the sidebar? Well, we hope you aren't already rusty since the last chapter. Here's all the information you need to compute the width of the sidebar. And here's the solution.

```
#sidebar {
        background:  #efe5d0 url(images/background.gif) bottom right;
        font-size:   105%;
        padding:     15px;
        margin:      0px 10px 10px 10px;
        width:       280px;
        float:       right;
}
```

$$15 + 15 + 280 + 0 + 0 + 10 + 10 = 330$$

left padding | right padding | content area | left border | right border | right margin | left margin

Sharpen your pencil
Solution

Time to put all this knowledge about floating and positioning to a test!
Take a look at the Web page below. There are four elements with
an id. Your job is to correctly match each of those elements with the
CSS rules on the right, and fill in the correct id selector for each one.
Here's the solution. Did you get them all correct?

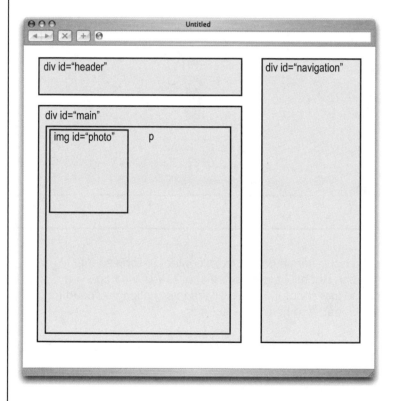

Fill in the selectors to
complete the CSS.

```
#main        {
    margin-top:    140px;
    margin-left:   20px;
    width:         500px;
}

#navigation  {
    position: absolute;
    top:        20px;
    left:       550px;
    width:      200px;
}

#photo       {
    float: left;
}

#header      {
    position: absolute;
    top:       20px;
    left:      20px;
    width:     500px;
    height:    100px;
}
```

Solution

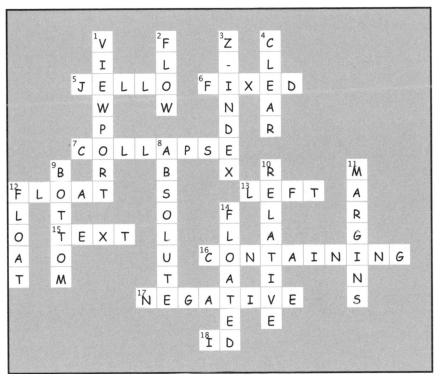

13 tables and more lists

Getting Tabular

If it walks like a table and talks like a table... There comes a time in life when we have to deal with the dreaded *tabular data*. Whether you need to create a page representing your company's inventory over the last year or a catalog of your Beanie Babies collection (don't worry, we won't tell), you know you need to do it in XHTML; but how? Well, have we got a deal for you: order now and in a single chapter we'll reveal the secrets that will allow you to put your very own data right inside XHTML tables. But there's more: with every order we'll throw in our exclusive guide to styling XHTML tables. And, if you act now, as a special bonus, we'll throw in our guide to styling XHTML lists. Don't hesitate, call now!

Hey guys, I just created this little table of the cities in my journal. I was going to put it on the Web site, but I couldn't find a good way to do it with headings or blockquotes or paragraphs. Can you help?

City	Date	Temperature	Altitude	Population	Diner Rating
Walla Walla, WA	June 15	75	1,204 ft	29, 686	4/5
Magic City, ID	June 25	74	5,312 ft	50	3/5
Bountiful, UT	July 10	91	4,226 ft	41, 173	4/5
Last Chance, CO	July 23	102	4,780 ft	265	3/5
Truth or Consequences, NM	August 9	93	4,242 ft	7, 289	5/5
Why, AZ	August 18	104	860 ft	480	3/5

How do you make tables with XHTML?

Tony's right; you really haven't seen a good way of using XHTML to represent his table, at least not yet. While you might think there's a way to use CSS and **<div>**s to create tables, XHTML has a **<table>** element to take care of all your tabular needs. Before we dive into the **<table>** element, let's first get an idea of what goes into a table:

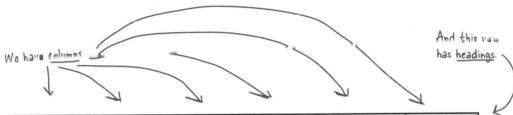

We have columns

And this row has <u>headings</u>.

And we have <u>rows</u>...

City	Date	Temp	Altitude	Population	Diner Rating
Walla Walla, WA	June 15th	75°	1,204 ft	29,686	4/5
Magic City, ID	June 25th	74°	5,312 ft	50	3/5
Bountiful, UT	July 10th	91°	4,.226 ft	41,173	4/5
Last Chance, CO	July 23rd	102°	4,780 ft	265	3/5
Truth or Consequences, NM	August 9th	93°	4,242 ft	7,289	5/5
Why, AZ	August 18th	104°	060 ft	480	3/5

We call each piece of data a <u>cell</u>, or sometimes just <u>table data</u>.

⚛ BRAIN POWER

If they put you in charge of XHTML, how would you design one or more elements that could be used to specify a table, including headings, rows, columns, and the actual table data?

How to create a table using XHTML

Before we pull out Tony's site and start making changes, let's get the table working like we want it in a separate XHTML file. We've started the table and already entered the headings and the first two rows of the table into an XHTML file called "table.html" in the "chapter13/journal/" folder. Check it out:

```
<!DOCTYPE html PUBLIC "-//W3C//DTD XHTML 1.0 Strict//EN"
    "http://www.w3.org/TR/xhtml1/DTD/xhtml1-strict.dtd">
<html xmlns="http://www.w3.org/1999/xhtml" lang="en" xml:lang="en">
<head>
    <meta http-equiv="content-type" content="text/html; charset=ISO-8859-1" />
    <style type="text/css">
        td, th {border: 1px solid black;}
    </style>
    <title>Testing Tony's Travels</title>
</head>
<body>
    <table>
        <tr>
            <th>City</th>
            <th>Date</th>
            <th>Temperature</th>
            <th>Altitude</th>
            <th>Population</th>
            <th>Diner Rating</th>
        </tr>
        <tr>
            <td>Walla Walla, WA</td>
            <td>June 15th</td>
            <td>75</td>
            <td>1,204 ft</td>
            <td>29,686</td>
            <td>4/5</td>
        </tr>
        <tr>
            <td>Magic City, ID</td>
            <td>June 25th</td>
            <td>74</td>
            <td>5,312 ft</td>
            <td>50</td>
            <td>3/5</td>
        </tr>
    </table>
</body>
</html>
```

Just a small bit of CSS so we can see the structure of the table in the browser. Don't worry about this for now.

We use a <table> tag to start the table.

Here's the first row, which we start with a <tr>.

Each <th> element is a table heading for a column.

Notice that the table headings are listed one after each other. While these look like they might make up a column in the HTML, we are actually defining the entire table headings row. Look back at Tony's list to see how his headings map to these.

Each <tr> element forms a table row.

Here's the start of the second row, which is for the city Walla Walla.

Each <td> element holds one cell of the table, and each cell makes a separate column.

All these <td>s make up one row.

And here's the third row. Again, the <td> elements each hold one piece of table data.

What the browser creates

Let's take a look at how the browser displays this XHTML table. We'll warn you now: this isn't going to be the *best-looking* table, but it *will* look like a table. We'll worry about how it looks shortly; for now let's make sure you've got the basics down.

Here's how the browser displays the table XHTML.

We've got three rows total, including the headings.

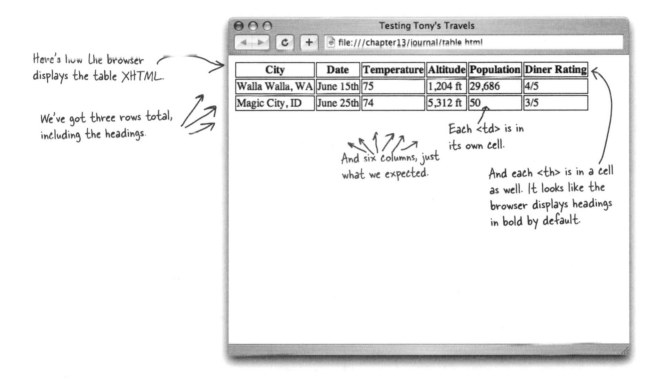

Testing Tony's Travels

file:///chapter13/journal/table.html

City	Date	Temperature	Altitude	Population	Diner Rating
Walla Walla, WA	June 15th	75	1,204 ft	29,686	4/5
Magic City, ID	June 25th	74	5,312 ft	50	3/5

And six columns, just what we expected.

Each <td> is in its own cell.

And each <th> is in a cell as well. It looks like the browser displays headings in bold by default.

Exercise

First type in the "Testing Tony's Travels" XHTML from the previous page. Typing this in, while tedious, will help get the structure of the <table>, <tr>, <th>, and <td> tags in your head. When you finish, give it a quick test, and then add the remaining items from Tony's table. Test that too.

Tables dissected

You've seen four elements used to create a single table: <table>, <tr>, <th> and <td>. Let's take a closer look at each one to see exactly what role it plays in the table.

The <table> tag is the tag that starts the whole thing off. When you want a table, start here.

The <th> element contains one cell in the heading of your table. It must be inside a table row.

<th>Date</th>

The </tr> tag ends a row of the table.

<table>

<tr> ....

</tr>

City	Date	Temp	Altitude	Population	Diner Rating
Walla Walla, WA	June 15th	75°	1,204 ft	29,686	4/5
Magic City, ID	June 25th	74°	5,312 ft	50	3/5
Bountiful, UT	July 10th	91°	4,226 ft	41,173	4/5
Last Chance, CO	July 23rd	102°	4,780 ft	265	3/5
Truth or Consequences, NM	August 9th	93°	4,242 ft	7,289	5/5
Why, AZ	August 18th	104°	860 ft	480	3/5

<tr> ....   **</tr>**

Each <tr> element specifies a table row. So, all the table data that goes in a row is nested inside the <tr> element.

<td>August 9th</td>

The <td> element contains one data cell in your table. It must be inside a table row.

</table>

The </table> tag ends the table.

Q: Why isn't there a table column element? That seems pretty important.

A: The designers of XHTML decided to let you specify tables by row, rather than by column. But notice that by specifying each row's <td> elements, you are implicitly specifying each column anyway.

Q: What happens if I have a row that doesn't have enough elements? In other words, I've got less things than the number of columns in the table?

A: The easiest way to deal with that is to just leave the content of the data cell empty, in other words, you write <td></td>. If you leave out the data cell, then the table won't line up properly, so all the data cells have to be there, even if they are empty.

Q: What if I want my table headings to be down the left side of the table, instead of across the top; can I do that?

A: Yes, you certainly can. You just need to put your table heading elements in each row instead of all in the first row. If your <th> element is the first item in each row, then the first column will consist of all table headings.

Q: My friend showed me a cool trick where he did all his page layout right within a table. He didn't even have to use CSS!

A: Go straight to CSS jail. Do not pass go; do not collect $200.

Using tables for layout was commonly done in the HTML era before CSS, when, frankly, there was no better way to do complex layouts. However, it is a poor way to do your layouts today. Using tables for layout is notoriously hard to get right and difficult to maintain. Tell your friend that his technique is old school, and he needs to get up to speed with the right way to do layout: CSS with XHTML.

Q: Isn't a table all about presentation? What happened to presentation versus structure?

A: Not really. With tables you are specifying the relationships between truly tabular data. We'll use CSS to alter the presentation of the table.

Tables give you a way to specify tabular data in your HTML.

Tables consist of data cells within rows. Columns are implicitly defined within the rows.

The number of columns in your table will be the number of data cells you have in a row.

In general, tables are not meant to be used for presentation; that's the job of CSS.

BE the Browser

On the left, you'll find the XHTML for a table. Your job is to play like you're the browser displaying the table. After you've done the exercise, look at the end of the chapter to see if you got it right.

```
<table><tr><th>Artist</th>
<th>Album</th></tr><tr>
<td>Enigma</td><td>Le Roi Est Mort,
Vive Le Roi!</td></tr> <tr><td>LTJ
Bukem</td>
<td>Progression Sessions 6</td>
</tr><tr>
<td>Timo Maas</td>
<td>Pictures</td></tr></table>
```

Here's just the table XHTML...

Argh! Someone needs to learn how to format their XHTML.

Draw the table here.

Adding a caption and a summary

There are a couple of things you can do right off the bat to improve your tables, like adding a caption and a summary.

```
    <table summary="This table holds data about the
cities I visited on my travels.  I've included the date
I was in each city, the temperature when I was there,
and altitude and population of each city.  I've also
included a rating of the diners where I had lunch, on a
scale from 1 to 5.">
        <caption>
                The cities I visited on my
                Segway'n USA travels
        </caption>
        <tr>
            <th>City</th>
            <th>Date</th>
            <th>Temperature</th>
            <th>Altitude</th>
            <th>Population</th>
            <th>Diner Rating</th>
        </tr>
        <tr>
            <td>Walla Walla, WA</td>
            <td>June 15th</td>
            <td>75</td>
            <td>1,204 ft</td>
            <td>29,006</td>
            <td>4/5</td>
        </tr>
        <tr>
            <td>Magic City, ID</td>
            <td>June 25th</td>
            <td>74</td>
            <td>5,312 ft</td>
            <td>50</td>
            <td>3/5</td>
        </tr>
        .
        .
        .
</table>
```

The summary doesn't appear in the Web page display. This is purely for accessibility, and acts as a bit of text a screen reader may read aloud to a user to describe the table.

The caption, on the other hand, is displayed in the browser. By default, most browsers display this above the table.

If you don't like the default location of the caption, you can use CSS to reposition it (we'll give that a try in a sec), although some browsers don't fully support repositioning the caption yet.

The rest of the table rows go here.

Test drive... and start thinking about style

Add the summary and caption to your table. Save and reload.

You won't see the summary; it's primarily for screen readers to read aloud to the visually impaired to help provide more information about the table data.

The caption is at the top of the table. It'll probably look better on the bottom.

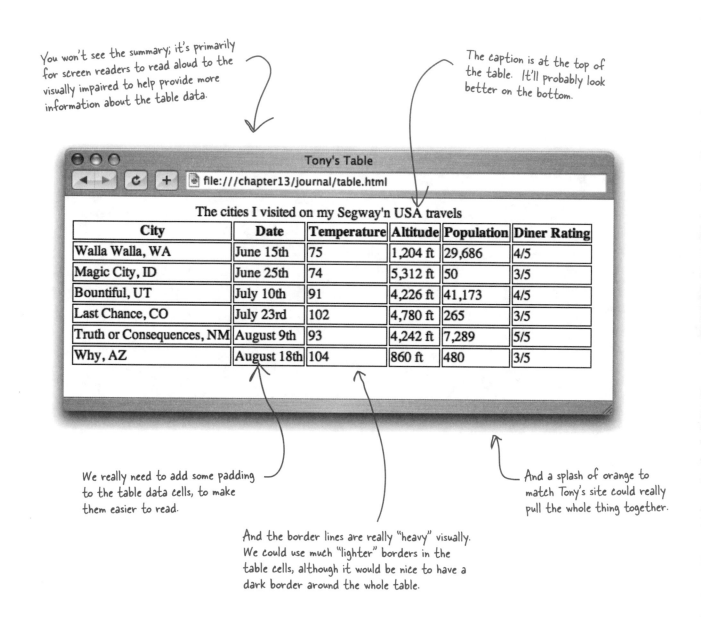

We really need to add some padding to the table data cells, to make them easier to read.

And the border lines are really "heavy" visually. We could use much "lighter" borders in the table cells, although it would be nice to have a dark border around the whole table.

And a splash of orange to match Tony's site could really pull the whole thing together.

Before we start styling, let's get the table into Tony's page

Before we start adding style to Tony's new table, we should really get the table into his main page. Remember that Tony's main page already has set a font-family, font-size, and a lot of other styles that our table is going to inherit. So without putting the table into his page we won't really know what the table looks like.

Start by opening the "journal.html" in the "chapter13/journal" folder, locate the August 20th entry, and make the following changes. When you've finished, move on to the next page before reloading.

```
<h2>August 20, 2005</h2>
<p>
    <img src="images/segway2.jpg" alt="Me and my Segway in New Mexico" />
</p>


<p>
Well, I made it 1200 miles already, and I passed through some interesting
places on the way:
</p>

<ol>
    <li>Walla Walla, WA</li>
    <li>Magic City, ID</li>
    <li>Bountiful, UT</li>
    <li>Last Chance, CO</li>
    <li>Truth or Consequences, NM</li>
    <li>Why, AZ</li>
</ol>
```

This is the old list of cities. Delete this because we're replacing it with the table.

```
<table summary="This table holds data about the cities I visited on my travels.  I've included
    the date I was in each city, the temperature when I was there, and altitude and population
    of each city.  I've also included a rating of the diners where I had lunch, on a
    scale from 1 to 5.">
    <caption>The cities I visited on my Segway'n USA travels</caption>
    <tr>
        <th>City</th>
        <th>Date</th>
        <th>Temperature</th>
        <th>Altitude</th>
        <th>Population</th>
        <th>Diner Rating</th>
    </tr>
        .
        .
        .
</table>
```

The new table goes here. Copying and pasting it from the previous file is the easiest way to get it here.

Now let's style the table

Now we need to copy the table styles into "journal.css". But, since we're going to change them anyway, let's just add new style instead. Add the new styles highlighted below at the bottom of the style sheet file.

```
body {
    font-family: Verdana, Geneva, Arial, sans-serif;
    font-size: small;
}
h1, h2 {
    font-weight: normal;
    color: #cc6600;
    border-bottom: thin dotted #888888;
}
h1 {
    font-size: 170%;
}
h2 {
    font-size: 130%;
}
blockquote {
    font-style: italic;
}
```

This is all the style that's currently in Tony's Web page. We added all this in Chapter 9. We're going to add the new style for the tables below it.

```
table {
    margin-left: 20px;
    margin-right: 20px;
    border: thin solid black;
    caption-side: bottom;
}

td, th {
    border: thin dotted gray;
    padding: 5px;
}

caption {
    font-style: italic;
    padding-top: 8px;
}
```

First, we'll style the table. We're going to add a margin on the left and right, and a thin, black border to the table.

And, we're going to move that caption to the bottom of the table.

Let's also change the border on the table data cells to be a much lighter, dotted border in gray.

And let's add some padding to the data cells so there's some space between the data content and the border.

This rule styles the caption. We're changing the font-style to italic and adding some top padding.

Taking the styled tables for a test drive

That's a lot of changes at once. Make sure you save them, and you should validate as well. Then load "journal.html" into your browser.

The table looks quite different now that you've styled it. We're also inheriting a few styles that were already in Tony's journal.

All the fonts are now sans-serif and a smaller size. We picked that up from the previous styles already in the file.

Now we've got a dark border and dotted lines.

And we've got some margin on the table and some padding in each table cell.

Those dotted lines are looking really busy and distracting though. It doesn't help that they are duplicated between each pair of table cells.

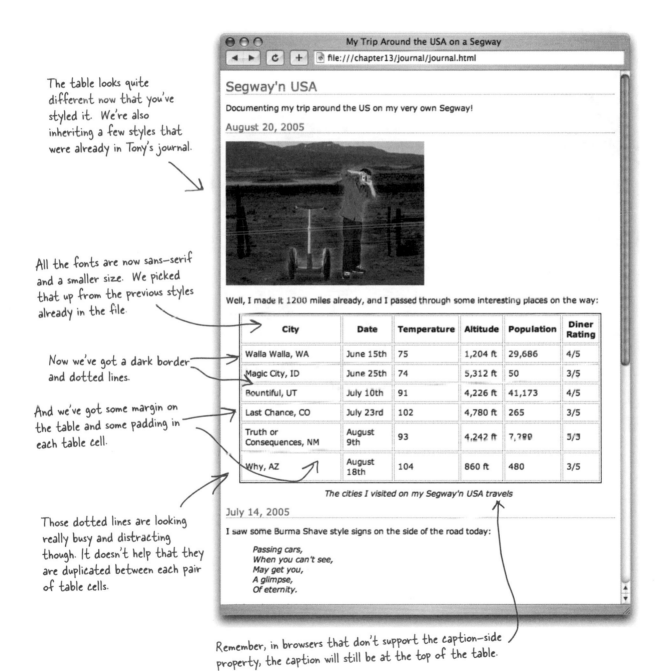

Remember, in browsers that don't support the caption-side property, the caption will still be at the top of the table.

Table cells look like they just use the box model too... they've got padding and a border. Do they also have a margin?

Table cells do have padding and a border – just like you've seen in the box model – but they are a little different when it comes to margins.

The box model is a good way to think about table cells, but they do differ when it comes to margins. Let's take a look at one of the cells in Tony's table:

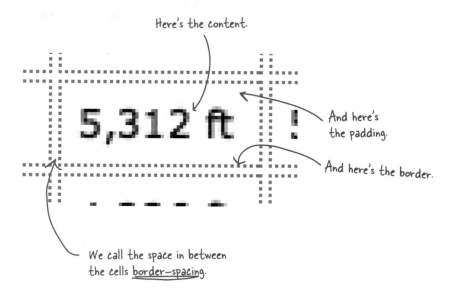

Here's the content.

And here's the padding.

And here's the border.

We call the space in between the cells <u>border-spacing</u>.

So instead of a margin, we have a **border-spacing** property, which is defined over the entire table. In other words, you can't set the "margin" of an individual table cell; rather, you set a common spacing around all cells.

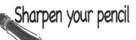

Sharpen your pencil

The double dotted lines are giving Tony's table a busy and distracting look. It would be much better, and wouldn't detract from the table, if we could just have one border around each table cell. Can you think of a way to do that with styling given what you've just learned? Give it a try and check your answer in the back of the chapter.

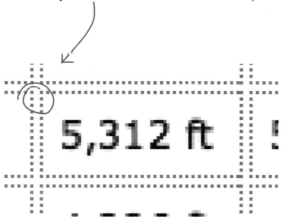

there are no
Dumb Questions

Q: So border spacing is defined for the entire table, while a margin can be set for an individual element?

A: Right. Table cells don't have margins; what they have is spacing around their borders, and this spacing is set for the entire table. You can't control the border spacing of each table cell separately.

Q: Well, is there any way to have different border spacing on the vertical than I have on the horizontal? That seems useful.

A: You sure can. You can specify your border spacing like this:

border-spacing: 10px 30px;

That sets ten pixels of horizontal border space and thirty pixels of vertical border space.

Q: The border-spacing doesn't seem to work in my browser.

A: Are you using Internet Explorer? We're sorry to report that IE version 6 doesn't support border-spacing. And, we're sorry we didn't tell you sooner. But, hey, you're not going to forget that now, are you?

Getting those borders to collaspe

There is another way to solve the border dilemma, besides the **border-spacing** property. You can use a CSS property called **border-collapse** to collapse the borders so that there is no border spacing at all. When you do this, your browser will ignore any border spacing you have set on the table. It will also combine two borders that are right next to each other into one border. This "collapses" two borders into one.

Here's how you can set the **border-collapse** property. Follow along and make this change in your "journal.css" file:

```
table {
    margin-left: 20px;
    margin-right: 20px;
    border: thin solid black;
    caption-side: bottom;
    border-collapse: collapse;
}
```

Add a border-collapse property and set its value to "collapse".

Save the file and reload; then check out the changes in the border.

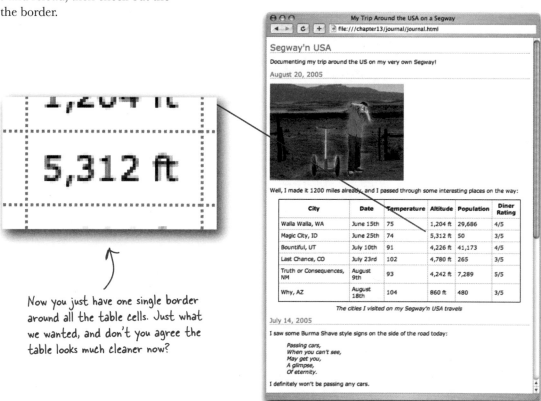

Now you just have one single border around all the table cells. Just what we wanted, and don't you agree the table looks much cleaner now?

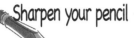

Sharpen your pencil

You're becoming quite the pro at XHTML and CSS, so we don't mind giving you a little more to play with in these exercises. How about this: we'd like to spruce this table up even a little more, starting with some text alignment issues. Let's say we want the date, temperature, and diner rating to be center-aligned. And how about right alignment on the altitude and population? How would you do that?

Here's a hint: create two classes, one for center-aligned and one for right-aligned. Then just use the text-align property in each. Finally, add the appropriate class to the correct <td> elements.

This may sound tough, but take it step by step; you already know everything you need to finish this one. And, of course, you can find the answer in the back of the chapter, but give yourself the time to solve it before you peek.

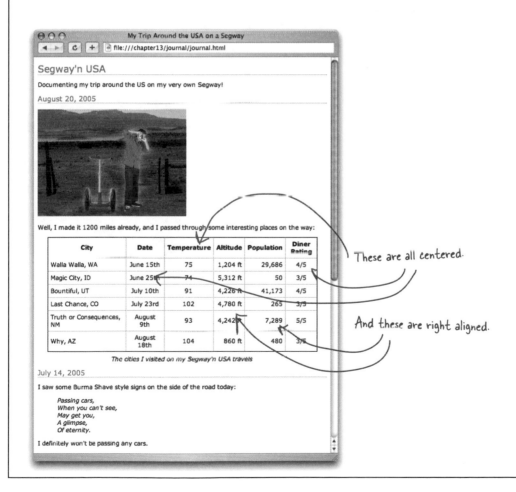

City	Date	Temperature	Altitude	Population	Diner Rating
Walla Walla, WA	June 15th	75	1,204 ft	29,686	4/5
Magic City, ID	June 25th	74	5,312 ft	50	3/5
Bountiful, UT	July 10th	91	4,226 ft	41,173	4/5
Last Chance, CO	July 23rd	102	4,780 ft	265	3/5
Truth or Consequences, NM	August 9th	93	4,242 ft	7,289	5/5
Why, AZ	August 18th	104	860 ft	480	3/5

These are all centered.

And these are right aligned.

Segway'n USA

Documenting my trip around the US on my very own Segway!

August 20, 2005

Well, I made it 1200 miles already, and I passed through some interesting places on the way:

The cities I visited on my Segway'n USA travels

July 14, 2005

I saw some Burma Shave style signs on the side of the road today:

Passing cars,
When you can't see,
May get you,
A glimpse,
Of eternity.

I definitely won't be passing any cars.

How about some color?

You know Tony loves his signature color and there's no reason not to add some color to his table; not only will it look great, but we can actually improve the readability of the table by adding some color. Just like for any other element, all you need to do is set the **background-color** property on a table cell to change its color (notice how everything you've learned about XHTML and CSS is starting to come together!). Here's how you do that:

```
th {
    background-color: #cc6600;
}
```

Add this new rule to your "journal.css" file and reload. Here's what you'll see:

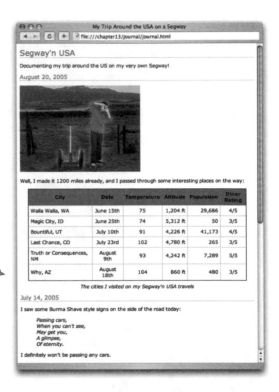

How about some color in the table rows?

So far the color is looking pretty nice. So let's take it to the next level. A common way to color tables is to give rows an alternating color, which allows you to more easily see each row without getting confused about which column goes with which row. Check it out:

Difficult to do in CSS? Nope. Here's how you can do this. First define a new class; let's call it "cellcolor":

```
.cellcolor {
    background-color: #fcba7a;
}
```

Now all you need to do is add this class attribute to each row you'd like to color. So in this case, you find the **<tr>** opening tags for Magic City, Last Chance, and Why, and add **class="cellcolor"** to each one.

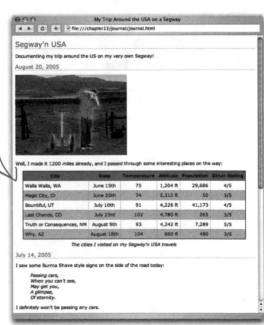

Did we mention that Tony made an interesting discovery in Truth or Consequences, New Mexico?

It's fair to say Tony found something interesting about Truth or Consequences, New Mexico; in fact, he found *her* so interesting that after going to Arizona, he turned around and came right back.

We're glad for Tony, but he's really given us a conundrum with the table. While we could just add a new row for Truth or Consequences, we'd really like to do it in a more elegant way. What are we talking about? Turn the page to find out.

Tess

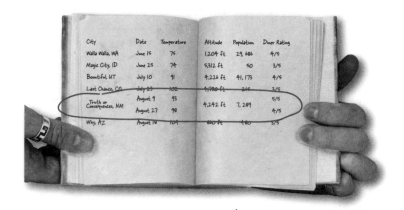

Another look at Tony's table

Based on his return trip to New Mexico, Tony's added a new entry for August 27th, just below the original Truth or Consequences entry. He's also reused a couple of cells where the information didn't change (a great technique for reducing the amount of information in a table). You can see that when he added the new row, all he needed to do was list the things that were different the second time around (the date, the temperature, and that he revisited the diner).

Here are both Tony's visits to Truth or Consequences.

City	Date	Temp	Altitude	Population	Diner Rating
Walla Walla, WA	June 15th	75°	1,204 ft	29,686	4/5
Magic City, ID	June 25th	74°	5,312 ft	50	3/5
Bountiful, UT	July 10th	91°	4,226 ft	41,173	4/5
Last Chance, CO	July 23rd	102°	4,780 ft	265	3/5
Truth or Consequences, NM	August 9th	93°	4,242 ft	7,289	5/5
	August 27th	98°			4/5
Why, AZ	August 18th	104°	860 ft	480	3/5

These table data cells span TWO rows now.

But where does this leave you with XHTML? It seems like you'd have to add a entirely new row and just duplicate the city, altitude and population, right? Well, not so fast. We have the technology... using XHTML tables, you can have cells span more than one row (or more than one column). Let's see how this works...

How to tell cells to span more than one row

What does it mean for a cell to span more than one row? Let's look at the entries for Truth or Consequences, NM in Tony's table again. The data cells for city, altitude, and population span *two rows*, not one, while the date, temp, and diner rating span one row, which is the normal, default behavior for data cells.

City	Date	Temp	Altitude	Population	Diner Rating
Walla Walla, WA	June 15th	75°	1,204 ft	29,686	4/5
Magic City, ID	June 25th	74°	5,312 ft	50	3/5
Bountiful, UT	July 10th	91°	4,226 ft	41,173	4/5
Last Chance, CO	July 23rd	102°	4,780 ft	265	3/5
Truth or Consequences, NM	August 9th	93°	4,242 ft	7,289	5/5
	August 27th	98°			4/5
Why, AZ	August 18th	104°	860 ft	480	3/5

These cells span two rows.

While the date, temp, and diner rating cells take up just one.

So, how do you do that in XHTML? It's easier than you might think: you use the **rowspan** attribute to specify how many rows a table data cell should take up, and then remove the corresponding table data elements from the other rows that the cell spans over. Have a look – it's easier to see than describe:

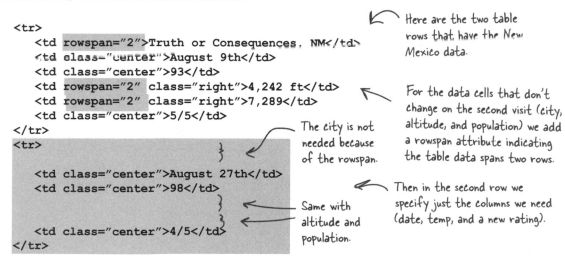

```
<tr>
    <td rowspan="2">Truth or Consequences, NM</td>
    <td class="center">August 9th</td>
    <td class="center">93</td>
    <td rowspan="2" class="right">4,242 ft</td>
    <td rowspan="2" class="right">7,289</td>
    <td class="center">5/5</td>
</tr>
<tr>

    <td class="center">August 27th</td>
    <td class="center">98</td>

    <td class="center">4/5</td>
</tr>
```

Here are the two table rows that have the New Mexico data.

For the data cells that don't change on the second visit (city, altitude, and population) we add a rowspan attribute indicating the table data spans two rows.

The city is not needed because of the rowspan.

Same with altitude and population.

Then in the second row we specify just the columns we need (date, temp, and a new rating).

WHO DOES WHAT?

Just to make sure you've got this down, draw an arrow from each <td> element to its corresponding cell in the table. Check your answers before moving on.

```
<tr>
   <td rowspan="2">Truth or Consequences, NM</td>
   <td class="center">August 9th</td>
   <td class="center">93</td>
   <td rowspan="2" class="right">4,242 ft</td>
   <td rowspan="2" class="right">7,289</td>
   <td class="center">5/5</td>
</tr>
<tr>

   <td class="center">August 27th</td>
   <td class="center">98</td>

   <td class="center">4/5</td>
</tr>
```

Truth or Consequences, NM	August 9th	93°	4,242 ft	7,289	5/5
	August 27th	98°			4/5

The new and improved table

Make the changes to the table in "journal.html" and give it a test run. Take a look at the table. Think about exactly what you're doing to the table: you're using XHTML to specify that certain cells should take up more than one row, and to do that, you're removing the **<td>**s they're displacing.

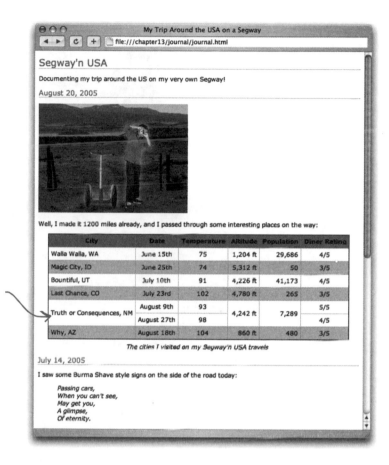

Now we've got a great-looking table that doesn't have any redundant information in it.

there are no
Dumb Questions

Q: You said you can have table data span columns too?

A: You sure can. Just add a colspan attribute to your <td> element and specify the number of columns. Unlike the rowspan, when you span columns, you remove table data elements that are in the *same* row (since you are spanning columns, not rows).

Q: Can I have a colspan and rowspan in the same <td>?

A: You sure can. Just make sure you adjust the other <td>s in the table to account for both the row and column spans. In other words, you'll need to remove the corresponding number of <td>s from the same row, *and* from the column.

Q: Do you really think these rowspans look better?

A: Well they certainly reduce the amount of information in the table, which is usually a good thing. And, if you look at a few tables out there in the real world you'll find that rowspans and colspans are quite common, so it's great to be able to do them in XHTML. But if you liked the table better before, feel free to change your XHTML and go back to the previous version.

Trouble in paradise?

It looks like we've got a disagreement on the diner rating for August 27th, and while we could ask Tony and Tess to come to a consensus, why should we? We've got tables and we should be able to get another rating in there. But how? We don't really want to add yet another entry just for Tess' review. Hmmm... why don't we do it like this?

City	Date	Temp	Altitude	Population	Diner Rating
Walla Walla, WA	June 15th	75°	1,204 ft	29,686	4/5
Magic City, ID	June 25th	74°	5,312 ft	50	3/5
Bountiful, UT	July 10th	91°	4,226 ft	41,173	4/5
Last Chance, CO	July 23rd	102°	4,780 ft	265	3/5
Truth or Consequences, NM	August 9th	93°	4,242 ft	7,289	5/5
	August 27th	98°			Tess 5/5 Tony 4/5
Why, AZ	August 18th	104°	860 ft	480	3/5

Why not put both their ratings in the table? That way we get more accurate information.

Hold on... that looks like a table within a table.

That's because it is. But, nested tables in XHTML are straightforward. All you need to do is put another **<table>** element inside a **<td>**. How do you do that? You create a simple table to represent both Tony's and Tess' ratings together, and when you have that working, put it inside the table cell that now holds Tony's 4/5 rating. Let's give it a try...

```
<tr>
   <td rowspan="2">Truth or Consequences, NM</td>
   <td class="center">August 9th</td>
   <td class="center">93</td>
   <td rowspan="2" class="right">4,242 ft</td>
   <td rowspan="2" class="right">7,289</td>
   <td class="center">5/5</td>
</tr>
<tr>
   <td class="center">August 27th</td>
   <td class="center">98</td>
   <td>
      4/5
      <table>
         <tr>
            <th>Tess</th>
            <td>5/5</td>
         </tr>
         <tr>
            <th>Tony</th>
            <td>4/5</td>
         </tr>
      </table>
   </td>
</tr>
```

First delete the old rating that represented Tony's rating...

... and put a table in its place. This table holds two diner ratings: one for Tess and one for Tony. We're using table headings for their names, and data cells for their ratings.

Test driving the nested table

Go ahead and type in the new table. Tables are easy to mistype, so make sure you validate and then reload your page. You should see the new, nested table.

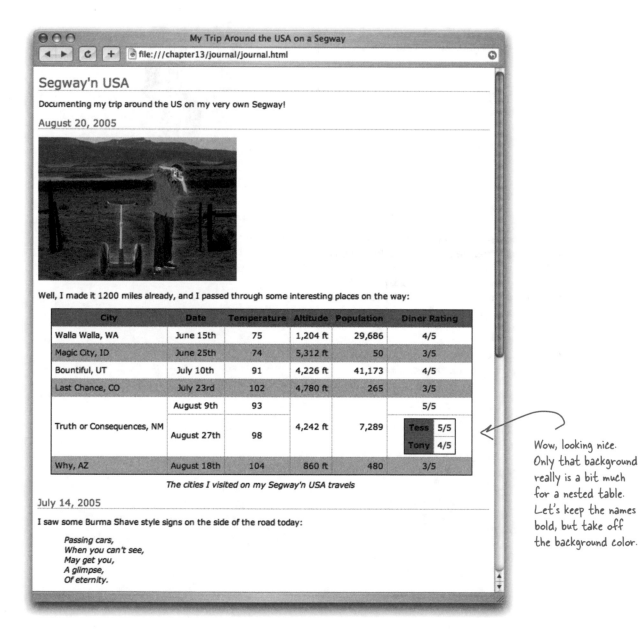

Wow, looking nice. Only that background really is a bit much for a nested table. Let's keep the names bold, but take off the background color.

BRAIN BARBELL

It's time to fall back on all that training you've done. What you need to do is change the table heading background color for just Tony and Tess, and do it without changing the background of the main table headings. How? You need to find a selector that selects only the nested table headings.

City	Date	Temperature	Altitude	Population	Diner Rating	
Walla Walla, WA	June 15th	75	1,204 ft	29,686	4/5	
Magic City, ID	June 25th	74	5,312 ft	50	3/5	
Bountiful, UT	July 10th	91	4,226 ft	41,173	4/5	
Last Chance, CO	July 23rd	102	4,780 ft	265	3/5	
Truth or Consequences, NM	August 9th	93	4,242 ft	7,289	5/5	
	August 27th	98			**Tess**	5/5
					Tony	4/5
Why, AZ	August 18th	104	860 ft	480	3/5	

The cities I visited on my Segway'n USA travels

We want to change the background color of the nested table headers to white.

Determine the selector to select only the nested table heading elements.

```
_____ {
    background-color: white;
}
```

Stop! Don't turn the page until you do this exercise.

Overriding the CSS for the nested table headings

You can target just the **`<th>`** elements in the nested table using a descendant selector. Add a new rule to your CSS that uses the "table table th" selector to change the background color of the nested table headers to white:

```
table table th {
    background-color: white;
}
```

Now save the changes to your "journal.css" file and reload.

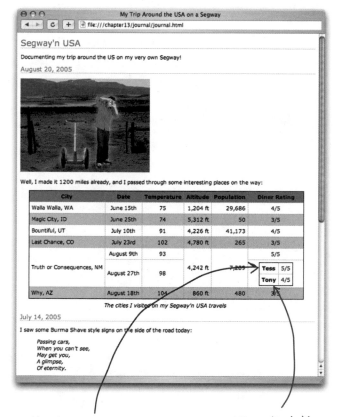

Now the `<th>` in the nested table has a white background.

But notice it still has the bold font weight since we didn't override that property.

there are no
Dumb Questions

Q: I used a class to solve the Brain Barbell. I created a class called "nestedtable" and assigned each table heading to it. Then I created a rule like this:

```
.nestedtable {
    background-color: white;
}
```

Is that an okay solution too?

A: There are lots of different ways to solve problems using CSS, and certainly your solution is an effective and perfectly valid way to use CSS. We'll just point out that by using the descendant selector instead, we didn't have to make any changes to our XHTML. What if Tony and Tess keep adding reviews for diners? Then for every review, you'd have to make sure and add the class to each `<th>`. With our solution, the styling happens automatically.

You want Tony and Tess to have different background colors on their table rows; say, blue and pink. Can you think of several ways to do that?

Giving Tony's site the final polish

Tony's page is really looking nice, but there's one more area we haven't spent any time styling yet: the list that contains the set of items he was preparing for his trip. You'll find this list in his June 2nd entry; check it out below:

> *We're looking at just the XHTML snippet from the June 2nd entry*

```
<h2>June 2, 2005</h2>

<p>
    <img src="images/segway1.jpg"
         alt="The first day of the trip" />
</p>

<p>
    My first day of the trip!  I can't
    believe I finally got everything
    packed and ready to go.  Because
    I'm on a Segway, I wasn't able
    to bring a whole lot with me:
</p>
<ul>
    <li>cellphone</li>
    <li>iPod</li>
    <li>digital camera</li>
    <li>a protein bar</li>
</ul>
<p>
    Just the essentials.  As Lao Tzu
    would have said, <q>A journey of
    a thousand miles begins with
    one Segway.</q>
</p>
</body>
</html>
```

> *Here's the bottom of Tony's journal, "journal.html". Remember his packing list in his first journal entry?*

> *Here's what the list looks like now.*

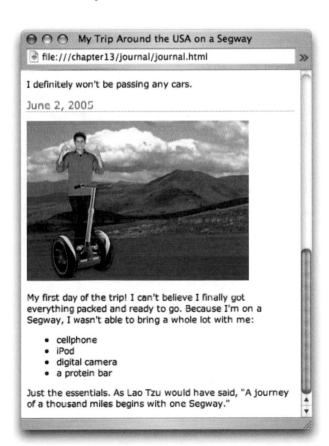

Giving the list some style

You're probably figuring out that once you know the basic CSS font, text, color, and other properties, you can style just about anything. The same is true for lists; in fact, there are only a couple of properties that are specific to lists. The main list property is called **list-style-type** and it allows you to control the bullets (or "markers", as they are called) used in your lists. Here are a few ways you can do that:

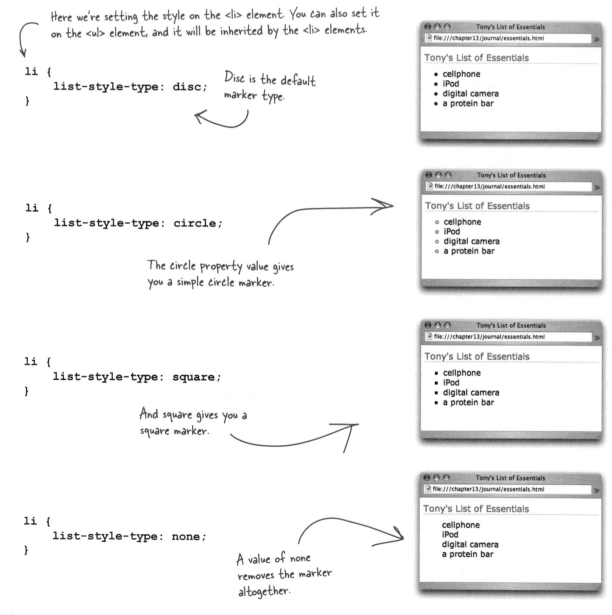

Here we're setting the style on the <li> element. You can also set it on the <ul> element, and it will be inherited by the <li> elements.

```
li {
    list-style-type: disc;
}
```

Disc is the default marker type.

```
li {
    list-style-type: circle;
}
```

The circle property value gives you a simple circle marker.

```
li {
    list-style-type: square;
}
```

And square gives you a square marker.

```
li {
    list-style-type: none;
}
```

A value of none removes the marker altogether.

What if you want a custom marker?

Do you really think Tony would want anything less than his own custom marker? Well, luckily CSS has a property called **list-style-image** that lets you set an image to be the marker for a list. Let's give it a try on Tony's list:

Here's the list-style-image property, which we're setting to a URL.

```
li {
    list-style-image: url(images/backpack.gif);
    padding-top: 5px;
    margin-left: 20px;
}
```

We're adding some margin to add space on the left of the list items, and also a little top padding to give each list item a bit of headroom.

The image "backpack.gif" is a small version of this backpack. Seems fitting doesn't it? And in Tony's signature color, too.

And, the final test drive...

This is it: your last change to Tony's site. Add the rule for the list item to your CSS and then reload.

Here's the list with the marker replaced with an image and some extra margin and padding spacing.

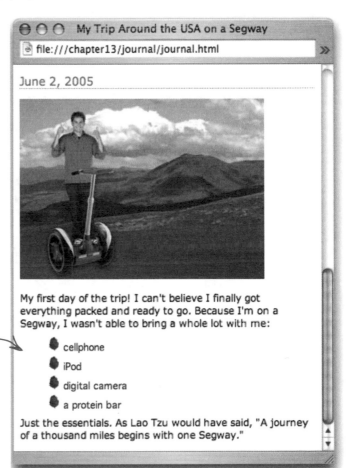

Q: What about ordered lists? What can I do to change their style?

A: You style ordered and unordered lists in the same way. Of course, an ordered list has a sequence of numbers or letters for markers, not bullets. Using CSS you can control whether an ordered lists' markers are decimal numbers, roman numerals, or alphabetic letters (like a, b, c) with the list-style-type property. Common values are decimal, upper-alpha, lower-alpha, upper-roman, and lower-roman. Consult a CSS reference for more options (there are many).

Q: How can I control the text wrap on lists? In other words, how can I control whether text wraps underneath the marker or just underneath the text?

A: There's a property called list-style-position. If you set this property to "inside" then your text will wrap under the marker. If you set it to "outside" then it will wrap just under the text above it.

Q: Are you sure that's right? That seems backwards.

A: Yes, and here's what inside and outside *really* mean: if you set your line-style-position to "inside" then the *marker is inside* your list item and so text will wrap under it. If you set it to "outside", then the *marker is outside* your list item and so text will just wrap under itself. And, by "inside your item" we mean inside the border of the list item's box.

Wow, who would have known we could take my site this far when we started?

We're going to get Tess a Segway of her own so she can go with me on the rest of my Segway'n USA trip. See ya somewhere... and we'll BOTH be updating the Web page. Thanks for everything!

BULLET POINTS

- XHTML tables are used to structure tabular data.

- Use the HTML table elements, <table>, <tr>, <th>, and <td> together to create a table.

- The <table> element defines and surrounds the entire table.

- Tables are defined in rows, using the <tr> element.

- Each row contains one or more data cells, defined with the <td> element.

- Use the <th> element for data cells that are row or column headings.

- Tables are laid out in a grid. Each row corresponds to a <tr>...</tr> row in your HTML, and each column corresponds to the <td>...</td> content within the rows.

- You can provide additional information about your tables with the table summary attribute, and the <caption> element.

- Table data cells can have padding, borders, and border spacing, which is the space between cells.

- Just like you can control the padding, borders, and margins of elements, you can control the padding, borders, and border spacing of table cells with CSS.

- The border-collapse property is a special CSS property for tables that allows you to combine cell borders into one border for a cleaner look.

- You can change the alignment of the data in your table cells with the text-align and vertical-align CSS properties.

- You can add color to your tables with the background-color property. Background color can be added to the entire table, to each row, or to a single data cell.

- If you have no data for a data cell, put no content into the <td> element. You need to use a <td>...</td> element to maintain the alignment of the table, however.

- If your data cell needs to span multiple rows or columns, you can use the rowspan or colspan attributes of the <td> element.

- You can nest tables within tables by placing the <table> element and all its content inside a data cell.

- Tables should be used for tabular data, not for laying out your pages. Use CSS positioning to create multi-column page layouts as we described in Chapter 12.

- Lists can be styled with CSS just like any other element. There are a few CSS properties specific to lists, such as list-style-type and list-style-image.

- list-style-type allows you to change the type of the marker used in your list.

- list-style-image allows you to specify an image for your list marker.

XHTMLcross

That crossword looks a bit like a table, doesn't it? Give your left brain a workout and solve this crossword. All the words are from this chapter.

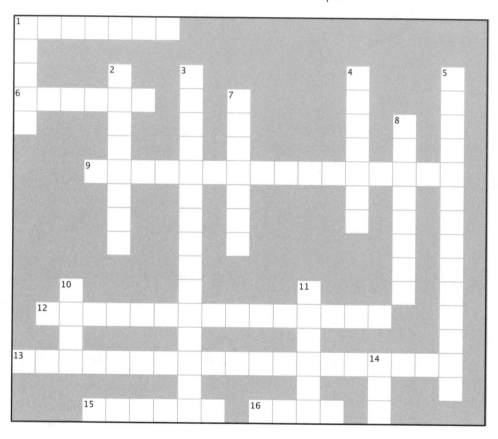

Across

1. Provides a longer description used for screen readers.
6. One table inside another is called _____.
9. Use this property to use an image instead of a built-in marker in your lists.
12. Used to merge borders.
13. Used to control whether the marker is inside or outside the list items border.
15. We call bullets a type of list _____.
16. <td> is for these.

Down

1. What a data cell does when it uses more than one row or column.
2. <th> is for these.
3. Use this property to change your list marker.
4. Table cells have padding and borders, but no _____.
5. Area between borders.
7. Adds a short description that is displayed with the table.
8. list-item-position can be used to control the behavior of text _____.
10. You specify HTML tables by _____, not columns.
11. Don't use tables for this.
14. Default position of the caption.

Exercise Solutions

First type in the "Testing Tony's Table" XHTML. Typing this in, while tedious, will help get the structure of the <table>, <tr>, <th>, and <td> elements in your head. When you finish, give it a quick test, and then add the remaining items from Tony's table. Test that too.

```
<!DOCTYPE html PUBLIC "-//W3C//DTD XHTML 1.0 Strict//EN"
    "http://www.w3.org/TR/xhtml1/DTD/xhtml1-strict.dtd">
<html xmlns="http://www.w3.org/1999/xhtml" lang="en" xml:lang="en">
<head>
    <meta http-equiv="Content-Type" content="text/html; charset=ISO-8859-1" />
    <style type="text/css">
        td, th {border: 1px solid black;}
    </style>
    <title>Testing Tony's Table</title>
</head>
<body>
    <table>
        <tr>
            <th>City</th>
            <th>Date</th>
            <th>Temperature</th>
            <th>Altitude</th>
            <th>Population</th>
            <th>Diner Rating</th>
        </tr>
        <tr>
            <td>Walla Walla, WA</td>
            <td>June 15th</td>
            <td>75</td>
            <td>1,204 ft</td>
            <td>29,686</td>
            <td>4/5</td>
        </tr>
        <tr>
            <td>Magic City, ID</td>
            <td>June 25th</td>
            <td>74</td>
            <td>5,312 ft</td>
            <td>50</td>
            <td>3/5</td>
        </tr>
        <tr>
            <td>Bountiful, UT</td>
            <td>July 10th</td>
            <td>91</td>
            <td>4,226 ft</td>
            <td>41,173</td>
            <td>4/5</td>
        </tr>
        <tr>
            <td>Last Chance, CO</td>
            <td>July 23rd</td>
            <td>102</td>
            <td>4,780 ft</td>
            <td>265</td>
            <td>3/5</td>
        </tr>
        <tr>
            <td>Truth or Consequences, NM</td>
            <td>August 9th</td>
```

Exercise
Solutions

```
            <td>93</td>
            <td>4,242 ft</td>
            <td>7,289</td>
            <td>5/5</td>
        </tr>
        <tr>
            <td>Why, AZ</td>
            <td>August 18th</td>
            <td>104</td>
            <td>860 ft</td>
            <td>480</td>
            <td>3/5</td>
        </tr>
    </table>
</body>
</html>
```

Testing Tony's Table

file:///chapter13/journal/table.html

City	Date	Temperature	Altitude	Population	Diner Rating
Walla Walla, WA	June 15th	75	1,204 ft	29,686	4/5
Magic City, ID	June 25th	74	5,312 ft	50	3/5
Bountiful, UT	July 10th	91	4,226 ft	41,173	4/5
Last Chance, CO	July 23rd	102	4,780 ft	265	3/5
Truth or Consequences, NM	August 9th	93	4,242 ft	7,289	5/5
Why, AZ	August 18th	104	860 ft	480	3/5

BE the Browser

On the left, you'll find the XHTML for a table. Your job is to play like you're the browser displaying the table. Here's the solution.

```
<table>
   <tr>
      <th>Artist</th>
      <th>Album</th>
   </tr>
   <tr>
      <td>Enigma</td>
      <td>Le Roi Est Mort, Vive Le Roi!</td>
   </tr>
   <tr>
      <td>LTJ Bukem</td>
      <td>Progression Sessions 6</td>
   </tr>
   <tr>
      <td>Timo Maas</td>
      <td>Pictures</td>
   </tr>
</table>
```

Artist	Album
Enigma	Le Roi Est Mort, Vive Le Roi!
LTJ Bukem	Progression Sessions 6
Timo Maas	Pictures

Sharpen your pencil
Solution

The double dotted lines are giving Tony's table a busy and distracting look. It would be much better, and wouldn't detract from the table, if we could just have one border around each table cell. Can you think of a way to do that with styling given that you've just learned? You can set the border-spacing property to 0 to remove the space between the borders.

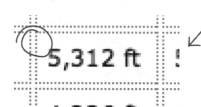

We could use border-spacing to set spacing to 0; then the two lines would be right next to each other.

```
table {
    margin-left: 20px;
    margin-right: 20px;
    border: thin solid black;
    caption-side: bottom;
    border-spacing: 0px;
}
```

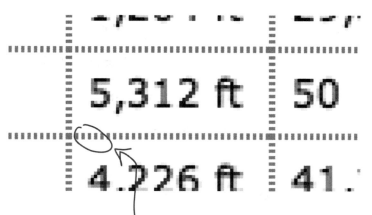

Better, but we have still two lines and they're right up against each other, so we have a double thick dotted border. We'd rather it just be ONE border between the cells. Wouldn't we?

Sharpen your pencil
Solution

```
.center {
    text-align: center;
}
.right {
    text-align: right;
}
```

Here are the two classes, one for center and one for right alignment.

```
<table summary="This table holds data about the cities I visited on my
travels.  I've included the date I was in each city, the temperature when
I was there, and altitude and population of each city.  I've also included
a rating of the diners where I had lunch, on a scale from 1 to 5.">
    <caption>The cities I visited on my Segway'n USA travels</caption>
    <tr>
        <th>City</th>
        <th>Date</th>
        <th>Temperature</th>
        <th>Altitude</th>
        <th>Population</th>
        <th>Diner Rating</th>
    </tr>
    <tr>
        <td>Walla Walla, WA</td>
        <td class="center">June 15th</td>
        <td class="center">75</td>
        <td class="right">1,204 ft</td>
        <td class="right">29,686</td>
        <td class="center">4/5</td>
    </tr>
    <tr>
        <td>Magic City, ID</td>
        <td class="center">June 25th</td>
        <td class="center">74</td>
        <td class="right">5,312 ft</td>
        <td class="right">50</td>
        <td class="center">3/5</td>
    </tr>
    .
    .
    .
</table>
```

And here you just add each <td> to the appropriate class!

Exercise Solution

To create alternating colors in the Magic City, Last Chance, and Why table rows, you just add the class="cellcolor" attribute to the <tr> opening tag in these rows, like this:

```
<tr class="cellcolor">
    <td>Magic City, ID</td>
    ...
</tr>
```

City	Date	Temperature	Altitude	Population	Diner Rating
Walla Walla, WA	June 15th	75	1,204 ft	29,686	4/5
Magic City, ID	June 25th	74	5,312 ft	50	3/5
Bountiful, UT	July 10th	91	4,226 ft	41,173	4/5
Last Chance, CO	July 23rd	102	4,780 ft	265	3/5
Truth or Consequences, NM	August 9th	93	4,242 ft	7,289	5/5
Why, AZ	August 18th	104	860 ft	480	3/5

WHO DOES WHAT?

Just to make sure you've got this down, draw an arrow from each <td> element to its corresponding cell in the table. Here are the answers.

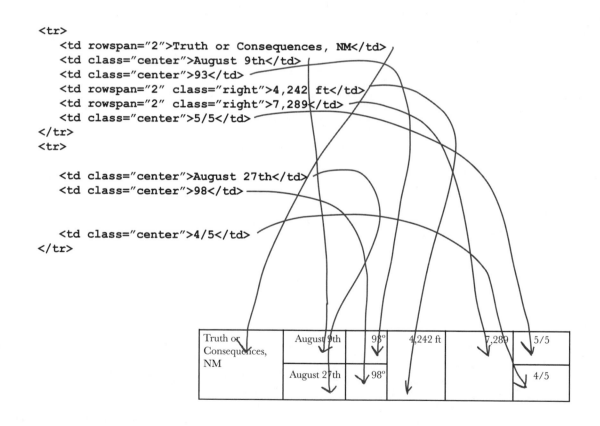

```
<tr>
    <td rowspan="2">Truth or Consequences, NM</td>
    <td class="center">August 9th</td>
    <td class="center">93</td>
    <td rowspan="2" class="right">4,242 ft</td>
    <td rowspan="2" class="right">7,289</td>
    <td class="center">5/5</td>
</tr>
<tr>

    <td class="center">August 27th</td>
    <td class="center">98</td>


    <td class="center">4/5</td>
</tr>
```

| Truth or Consequences, NM | August 9th | 98° | 4,242 ft | 7,289 | 5/5 |
| | August 27th | 98° | | | 4/5 |

Exercise
Solutions

BRAIN BARBELL

It's time to fall back on all that training you've done. What you need to do is change the table heading background color just for Tony and Tess, and do it without changing the background of the main table headings. How? You need to find a selector that selects only the nested table headings.

We can use a descendant selector to select just the nested table header. Here's how you can do that:

(1) Start by selecting the outer table...

City	Date	Temperature	Altitude	Population	Diner Rating
Walla Walla, WA	June 15th	75	1,204 ft	29,686	4/5
Magic City, ID	June 25th	74	5,312 ft	50	3/5
Bountiful, UT	July 10th	91	4,226 ft	41,173	4/5
Last Chance, CO	July 23rd	102	4,780 ft	265	3/5
Truth or Consequences, NM	August 9th	93	4,242 ft	7,289	5/5
	August 27th	98			Tess 5/5 / Tony 4/5
Why, AZ	August 18th	104	860 ft	480	3/5

The cities I visited on my Segway'n USA travels

(2) Then select the inner table...

(3) Then select the table heading.

    (1)   (2)   (3)

table table th {
    background-color: white;
}

Exercise
Solutions

```
S U M M A R Y
P
A           H       L               M           B
N E S T E D I       C               A           O
S           A   S   C       W       R           R
            D   T   A       R       G           D
        L I S T - S T Y L E - I M A G E
            N   S   I               N   P       R
            G   T   O                   P       -
            S   Y   N                   I       S
                L                       N       P
            R       E           L       G       A
        B O R D E R - C O L L A P S E           C
        W       T           Y                   I
    L I S T - S T Y L E - P O S I T I O N G
                P           U       O
            M A R K E R   D A T A   P
```

14 xhtml forms

Getting Interactive

Yeah, just got your form. We're checking it with the server now, and then we'll get a response right back to you.

So far all your Web communication has been one way: from your page to your visitors. Golly, wouldn't it be nice if your visitors could talk back? That's where XHTML forms come in: once you enable your pages with forms (along with a little help from a Web server), your pages are going to be able to gather customer feedback, take an online order, get the next move in an online game, or collect the votes in a "hot or not" contest. In this chapter you're going to meet a whole team of XHTML elements that work together to create Web forms. You'll also learn a bit about what goes on behind the scenes in the server to support forms, and we'll even talk about keeping those forms stylish (a controversial topic; read on and see why).

How forms work

If you use the Web at all, then you know what a form is. But you might not have really thought about what they have to do with XHTML. A form is basically a Web page with input fields that allows you to enter information. When the form is *submitted*, that information is packaged up and sent off to a Web server to be processed by a Web application. When the processing is done, what do you get? Another Web page, of course, as a response. Let's take a closer look at how this works:

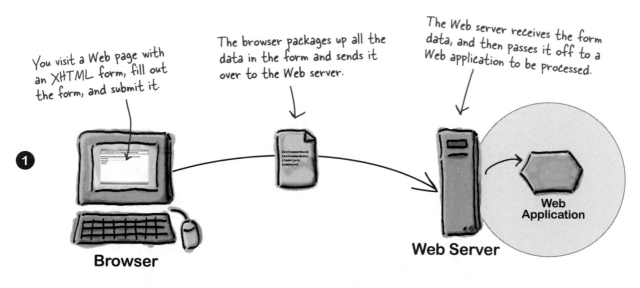

❶

You visit a Web page with an XHTML form, fill out the form, and submit it.

The browser packages up all the data in the form and sends it over to the Web server.

The Web server receives the form data, and then passes it off to a Web application to be processed.

Browser

Web Server

Web Application

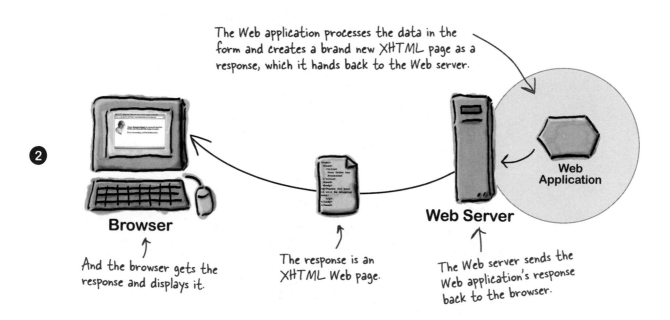

❷

The Web application processes the data in the form and creates a brand new XHTML page as a response, which it hands back to the Web server.

Browser

Web Server

Web Application

And the browser gets the response and displays it.

The response is an XHTML Web page.

The Web server sends the Web application's response back to the browser.

How forms work in the browser

To a browser, a form is just a bit of XHTML in a page. You'll see that you can easily create forms in your pages by adding a few new elements. Here's how a form works from the browser's perspective:

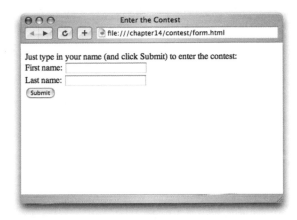

The browser loads the page

The browser loads the XHTML for a page like it always does, and when it encounters form elements, it creates *controls* on the page that allow you to input various kinds of data. A control is just something like a button or a text input box or a drop down menu – basically something that allows you to input data.

You enter data

You use the controls to enter data. Depending on the type of control, this happens in different ways. You can type a single line of text into a text control, or you might click one option of many in a checkbox control. We'll look at the different kinds of controls shortly.

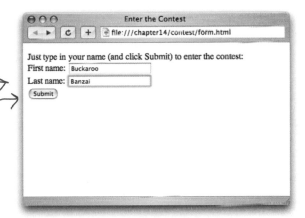

You submit the form

You *submit* the form by clicking on a submit button control. That's the browser's cue that it needs to package up all the data and send that data off to the server.

The server responds

Once the server has the form data, it passes it off to the appropriate Web application for processing. This processing results in a brand new XHTML page that is returned to the browser, and since it's just XHTML, the browser displays it for you.

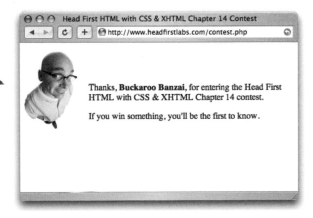

What you write in XHTML

There's no deep mystery to creating forms with XHTML. In fact, in this chapter you're going to meet a whole new set of XHTML elements that all work together to create forms. The best way to get a feel for forms is to look at a little XHTML and then to give it a try. Check out this form:

```
<!DOCTYPE html PUBLIC "-//W3C//DTD XHTML 1.0 Strict//EN"
    "http://www.w3.org/TR/xhtml1/DTD/xhtml1-strict.dtd">
<html>
    <head>
```

← This stuff is all old hat for you now.

```
        <meta http-equiv="Content-Type"
            content="text/html; charset=ISO-8859-1" />
        <title>Enter the Contest</title>
    </head>
    <body>
```

Here's the form.

```
<form action="http://www.headfirstlabs.com/contest.php" method="POST">
    <p>Just type in your name (and click Submit) to
        enter the contest: <br />
```

We've got the `<form>` element itself.

```
    First name: <input type="text" name="firstname" value="" /> <br />
    Last name: <input type="text" name="lastname" value="" /> <br />
    <input type="submit" />
```

And a bunch of elements nested inside it.

```
    </p>
</form>
```

```
    </body>
</html>
```

(A) (B) (C) (D)

Relax For now just take a good look at the form and what's in it; we'll be going into all the details throughout the chapter.

What the browser creates

Big surprise; to create a form you use a **<form>** element. Now, just about any block level element can go inside the **<form>** element, but there's a whole new set of elements that are made especially for forms. Each of these form elements provides a different way for you to enter information: text boxes, checkboxes, menus of options, and more. We'll examine all these elements, but first take another look back at the XHTML on the previous page and see how the elements and content inside the **<form>** element are displayed in the page below:

Here's just normal paragraph text in a form.

And here are two text controls for entering a first and last name. In XHTML you use the <input> element to create these.

And here's the submit button. (Your button might say "Submit Query" instead.)

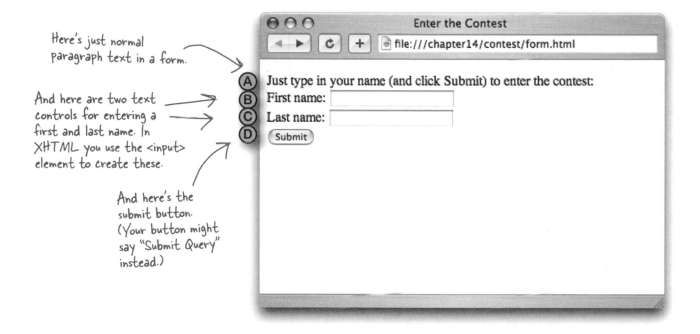

Enter the Contest

file:///chapter14/contest/form.html

(A) Just type in your name (and click Submit) to enter the contest:
(B) First name: [   ]
(C) Last name: [   ]
(D) Submit

Exercise

You'll find the contest form in your "chapter14/contest" folder. Open it, take another look around, then load it in your browser and enter the contest.

How the form element works

Let's take a closer look at the **\<form\>** element – not only does it hold all the elements that make up the form, but it also tells the browser where to send your form data when you submit the form (and the method the browser should use to send it).

Here's the opening tag. Everything in the form goes inside.

The action attribute holds the URL of the Web server...

...and the name of the Web application that will process the form data.

The method attribute determines how the form data will be sent to the server. We're going to use the most common one: POST. Later in the chapter we'll talk about other ways to send data, and why you might or might not use POST.

`<form action="http://www.headfirstlabs.com/contest.php" method="POST">`

Everything inside your form goes here.

`</form>`

And the closing tag ends the form.

Hey "www.headfirstlabs.com", my user just clicked a button to submit a form. I've got some form data I'm sending you via POST. It's addressed to the "contest.php" application.

Bring it on. We're ready!

Submit

Browser

contest.php

www.headfirstlabs.com

Okay, so I have an XHTML form - that seems like the easy part. But where do I get a Web application, or how do I make one?

Good question. Creating Web applications is a whole topic unto itself and far beyond what we cover in this book. Well, we tried to cover them, but the book ended up weighing more than you do (not good). So, anyway...

To create Web applications you need to know a scripting or programming language, and one that is supported by your hosting company. Most hosting companies support languages like PHP, Perl, Python, and Java, and if you're interested, you'll definitely want to pick up a book specifically for creating Web applications. Also, check with your hosting company; they sometimes provide simple scripts to their customers, which takes the work out of developing Web applications yourself.

As for this chapter, we've already developed all the Web applications you'll need. All you'll need to do is put the URL of these applications in the **action** attribute of your **<form>** element.

What can go in a form?

You can put just about any block element into a form, but that's not what we really care about right now; we're interested in the *form elements that create controls in the browser*. Here's a quick rundown of all the commonly used form elements. We're going to start with the **`<input>`** form element, which plays a lot of roles in the form's world.

text input

The text <input> element is for entering one line of text. Optional attributes let you set a maximum number of characters and the width of this control.

Name: Buckaroo Banzai

An <input> element with a type attribute of "text" creates a one line control in the browser page.

Most form elements require a name that is used by the Web application. We'll see how this works in a bit.

Use the type attribute to indicate you want a "text" input.

```
<input type="text" name="fullname" />
```

The <input> element is an empty element, so you end it with a " />"

Notice that both of these use the same XHTML element, but with different values in their type attribute.

submit input

The submit <input> element creates a button that allows you to submit a form. When you click this button, the browser sends the form to the Web application for processing.

Submit

The button is labelled "Submit" (or "Submit Query") by default, although you can change that (we'll show you how later).

```
<input type="submit" />
```

For a submit button, specify "submit" as the <input> element's type.

radio input

The radio <input> element creates a single control with several buttons, only one of which can be selected at any time. These are like old time car radio buttons; you "push" one in, and the rest "pop out".

 hot

◯ not

The radio control allows only one of a set of choices.

Use a radio <input> for each choice.

All the radio buttons associated with a given set of choices must have the same name...

...but each choice has a different value.

Same here, we're still using the <input> element, just with different type values.

```
<input type="radio" name="hotornot" value="hot" />
<input type="radio" name="hotornot" value="not" />
```

checkbox input

A checkbox <input> element creates a checkbox control that can be either checked or unchecked. You can use multiple checkboxes together, and if you do, you can check as many or few as you like.

☑ Salt
☑ Pepper
☐ Garlic

Unlike radio buttons, a checkbox allows zero or more of a set of choices.

Like radio, you use one checkbox <input> element for each choice.

Related checkboxes also share a common name.

Each checkbox has a different value.

```
<input type="checkbox" name="spice" value="Salt" />
<input type="checkbox" name="spice" value="Pepper" />
<input type="checkbox" name="spice" value="Garlic" />
```

What can go in a form? (Part II)

Okay, not every form element is an **<input>** element. There are a few others, like **<select>** for menus and **<textarea>** for typing in more than one line of text. So, why don't you get familiar with these as well before moving on? Oh, and by the way, once you do that, you'll know 90% of the form elements (and 99% of the form elements that are commonly used).

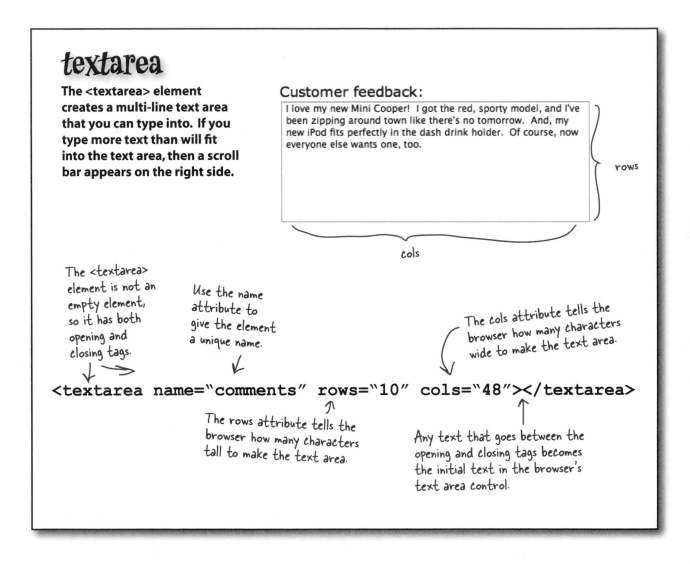

textarea

The <textarea> element creates a multi-line text area that you can type into. If you type more text than will fit into the text area, then a scroll bar appears on the right side.

Customer feedback:

> I love my new Mini Cooper! I got the red, sporty model, and I've been zipping around town like there's no tomorrow. And, my new iPod fits perfectly in the dash drink holder. Of course, now everyone else wants one, too.

rows

cols

The <textarea> element is not an empty element, so it has both opening and closing tags.

Use the name attribute to give the element a unique name.

The cols attribute tells the browser how many characters wide to make the text area.

```
<textarea name="comments" rows="10" cols="48"></textarea>
```

The rows attribute tells the browser how many characters tall to make the text area.

Any text that goes between the opening and closing tags becomes the initial text in the browser's text area control.

select

The **<select>** element creates a menu control in the Web page. The menu provides a way to choose between a set of choices. The **<select>** element works in combination with the **<option>** element below to create a menu.

> Buckaroo Banzai ⬍

The select element creates a menu that looks like this (although the look will vary depending on the browser you're using).

The <select> element goes around all the menu options to group them into one menu.

Just like the other form elements, give the select element a unique name using the name attribute.

```
<select name="characters">
    <option value="Buckaroo">Buckaroo Banzai</option>
    <option value="Tommy">Perfect Tommy</option>
    <option value="Penny">Penny Priddy</option>
    <option value="Jersey">New Jersey</option>
    <option value="John">John Parker</option>
</select>
```

option

The **<option>** element works with the **<select>** element to create a menu. Use an **<option>** element for each menu item.

After clicking on the menu, the menu items drop down.

> ✓ Buckaroo Banzai
> Perfect Tommy
> Penny Priddy
> New Jersey
> John Parker

The content of the <option> element is used for the menu items' description. Each menu option also includes a value representing the menu item.

```
<select name="characters">
    <option value="Buckaroo">Buckaroo Banzai</option>
    <option value="Tommy">Perfect Tommy</option>
    <option value="Penny">Penny Priddy</option>
    <option value="Jersey">New Jersey</option>
    <option value="John">John Parker</option>
</select>
```

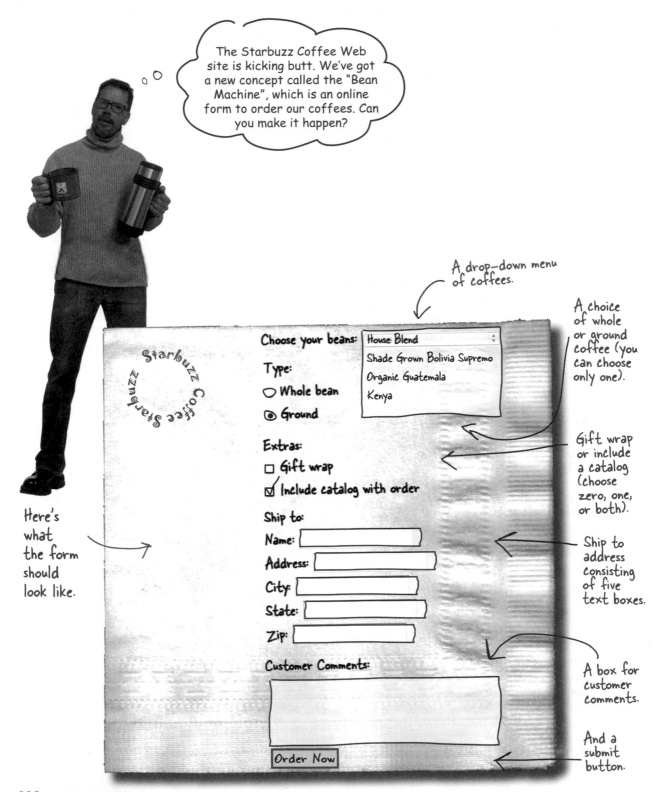

The Starbuzz Coffee Web site is kicking butt. We've got a new concept called the "Bean Machine", which is an online form to order our coffees. Can you make it happen?

A drop-down menu of coffees.

A choice of whole or ground coffee (you can choose only one).

Choose your beans: House Blend
Shade Grown Bolivia Supremo
Organic Guatemala
Kenya

Type:
○ Whole bean
◉ Ground

Extras:
☐ Gift wrap
☑ Include catalog with order

Gift wrap or include a catalog (choose zero, one, or both).

Here's what the form should look like.

Ship to:
Name:
Address:
City:
State:
Zip:

Ship to address consisting of five text boxes.

Customer Comments:

A box for customer comments.

Order Now

And a submit button.

Markup Magnets

Your job is to take the form element magnets and lay them on top of the corresponding controls in the sketch. You won't need all the magnets below to complete the job; some will be left over. Check your answer in the back of the chapter before moving on.

```
<input type="text" ... />
```

```
<input type="checkbox" ... />
```

```
<input type="radio" ... />
```

```
<textarea>...</textarea>
```

```
<select>...</select>
```

```
<option>...</option>
```

```
<input type="submit" ... />
<input type...
```

Choose your beans:

| House Blend |
| Shade Grown Bolivia Supremo |
| Organic Guatemala |
| Kenya |

Type:

◯ Whole bean

◯ Ground

Extras:

☐ Gift wrap

☑ Include catalog with order

Ship to:

Name:

Address:

City:

State:

Zip:

Order Now

Getting ready to build the Bean Machine form

Before we start building that form, take a look inside the "chapter14/starbuzz" folder and you'll find the file "form.html". Open it and have a look around. All this file has in it are the XHTML basics:

```
<!DOCTYPE html PUBLIC "-//W3C//DTD XHTML 1.0 Strict//EN"
                "http://www.w3.org/TR/xhtml1/DTD/xhtml1-strict.dtd">
<html xmlns="http://www.w3.org/1999/xhtml" lang="en" xml:lang="en" >
    <head >
        <meta http-equiv="Content-Type" content="text/html; charset=ISO-8859-1" />
        <title>The Starbuzz Bean Machine</title>
    </head>
    <body>

        <h1>The Starbuzz Bean Machine</h1>
        <h2>Fill out the form below and click submit to order</h2>



    </body>
</html>
```

The form is going to go here.

All we've got so far is a heading identifying the page, along with instructions.

For now, we're going to build these forms without all the style we've been using on the Starbuzz site. That way we can concentrate on the form XHTML. We'll add the style in later.

Figuring out what goes in the form element

It's time to add your very first **<form>** element. The first thing you have to know when creating a **<form>** element is the URL of the Web application that is going to process your form data. We've already taken care of that for you; you'll find the Web application that processes Starbuzz orders here:

http://www.starbuzzcoffee.com/processorder.php

This URL points to the starbuzzcoffee Web site...

...and to the processorder.php Web application that's on the server there. This application already knows how to take orders from the form we're going to build.

Adding the form element

Once you know the URL of the Web application that will process your form, all you
need to do is plug it into the **action** attribute of your **<form>** element, like this
(follow along and type the changes into your XHTML):

```
<!DOCTYPE html PUBLIC "-//W3C//DTD XHTML 1.0 Strict//EN"
                       "http://www.w3.org/TR/xhtml1/DTD/xhtml1-strict.dtd">
<html xmlns="http://www.w3.org/1999/xhtml" lang="en" xml:lang="en" >
   <head>
      <meta http-equiv="Content-Type" content="text/html; charset=ISO-8859-1" />
      <title>The Starbuzz Bean Machine</title>
   </head>
   <body>

      <h1>The Starbuzz Bean Machine</h1>
      <h2>Fill out the form below and click submit to order</h2>

      <form action="http://www.starbuzzcoffee.com/processorder.php" method="POST">



      </form>
   </body>
</html>
```

Here's the
form element.

The action attribute contains the
URL of the Web application.

And remember we're using the
"POST" method to deliver
the form data to the server.
More on this later.

Go ahead and add the
form closing tag too.

So far so good, but an empty **<form>** element isn't going to get you very far.
Looking back at the sketch of the form, there's a lot there to add, but we're going
to start simple and get the "Ship to:" part of the form done first, which consists of
a bunch of text inputs. You already know a little about text inputs, but let's take a
closer look. Here's what the text inputs for the Starbuzz form look like:

We use the <input>
element for a few
different controls.
The type attribute
determines what kind
of control it is.

```
<input type="text" name="name" />
<input type="text" name="address" />
<input type="text" name="city" />
<input type="text" name="state" />
<input type="text" name="zip" />
```

We've got one
text input for
each input area in
the form: Name,
Address, City,
State, and Zip.

Here the type is "text" because this
is going to be a text input control.

The name attribute acts as an identifier for the
data the user types in. Notice how each one is set to
a different value. Let's see how this works...

How form element names work

Here's the thing to know about the **name** attribute: it acts as the glue between your form and the Web application that processes it. Here's how this works:

Each input control in your form has a name attribute

When you type the elements for a form into your XHTML file, you give them unique names. You saw this with the text inputs:

```
<input type="text" name="name" />
<input type="text" name="address" />
<input type="text" name="city"  />
<input type="text" name="state"  />
<input type="text" name="zip"  />
```

Notice here we've got an element whose name is "name" (which is perfectly fine).

Each <input> element gets its own name.

When you submit a form, the browser packages up all the data using the unique names:

Say you type your name, address, city, state, and zip into the form and click submit. The browser takes each of these pieces of data and labels them with your unique name attribute values. The browser then sends the names and values to the server. Like this:

What you enter into the form.

Name: Buckaroo Banzai
Address: Banzai Institute
City: Los Angeles
State: CA
Zip: 90050

The unique names for each form element.

```
name = Buckaroo Banzai
address = Banzai Institute
city = Los Angeles
state = CA
zip = 90050
```

Each unique name gets a value from the data you type into the form.

What the browser packages up for the server.

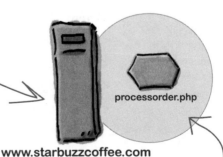

processorder.php

www.starbuzzcoffee.com

The Web application needs the form data to be labelled so it can tell what is what.

Q: What's the difference between a text <input> and a <textarea>?

A: You want to use a text <input> for entering text that is just a single line, like a name or zip code, and a <textarea> for longer, multi-line text.

Q: Can I make the submit button say something other than "Submit"?

A: Yes, just put a value attribute in the element and give it a value like "Order Now". You can also use the value attribute of text input to give that input some default text.

Q: Is there a limit to how much text I can type into a text <input> or a <textarea>?

A: Browsers do place a limit on the amount of text you can type into either a text <input> or a <textarea>; however, it's usually way more than you'd ever need to type. If you'd like to limit how much your users can type into a text <input>, you can use the maxlength attribute and set it to a specific number of characters. For example, maxlength="100" would limit users to typing at most 100 characters. However, for a <textarea>, there is no way with XHTML to limit how much your users can type.

Q: I still don't get how the names get matched up with the form data.

A: Okay, you know each form element has a unique name, and you also know that the element has a corresponding value. When you click the submit button the browser takes all the names along with their values and sends them to the server. For instance, when you type the zip code "90050" into a text <input> element with the name "zip", the browser sends "zip = 90050" to the server when the form is submitted.

Q: How does the Web application know the names I'm going to use in my form? In other words, how do I pick the names for my form elements?

A: Good question. It really works the other way around: you have to know what form names your Web application is expecting and write your form to match it. If you're using a Web application that someone else wrote, they'll have to tell you what names to use, or provide that information in the documentation for the application. A good place to start is to ask your hosting company for help.

Q: Why doesn't the <option> element have a name attribute? Every other form element does.

A: Good catch. All <option> elements are actually part of the menu that is created by the <select> element. So, we only really need one name for the entire menu, and that is already specified in the <select> element. In other words, <option> elements don't need a name attribute because the <select> has already specified the name for the entire menu. Keep in mind that when the form is submitted, only the value of the currently selected option is sent along with this name to the server.

Q: Didn't you say that the name for each form element needs to be unique? But the radio <input> elements all have the same name.

A: Right. Radio buttons come as a set. Think about it: if you push one button in, the rest pop out. So, for the browser to know the radio buttons belong together, you use the same name. Say you have a set of radio buttons named "color" with values of "red", "green", and "blue". They're all colors, and only one color can be selected at a time, so a single name for the set makes sense.

Q: What about checkboxes? Do they work like radio buttons?

A: Yes; the only difference is that you are allowed to select more than one choice with a checkbox.

When the browser sends the form data to the server, it combines all the checkbox values into one value and sends them along with the checkbox name. So, say you had "spice" checkboxes for "salt", "pepper", and "garlic", and you checked them all; then the server would send "spice = salt&pepper&garlic" to the server.

Q: Geez, do I really need to know all this stuff about how data gets to the server?

A: All you need to know is the names and types of the form elements your Web application is expecting. Beyond that, knowing how it all works sometimes helps, but, no, you don't need to know all the gory-behind-the-scenes details of what is being sent to the server.

Back to getting those <input> elements into your XHTML

Now we've got to get those **<input>** elements inside the form.
Check out the additions below, and then make the changes in
your "form.html".

We're going to start by putting everything inside a <p> element.

You can only nest block elements directly inside a form.

Here's JUST the form snippet from "form.html". Hey, we've got to save a few trees here!

```
<form action="http://www.starbuzzcoffee.com/processorder.php" method="POST">
   <p>Ship to: <br />

      Name: <input type="text" name="name" /> <br />

      Address: <input type="text" name="address" /> <br />

      City: <input type="text" name="city" /> <br />

      State: <input type="text" name="state" /> <br />

      Zip: <input type="text" name="zip" /> <br />
   </p>
   <p>

      <input type="submit" value="Order Now" />

   </p>

</form>
```

Here are all the <input> elements: one for each text input in the "Ship to" section of the form.

We've added a label for each input so the user knows what goes in the text input.

*And you should also know that <input> is an inline element, so if you want some linebreaks between the <input> elements, you have to add
s. That's also why you need to nest them all inside a paragraph.*

Finally, don't forget that users need a submit button to submit the form. So add a submit button by inserting an <input> at the bottom with a type of "submit". Also add a value of "Order Now", which will change the text of the button from "Submit" to "Order Now".

After you've made all these changes, save your "form.html" file
and let's give this a whirl.

Don't forget to validate your XHTML. Forms elements need validation too!

A form-al test drive

Reload the page, fill in the text inputs, and submit the form. When you do that, the browser will package up the data and send it to the URL in the **action** attribute, which is at www.starbuzzcoffee.com.

You don't think we'd give you a toy example that doesn't really work, do you? Seriously, starbuzzcoffee.com is all ready to take your form submission. Go for it!

Notice the change in the URL of your address bar after you submit the form (you'll see the URL in the action attribute in the address bar).

Here's the form.

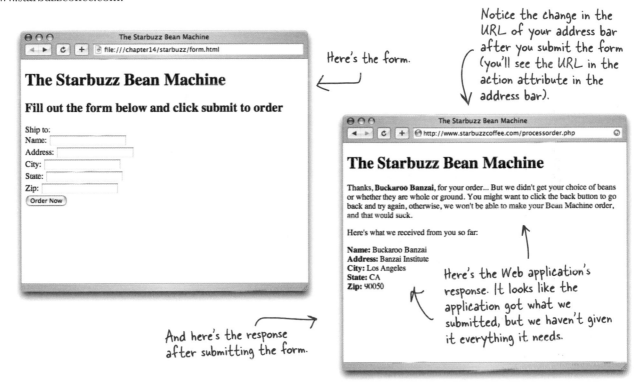

And here's the response after submitting the form.

Here's the Web application's response. It looks like the application got what we submitted, but we haven't given it everything it needs.

Adding some more input elements to your form

It looks like the Web application isn't going to let us get very far without telling it the beans we want, as well as the bean type (ground or whole). Let's add the bean selection first by adding a **<select>** element to the form. Remember that the **<select>** element contains a list of options, each of which becomes a choice in a drop-down menu. Also, associated with each choice is a value; when the form is submitted, the value of the chosen menu option is sent to the server. Turn the page and let's add the **<select>** element.

Adding the <select> element

```
<form action="http://www.starbuzzcoffee.com/processorder.php" method="POST">
    <p> Choose your beans:

    <select name="beans">

        <option value="House Blend">House Blend</option>

        <option value="Bolivia">Shade Grown Bolivia Supremo</option>

        <option value="Guatemala">Organic Guatemala</option>

        <option value="Kenya">Kenya</option>

    </select>

</p>
```

Here's our brand new <select> element. It gets a unique name too.

Inside we put each <option> element, one per choice of coffee.

```
    <p>Ship to: <br />
        Name: <input type="text" name="name" /> <br />
        Address: <input type="text" name="address" /> <br />
        City: <input type="text" name="city" /> <br />
        State: <input type="text" name="state" /> <br />
        Zip: <input type="text" name="zip" /> <br />
    </p>
    <p>
        <input type="submit" value="Order Now" />
    </p>
</form>
```

HTML Up Close

Let's take a closer look at the **<option>** element.

The content of the element is used as the label in the drop down menu.

Each option has a value.

<option value="House Blend">House Blend**</option>**

When the browser packages up the names and values of the form elements, it uses the name of the <select> element along with the value of the chosen option.

← In this case, the browser would send the server beans = "House Blend".

Test driving the <select> element

Let's give the **<select>** element a spin now. Reload your page and you should have a nice new menu waiting on you. Choose your favorite coffee, fill in the rest of the form, and submit your order.

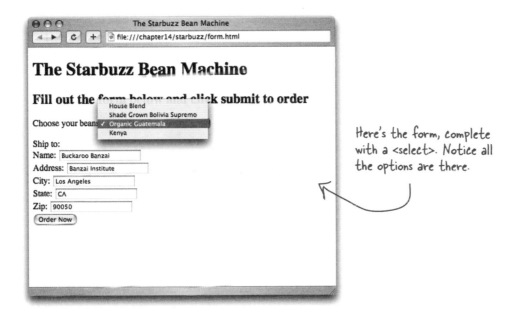

Here's the form, complete with a <select>. Notice all the options are there.

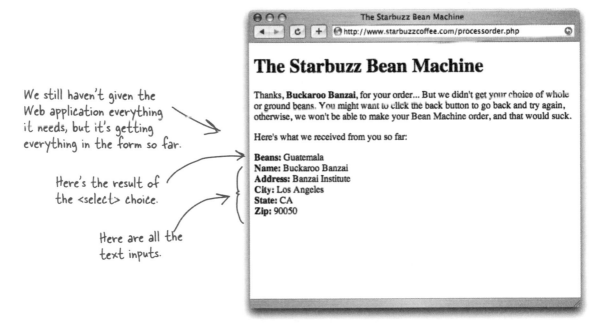

We still haven't given the Web application everything it needs, but it's getting everything in the form so far.

Here's the result of the <select> choice.

Here are all the text inputs.

BRAIN POWER

Change the <select> element name attribute to "thembeans". Reload the form and resubmit your order. How does this affect the results you get back from the Web application?

Make sure you change the name back to "beans" when you're done with this exercise.

Give the customer a choice of whole or ground beans

The customer needs to be able to choose whole or ground beans for their order. For those, we're going to use radio buttons. Radio buttons are like the buttons on old car radios – you can push only one in at a time. The way they work in XHTML is that you create one **<input>** of type "radio" for each button; so, in this case you need two buttons: one for whole beans and one for ground. Here's what that looks like:

There are two radio buttons here: one for whole beans, and one for ground.

```
<p>Type: <br />

    <input type="radio" name="beantype" value="whole"  /> Whole bean <br />
    <input type="radio" name="beantype" value="ground" /> Ground

</p>
```

We're using the <input> element for this, with its type set to "radio".

Here's the unique name. All radio buttons in the same group share the same name.

And here's the value that will be sent to the Web application. Only one of these will be sent (the one that is selected when the form is submitted).

Notice that we often label radio buttons on the right-hand side of the element.

Punching the radio buttons

Take the radio button XHTML on the previous page and insert it into
your XHTML just below the paragraph containing the **<select>**
element. Make sure you reload the page, and then submit it again.

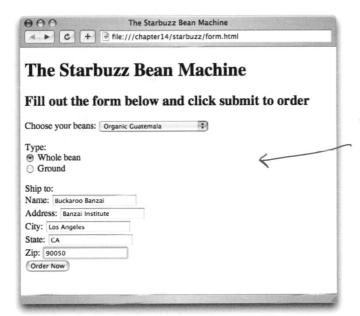

Depending on your browser,
you may have noticed that
no radio button was pressed
when you reloaded the page.

Wow! Starbuzz took our order, and
we're not even done with it yet. We've
still got to add the gift options and
an area for customer comments.

How could the order work without all
the elements being in the form? Well, it
all depends on how the Web application is
programmed. In this case, it is programmed
to process the order even if the gift
wrap and catalog options and the customer
comments are not submitted with the rest
of the form data. The only way you can
know if a Web application requires certain
form elements is to talk to the person who
developed it, or to read the documentation.

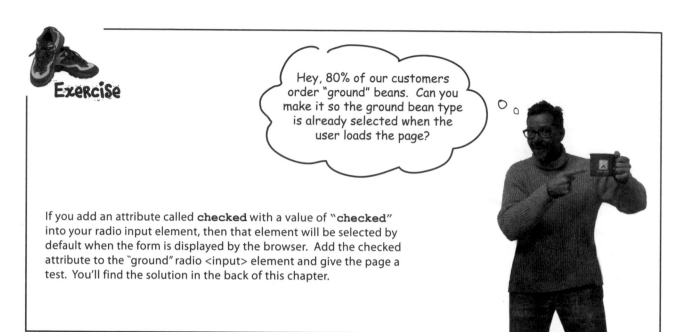

Exercise

Hey, 80% of our customers order "ground" beans. Can you make it so the ground bean type is already selected when the user loads the page?

If you add an attribute called **checked** with a value of "**checked**" into your radio input element, then that element will be selected by default when the form is displayed by the browser. Add the checked attribute to the "ground" radio <input> element and give the page a test. You'll find the solution in the back of this chapter.

Completing the form

You're almost there. You've just got two sections to add to the form: the "Extras" section with the two checkboxes and the customer comment section. Since you're getting the hang of forms, we're going to speed up a bit and add them both at the same time.

The extras section consists of two checkboxes, one for gift wrap and another to include a catalog.

It looks like the "include catalog" option should be checked by default.

The customer comment section is just a <textarea>.

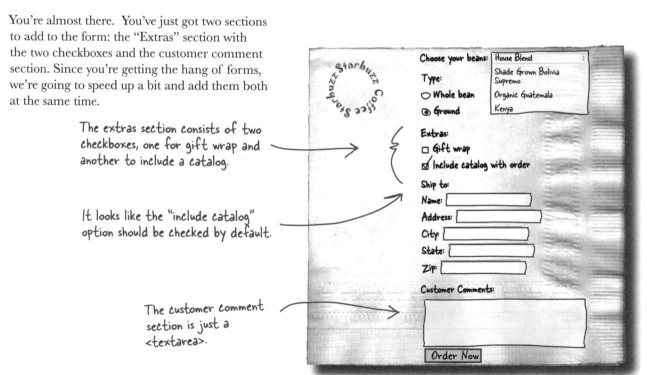

Adding the checkboxes and text area

You know the drill: look over the new XHTML and add
it to your "form.html".

```
<form action="http://www.starbuzzcoffee.com/processorder.php" method="POST">
  <p> Choose your beans:

        <select name="beans">

          <option value="House Blend">House Blend</option>

          <option value="Bolivia">Shade Grown Bolivia Supremo</option>

          <option value="Guatemala">Organic Guatemala</option>

          <option value="Kenya">Kenya</option>

        </select>
  </p>

  <p>Type: <br />

      <input type="radio" name="beantype" value="whole"  /> Whole bean <br />
      <input type="radio" name="beantype" value="ground" checked="checked" /> Ground

  </p>

  <p>Extras: <br />
      <input type="checkbox" name="extras[]" value="giftwrap" /> Gift wrap <br />
      <input type="checkbox" name="extras[]" value="catalog" checked="checked" /> Include
      catalog with order
  </p>

  <p>Ship to: <br />
      Name: <input type="text" name="name" /> <br />
      Address: <input type="text" name="address" /> <br />
      City: <input type="text" name="city" /> <br />
      State: <input type="text" name="state" /> <br />
      Zip: <input type="text" name="zip" /> <br />

  <p>Customer Comments: <br />
      <textarea name="comments" rows="10" cols="48"></textarea>
  </p>

  <p>
      <input type="submit" value="Order Now" />
  </p>

</form>
```

Here we've added a checkbox for each option. Notice that these share the same name, "extras[]"...

...but have different values.

We're using the checked attribute to specify that the catalog option should be checked by default. You can add a checked attribute to more than one checkbox.

Like the radio buttons, we've put these labels to the right of the checkboxes.

Here's the text area.

We've specified that we want it to be 10 characters high and 48 characters wide.

The final test drive

Save your changes, reload, and check out the new form. Don't you think it's looking quite nice?

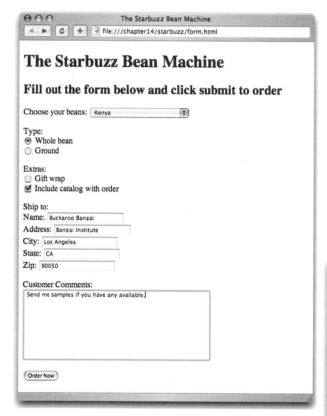

Here's what you get when you submit. The Web application has received all the form data on the page and has incorporated it into the response page. See if you can locate all the form data you submitted.

Be sure and try out all the various combinations of sending this form (with gift wrap, without, with a catalog, without, different coffees, and so on) and see how it all works.

Stop right there. Do you think I didn't see the way you slipped in that element name of "extras[]"? What's with those square brackets! You have to explain that.

Believe it or not, "extras[]" is a perfectly valid name for a form element.

But even if it's *valid*, it doesn't exactly look *normal*, does it? Here's the deal: from the perspective of XHTML, this is a normal form element name; it doesn't have any effect on the browser at all if it has square brackets in the name.

So why did we use them? It turns out that the scripting language that the processorder.php Web application is written in likes a little hint that a form variable may have multiple values in it. The way you give it this hint is to add "[ ]" on the end of the name.

So, from the perspective of learning XHTML, you can pretty much forget about all this, but you might just tuck this into the back of your mind in case you ever write a form that uses a PHP Web application in the future.

BE the Browser

Below, you'll find an XHTML form, and on the right the data a user entered into the form. Your job is to play like you're the browser and match each form element name with the values the user entered. After you've done the exercise, look at the end of the chapter to see if you matched up the form names with the values correctly.

```
<form action="http://www.chooseyourmini.com/choice.php" method="POST">
    <p>Your information: <br />

        Name: <input type="text" name="name" /><br />
        Zip: <input type="text" name="zip" /><br />

    </p>
    <p>Which model do you want? <br />
        <select name="model">
            <option value="cooper">Mini Cooper</option>
            <option value="cooperS">Mini Cooper S</option>
            <option value="convertible">Mini Cooper Convertible</option>
        </select>
    </p>
    <p>Which color do you want? <br />
        <input type="radio" name="color" value="chilired" /> Chili Red  <br />
        <input type="radio" name="color" value="hyperblue" /> Hyper Blue
    </p>
    <p>Which options do you want?  <br />
        <input type="checkbox" name="caroptions[]" value="stripes" /> Racing Stripes
        <br />
        <input type="checkbox" name="caroptions[]" value="sportseats" /> Sport Seats
    </p>

    <p>
        <input type="submit" value="Order Now" />
    </p>

</form>
```

Here's the form.

And here's the form filled out.

Match each piece of form data with its form name and put your answers here.

name = "Buckaroo Banzai" _____

zip = _____

model = _____

color = _____

caroptions[] = _____

Extra credit...

> Now that we've got the form finished, can we talk about the method the browser uses to send this data to the server? We've been using "POST", but you said there are other methods, too.

There are two primary methods the browser uses: POST and GET.

POST and **GET** accomplish the same thing – getting your form data from the browser to a server – but in two different ways. **POST** packages up your form variables and sends them behind the scenes to your server, while **GET** also packages up your form variables, but appends them on the end of the URL before it sends a request to the server.

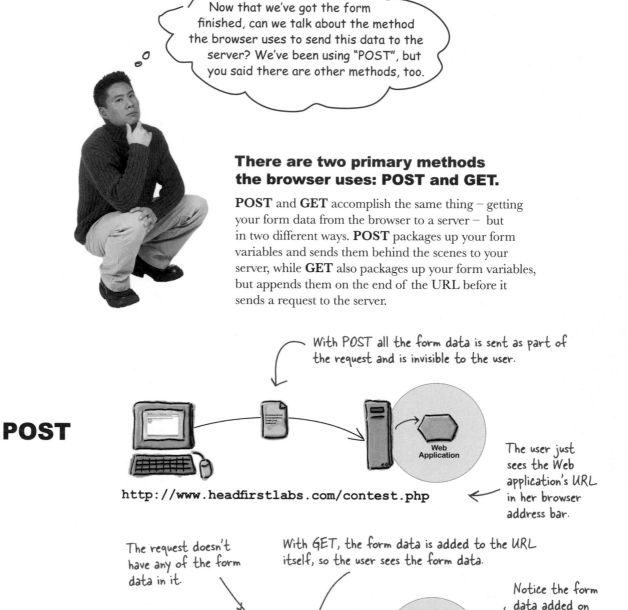

With POST all the form data is sent as part of the request and is invisible to the user.

POST

`http://www.headfirstlabs.com/contest.php`

The user just sees the Web application's URL in her browser address bar.

The request doesn't have any of the form data in it.

With GET, the form data is added to the URL itself, so the user sees the form data.

Notice the form data added on to the end of the URL. This is what the user sees in the address bar.

GET

`http://www.headfirstlabs.com/contest.php?firstname=buckaroo&lastname=banzai`

Watching GET in action

There's no better way to understand GET than to see it in action. Open up your "form.html" file and make the following small change:

Just change the method from "POST" to "GET".

```
<form action="http://www.starbuzzcoffee.com/processorder.php" method="GET">
```

Save and reload the page; then fill out the form and submit it. You should see something like this:

You'll see this URL in your browser.

```
http://www.starbuzzcoffee.com/processorder.php?beans=Kenya&beantype=gro
    und&extras%5B%5D=catalog&name=Buckaroo+Banzai&address=Banzai+Instit
    ute&city=Los+Angeles&state=CA&zip=90050&comments=Great+coffee
```

The Starbuzz Bean Machine

Thanks, **Buckaroo Banzai**, for your order from the Starbuzz Bean Machine.

Your order of ground House Blend, catalog included has been sent to:

Buckaroo Banzai
Banzai Institute
Los Angeles
CA, 90050

Thank you for submitting your comments to Starbuzz! We love getting comments from our Bean Machine users. You said,

    Great coffee!

Now you can see every form element name and their values right here in the URL.

Notice that the browser encodes various characters, like spaces. The Web application will automatically decode these when it receives them.

there are no Dumb Questions

Q: Why is it called "GET" if we're sending something to the server?

A: Good question. What's the main job of a browser? To *get* Web pages from a server. And, when you are using GET, the browser is just going about getting a Web page in the normal way it always does, except that, in the case of a form, it has appended some more data to the end of the URL. Other than that, the browser just acts like it's a normal request.

With POST, on the other hand, the browser actually creates a little data package and sends it to the server.

Q: So why would I use POST over GET, or vice versa?

A: There's a couple of big differences that really matter. If you want users to be able to bookmark pages that are the result of submitting a form, then you have to use GET, because there is no way to bookmark a page that has been returned as a result of a POST. When would you want to do that? Say you have a Web application that returns a list of search results; you might want users to be able to bookmark those results so they can see them again without having to fill out a form.

On the other hand, if you have a Web application that processes orders, then you wouldn't want users to be able to bookmark the page. (Otherwise, every time they returned to the bookmark, the order would be resubmitted.)

A situation when you'd *never* want to use a GET is when the data in your form is private, like a credit card or a password. Because the URL is in plain view, the private information is easily found by others if they look through your browser history or if the GET somehow gets bookmarked.

Finally, if you use a <textarea>, you should use POST, because you're probably sending a lot of data. GET requests have a limit of 256 characters; POST has no limit on the size of the data package you send.

Sharpen your pencil

GET or POST

For each description, circle either GET or POST depending on which method would be more appropriate. If you think it could be either, circle both. But be prepared to defend your answers...

GET   POST   *A form for typing in a username and password.*

GET   POST   *A form for ordering CDs.*

GET   POST   *A form for looking up current events.*

GET   POST   *A form to post book reviews.*

GET   POST   *A form for retrieving benefits by your government ID number.*

GET   POST   *A form to send customer feedback.*

I've been meaning to say, great job on the Bean Machine! This is really going to boost our coffee bean sales. All you need to do is give this a little style and we're ready to launch it for our customers.

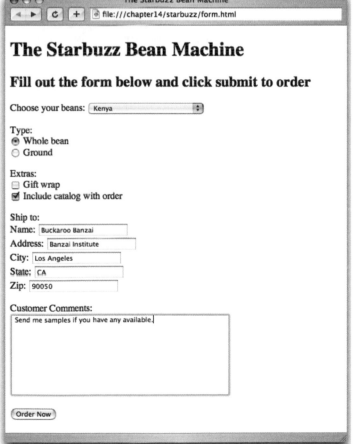

Given everything you know about XHTML and CSS, how would you approach styling this form?

Fireside Chats

Tonight's talk: **Table and CSS spar over how to lay out forms.**

Table	CSS
Hey CSS, what's happening?	
	What on earth are you doing in this chapter, Table?
What do you mean? I dropped by to help get these forms in shape. They're looking a bit... well, ragged, if you ask me.	
	I agree the forms need some fixing up in the looks department, but that's *my* job. You're for tabular data, remember?
Yes, and some people consider form elements to be tabular data, you know. Besides, I'm much better at making forms look good than you are.	
	Says who?
Says me. I get forms looking nice and neat, with the labels and form elements all aligned properly.	
	I can position things too, you know. These readers have read the chapter on positioning; they know how to get things "all aligned properly" using CSS. Anyway, even if you can align the form elements properly, you certainly can't do things like add color and padding and change the font family.
Well, I agree I can't add those little extra touches like you can, but that stuff doesn't really matter anyway. That's just the icing on the cake. The real trick to making forms user-friendly is getting the labels and elements presented in a way that makes sense, so there's no confusion about what goes with what. Users don't really care about all that other stuff.	

Table

CSS

Dude, you have *no* idea what you're talking about. Forms should match the look and feel of the rest of the Web site. Users will be confused if they go to fill out a form and it doesn't look like part of the site.

I guess. But when it comes to laying out a table properly, I'm the way to go. The last time I saw someone trying to lay out a form using CSS, there were <div>s and <span>s all over the place; it was a mess. And all that positioning and messing with margins to get the widths just right... it gave me a headache just looking at it all.

Well, what about all your <tr>s and <td>s littering up the XHTML? That's no different.

At least with my table rows and data cells, it's easier to figure out what's going to end up where; with your positioning tricks, I never know where stuff is going to end up.

You obviously haven't read Chapter 12. And I just don't buy that form elements are tabular data... they're XHTML elements, not data.

But the users are entering *data* into the form controls, aren't they? A form is used for gathering data from the person using the form. How is that *not* tabular data?

Hmm... I suppose I can sort of see that... but it just seems so wrong to use a table to do layout. Layout is *presentation*, and presentation is *my* job.

Well, I say if I can do a job better than you, then, hey, use me to do it. I'm happy to oblige.

Better than me? Whoa now, that's going too far...

Tell you what, why don't we just let the readers decide?

To Table or Not to Table? That's the question...

You're going to find people on both sides of this issue. Should you use CSS to layout your forms? Or tables? The harsh reality is that laying out forms with CSS is difficult. And, if you'd like to bend space and time to lay out your forms with CSS, we'll gladly get out of your way and look on in admiration. However, many forms *are* tabular in their layout, so why not use tables to do the layout of your forms and let CSS do the styling? That way, we get the best of *both* worlds.

Let's start with the layout...

We'll start by getting the form into a table. Check out the sketch below and you'll see the form fits pretty nicely in a table, and even better, it looks like a form rather than a ragged collection of input elements. Also notice that we've used a nested table in the "Ship to:" section.

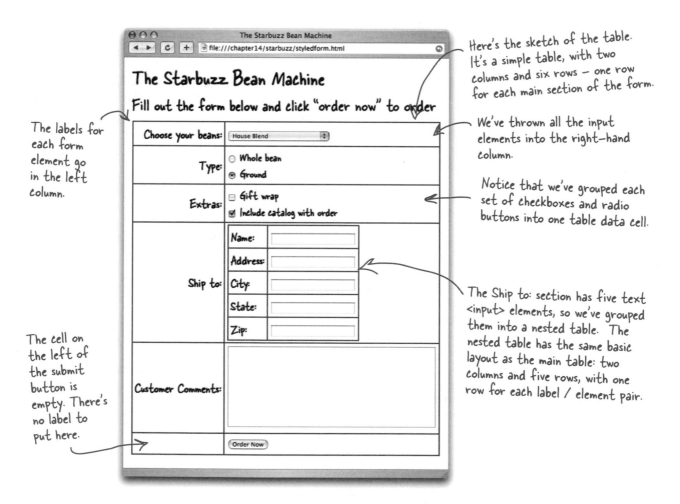

The labels for each form element go in the left column.

Here's the sketch of the table. It's a simple table, with two columns and six rows – one row for each main section of the form.

We've thrown all the input elements into the right-hand column.

Notice that we've grouped each set of checkboxes and radio buttons into one table data cell.

The Ship to: section has five text <input> elements, so we've grouped them into a nested table. The nested table has the same basic layout as the main table: two columns and five rows, with one row for each label / element pair.

The cell on the left of the submit button is empty. There's no label to put here.

Ready Bake XHTML

Getting the form elements into a table

Now that you know how to organize the form elements in a table, you need to put your XHTML table writing skills to the test. So get typing!

Just kidding. We wouldn't make you type all this... after all, this chapter is really about forms, not tables. We already typed this in for you; it's in the file "styledform.html" in the "chapter14/starbuzz" folder. Even though it looks complicated, it's really not that bad. We've added a few annotations below to point out the main parts.

Here's the <form> element; we don't need to put this part into the table.

```
<form action="http://www.starbuzzcoffee.com/processorder.php" method="POST">

<table>          Here's where the table begins.
    <tr>
        <th>Choose your beans:</th>
        <td>
            <select name="beans">
                <option value="House Blend">House Blend</option>
                <option value="Bolivia">Shade Grown Bolivia Supremo</option>
                <option value="Guatemala">Organic Guatemala</option>
                <option value="Kenya">Kenya</option>
            </select>
        </td>
    </tr>

    <tr>
        <th>Type:</th>
        <td>
            <input type="radio" name="beantype" value="whole" />
            Whole bean
            <br />
            <input type="radio" name="beantype" value="ground" checked="checked" />
            Ground
        </td>
    </tr>

    <tr>
        <th>Extras:</th>
        <td>
            <input type="checkbox" name="extras[]" value="giftwrap" />
            Gift wrap
            <br />
            <input type="checkbox" name="extras[]" value="catalog" checked="checked" />
            Include catalog with order
        </td>
    </tr>
```

Each of the main table rows has two data cells: a <th> for the label, and a <td> for the form element.

Each section of the form goes into a separate row.

For the bean selection menu, the "beantype" radio buttons, and the "extras" checkbox, we put all the form elements for each menu in one data cell.

```
<tr>
   <th>Ship to:</th>
   <td>
      <table>
         <tr>
            <td>Name:</td>
            <td>
               <input type="text" name="name" value="" />
            </td>
         </tr>
         <tr>
            <td>Address:</td>
            <td>
               <input type="text" name="address" value="" />
            </td>
         </tr>
         <tr>
            <td>City:</td>
            <td>
               <input type="text" name="city" value="" />
            </td>
         </tr>
         <tr>
            <td>State:</td>
            <td>
               <input type="text" name="state" value="" />
            </td>
         </tr>
         <tr>
            <td>Zip:</td>
            <td>
               <input type="text" name="zip" value="" />
            </td>
         </tr>
      </table>
   </td>
</tr>

<tr>
   <th>Customer Comments:</th>
   <td>
      <textarea name="comments" rows="10" cols="48"></textarea>
   </td>
</tr>

<tr>
   <th></th>
   <td><input type="submit" value="Order Now" /></td>
</tr>
</table>
</form>
```

But for the shipping data, we are creating a nested table – a table in a data cell. We did this so we could align the labels on each text <input> in the "Ship to" part of the form properly.

Here's the end of the nested table for the shipping data.

And here are the rows in the main table with the <textarea> and submit <input> elements.

Test driving a very tabular form

Open "styledform.html" in your browser and take a look at the Starbuzz Bean Machine form in table format. It looks better, doesn't it? All the labels and form elements are aligned, and it looks more professional.

Now, we can use CSS to make it look even better, by tweaking some things here and there. Let's take a look at what you might want to change.

We'll do some basic styling that you're well familiar with by now, like changing the font, and adding a background color.

We can align all these labels to the right so they line up nicely against the form elements.

A border around the table would look nice.

Notice how the rows are a little too close together? We can add space between the cells in the rows so the form is easier to read.

We can also align the labels and the form elements vertically so they both align to the top of the data cells.

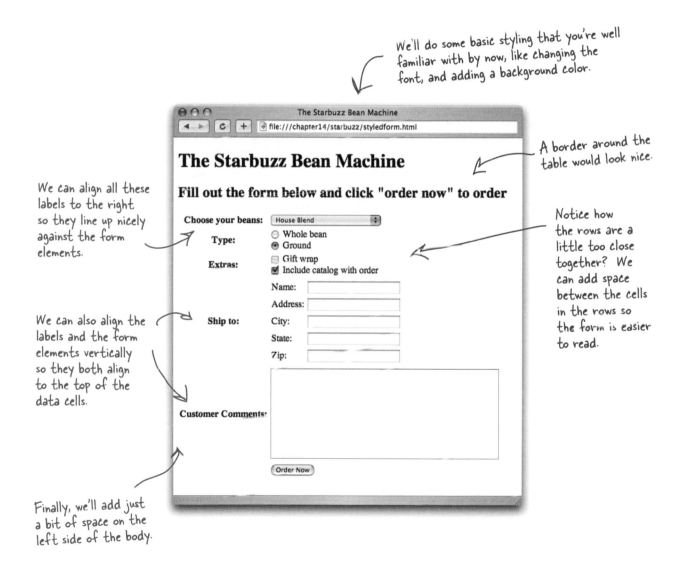

Finally, we'll add just a bit of space on the left side of the body.

Styling the form and the table with CSS

We just need to add a few styling rules to the XHTML, and we'll be done. Because this form is part of the Starbuzz site, we're going to reuse the style in the "starbuzz.css" style sheet, and create a new style sheet, "styledform.css", to add new style rules for the Bean Machine form. All of this CSS should be familiar to you now. We're not using any rules unique to tables or forms; it's all just the same stuff you've been using in the last few chapters.

Ready Bake CSS

You'll find this CSS in the file "styledform.css" in the folder "chapter14/starbuzz".

We're going to rely on the Starbuzz CSS for some of our style, but we're changing the body font to a sans-serif font, adding the Starbuzz background image, and adding a margin to the body.

```
body {
    background: #efe5d0 url(images/background.gif) top left;
    font-family: Verdana, Helvetica, Arial, sans-serif;
    margin: 20px;
}
```

These font properties will be inherited by all the elements on the page, including the text in the table and the form.

```
table {
    border: thin dotted #7e7e7e;
    padding: 10px;
}
```

We're adding a border around the table, and some padding between the table content and the border.

```
th {
    text-align: right;
    vertical-align: top;
    padding-right: 10px;
    padding-top: 2px;
}
```

The form labels are in the table headings. We want to align these to the top and right so they align nicely with the form elements in the right column. We're also adding a bit of padding to give them a little bit more space.

```
td {
    vertical-align: top;
    padding-bottom: 15px;
}
```

The content of the data cells is already aligned to the left by default, which is what we want, but we have to align them vertically too, to match the table headings. We're adding a bit of padding here too, to add space between the rows.

```
table table {
    border: none;
    padding: 0px;
}

table table td {
    text-align: right;
    padding-bottom: 0px;
}
```

These two rules override some of the other properties we set in the rules for table and td above. Why? Because we don't want the nested table to have a border, and we want the spacing to be tighter, so we're removing the padding. We also need to align the form labels in the nested data cells to the right (those aren't in table headings, like the others are, so they're not aligned with the th rule above).

The final test drive

You're going to add *two* **<link>** elements to the **<head>** of your XHTML in "styledform.html", linking in the Starbuzz style sheet from Chapter 12, "starbuzz.css", and your new style sheet, "styledform.css". Make sure you get the order correct: link the "starbuzz.css" file first, then the "styledform.css". Once you've got the two style sheets linked, save and reload your page. You should see the snazzy, styled version of the Starbuzz Bean Machine in your browser.

Wow, what a difference a little style makes!

← If you want to stretch your XHTML and CSS skills a bit, see if you can add the Starbuzz header and footer to the Bean Machine page and make the Bean Machine look really nice with those elements.

The bean machine form now matches the rest of the Starbuzz site.

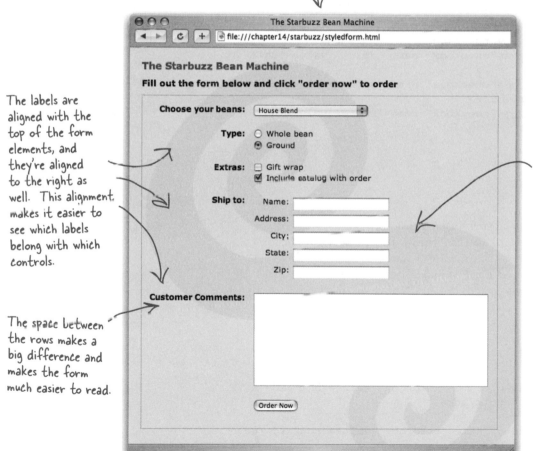

The labels are aligned with the top of the form elements, and they're aligned to the right as well. This alignment makes it easier to see which labels belong with which controls.

The space between the rows makes a big difference and makes the form much easier to read.

Notice that the nested table doesn't have a border, and the spacing is tighter; that's because of those rules that override the properties set for the main table.

What more could possibly go into a form?

We've covered just about everything you'll regularly use in your forms, but there's a few more elements you might want to consider adding to your form répertoire; so, we're including them here just in case you want to take your own form studies even further.

Fieldsets and legends

When your forms start getting large, it can be helpful to visually group elements together. While you might use **\<div\>**s and CSS to do this, XHTML also provides a **\<fieldset\>** element that can be used to group together common elements. **\<fieldset\>** makes use of a second element, called **\<legend\>**. Here's how they work together:

The \<fieldset\> element surrounds a set of input elements.

The \<legend\> provides a label for the group.

```
<fieldset>
    <legend>Condiments</legend>
        <input type="checkbox" name="spice" value="salt" />
            Salt  <br />
        <input type="checkbox" name="spice" value="pepper" />
            Pepper <br />
        <input type="checkbox" name="spice" value="garlic" />
            Garlic
</fieldset>
```

┌─ Condiments ──────────────────┐
│ ☑ Salt   │
│ ☑ Pepper   │
│ ☐ Garlic   │
└───────────────────────────────┘

Here's how the fieldset and legend look in one browser. You'll find that browsers display them differently.

Labels

So far you've been labeling your form elements with simple text, but XHTML also provides a **\<label\>** element. This element provides further information about the structure of your page, allows you to style your labels using CSS more easily, and can even help screen readers for the visually impaired correctly identify form elements.

⦿ hot
◯ not

Labels don't look different from just plain text, by default. However, they can make a big difference when it comes to accessibility.

To use a \<label\> element, first add an id attribute to your form element.

```
<input type="radio" name="hotornot" value="hot" id="hot" />
<label for="hot">hot</label>

<input type="radio" name="hotornot" value="not" id="not" />
<label for="not">not</label>
```

Then add a \<label\> and set its "for" attribute to the corresponding id.

You can use a \<label\> element with any form element.

Passwords

The password **\<input\>** element works just like the text
\<input\> element, except that the text you type is masked. This
is useful for forms that require you to type in a password, a secret
code, or other sensitive information that you may not want other
people to see as you type. Keep in mind, however, that the
form data is *not* sent from the browser to the Web application
in a secure way, unless you make it secure. For more on security,
contact your hosting company.

```
<input type="password" name="secret" />
```

The password <input> element works
exactly like the text <input> element,
except the text you type is masked.

File input

Here's a whole new input element we haven't talked about. If
you need to send an entire file to a Web application, you'll once
again use the **\<input\>** element, but this time set its type to
"file". When you do that, the **\<input\>** element creates a control
that allows you to select a file and – when the form is submitted
– the contents of the file are sent with the rest of your form data
to the server. Remember, your Web application will need to
be expecting a file upload, and also note that you must use the
POST method to use this element.

```
<input type="file" name="doc" />
```

Choose File

Browse...

Here's what the file input
element looks like in a couple
of different browsers.

To create a file input element, just set the
type of the <input> element to "file".

Multiple selection

This isn't a new element, but a new way to use an element you
already know. If you add the attribute **multiple** with a value
of "multiple" to your **\<select\>** element, you turn your single
choice menu into a multiple choice menu. Instead of a pop-
down menu, you'll get a multiple choice menu that shows all
the options on the screen (with a scrollbar if there are a lot of
them); you can choose more than one by holding down the Ctrl
(Windows) or Command (Mac) key as you select.

With multiple
selection, you
can choose more
than one option
at a time.

Buckaroo Banzai
Perfect Tommy
Penny Priddy
New Jersey
John Parker

```
<select name="characters" multiple="multiple">
    <option value="Buckaroo">Buckaroo Banzai</option>
    <option value="Tommy">Perfect Tommy</option>
    <option value="Penny Priddy">Penny</option>
    <option value="New Jersey">Jersey</option>
    <option value="John Parker">John</option>
</select>
```

Just add the attribute
multiple with a value of
"multiple" to turn a single
selection menu into a multiple
selection menu.

BULLET POINTS

- The <form> element defines the form, and all form input elements are nested inside it.

- The action attribute contains the URL of the Web Application.

- The method attribute contains the method of sending the form data: either POST or GET.

- A POST packages form data and sends it as part of the request.

- A GET packages form data and appends it to the URL.

- Use POST when the form data should be private, or when it is large, such as when a <textarea> or file <input> element is used.

- Use GET for requests that might be bookmarked.

- The <input> element can act as many different input controls on the Web page, depending on the value of its "type" attribute.

- A type of "text" creates a single line text input.

- A type of "submit" creates a submit button.

- A type of "radio" creates one radio button. All radio buttons with the same name make up a group of mutually exclusive buttons.

- A type of "checkbox" creates one checkbox control. You can create a set of choices by giving multiple checkboxes the same name.

- A <textarea> element creates a multi-line text input area.

- A <select> element creates a menu, which contains one or more <option> elements. <option> elements define the items in the menu.

- If you put text into the content of a <textarea> element, it will become the default text in a text area control on the Web page.

- The value attribute in the text <input> element can be used to give a single-line text input an initial value.

- Setting the value attribute on a submit button changes the text of the button.

- When a Web form is submitted, the form data values are paired with their corresponding names, and all names and values are sent to the server.

- Tables are often used to layout forms, given that forms have a tabular structure. Once laid out, CSS should be used to style forms to provide the presentation, including color, font styles, etc.

- XHTML allows form elements to be organized with the <fieldset> element.

- The <label> element can be used to attach labels to form elements in a way that aids accessibility.

Markup Magnets Solution

Your job is to take the form element magnets and lay them on top of the corresponding controls in the sketch. You won't need all the magnets below to complete the job; some will be left over. Here's the solution.

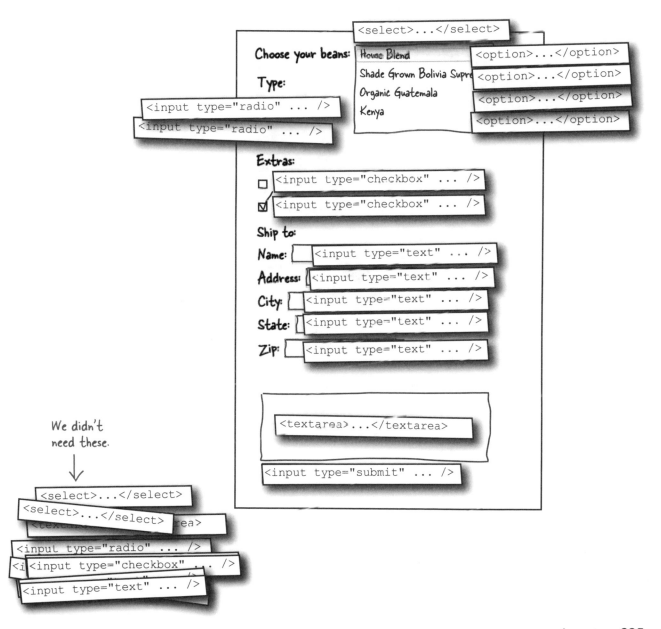

Choose your beans:

Type:

`<select>...</select>`

House Blend
Shade Grown Bolivia Supre
Organic Guatemala
Kenya

`<option>...</option>`
`<option>...</option>`
`<option>...</option>`
`<option>...</option>`

`<input type="radio" ... />`
`<input type="radio" ... />`

Extras:

☐ `<input type="checkbox" ... />`
☑ `<input type="checkbox" ... />`

Ship to:

Name: `<input type="text" ... />`
Address: `<input type="text" ... />`
City: `<input type="text" ... />`
State: `<input type="text" ... />`
Zip: `<input type="text" ... />`

`<textarea>...</textarea>`

`<input type="submit" ... />`

We didn't need these.
↓

`<select>...</select>`
`<select>...</select>` rea>
`<text` `ea>`
`<input type="radio" ... />`
`<i` `<input type="checkbox" ... />`
`<input type="text" ... />`

```
name = "Buckaroo Banzai"
zip = "90050"
model = "convertible"
color = "chilired"
caroptions[] = "stripes"
```

Sharpen your pencil
Solution

GET or POST

For each description, circle either GET or POST depending on which method would be more appropriate. If you think it could be either circle both. But be prepard to defend your answers...

GET **POST** *A form for typing in a username and password.*

GET **POST** *A form for ordering CDs.*

GET POST *A form for looking up current events.*

GET **POST** *A form to post book reviews.*

GET **POST** *A form for retrieving benefits by your government ID number.*

GET **POST** *A form to send customer feedback.*

Exercise
Solutions

Hey, 80% of our customers order "ground" beans. Can you make it so the ground bean type is already selected when the user loads the page?

If you add an attribute **checked** with a value of "**checked**" into your radio input element, then that element will be selected by default when the form is displayed by the browser. Add the checked attribute to the "ground" radio input element and give the page a test. Here's the solution.

Here's just the form section of "form.html".

```
<form action="http://www.starbuzzcoffee.com/processorder.php" method="POST">
    <p> Choose your beans:

        <select name="beans">

          <option value="House Blend">House Blend</option>

          <option value="Bolivia">Shade Grown Bolivia Supremo</option>

          <option value="Guatemala">Organic Guatemala</option>

          <option value="Kenya">Kenya</option>

        </select>

    </p>

    <p>Type: <hr />

        <input type="radio" name="beantype" value="whole"  /> Whole bean <br />
        <input type="radio" name="beantype" value="ground" checked="checked" /> Ground

    </p>
    <p>Ship to: <br />
        Name: <input type="text" name="name" /> <br />
        Address: <input type="text" name="address" /> <br />
        City: <input type="text" name="city" /> <br />
        State: <input type="text" name="state" /> <br />
        Zip: <input type="text" name="zip" /> <br />
        <input type="submit" value="Order Now" />
    </p>
</form>
```

And here's the new attribute that selects the "Ground" radio button.

Wouldn't it be dreamy if this were the end of the book? If there were no bullet points or puzzles or XHTML listings or anything else? But that's probably just a fantasy...

Congratulations!
You made it to the end.

Of course, there's still an appendix.

And the index.

And the colophon.

And then there's the Web site...

There's no escape, really.

Appendix: leftovers

The Top Ten Topics (we didn't cover)

We covered a lot of ground, and you're almost finished with this book. We'll miss you, but before we let you go, we wouldn't feel right about sending you out into the world without a little more preparation. We can't possibly fit everything you'll need to know into this relatively small chapter. Actually, we *did* originally include everything you need to know about XHTML and CSS (not already covered by the other chapters), by reducing the type point size to .00004. It all fit, but nobody could read it. So, we threw most of it away, and kept the best bits for this Top Ten appendix.

This really *is* the end of the book. Except for the index, of course (a must-read!).

#1 More Selectors

While you've already learned the most common selectors, here are a few more you might want to know about...

Pseudo-elements

You know all about pseudo-classes, and pseudo-elements are similar. Pseudo-elements can be used to select *parts of an element* that you can't conveniently wrap in a **<div>** or a **<span>** or select in other ways. For example, the **first-letter** pseudo-element can be used to select the first letter of the text in a block element, allowing you to create effects like initial caps and drop caps. There's one other pseudo-element called **first-line**, which you can use to select the first line of a paragraph. Here's how you'd use both to select the first letter and line of a **<p>** element:

```
p:first-letter {
        font-size: 3em;
}

p:first-line {
        font-style: italic;
}
```

Pseudo-elements use the same syntax as pseudo-classes.

Here we're making the first letter of the paragraph large, and the first line italics.

Attribute selectors

Attribute selectors are not currently well supported in current browsers; however, they could be more widely supported in the future. Attribute selectors are exactly what they sound like: selectors that allow you to select elements based on attribute values. You use them like this:

```
img[width] { border: black thin solid; }

img[height="300"] { border: red thin solid; }

image[alt~="flowers"] { border: #ccc thin solid; }
```

This selector selects all images that have a width attribute in their XHTML.

This selector selects all images that have a height attribute with a value of 300.

This selector selects all images that have an alt attribute that includes the word "flowers".

Selecting by Siblings

You can also select elements based on their preceding sibling. For example, say you want to select only paragraphs that have an **<h1>** element preceding them, then you'd use this selector:

Write the preceding element, a "+" sign, and then the sibling element.

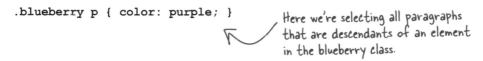

```
h1+p {
    font-style: italic;
}
```

This selector selects all paragraphs that come immediately after an <h1> element.

Combining Selectors

You've already seen examples of how selectors can be combined in this book. For instance, you can take a class selector and use it as part of a descendant selector, like this:

```
.blueberry p { color: purple; }
```

Here we're selecting all paragraphs that are descendants of an element in the blueberry class.

There's a pattern here that you can use to construct quite complex selectors. Let's step through how this pattern works:

(1) Start by defining the context for the element you want to select, like this:

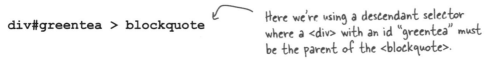

```
div#greentea > blockquote
```

Here we're using a descendant selector where a <div> with an id "greentea" must be the parent of the <blockquote>.

(2) Then supply the element you want to select:

```
div#greentea > blockquote p
```
context   element

Next we add the <p> element as the element we want to select in the context of the <blockquote>. The <p> element must be a descendant of <blockquote>, which must be a child of a <div> with an id of "greentea".

(3) Then specify any pseudo-classes or pseudo-elements:

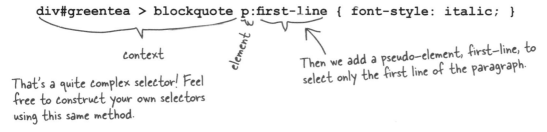

```
div#greentea > blockquote p:first-line { font-style: italic; }
```
context   element   pseudo

Then we add a pseudo-element, first-line, to select only the first line of the paragraph.

That's a quite complex selector! Feel free to construct your own selectors using this same method.

#2 Frames

HTML allows you to divide a Web page into a set of *frames*, where each frame is capable of displaying one embedded Web page. You may have noticed pages with frames that allow you to visit a third party page while leaving the header and navigation of the original site intact. These days frames are, for the most part, considered "old school" because they cause navigation and usability problems, and they are not recommended by the W3C. However, you will still find them in use in some situations.

To create a set of frames in a page, use the **<frameset>** and **<frame>** elements:

Creates a set of frames as three rows, where the first frame takes up 30% of the browser, the last part takes up 20%, and the middle part takes up the remaining space.

You can also specify framesets as columns of frames, or as rows and columns.

```
<frameset rows="30%, *, 20%">
    <frame name="header" src="header.html" />
    <frame name="content" src="content.html" />
    <frame name="footer" src="footer.html" />
</frameset>
```

For each frame we use a <frame> element. Each frame specifies a name for the frame and the source HTML file that goes in the frame.

You can also target individual names with your **<a>** elements by specifying the frame's name in the target of the link, like this:

<a href="newpage.html" target="content">new content**</a>**.

There is also a related element called an **<iframe>** that is widely supported in newer browsers. The inline element **<iframe>** allows you to place a frame anywhere within a page. Here's how you use **<iframe>**:

Creates an inline frame for the page "newcontent.html".

```
<iframe name="inlinecontent" src="newcontent.html"
        width="500" height="200" />
```

Finally, you should know that to use frames you'll need to use a DOCTYPE in the page that contains the frameset. The frameset DOCTYPEs are considered to be transitional, so you can't have frames and be strict. For HTML 4.01 use:

```
<!DOCTYPE html PUBLIC "-//W3C//DTD HTML 4.01 Frameset//EN"
                    "http://www.w3.org/TR/html4/frameset.dtd">
```

and for XHTML 1.0 use:

```
<!DOCTYPE html PUBLIC "-//W3C//DTD XHTML 1.0 Frameset//EN"
            "http://www.w3.org/TR/xhtml1/DTD/xhtml1-frameset.dtd">
```

#3 Multimedia & Flash

Browsers can play sounds and display videos or even interactive content like Flash applications in a Web page. HTML supports these types of media through an element called **<object>** that is responsible for embedding external content into your Web page (your page will also need the help of a plugin viewer that knows how to display the content).

We should mention the **<object>** element and a close cousin – the **<embed>** element – have never fully recovered from the browser wars, so using them is somewhat more complicated than it should be. If you'd like to include multimedia in your own pages, we encourage you to visit the Web site of the author of your media type and make sure you use their recommended settings. While embedding multimedia is more complicated than it needs to be, don't let that scare you off – given how much you know about HTML, it won't take you long to get your sounds, animations, and movies into your pages.

Here's a simple example of embedding a Quicktime movie using an **<object>** element:

Here's the object opening tag. As you can see, it requires a lot of specialized tags and attributes to specify the correct viewer to embed in the page.

```
<object classid="clsid:02BF25D5-8C17-4B23-BC80-D3488ABDDC6B"
        codebase="http://www.apple.com/qtactivex/qtplugin.cab"
        height="200"
        width="300">
    <param name="src" value="buckaroo.mov">
    <param name="autoplay" value="true">
    <param name="controller" value="true">
    <embed height="200"
           width="300"
           src="buckaroo.mov"
           pluginspage="http://www.apple.com/quicktime/download/"
           type="video/quicktime"
           controller="true"
           autoplay="true">Sorry your browser does not support this movie type</embed>
</object>
```

You can nest object elements to provide a set of choices. If the browser can't support the outer <object>, it tries the <embed>

The legacy <embed> element is nested for support of old browsers.

Embedding multimedia content into your pages can help to create a compelling and more immersive experience for your users, but specifying **<object>** elements can be a tricky business, so make sure you consult the viewer manufacturer's documentation on how to embed their viewers into your pages.

#4 Tools for Creating Web Pages

Now that you know XHTML and CSS you're in a good position to decide if tools like Dreamweaver, GoLive, and FrontPage are for you. All these applications attempt to provide what-you-see-is-what-you-get (WYSIWYG) tools for creating Web pages. We're sure you know enough about XHTML and browser support to know that this goal, while worthwhile, also comes up short from time to time. But, that said, these tools also provide some very handy features, even if you're writing a lot of the XHTML yourself:

- A "code" window for entering XHTML and CSS with syntax checking to catch common mistakes and suggest common names and attributes as you type.

- A preview and publish functionality that allows you to test pages before making them "live" on the Web.

- A site manager that allows you to organize your site, and also keeps your local changes in synch with your Web site on the server. Note that this usually takes care of all the FTP work for you.

These tools are also not without their downsides:

- Often these tools lag behind standards in terms of support, so to keep your XHTML and CSS current – you'll need to write the XHTML yourself.

- Often these tools don't enforce strict standards, and may allow you to get sloppy with your XHTML and CSS, so don't forget to validate (some tools help you validate as well).

Keep in mind you can use a combination of simple editors along with these more sophisticated tools; one solution doesn't have to fit all your needs. So use a page creation tool when it makes sense.

Some tools to consider:

- Apple iWeb
- Macromedia Dreamweaver
- Adobe GoLive
- Microsoft FrontPage
- GNU Emacs (open source)

#5 Client-side Scripting

HTML pages don't have to be passive documents; they can also have content that is *executable*. Executable content gives your pages behavior. You create executable content by writing programs or scripts using a scripting language. While there are a quite a few scripting languages that work with browsers, JavaScript is the reigning king. Here's a little taste of what it means to put executable content into your pages.

```
<script type="text/javascript">
    function validBid(form) {
        if (form.bid.value > 0) return true;
        else return false;
    }
</script>
```

Here's a new HTML element, <script>, which allows you to write code right inside of HTML. Notice we've set the type to JavaScript.

And here's a bit of JavaScript script that checks a user's bid to make sure it's not zero dollars or less.

Then in XHTML, you can create a form that uses this script to check the bid before the form is submitted. If the bid is more than zero, the form gets submitted.

```
<form onsubmit="return validBid(this);" method="post" action="contest.php">
```

Here's a new attribute in the form called onsubmit that invokes a script when the submit button is pressed.

What else can scripting do?

As you see above, form input validation is a common and useful task that is often done with JavaScript (and the types of validation you can do go far beyond this example). But that's just the beginning of what you can do with JavaScript. JavaScript actually has access to the entire document tree of elements (the same element tree you worked with in Chapter 3) and can programatically change values and elements in the tree. What does that mean? It means you can have a script change various aspects of your Web page based on a user's actions. Here are a few things you might do with JavaScript:

- Create an interactive game, like a crossword puzzle.

- Dynamically change images as the user passes their mouse over the image.

- Set local information in the user's browser so you can remember them next time they visit.

- Let users choose between different stylings of a page.

- Display a random quote from a set of quotes.

- Display the number of shopping days before Christmas.

#6 Server-side Scripting

Many Web pages aren't created by hand, but are generated by Web applications running on a server. For example, think about an online order system where a server is generating pages as you step through the order process. Or, an online forum, where there's a server generating pages based on forum messages that are stored in a database somewhere. We used a Web application to process the form you created in Chapter 14 for the Starbuzz Bean Machine.

Many hosting companies will let you create your own Web applications by writing server-side scripts and programs. Here's a few things server-side scripting will allow you to do:

- Build an online store complete with products, a shopping cart, and an order system.

- Personalize your pages for each user based on their preferences.

- Deliver up to date news, events, and information.

- Allow users to search your site directly.

- Allow your users to help build the content of your site.

To create Web applications, you'll need to know a server-side scripting or programming language. There are a lot of competing languages for Web development and you're likely to get differing opinions on which language is best depending on who you ask. In fact, Web languages are a little like automobiles: you can drive anything from a Yugo to a Hummer, and each has its own strengths and weaknesses (cost, ease of use, size, economy, and so on).

Web languages are constantly evolving; PHP, Python, Perl, Ruby on Rails, and JavaServer Pages (JSPs) are all commonly used. If you're new to programming, PHP may be the easiest language to start with, and there are millions of PHP-driven Web pages, so you'd be in good company. If you have some programming experience, you may want to try JSPs. If you're more aligned with the Microsoft technologies, then you'll want to look at VB.NET and ASP.NET as a server-side solution.

Here are a few books that can get you started:

Coming in late 2008

#7 Tuning for Search Engines

Many users will find your site through search engines (like Google and Yahoo!). In some cases you may not want your site to be listed in the search engine rankings, and you can use XHTML to request that they not be listed. But, in other cases, you'll want to do everything you can to tune your site so it appears high in the rankings when particular terms are searched for. Here are some general tips for improving the search engine results for your pages. But keep in mind that every search engine works differently and each considers different factors when deciding the order of its rankings.

Improving your rankings

Search engines use a combination of the words and phrases in your pages in their search rankings. To improve your rankings and help search engines determine what your page is about, start with two **<meta>** tags in your **<head>** element: one to list keywords and the other to provide a description of your content. A keyword is a simple word or two that describes your site, like "coffee" or "travel journal".

```
<meta name="description" content="This would be your description of what
is on your page. Your most important keyword phrases should appear in this
description." />

<meta name="keywords" content="keyword phrase 1, keyword phrase 2, keyword
phrase 3, etc." />
```

Many search engines treat the words in your headings and the **alt** and **title** attributes with more weight than the rest of your text, so be sure to write concise and meaningful text in these elements and attributes.

Finally, many search engines factor in the number of links to your site from other sites; the more sites that link to you, the more important your site must be. So, anything you can do to encourage others to link to your site can improve your search engine rankings.

How do I keep my site from being listed?

You can request that search engines ignore your pages, but there is no guarantee that all of them will. The only way to truly prevent others from finding your site is to make it private (discuss that with your hosting company). But if you want to request that your site not be listed, which works with most of the major search engines, just put a **<meta>** tag in the head of your XHTML, like this:

```
<meta name="robots" content="noindex,nofollow" />
```

This meta tag tells search engines to ignore this page, and any other pages on the same site that this page happens to link to.

#8 More about Style Sheets for Printing

As you saw in Chapter 10, you can use the **media** attribute of the **<link>** element to specify an alternative media type. If you specify a value of "print" in the **media** attribute of a style sheet, then that style sheet is used when your page is printed. Here's how you use the **<link>** element to do that:

```
<link rel="stylesheet" type="text/css" media="print" href="forprint.css" />
```

The media attribute on the link element tells the browser that it should use this style sheet when it prints the Web page.

Here's the link to the print stylesheet. This won't be used when your Web page is viewed on a monitor; it will only be used when you use the browser to print your Web page.

Then, as you've already seen, when a user visits your page and selects the browser's print function, the browser applies the "forprint.css" style sheet before the page is printed. This allows you to style your pages so they are more appropriate for the printed page. Here are a few considerations to keep in mind when developing styles for print:

- Change your background color to white for areas of printed text to make the text easier to read on the printed page.

- You can specify font sizes in points rather than pixels, percentages, or ems in your print style sheet. Points are designed specifically for printed text. A typical point size for most fonts is 12pt.

- While sans-serif fonts are easier to read on the screen, serif fonts are considered easier to read on the printed page. You can use your print style sheet to change the font-family too.

- If you have navigation menus, sidebars, or other content around the main content of the page, you can hide those elements for the printed version of the page if they are not essential for understanding the main content. This can be done by setting the display property on any element to "none".

- If you have positioned elements in your Web page, you may want to consider removing the positioning properties so your page prints the content in a top-down manner that makes the most sense when reading the content.

- If you have set specific widths for elements in your Web page, you might have to change those to flexible widths using margins or other methods. If your Web page has a specific width, then it may not fit properly on the printed page.

The key to making good print style sheets is to look at the primary content of the page, and make sure that this content prints clearly, fits on the printed page, and is easy to read. The best way to know if your Web page will look good when it's printed out is to test your print style sheet by printing the page.

#9 Pages for Mobile Devices

Do you want your Web pages to be usable on mobile devices, like cell phones and personal digital assistants (PDAs)? If you do, then you need to keep some things in mind when creating your pages. While mobile devices are getting more sophisticated, their support for XHTML and CSS still varies widely among the various devices. Some support CSS, some don't; some display XHTML really well, others make a mess of it. The best thing you can do is anticipate potential problems and plan for the future when support will be better.

First, remember that you can write a "handheld" specific style sheet by using the **media** attribute of the **<link>** element.

```
<link rel="stylesheet" type="text/css" media="handheld" href="formobile.css" />
```

To create a style sheet for mobile devices, use the media attribute with a value of "handheld".

Unfortunately, support for the "handheld" style sheet media type is still limited, so even if you've got a handheld style sheet link in your Web page, that doesn't mean the browser on your phone will actually use it. So, you need to keep some general design techniques in mind so your Web page looks good on both computer monitors and small devices:

- Remember that many mobile services still charge by the amount of data transmitted to the device. This is a good reason to write simple, correct XHTML and use CSS to style your Web pages.

- Keep navigation simple and obvious. That means you should use text links and avoid special scripting effects that require a mouse and keyboard to use.

- Scale down your page as much as you can. If you have a handheld style sheet, use it to reduce your font sizes, margins and padding as much as possible.

- Keep in mind that your multi-column layouts will often be ignored on small devices, so pay careful attention to the ordering of elements in your XHTML.

- Many mobile devices lack support for frames and pop-up windows, so avoid these.

- Finally, the best solution is always to test your Web pages on as many devices as you can to know how they truly perform on small devices.

And while support may currently be limited, if you get in the habit now of writing alternative style sheets for the "handheld" media type, you'll be well prepared for the future when there's more support for them.

#10 Blogs

Weblogs – or "blogs" as they are commonly known – are like personal Web pages, except they are written in journal style, like Tony's Web journal. Many people who create blogs use online services that take care of the details of managing the blog entries. These services also provide pre-made templates that allow you to pick from a variety of looks for your blog. They offer different background colors, font styles, and even background images you can use. But they also allow you to customize your blog template and create your own unique look for your blog, with, you guessed it – XHTML and CSS.

Here's a snippet of XHTML and CSS from the blog template of a popular online blogging service, Blogger.com. As you can see, they're using all the same elements and properties you've learned about in this book. And they're even on top of the new standards: their templates use XHTML 1.0 Strict, so it's a good thing you've learned how to write strict XHTML, right? Let's take a closer look...

```
<!DOCTYPE html PUBLIC "-//W3C//DTD XHTML 1.0 Strict//EN"
        "http://www.w3.org/TR/xhtml1/DTD/xhtml1-strict.dtd">
<html xmlns="http://www.w3.org/1999/xhtml" xml:lang="en" lang="en">

<head>

  <title><$BlogPageTitle$></title>

  <$BlogMetaData$>

  <style type="text/css">
    body {
        margin: 0px;
        padding: 0px;
        text-align: center;
        color: #554;
        background: #689C54 url(http://www.blogblog.com/dots_dark/bg_minidots.gif) top center repeat;
        font-family: "Lucida Grande", lucida, helvetica, sans-serif;
        font-size: small;
    }
    .
    .
    .
  </style>
</head>
<body>
    .
    .
    .
</body>
</html>
```

This blogging service uses XHTML 1.0 Strict, so here's the DOCTYPE and <html> attributes you've seen before.

These <$...$>s are template variables; they are filled in with the name of your blog and other content when you create your blog, and whenever you add a new post. You should leave these variables like they are, as they're needed to correctly display your blog content.

Here's the top of the style sheet that gives your blog its look. This template is removing the margins and padding from the body, giving the text a default color, putting an image in the background of the page, and setting font properties.

There are lots more style rules here. Each style rule controls things like the font used for your blog entries, the headings, the colors,... in other words, all the same stuff you're used to styling now.

The XHTML contains all the parts you need for your blog: headings, entries, dates, etc. Each content area will also have a <$...$> variable for plugging in the content from your post.

Index

Symbols

!important 477
#d2b48c (color in hex code) 32
& entity 114, 272
& character 114, 272
> entity 114
< entity 114
.. (dot dot) notation 64, 65
/* and */ 315
:8000 port 147
<!-- and --> (see comments)
< character 114
> character 114
[] (square brackets) 617
{ } braces 331

A

absolute layout 526
    versus floating layout 530–531
absolute paths 138–139
    versus relative paths 139
absolute positioning 519–526, 532, 542
accessibility
    alt attribute 176, 255
    forms 632, 634
    linking 149, 161
    scaling fonts using pixels 355
    table summaries 557
action attribute 596, 597
<a> element 47–49
    destination anchors 151–155
    frames 642
    href attribute (see href attribute)

new window 157–159
rendering in browser 49–50
state 468–470
strict HTML 4.01 254
target attribute 158–159
title attribute 149
(see also linking)
alt attribute 176, 237
    images 255
anchors 151–155
    finding 153
    name 154
anti-aliasing 213
ASP 646
attributes 51–52
    Attributes Exposed 53
    order 155
    required 255
    selectors 640
    supported 52
Attributes Exposed 53

B

background-color property 289, 367–368, 399
    tables 566
background-image property 404–408, 447
background-position property 406, 407
background-repeat property 406, 407, 447
background property 459
backups 127
backwards compatibility of XHTML with HTML 276
Behind the Scenes
    browsers and images 167–168
    default pages 141
    HTML links 48–50
blink decoration 377

F

O

P

X

Y